Guide to
UNIX Using Linux

FOURTH EDITION

Michael Palmer

COURSE TECHNOLOGY
CENGAGE Learning™

Australia • Brazil • Japan • Korea • Mexico • Singapore • Spain • United Kingdom • United States

COURSE TECHNOLOGY
CENGAGE Learning

Guide to UNIX Using Linux, Fourth Edition
Michael Palmer

Acquisitions Editor: Nick Lombardi

Publisher, Senior Vice President: Kristen Duerr

Senior Editor: Lisa Egan

Senior Product Manager: Alyssa Pratt

Product Managers: Molly Belmont and Alyssa Pratt

Development Editor: Deb Kaufmann

Technical Editor: John Bosco

Executive Editor: Steve Helba

Content Project Manager: Philippa Lehar

Editorial Assistant: Claire Jeffers

Marketing Manager: Gayathri Baskaran

Cover Design: Course Technology Design Department

Text Designer: GEX Publishing Services

Compositor: GEX Publishing Services

For product information and technology assistance, contact us at
Cengage Learning Customer & Sales Support, 1-800-354-9706
For permission to use material from this text or product, submit all requests online at **cengage.com/permissions**
Further permissions questions can be emailed to
permissionrequest@cengage.com

ISBN-13: 978-1-4188-3723-5
ISBN-10: 1-4188-3723-7

Course Technology
25 Thomson Place
Boston, Massachusetts 02210
USA

Cengage Learning is a leading provider of customized learning solutions with office locations around the globe, including Singapore, the United Kingdom, Australia, Mexico, Brazil, and Japan. Locate your local office at: **international.cengage.com/region**

Cengage Learning products are represented in Canada by Nelson Education, Ltd.

For your lifelong learning solutions, visit **course.cengage.com**

Purchase any of our products at your local college store or at our preferred online store **www.ichapters.com**

Printed in Canada
3 4 5 6 7 8 9 TW 12 11 10 09

TABLE OF

Contents

CHAPTER FOUR
UNIX/Linux File Processing   157

Preface

Guide to UNIX Using Linux, Fourth Edition is updated to include new UNIX/Linux distributions, networking utilities, new UNIX/Linux capabilities, and coverage of both the GNOME and KDE desktops. The large array of commands, utilities, file systems, and other information you learn here applies to any Linux system and most UNIX systems. Within the book four modern Linux operating systems are spotlighted as examples: Fedora, Red Hat Enterprise Linux, SUSE, and Knoppix.

Today UNIX and Linux operating systems are popularly used on all types of computers including desktops, portables, and servers. UNIX was the first popular operating system used with the extensive computer network that has become the Internet, and remains a staple of computing. Linux is a UNIX-like operating system first released in 1991 and has become immensely popular for all types of computing applications. Chances are that the next time you access an Internet server it will be running UNIX or Linux. Also, because of strong customer demand, many computer manufacturers offer pre-installed Linux versions on desktop and server computers.

A huge range of software is available for UNIX and Linux systems, including many free or low-cost applications. Through the X Window System and desktop software such as GNOME and KDE, UNIX and Linux provide a graphical user interface that is as versatile and easy to use as on any operating system. At the same time, UNIX and Linux have retained powerful capabilities that can be accessed through time-tested command line interfaces. In short, UNIX and Linux give you the best of two worlds, comprehensive command features and unbeatable graphical interface options.

The concepts you learn in this book help prepare you to use UNIX and Linux on all types of computer systems, including PCs, workstations, servers, and mainframe computers. Through this book you learn to use command-line features, run utilities, create your own applications, and use the GNOME and KDE desktops—giving you a comprehensive foundation in UNIX and Linux.

Taking a hands-on, practical approach, this book guides you through UNIX and Linux system and programming concepts. You practice what you learn through self-guided Hands-On Projects, Review Questions, and Discovery Exercises. Your learning is facilitated by a proven combination of tools that powerfully reinforce both concepts and real-world experience.

This book includes:

- Fedora Core 6 (on the DVD bundled with this book), which is a full-featured Linux operating system along with installation instructions

- Knoppix 5.1.1, which is a Linux operating system with the KDE desktop that you can run from the CD bundled with this book (there is nothing to install)

- Step-by-step hands-on projects to learn UNIX/Linux commands and utilities, shell programming, data management, text editing, Perl scripts, CGI scripts, Web programming, and C and C++ programming

- Comprehensive review and end-of-chapter materials, including point-by-point summaries, command summaries, review questions, and discovery exercises—all of which reinforce your learning and enable you to practice and master skills

- Presentation of the X Window graphical user interface, with a focus on the popular GNOME and KDE desktops and open source applications

- Review of UNIX/Linux security for all types of situations

- Extensive screen captures and graphics to visually reinforce the text and hands-on exercises

Intended Audience

This book is designed to serve anyone who wants to learn UNIX/Linux and how to use the command, desktop, and programming features built into UNIX/Linux. It provides a solid beginning for general UNIX/Linux users, programmers, and system administrators. General users will appreciate learning how to use UNIX/Linux utilities, how to employ command-line commands, and how to use the X Window-based GNOME and KDE interfaces. Programmers and system administrators will be interested in learning how to use all types of powerful programming capabilities in UNIX/Linux. When you finish this book, you will have a valuable foundation in UNIX/Linux skills on which to build for general, personal, or professional use.

Chapter Descriptions

The chapter coverage is balanced, with each chapter building on the skills and knowledge acquired in the preceding chapters. Here is a summary of what you will learn in each chapter:

Chapter 1: The Essence of UNIX and Linux gives you a basic introduction to UNIX and Linux, including how to access a UNIX/Linux system, how to use basic UNIX/Linux commands, and how to choose a shell in which to work. You also learn about the roles of general users and system administrators and how to protect your account through password configuration.

Chapter 2: Exploring the UNIX/Linux File Systems and File Security introduces you to the standard tree structure of files and directories, how to navigate the file system, and how partitions are deployed. You also gain hands-on experience with basic UNIX/Linux utilities to create files and directories, manage them, and make them secure.

Chapter 3: Mastering Editors enables you to learn the most commonly used UNIX/Linux editors, vi and Emacs. After you learn how to use these editors, you employ them in later chapters to process data, create scripts, and write programs.

Chapter 4: UNIX/Linux File Processing gives you basic techniques for handling data stored in files and for manipulating files. You use file creation and manipulation utilities, including the following: input, output, and error redirection utilities; utilities for creating, finding, moving, and deleting files; utilities for cutting, pasting, and sorting file contents; and the *join* and *awk* utilities for file processing.

Chapter 5: Advanced File Processing builds on the knowledge you learned in Chapter 4, while introducing a more advanced range of file processing utilities that include selection commands, manipulation and transformation commands, and file processing commands.

Chapter 6: Introduction to Shell Script Programming gives you an introduction to using shell scripts, which are powerful files containing commands that can be executed as a group. You begin creating shell scripts that use different forms of programming logic. Next, you progress to create a menu, a simple database, and a report—all steps to building your own application. You also learn how to debug scripts.

Chapter 7: Advanced Shell Programming builds on the skills you learned in Chapter 6 and enables you to add more functionality to the scripts you have created. You learn advanced techniques for managing data files, testing scripts, formatting screens, and creating shell functions.

Chapter 8: Exploring the UNIX/Linux Utilities summarizes many of the utilities you have already learned and introduces you to new utilities for processing files, managing disk usage, monitoring the system status, working with text files, backing up a system, using mail, and using a network. You also create your own manual documentation page for a script-based application you created in Chapters 6 and 7.

Chapter 9: Perl and CGI Programming gives you a taste of how to program in Perl, CGI, and HTML to manipulate data, access disk files, and create an interactive Web page.

Chapter 10: Developing UNIX/Linux Applications in C and C++ is an introduction to writing C and C++ programs in UNIX/Linux. You build on knowledge of data and logic structures that you have learned earlier in the book and put it to work creating C and C++ programs.

- *Chapter 11: The X Window System* enables you to learn about the UNIX/Linux X Window graphical interface. In this chapter, you discover how to use and customize the X Window GNOME and KDE desktops.

- *Appendix A: How to Access a UNIX/Linux Operating System* shows you how to remotely access a UNIX/Linux system using a terminal, a Microsoft Windows operating system, or a computer running UNIX/Linux, including a computer running Mac OS X.

- *Appendix B: Syntax Guide to UNIX/Linux Commands* provides a quick reference and review of the utilities and commands you have learned in this book, including the commands for the vi and Emacs editors.

- *Appendix C: How to Install Fedora and How to Use the Knoppix CD* shows you, step-by-step, how to successfully install the Fedora Linux operating system from scratch using the DVD provided with this book. You also learn how to boot from and use the Knoppix CD included with this book.

- *Appendix D: UNIX/Linux Variants* provides an overview of some of the most popular UNIX and Linux variants, including the different free and commercial versions of UNIX and Linux.

- *Appendix E: UNIX/Linux Security: Network and Internet Connectivity* focuses on security measures you can take to protect your UNIX or Linux operating system.

Features

To ensure a successful learning experience, this book includes the following learning features:

- **Chapter Objectives.** Each chapter in this book begins with a detailed list of the concepts to be mastered within that chapter. This list provides you with a quick reference to the contents of that chapter, as well as a useful study aid.

- **Screen Captures, Illustrations, and Tables.** Numerous reproductions of screens and illustrations of concepts aid you in the visualization of theories, concepts, and how to use commands and desktop features. In addition, many tables provide details and comparisons of both practical and theoretical information and can be used for a quick review of topics.

- **Syntax Boxes.** Commands are summarized in Syntax boxes that provide the format of a command and a dissection of the command's purpose plus useful options for that command.

- **End of Chapter Material.** The end of each chapter includes the following features to reinforce the material covered in the chapter:

  - **Chapter Summary.** A bulleted list gives a point-by-point summary of the chapter, which can be used as a valuable study aid.

- **Command Summary.** A summary table is provided that lists the commands, their purpose, and any command options covered in the chapter. If a chapter includes a large number of tables for commands, then the Command Summary provides a reference to the appropriate tables for review.

- **Key Terms.** Key terms are placed in bold within each chapter and at the end of the chapter, a summary of each key term is provided.

- **Review Questions.** A list of review questions tests your knowledge of the most important concepts covered in the chapter.

- **Hands-On Projects.** One of the best ways to reinforce learning about UNIX/Linux is to practice the commands, utilities, and programming features. Each chapter in this book contains many Hands-On Projects that give you experience implementing what you have learned.

- **Discovery Exercises.** Each chapter concludes with Discovery Exercises, which provide you with additional hands-on practice using the skills and concepts you have learned in the chapter.

Text and Graphic Conventions

Wherever appropriate, additional information and exercises have been added to this book to help you better understand what is being discussed in the chapter. Icons throughout the text alert you to additional materials. The icons used in this book are as follows:

The Note icon is used to present additional helpful material related to the subject being described.

Each Hands-On Project in this book is preceded by the Hands-On icon.

Tips are used to present extra information about how to use a command or how to address a particular need.

The Cautions are provided to help you anticipate potential problems or mistakes so that you can prevent them from happening.

INSTRUCTOR'S MATERIALS

The following supplemental materials are available when this book is used in a classroom setting. All of the supplements available with this book are provided to the instructor on a single CD, and are also available online at *www.course.com*.

Electronic Instructor's Manual. The Instructor's Manual that accompanies this textbook includes:

- Additional instructional material to assist in class preparation, including suggestions for classroom activities, discussion topics, quizzes, and additional exercises.

- Solutions to all end-of-chapter materials, including the Review Questions and Discovery Exercises.

ExamView®. This textbook is accompanied by ExamView, a powerful testing software package that allows instructors to create and administer printed, computer (LAN-based), and Internet exams. ExamView includes hundreds of questions that correspond to the topics covered in this text, enabling students to generate detailed study guides that include page references for further review. The computer-based and Internet testing components allow students to take exams at their computers and save the instructor time by grading each exam automatically.

PowerPoint presentations. This book comes with Microsoft PowerPoint slides for each chapter. These are included as a teaching aid for classroom presentation, to make available to students on the network for chapter review, or to be printed for classroom distribution. Instructors, please feel at liberty to add your own slides for additional topics you introduce to the class.

Figure files. All of the figures and tables in the book are reproduced on the Instructor's Resource CD, in bitmap format. Similar to the PowerPoint presentations, these are included as a teaching aid for classroom presentation, to make available to students for review, or to be printed for classroom distribution.

Script and program files. Files of the scripts and programs used in this book are provided on the Instructor's Resource CD.

System Requirements

The following system requirements are recommended to install Fedora Core 6 which comes with this book:

- A high-end Intel/AMD-class computer that operates at 500 MHz or faster

- 128 MB of RAM or more (more is preferred for faster response)

- At least 5 GB of disk space (to install X Window interfaces and applications)

- CD or CD/DVD drive
- Mouse or pointing device

The requirements to use the Knoppix CD which comes with this book are:

- An Intel/AMD-class computer
- A bootable CD, DVD, or CD/DVD drive
- 96 MB of RAM to run the operating system and the X Window interface
- Mouse or pointing device

To access a UNIX/Linux host on a local area network to which your computer is connected, you need the following software and information:

- Telnet or SSH installed
- Either an IP address or the host and domain name of the remote UNIX/Linux system

To access a UNIX/Linux host via the Internet, you need the following software and information:

- Connection to an Internet service provider (ISP)
- Telnet or SSH installed
- Either an IP address or the host and domain name of the remote UNIX/Linux system

Read This Before You Begin

There are several ways to set up a lab for the hands-on projects in this text. One is to provide students with their own PCs equipped with a Linux operating system, such as Fedora. This enables students to have the full experience of working with UNIX/Linux, including access to the X Window interface and the GNOME or KDE desktops.

Another way to perform the hands-on activities in this book is to provide students with access to a computer running Linux, such as Fedora, Red Hat Enterprise Linux, or SUSE that is configured as a server and connected to a network. Students can access the server remotely from a networked lab equipped with computers running a Microsoft Windows operating system, UNIX/Linux, or Mac OS X, and using the Telnet or SSH capabilities built into these systems. Students can also use computers with any of these operating systems and access the server over an Internet connection from a lab or from home.

Yet another way to perform the hands-on activities is for students and readers to install on their own computers the Fedora Core 6 operating system that accompanies this book on a DVD. The book also comes with the Knoppix CD that requires no installation, because it runs from a CD/DVD drive. Students can conveniently use the Knoppix CD on their own computers or on computers in a lab, without installing anything—so the computer is not altered in any way. A few projects cannot be completed via the Knoppix CD, which are those in Chapter 3 involving the Emacs editor and the GNOME desktop projects in Chapter 11. The Knoppix CD does, however, enable students and readers to complete the projects in Chapter 11 for the KDE desktop.

ACKNOWLEDGMENTS

It has been a great experience to update this book and to work with the people at Delmar/Course Technology who take publications to the highest level. I am grateful to Nick Lombardi, the Acquisitions Editor, for his interest in and support of this book. Deb Kaufmann, with whom I have worked on many books, has been outstanding as the Development Editor. Deb lights up a project with encouragement, wisdom, good will, and unfailing masterful editing. I'm also very grateful to the Product Managers Molly Belmont and Alyssa Pratt for their support and for ably guiding the teams that have produced this book. Philippa Lehar is the Content Product Manager who has skillfully worked to ensure the success of each step through the production process. Further, I am grateful to Sandra Mitchell, the Product Manager for GEX Publishing Services.

On a technical level, special thanks go to John Bosco of Greenpen Quality Assurance, the Technical Editor for this book. John has been amazing in his close reading and thorough testing (two complete passes) of all text, projects, review questions, and discovery exercises— a process that takes hours of work. I am also very indebted to the four peer reviewers Desmond Chun (Chabot College), Robert Guess (Tidewater Community College), Bradley Rounding (Clayton State University), and Diana Stinson (Southwest Virginia Community College) who have conscientiously examined and evaluated this book providing vital insights for improvements and additions. Further, the Copyeditor Dan Marinis has done fine work to tune the language for clearer presentation.

Finally, and very importantly, my thanks go to you the reader for using this book and for your interest in UNIX and Linux.

DEDICATION

I dedicate this book to my family who are a constant source of joy and support.

— Michael Palmer

1

THE ESSENCE OF **UNIX** AND LINUX

After reading this chapter and completing the exercises, you will be able to:

♦ Explain operating systems, including PC and server operating systems

♦ Describe the UNIX and Linux operating systems

♦ Explain the purpose of UNIX/Linux shells

♦ Understand how to select user names and passwords

♦ Connect to UNIX/Linux using Telnet or SSH

♦ Use basic UNIX/Linux commands and command-line editing features

♦ Explain the role of a system administrator

♦ Change your password for security

♦ Use multiple commands to view the contents of files

♦ Redirect output to a file

U NIX and the UNIX look-alike system Linux both have something for everyone. For the everyday user, these are friendly systems that offer a huge array of commercial and free software, including a free office suite. For the programmer, UNIX and Linux are ideal for collaborative development of software because they offer powerful tools and utilities. For the system administrator, UNIX and Linux contain time-tested and leading-edge tools for networking and multiuser management. In this book, you learn UNIX through the eyes of Linux. Linux is a modern operating system that has generated significant interest among all kinds of computer users—from general users to computer professionals. Also, it is a popular server system on the Web and in businesses. If you use Google to find something on the Internet, you are using a Linux Web server.

This chapter introduces you to operating systems in general and then explains the UNIX and Linux operating systems in particular. You also get an introduction to UNIX/Linux commands and command-line editing. As a variant of UNIX, Linux runs on PCs with Intel-type processors, but uses the same file systems and commands as other UNIX versions. Linux can be run from an individual PC workstation or as a server operating system that is accessed through a network. When you access it through a network, you might use an old-fashioned UNIX terminal, a modern UNIX or Linux workstation, or a Windows-based workstation. Several versions of Linux are available, but this book uses Fedora, Red Hat Enterprise Linux, SUSE Linux, and Knoppix as examples (Knoppix examples are mentioned in the Hands-on Projects). These are among the most popular versions of Linux. Red Hat Enterprise Linux is a commercial version of Linux, and Fedora is a Red Hat-sponsored development project offering a free Linux version. SUSE Linux is sponsored by Novell in the commercial SUSE Linux Enterprise version and in the free openSUSE version. Knoppix is a free version of Linux that can be run from a CD/DVD and is well suited for educational use, but is also used in home and production environments. The commands and programming techniques you learn in this book can be applied to other UNIX and Linux versions.

NOTE

You can learn more about Fedora at *fedora.redhat.com*. To find out more about Red Hat Enterprise Linux, go to *www.redhat.com*, and you can learn more about openSUSE Linux at *en.opensuse.org/Welcome_to_openSUSE.org*. For information about SUSE Linux Enterprise, visit *www.novell.com*.

UNDERSTANDING OPERATING SYSTEMS

An **operating system (OS)** is the most important program that runs on a computer. Operating systems enable you to store information, process raw data, use application software, and access all hardware attached to a computer, such as a printer or keyboard. In short, the operating system is the most fundamental computer program. It controls all the computer's resources and provides the base upon which application programs can be used or written. Figure 1-1 shows the relationship between an operating system and other parts of a computer system.

Different computer systems can have different operating systems. For example, the most common operating systems for desktop personal computers are Microsoft Windows, Mac OS, and Linux. Popular network and Web server computer operating systems are Microsoft Windows Server, UNIX/Linux, Novell NetWare, Novell Open Enterprise Server (which combines Netware and SUSE Linux Enterprise), and Mac OS X Server. Very large servers that are mainframe-class computers might use UNIX/Linux or the IBM z/OS operating system.

PC Operating Systems

A **personal computer** system, or **PC**, is usually a stand-alone machine, such as a desktop or laptop computer. A PC operating system conducts all the input, output, processing, and storage operations on a single computer. Figure 1-2 identifies some popular PC operating systems.

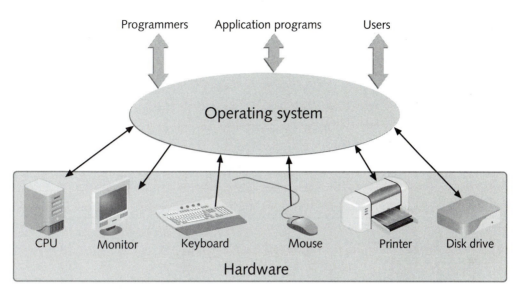

Figure 1-1 Operating system model

Microsoft Windows   Linux   Mac OS

Figure 1-2 Common PC operating systems

Server Operating Systems and Networks

Server operating systems are at the heart of a computer network. A computer **network** combines the convenience and familiarity of the personal computer with the ability to share files and other computer resources. With a network, you can share resources and exchange information with someone in the next room or on the other side of the world. Networked computers are connected by cables and through wireless communications. The Internet is one of the best examples of a network.

A **server operating system** controls the operations of a **server** computer, sometimes called a **host** computer, which accepts requests from user programs running on other machines, called **clients**. A server provides multiuser access to network resources, including shared files, hard disks, and printers. Figure 1-3 shows the relationship of a server and its clients on a network. Servers can be PC-type computers, clusters of PC-type computers working as one or several units, or mainframes. A **mainframe** is a large computer that has historically offered extensive processing, mass storage, and client access for industrial-strength computing. Mainframes are still in use today, but many have been replaced by PC-type computers that are designed as servers with powerful processing and disk storage capabilities—and cost considerably less than mainframes.

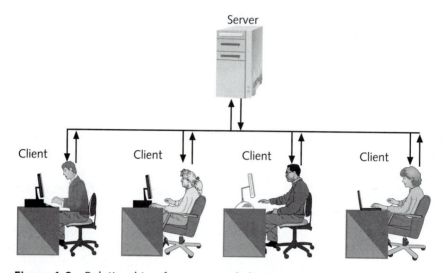

Figure 1-3   Relationship of a server and clients on a network

A server can be on a private or public network. For example, a server that stores legal files and accounting information in a law office is on a private network. A Web server, such as the one at *www.redhat.com* for Red Hat's Web site, is an example of a server on a public network.

In a centralized approach, the users' data and applications reside on the server. This type of network is called a **server-based network**. The system administrator secures all the information on the network by securing the server. The system administrator easily maintains the users' applications and performs backup operations directly on the server. If the server fails, however, clients cannot do their work until the server is returned to service.

Peer-to-peer networks, which are often used on small networks, are more distributed than server-based networks. In a peer-to-peer configuration, each system on the network is both a server and a client. There is no central server to manage user accounts; instead, each peer offers its own shared resources and controls access to those resources, such as through a workgroup of designated members or through accounts created on that peer workstation. Data and applications reside on the individual systems in the network. Software upgrades and backup operations must be performed locally at each computer. Security, which is implemented on each computer, is not uniform. Each user of the network is, to some degree, responsible for administering his or her own system. Despite the disadvantages a peer-to-peer network presents to the system administrator, the individual users do not depend on a central server. If one computer in the network fails, the other systems continue to operate.

Introducing the UNIX and Linux Operating Systems

UNIX and Linux are multiuser, multitasking operating systems with built-in networking functions. UNIX/Linux can be used on systems functioning as:

- Dedicated servers in a server-based network
- Client workstations connected to a server-based network
- Client/server workstations connected to a peer-to-peer network
- Stand-alone workstations not connected to a network

UNIX/Linux are **multiuser systems**, which let many people simultaneously access and share the resources of a server computer. Users must **log in** by typing their user name and a password before they are allowed to use a multiuser system. This validation procedure protects each user's privacy and safeguards the system against unauthorized use. UNIX and Linux are **multitasking systems** that allow one user to execute more than one program at a time. For example, you can update records in the foreground while your document prints in the background.

UNIX/Linux are also portable operating systems. **Portability** means these systems can be used in a variety of computing environments. In fact, they run on a wider variety of computers than any other operating system. They connect to the Internet, executing popular programs such as **File Transfer Protocol (FTP)**, an Internet protocol used for sending files, and **Telnet**, an Internet terminal emulation program. A terminal emulation program is one that enables a PC to respond like a **terminal** (sometimes called a dumb terminal), which is a device that has a monitor and keyboard, but no CPU.

In addition to Telnet, most UNIX/Linux systems now employ Secure Shell (SSH), which is a form of **authentication** (a process of verifying that a user is authorized to access a computer) developed for UNIX/Linux systems to provide security for communications over a network, including FTP applications. You learn about SSH later in this chapter.

Many organizations choose UNIX and Linux because these operating systems:

- Enable employees to work on a range of computers (portability)
- Are stable, reliable, and versatile
- Have thousands of applications written for them, both commercial and free
- Offer many security options
- Are well suited for networked environments (UNIX was one of the first server operating systems to be used on a network in the late 1960s.)

A Brief History of UNIX

A group of programmers at AT&T Bell Labs originally developed UNIX in the late 1960s and early 1970s. Bell Labs distributed UNIX in its source code form, so anyone who used

UNIX could customize it as needed. Attracted by its portability and low cost, universities began to modify the UNIX code to make it work on different machines. Eventually, two standard versions of UNIX evolved: AT&T Bell Labs produced **System V (SysV)**, and the University of California at Berkeley developed **Berkeley Software Distribution (BSD)**. Using features of both versions, Linux might be considered a more integrated version of UNIX than its predecessors. Currently, the **Portable Operating System Interface for UNIX (POSIX)** project, a joint effort of experts from industry, academia, and government, is working to standardize UNIX.

NOTE   At this writing, Bell Labs is now part of Alcatel Lucent. For a review of the Bell Labs inventions that have had a profound impact on the world, including the UNIX operating system and the transistor, go to *www.alcatel-lucent.com/wps/ portal/BellLabs/Top10Innovations*. You can also learn more about Bell Labs and its discoveries at en.*wikipedia.org/wiki/Bell_Labs*.

TIP   For a more complete look at the history of UNIX, visit *www.unix.org/what_is_ unix/history_timeline.html*. You can also read an historic paper about UNIX by Dennis Ritchie at *cm.bell-labs.com/cm/cs/who/dmr/hist.html*. Dennis Ritchie has played key roles in the development of UNIX and the C programming language.

UNIX Concepts

UNIX pioneered concepts that have been applied to other operating systems. For example, Microsoft DOS (Microsoft's early PC operating system) and Microsoft Windows adopted original UNIX design concepts, such as the idea of a **shell**, which is an interface between the user and the operating system, and the hierarchical structure of directories and subdirectories.

The concept of layered components that make up an operating system also originated with UNIX. Layers of software surround the computer system's inner core to protect its vital hardware and software components and to manage the core system and its users. Figure 1-4 shows how the layers of a UNIX system form a pyramid structure.

At the bottom of the pyramid is the hardware. At the top are the users. The layers between them provide insulation, ensuring system security and user privacy. The **kernel** is the base operating system, and it interacts directly with the hardware, software services, application programs, and user-created scripts (which are files containing commands to execute). It is accessible only through **Kernel mode**, which is reserved for the system administrator. This prevents unauthorized commands from invading basic operating system code and hardware, resulting in actions that might hang or disrupt smooth operating system functions. **User mode** provides access to higher layers where all application software resides.

This layered approach, and all other UNIX features, were designed by programmers for use in complex software development. Because the programmers wrote UNIX in the C

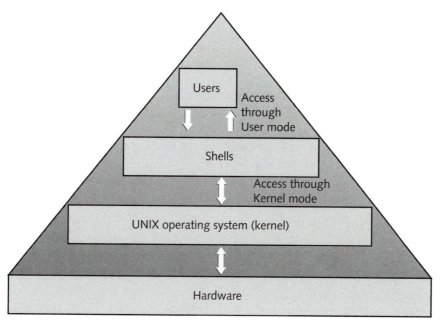

Figure 1-4   Layers of a UNIX system

programming language, this operating system can be installed on any computer that has a C compiler. This portability, flexibility, and power make UNIX a logical choice for a network operating system. In addition, with the growth in popularity of Linux, more and more organizations are moving from UNIX and Windows to Linux.

Linux and UNIX

Linux is a UNIX-like operating system because it is not written from the traditional UNIX code. Instead, it is original code (the kernel) created to look and act like UNIX, but with enhancements that include the POSIX standards. Linus Torvalds, who released it to the public free of charge in 1991, originally created Linux. A number of organizations and companies now offer free and commercial distributions or versions of Linux. The following list is a sampling of Linux distributions:

- Debian GNU/Linux (free, see *www.debian.org*)
- Fedora (free, see *fedoraproject.org*)
- Knoppix (free, see *www.knoppix.org*)
- Mandriva (commercial and free versions, see *www.mandriva.com*)
- Red Hat Enterprise Linux (commercial, see *www.redhat.com*)
- openSUSE Linux (free, see *en.opensuse.org/Welcome_to_openSUSE.org*)
- SUSE Linux Enterprise (commercial, see *www.novell.com*)

- Turbo Linux (commercial and free versions, see *www.turbolinux.com*)

- Ubuntu (free, see *www.ubuntu.com*)

Linux offers all the complexity of UNIX and can be obtained at no cost; or, for a relatively small amount of money, you can purchase commercial versions that have specialized tools and features. With all the networking features of commercial UNIX versions, Linux is robust enough to handle large tasks. You can install Linux on your PC, where it can coexist with other operating systems, and test your UNIX skills. All these features make Linux an excellent way to learn UNIX, even when you have access to other computers running UNIX.

Introducing UNIX/Linux Shells

The shell is a UNIX/Linux program that interprets the commands you enter from the keyboard. UNIX/Linux provide several shells, including the Bourne shell, the Korn shell, and the C shell. Stephen Bourne at AT&T Bell Labs developed the **Bourne shell** as the first UNIX command processor. Another Bell employee, David Korn, developed the Korn shell. Compatible with the Bourne shell, the **Korn shell** includes many extensions, such as a history feature that lets you use a keyboard shortcut to retrieve commands you previously entered. The **C shell** is designed for C programmers' use. Linux uses the freeware **Bash shell** as its default command interpreter. Its name is an acronym for "Bourne Again Shell," and it includes the best features of the Korn and Bourne shells. No matter which shell you use, your initial communications with UNIX/Linux always take place through a shell interpreter. Figure 1-5 shows the role of the shell in UNIX/Linux.

If you use a **graphical user interface (GUI)** desktop (similar to Microsoft Windows with graphics and icons), which you learn about later in this chapter and in Chapter 11, then your communications occur through the GUI desktop. To use commands, you open a special window, called a **terminal window**, and your communications with the operating system occur through a shell interpreter within the terminal window. Most versions of UNIX and Linux that support using a GUI desktop offer a terminal window. This is a powerful feature because it is literally your window to using commands.

All of the commands that you learn in this book can be used in a terminal window or directly from the command line on a system that does not use a GUI desktop.

Choosing Your Shell

Before working with a UNIX/Linux system, you need to determine which shell to use as your command interpreter. Shells do much more than interpret commands: Each has extensive built-in commands that, in effect, turn the shells into first-class programming languages. (You pursue this subject in depth in Chapter 6, "Introduction to Shell Script Programming," and Chapter 7, "Advanced Shell Programming.") A default shell is associated with your account when it is created, but you have the option to switch to a different shell

Figure 1-5   Shell's relationship to the user, operating system, and computer

after you log in. Bash is the default shell in Linux, and it is the shell many users prefer. The following is a list of shells:

- Bourne
- Korn (ksh)
- C shell (csh)
- Bash
- ash (a freeware shell derived from the Bourne and C shells)
- tcsh (a freeware shell derived from the C shell)
- zsh (a freeware shell derived from the Korn shell)

Switching from Shell to Shell

After you choose your shell, the system administrator stores your choice in your account record, and it becomes your assigned shell. UNIX/Linux use this shell any time you log in. However, you can switch from one shell to another by typing the shell's name (such as *tcsh*, *bash*, or *ash*) on your command line. You work in that shell until you log in again or type another shell name on the command line. Users often use one shell for writing shell scripts (programs) and another for interacting with a program. (In Hands-on Project 1-8 later in this chapter, you learn how to switch shells, and in Chapter 7, you learn how to set your own default shell.)

Choosing User Names and Passwords

Before you can work with UNIX/Linux, you must log in by providing a unique user name and password. Decide on a name you want to use to identify yourself to the UNIX/Linux system, such as "aquinn." This is the same name others on the UNIX/Linux system use to send you electronic mail. Some UNIX versions recognize only the first eight characters of a user name, but most versions of Linux, such as Fedora, Red Hat Enterprise Linux, and SUSE, recognize up to 32 characters.

You must also choose a password, which must contain six or more characters when using newer versions of UNIX/Linux, such as Fedora, Red Hat Enterprise Linux, and SUSE. The password should be easy for you to remember but difficult for others to guess, such as a concatenation of two or more words that have meaning to you—a combination of hobbies or favorite places, for example—written in a mix of uppercase and lowercase letters, numbers, and other characters. The password can contain letters, numbers, and punctuation symbols, but not control characters, such as Ctrl+x. (Control characters are codes that are a combination of the Control key and a letter, such as x, and that offer services to perform a specific action on a computer.)

 The default minimum password length depends on your version of UNIX/Linux. Some earlier versions of Linux have a minimum length of five characters, but Fedora, Red Hat Enterprise Linux, and SUSE require a minimum length of six characters, which is the practice used in this book.

You can log in to any UNIX or Linux system as long as you have a user account and password on the workstation or host (server) computer. A UNIX/Linux system administrator creates your account by adding your user name (also called a login name or user ID) and your password. You can change your password at any time by using the *passwd* command. You'll learn how to use the *passwd* command later in this chapter.

To use this book and the Hands-on Projects, you must have an account on a UNIX or Linux system along with some means to connect to that system. Some of the common ways to connect or to access a UNIX/Linux system are:

- Through a Telnet or SSH connection to a remote computer, such as from another UNIX/Linux or a Windows-based operating system (Not all versions of Windows implement SSH, but you can obtain SSH from a third-party source, such as SSH Communications Security at *www.ssh.com*.)

- Through client software on a UNIX/Linux client/server network

- As a peer on a peer-to-peer, local area network in which each computer has the UNIX/Linux operating system installed

- On a stand-alone PC that has the UNIX/Linux operating system installed

- Through a dumb terminal connected to a communications port on a UNIX/Linux host

NOTE   Appendix A, "How to Access a UNIX/Linux Operating System," describes several access methods, including how to set up and use Telnet or SSH. Also, see Appendix C, "How to Install Fedora and How to Use the Knoppix CD" for instructions on how to install the Fedora version of Linux on your computer and how to run Knoppix from the CD included with this book.

The steps you take to connect to a UNIX/Linux system vary according to the kind of connection you use. Connecting via a dumb terminal or accessing the OS through a stand-alone system are two of the easiest methods. In both cases, you need to log in to your account. Connecting by using client software for a client/server network might take special instructions or training from a network administrator.

If you connect on a peer-to-peer network, you can use Telnet or SSH. Connecting through Telnet or SSH are common methods and are described in the next section. You can use Telnet or SSH to access a UNIX/Linux peer or server computer over a local area network and through the Internet. Appendix A also discusses how to connect over a network using different methods.

Connecting to UNIX/Linux Using Telnet or SSH

Telnet is a terminal emulation program. It runs on your computer and connects your PC to a server, or host, on the network. The PC from which you connect can be running UNIX, Linux, a Windows-based operating system, or Mac OS. You can then log in to a UNIX/Linux host and begin working. Most UNIX/Linux versions include Telnet, as do most versions of Microsoft Windows and later versions of Mac OS.

Each computer on the Internet has an **Internet Protocol (IP) address**. An IP address is a set of four numbers (in the commonly used IP version 4) separated by periods, such as *172.16.1.61*. Most systems on the Internet also have a **domain name**, which is a name that identifies a grouping of computer resources on a network. Internet-based domain names consist of three parts: a top-level domain (such as a country or organization type), a subdomain name (such as a business or college name), and a host name (such as the name of a host computer). An example using the three-part identification is *research.campus.edu*, in which "research" is the host name, "campus" is the subdomain name, and "edu" is the top-level domain. Both the IP address and the domain name identify a system on the network. Programs such as Telnet use IP addresses or domain names to access remote systems.

The general steps used to access a UNIX/Linux host via Telnet are:

1. Determine the remote host's IP address or domain name.

2. Connect to your network or the Internet.

3. Start your Telnet program, and connect to the UNIX/Linux system. For example, to start Telnet in Windows XP or Vista, open a Command Prompt window, type telnet, and press Enter. To connect to Telnet in Fedora, Red Hat Enterprise Linux, or SUSE, open a terminal window, type telnet, and press Enter.

4. Follow the instructions in your Telnet program to connect to a remote host. Usually, you must provide the host name or IP address to connect to a UNIX/Linux system. For example, after the command prompt in a Windows 2000/XP/Server 2003/Vista Command Prompt window or at the UNIX/ Linux command line to access the system *lunar.campus.edu*, you can type the following command:
   `telnet lunar.campus.edu`

   Press Enter after you type the command.

5. Provide a user name and password to log in to the remote UNIX/Linux computer.

Secure Shell (SSH) was developed for UNIX/Linux systems to provide authentication security for TCP/IP applications, such as FTP and Telnet. Historically, the authentication for these applications has largely consisted of providing an unencrypted account and password, making both extremely vulnerable. SSH applies modern security techniques to ensure the authentication of a communications session. SSH can encrypt communications as they go across a network or the Internet.

In Fedora, Red Hat Enterprise Linux, SUSE, and other versions of UNIX/Linux, the *ssh* command can be used instead of *telnet* to establish a secure connection to a remote computer also running UNIX/Linux and that is compatible with openSSH. openSSH is a version of SSH that includes protocols and software intended for free distribution and which can be used on many UNIX/Linux systems.

To use *ssh*, you open a terminal window (or access the command line) and enter *ssh -l* on the command line along with the user account name and the name of the host computer. Two other options are to enter *ssh* with *user@hostname* or *ssh* with the IP address.

Hands-on Project 1-1 shows you how to use Telnet in Windows 2000/XP/Vista, and Hands-on Project 1-2 shows you how to access a terminal window in Fedora, Red Hat Enterprise Linux, or SUSE and use *ssh* to access a remote computer.

To use Telnet or SSH, you need to enable them on your system. See the note with Hands-on Project 1-1 to learn how to enable Telnet or SSH in different UNIX/Linux systems.

Logging In to UNIX/Linux

After you boot or connect to a UNIX/Linux system, you must log in by specifying your user name and password. You should see either a command line or a login dialog box if you are using a **graphical user interface (GUI)**. For security, the password does not appear on the screen as you type it.

When you connect through the network or a dumb terminal, you log in and execute commands using a command-line screen. If you are on a stand-alone PC, the system might be configured to use only the command-line (text) mode, or it might be configured using a GUI. In UNIX/Linux, the foundation of a GUI is called the X Window interface. The X Window interface can have a different look and feel depending on what desktop environment is used with it. The Fedora examples and figures in this book use the popular (and free) GNU Network Object Model Environment (GNOME) desktop. GNU stands for "Gnu's Not Unix," which was an endeavor started in 1983 to develop a free, open-standards, UNIX-like operating system (and additional operating system utilities). In the beginning, they were typically written in the C language.

To learn more about the GNOME Project, visit the Web site at *www.gnome.org*. Also, you learn more about the X Window interface and GNOME desktop in Chapter 11, "The X Window System."

You cannot log in without an authorized user account. If your password fails, or if you wait too long before entering your user name and password, contact your system administrator for help.

After you log in, you are ready to begin using the system. If you access UNIX/Linux through a network or a dumb terminal—or if your stand-alone system is configured for the command-line text mode—you can immediately enter commands at the command prompt. However, if you are using a stand-alone computer and an X Window desktop such as GNOME, you must open a terminal window (see Figure 1-6) to access the command prompt. Hands-on Project 1-2 demonstrates how to access a terminal window in Fedora, Red Hat Enterprise Linux, or SUSE (to execute the *ssh* command).

Figure 1-6   Terminal window in Fedora

Using Commands

To interact with UNIX/Linux, you enter a **command**, which is text you type after the command prompt. When you finish typing the command, press Enter. UNIX/Linux are **case sensitive**; that is, they distinguish between uppercase and lowercase letters, so *John* differs from *john*. You type most UNIX/Linux commands in lowercase.

Commands are divided into two categories: user-level commands that you type to perform tasks, such as retrieve information or communicate with other users, and system-administration commands, which the system administrator uses to manage the system.

You must know a command's syntax to enter it properly. **Syntax** refers to a command's format and wording, as well as the **options** and **arguments** you can use to extend and modify its functions. Most commands are single words, such as the command *clear*. If you enter a command using correct syntax, UNIX/Linux execute the command. Otherwise, you receive a message that UNIX/Linux cannot interpret your command.

Appendix B, "Syntax Guide to UNIX/Linux Commands," alphabetically lists all the commands in this book and tells you how to enter each command and use its options.

NOTE

The place on the screen where you type the command is called the **command line** (refer to Figure 1-6). Commands use the following syntax:

Syntax **command_name** [-option] [*argument*]

Dissection

- The **command_name** specifies what operation to perform. In the syntax illustrations in this book, command names appear in boldface. (In regular text, command names appear in italic.)

- Command *options* are ways to request that UNIX/Linux carry out a command in a specific style or variation. Options follow command names, separated by a space. They usually begin with a hyphen (-). Options are also case sensitive. For example, *-R* differs from *-r*. You do not need to type an option after every command; however, some commands do not work unless you specify an option. The syntax illustrations in this book list options in square brackets ([ ]) when the command does not require them.

- Command *arguments* follow command options, separated by white space (blank space). Command arguments are usually file and directory names. In the syntax illustrations in this book, arguments appear in italic. Square brackets surround arguments if the command does not require them.

In the following sections, you start your journey learning UNIX/Linux with an introduction to the following basic commands:

- *date*
- *cal*
- *who*
- *clear*
- *man*
- *whatis*

You also learn command-line editing techniques, how to enter multiple commands, and how to recall commands you've used previously. And, you learn how to log out of an active session.

The date Command

The UNIX/Linux *date* command displays the system date, which the system administrator maintains (see Figure 1-7). Because the date and time on a multiuser system are critical for applications, only the system administrator can change the date. For example, the Accounting Department might need to associate a date with a specific file used for reporting tax information, or the Publications Department might have to date stamp a document to ensure a specific copyright date.

```
                            mpalmer@localhost:~                    _  □  X
File  Edit  View  Terminal  Tabs  Help
[mpalmer@localhost ~]$ date
Sat Nov 21 10:29:56 MST 2009
[mpalmer@localhost ~]$ █
```

Figure 1-7   Using the *date* command

The *date* command has an option, *-u*, which displays the time in Greenwich Mean Time (GMT).

GMT is also known as Greenwich Meridian Time and Coordinated Universal Time (UTC). UTC is considered the international time standard. To learn more about UTC, visit NASA's Web page at *www.ghcc.msfc.nasa.gov/utc.html*.

TIP

Hands–on Project 1–3 enables you to use the *date* command.

Syntax **date** [–option]

Dissection

- Displays the system date and time
- Commonly used options include:
    - *-u* view Greenwich Mean Time
    - *-s* to reset the date or time

The cal Command

Use the *cal* command to show the system calendar. This command can be useful for scheduling events or determining a specific date of a project you completed in the past or intend to complete in the future. The *cal* command can also be used to determine the Julian date, by using *cal -j* at the command line. The Julian date is the number of the date from the beginning of the year, and is a value between 1 and 366 (including leap year). Programmers sometimes use the Julian date for specific programming functions, such as determining the number of days an employee has worked in an organization for the current year. Figure 1-8 shows the results of the command *cal -j 2009*, showing the Julian date for monthly calendars in 2009. Hands-on Project 1-4 enables you to use the *cal* command.

```
                                          mpalmer@localhost:~                         _ □ x
 File  Edit  View  Terminal  Tabs  Help
                182 183 184 185                                        213
 186 187 188 189 190 191 192      214 215 216 217 218 219 220
 193 194 195 196 197 198 199      221 222 223 224 225 226 227
 200 201 202 203 204 205 206      228 229 230 231 232 233 234
 207 208 209 210 211 212          235 236 237 238 239 240 241
                                  242 243
          September                         October
 Sun Mon Tue Wed Thu Fri Sat      Sun Mon Tue Wed Thu Fri Sat
             244 245 246 247 248                      274 275 276
 249 250 251 252 253 254 255      277 278 279 280 281 282 283
 256 257 258 259 260 261 262      284 285 286 287 288 289 290
 263 264 265 266 267 268 269      291 292 293 294 295 296 297
 270 271 272 273                  298 299 300 301 302 303 304

          November                          December
 Sun Mon Tue Wed Thu Fri Sat      Sun Mon Tue Wed Thu Fri Sat
 305 306 307 308 309 310 311                  335 336 337 338 339
 312 313 314 315 316 317 318      340 341 342 343 344 345 346
 319 320 321 322 323 324 325      347 348 349 350 351 352 353
 326 327 328 329 330 331 332      354 355 356 357 358 359 360
 333 334                          361 362 363 364 365

 [mpalmer@localhost ~]$ █
```

Figure 1-8   Using the *cal* command to determine the Julian date

---

Syntax **cal** [-option]

Dissection

- Generates a calendar for the current year or for a year specified by the user
- Commonly used options include:
    - *-j* for Julian date
    - *-s* to show Sunday as the first day in the week
    - *-m* to show Monday as the first day in the week
    - *-y* to show all of the months for the current year

The who Command

To determine information about who is logged in, use the *who* command. In a multiuser system, knowing who is logged in to the system is important for the administrator, so the administrator can periodically verify authorized users and levels of use. Knowing who is logged in is also valuable for ordinary users, who can use that information to judge how busy the system is at a given time or who might want to contact another user.

Syntax **who** [-option]

Dissection

- Provides a listing of those logged in to the operating system
- Commonly used options include:

  am i (type *who* in front, as in *who am i*) for information about your own session

  whoami (type *whoami* as all one word) to see what account you are using

  -H to show column headings

  -u to show idle time for each user (the older *-i* is being retired from the *who* options)

  -q for a quick list and total of users logged in

  -b used by system administrators and others to verify when the system was last booted

Try Hands-on Project 1-5 to learn how to use the *who* command.

The clear Command

As you continue to enter commands, your screen might become cluttered. Unless you need to refer to commands you previously entered and to their output, you can use the *clear* command to clear your screen. It has no options or arguments.

You use the *clear* command in Hands-on Project 1-6.

Syntax **clear**

- Clears the terminal screen, display, or terminal window

The man Program

For reference, UNIX/Linux include an online manual that contains all commands, including their options and arguments. The *man* program in UNIX/Linux displays this online manual, called the **man pages**, for command-line assistance. Although the man pages for some commands contain more information than others, most man pages list the following items:

- *Name*—The name of the command and a short statement describing its purpose

- *Synopsis*—A syntax diagram showing the usage of the command
- *Description*—A more detailed description of the command than the name item gives as well as a list of command options and their descriptions
- *Author*—The name or names of the author or authors who developed the command or program (if available)
- *Reporting Bugs*—The information about how to report bugs or problems
- *History*—The information that is sometimes included to show where the command originated
- *Other Versions*—The information that is sometimes included to indicate there are other versions of the command available
- *See Also*—The other commands or man pages that provide related information

The *man* program usually accepts only one argument—the name of the command about which you want more information. The online manual shows the valid command formats that your system accepts. To close the online manual, type *q*.

Syntax **man** [–option] *argument*

Dissection

- Shows information from the online documentation
- Example options include:

  -d to print information for debugging

  -f displays a short description of a command (produces the same information as using the *whatis* command described in the next section)

  -K to find a certain string by searching through all of the man information

- The argument is to supply the name of the command or program you want to learn more about, such as *man who*

As an example, consider the man pages for the *cal* command, as shown in Figures 1-9 and 1-10. In this example, the top line shows the name of the command, which is *cal*, and a brief description, which is "displays a calendar." Next, the Synopsis section provides information about the way in which the command is used, showing that it can be used with options, such as any of *-smjyl3*, as well as specifying the month or year as arguments. The Description section provides more information about the purpose of the *cal* command and explains the default usage, such as that the current month is displayed if there are no arguments used. The Description section also shows the options, such as *-s* to display the calendar starting with Sunday.

In Figure 1-10, more information about the use of the *cal* command appears at the end of the Description section. The History section shows that this command appeared in Version 6 AT&T UNIX. Finally, the Other Versions section contains information about other versions of *cal* that you can obtain and use, and at the end a date shows when this man page was written or updated.

```
┌─────────────────────────────────────────────────────────────────────┐
│ ▣                    mpalmer@localhost:~                    _ □ ✕     │
├─────────────────────────────────────────────────────────────────────┤
│ File  Edit  View  Terminal  Tabs  Help                                │
│ CAL(1)                 BSD General Commands Manual             CAL(1)  │
│                                                                        │
│ NAME                                                                   │
│      cal - displays a calendar                                         │
│                                                                        │
│ SYNOPSIS                                                               │
│      cal [-smjy13] [[month] year]                                      │
│                                                                        │
│ DESCRIPTION                                                            │
│      Cal displays a simple calendar.  If arguments are not specified,  │
│      the cur-                                                          │
│      rent month is displayed.  The options are as follows:            │
│                                                                        │
│      -1      Display single month output.  (This is the default.)      │
│                                                                        │
│      -3      Display prev/current/next month output.                   │
│                                                                        │
│      -s      Display Sunday as the first day of the week.  (This is    │
│              the default.)                                             │
│                                                                        │
│      -m      Display Monday as the first day of the week.              │
│                                                                        │
│      -j      Display Julian dates (days one-based, numbered from       │
│              January 1).                                               │
│                                                                        │
│ :▮                                                                     │
└─────────────────────────────────────────────────────────────────────┘
```

Figure 1-9   man page for the *cal* command

```
┌─────────────────────────────────────────────────────────────────────┐
│ ▣                    mpalmer@localhost:~                    _ □ ✕     │
├─────────────────────────────────────────────────────────────────────┤
│ File  Edit  View  Terminal  Tabs  Help                                │
│      A single parameter specifies the year (1 - 9999) to be displayed; │
│      note the year must be fully specified: "cal 89" will not display  │
│      a calendar for 1989.  Two parameters denote the month (1 - 12)    │
│      and year.  If no parameters are specified, the current month's    │
│      calendar is displayed.                                            │
│                                                                        │
│      A year starts on Jan 1.                                           │
│                                                                        │
│      The Gregorian Reformation is assumed to have occurred in 1752 on  │
│      the 3rd of September.  By this time, most countries had recognized│
│      the reforma-                                                      │
│      tion (although a few did not recognize it until the early 1900's.)│
│      Ten days following that date were eliminated by the reformation,  │
│      so the cal-                                                       │
│      endar for that month is a bit unusual.                            │
│                                                                        │
│ HISTORY                                                                │
│      A cal command appeared in Version 6 AT&T UNIX.                     │
│                                                                        │
│ OTHER VERSIONS                                                         │
│      Several much more elaborate versions of this program exist, with  │
│      support for colors, holidays, birthdays, reminders and            │
│      appointments, etc. For example, try the cal from                  │
│      http://home.sprynet.com/~cbagwell/projects.html or GNU gcal.      │
│                                                                        │
│ BSD                        June 6, 1993                         BSD    │
│ (END) ▮                                                                │
└─────────────────────────────────────────────────────────────────────┘
```

Figure 1-10   Additional information from the man documentation for the *cal* command

TIP

Many systems also offer info pages in addition to the man pages. Sometimes the info pages provide more information about commands, and sometimes the man pages do. Further, a new command might only be covered in *man* or *info*. If you need help with a particular command, consider checking both sources. For example, to find out about the *who* command, enter *info* who.

The whatis Command

Sometimes you find that the man pages contain more information than you want to see. To display a brief summary of a command, use the *whatis* command (see Figure 1-11). The *whatis* command shows only the name and brief description that appears near the top of a command's man page.

```
mpalmer@localhost:~
File  Edit  View  Terminal  Tabs  Help
[mpalmer@localhost ~]$ whatis cal
cal                 (1)   - displays a calendar
cal                 (1p)  - print a calendar
[mpalmer@localhost ~]$
```

Figure 1-11   Using *whatis* for a quick summary of the *cal* command

TIP

The *whatis* command relies on information stored in a database. On some UNIX/Linux systems, the administrator must execute the *whatis* command, which creates the database, before the *whatis* command operates properly. In Fedora and Red Hat Enterprise Linux, log in to the root account and type */usr/sbin/makewhatis* to create the database—although recent versions of these operating systems and of SUSE Linux already come with the database. (SUSE Linux does not include *makewhatis* in the /usr/sbin directory.)

Syntax **whatis** *argument*

Dissection

- Displays the short descriptions of commands as obtained from a whatis database

- In many UNIX/Linux versions, including Fedora and Red Hat Enterprise Linux, the *whatis* command only takes an argument (the name of a command or program) and there are no options. In SUSE, *whatis* offers several options. One important option is -*w* to search the whatis database using a wildcard in the spelling, such as * and ? when using the Bash shell (for example, enter *whatis -w ma?* when searching for *man*). Another useful option is -*m system* to enable SUSE to search the whatis database on a different UNIX/Linux system on the same network, such as on a BSD UNIX computer.

Hands-on Project 1-7 enables you to use the *man* and *whatis* commands.

Command-line Editing

Shells support certain keystrokes for performing command-line editing. For example, Bash (which is the default Linux shell) supports the left and right arrow keys, which move the cursor on the command line. For instance, if you misspell a command or argument, you can use the left and right arrows to move around on the active command line to the misspelling, correct it, and then execute the command—all without retyping it. Other keys, used in combination with the Alt or Ctrl key, are used for other editing operations, and the Del key is used to delete a character. Table 1-1 illustrates common Alt, Ctrl, and Del key combinations you can use for command-line editing. Also, try Hands-on Project 1-8 to practice editing on the command line.

Table 1-1   Common Alt, Ctrl, and Del key combinations for command-line editing

Key Combination	Description
Ctrl+b	Moves the cursor to the previous letter
Alt+d	Deletes a word or consecutive characters
Alt+l	Moves the cursor to the position just before the first character of the next word
Ctrl+a	Moves the cursor to the beginning of the command line
Ctrl+k	Deletes the content of the command line from the current cursor position to the end of the command line
Del	Deletes a character

Not all shells support command-line editing in the same manner. Table 1-1 applies to the Bash shell in Linux.

Hands-on Project 1-8 enables you to practice command-line editing, and to determine whether you are employing the Bash shell.

Multiple Command Entries

You can type more than one command on the command line by separating commands with a semicolon (;). When you press Enter, the commands execute in the order in which you entered them. For example, if you type *date ; cal*, you see today's date and then the calendar for the current month. As you learn in later chapters, this is an important capability for completing several operations at a time, such as working on the data in a file and then printing or displaying specific data. Try Hands-on Project 1-9 to execute multiple commands from a single command-line entry.

The Command-line History

Often, you find yourself entering the same command several times within a short period of time. Most shells keep a list of your recently used commands and allow you to recall a command without retyping it. You can access the command history with the up and down arrow keys. Pressing the up arrow key once recalls the most recently used command. Pressing the up arrow key twice recalls the second most recently used command. Each time you press the up arrow key, you recall an older command. Each time you press the down arrow key, you scroll forward in the command history. When you locate the command you want to execute, press Enter. This capability can save time and frustration when you need to enter the same or similar commands in one session. Hands-on Project 1-10 enables you to use the command-line history capability.

Logging Out of UNIX/Linux

When you finish your day's work or leave your computer or terminal for any reason, log out of the UNIX/Linux system to ensure security. Logging out ends your current process and indicates to the OS you are finished. How you log out depends on the shell you are using. For the Bourne, Korn, or Bash shells, enter *exit* on the command line or press Ctrl+d. In the C shell, enter *logout* on the command line. These commands log you out of your system, if you are not using a desktop environment.

If you are working in an X Window desktop environment, such as GNOME, typing *exit* and pressing Enter or using Ctrl+d only closes the terminal window. To log out, use the Log Out option for the desktop. For example, if you are using GNOME in Fedora or Red Hat Enterprise Linux, click the System menu in the Panel at the top of the screen, click Log Out *username*, and click Log Out to verify that is what you want to do. In openSUSE version 10.2 and higher, click the Computer menu in the Panel at the bottom of the screen, click Log Out, click Log out on the next menu, and click OK. In SUSE versions up through 10.0 with the GNOME desktop, click the Desktop menu in the Panel at the top of the screen, click Log Out, click Log out on the next menu, and click OK.

Understanding the Role of the UNIX/Linux System Administrator

There are two types of users on a UNIX/Linux system: system administrators and ordinary users. As the name suggests, a **system administrator** manages the system by adding new users, deleting old accounts, and ensuring that the system performs services well and efficiently for all users. **Ordinary users** are all other users. The system administrator is also called the **superuser**, because the system administrator has unlimited permission to alter the system. UNIX/Linux grant this permission when the operating system is initially installed. The system administrator grants privileges and permissions to ordinary users.

The system administrator has a unique user name: **root**. This account has complete access to a UNIX/Linux system. The password for the root account is confidential; only the system administrator and a backup person know it. If the root's password is lost or forgotten, the system administrator uses an emergency rescue procedure to reset the password.

The System Administrator's Command Line

Although ordinary users type their commands after the $ (dollar sign) command prompt, the system administrator's prompt is the # (pound) symbol. The UNIX/Linux system generates a default setting for the command prompt for the system administrator in the following format:

```
[root@hostname root]#
```

In the prompt, *hostname* is the name of the computer the system administrator logged in to. On some computers the hostname is simply localhost to refer to the local computer, or localhost is used when the computer does not have a name. Besides the reference to the root account, there are two other meanings of root which you learn more about later in this book. One meaning is the base level for all directories and another is the default home directory for the root account.

NOTE

When you use the GNOME terminal window in SUSE, the user's prompt is a right-pointing arrow with the account name and computer name (or operating system name) appearing before the arrow, such as mpalmer@aspen: → (where mpalmer is the user name and aspen is the computer name). Also, the system administrator's prompt in SUSE consists of the computer name, a colon, a tilde (for the current directory), and the pound sign, such as aspen: ~ #.

The Ordinary User's Command Line

The $ (dollar sign) (or the right-pointing arrow in SUSE) is traditionally associated with ordinary users. The UNIX/Linux system generates a default setting for the command prompt for ordinary users. The following formats are common on Linux systems:

```
[username@hostname username] $
[username@hostname ~] $
username@hostname: →
```

In the prompt, *username* is the user's login name, such as jean, and *hostname* is the name of the computer to which the user is logged in (or localhost is used). In the first example of the

1

prompt shown above, the second instance of *username* refers to the name of the user's home directory (which by default has the same name as the user name). When a tilde (~) is used, this also refers to the user's home directory (in this instance); and if you change directories, the name of the directory you change to is shown instead of the tilde.

CHANGING PASSWORDS

Your user name, or login name, identifies you to the system. You can choose your own user name and give it to the system administrator, who then adds you as a new user. As mentioned earlier, some UNIX/Linux versions recognize up to eight characters, while other versions, such as Fedora, Red Hat Enterprise Linux, SUSE, and Knoppix, recognize up to 32 characters in your user name—which is often your first initial and last name, your last name and first initial, your last name, or sometimes a nickname.

A user name is unique but not confidential, and can be provided to other users. The password, on the other hand, is confidential and secures your work on the system. You can change your password, if necessary, by using the *passwd* command, but you must know your current password to change it. If your account does not have a password, use the *passwd* command to create one.

Syntax **passwd** [-option] [*argument*]

Dissection

Used by an account owner or system administrator to change a password.

    -e used by the system administrator to expire a password so the user has to create a new password the next time she logs in

    -l locks an account and is used by the system administrator

    -S typically used by a system administrator to view the password status of an account, such as to ensure that an account has a password

UNIX/Linux system administrators can apply rules for passwords, such as they must have a minimum number of characters, contain a combination of letters, numbers, and other characters, or cannot be the same as recent passwords you have used. Hands-on Project 1-11 enables you to change your password.

After changing your password, you should log out and log in again to make certain UNIX/Linux recognizes your new password.

TIP

Remember your password! You need your password every time you log in to UNIX/Linux. For more information about the *passwd* command and for tips about keeping your password secure, enter the *man passwd* command.

Viewing Files Using the cat, more, less, head, and tail Commands

Three UNIX/Linux commands allow you to view the contents of files: *cat*, *more*, and *less*. The *more* and *less* commands display a file one screen at a time. The *more* command scrolls only down, whereas *less* enables you to scroll down and up. The *cat* command displays the whole file at one time. Two other commands, *head* and *tail*, allow you to view the first few or last few lines of a file (ten lines by default).

The *cat* command gets its name from the word concatenate, which means to link. You can display multiple files by entering their file names after the *cat* command and separating them with spaces. UNIX/Linux then display the files' contents in the order in which you entered them.

Try Hands-on Projects 1-12, 1-13, and 1-14 to use the *cat* command, the *more* and *less* commands, and, finally, the *head* and *tail* commands.

Redirecting Output

In UNIX/Linux, the greater-than sign (**>**) is called an **output redirection operator**. You can use this redirection operator to create a new file or overwrite an existing file by attaching it to a command that produces output. In effect, you redirect the output to a disk file instead of to the monitor. For example, if you type *who > current_users* and press Enter, this creates a file called current_users that contains the information from the *who* command.

Redirecting output is useful in many circumstances. For example, when you monitor a system, you might redirect output to a file that you can examine later. Or, you might have a program or report-generating utility that manipulates data so that you can redirect the results to a file instead of to the screen. You learn about other redirection operators later in this book, but, for now, the > operator is a good starting point.

Try Hands-on Projects 1-15 and 1-16 to use the > output redirection operator.

You can also use the *cat* command combined with the output redirection operator to create files from information you type at the keyboard. Type *cat > filename* after the command prompt, where *filename* is the name of the file you are creating. Enter the data in the file, and then press Ctrl+d to end data entry from the keyboard. Hands-on Project 1-17 enables you to use the *cat* command with the > redirection operator.

TIP   Use the output redirection operator (>) to send output to a file that already exists only if you want to overwrite the current file. To append output to an existing file, use two redirection operators (>>). This adds information to the end of an existing file without overwriting that file.

CHAPTER SUMMARY

1

- ❏ The operating system is the most fundamental computer program. It controls all computer resources and provides the base upon which application programs can be used or written.

- ❏ In a centralized server-based network, all the users' data and applications reside on the server, which is secured, maintained, and backed up by the system administrator. Each computer in a server-based network relies on the server. All systems in a peer-to-peer network function as both server and client. The security and maintenance of the network are distributed to each system. If one of the systems in a peer-to-peer network fails, the other systems continue to function.

- ❏ UNIX/Linux operating systems are multiuser systems, enabling many people to access and share the computer simultaneously. These are also multitasking operating systems, which means they can perform more than one task at one time.

- ❏ UNIX/Linux systems can be configured as dedicated servers in a server-based network, client workstations in a server-based network, client/server workstations in a peer-to-peer network, or stand-alone workstations not connected to a network.

- ❏ The concept of the layered components that make up an operating system originated with UNIX. Layers of software surrounding the computer system's inner core protect the vital hardware and software components and manage the core system for users.

- ❏ Linux is a UNIX-like operating system that you install on your PC. It can run alone or it can coexist with other operating systems such as Windows. Like UNIX, Linux is portable, which means it runs on computers from PCs to mainframes.

- ❏ In UNIX/Linux, you communicate with the operating system programs through an interpreter called the shell, which interprets the commands you enter from the keyboard. UNIX/Linux provide several shell programs, including the Bourne, Korn, and C shells. The Bash shell provides enhanced features from the Bourne and the Korn shells. It is the most popular shell on the Linux system.

- ❏ In UNIX/Linux, the system administrator sets up accounts for ordinary users. To set up your account and to protect the privacy and security of the system, you select and give the system administrator your user name and password. You can log in to any UNIX or Linux system anywhere as long as you have a user account and password on the host (server) computer. You can also use UNIX/Linux, Microsoft Windows, and Mac OS Telnet or SSH programs to log in to a remote UNIX/Linux system.

- ❏ The commands you type to work with UNIX/Linux have a strict syntax that you can learn by referring to the online manual called the man pages. Use the *man* program to display the syntax rules for a command. Use the *whatis* command to see a brief description of a command. Use the *who* command to list who is logged in and where they are located. Use the *cal* command to display the system calendar for all or selected months. Use the *passwd* command to change your account's password. To log out when you decide to stop using UNIX/Linux, use the *exit* or *logout* command from a system that does not use a GUI. Or, on a GUI-based system, use the Log Out option that you access from the menus.

❏ Most shells provide basic command-line editing capabilities and keep a history of your most recently used commands. Use the up and down arrow keys to scroll backward and forward through the list of recently used commands. You can enter multiple commands on a single command line by separating them with a semicolon. UNIX/Linux execute the commands in the order in which you enter them.

❏ You can use the "view" commands to examine the contents of files. Use the *cat* command to create a file by typing information from the keyboard. Use the *less* and *more* commands to display multipage documents. Use the *head* and *tail* commands to view the first or last few lines of a file.

COMMAND SUMMARY: REVIEW OF CHAPTER 1 COMMANDS

Command	Purpose	Options Covered in This Chapter
cal	Shows the system calendar	**-j** displays the Julian date format. **-s** shows Sunday as the first day in the week. **-m** shows Monday as the first day in the week. **-y** shows all of the months for the current year.
cat	Displays multiple files	**-n** displays line numbers.
clear	Clears the screen	
date	Displays the system date	**-u** displays the time in Greenwich Mean Time. **-s** resets the date and time.
exit or **logout**	Exits UNIX/Linux when a GUI is not used	
head	Displays the first few lines of a file	**-n** displays the first *n* lines of the specified file.
less	Displays a long file one screen at a time, and you can scroll up and down	
man	Displays the online manual for the specified command	**-d** prints information for debugging. **-f** gives a short description of the command (same as using the *whatis* command) **-K** finds a certain string by searching through all of the *man* information.
more	Displays a long file one screen at a time, and you can scroll down	
passwd	Changes your UNIX/Linux password	**-e** expires a password causing the user to have to re-create it **-l** locks an account **-S** displays the password status of an account

Command	Purpose	Options Covered in This Chapter
tail	Displays the last few lines of a file	**-n** displays the last *n* lines of the specified file.
whatis	Displays a brief description of a command	
who	Allows you to see who is logged in (also *whoami* shows the account currently logged in and *who am i* displays information about the account session)	**-H** displays column headings. **-u** displays session idle times. **-q** displays a quick list of users. **-b** verifies when the system was last booted.

KEY TERMS

argument — Text that provides UNIX/Linux with additional information for executing a command. On the command line, an argument name follows an option name, and a space separates the two. Examples of arguments are file and directory names.

authentication — The process of verifying that a user is authorized to access a particular computer, server, network, or network resource, such as Telnet or FTP.

Bash shell — A UNIX/Linux command interpreter (and the default Linux shell). Incorporates the best features of the Bourne shell and the Korn shell. Its name is an acronym for "Bourne Again Shell."

Berkeley Software Distribution (BSD) — A distribution of UNIX developed through the University of California at Berkeley, which first distributed the BSD UNIX version in 1975.

Bourne shell — The first UNIX/Linux command interpreter, developed at AT&T Bell Labs by Stephen Bourne.

C shell — A UNIX/Linux command interpreter designed for C programmers.

case sensitive — A property that distinguishes uppercase letters from lowercase letters—for example, *John* differs from *john*. UNIX is case sensitive.

client — A computer on a network running programs or accessing files from a mainframe, network server, or host computer.

command — Text typed after the command-line prompt which requests that the computer take a specific action.

command line — The onscreen location for typing commands.

domain name — A name that identifies a grouping of computer resources on a network. Internet-based domain names consist of three parts: a top-level domain (such as a country or organization type), a subdomain name (such as a business or college name), and a host name (such as the name of a host computer).

File Transfer Protocol (FTP) — An Internet protocol for sending and receiving files.

graphical user interface (GUI) — Software that transforms bitmaps into an infinite variety of images, so that when you use an operating system you see graphical images.

host — *See* server.

Internet Protocol (IP) address — A set of four numbers (for the commonly used IP version 4) separated by periods—for example, 172.16.1.61—and used to identify and access remote computers on a network or over the Internet.

kernel — The basic operating system, which interacts directly with the hardware and services user programs.

Kernel mode — A means of accessing the kernel. Its use is limited to the system administrator to prevent unauthorized actions from interfering with the hardware that supports the entire UNIX/Linux structure.

Korn shell — A UNIX/Linux command interpreter that offers more features than the original Bourne shell. Developed by David Korn at AT&T Bell Laboratories.

log in — A process that protects privacy and safeguards a multiuser system by requiring each user to type a user name and password before using the system.

mainframe — A large computer that has historically offered extensive processing, mass storage, and client access for industrial-strength computing. Mainframes are still in use today, but many have been replaced by PC-type computers that are designed as servers with powerful processing and disk storage capabilities.

man pages — The online manual pages for UNIX/Linux commands and programs that can be accessed by entering *man* plus the name of the command or program.

multitasking system — An operating system that enables a computer to run two or more programs at the same time.

multiuser system — A system in which many people can simultaneously access and share a server computer's resources. To protect privacy and safeguard the system, each user must type a user name and password in order to use, or log in to, the system. UNIX and Linux are multiuser systems.

network — A group of computers connected by network cable or wireless communications to allow many users to share computer resources and files. It combines the convenience and familiarity of the personal computer with the processing power of a mainframe.

operating system (OS) — The most fundamental computer program, it controls all the computer's resources and provides the base upon which application programs can be used or written.

options — The additional capabilities you can use with a UNIX/Linux command.

ordinary user — Any person who uses the system, except the system administrator or superuser.

output redirection operator — The greater-than sign (>) is one example of a redirection operator. Typing > after a command that produces output creates a new file or overwrites an existing file and then sends output to a disk file, rather than to the monitor.

peer-to-peer network — A networking configuration in which each computer system on the network is both a client and a server. Data and programs reside on individual systems, so users do not depend on a central server. The advantage of a peer-to-peer network is that if one computer fails, the others continue to operate.

personal computer (PC) — A single, stand-alone machine, such as a desktop or laptop computer, that performs all input, output, processing, and storage operations.

portability — A characteristic of an operating system that allows the system to be used in a number of different environments, particularly on different types of computers. UNIX and Linux are portable operating systems.

Portable Operating System Interface for UNIX (POSIX) — Standards developed by experts from industry, academia, and government through the Institute of Electrical and Electronics Engineers (IEEE) for the portability of applications, including the standardization of UNIX features.

root — The system administrator's unique user name; a reference to the system administrator's ownership of the root account and unlimited system privileges. Also, root has two other meanings: (1) the basis of the treelike structure of the UNIX/Linux file system and the name of the file (root directory) located at this level and (2) the home directory for the root account.

Secure Shell (SSH) — A form of authentication developed for UNIX/Linux systems to provide authentication security for TCP/IP applications, including FTP and Telnet.

server — The computer that has a network operating system and, as a result, can accept and respond to requests from user programs running on other computers (called clients) in the network. Also called a host.

server-based network — A centralized approach to networking, in which client computers' data and programs reside on the server.

server operating system — An operating system that controls the operations of a server or host computer, which accepts and responds to requests from user programs running on other computers (called clients) on the network.

shell — An interface between the user and the operating system.

superuser — *See* system administrator.

System V (SysV) — A version of UNIX originating from AT&T Bell Labs and first released as System 3 in the early 1980s as a commercial version of UNIX. Today, commercial and free versions based on System V are available.

syntax — A command's format, wording, options, and arguments.

system administrator — A user who has an account that can manage the system by adding new users, deleting old accounts, and ensuring that the system performs services well and efficiently for all users.

Telnet — An Internet terminal emulation program.

terminal — A device that connects to a server or host, but consists only of a monitor and keyboard and has no CPU. Sometimes called a dumb terminal.

terminal window — A special window that is opened from a UNIX or Linux GUI desktop and that enables you to enter commands using a shell, such as the Bash shell.

User mode — A means of accessing the areas of a system where program software resides.

REVIEW QUESTIONS

1. Your boss drops by your office in a hurry to ask you to attend a meeting at 10:30 on Friday morning and you can't find a pen to make a note as a reminder. What Linux command can you use to make a quick note to store in a file called Meeting?

   a. *note: Meeting*

   b. *cat > Meeting*

   c. *Meeting >> note*

   d. *record = Meeting*

2. Before you make the note in Question 1, you decide to determine Friday's date, so that you can include it in your note. What Linux command can you use to quickly determine Friday's date?

   a. *cal*

   b. *date -cal*

   c. *weekday*

   d. *time -d*

3. While you are typing a command, you misspell the name of a file you want to specify with the command. Which of the following command-line key combinations enables you to go back and fix your error?

   a. Ctrl+b

   b. Alt+End

   c. Ctrl+2

   d. Shift+Alt+m

4. You haven't changed your user account password for several months and now decide to create a new password. Which of the following commands should you use?

   a. *changepass*

   b. *newpass*

   c. *cat -p*

   d. *passwd*

5. You have forgotten the purpose of the *-n* option in the *cat* command. Which of the following can you enter at the Linux command line to find out what the *-n* option does when used with *cat*?

   a. *what's cat -n*

   b. *? cat*

   c. *man cat*

   d. *find -n for cat*

1

6. Which of the following is the UNIX distribution originally developed through AT&T Bell Labs?

   a. SUSE

   b. BSD

   c. TurboUNIX

   d. System V

7. Which shell is used by Linux as the default command interpreter?

   a. Bash shell

   b. Korn shell

   c. Bourne shell

   d. C shell

8. You need to type in a line of text to the end of a file called Annual_Report. Which of the following commands enables you to add the text?

   a. *add = Annual_Report*

   b. *append < Annual_Report*

   c. *cat >> Annual_Report*

   d. *append @ Annual_Report*

9. SSH can be used to _____ .

   a. analyze the security on a UNIX or Linux computer

   b. log in remotely to another computer on a network

   c. quiet the volume of the sound card

   d. quickly switch to another user account on the local computer

10. This is your first day on the job as a Linux server administrator and your boss gives you the password for root. What is root?

    a. the name of a practice user account

    b. a program used to determine the users on a Linux server and what they are doing

    c. the lowest layer or branch of security, because you must work your way up in levels of security to prove to a UNIX/Linux system that you have the skills to be an administrator

    d. the administrative account that has complete access to a UNIX/Linux system

11. In your document files, you often put the date you created the file and the date you last modified it in the last two lines of the file. What command can you use to look at only the last two lines of the file, called project?

    a. *show -l 2 project*

    b. *display project -2*

    c. *tail -n 2 project*

    d. *less/2 project*

12. You are working with a new colleague who has entered the *man* command, but who does not know how to end the *man* session to return to the regular command prompt. What keystrokes do you show your colleague to end the *man* session? (Choose all that apply.)

    a. q

    b. Alt+s

    c. Shift+Spacebar

    d. Ctrl+Alt+Del

13. Which of the following are examples of Linux distributions? (Choose all that apply.)

    a. SUSE Linux Enterprise

    b. Mandriva

    c. Fedora

    d. Red Hat Enterprise Linux

14. Which of the following commands enable you to view the contents of a file? (Choose all that apply.)

    a. *less*

    b. *cat*

    c. *grok*

    d. *whatis*

15. When you enter the *who* command, what information do you see? (Choose all that apply.)

    a. the users on the local system

    b. the owner of the local system

    c. a listing of all authorized users on a system, regardless of whether or not they are logged in

    d. a listing of all computers on your local network

16. You have been entering lots of commands and now your terminal window is cluttered will all kinds of activity. What command can you use to clear your window of the clutter?

    a. clean

    b. freshstart

    c. new

    d. clear

17. You share a Linux computer with a coworker. What is the best way to exit your UNIX or Linux session when you are done?

   a. Turn off the computer using the on/off switch.

   b. Use the Shut Down option even though your coworker may want to access the computer after you, because this is the best way to fully reinitialize security for the next user session.

   c. Use the *over >> out* command.

   d. Use a GUI menu option to log out or enter an appropriate command for the shell you are using, such as *exit* or *logout* (if there is no GUI desktop in use).

18. You work at a law firm with eight other people. All of the eight computers on the firm's network use wireless connections to communicate with one another without a server. This is an example of which of the following?

   a. a central network

   b. a peer-to-peer network

   c. a stand-alone serial network

   d. a Telnet spoke network with no hub

19. On which of the following types of computers might you find a UNIX or Linux operating system? (Choose all that apply.)

   a. a mainframe computer

   b. a desktop PC

   c. a server

   d. a workstation used for scientific research

20. You're in a hurry and have just executed a command to print the contents of a file, and you decide you want another copy of the printout. What key sequence can you use to repeat the last command, which was used to print the file?

   a. Press Alt+P.

   b. Press the Backspace key.

   c. Press the up arrow key one time.

   d. Press Shift+R.

21. Your international company is scheduling a meeting among managers in Canada, the United States, Spain, Sweden, and Hong Kong on the basis of Greenwich Mean Time (GMT). What command enables you to display the current time in GMT?

   a. *time -g*

   b. *date -u*

   c. *cal -t*

   d. *hour -g*

22. How would you describe the purpose of the *more* command?

23. What is the purpose of Telnet?

24. You enter *Cal* on the command line to view a calendar but only see an error message. Explain why you got the error message.

25. Explain how you can run more than one command on a single command line.

HANDS-ON PROJECTS

A valuable way to enhance your understanding of the UNIX and Linux operating systems is to experience them through Hands-on Projects. Each chapter in this book offers many Hands-on Projects to give you a variety of ways to practice what you learn. For these projects, you need your own user account. Also, for a few projects, you need access to the root account, which is the administrative account used in UNIX and Linux. Unless the introduction to a project specifies that you need to be logged in as root, you should use your own account by default. This follows the practice of UNIX/Linux administrators, who typically only use the root account when necessary.

HANDS-ON PROJECTS

Project 1-1

You can remotely access a computer running UNIX/Linux from another computer by using Telnet. In this project, you learn how to access a UNIX/Linux computer from a Windows 2000, Windows XP (Home, Professional, or Media Center), or Windows Vista computer using Telnet. The Telnet service should be started on your Windows 2000/XP/Vista computer. (See the following Tip or check with your instructor for help, if it is not.) Also, if your computer has firewall software, this should be configured to enable Telnet. (Check the documentation for your firewall.) Further, Telnet should be enabled on the UNIX/Linux computer you access. (See the following note.) Appendix A explains more about using and configuring Telnet. Ask your instructor for the name and domain designation or the IP address for the remote UNIX/Linux computer. You also need an account and password on a computer running Windows 2000/XP/Vista and an account and password on the remote UNIX/Linux computer.

To use Telnet to access a UNIX/Linux computer remotely:

1. Click **Start**, point to **Programs** (in Windows 2000) or **All Programs** (in Windows XP/Vista), point to **Accessories**, and click **Command Prompt**.

2. In Windows 2000/XP/Vista, type **telnet** and the name and domain or IP address of the remote UNIX/Linux computer, such as telnet 169.254.42.2 (see Figure 1-12). Press **Enter**.

3. Type the account name and press **Enter**.

4. Type the password and press **Enter**.

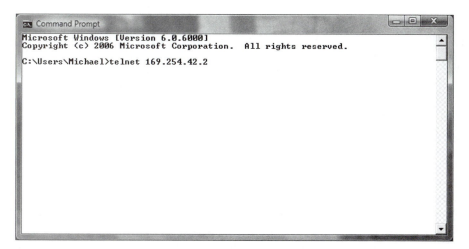

Figure 1-12   Using Telnet from Windows Vista

5. After you are logged in, close the session. Depending on the system you access, you might need to log out in one of two ways. One way is by typing **c** and pressing **Enter** to close the connection. Next, type **exit** and press **Enter** to exit Telnet. The second way to end the session is to type **logout** and press **Enter**. Then, if necessary, type **c** and press **Enter**, and then type **exit** and press **Enter**.

6. Close the Command Prompt window.

TIP   Telnet is disabled by default in Windows Vista. To enable Telnet in Windows Vista, log on to an account with administrator privileges, click Start, click Control Panel, click Programs (from Control Panel Home display mode), under Programs and Features click Turn Windows features on or off, click Continue, check the box for Telnet Client, and click OK.

NOTE   On the UNIX/Linux host server, Telnet should also be enabled, such as by editing the /etc/xinetd.d/telnet file and changing disable=yes to disable=no. On many UNIX/Linux systems, you can also log in to the root and enter ~/ .telnetrc to configure Telnet parameters. Further, you may need to start the Telnet or SSH service. On many UNIX/Linux systems, to start Telnet or SSH services, log in to root and enter either *service telnet start* or *telnet start* for Telnet, or to start the SSH service, enter *service sshd start* or *sshd start*. Keep in mind that Telnet is not very secure and so, if possible, it is better to use SSH.

NOTE

In terms of firewall security on the host server, you can enable Telnet and SSH communications through the firewall in Fedora and Red Hat Enterprise Linux (with the GNOME desktop installed) by using these steps: Click the System menu, point to Administration, click Security Level and Firewall, enter the root password (if requested) and click OK, check the boxes for Telnet and SSH, click OK, and click Yes. If you are using SUSE Linux 10.0 or earlier (with GNOME), click the Desktop menu, click Yast, enter the root password (if requested) and click Continue, click Security and Users in the left pane, click Firewall in the right pane, click Allowed Services in the left pane, and ensure that SSH is listed under the Allowed Service column. If SSH is not listed, open the Service to Allow list box, select SSH (Telnet is not listed as an option), click the Add button, click Next, and click Accept. In SUSE Linux 10.2 and later, click the Computer menu in the Panel at the bottom of the desktop, click Control Center, click Yast, enter the root password (if requested), and click Continue. Click Security and Users in the left pane, click Firewall in the right pane, click Allowed Services in the left pane, and ensure that SSH is listed under the Allowed Service column. If SSH is not listed, open the Service to Allow list box, select SSH (Telnet is not listed as an option), click the Add button, click Next, and click Accept. If none of these steps work, consult Appendix A.

HANDS-ON PROJECTS

Project 1-2

In this project, you use SSH from Fedora, Red Hat Enterprise Linux, or SUSE. For this project, you need the name of the remote account and host name of the remote computer. You also need the password for the remote account. Further, SSH should be enabled via the Fedora, Red Hat Enterprise Linux, or SUSE firewall software (see the preceding note). Step 1 provides instructions for opening a terminal window on systems using the GNOME desktop. If your system does not use a desktop, such as GNOME, go to Step 2.

To use SSH from Fedora, Red Hat Enterprise Linux, or SUSE to access another UNIX/Linux computer remotely:

1. On newer Fedora and Red Hat Enterprise Linux systems (such as Fedora Core 2 and later), click **Applications**, point to **Accessories**, and click **Terminal**. On older Fedora or Red Hat Enterprise Linux systems, click **Main Menu**, point to **System Tools**, and click **Terminal**. In SUSE Linux 10.0 and earlier, click **Applications**, point to **System**, point to **Terminal**, and click **Gnome Terminal** (or you can click other terminal window options, such as Konsole or X Terminal). In SUSE Linux 10.2 and later, click the **Computer** menu in the Panel, click **More Applications**, click **System** in the left pane (or scroll to the System section in the right pane), and click **Gnome Terminal**.

2. At the command prompt, type **ssh –l** plus the account name and IP address or host name, such as *ssh -l trbrown 192.168.0.5*, and press **Enter**. (If this is a first-time connection and you are asked whether you want to continue connecting, type **yes** and press **Enter**.)

3. Type the account's password and press **Enter** to view a terminal window, as shown in Figure 1-13. (Depending on the configuration of the network and SSH, you might see the following message after entering the password: "No xauth data; using fake authentication data for X11 forwarding.")

4. Type **logout** and press **Enter** to log out of the remote computer.

5. Type **exit** and press **Enter** to exit the terminal window.

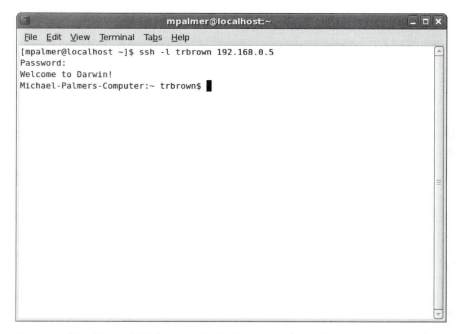

Figure 1-13   Using SSH from a GNOME terminal window to access another account on a remote UNIX/Linux computer

TIP

To open a terminal window and use SSH from Knoppix, click the Konsole icon in the Panel or click the K Menu (the left-most icon on the Panel in the bottom of the screen), point to Utilities, and click Terminal. Use the ssh command as described in Steps 2 through 5. To use SSH from a Mac OS X Panther or Tiger computer, click the Go menu, click Utilities, and double-click Terminal. Use the ssh command as you did in Steps 2 through 4. To close the terminal window, click the Terminal menu and click Quit Terminal.

Project 1-3

This project shows you how to use the *date* command. You should already be at the command line or have a terminal window open for the project. (See Project 1-2, Step 1, for instructions to open a terminal window.)

To display your system date:

1. Type **date** in the command line, and press **Enter**.

   A date similar to the following appears:

   ```
   Sat Nov 21 21:30:09 EST 2009
   ```

   You might see the abbreviation EDT (Eastern Daylight Time) instead of EST (Eastern Standard Time), or another time zone abbreviation, such as PDT (Pacific Daylight Time) or CST (Central Standard Time). Notice also that UNIX/Linux use a 24-hour clock.

2. Type **Date** in the command line, and press **Enter**. You see the following system error message:

   ```
   bash: Date: command not found
   ```

   The system error message appears because you must enter the *date* command, like most UNIX/Linux commands, in lowercase letters.

To display your system date in UTC:

1. Type **date –u** in the command line, and press **Enter**.

   A date similar to the following appears:

   ```
   Sat Nov 21 23:43:148 UTC 2009
   ```

Project 1-4

In this project, you use the *cal* command to display the current calendar, a Julian date calendar, and the historical calendar for July 1776.

To use the *cal* command:

1. Type **cal** in the command line, and press **Enter**. What calendar do you see?

2. Type **cal –j 2009** in the command line, and press **Enter**. What type of calendar appears?

3. To determine the day of the week when the Declaration of Independence was signed, type **cal 7 1776** in the command line, and press **Enter**. You should see a calendar similar to the one in Figure 1-14. In this case, the month and year are the command arguments.

```
mpalmer@localhost:~
File  Edit  View  Terminal  Tabs  Help
[mpalmer@localhost ~]$ cal 7 1776
      July 1776
Su Mo Tu We Th Fr Sa
       1  2  3  4  5  6
 7  8  9 10 11 12 13
14 15 16 17 18 19 20
21 22 23 24 25 26 27
28 29 30 31

[mpalmer@localhost ~]$ █
```

Figure 1-14   Using the *cal* command to show the calendar for July,1776

If you type *cal july 1776*, you see an error message similar to the following because you must use numbers, such as 7, to indicate months, such as July.

`cal: illegal month value: use 1-12`

TIP

HANDS-ON PROJECTS

Project 1-5

The *who* command is valuable for determining who is currently logged in to a system. In this project, you try out the *who* command using several options.

To use the *who* command to determine who is logged in to the system:

1. Type **who** in the command line, and press **Enter**.

2. You see a list showing user names, the terminals (lines) they are using, and the dates and the times they logged in. For example, for your connection you will likely see the lines pts/1, :0, or both, which show you are logged on locally. Users who are logged on remotely will have lines that begin with tty, such as tty1, tty2, and so on.

3. To display a line of column headings with the *who* command's output, type **who -H** and press **Enter**.

   If any current users are logged in from a remote host, the COMMENT column shows the name of the host.

4. Idle time is the amount of time that has elapsed with no activity in a user's session. Type **who –u** and press **Enter** to see each user's idle time. The following is a sample listing of *who* information. (The final value is the process ID, but you might also see a comment after the process ID.)

```
mpalmer    pts/1   2009-11-22   08:15   4230   (:0.0)
sjones     tty1    2009-11-22   07:56   4229   (:29.0)
rsanchez   tty3    2009-11-22   08:21   4238   old
```

The output shows that the person logged in as mpalmer has been active in the last minute. The account sjones has no activity in the last 29 minutes. The word "old" on rsanchez's line indicates no activity in the past 24 hours.

5. If you want to use multiple options on the same command line, type them all after a single hyphen. For example, type **who –uH** and press **Enter** to see a list of users with idle times and column headings.

6. Type **who –q** and press **Enter** to see a quick list of current users. You see a list similar to the following, which shows only login names and the total number of users on the system.

```
mpalmer sjones rsanchez
# users=3
```

7. To determine which terminal you are using or what time you logged in, type **who am i** in the command line, and press **Enter** (see Figure 1-15). What information appears? If you are not certain, type **who am i –H** and press **Enter** to view column headings. (Another option is to type **whoami** as one word, which only displays your account name or user ID, in case you are not certain which account you are currently using; this option is often used by system administrators. Also try entering *who mom likes* to see what you find out.)

TIP   If you provide two arguments to the *who* command, you see the output described in Step 7. For example, you can type *who are you* or *who x x* to see the same information. Traditionally, UNIX/Linux users type *who am i* to see information describing their session.

TIP   Another command that is similar to who is the *w* command. System administrators often use the *w* command to see not only who is logged in, but also what system resources, such as CPU resources, are being used.

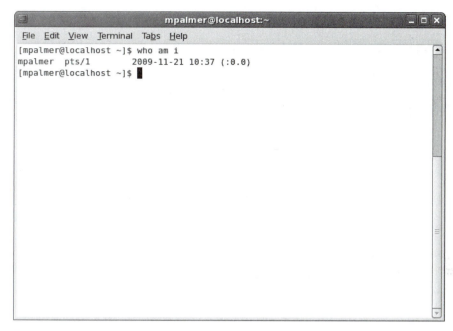

Figure 1-15   Using *who am i*

Project 1-6

At this point, your screen might seem filled with commands and their results. Use the *clear* command anytime you want a clean slate. This project enables you to clear the screen now.

To clear the screen:

1. Type **clear** on the command line, and press **Enter**. The command prompt is now in the upper-left corner of your screen.

Project 1-7

You can use the manual pages to learn more about a command or program (if the program is documented in the manual pages). In addition, the *whatis* command provides a quick summary of specific commands and programs. You use both the *man* and *whatis* commands in this project. The database for the *whatis* command should already be created prior to using the command.

To display online help using *man*:

1. Type **man who** in the command line, and press **Enter**. You see the explanation of the *who* command illustrated in Figure 1-16.

2. Press **Enter** one or more times to view additional lines of text. Next press the **Spacebar** to view additional pages of documentation.

3. Type **q** to exit the man program.

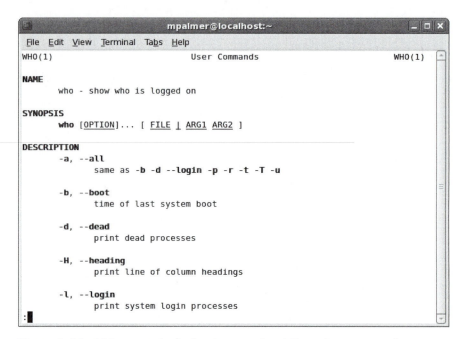

Figure 1-16   Using *man* to find out more about the *who* command

4. Type **man man** and press **Enter**. You see the man pages describing the *man* command. What is the purpose of the *-M* option?

5. Type **q** to exit the *man* program.

To display a brief description of a command with the *whatis* command:

1. Type **whatis who** and press **Enter**.

2. You see a summary of the *who* command, as follows:

```
who    (1p) - display who is on the system
who    (1) - show who is logged on
```

**HANDS-ON
PROJECTS**

Project 1-8

When you type a command and make a spelling or other mistake, you do not need to retype the entire command. You can use the command-line edit functions instead. In this project, you practice using the edit functions.

To edit a command typed on the command line:

1. Begin by determining the shell you are using. To determine the shell, type **echo $SHELL** and press **Enter**. If you are using the Bash shell, you see the following output:

   `/bin/bash`

   If you are not using the Bash shell, type **bash** and press **Enter**.

2. Type **who am I**, but do *not* press Enter.

3. Press the **left arrow** key to move the cursor to the letter **a** in the word "am."

4. Press **Alt+d** to delete the word "am."

5. Press **Ctrl+k** to delete the command line from the current cursor position.

6. Press **Ctrl+a** to move the cursor to the beginning of the command line.

7. Press **Ctrl+k** again to delete the command line.

8. Retype the command **who am I** but do *not* press Enter.

9. Press **Ctrl+b** eight times or until the cursor is positioned at the beginning of the line.

10. Press **Alt+l** three times. Each time you press the key combination, the cursor moves to the position just before the first character of the next word.

11. Press **Ctrl+a**, and then press **Ctrl+k** to clear the command line.

HANDS-ON PROJECTS

Project 1-9

You can execute multiple commands on one command line by using a semicolon between commands. You practice running multiple commands in this project.

To enter multiple commands on the command line:

1. Type **date ; cal** and press **Enter** to view the current date and this month's calendar. (Using the semicolon between commands works whether or not you put spaces before and after it. For example, you can enter either *date ; cal* or *date;cal*.)

2. Type **date ; who –uH** and press **Enter** (see Figure 1-17). The *date* command produces the first line of the output; the remainder of the output is the result of the *who* command.

HANDS-ON PROJECTS

Project 1-10

In this project, you use the command history capability of the Bash shell to recall commands you have used earlier. As you'll discover the more you use UNIX/Linux, this command-line capability saves lots of time otherwise spent on repeated typing.

To use the command-line history:

1. Type **date** and press **Enter**.

2. Type **who** and press **Enter**.

3. Type **who –uH** and press **Enter**.

4. Type **clear** and press **Enter**.

5. Press the **up arrow** key four times. The *date* command is recalled to the command line. Do not press Enter.

6. Press the **down arrow** key twice. What command do you see? Press **Enter** to execute the command.

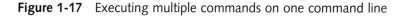

```
                        mpalmer@localhost:~                    _ □ ✕
File  Edit  View  Terminal  Tabs  Help
[mpalmer@localhost ~]$ date ; cal
Sat Nov 21 10:57:22 MST 2009
    November 2009
Su Mo Tu We Th Fr Sa
 1  2  3  4  5  6  7
 8  9 10 11 12 13 14
15 16 17 18 19 20 21
22 23 24 25 26 27 28
29 30

[mpalmer@localhost ~]$ date ; who -uH
Sat Nov 21 10:57:56 MST 2009
NAME     LINE        TIME             IDLE       PID COMMENT
mpalmer  pts/1       2009-11-21 10:57   .        2978 (:0.0)
[mpalmer@localhost ~]$ ▮
```

Figure 1-17   Executing multiple commands on one command line

Project 1-11

Your password is your means to protect your user account from others who might attempt to access it without your authorization. Plan to change your password often to keep your account secure. In this project, you learn how to change your password.

To change your password:

1. Type **passwd** after the command prompt, and press **Enter**.

2. Type your current password and press **Enter**. (On some systems, if you are logged in to the root account, you skip this step and go directly to Step 3.)

3. Type your new password and press **Enter**. Your new password does not appear on the screen as you type.

4. Retype your new password and press **Enter** so that UNIX/Linux can confirm the new password.

TIP

If the password you retype as confirmation does not match your new password, UNIX/Linux asks you to enter the password again. UNIX/Linux might also ask you to choose a different password because you chose one that is too short, too easily guessed, or one you have used previously.

HANDS-ON PROJECTS

Project 1-12

The *cat* command has several purposes, but one of the most commonly used is to view the contents of a file. For example, in this project, you use the *cat* command to view a file called shells that resides in the /etc directory. This file contains a list of valid shell programs available through UNIX/Linux.

To use *cat* to view the shells file:

1. Type **cat /etc/shells** after the command prompt, and press **Enter** (see Figure 1-18). (The forward slash (/) is used to indicate a directory or folder change.) What shells do you see on your system?

```
mpalmer@localhost:~

File  Edit  View  Terminal  Tabs  Help
[mpalmer@localhost ~]$ cat /etc/shells
/bin/sh
/bin/bash
/sbin/nologin
/bin/tcsh
/bin/csh
/bin/ksh
[mpalmer@localhost ~]$ █
```

Figure 1-18   Using the *cat* command to view the contents of a file

2. Sometimes, it is helpful to see a file's contents displayed with line numbers. The *-n* option causes the *cat* command to display a number at the beginning of each line of output. Type **cat –n /etc/shells** and press **Enter**. You see the same list of shells as before, but this time a number precedes each line.

Project 1-13

You can also view another file in the /etc directory called termcap. This multiple-page file contains many specifications about all terminals supported on a Linux system. The *cat* command is not a practical way to view this file, which is longer than one screen. However, as you learn in this project, you can use the *more* and *less* commands to read a large file, screen by screen.

To view the contents of large files on the screen with the *more* command:

1. Type **more /etc/termcap** after the command prompt, and press **Enter** (see Figure 1-19).

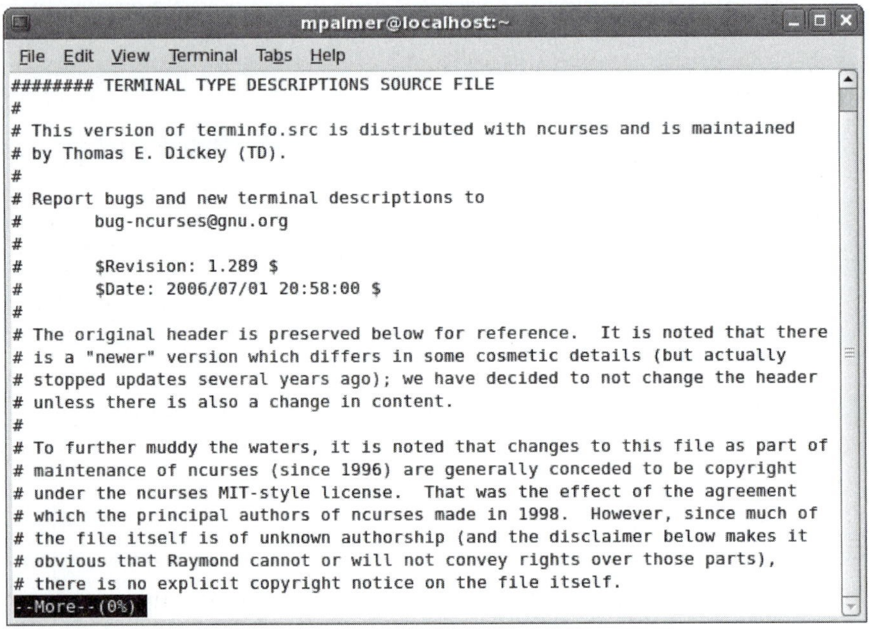

```
######## TERMINAL TYPE DESCRIPTIONS SOURCE FILE
#
# This version of terminfo.src is distributed with ncurses and is maintained
# by Thomas E. Dickey (TD).
#
# Report bugs and new terminal descriptions to
#        bug-ncurses@gnu.org
#
#        $Revision: 1.289 $
#        $Date: 2006/07/01 20:58:00 $
#
# The original header is preserved below for reference.  It is noted that there
# is a "newer" version which differs in some cosmetic details (but actually
# stopped updates several years ago); we have decided to not change the header
# unless there is also a change in content.
#
# To further muddy the waters, it is noted that changes to this file as part of
# maintenance of ncurses (since 1996) are generally conceded to be copyright
# under the ncurses MIT-style license.  That was the effect of the agreement
# which the principal authors of ncurses made in 1998.  However, since much of
# the file itself is of unknown authorship (and the disclaimer below makes it
# obvious that Raymond cannot or will not convey rights over those parts),
# there is no explicit copyright notice on the file itself.
--More--(0%)
```

Figure 1-19 Using the *more* command to view, screen by screen, the contents of a large file

2. Press the **Spacebar** to scroll to the next screen.

3. Terminate the display by typing **q** (for quit).

To view the contents of large files on the screen with the *less* command:

1. Type **less /etc/termcap** after the command prompt, and press **Enter**. You see a long file of text on your screen.

2. Press the **down arrow** key several times to scroll forward in the file one line at a time.

3. Press the **up arrow** key several times to scroll backward in the file one line at a time.

4. Press **Pg Dn** (or Page Down), **Spacebar**, **z**, or **f** to scroll forward one screen.

5. Press **Pg Up** (or Page Up) or **b** to return to a previous screen.

6. Terminate the display by typing **q** (for quit).

For Knoppix users, there is no termcap file in the /etc directory. Replace termcap with mailcap by using /etc/mailcap in the steps for this project and in Project 1-14.

Project 1-14

Sometimes, you only need to glimpse part of a file's contents to determine what is stored in the file. In this project, you use the *head* command to view the beginning 10 lines in a file, and then you use the *tail* command to view the final 10 lines in the file.

To view the first and final few lines of a file:

1. Type **head /etc/termcap** and press **Enter** to see the first 10 lines of the /etc/termcap file.

2. The *-n* option specifies the number of lines the *head* command displays. Type **head –n 5 /etc/termcap** and press **Enter**. You see the first five lines of the /etc/termcap file.

3. The *tail* command shows you the final few lines of a file. Like the *head* command, *tail* displays 10 lines by default. Type **tail /etc/termcap** and press **Enter** to see the final 10 lines of the /etc/termcap file.

4. The *-n* option specifies the number of lines the *tail* command displays. Type **tail –n 5 /etc/termcap** and press **Enter**. You see the final five lines of the /etc/termcap file.

Project 1-15

You already used the *who* command to find out who is logged in to a computer. In this project, you use the same command with the > redirection operator to save this information in a text file.

To save to a file that lists persons logged in to the system:

1. Type **who > current_users** after the command prompt, and press **Enter**. The *who* command output does not appear on the screen, but is redirected to a new disk file called current_users. UNIX/Linux places this text file in the active directory (the directory on the disk where you are currently using the system).

2. Type **cat current_users** after the command prompt, and press **Enter** to see a list of users currently using the system, such as the following:

```
mpalmer  pts/1  2009-11-23  15:14  (:0.0)
```

Project 1-16

You can also use the output redirection operator with the *cal* command to save a calendar in a text file. For example, assume that you are involved in a development project with a projected deadline in the year 2009. You can save the calendar in a text file.

To save the year 2009 calendar in a file:

1. Type **cal 2009 > year_2009** after the command prompt, and press **Enter**. This creates a text file called year_2009.

2. Type **less year_2009** and press **Enter** to see the calendar created by the previous command. Use the arrow keys, Pg Dn (or Page Down), Pg Up (or Page Up), and other keys to scroll through the file.

3. Terminate the display by typing **q** (for quit).

Project 1-17

As you work with UNIX/Linux, you remember that your supervisor asked you to complete a few tasks by the end of the week. In this project, you decide to create a notes file of task reminders by using the *cat* command with the > redirection operator.

To create a new file:

1. Type **cat > notes** after the command prompt, and press **Enter**.

2. Type the following: **Remember to order a new CD-ROM, and send the report by Thursday**, and press **Enter**.

3. Press **Ctrl+d**.

4. To review the file you just created, type **cat notes** after the command prompt, and press **Enter**. The sentence you typed in Step 2 appears on the screen.

After you create the notes file, you remember that your supervisor asked you to complete another task. You can append the reminder to the existing notes file. You also want to include the appropriate monthly calendar in the file for reference.

To add information to an existing file:

1. Type **cat >> notes** after the command prompt, and press **Enter**.

2. Type the following: **Also remember to make reservations for Sept. conference**, and press **Enter**.

3. Press **Ctrl+d**.

4. To add the September calendar to your notes, type **cal 9 2009 >> notes** and press **Enter**.

5. Type **less notes** and then press **Enter** to review the file (see Figure 1-20).

6. Type **q** to exit the file.

7. Exit the command-line display by closing the terminal window or by terminating your Telnet or SSH session.

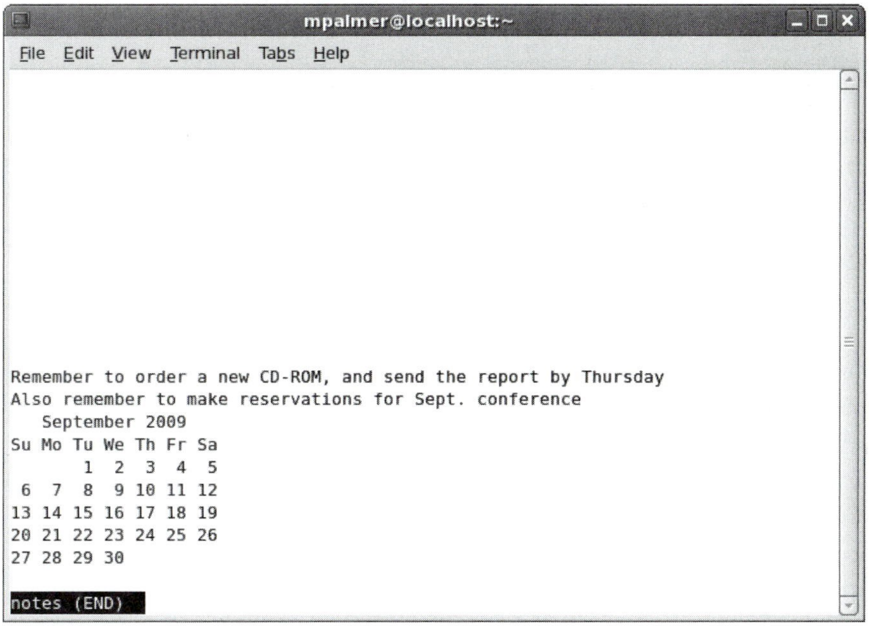

```
mpalmer@localhost:~

File  Edit  View  Terminal  Tabs  Help




Remember to order a new CD-ROM, and send the report by Thursday
Also remember to make reservations for Sept. conference
    September 2009
Su Mo Tu We Th Fr Sa
       1  2  3  4  5
 6  7  8  9 10 11 12
13 14 15 16 17 18 19
20 21 22 23 24 25 26
27 28 29 30
notes (END)
```

Figure 1-20 Viewing the contents of the notes file

DISCOVERY EXERCISES

1. Use the *whatis* command to determine the purpose of the *ls* command.

2. Use the *man* program to find out what the *-R* option does when used with the *date* command.

3. Use the *man* program to determine what other commands you should also see in relation to the *clear* command.

4. Use the *cal* command to determine on what day of the week you were born.

5. Use the *cal* command to determine which years between 2006 and 2015 are leap years.

6. Clear the screen, and view the online manual to determine how to display today's date in UTC.

7. Display the current UTC.

8. Create a file called month containing the current month.

9. View the contents of the month file you created in Exercise 8.

10. Use the *who* command to determine the idle time for users currently logged in, but output that information to a file called users_info. Next, view the file you created.

11. View the files, month and users_info, in sequence using only one command-line sequence of commands.

12. View the files month and users_info in sequence by using:

    ❏ The *less* command

    ❏ The *more* command

13. Create a file called who_info that contains the documentation for the *who* command. Next, use the *less* command to view the who_info file contents, and scroll forward and backward through the information. Then use the *tail* command to view the final 12 lines of the who_info file. Finally, use the *head* command to view the first 12 lines of the who_info file.

14. Create a file called favorite_foods, and list your favorite foods, entering five or six or more. Press Enter after each favorite food so it appears on its own line (make certain you also press Enter after the final food item). After the file is created, add two more foods you like that are not on the list (press Enter after the final food item). View the list of foods to make certain the two items you added appear at the end of the list.

15. View the documentation for *who*, and then view the documentation for *w*. How are these commands similar?

16. Run the *who -uH* and *w* commands using one command-line sequence to compare the results.

17. Determine when the computer on which you are working was last booted.

18. Use the command-line history function to determine the most recent two commands you entered.

19. Run the *who -H*, *cal 2009*, and *clear* commands using one command-line sequence. What do you end up with on the screen?

20. Use the history function to retrieve the command line you used in Exercise 19. Use the edit function to remove the word "clear" and replace it with "date." Next, go to the beginning of "cal" and delete the text on the line from "cal" to the end. Now, change the *-H* to *-u*. Finally, add "*date -u*" so that your final command-line entry is *who -u ; date -u*. Execute the command-line entries.

2

EXPLORING THE UNIX/LINUX FILE SYSTEMS AND FILE SECURITY

After reading this chapter and completing the exercises, you will be able to:

♦ Discuss UNIX/Linux file systems

♦ Explain partitions and inodes

♦ Understand the elements of the root hierarchy

♦ Use the *mount* command

♦ Explain and use paths, pathnames, and prompts

♦ Navigate the file system

♦ Create and remove directories

♦ Copy and delete files

♦ Configure file permissions

An essential reason for deploying UNIX/Linux is to store and use information. A file system enables you to create and manage information, run programs, and save information to use later. Through a file system, you can protect information and programs to ensure that only specific users have access. You can also copy information from one location to another, and you can delete information you are no longer using.

In this chapter, you explore UNIX/Linux file systems, including the basic concepts of directories and files and their organization in a hierarchical tree structure. You learn to navigate the file system, and then you practice what you've learned by creating directories and files and copying files from one directory to another. You also have the opportunity to set directory and file permissions, which is vital for security in a UNIX/Linux multiuser system.

Understanding UNIX/Linux File Systems

In UNIX/Linux, a **file** is the basic component for data storage. UNIX/Linux consider everything with which they interact a file, even attached devices such as the monitor, keyboard, and printer. A **file system** is the UNIX/Linux system's way of organizing files on storage devices, such as hard disks and CDs or DVDs. A **physical file system** is a section of the hard disk that has been formatted to hold files. UNIX/Linux consist of multiple file systems that form virtual storage space for multiple users. **Virtual storage** in this sense is storage that can be allocated using different disks or file systems (or both), but that is transparently accessible as storage to the operating system and users. The file system's organization is a hierarchical structure similar to an inverted tree; that is, it is a branching structure in which top-level files contain other files, which in turn contain other files. Figure 2-1 illustrates a typical UNIX/Linux hierarchical structure.

One reason why UNIX and Linux systems are so versatile is that they support many different file systems. Some file systems are native to UNIX/Linux and others provide compatibility with different operating systems, such as Windows.

Most versions of UNIX and Linux support the **UNIX file system (ufs)**, which is the original native UNIX file system. ufs is a hierarchical (tree structure) file system that is expandable, supports large amounts of storage, provides excellent security, and is reliable. In fact, many qualities of other file systems are modeled after ufs. ufs supports **journaling**, so that if a system crashes unexpectedly, it is possible to reconstruct files or to roll back recent changes for minimal or no damage to the integrity of the files or data. Journaling means that the file system keeps a log (journal) of its own activities. If the operating system crashes or is not properly shut down, such as during a power failure, the operating system reads the journal file when it is restarted. The information in the journal file enables files to be brought back to their previous or stable state before the crash. This is particularly important for files that were being updated before the crash and that did not have time to finish writing the updates to disk. ufs also supports **hot fixes**, which automatically move data on damaged portions of disks to areas that are not damaged.

In Linux, the native file system is called the **extended file system** (**ext** or **ext fs**), which is installed by default. ext is modeled after ufs, but the first version contained some bugs, supported files up to only 2 GB, and did not offer journaling. However, in Linux, ext provides an advantage over all other file systems because it enables the use of the full range of built-in Linux commands, file manipulation, and security. Newer versions of Linux use either the second (ext2), third (ext3), or fourth (ext4) versions of the extended file system. ext2 is a reliable file system that handles large disk storage. ext3 has the enhancements of ext2, with the addition of journaling.

Appearing in October 2006, ext4 is the newest version of ext. ext4 allows a single volume to hold up to 1 exabyte (1,152,921,504,606,846,976 bytes, which is over 1.1 quintillion bytes) of data and it enables the use of extents. An **extent** is used to reduce file fragmentation, because a block of contiguous disk storage can be reserved for a file. For example, consider a file of names and addresses that continuously grows as you add more people. Each

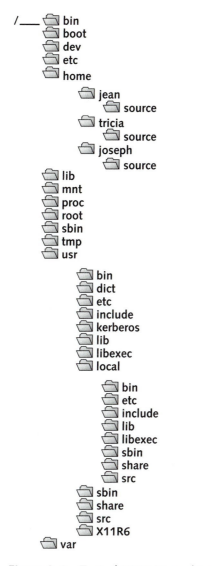

Figure 2-1 Typical UNIX/Linux hierarchical structure

time you add more people to the file, the new data is stored right next to the old in the extent of contiguous disk space reserved for that file. This is an improvement over other file systems in which the new data may be stored in a different location on the disk. Over time the data in a file (without the use of an extent) may be spread all over the disk, resulting in more time to locate data and more disk wear.

NOTE

ext3 and ext4 are compatible unless extents are used in ext4. ext3 is also compatible with ext2. This means that many disk utilities that work with ext2 are likely to work with ext3 and ext4 (without the use of extents in ext4). Also note that a gigabyte is 2^{30}, whereas an exabyte is significantly larger at 2^{60} in binary, or 10^9 compared to 10^{18} in decimal.

Table 2-1 summarizes ufs, ext, and other file systems typically supported by UNIX/Linux. Also, Table 2-2 compares FAT, NTFS, ext4, and ufs to give you a taste of what to consider when using a file system. As you consider a file system, keep in mind that the actual capabilities of that file system are also contingent on what is supported by the UNIX/Linux operating system you use, and even the version of the kernel in that particular operating system.

Table 2-1 Typical file systems supported by UNIX/Linux

File System	Description
Extended file system (ext or ext fs) and the newer versions: second extended file system (ext2 or ext2 fs), third extended file system (ext3 or ext3 fs), and fourth extended file system (ext4 or ext4 fs)	Comes with Linux by default (compatible with Linux and FreeBSD); ext3 offers journaling, which is important for reliability and recovery when a system goes down unexpectedly; ext4 adds larger volume sizes plus extents
High-performance file system (HPFS)	Developed for use with the OS/2 operating system
International Organization for Standardization (ISO) Standard Operating System 9660 (iso9660 in Linux, hsfs in Solaris, cd9660 in FreeBSD)	Developed for CD and DVD use; does not support long file names
Journaled File System (JFS)	Modeled after IBM's JFS; offers mature journaling features, fast performance for processing larger files, dynamic inode allocation for better use of free space, and specialized approaches for organizing either small or large directory structures
msdos	Offers compatibility with FAT12 and FAT16 (does not support long file names); typically installed to enable UNIX to read floppy disks made in MS-DOS or Windows
Network file system (NFS)	Developed by Sun Microsystems for UNIX systems to support network access and sharing of files (such as uploading and downloading); supported on virtually all UNIX/Linux versions as well as many other operating systems
NT file system (NTFS)	Used by Windows NT, Windows 2000, Windows XP, Windows Vista, and Windows Server systems
Proc file system	Presents information about the kernel status and the use of memory (not truly a physical file system, but a logical file system)

Table 2-1 Typical file systems supported by UNIX/Linux (continued)

File System	Description
ReiserFS	Developed by Hans Reiser and similar to ext3 and ext4, with journaling capabilities; designed to be faster than ext3 and ext4 (up to 15 times) for handling small files; intended to encourage programmers to create efficient code through use of smaller files
Swap file system	File system for the swap space—that is, disk space used exclusively to store spillover information from memory when memory is full (called virtual memory) and used by virtually all UNIX/Linux systems; on newer UNIX/Linux systems, the swap file system is encrypted for improved security
Universal Disk Format (UDF)	Developed for CD and DVD use and broadly replacing iso9660. UDF read capability is supported in Windows, UNIX/Linux, and Mac OS systems prior to 2006; read/write capability is supported in Windows Vista, UNIX/Linux versions after 2005, and Mac OS Tiger and the newer Leopard.
uMS/DOS	Compatible with extended FAT16 as used by Windows NT, 2000, XP, Vista, and Server, but also supports security permissions, file ownership, and long file names
UNIX file system (ufs; also called the Berkeley Fast File System)	Original file system for UNIX; compatible with virtually all UNIX systems and most Linux systems
vfat	Compatible with FAT32 and supports long file names
XFS	Silicon Graphics' file system for the Irix version of UNIX; offers many types of journaling features and is targeted for use with large disk farms (multiple disk storage devices available through high-speed connections)

Table 2-2 Comparison of typical file systems supported by UNIX/Linux

Feature	FAT	NTFS	ext4	ufs
Total volume or partition size	2 GB to 2 TB	2 TB	1 exabyte in Linux depending on the kernel version*	1 TB in Linux; 4 GB to 2 TB in UNIX depending on the version

Table 2-2 Comparison of typical file systems supported by UNIX/Linux (continued)

Feature	FAT	NTFS	ext4	ufs
Maximum file size	2 GB for FAT16; 4 GB for FAT32	Potentially 16 TB, but limited by the volume size (up to 2 TB)	16 GB to 2 TB in Linux depending on the kernel version*	2 GB in Linux; 2 GB to 16 TB in UNIX depending on the version
Security	Limited security based on attributes and shares	Extensive security through permissions, groups, and auditing options	Extensive security through permissions and groups	Extensive security through permissions and groups
Reliability through file activity tracking or journaling	None	Journaling	Journaling	Journaling
POSIX support	None (FAT16); limited (FAT32)	Yes	Yes	Yes
Reliability through hot fix capability	Limited	Supported	Supported	Supported
Support for extents	No	Yes, when pre-allocated via a program	Yes, when enabled	No
*These maximums are limited by the kernel version and are based on Linux kernel version 2.6.19.				

Understanding the Standard Tree Structure

The treelike structure for UNIX/Linux file systems starts at the root file system level. Root is the name of the file at this basic level, and it is denoted by the slash character (/). The slash represents the **root file system directory**. Notice in Figure 2-1 that there is also a directory that is used to store files for the root account, but this is designated as /root and is under the main root file system directory (/).

A **directory** is a special kind of file that can contain other files and directories. Regular files store information, such as records of employee names and addresses or payroll information, while directory files store the names of regular files and the names of other directories, which are called **subdirectories**. The subdirectory is considered the **child** of the **parent** directory because the child directory is created within the parent directory. In Figure 2-1, the root system directory (/) is the parent of all the other directories, such as /bin, /boot, /dev, /etc, /home, and so on. The /home directory is the parent of the /jean, /tricia, and /joseph subdirectories; /usr is the parent of the /bin, /dict, and /etc subdirectories.

2

Using UNIX/Linux Partitions

The section of the disk that holds a file system is called a **partition**. One disk might have many partitions, each separated from the others so that it remains unaffected by external disturbances such as structural file problems associated with another partition. When you install UNIX/Linux on your computer, one of your first tasks is deciding how to partition your hard drive (or hard drives, if you have more than one).

UNIX/Linux partitions are identified with names; for example, Linux uses "hda1" and "hda2" for some types of disks. In this case, the first two letters tell Linux the device type; "hd," for instance, identifies the commonly used IDE type of hard disk. The third letter, "a" in this case, indicates whether the disk is the primary or secondary disk (a=primary, b=secondary).

Partitions on a disk are numbered starting with 1. The name "hda1" tells Linux that this is the first partition on the disk, and the name "hda2" indicates it is the second partition on the same disk. If you have a second hard disk with two partitions, the partitions are identified as "hdb1" and "hdb2."

Computer storage devices such as hard disks are called peripheral devices. Computer **peripherals** connect to the computer through electronic interfaces. The two most popular hard disk interfaces are **Integrated Drive Electronics (IDE)** and **Small Computer System Interface (SCSI)**. **Enhanced IDE (EIDE)**, which is IDE with built-in speed improvements, is now used more commonly than the original IDE technology, but often appears in computer system information as IDE.

On PCs used by individuals, IDE/EIDE hard disk drives (identified as hd*x*) are more common than SCSI (pronounced "scuzzy"). SCSI is faster and more reliable, so it is often used on servers. If you have a primary SCSI hard disk with two partitions, the two partitions are named "sda1" and "sda2." Figure 2-2 shows two partition tables: one with an IDE drive and the other with a SCSI drive.

TIP

IDE is sometimes referred to as Integrated Device Electronics. The American National Standards Institute (ANSI) standard for IDE is actually named Advanced Technology Attachment (ATA). ATA and SCSI are standards developed by the ANSI-sponsored T10 and T13 committees; you can find out more about them by visiting *www.T10.org* and *http://www.t13.org/*.

NOTE

Modern computers come with one or more Universal Serial Bus (USB) connections for connecting keyboards, pointing devices, printers, and external hard drives. An external hard drive (that you plug into a USB port on your computer) may be referred to as a Serial ATA, SATA, or eSATA drive. SATA/eSATA is a newer technology than ATA, and the bottom line for the user is that it is generally faster than ATA (when used with a USB 2.0 port). Also, internal SATA drives are in many new PCs.

```
Disk/dev/hda: 128 heads, 63 sectors, 767 cylinders
Units = cylinders of 8064 * 512 bytes

Device      Boot  Begin   Start     End     Blocks   Id  System
/dev/hda1    *       1       1       242    975712+    6  DOS 32-bit >=32M
/dev/hda2           243     243      767   2116899     5  Extended
/dev/hda3           243     243      275    127024+   83  Linux native
/dev/hda6           276     276      750   1028224+   83  Linux native
/dev/hda7           751     751      767     68512+   82  Linux swap

Command (m for help):  _
```
This partition table is from a Linux system with an IDE drive

```
Disk /dev/sda: 255 heads, 63 sectors, 1106 cylinders
Units = cylinders of 16065 * 512 bytes

Device      Boot  Begin   Start     End     Blocks   Id  System
/dev/sda1            1       1        64    514048+   83  Linux native
/dev/sda2           65      65      1106   8369865     5  Extended
/dev/sda5           65      65      1084   8193118+   83  Linux native
/dev/sda6         1085    1085      1100    128488+   82  Linux swap

Command (m for help):  _
```
This partition table is from a Linux system with a SCSI drive

Figure 2-2   Sample Linux partition tables

Note that the first table in Figure 2-2 identifies "hda" as the device, which indicates an IDE drive. The second table identifies "sda" as the device, which indicates a SCSI drive.

Fedora, Red Hat Enterprise Linux, and SUSE have an Automatic Partitioning option that you can select as you are installing these systems. This tool automatically allocates space to create the swap, /boot, and root partitions described in the next section of this book.

Setting Up Hard Disk Partitions

Partitioning your hard disk provides organized space to contain your file systems. If one file system fails, you can work with another. This section provides general guidelines on how to partition hard disks. These recommendations are suggestions only. How you partition your hard disk might vary depending on your system's configuration, number of users, and planned use. Partition size is measured in megabytes (MB, about a million characters) or gigabytes (GB, about a billion characters). Some UNIX/Linux vendors recommend at least three partitions: root, swap, and /boot.

You can begin the process by setting up a partition for the root file system, which holds the root file system directory (remember that this is referred to as "/"). A partition must be mounted before it becomes part of the file system. The kernel mounts the root file system when the system starts.

TIP References to the root file system directory (/) and to the directory used by the root account (/root) can get confusing. Some UNIX/Linux users refer to the root file system directory as "slash" and to /root as the "root directory" to help avoid confusion.

2

The size of the root partition depends on the type of installation you are performing. For example, in Fedora, Red Hat Enterprise Linux, or SUSE, the root partition should be a minimum of 1.2 GB to load the basic operating system required for a workstation or portable computer installation. A 1.2 GB partition for a basic system does not include enough space to load the GNOME desktop or many software packages. If you are setting up a server or loading the full complement of software packages that come with Fedora, Red Hat Enterprise Linux, or SUSE, use a partition of 5-10 GB or larger. Besides loading the software packages, this allows space for a desktop, such as GNOME, KDE, or a combination of both. (You learn more about desktops in Chapter 11, "The X Window System.")

After creating the root partition, you should set up the swap partition. The **swap partition** acts like an extension of memory, so that UNIX/Linux have more room to run large programs. As a general rule, the swap partition should be the same size as the amount of RAM in your computer. For instance, if you have 256 MB of RAM, make your swap space 256 MB. If you have a large amount of RAM, such as 1 GB, but your disk space is limited, you can make the swap space smaller than 1 GB. However, before configuring the swap partition, check the documentation for your version of UNIX/Linux. For example, for Fedora and Red Hat Enterprise Linux, Red Hat suggests that your swap space be a minimum of 256 MB, or two times the size of the RAM in the computer (use the larger figure). For SUSE, consider a swap partition of about 500 MB or a little larger. However, the swap space should not be too large, such as over 2 GB, because then you begin sacrificing speed because disk access is slower than direct RAM access. For instance, if you have 256 MB of RAM in a Fedora system, it doesn't make sense to allocate 2 GB of disk for the swap partition. From the standpoint of performance, it makes more sense to install 256 MB more RAM for a total of 512 MB and then allocate 1 GB for the swap partition.

A swap partition enables virtual memory. **Virtual memory** means you have what seem to be unlimited memory resources. Swap partitions accomplish this by providing swap space on a disk and treating it like an extension of memory (RAM). It is called swap space because the system can use it to swap information between disk and RAM. Setting up swap space makes your computer run faster and more efficiently.

TIP You can create and use more than one swap partition in Linux. Having multiple swap partitions spread across several hard disks can sometimes improve application performance on busy systems. Also note that you can often improve the speed of a server by installing higher amounts of RAM, such as 1 GB or more.

The **/boot partition** is used to store the operating system files that compose the kernel. The size of this partition depends on how much space is needed for the operating system files in your version of UNIX/Linux. Generally, this is a relatively small partition. For example, if you are installing Fedora, Red Hat Enterprise Linux, or SUSE, consider creating a /boot partition that is about 100 to 200 MB in size.

If you plan to have multiple users accessing your system, consider having a **/usr partition** in which to store some or all of the nonkernel operating system programs that are accessed by users. These programs include software development packages that support computer programming, networking, Internet access, graphical screens (including desktop software), and the large number of UNIX/Linux utilities. **Utilities** are programs that perform operations such as copying files, listing directories, and communicating with other users. The /usr partition should be large enough—such as 10 GB or more—to accommodate all of the software that you install.

Also, if you plan to have multiple users access the system, you can create a **/home partition**, which is the home directory for all users' directories. Having separate /usr and /home partitions makes many system administration tasks, such as backing up only software or only data, much easier.

The /home partition is the storage space for all users' work. If the root partition (/)—or any other partition—crashes, having a /home partition ensures that you do not lose all the users' information. Although regular user accounts are restricted from reading information in other partitions, you own and can access most files in your home directory. You can grant or deny access to your files as you choose. See "Configuring File Permissions for Security" later in this chapter for more information on file ownership.

Finally, you can create a **/var partition** to hold files that are created temporarily, such as files used for printing documents (spool files) and files used to record monitoring and adminis-tration data, often called log files. Fedora, Red Hat Enterprise Linux, and SUSE also use the /var partition for files used to update the operating system. Plan on using a /var partition that is over 5 GB.

Consider a small geological research company that plans to set up a Red Hat Enterprise Linux server that has 512 MB of RAM. The company might set up a swap partition at 1024 MB. The /boot partition would be 150 MB. They plan to install 20 GB of nonkernel programs for users, so there might be a 25 to 50 GB /usr partition (allowing for programs not currently anticipated). Each of the 15 users will be allocated 10 GB of space in their home directories, which means the /home partition must be at least 150 GB (adding another 20 GB or more would provide some margin for extra needs). Finally, a 10 GB /var partition should be created because all of the users print large documents, often at the same time.

TIP Setting up partitions might seem like a big task when you are learning UNIX/Linux. Fortunately, many operating systems, including Fedora, Red Hat Enter-prise Linux, and SUSE, offer tools to automatically set up partitions during installation (see Appendix C, "How to Install Fedora and How to Use the Knoppix CD"). Consider using these tools until you have more experience with UNIX/Linux.

Using Inodes

Partitions containing directories and files in the ufs and ext file systems are built on the concept of **information nodes**, or **inodes**. Each directory or file has an inode and is identified by an inode number. Inode 0 contains the root of the directory structure (/) and is the jumping-off point for all other inodes.

An inode contains (1) the name of a directory or file, (2) general information about that directory/file, and (3) information (a pointer) about how to locate the directory/file on a disk partition. In terms of general information, each inode indicates the user and group ownership, the access mode (read, write, and execute security permissions, discussed later in this chapter), the size and type of the file, the date the file was created, and the date the file was last modified and read.

The pointer information is based on logical blocks. Each disk is divided into logical blocks ranging in size (depending on the version of UNIX/Linux) from 512 to 8,192 bytes or more (blocks can also be divided into multiple subblocks or fractions as needed by the file system). The inode for a file contains a pointer (number) that tells the operating system how to locate the first in a set of one or more logical blocks that contain the specific file contents (or, it specifies the number of blocks or links to the first block used by the directory or file). In short, the inode tells the operating system where to find a file on the hard disk.

Everything in the UNIX/Linux file system is tied to inodes. Space is allocated one block, or fraction of a block, at a time. Directories are really simple files that have been marked with a directory flag in their inodes. The file system itself is identified by the superblock. The **superblock** contains information about the layout of blocks on a specific partition. This information is the key to finding anything on the file system, and it should never change. Without the superblock, the file system cannot be accessed. For this reason, many copies of the superblock are written into the file system at the time the file system is created through partitioning and formatting. If the superblock is destroyed, you can copy one of the superblock copies over the original, damaged superblock to restore access to the file system.

TIP

You can display inode information for directories and files by using the *ls –i* command, which you will learn later in this chapter.

EXPLORING THE ROOT HIERARCHY

The root (/) file system is mounted by the kernel when the system starts. To **mount** a file system is to connect it to the directory tree structure. The system administrator uses the *mount* command to mount a file system.

UNIX/Linux must mount a file system before any programs can access files on that file system. After mounting, the root file system is accessible for reading only during the initial systems check and boot-up sequence—after that, it is remounted as read and write. The root file system contains all essential programs for file system repair: restoring from a backup, starting the system, and initializing all devices and operating resources. It also contains the information for mounting all other file systems. Nothing beyond these essentials should reside in the root partition.

 You can restore a crashed root partition using rescue files stored on disks, CDs, DVDs, tapes, or other removable media. The installation media that comes with Fedora, Red Hat Enterprise Linux, and SUSE can be used to create rescue discs, **TIP** or your installation CDs/DVDs can double as rescue discs.

The following sections describe commonly used directories under the root file system.

The /bin Directory

The /bin directory contains **binaries**, or **executables**, which are the programs needed to start the system and perform other essential system tasks. This directory holds many programs that all users need to work with UNIX/Linux.

The /boot Directory

The /boot directory normally contains the files needed by the **bootstrap loader** (the utility that starts the operating system); it also contains the kernel (operating system) images.

The /dev Directory

Files in /dev reference system devices. They access system devices and resources, such as the hard disks, mice, printers, consoles, modems, memory, and CD/DVD drives. UNIX/Linux versions include many device files in the /dev directory to accommodate separate vendor devices that can be attached to the computer.

UNIX/Linux devices are managed through the use of **device special files**, which contain information about I/O devices that are used by the operating system kernel when a device is accessed. In many UNIX/Linux systems, two types of device special files exist:

- **Block special files** (also called block device files) are used to manage random access devices that involve handling blocks of data, including CD/DVD drives, hard disk drives, tape drives, and other storage devices.
- **Character special files** (also called character device files) handle byte-by-byte streams of data, such as through serial or universal serial bus (USB) connections, including terminals, printers, and network communications. USB is a relatively high-speed I/O port found on most modern computers. It is used to interface mice, keyboards, monitors, digital sound cards, disk drives, and other external computer hardware, such as printers and digital cameras.

TIP Another method for managing devices is the use of a named pipe, which offers a method for handling internal communications, such as redirecting file output to a monitor. You learn about piping in Chapter 5.

2

When you install a UNIX/Linux operating system, device special files are created for the devices already installed on the system. Table 2-3 shows a sampling of device special files.

Table 2-3   UNIX/Linux device special files

File	Description
/dev/console	For the console components, such as the monitor and keyboard attached to the computer (/dev/tty0 is also used at the same time on many systems)
/dev/fd*n*	For floppy disk drives, where *n* is the number of the drive, such as fd0 for the first floppy disk drive
/dev/hd*xn*	For IDE and EIDE hard drives, where *x* represents the disk and the *n* represents the partition number, such as hda1 for the first disk and partition
/dev/modem	For a modem, a symbolic link to the device special file (typically linked to /dev/ttys1), where a symbolic link enables one file or directory to point to another (in later versions of Fedora/Red Hat Enterprise Linux, the modem file may be in /usr/share/applications, and in SUSE this file may be under /usr/share/applications/YaST2 because it is managed using the YaST management tool)
/dev/mouse	For a mouse or other pointing device, a symbolic link to the device special file (typically linked to /dev/ttys0)—in Fedora/Red Hat Enterprise Linux, the mouse file may be under /usr/share/applications, and in SUSE it may be under /opt/gnome/share/applications
/dev/sd*xn*	For a hard drive connected to a SCSI interface, where *x* represents the disk and the *n* represents the partition, such as sda1 for the first SCSI drive and first partition on that drive
/dev/st*n*	For a SCSI tape drive, where *n* represents the number of the drive, such as st0 for the first tape drive
/dev/tty*n*	For serial terminals connected to the computer
/dev/ttys*n*	For a serial device connected to the computer, such as ttys0 for the mouse

TIP

If you need to create a device special file for a new device, you can do so by using the *mknod* command as in the following general steps: 1. Log in to the root account. 2. Access a terminal window or the command prompt. 3. Type *cd /dev* and press Enter to switch to the /dev folder. 4. Use the *mknod* command plus the device special file name, such as ttys42, and the type of file, such as character (c) or block (b), and a major and minor node value used by the kernel (check with the device manufacturer for these values). For example, you might type *mknod ttys20 c 8 68*, and press Enter for a new serial device.

You can see the list of device files by typing *ls -l /dev* and pressing Enter after the command prompt. (See "Listing Directory Contents" later in this chapter for more information on the *ls* command.) The far-left character in the list tells you whether the file is a character device (c) or a block device (b), as shown in Figure 2-3. Try Hands-on Project 2-8 to view the contents of the /dev directory on your computer. Hands-on Project 2-8 also teaches you to use the *ls* command.

Explanations of the kinds of items you will see in the /dev directory are as follows:

- *console* refers to the system's console, which is the monitor connected directly to your system.

- *ttyS1* and *cua1* are devices used to access serial ports. For example, /dev/ttyS1 refers to COM2, the communication port on your PC.

- *cua* devices are callout devices used in conjunction with a modem.

- Device names beginning with *hd* access IDE hard drives.

- Device names beginning with *sd* are SCSI drives.

- Device names beginning with *lp* access parallel ports. The lp0 device refers to LPT1, the line printer.

- *null* is a "black hole"; any data sent to this device is gone forever. Use this device when you want to suppress the output of a command appearing on your screen. Chapters 6 and 7 ("Introduction to Shell Script Programming" and "Advanced Shell Programming," respectively) discuss this technique.

- Device names beginning with *tty* refer to terminals or consoles. Several "virtual consoles" are available on your Linux system. (You access them by pressing (Ctrl+Alt+F1, Ctrl+Alt+F2, and so on.) Device names beginning with *pty* are "pseudoterminals." They are used to provide a terminal to remote login sessions. For example, if your machine is on a network, incoming remote logins would use one of the *pty* devices in /dev.

The /etc Directory

The /etc directory contains configuration files that the system uses when the computer starts. Most of this directory is reserved for the system administrator, and it contains system-critical information stored in the following files:

- *fstab*—The mapping information about file systems to devices (such as hard disks and CDs/DVDs)

Some block devices in /dev

```
brw-rw-r--   1 root   floppy    2,     0 May 5 2008 fd0
brw-rw----   1 root   disk      3,     0 May 5 2008 hda
brw-rw----   1 root   disk      3,     1 May 5 2008 hda1
brw-rw----   1 root   disk      3,    64 May 5 2008 hdb
brw-rw----   1 root   disk      3,    65 May 5 2008 hdb1
brw-r-----   1 root   disk      1,     1 May 5 2008 ram
brw-rw----   1 root   disk     11,     0 May 5 2008 scd0
brw-rw----   1 root   disk     11,     1 May 5 2008 scd1
brw-rw----   1 root   disk      8,     0 May 5 2008 sda
brw-rw----   1 root   disk      8,     1 May 5 2008 sda1
brw-rw----   1 root   disk      8,    16 May 5 2008 sdb
brw-rw----   1 root   disk      8,    17 May 5 2008 sdb1
```

File type	Meaning
-	Normal
d	Subdirectory
b	Block device
c	Character device

Some character devices in /dev

```
crw-------   1 root    root      4,     0 Jan 4 01:07 console
crw-rw----   1 root    uucp      5,    64 Jan 4 01:07 cua0
crw-rw----   1 root    uucp      5,    65 May 5 2008 cua1
crw-rw----   1 root    uucp      5,    66 May 5 2008 cua2
crw-rw----   1 root    uucp      5,    67 May 5 2008 cua3
crw-rw-rw-   1 root    root     44,     0 May 5 2008 cui0
crw-rw----   1 root    daemon    6,     0 May 5 2008 lp0
crw-rw----   1 root    daemon    6,     1 May 5 2008 lp1
crw-r-----   1 root    kmem      1,     1 May 5 2008 mem
crw-rw-rw-   1 root    root      1,     3 May 5 2008 null
crw-rw-rw-   1 root    tty       2,   176 May 5 2008 ptya0
crw-rw-rw-   1 root    tty       2,   177 May 5 2008 ptya1
crw-rw-rw-   1 root    root      5,     0 May 5 2008 tty
crw-------   1 jdent   jdent     4,     0 May 5 2008 tty0
crw-r--r--   1 root    root      4,    65 Jan 4 18:29 ttyS1
```

Figure 2-3   Device files in /dev

- *group*—The user group information file

- *inittab*—The configuration file for the init program, which performs essential chores when the system starts

- *login.defs*—The configuration file for the login command

- *motd*—The message-of-the-day file

- *passwd*—The user information file

- *printcap*—The printer-capability information file

- *profile* and *bashrc*—The files executed at login that let the system administrator set global defaults for all users

- *rc*—The scripts or directories of scripts to run when the system starts

- *termcap*—The terminal capability information file

To get a taste of what is in the /etc directory, try viewing the contents of the fstab file. Enter *more /etc/fstab* and you'll see default setup information for file systems and devices such as CD/DVD drives.

The /home Directory

The /home directory is often on the /home partition and is used to offer disk space for users, such as on a system that has multiple user accounts. In Figure 2-1, for example, three home directories exist for three user accounts: /home/jean, /home/tricia, and /home/joseph.

The /lib Directory

This directory houses kernel modules, security information, and the **shared library images**, which are files that programmers generally use to share code in the libraries rather than creating copies of this code in their programs. This makes the programs smaller and, in some cases, they can run faster using this structure. Many files in this directory are symbolic links to other library files. A **symbolic link** is a name, file name, or directory name that contains a pointer to a file or directory in the same directory or in another directory on your system. Another related use of a symbolic link is to create a name or shortcut notation for accessing a directory. In a directory's long listing, *l* in the far-left position identifies files that are symbolic links.

One way to save typing time is to create a symbolic link to a directory that has a long path. For example, assume that you store many files in the /data/manufacturing/inventory/parts subdirectory. Each time you want to perform a listing of that subdirectory, you must type *ls /data/manufacturing/inventory/parts*. If you enter *ln -s /data/manufacturing/inventory/parts* to create a symbolic link (*ln* is the command to create a link and *-s* is the option for a symbolic link) to that directory; in the future you only have to type *ls parts* to see the contents. To learn more about the *ln* command, type *man ln* or *info ln* and press Enter.

The /mnt Directory

Mount points for temporary mounts by the system administrator reside in the /mnt directory. A temporary mount is used to mount a removable storage medium, such as a CD/DVD or USB/flash storage so that it can be easily unmounted for quick removal. For example, you might mount a CD to burn a disc and then quickly unmount it to give the disc to an office associate. The /mnt directory is often divided into subdirectories, such as /mnt/cdrom, to clearly specify device types.

The /media Directory

In newer distributions of UNIX/Linux, mount points for removable storage are in the /media directory, which is a relatively new recommendation of the Filesystem Hierarchy Standard (FHS). Modern Linux distributions include both /mnt and /media directories, but automated software to detect insertion of a CD/DVD typically uses /media. Linux users and programmers are often encouraged to use /media instead of /mnt as a way to follow the newer FHS recommendation.

NOTE Guidelines for the file hierarchy in UNIX/Linux are provided by the Filesystem Hierarchy Standard (FHS). You can learn more about FHS at the official Web site: *http://www.pathname.com/fhs*. Also, Wikipedia offers an introduction to FHS at *en.wikipedia.org/wiki/Filesystem_Hierarchy_Standard*.

The /proc Directory

The /proc directory occupies no space on the disk; it is a **virtual file system** allocated in memory only. Files in /proc refer to various processes running on the system as well as details about the operating system kernel.

The /root Directory

The /root directory is the home directory for the root user—the system administrator.

The /sbin Directory

The /sbin directory is reserved for the system administrator. Programs that start the system, programs needed for file system repair, and essential network programs are stored here.

The /tmp Directory

Many programs need a temporary place to store data during processing cycles. The traditional location for these files is the /tmp directory. For example, a payroll program might create several temporary data files as it processes a payroll for 5,000 people. The temporary files might hold data briefly needed for calculating withholdings for taxes and retirement and then be deleted after the withholding information is written to tape or CD to send to federal and state agencies.

The /usr Directory

Frequently on the /usr partition, this directory houses software offered to users. The software might be accounting programs, manufacturing programs, programs for research applications, or office software.

The /var Directory

Located on the /var partition, the /var directory holds subdirectories that often change in size. These subdirectories contain files such as error logs and other system performance logs that are useful to the system administrator. The /var/spool/mail subdirectory can contain incoming mail from the network, for example. Another example is the /var/spool/lpd subdirectory, which is the default directory for holding print files until they are fully transmitted to a printer.

TIP   Try viewing the contents of a log to get an idea of what is in the /var directory. For example, log in as root and enter more */var/log/boot.log* to see how information about booting the system is retained for informational purposes and troubleshooting. (If the boot.log file is empty, try entering a log version number, such as boot.log.2.)

USING THE MOUNT COMMAND

As you learned, UNIX/Linux use the *mount* command to connect the file system partitions to the directory tree when the system starts. Users can access virtually any file system that has been mounted and to which they have been granted permission. Additional file systems can be mounted at any time using the *mount* command. The CD and DVD drives are the file system devices beyond the hard disk that are most commonly mounted. The syntax for the *mount* command is as follows:

Syntax **mount** [–option] [*device-name mount-point*]

Dissection

- Use the *-t* option to specify a file system to mount.

- *device-name* identifies the device to mount.

- *mount-point* identifies the directory in which you want to mount the file system.

TIP   To ensure security on the system, only the root user can normally use the *mount* command. Ordinary users can sometimes mount and unmount file systems located on floppy disks and CDs/DVDs, but some operating systems require the root account to mount one or both.

Suppose you want to access files on a CD for your organization. You or the system administrator can mount a CD by inserting a disk in the CD drive, and then using one of the following *mount* commands (depending on whether your UNIX/Linux distribution and version use /mnt or /media):

```
mount -t iso9660 /dev/cdrom /mnt/cdrom
```

or

```
mount -t iso9660 /dev/cdrom /media/cdrom
```

This command mounts the CD on a device called "cdrom" located in the /dev directory. The actual mount point in UNIX/Linux is /mnt/cdrom or /media/cdrom, a directory that references the CD device. After the CD is mounted, you can access its files through the /mnt/cdrom or /media/cdrom directory.

UNIX/Linux support several different types of file systems. The type of file system is specified with the *-t* option. CDs are classified as iso9660 or udf devices, so the system administrator types *-t*, followed by the argument, such as *iso9660*, to specify the file system for CDs. On some newer versions of Linux, CDs/DVDs are mounted automatically through program software. The contents of CDs/DVDs can be viewed by double-clicking the CD's/DVD's icon on the desktop or as a subdirectory in the /media directory under the root (/).

TIP

After a CD is mounted, you can view the device paths, file system, and permissions by typing the *mount* command without options or arguments.

NOTE

Some systems still include legacy floppy disk drives. To mount a floppy disk, first insert it and then use one of the following commands (where filesystem is the floppy disk file system, such as vfat for porting a floppy to a Windows system):

```
mount -t filesystem /dev/fd0 /mnt/floppy
```

or

```
mount -t filesystem /dev/fd0 /media/floppy
```

After accessing manually mounted file systems, the system administrator unmounts them using the *umount* command before removing the storage media, as in the following example:

umount /mnt/cdrom (or umount /media/cdrom)

Syntax **umount** *mount-point*

Dissection

- *mount-point* identifies the directory to unmount.

Notice that the command is *umount*, not *unmount*; there is only one "n" in *umount*.

TIP

Try Hands-on Project 2-1 to use the *mount* command to view the file systems you can mount in your version of UNIX/Linux and to view what file systems are currently mounted. Also, Hands-on Project 2-2 enables you to mount or load a CD and view the files on the CD. See Appendix B, "Syntax Guide to UNIX/Linux Commands," for a brief description of the *mount* and *umount* commands.

USING PATHS, PATHNAMES, AND PROMPTS

As you've learned, all UNIX/Linux files are stored in directories in the file system, starting from the root file system directory. To specify a file or directory, use its **pathname**, which follows the branches of the file system to the desired file. A forward slash (/) separates each directory name. For example, suppose you want to specify the location of the file named phones.502. You know that it resides in the source directory in Jean's home directory, /home/jean/source, as illustrated in Figure 2-1. You can specify this file's location as /home/jean/source/phones.502.

Using and Configuring Your Command-Line Prompt

The UNIX/Linux command prompt can be configured to show your directory location within the file system. For example, in Fedora the prompt [jean@localhost ~]$ is the default prompt that the system generated when the system administrator first created the user account called "jean." The prompt [jean@localhost ~]$ means that "jean" is the user working on the host machine called "localhost" in her home directory, which is signified by the tilde (~). The ~ is shorthand for the home directory, which typically has the same name as the user's account name. The account jean would typically have a home directory also called jean that is located at /home/jean. When Jean changes her location to /home/jean/source, her prompt looks like:

[jean@localhost source]$

TIP When the system is initially installed, the default root prompt looks like this: [root@localhost root]#. To simplify the meaning of the command prompts in this book, the steps use $ to represent the ordinary user's command prompt and # to represent the system administrator's command prompt.

Your command prompt is configured automatically when you log in. An environment variable, PS1, contains special formatting characters that determine your prompt's configuration. An environment variable is a value in a storage area that is read by UNIX/Linux when you log in. Environment variables can be used to create and store default settings, such as the shell that you use or the command prompt format you prefer. You learn more about environment variables and how to configure them in Chapter 6. Figure 2-4 illustrates how the PS1 variable is configured by default for a user account in Fedora.

```
mpalmer@localhost:~

File  Edit  View  Terminal  Tabs  Help

[mpalmer@localhost ~]$ echo $PS1
[\u@\h \W]\$
[mpalmer@localhost ~]$ █
```

Figure 2-4 Viewing the contents of the PS1 variable

In Figure 2-4, the PS1 variable contains: [\u@\h \W]\$. Characters that begin with \ are special Bash shell formatting characters. \u prints the username, \h prints the system host name, and \W prints the name of the working (current) directory. The characters \$ print either a # or a $, depending on the type of user logged in. The brackets, [and], and the space that separates \h and \W are not special characters, so they are printed just as they appear. When Jean is logged into the system localhost and working in her home directory, her prompt appears as [jean@localhost ~]$ in the format shown previously.

Table 2-4 shows other formatting characters for configuring your Bash shell prompt.

Table 2-4   Formatting characters for configuring a Bash shell prompt

Formatting Character	Purpose
\a	Sounds an alarm
\d	Displays the date
\e	Uses an escape character
\h	Displays the host name
\j	Shows the number of background jobs
\n	Displays a new line
\nnn	Displays the ASCII character that corresponds to the octal number nnn
\r	Places a carriage return in the prompt
\s	Displays the shell name
\t	Displays the time
\u	Displays the username
\v	Displays the Bash version and release number
\w	Displays the path of the working directory
\A	Displays the time in 24-hour format
\D(format)	Displays the time in a specific format
\H	Has the same effect as \h
\T	Displays the time in 12-hour format
\V	Displays the Bash version, release number, and patch level
\W	Displays the name of the working directory without any other path information
\!	Displays the number of the current command in the command history
\#	Displays the number of the command in the current session
\$	Displays a # if root is the user, otherwise displays a $
\@	Displays the time in 12-hour format
$PWD	Displays the path of the current working directory
\[	Marks the beginning of a sequence of nonprinting characters, such as a control sequence
\]	Marks the end of a sequence of nonprinting characters
\\	Displays a \ character

Hands–On Project 2-3 gives you the opportunity to view the contents of the PS1 environment variable for your user account and then to configure your Bash shell prompt.

The pwd Command

If you have configured your prompt so that it does not show your working directory, you can use the *pwd* command (*pwd* stands for print working directory) to verify in what directory you are located, along with the directory path. This command can be important for several reasons. One is that you can list the contents of a directory and not find the files you are expecting, and so it can help to ensure that you are in the right directory before doing anything else (such as restoring the files). In other situations, you might have created a script or program that you can only run from a specific directory. If the script or program is not working, first use *pwd* to verify you are in the right directory. Hands-on Project 2-4 enables you to use *pwd*.

Syntax **pwd**

Dissection

- Use *pwd* to determine your current working directory.
- Typically, there are no options with this command.

TIP *pwd* is a simple but important command for all users. Often, users, programmers, and administrators alike experience errors or misplace a file because they are working in the wrong directory. Periodically using *pwd* can be invaluable for making certain you are in the right place.

Navigating the File System

To navigate the UNIX/Linux directory structure, use the *cd* (change directory) command. Its syntax is:

Syntax **cd** [*directory*]

Dissection

- *directory* is the name of the directory to which you want to change. The directory name is expressed as a path to the destination, with slashes (/) separating subdirectory names.

When you log in, you begin in your home directory, which is under the /home main directory. When you change directories and then want to return to your home directory, type *cd*, and press Enter. (Some shells also use the tilde character (~) to denote the user's home directory.) Try Hands-on Project 2-5 to use the *cd* command.

In UNIX/Linux, you can refer to a path as either an absolute path or a relative path. An **absolute path** begins at the root level and lists all subdirectories to the destination file. For example, assume that Becky has a directory named lists located under her home directory. In the lists directory, she has a file called todo. The absolute path to the todo file is /home/becky/lists/todo. This pathname shows each directory that lies in the path to the todo file.

NOTE

Any time the / symbol is the first character in a path, it stands for the root file system directory. All other / symbols in a path serve to separate the other names.

A **relative path** takes a shorter journey. You can enter the relative path to begin at your current working directory and proceed from there. In Figure 2-1, Jean, Tricia, and Joseph each have subdirectories located in their home directories. Each has a subdirectory called "source." Because Jean is working in her home directory, she can change to her source directory by typing the following command and pressing Enter:

```
cd source
```

In this example, which is called relative path addressing, Jean is changing to her source directory directly from her home directory, /home/jean. Her source directory is one level away from her current location, /home/jean. As soon as she enters the change directory command, *cd source*, the system takes her to /home/jean/source because it is relative to her current location.

If Tricia, who is in the /home/tricia directory, enters the command *cd source*, the system takes her to the /home/tricia/source directory. For Tricia to change to Jean's source directory, she can enter:

```
cd /home/jean/source
```

This example uses absolute path addressing because Tricia starts from the root file system directory and works through all intervening directories. (Tricia, of course, needs permission to access Jean's source directory, which is discussed later in this chapter.)

Hands-on Project 2-6 enables you to practice absolute and relative path addressing.

Using Dot and Dot Dot Addressing Techniques

UNIX/Linux interpret a single dot character to mean the current working directory, and dot dot (two consecutive dots) to mean the parent directory. Entering the following command keeps you in the current directory:

```
cd .
```

TIP

When you use UNIX/Linux commands, always pay close attention to spaces. For example, in *cd .* and *cd ..* there is one space between *cd* and the single or double dot characters. Remember, you must always use a space after a UNIX/Linux command before including options or arguments with that command.

If you use two dots, you move back to the parent directory. Do not type a space between the two dots. The next example shows how the user jean, who is currently in the /home/jean/source directory, returns to her home directory, which is /home/jean:

```
cd ..
```

Assume you are Jean in her home directory and want to go to Tricia's source directory. Use the following command:

```
cd ../tricia/source
```

In the preceding example, the dot dot tells the operating system to go to the parent directory, which is /home. The first / separator followed by the directory name tells the operating system to go forward to the tricia subdirectory. The second / separator followed by the directory name tells UNIX/Linux to go forward to the source subdirectory, the final destination. If no name precedes or follows the slash character, UNIX/Linux treat it as the root file system directory. Otherwise, / separates one directory from another. Hands-on Project 2-7 gives you practice using the dot and dot dot conventions.

Listing Directory Contents

Use the *ls* (list) command to display a directory's contents, including files and other directories. When you use the *ls* command with no options or arguments, it displays the names of regular files and directories in your current working directory. You can provide an argument to the *ls* command to see the listing for a specific file or to see the contents of a specific directory, such as *ls myfile* or *ls /etc*.

Syntax **ls** [–option] [*directory or filename*]

Dissection

- Common arguments include a directory name (including the path to the directory) or a file name.
- Useful options include:

    -l to view detailed information about files and directories

    -S to sort by size of the file or directory

    -X to sort by extension

    -r to sort in reverse order

    -t to sort by the time when the file or directory was last modified

    -a to show hidden files

    -i to view the inode value associated with a directory or file

---

Remember, when you log in, you begin in your home directory, which is /home/*username*.

You can also use options to display specific information or more information than the command alone provides. The *-l* option for the *ls* command generates a long directory listing, which includes more information about each file, as shown in Figure 2-5.

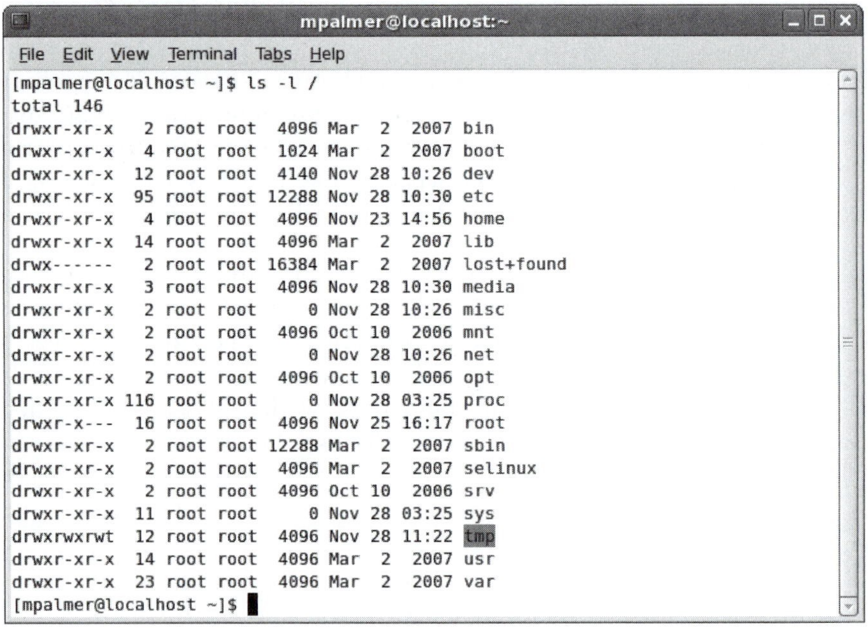

```
                                mpalmer@localhost:~                          _ □ ✕

 File  Edit  View  Terminal  Tabs  Help
 [mpalmer@localhost ~]$ ls -l /
 total 146
 drwxr-xr-x    2 root root  4096 Mar  2  2007 bin
 drwxr-xr-x    4 root root  1024 Mar  2  2007 boot
 drwxr-xr-x   12 root root  4140 Nov 28 10:26 dev
 drwxr-xr-x   95 root root 12288 Nov 28 10:30 etc
 drwxr-xr-x    4 root root  4096 Nov 23 14:56 home
 drwxr-xr-x   14 root root  4096 Mar  2  2007 lib
 drwx------    2 root root 16384 Mar  2  2007 lost+found
 drwxr-xr-x    3 root root  4096 Nov 28 10:30 media
 drwxr-xr-x    2 root root     0 Nov 28 10:26 misc
 drwxr-xr-x    2 root root  4096 Oct 10  2006 mnt
 drwxr-xr-x    2 root root     0 Nov 28 10:26 net
 drwxr-xr-x    2 root root  4096 Oct 10  2006 opt
 dr-xr-xr-x  116 root root     0 Nov 28 03:25 proc
 drwxr-x---   16 root root  4096 Nov 25 16:17 root
 drwxr-xr-x    2 root root 12288 Mar  2  2007 sbin
 drwxr-xr-x    2 root root  4096 Mar  2  2007 selinux
 drwxr-xr-x    2 root root  4096 Oct 10  2006 srv
 drwxr-xr-x   11 root root     0 Nov 28 03:25 sys
 drwxrwxrwt   12 root root  4096 Nov 28 11:22 tmp
 drwxr-xr-x   14 root root  4096 Mar  2  2007 usr
 drwxr-xr-x   23 root root  4096 Mar  2  2007 var
 [mpalmer@localhost ~]$ ▮
```

Figure 2-5   Using *ls -l* to view the root file system directory contents

Notice the first line in Figure 2-5 for the /bin directory:

`drwxr-xr-x 2 root root 4096 Mar 2 2007 bin`

If you look in the far-right column, you see bin, the name of a file. All of the columns to its left contain information about the file bin. Here is a description of the information in each column, from left to right.

- *File type and access permissions*—The first column of information shown is the following set of characters:

  `drwxr-xr-x`

  The first character in the list, d, indicates that the file is actually a directory. If bin were an ordinary file, a hyphen (-) would appear instead. The rest of the characters indicate the file's access permissions. You learn more about these later in this chapter, in the section "Configuring File Permissions for Security."

- *Number of links*—The second column is the number of files that are hard-linked to this file. (You learn more about links in Chapter 5, "Advanced File Processing.") If the file is a directory, this is the number of subdirectories it contains. The listing for bin shows it contains two (2) entries. (A directory always contains at least two entries: dot and dot dot.)

- *Owner*—The third column is the owner of the file. The root user owns the /bin directory.

- *Group*—The fourth column is the group that owns the file. The root group owns the /bin directory.

- *Size*—The fifth column shows the size of the file in bytes, which is 4096 for the /bin directory.

- *Date and time*—The sixth and seventh columns show the date when a directory or file was created, or if information has been changed for a directory or file, it shows the date and time of the last modification.

- *Name*—The eighth column shows the directory or file name.

You can also use the *-a* option with the *ls* command to list **hidden files**. Hidden files appear with a dot at the beginning of the file name. The operating system normally uses hidden files to keep configuration information, among other purposes. To view the inode value for a directory or file, use the *-i* option.

Try Hands-on Project 2-8 to use the *ls* command. Also, see Appendix B for a brief description of the *ls* command.

Using Wildcards

A **wildcard** is a special character that can stand for any other character or, in some cases, a group of characters. Wildcards are useful when you want to work with several files whose names are similar or with a file whose exact name you cannot remember. UNIX/Linux support several wildcard characters. In this section, you learn about two: * and ?.

The * wildcard represents any group of characters in a file name. For example, assume Becky has these 10 files in her home directory:

```
friends
instructions.txt
list1
list2
list2b
memo_to_fred
memo_to_jill
minutes.txt
notes
readme
```

If she enters *ls *.txt* and presses Enter, she sees the following output:

```
instructions.txt minutes.txt
```

The argument *.txt causes *ls* to display the names of all files that end with .txt. If she enters *ls memo**, she sees the following output:

```
memo_to_fred memo_to_jill
```

If she enters the command *ls **s and presses Enter, *ls* displays all file names that end with "s". She sees the output:

```
friends notes
```

The ? wildcard takes the place of only a single character. For example, if Becky types *ls list?* and presses Enter, *ls* displays all files whose names start with "list" followed by a single character. She sees the output:

```
list1 list2
```

She does not see the listing for the file list2b, because two characters follow the word "list" in its name. To see the list2b file in the listing, Becky could use two wildcard characters as in *ls list??*. Further, she can combine wildcard characters. For instance, if she wants to include the readme file in a listing, she might enter *ls ??a** .

You work again with wildcard characters in Chapter 6. In this chapter, Hands-on Project 2-9 enables you to use wildcards with the *ls* command.

NOTE
Wildcards are connected to the shell that you are using. The* and ? wildcards are available in the Bash shell. You can determine what wildcards are supported by a shell by reading the man documentation for that shell. For example, to read the documentation about the Bash shell, enter *man bash* at the command line.

CREATING AND REMOVING DIRECTORIES

You sometimes need to organize information by creating one or more new directories, such as under your home directory. System administrators also create new directories to hold programs, data, utilities, and other information. The *mkdir* command is used to create a new directory.

Syntax **mkdir** [-option] *directory*

Dissection

- The argument used with *mkdir* is a new directory name.

- There are only a few options used with *mkdir*. One option is to use *-v* to display a message that verifies the directory has been made.

Hands-on Project 2-10 enables you to make a directory and begin a set of projects in which you create a telephone database.

You can delete empty directories by using the remove directory command, *rmdir*. First, use the *cd* command to change to the parent directory of the subdirectory you want to delete. For example, if you want to delete the old directory in /home/old, first change to the home directory. Then type *rmdir old* and press Enter. In many versions of UNIX/Linux, including Fedora, Red Hat Enterprise Linux, and SUSE, *rmdir* will not delete a directory that contains files and you must delete, or move and delete, the files before you can delete the directory. Also, the *rm -r* command can be used to delete a directory that is not empty. You learn more about deleting directories in Chapter 4, "UNIX/Linux File Processing."

Syntax **rmdir** [–option] *directory*

Dissection

- The argument used with *rmdir* is a directory.

- As is true for *mkdir*, *rmdir* has only a few options. Consider using the *-v* option to display a message that verifies the directory has been removed.

COPYING AND DELETING FILES

The UNIX/Linux copy command is *cp*, which is used to copy files from one directory to another. The *-i* option provides valuable insurance because it warns you that the *cp* command overwrites the destination file, if a file of the same name already exists. You can also use the dot notation (current directory) as shorthand to specify the destination of a *cp* command. Try Hands-on Project 2-11 to use the *cp* command.

Syntax **cp** [–option] *source destination*

Dissection

- The argument consists of the source and destination directories and files, such as *cp /home/myaccount/myfile /home/youraccount*.

- Common options include:

  -b makes a backup of the destination file if the copy will overwrite a file

  -i provides a warning when you are about to overwrite a file

  -u specifies to only overwrite if the file you are copying is newer than the one you are overwriting

To delete files you do not need, use the remove command, *rm*. First, use the *cd* command to change to the directory containing the file you want to delete. Then type *rm filename*. For example, to delete the file "old" in the current working directory, type *rm old*. Depending on your version of UNIX/Linux, you might or might not receive a warning before the file is deleted. However, you can have the operating system prompt to make certain you want to perform the deletion by using the *-i* option. The best insurance, though, is to be certain you want to remove a file permanently before using this command. You learn more about the *rm* command in Chapter 4.

Syntax **rm** [–option] *filename*

Dissection

- The argument consists of the name of the file to delete.

- The *-i* option causes the operating system to prompt to make certain you want to delete the file before it is actually deleted.

CONFIGURING FILE PERMISSIONS FOR SECURITY

Early in computing, people didn't worry much about security. Stolen files and intrusions were less of a concern, in part because networks were rare and there was no Internet. As you have probably learned through the media, friends, and school, times are different and you need to protect your files. Security is important on UNIX/Linux systems because they can house multiple users and are connected to networks and the Internet, all potential sources of intrusion.

Users can set **permissions** for files (including directories) they own so as to establish security. System administrators also set permissions to protect system and shared files. Permissions manage who can read, write, or execute files.

The original owner of a file is the account that created it; however, file ownership can be transferred to another account. The permissions the owner sets are listed as part of the file description. Figure 2-6 shows directory listings that describe file types.

Notice the long listing of the two directories. (Remember that the directory is just another file.) An earlier section of this chapter, "Listing Directory Contents," describes the information presented in a long listing. Now, you can look closer at the file permissions. For the first file described, the column on the far left shows the string of letters drwxr-xr-x. You already know the first character indicates the file type, such as – for a normal file and d for a directory/subdirectory. The characters that follow are divided into three sections of file permission specifiers, as illustrated in Figure 2-7.

The first section of file permission specifiers indicates the owner's permissions. The owner, like all users, belongs to a group of users. The second section indicates the group's permissions. This specification applies to all users (other than the owner) who are members of the owner's group. The third section indicates all others' permissions. This specification applies to all users who are not the owner and not in the owner's group. In each section, the

File type	Meaning
-	Normal file
d	Subdirectory
l	Symbolic link
b	Block device file
c	Character device file

```
Excerpt from ls -l /etc

drwxr-xr-x   16 root     root         4096  Jan  17    9:29   X11
-rw-r--r--    1 root     root           46  Jan  15   19:11   adjtime
drwxr-xr-x    1 root     root         1024  Feb  27    2007   cron.daily
```

```
Excerpt from ls -l /home/jean/source

rw-rw-r--     1 jean     jean          387  Dec  12   23:11   phones.502
```

Figure 2-6   File types described in directory listings

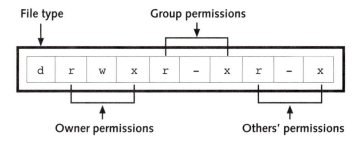

Figure 2-7   Example of the file type and the file permissions for a file

first character indicates read permissions. If an "r" appears there, that category of users has permission to read the file. The second character indicates write permission. If a "w" appears there, that category of users has permission to write to the file. The third character indicates the execute permission. If an "x" appears there, that category of users has permission to execute the file, such as a program file. If a dash (-) appears in any of these character positions, that type of permission is denied.

If a user is granted read permission for a directory, the user can see a list of its contents. Write permission for a directory means the user can rename, delete, and create files in the directory. Execute permission for a directory means the user can make the directory the current working directory.

From left to right, the letters rwxr-xr-x mean:

> r — File's owner has read permission
>
> w — File's owner has write permission

x — File's owner has execute permission (can run the file as a program)

r — Group has read permission

- — Group does not have write permission

x — Group has execute permission

r — Others have read permission

- — Others do not have write permission

x — Others have execute permission

You can change the pattern of permission settings by using the *chmod* command. For example, setting others' permissions to --- removes all permissions for others. They cannot read, write, or execute the file. In the first line of Figure 2-6, notice that the owner has read, write, and execute (rwx) permissions for the subdirectory X11. The first character is the file type, in this case, a "d" for a subdirectory. The rwx gives the owner read, write, and execute permissions. The next r-x indicates that the group of users that shares the same group id as the owner has only read and execute permissions; the final r-x gives read and execute permissions to others.

The system administrator assigns group ids when he or she adds a new user account. A **group id (GID)** gives a group of users equal access to files that they all share. Others are all other users who are not associated with the owner's group by a group id, but who have read and execute permissions.

NOTE   In many UNIX/Linux distributions, when the system administrator creates an account, a group with the same name as the user account is created. The system administrator can choose to suppress the creation of the group with the same name as the account and instead assign new accounts to a general group called users or to another group (or groups) the administrator has previously created. Groups are simply a tool the administrator uses to manage security.

Syntax **chmod** [-option] *mode filename*

Dissection

- The argument can include the mode (permissions) and must include the file name. You can also use a wildcard to set the permissions on multiple files.

- Permissions are applied to owner (u), group (g), and others (o). The permissions are read (r), write (w), and execute (x). Use a plus sign (+) before the permissions to allow them or a hyphen (-) to disallow permissions. Octal permissions are assigned by a numeric value for each owner, group, and others.

Use the UNIX/Linux *chmod* command to set file permissions. In its simplest form, the *chmod* command takes as arguments a symbolic string (individual characters that are abbreviations for permissions) followed by one or more file names. The symbolic string specifies permissions that should be granted or denied to categories of users. Here is an example: ugo+rwx. In the string, the characters ugo stand for user (same as owner), group, and others. These categories of users are affected by the *chmod* command. The next character, the + sign, indicates that permissions are being granted. The last set of characters, in this case rwx, indicates the permissions being granted. The symbolic string ugo+rwx indicates that read, write, and execute permissions are being granted to the owner, group, and others. The following is an example of how the symbolic string is used in a command to modify the access permissions of myfile:

```
chmod ugo+rwx myfile
```

The following command grants group read permission to the file customers:

```
chmod g+r customers
```

It is also possible to deny permissions with a symbolic string. The following command denies the group and others write and execute permissions for the file account_info.

```
chmod go-wx account_info
```

NOTE
From your home directory, you can create any subdirectory and set permissions for it. However, you cannot create subdirectories outside your home directory unless the system administrator makes a special provision.

The octal permission format is another way to assign permissions; it assigns a number on the basis of the type of permission and on the basis of owner, group, and other. The type of permission is a number. For example, execute permission is assigned 1, write is 2, and read is 4. These permission numbers are added together for a value between 0 and 7. For instance, a read and write permission is a 6 (4 + 2) and read and execute is a 5 (4 + 1), as shown in the following list:

- 0 is no permissions.
- 1 is execute (same as *x*).
- 2 is write (same as *w*).
- 3 is write and execute (same as *wx*).
- 4 is read (same as *r*).
- 5 is read and execute (same as *rx*).
- 6 is read and write (same as *rw*).
- 7 is read, write, and execute (same as *rwx*).

One of these numbers is associated with each of three numeric positions (xxx) after the *chmod* command. The first position gives the permission number of the owner, the second position gives the permission number of the group, and the final position gives the permission number of other. For example, the command *chmod 755 myfile* assigns read, write, and execute permissions to owner (7) for myfile; it assigns read and execute permissions to both group and other (5 in both positions). Here are some other examples:

- *chmod 711 data*—For the file data, this command assigns read, write, and execute to owner; execute to group; and execute to other (programmers often use this for programs they write, enabling users to execute those programs).

- *chmod 642 data*—For the file data, this command assigns read and write to owner; read to group; and write to other.

- *chmod 777 data*—For the file data, this command assigns read, write, and execute to owner, group, and other.

- *chmod 755 data*—For the file data, this command assigns read, write, and execute to owner; read and execute to group; and read and execute to other (another permission often used by programmers).

- *chmod 504 data*—For the file data, this command assigns read and execute to owner; no permissions to group; and read permission to other.

TIP

If you want to set security on a directory to ensure that users must know the exact path to a file in that directory—so they can execute a program, but not snoop—configure the directory to have 711 permissions. This gives all permissions to the owner (you) and only the execute permission to group and others.

TIP

Some versions of UNIX/Linux include the *umask* command, which enables you to set permissions on multiple files at one time. This command is more complex than using *chmod* octal commands, but can save time for system administrators. For example, *umask 022* grants rwx permissions for all users. However, you can also grant permissions on multiple files by using the wildcard asterisk (*) with *chmod*. For example, *chmod 777 ** grants full permission on all files in the current directory to all users and groups.

Now that you've learned about permissions, check out Table 2-5 for suggestions about setting permissions. Also, try Hands-on Project 2-12 to configure permissions. See Appendix B for a brief description of the *chmod* command.

Table 2-5 Suggestions for setting permissions

Type of File or Directory	Permissions Suggestion
System directories such as /bin, /boot, /dev, /etc, /sbin, /sys, and /usr	Give all permissions to root (the owner), rx to group and others—*chmod 755*.
/root directory for the root account	Give all permissions to root (the owner), rx to group, and no permissions to others—*chmod 750*.

Table 2-5   Suggestions for setting permissions (continued)

Type of File or Directory	Permissions Suggestion
Your home directory	Give all permissions to owner (your account), x or no permissions to group, and no permissions to others—*chmod 710* or *chmod 700*. (If you are a student and need to give your instructor access to your home directory, consider using *chmod 705* so your instructor has rx permissions.)
A subdirectory under your home directory that you want to share with others so they can access and create files	Give all permissions to owner (your account), group, and others—*chmod 777*.
A file in your home directory that you want people to be able to view, but not change	Give all permissions to owner (your account), rx to group, and rx to others—*chmod 755*.
A file that should only be accessed by you	Give all permissions to owner and no permissions to group and others—*chmod 700*.
An archived file in your home directory that should not be changed (just preserved) and that only you should be able to view	Give rx permissions to owner and no permissions to group and others—*chmod 500*.

There are three advanced permissions that deserve brief mention so that you are aware of them: **sticky bit**, **set user id (SUID) bit**, and **set group ID (SGID) bit**. All three permissions are typically used by a system administrator for special purposes.

On older UNIX and Linux distributions, the sticky bit has been used to cause an executable program (a file you run as a program) to stay resident in memory after it is exited. This action ensures that the program is immediately ready to use the next time around or that it stays ready for multiple users on a server. In current operating systems, the sticky bit is used instead to enable a file to be executed, but only the file's owner or root have permission to delete or rename it. The symbol for the sticky bit is t (used in place of x), such as when you view permissions using *ls -l*. For example, when the sticky bit is set on a file, the permissions might look like: -rwxr-xr-t.

The SUID bit is generally used on programs and files used by programs. SUID gives the current user (user ID) temporary permissions to execute program-related files as though they are the owner. For example, programs on a multiuser system or server are usually installed by root. However, an ordinary user may need capabilities to execute and possibly modify files to run those programs as though they are the root account. Setting the SUID bit gives them the access they need to use the programs—temporarily treating the user as root (the owner). Even though someone is using the program with the SUID bit permission, root still retains actual ownership.

The SGID bit works similarly to SUID, but it applies to groups. For example, your company might have a group of people who use accounting files on a computer. The system administrator can create a group called accounting and, through the SGID bit, give temporary access as an owner to each member of the group while she or he is using the accounting programs and files. The symbol for SUID or SGID is an s. For example, when both SUID and SGID are set, the permissions on a file might look like –rwsr-sr-x (notice that the x permission is replaced with s for the owner and group).

Chapter Summary

❐ In UNIX/Linux, a file is the basic component for data storage. UNIX/Linux consider everything to be a file, even attached devices such as the monitor, keyboard, and printer. Even a directory, which can contain both files and subdirectories, is really just a special file in UNIX/Linux.

❐ A file system is the UNIX/Linux systems' way of organizing files on storage devices such as hard disks and removable media such as CDs/DVDs. Files are stored in a file system, which is a hierarchical, treelike structure in which top-level directories contain subdirectories, which in turn can contain other subdirectories. Every file can be located by using a pathname—a listing of names of directories leading to a particular file.

❐ The standard tree structure starts with the root (/) file system directory, which serves as the foundation for a hierarchical group of other directories and subdirectories.

❐ The section of the disk that holds a file system is called a partition. One disk might have many partitions, each separated from the others so that it remains unaffected by external disturbances such as structural file problems associated with another partition. The UNIX/Linux file system is designed to allow access to multiple partitions after they are mounted in the tree structure.

❐ A path, as defined in UNIX/Linux, serves as a map to access any file on the system. An absolute path is one that always starts at the root level. A relative path is one that starts at your current location.

❐ You can customize your command prompt to display the current working directory name, the date, the time, and several other items.

❐ The *ls* command displays the names of files and directories contained in a directory. The *ls -l* command, or long listing, displays detailed file information. The *ls -a* command shows hidden files.

❐ Wildcard characters can be used in a command, such as *ls*, and take the place of other characters in a file name. In the Bash shell, the * wildcard can take the place of any string of characters, and the ? wildcard can take the place of any single character. The specific wildcards you can use are related to the shell.

❐ You can use the *mkdir* command to create a new directory as long as you own the parent directory. A file's original owner is the person who creates it, and he becomes the one who controls access to it (although the root account also can control access).

2

□ Use the *cp* command to copy a source file to a destination file. UNIX/Linux might overwrite the destination file without warning unless you use the *-i* option. The dot notation (current directory) is a shorthand way to specify the destination in a *cp* command.

□ You can use the *chmod* command to set permissions for files that you own. The basic permission settings are *rwx*, which mean read, write, and execute, respectively. File permissions are set to control file access by three types of users: the owner (u), the group (g), and others (o). You must remember to change permission settings on any directories you own if you want others to access information in those directories. Also, to run a program file, the intended users (owner, group, others) must have execute permissions.

COMMAND SUMMARY: REVIEW OF CHAPTER 2 COMMANDS

Command	Purpose	Options Covered in This Chapter
cd	Changes directories (with no options, *cd* goes to your home directory)	. Changes to the current working directory. .. Changes to the parent directory.
chmod	Sets file permissions for specified files	+ assigns permissions. -removes permissions.
cp	Copies files from one directory to another	-b makes a backup of the destination file, if an original one already exists (so you have a backup if overwriting a file). -i prevents overwriting of the destination file without warning. -u overwrites an existing file only if the source is newer than the file in the current destination.
ls	Displays a directory's contents, including its files and subdirectories	-a lists the hidden files. -l (lowercase L) generates a long listing of the directory. -r sorts the listing in reverse order. -S sorts the listing by file size. -t sorts by the time when the file or directory was last modified. -X sorts by extension.
mkdir	Makes a new directory	-v verifies that the directory is made.
mount	Connects the file system partitions to the directory tree when the system starts, and mounts additional devices, such as the CD/DVD drive	-t specifies the type of file system to mount.
pwd	Displays your current path	

Command	Purpose	Options Covered in This Chapter
rm	Removes a file	**-i** prompts before you delete the file.
rmdir	Removes an empty directory	**-v** provides a message to verify the directory is removed.
umask	Sets file permissions for multiple files	
umount	Disconnects the file system partitions from the directory tree	

Key Terms

/boot partition — A partition that is used to store the operating system files that compose the kernel.

/home partition — A partition that is on the home directory and provides storage space for all users' directories. A separate section of the hard disk, it protects and insulates users' personal files from the UNIX/Linux operating system software.

/usr partition — A partition in which to store some or all of the nonkernel operating system programs that will be accessed by users.

/var partition — A partition that holds temporarily created files, such as files used for printing documents and log files used to record monitoring and administration data.

absolute path — A pathname that begins at the root file system directory and lists all subdirectories to the destination file.

binaries — The programs residing in the /bin directory and elsewhere that are needed to start the system and perform other essential tasks. *See also* executables.

block special file — In UNIX/Linux, a file used to manage random access devices that involve handling blocks of data, including CD/DVD drives, hard disk drives, tape drives, and other storage devices. Also called a block device file.

bootstrap loader — A utility residing in the /boot directory that starts the operating system.

character special file — A UNIX/Linux I/O management file used to handle byte-by-byte streams of data, such as through serial or USB connections, including terminals, printers, and network communications. Also called a character device file.

child — A subdirectory created and stored within a (parent) directory.

device special file — A file used in UNIX/Linux for managing I/O devices. It can be one of two types: *block special file* or *character special file*.

directory — A special type of file that can contain other files and directories. Directory files store the names of regular files and other directories, called *subdirectories*.

Enhanced IDE (EIDE) — An improved version of IDE that offers faster data transfer speeds and is commonly used in modern computers. *See also* Integrated Drive Electronics.

executables — The programs residing in the /bin directory that are needed to start the system and perform other essential tasks. *See also* binaries.

extended file system (ext or **ext fs)** — The file system designed for Linux that is installed, by default, in Linux operating systems. It enables the use of the full range of built-in Linux

2

commands, file manipulation, and security. Released in 1992, ext had some bugs and supported only files of up to 2 GB. In 1993, the second extended file system (ext2 or ext2 fs) was designed to fix the bugs in ext, and supported files up to 4 TB. In 2001, ext3 (or ext3 fs) was introduced to enable journaling for file and data recovery. ext4 was introduced in 2006, enabling a single volume to hold up to 1 exabyte of data and supporting the use of extents. ext, ext2, ext3, and ext4 support file names up to 255 characters.

extent — A portion of a disk, such as a block or series of blocks, that is reserved for a file and that represents contiguous space, so that as the file grows, all of it remains in the same location on disk. The use of extents reduces file fragmentation on a disk, which reduces disk wear and the time it takes to retrieve information.

file — The basic component for data storage.

file system — An operating system's way of organizing files on mass storage devices, such as hard and floppy disks. The organization is hierarchical and resembles an inverted tree. In the branching structure, top-level files (or folders or directories) contain other files, which in turn contain other files.

group id (GID) — A number used to identify a group of users.

hidden file — A file that the operating system uses to keep configuration information, among other purposes. The name of a hidden file begins with a dot.

hot fixes — The ability to automatically move data on damaged portions of disks to areas that are not damaged.

information node, or **inode** — A system for storing essential information about directories and files. Inode information includes (1) the name of a directory or file, (2) general information about that directory/file, and (3) information (a pointer) about how to locate the directory/file on a disk partition.

Integrated Drive Electronics (IDE) — Sometimes called Integrated Device Electronics, the most popular electronic hard disk interface for personal computers. This is the same as the ANSI Advanced Technology Attachment (ATA) standard.

journaling — The process of keeping chronological records of data or transactions so that if a system crashes without warning, the data or transactions can be reconstructed or backed out to avoid data loss or information that is not properly synchronized.

mount — The process of connecting a file system to the directory tree structure, making that directory accessible.

parent — The directory in which a subdirectory (child) is created and stored.

partition — A separate section of a disk that holds a file system and that is created so activity and problems occurring in other partitions do not affect it.

pathname — A means of specifying a file or directory that includes the names of directories and subdirectories on the branches of the tree structure. A forward slash (/) separates each directory name. For example, the pathname of the file phones (the destination file) in the source directory of Jean's directory within the /home directory is /home/jean/source/phones.

peripherals — The equipment connected to a computer via electronic interfaces. Examples include hard and floppy disk drives, printers, and keyboards.

permission — A specific privilege to access and manipulate a directory or file, for example, the privilege to read a file.

physical file system — A section of the hard disk that has been formatted to hold files.

relative path — A pathname that begins at the current working directory and lists all subdirectories to the destination file.

root file system directory — The main or parent directory (/) for all other directories (the highest level of the file system); also can refer to the directory in which the system administrator's files are stored (/root).

set group ID (SGID) bit — Enables the owner of a program to keep full ownership, but also gives members of a group temporary ownership while executing that program.

set user ID (SUID) bit — Enables the owner of a program to retain full ownership, but also gives an ordinary user temporary ownership while executing that program.

shared library images — The files residing in the /lib directory that programmers use to share code, rather than copying this code into their programs. Doing so makes their programs smaller and faster.

Small Computer System Interface (SCSI) — Pronounced "*scuzzy*," a popular and fast electronic hard disk interface commonly used on network servers. SCSI is actually a set of standards that defines various aspects of fast communications with a hard disk.

sticky bit — An executable permission that either causes a program to stay resident in memory (on older UNIX/Linux systems) or ensures that only root or the owner can delete or rename a file (on newer systems).

subdirectory — A directory under a higher or parent directory.

superblock — A special data block on a partition that contains information about the layout of blocks. This information is the key to finding anything on the file system, and it should never change.

swap partition — A section of the hard disk separated from other sections so that it functions as an extension of memory, which means it supports virtual memory. A computer system can use the space in this partition to swap information between disk and RAM so the computer runs faster and more efficiently.

symbolic link — A name or file name that points to and lets you access a file using a different name in the same directory or a file using the same or a different name in a different directory.

UNIX file system (ufs) — A hierarchical (tree structure) file system supported in most versions of UNIX/Linux. It is expandable, supports large storage, provides excellent security, is reliable, and employs information nodes (inodes).

utility — A program that performs useful operations such as copying files, listing directories, and communicating with other users. Unlike other operating system programs, a utility is an add-on and not part of the UNIX/Linux shell, nor a component of the kernel.

virtual file system — A system that occupies no disk space, such as the /proc directory. The virtual file system references and lets you obtain information about which programs and processes are running on a computer.

virtual memory — A memory resource supported by the swap partition, in which the system can swap information between disk and RAM, allowing the computer to run faster and more efficiently.

virtual storage — The storage that might be allocated via different disks or file systems (or both), but that is transparently accessible as storage to the operating system and users.

wildcard — A special character that can stand for any other character or, in some cases, a group of characters and is often used in an argument, such as *ls file.* * .

REVIEW QUESTIONS

1. Your company is discussing plans to migrate desktop and laptop users to Linux. One concern raised by the users is whether Linux supports the use of CDs and DVDs for both work files and for listening to music. Which of the following is an appropriate answer?

    a. Linux only supports hard disk file systems, such as extended file system (ext) and UNIX file system, but users can copy music (MP3) files to the hard disk to play.

    b. Linux can use the Reiser File System, which supports CD and DVD files of all types.

    c. Linux supports both the UDF and iso9660 file systems for CD and DVD use.

    d. Linux supports mounting CDs and DVDs by using the /removable partition.

2. You receive a message that you've successfully backed up hda2 on your Linux system. What is hda2?

    a. the second disk on a two-disk system

    b. the second partition on your main hard disk

    c. the files on a CD

    d. the subdirectory under the /root directory that houses the kernel

3. You have purchased a special monitor for your computer and the instructions tell you to make a minor modification to the inittab file. Where would you locate this file on a typical Linux system?

    a. /var

    b. /fastboot

    c. /home/users

    d. /etc

4. You're frantically trying to get ready for a meeting and want to access a file in your home directory, but you are currently working in a public directory open to all users. What command can you enter to instantly go to your home directory?

    a. *cd*

    b. *home*

    c. *go*

    d. *fetch*

5. Your new colleague asks which partitions vendors recommend setting up on a Linux system. Which of the following partitions do you include in your response? (Choose all that apply.)

   a. /backup

   b. root

   c. swap

   d. /boot

6. You have mounted a remote network drive and now you want to unmount that drive. Which of the following commands do you use? (Choose all that apply.)

   a. *bye*

   b. *umount*

   c. *driveoff*

   d. *disconnect*

7. When you connect a printer via a USB port on your Linux computer, which type of device special file is used to handle streams of data sent to and from the printer?

   a. character special file

   b. block special file

   c. root device file

   d. port device file

8. Some of the users in your company create and delete so many files that they have problems with fragmented disks. Which of the following new features in the ext4 file system help to reduce fragmentation problems?

   a. hot swap

   b. fragmonitor

   c. smaller file sizes

   d. extents

9. In UNIX and Linux systems, what source of extra memory space is used when working on tasks and files that exceed the RAM capacity on chips in the computer?

   a. register memory contained on the circuit board used to run the monitor

   b. swap partition

   c. /mem directory

   d. memory subdirectory under the /users directory (/users/mem)

10. You are always scheduled for two or three meetings each day and need to keep an eye on the time. What PS1 variable parameter can you set in order to have your command prompt display the current time?

    a. \t

    b. \v

    c. /time

    d. /date

11. You have been working in several directories for the past hour and right now you don't remember which directory you're in currently. What command can you use to show your current working directory?

    a. *showme*

    b. *where am i*

    c. *pwd*

    d. *dir -w*

12. A member of your department has given you permissions to view the contents of the accounting directory under his home directory. The name of his home directory is bramirez. Which of the following commands should you use to display the contents of the accounting directory?

    a. *dir accounting*

    b. *ls ~/accounting*

    c. *ls /home/bramirez/accounting*

    d. *cd -l /bramirez/accounting*

13. It's late and you have been working all day to finish a report. Before you go home, you want to copy several files, including your report file. What copy command should you use to ensure that you don't inadvertently copy an older report file over the newer report file you've been working on for the last four hours?

    a. *cp -u*

    b. *cp --warn*

    c. *copy -w*

    d. *copy --caution*

14. Which of the following are file systems supported by UNIX and Linux operating systems? (Choose all that apply.)

    a. NTFS

    b. vfat

    c. PICK

    d. ufs

    e. ext

15. You are helping a friend who is new to Linux. You want to determine which entries under her home directory are directories instead of files. When you perform a long listing of the home directory's contents, what do you use to distinguish a directory from a file?

   a. The very first character in the line for an entry will be either "~" for a directory or "$" for an ordinary file.

   b. The very last word in the line for an entry will be "file" or "directory."

   c. The last character appended to the entry's name will be either "1" for an ordinary file or "2" for a directory.

   d. The very first character in the line for an entry will be "d" for directory or "–" for an ordinary file.

16. Your boss is planning to do some house cleaning by deleting several old files. However, she mentions that she doesn't want to delete an important file inadvertently. What command can she use so that she is prompted to make sure she wants to delete a particular file?

   a. *del ?*

   b. *cp -d*

   c. *write -del -q*

   d. *rm -i*

17. You are curious about the error and system logs kept by your operating system. In what main directory under the root (/) would you most likely find these logs?

   a. /var

   b. /sbin

   c. /tmp

   d. /sys

18. A friend of yours is trying to make more space on his hard disk drive and is considering deleting the /lib directory because he has heard it mostly contains games that he doesn't use. What is your recommendation?

   a. Delete the /lib directory because it mainly contains old games anyway.

   b. Before deleting the /lib directory, copy the config file to another directory, because this file is used to configure games and other software.

   c. Delete the /mnt directory instead, because it contains backups of changed maintenance and log files.

   d. Keep the /lib directory because it holds security information, shared library images, kernel modules and other important files.

2

19. Which of the following are permissions that can be granted to a file? (Choose all that apply.)

    a. start

    b. write

    c. execute

    d. manage

    e. read

20. Which of the following commands enable(s) you to set permissions on a directory after you create it? (Choose all that apply.)

    a. *mkdir -p*

    b. *cpdir --permissions*

    c. *chmod*

    d. *catperm*

21. You have created many notes to yourself that end in .txt. Which of the following commands enables you to list all of the .txt files in your home directory while you are in the Bash shell?

    a. *dir ##.txt*

    b. *ls *.txt*

    c. *cp .txt -all*

    d. *cat $.txt*

22. Where is virtual memory located?

23. When you see the permissions rwx--x--x associated with a file, what permissions are granted?

24. Your boss wants to use the command to view hidden files and also wants to know how to find them among other files. What do you tell her?

25. You have many files that begin with the word "account" and that end with two digits to designate a year, such as account00, account 01, and so on. What is the command that enables you to view all of these files that start with account?

HANDS-ON PROJECTS

All projects in this chapter are performed from the command line, such as from a terminal window.

NOTE

Project 2-1

UNIX/Linux support many different file systems that can be mounted using the *mount* command. In this project, you will use the *mount* command to determine what file systems are available in your version of UNIX/Linux. For this and all projects in this chapter, unless otherwise specified as in Hands-on Project 2-2, you should be logged in to your own account.

To view the available file systems:

1. At the command prompt, type **man mount** and press **Enter**. Continue pressing the **Spacebar**, as necessary, to view the documentation for the *-t* parameter for the *mount* command. (If you are using a terminal window, you might need to press **q** to exit the text display mode when you are finished.)

2. What file systems can be mounted?

3. Next, type **mount** and press **Enter** to determine what file systems are actually mounted. (See Figure 2-8.) What file systems do you see mounted on your system?

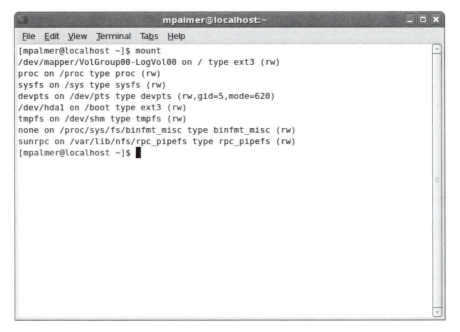

```
[mpalmer@localhost ~]$ mount
/dev/mapper/VolGroup00-LogVol00 on / type ext3 (rw)
proc on /proc type proc (rw)
sysfs on /sys type sysfs (rw)
devpts on /dev/pts type devpts (rw,gid=5,mode=620)
/dev/hda1 on /boot type ext3 (rw)
tmpfs on /dev/shm type tmpfs (rw)
none on /proc/sys/fs/binfmt_misc type binfmt_misc (rw)
sunrpc on /var/lib/nfs/rpc_pipefs type rpc_pipefs (rw)
[mpalmer@localhost ~]$
```

Figure 2-8   Mounted file systems

Project 2-2

Most systems have a CD or CD/DVD drive enabling you to mount CDs. Ask your instructor if your system supports using the mount command to mount a CD from the command line. This project allows you to mount and then unmount a CD. You need a CD that can be inserted (by you or by a server operator) in the CD/DVD drive.

If your system supports mounting a CD from the command line, try the following project. Also, note that on newer systems the /mnt/cdrom mount point may be replaced with /media/cdrom. Ask your instructor about whether to use /mnt/cdrom or /media/cdrom.

To mount and unmount a CD:

1. Log in to root.

2. Insert the CD or request the server operator to insert the CD.

3. If your system automatically mounts the CD, type **umount/mnt/cdrom** (or replace mnt with media) and press **Enter** to unmount it. (Close the CD drive with the CD loaded, if the drive opens.)

4. Type **mount –t iso9660 /dev/cdrom /mnt/cdrom** (or replace mnt with media) and press **Enter**. (Note that */mnt/cdrom* or */media/cdrom* is used as a mount point for the CD, and after the CD is mounted, you can view its files in the /mnt/cdrom or /media/cdrom subdirectory. Also, if your system does not have a /mnt/cdrom or /media/cdrom directory, you will need to create it for this step.)

5. Type **mount** and press **Enter** to verify that the CD is mounted.

6. Type **ls /mnt/cdrom** (or replace mnt with media) and press **Enter** to view the contents of the CD.

7. Type **umount /mnt/cdrom** (or replace mnt with media) and press **Enter**. (On some systems, the CD drive now opens for you or the server operator to remove the CD.)

8. What commands would you use to mount and unmount a floppy disk for use with a Windows-based system?

If your system does not support using the *mount* command to mount a CD from the command line, try this project using the GNOME or KDE desktop. You'll need a CD that is configured to automount (which can be a program, music, or video CD, for example).

To load a CD:

1. Log in to your individual account.

2. Insert a CD.

3. Notice that an icon appears on the desktop for the CD. (The icon may display the label of the CD and the type of CD, such as CD-R.)

4. Double-click the CD's icon to view its contents in a window.

5. Close the window when you are finished viewing the contents.

**HANDS-ON
PROJECTS**

Project 2-3

The PS1 variable contains the configuration parameters for how your command-prompt line appears. In this project, you will view the contents of the PS1 variable and then you configure the PS1 variable. You should be using the default Bash shell and be logged in using your own account and home directory.

To view the PS1 variable's contents and then to configure the variable:

1. Type **echo $PS1** and press **Enter**. (Refer to Figure 2-4.)

2. You see the contents of the PS1 variable, which in Red Hat Enterprise Linux and Fedora appear as:

   [\u@\h \W]\$

3. To change your prompt to display the date and time, type **PS1='\d \t>'** and press **Enter**. Type the command with no spaces between the characters, other than one space between \d and \t. Your prompt now looks similar to:

   Tue Jul 5 09:18:33>

4. To change your prompt to display the current working directory, type **PS1='\w>'** and press **Enter**. Your prompt now looks similar to:

   ~>

   The \w formatting character displays the ~ to represent the user's home directory.

5. To change your prompt to display the full path of the current working directory, you must use another environment variable, PWD. The PWD variable contains the full pathname of the current working directory. To display the PWD variable in the prompt, type **PS1='$PWD>'** and press **Enter**. (Notice that you must place the $ in front of the environment variable name to extract its contents.) Your prompt now looks similar to:

   /home/jean>

6. If you are using a terminal window, close and open a new terminal window session, or log out and log back in and then access the command line. How does your prompt change from what you saw in Step 5?

Project 2-4

In this project, you will use the *pwd* command to view your working directory.

To display your current path:

1. Type **pwd** and press **Enter**.

2. What is your current directory path?

Project 2-5

For this project, you will practice more with changing the PS1 variable, and you use the *cd* command.

To use the *cd* command:

1. First, change your prompt so that you can view the directory path. At the $ command prompt, type **PS1='$PWD>'** and press **Enter**.

2. Type **cd /var/spool/mail** and press **Enter**. This moves you to the /var/spool/mail subdirectory.

3. Type **cd** and press **Enter**. The change directory command (*cd*) without arguments returns you to your home directory. (See Figure 2-9.)

4. If you are using a terminal window, close that terminal window and open another terminal window for the next project. If you are logged in remotely or are not using a terminal window to access the command prompt, log out and then log back in to reset your prompt.

```
                          mpalmer@localhost:~                      _ □ ✕

File  Edit  View  Terminal  Tabs  Help
[mpalmer@localhost ~]$ PS1='$PWD>'
/home/mpalmer>cd /var/spool/mail
/var/spool/mail>cd
/home/mpalmer>█
```

Figure 2-9 Using the *cd* command

Project 2-6

Comparing the use of absolute versus relative paths can be handy for understanding how each works. In this project, you will use both types of path addressing to navigate through a file system.

To navigate directories:

1. If you are not in your home directory, type **cd** and press **Enter**.

2. The parent directory of your home directory is /home. /home is an absolute path name. Type **cd /home** and press **Enter**. The system takes you to the /home directory.

3. Type **cd** plus your username, such as *cd joseph,* and press **Enter**. This step uses relative path addressing to return to your home directory.

Project 2-7

Navigating a file system using the dot and dot dot options can save you typing time. In this project, you practice using both conventions. Make certain you are logged in to your own account for this project and not as root.

To use dot and dot dot to change your working directory:

1. If you are not in your home directory, type **cd** and press **Enter**.

2. Type **cd .** and press **Enter**. Because the . (dot) references your current directory, the system did not change your working location.

3. Type **cd ..** and press **Enter**. The system takes you to the parent directory, which is /home.

4. Type **cd ..** and press **Enter**. The system takes you to the root file system directory (/). Type **cd** and press **Enter**. The system takes you to your home directory.

On any of the steps in this project, you can enter *pwd* to verify which directory you are in currently.

Project 2-8

The *ls* command is one of the most useful commands. In this project, you will start by using *ls* to view your working directory. Next, you use *ls* with an argument to view a file and then a directory. For a more complete listing of information about the contents of a directory, you use the *-l* option, and finally you use the *-a* option to include hidden files in a directory listing.

To see a list of files and directories in your current working directory:

1. Type **ls** and press **Enter**. You see a list of file and directory names.

To see a listing for a specific file or directory:

1. If you are not in your home directory, type **cd** and press **Enter**.

2. In Chapter 1, "The Essence of UNIX and Linux," you used the *cat* command to create a notes file. You should still have that file in your home directory. (If not, use *cat* again to create a notes file.) Type **ls notes** and press **Enter**. The system displays the listing for the notes file.

3. To see the contents of a directory other than your current working directory, give the directory name as an option to the *ls* command. For example, to see the contents of the /var directory, type **ls /var** and press **Enter**. You see a listing similar to the one in Figure 2-10.

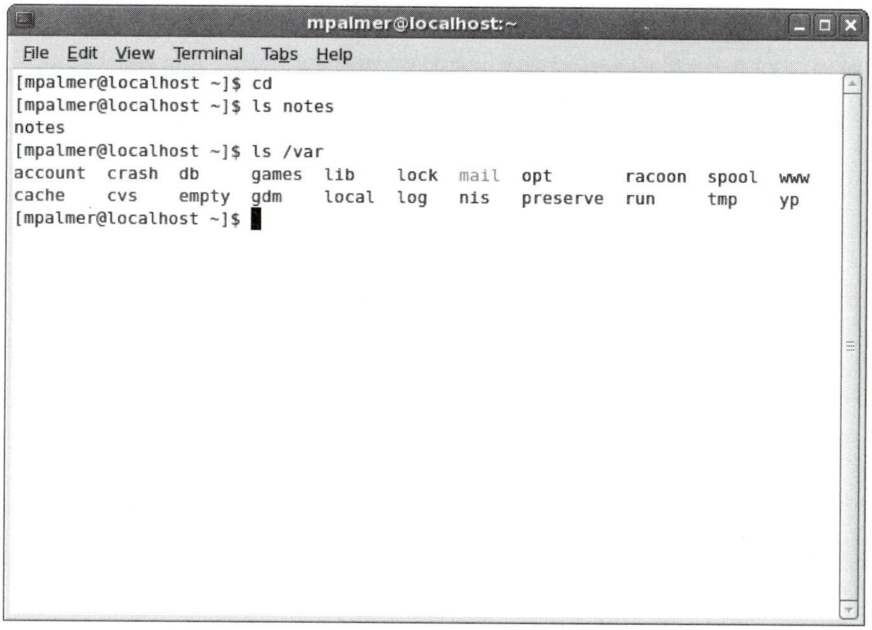

2

```
                          mpalmer@localhost:~
File  Edit  View  Terminal  Tabs  Help
[mpalmer@localhost ~]$ cd
[mpalmer@localhost ~]$ ls notes
notes
[mpalmer@localhost ~]$ ls /var
account  crash  db      games  lib    lock  mail  opt             racoon  spool  www
cache    cvs    empty   gdm    local  log   nis   preserve  run           tmp    yp
[mpalmer@localhost ~]$
```

Figure 2-10   Viewing the contents of the /var directory

To use the *ls* command with the *-l* option:

1. Type **ls –l /dev** and press **Enter**. You see information similar to that in Figure 2-11. This shows a listing of block special and character special files in the /dev directory. Notice in the first column of information that the block special files begin with a "b". (You may need to scroll up to find a block special file.) What designates a character special file?

2. Type **ls –l /** and press **Enter** to view the contents of the root file system directory. (Refer to Figure 2-5 earlier in this chapter.)

To list hidden files in your home directory:

1. Type **clear** and press **Enter** to clear the screen.

2. Type **ls –a** after the command prompt and press **Enter**. (See Figure 2-12.)

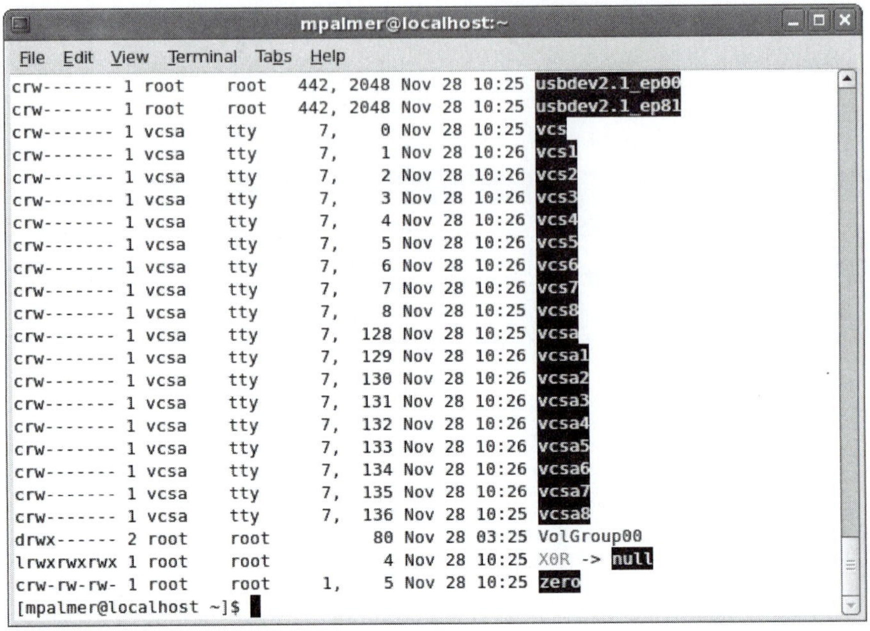

```
                          mpalmer@localhost:~                        _  □  x
File  Edit  View  Terminal  Tabs  Help
crw------- 1 root    root    442, 2048 Nov 28 10:25 usbdev2.1_ep00
crw------- 1 root    root    442, 2048 Nov 28 10:25 usbdev2.1_ep81
crw------- 1 vcsa    tty      7,    0 Nov 28 10:25 vcs
crw------- 1 vcsa    tty      7,    1 Nov 28 10:26 vcs1
crw------- 1 vcsa    tty      7,    2 Nov 28 10:26 vcs2
crw------- 1 vcsa    tty      7,    3 Nov 28 10:26 vcs3
crw------- 1 vcsa    tty      7,    4 Nov 28 10:26 vcs4
crw------- 1 vcsa    tty      7,    5 Nov 28 10:26 vcs5
crw------- 1 vcsa    tty      7,    6 Nov 28 10:26 vcs6
crw------- 1 vcsa    tty      7,    7 Nov 28 10:26 vcs7
crw------- 1 vcsa    tty      7,    8 Nov 28 10:25 vcs8
crw------- 1 vcsa    tty      7,  128 Nov 28 10:25 vcsa
crw------- 1 vcsa    tty      7,  129 Nov 28 10:25 vcsa1
crw------- 1 vcsa    tty      7,  130 Nov 28 10:26 vcsa2
crw------- 1 vcsa    tty      7,  131 Nov 28 10:26 vcsa3
crw------- 1 vcsa    tty      7,  132 Nov 28 10:26 vcsa4
crw------- 1 vcsa    tty      7,  133 Nov 28 10:26 vcsa5
crw------- 1 vcsa    tty      7,  134 Nov 28 10:26 vcsa6
crw------- 1 vcsa    tty      7,  135 Nov 28 10:26 vcsa7
crw------- 1 vcsa    tty      7,  136 Nov 28 10:25 vcsa8
drwx------ 2 root    root          80 Nov 28 03:25 VolGroup00
lrwxrwxrwx 1 root    root           4 Nov 28 10:25 X0R -> null
crw-rw-rw- 1 root    root      1,    5 Nov 28 10:25 zero
[mpalmer@localhost ~]$
```

Figure 2-11   Using *ls -l* to view the /dev directory

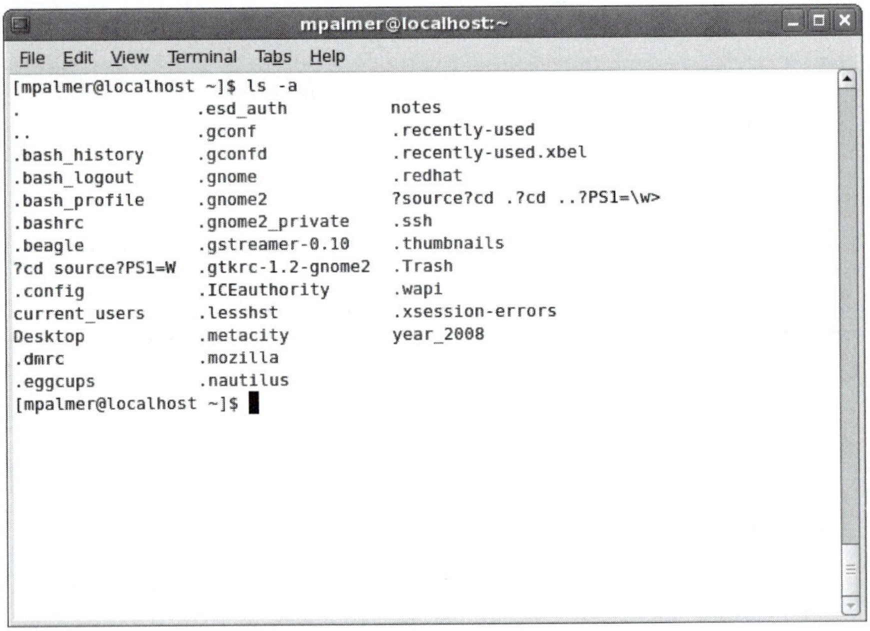

```
                          mpalmer@localhost:~                        _  □  x
File  Edit  View  Terminal  Tabs  Help
[mpalmer@localhost ~]$ ls -a
.                    .esd_auth            notes
..                   .gconf               .recently-used
.bash_history        .gconfd              .recently-used.xbel
.bash_logout         .gnome               .redhat
.bash_profile        .gnome2              ?source?cd .?cd ..?PS1=\w>
.bashrc              .gnome2_private      .ssh
.beagle              .gstreamer-0.10      .thumbnails
?cd source?PS1=W     .gtkrc-1.2-gnome2    .Trash
.config              .ICEauthority        .wapi
current_users        .lesshst             .xsession-errors
Desktop              .metacity            year_2008
.dmrc                .mozilla
.eggcups             .nautilus
[mpalmer@localhost ~]$
```

Figure 2-12   Viewing hidden files

Project 2-9

Wildcards are handy when you want to find or work on files that have a specific sequence of characters or when you are searching for a file and are not certain of the correct spelling of that file name. In this project, you will use the * and ? wildcards with the *ls* command.

2

To work with wildcards:

1. To practice using wildcards, you first must create a set of files with similar names. In Chapter 1, you used the *cat* command to create the notes file. Use the *cat* command now to create these five files:

   ❑ **first_name**—A file containing your first name

   ❑ **middle_name**—A file containing your middle name

   ❑ **last_name**—A file containing your last name

   ❑ **full_name1.txt**—A file containing your full name

   ❑ **full_name22.txt**—Another file containing your full name

2. For example, type **cat > first_name**, press **Enter**, type your first name, press **Enter**, and press **Ctrl+d**.

3. Type **ls *name** and press **Enter**. You see first_name, last_name, and middle_name listed.

4. Type **ls full_name?.txt** and press **Enter**. You see full_name1.txt listed.

5. Type **ls *.txt** and press **Enter**. Now, you see full_name1.txt and full_name22.txt listed.

Project 2-10

Assume that you work for a company that is developing a telephone database, and in this project you will be creating directories for the Mail and Receiving Departments, which are referenced in the company's budget and accounting systems as departments 4540 and 4550. After you create the directories, you will begin creating files of department phone numbers to store in those directories. You will use the *mkdir* (make directory) command to create new directories, and then you use the *cat* command to create the phone files. Also, don't delete the files you create because you use them in other projects.

To create new directories and phone files:

1. Type **cd** and press **Enter** to make certain you are in your home directory.

2. Type **mkdir dept_4540** and press **Enter** to make a new directory called dept_4540.

3. Type **ls** and press **Enter**. You see the dept_4540 directory in the listing.

4. Type **cd dept_4540** and press **Enter** to change to the new directory. Now, you can use the *cat* command to create a file called phones1. The phones1 file contains fields

for area code, phone prefix, phone number, last name, and first name. A colon (:) separates each field.

5. Type these commands, pressing **Enter** at the end of each line:

   cat > phones1

   219:432:4567:Harrison:Joel

   219:432:4587:Mitchell:Barbara

   219:432:4589:Olson:Timothy

6. Press **Ctrl+d**.

7. Type **cat phones1** and press **Enter** to view and verify the contents of the file you created.

8. Type **cd** and press **Enter** to return to your /home directory.

9. Type **mkdir dept_4550** and press **Enter** to make a new directory called dept_4550.

10. Type **ls** and press **Enter**. You see the dept_4550 directory in the listing.

11. Type **cd dept_4550** and press **Enter** to change to the new directory. Now you can use the *cat* command to create the file phones2, which contains the same fields as the phones1 file.

12. Type these commands, pressing **Enter** at the end of each line:

    cat > phones2

    219:432:4591:Moore:Sarah

    219:432:4522:Polk:John

    219:432:4501:Robinson:Lisa

13. Press **Ctrl+d**.

14. Type **cat phones2** and press **Enter** to view and verify the contents of the phones2 file.

15. Type **clear** and press **Enter** to clear the screen for the next project.

HANDS-ON PROJECTS

Project 2-11

After you create the phones files, you will need to create a new central directory called corp_db for general access to the information, and you will copy the phones1 file into the new directory. Next, using > you merge phones1 and phones2 into one file, called corp_phones in your new directory. Note that you can use the tilde character (~) to represent the location of your home directory.

To copy the phones1 file into a new directory, corp_db:

1. Type **cd** and press **Enter** to return to your home directory.

2. Type **mkdir corp_db** and press **Enter** to make a new directory.

3. Type **cd corp_db** and press **Enter** to change to the new directory.

4. To copy the phones1 file from the dept_4540 directory to the current directory, type **cp ~/dept_4540/phones1 .** and press **Enter**.

5. To copy the phones2 file from the dept_4550 directory to the current directory, type **cp ~/dept_4550/phones2 .** and press **Enter**. (See Figure 2-13.)

6. Type **ls** and press **Enter** to ensure that phones1 and phones2 are now in the new directory.

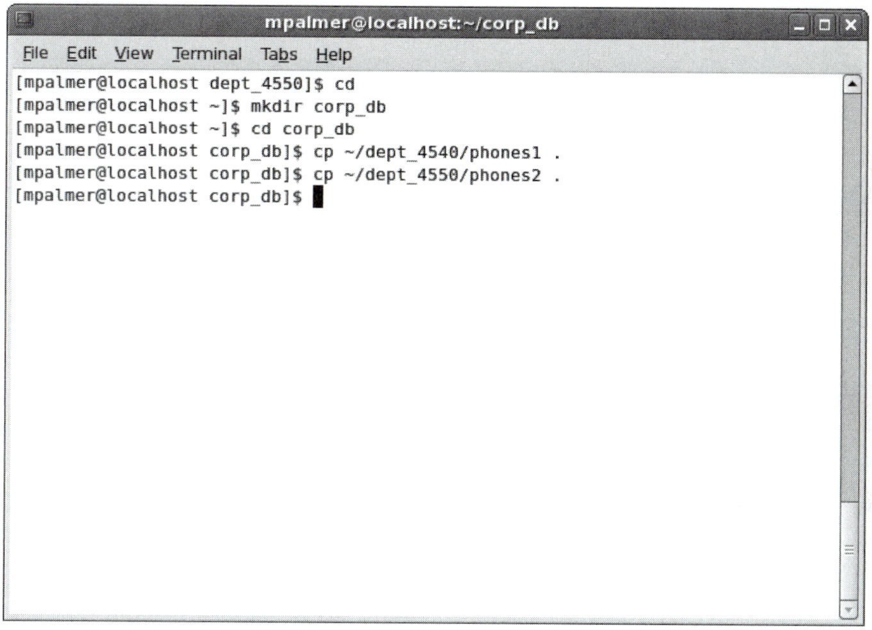

```
mpalmer@localhost:~/corp_db

File  Edit  View  Terminal  Tabs  Help
[mpalmer@localhost dept_4550]$ cd
[mpalmer@localhost ~]$ mkdir corp_db
[mpalmer@localhost ~]$ cd corp_db
[mpalmer@localhost corp_db]$ cp ~/dept_4540/phones1 .
[mpalmer@localhost corp_db]$ cp ~/dept_4550/phones2 .
[mpalmer@localhost corp_db]$ █
```

Figure 2-13   Creating a directory and copying files into it

To concatenate the phones1 and phones2 files into one file:

1. Type **cat phones1 phones2 > corp_phones** and press **Enter** to add the contents of the two phone files to one new file called corp_phones.

2. Type **clear** and press **Enter** to clear the screen.

3. Type **more corp_phones** and press **Enter** to view the new file's contents, as shown in Figure 2-14.

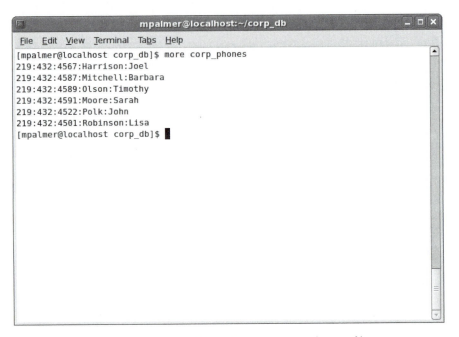

Figure 2-14   Viewing the contents of the new corp_phones file

 As you recall from Chapter 1, the *more* command, which lets you display files one screen at a time, is especially useful for reading long files.

NOTE

HANDS-ON PROJECTS

Project 2-12

Assume that you want all users to have access to the corp_phones file. In this project, you first grant access to your home directory. Next, you allow access to the corp_db directory, and then set the permissions for everyone to read the corp_phones file. You use the *chmod* command with the *x* argument to grant access to directories.

To change file and directory permissions:

1. Make certain that you are in your home directory. (Type **cd** and press **Enter.**)

2. Type **clear** and press **Enter** to clear the screen.

3. Type **chmod go+x ~** and press **Enter** to allow access to your home directory.

   This command means "make your home directory (~) accessible (+x) to the group (g) and others (o)."

4. Type **chmod ugo+x ~/corp_db** and press **Enter** to allow access to the corp_db directory.

   This command means "make the corp_db directory accessible (+x) for the owner (u), group (g), and others (o)."

5. Type **chmod o+w ~/corp_db/*** and press **Enter** to set permissions so that others can write to the files in the corp_db directory. (Owner and group already have write permission by default.)

This command means "make all files in the corp_db directory so that others (o) can write (+w) to them."

6. Type **ls -l ~/corp_db** to check the permissions you have set. (See Figure 2-15.)

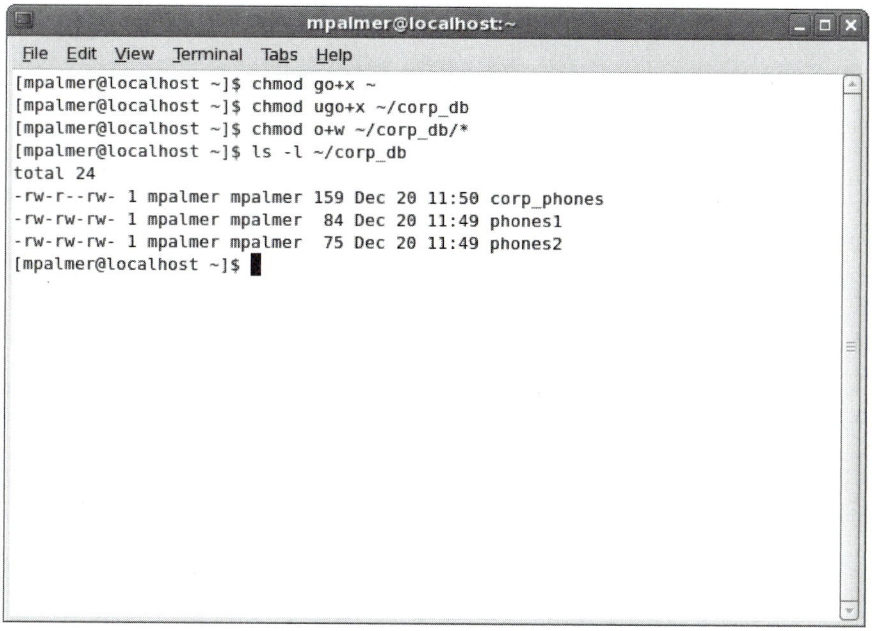

```
                              mpalmer@localhost:~

 File  Edit  View  Terminal  Tabs  Help
[mpalmer@localhost ~]$ chmod go+x ~
[mpalmer@localhost ~]$ chmod ugo+x ~/corp_db
[mpalmer@localhost ~]$ chmod o+w ~/corp_db/*
[mpalmer@localhost ~]$ ls -l ~/corp_db
total 24
-rw-r--rw- 1 mpalmer mpalmer 159 Dec 20 11:50 corp_phones
-rw-rw-rw- 1 mpalmer mpalmer  84 Dec 20 11:49 phones1
-rw-rw-rw- 1 mpalmer mpalmer  75 Dec 20 11:49 phones2
[mpalmer@localhost ~]$ █
```

Figure 2-15   Permissions changes to enable users' access

DISCOVERY EXERCISES

1. Use the *ls* command to list the contents of the root file system directory (/) on your system.

2. Use the *ls -l* command to view the contents of the root file system directory (/).

3. Determine the inode value for the /etc directory.

4. Make /etc your current working directory and then go back to your home directory.

5. Make the root file system directory your current working directory. What command can you use to verify that you are in the root file system directory? Return to your home directory.

6. The file info.txt is in the help directory, which is a subdirectory of the /dev directory. What is the absolute path to info.txt?

7. Change to the /dev directory. Next, access your home directory using a tilde (~) in the command that you employ.

8. Determine whether there are any hidden files in the /home directory.

9. Make a directory under your home directory called documents. Next, make a directory under the documents directory called spreadsheets. What is the absolute path for the spreadsheets directory?

10. Make certain you are in your home directory. Use a relative path to make your new documents directory the current working directory. Next, use a relative path to make the spreadsheets directory your current working directory. Now use a command with dots in it to make the documents directory your current working directory.

11. With your home directory as your current directory, use the command to remove read, write, and execute permissions from group and others for the spreadsheets directory. Next, verify that your change has taken place.

12. Use the *cat* command to create a two-line file in your home directory called datainfo. On the first line, enter 144, and on the second line, enter 288. After the file is created, copy it from your home directory to the spreadsheets directory you created.

13. Determine the default permissions on the datainfo file you created. Next, set the permissions on the datainfo file so that the owner, group, and others can read and execute the file. (Otherwise, leave the default settings as is.)

14. Append the current month's calendar to the datainfo file that is in your home directory. Next, copy your changed datainfo file over the older datainfo file in the spreadsheets directory, but use the copy option that prompts you before you overwrite the file in the spreadsheets directory. Check the contents of the datainfo file in the spreadsheets directory to make certain your copy was successful.

15. Make the spreadsheets directory your working directory. Make copies of the datainfo file in the spreadsheets directory, so that one copy is named myinfo and one is named datadata. Next, use a wildcard character to list all files that start with "data." Use a wildcard character to list all files that end with "info." Use a wildcard character combination to list all files that have "ata" as the second, third, and fourth characters.

16. Make certain you are in your home directory. Change your command prompt so that it shows your current working directory with an exclamation point, such as *mydirectory!* Change to the spreadsheets and then to the documents directory and notice how the prompt changes.

17. Change to your home directory. Use the *rmdir* command to delete the spreadsheets directory. What happens?

18. Delete the datainfo files in both your home directory and in the spreadsheets directory. Also, delete the myinfo and datadata files in the spreadsheets directory.

19. Change to your home directory. Delete the spreadsheets directory and then delete the documents directory.

20. Create a directory called secure under your home directory. Next, using the octal permission format, set security on the secure directory so that you have all permissions and no one else has any permissions.

3

MASTERING EDITORS

After reading this chapter and completing the exercises, you will be able to:

♦ Explain the basics of UNIX/Linux files, including ASCII, binary, and executable files

♦ Understand the types of editors

♦ Create and edit files using the vi editor

♦ Create and edit files using the Emacs editor

The ability to create and modify the contents of files is a fundamental skill not only in producing documents such as memos, reports, and letters, but also in writing programs and customizing system configuration files. All operating systems, including UNIX/Linux, provide one or more editors that enable you to work with the contents of files.

This chapter introduces two important UNIX/Linux editors, which you use throughout the rest of this book. The vi editor provides basic editing functions and is often preferred by UNIX/Linux administrators and programmers for its simplicity. The Emacs editor offers more sophisticated editing capabilities for writing all kinds of documents as well as programs. Both of these popular editors can be started from the command line and are included in most versions of UNIX/Linux.

Understanding UNIX/Linux Files

Almost everything you create in UNIX/Linux is stored in a file. All information stored in files is in the form of binary digits. A binary digit, called a **bit** for short, is in one of two states. The states are 1 (on) and 0 (off). They can indicate, for example, the presence or absence of voltage in an electronic circuit. Because the computer consists of electronic circuits that are either in an on or off state, binary numbers are perfectly suited to report these states. The exclusive use of 0s and 1s as a way to communicate with the computer is known as **machine language**. The earliest programmers had to write their programs using machine language, a tedious and time-consuming process.

ASCII Text Files

To make information stored in files accessible, computer designers established a standard method for translating binary numbers into plain English. This standard uses a string of eight binary digits, called a **byte**, which is the abbreviation for binary term. A byte can be configured into fixed patterns of bits, and these patterns can be interpreted as an alphabetic character, decimal number, punctuation mark, or a special character, such as &, *, or @. Each byte, or code, has been standardized into a set of bit patterns known as ASCII. **ASCII** stands for the American Standard Code for Information Interchange. Computer files containing nothing but printable characters are called **text files**, and files that contain nonprintable characters, such as machine instructions, are called **binary files**. The ASCII character set represents 256 characters. Figure 3-1 lists the printable and nonprintable ASCII characters.

NOTE   Many nonprintable ASCII characters are available. Some examples are characters used to control printers, such as the escape (ESC) character to show the start of a printing command, a form feed (FF) character, and a line feed (LF) character. If you use Microsoft Word or OpenOffice.org Writer, you are familiar with other nonprinting characters, such as the paragraph symbol. You can view nonprinting characters in Microsoft Word or OpenOffice.org Writer by clicking the Show/Hide ¶ or Nonprinting Characters button (paragraph symbol) on the Standard toolbar.

Some operating systems also support **Unicode**. Unicode offers up to 65,536 characters, although not all of the possible characters are currently defined. Unicode was developed because the 256 characters in ASCII are not enough for some languages, such as Chinese, that use more than 256 characters. Visit *www.unicode.org* to learn more about Unicode.

Binary Files

Computers are not limited to processing ASCII codes. To work with graphic information, such as icons, illustrations, and other images, binary files can include strings of bits representing white and black dots, in which each black dot represents a 1 and each white dot

Printing Characters (Punctuation Characters)

Dec	Octal	Hex	ASCII
32	040	20	(Space)
33	041	21	!
34	042	22	"
35	043	23	#
36	044	24	$
37	045	25	%
38	046	26	&
39	047	27	'
40	050	28	(
41	051	29	)
42	052	2A	*
43	053	2B	+
44	054	2C	,
45	055	2D	-
46	056	2E	.
47	057	2F	/

(Decimal Numbers—Print)

Dec	Octal	Hex	ASCII
48	060	30	0
49	061	31	1
50	062	32	2
51	063	33	3
52	064	34	4
53	065	35	5
54	066	36	6
55	067	37	7
56	070	38	8
57	071	39	9

(Special Characters—Print)

Dec	Octal	Hex	ASCII
58	072	3A	:
59	073	3B	;
60	074	3C	<
61	075	3D	=
62	076	3E	>
63	077	3F	?
64	080	40	@

Printing Characters (Alphabet—Uppercase)

Dec	Octal	Hex	ASCII
65	101	41	A
66	102	42	B
67	103	43	C
68	104	44	D
69	105	45	E
70	106	46	F
71	107	47	G
72	110	48	H
73	111	49	I
74	112	4A	J
75	113	4B	K
76	114	4C	L
77	115	4D	M
78	116	4E	N
79	117	4F	O
80	120	50	P
81	121	51	Q
82	122	52	R
83	123	53	S
84	124	54	T
85	125	55	U
86	126	56	V
87	127	57	W
88	130	58	X
89	131	59	Y
90	132	5A	Z

Printing Characters (Alphabet—Lowercase)

Dec	Octal	Hex	ASCII
97	141	61	a
98	142	62	b
99	143	63	c
100	144	64	d
101	145	65	e
102	146	66	f
103	147	67	g
104	150	68	h
105	151	69	i
106	152	6A	j
107	153	6B	k
108	154	6C	l
109	155	6D	m
110	156	6E	n
111	157	6F	o
112	160	70	p
113	161	71	q
114	162	72	r
115	163	73	s
116	164	74	t
117	165	75	u
118	166	76	v
119	167	77	w
120	170	78	x
121	171	79	y
122	172	7A	z

Nonprinting Characters (Abridged) Control Characters

Dec	Octal	Hex	ASCII
0	000	00	^@ (Null)
7	007	07	Bell
8	010	08	Backspace
9	011	09	Tab
10	012	0A	Line Feed, Newline
11	013	0B	Vertical tab
12	014	0C	Form feed
13	015	0D	Carriage return

Figure 3-1 ASCII characters

represents a 0. Graphics files include bit patterns—rows and columns of dots called a **bitmap**—that must be translated by graphics software, commonly called a graphics viewer, which transforms a complex array of bits into an image.

Executable Program Files

Many programmers develop source code for their programs by writing text files; then, they compile these files to convert them into executable program files. **Compiling** is a process of translating a program file into machine-readable language. Programmers and users also develop scripts, which are files containing commands. Scripts are typically not compiled into machine code prior to running, but are executed through an interpreter. At the time the script is run, the interpreter looks at each line and converts the commands on each line into actions taken by the computer. Scripts are interpreted program files that are executable. You learn more about writing program code, scripts, compilers, and interpreters later in this book.

NOTE

Compiled and interpreted files that can be run are called **executable program files** (or sometimes just **executables**). These files can be run from the command line.

USING EDITORS

An **editor** is a program for creating and modifying files containing source code, text, data, memos, reports, and other information. A **text editor** is like a simplified word-processing program; you can use a text editor to create and edit documents, but many text editors do not allow you to format text using boldface text, centered text, or other text-enhancing features.

Editors let you create and edit ASCII files. UNIX/Linux normally include the two editors vi and Emacs. They are **screen editors**, because they display the text you are editing one screen at a time and let you move around the screen to change and add text. Both are text editors as well, because they work like simple word processors. You can also use a line editor to edit text files. A **line editor** lets you work with only one line or group of lines at a time. Although line editors do not let you see the context of your editing, they are useful for general tasks, such as searching, replacing, and copying blocks of text. In UNIX/Linux, however, most users prefer vi or Emacs to using a simple line editor, which is another reason why vi and Emacs are included with UNIX/Linux systems.

NOTE

The vi and Emacs editors do not offer the same functionality as GUI-based editors such as Microsoft Word (although Emacs now has lots of functionality and "snap-ins" for extra functions like editing Web documents). Also, UNIX/Linux systems can use more sophisticated GUI editors, such as OpenOffice.org Writer, gedit in the GNOME desktop, and KEdit in the KDE desktop. However, both vi and Emacs are typically preferred for system, configuration, and programming activities, because they are quickly initiated from the command line and offer a simple, direct way to perform critical editing tasks.

USING THE VI EDITOR

The vi editor is so called because it is visual—it immediately displays on screen the changes you make to text. It is also a **modal editor**; that is, it works in three modes: insert mode, command mode, and extended (ex) command set mode. **Insert mode**, which lets you enter text, is accessed by typing the letter "i" after the vi editor is started. **Command mode**, which is started by pressing Esc, lets you enter commands to perform editing tasks, such as moving through the file and deleting text. **Ex mode** employs an extended set of commands that were initially used in an early UNIX editor called ex. You can access this mode by pressing Esc to enter command mode, and then typing a colon (:) to enter extended commands at the bottom of the screen.

NOTE

You can simulate a line editor using vi by starting the vi editor with the -e option (*vi -e filename*), which places vi exclusively in ex mode. Also, when you open vi, it is set up by default to edit a text file. You can edit a binary file by using the -b option with vi.

To use the vi editor, it is important to master the following tasks:

- Creating a file
- Inserting, editing, and deleting text
- Searching and replacing text
- Adding text from other files
- Copying, cutting, and pasting text
- Printing a file
- Saving a file
- Exiting a file

NOTE

Different versions of the vi editor are included in different versions of UNIX/Linux. The commands described in this chapter generally apply to most UNIX/Linux vi editor versions. However, they particularly apply to the vi editor in Fedora, Red Hat Enterprise Linux, and SUSE, which is technically called the vim (vi improved) editor.

Creating a New File in the vi Editor

To create a new file in the vi editor:

1. Access the command line.
2. Enter *vi* plus the name of the file you want to create, such as *vi data*.

These steps open the vi editor and enable you to begin entering text in the file you specify. Remember, though, at this point the file is in memory and is not permanently saved to the disk until you issue the command to save it.

As you enter text, the line containing the cursor is the current line. Lines containing a tilde (~) are not part of the file; they indicate lines on the screen only, not lines of text in the file. (See Figure 3-2.)

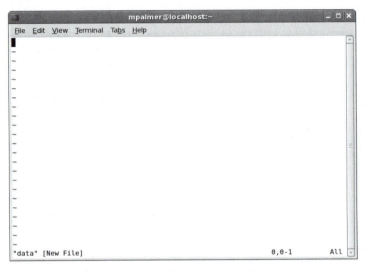

Figure 3-2 Creating a new file in the vi editor

Hands-on Project 3-1 enables you to create a new file using the vi editor.

Sometimes you might open the vi editor without specifying the file name with the vi command on the command line. You can save the file and specify a file name at any time by pressing Esc, typing *:w filename*, and pressing Enter.

Inserting Text

When you start the vi editor, you're in command mode. This means that the editor interprets anything you type on the keyboard as a command. Before you can insert text in your new file, you must use the *i* (insert) command. In insert mode, every character you type appears on the screen. You can return to command mode at any time by pressing the Esc key.

Try Hands-on Project 3-2 to insert text in the vi editor.

Repeating a Change

The vi editor offers features that can save you time. One such feature is the ability to replicate any changes you make. When you are in command mode, you can use a period (.) to repeat the most recent change you made. This is called the repeat command and it can save you time when typing the same or similar text. Hands-on Project 3-3 uses the repeat command.

Moving the Cursor

When you want to move the cursor to a different line or to a specific position on the same line, use command mode (press Esc). In command mode, you can move forward or back one word, move up or down a line, go to the beginning of the file, and so on. Table 3-1 summarizes useful cursor-movement commands. You can practice moving the cursor in Hands-on Project 3-4.

Table 3-1   vi editor's cursor movement keys

Key	Movement
h or left arrow	Left one character position
l or right arrow	Right one character position
k or up arrow	Up one line
j or down arrow	Down one line
H	Upper-left corner of the screen
L	Last line on the screen
G	Beginning of the last line
nG	The line specified by a number, *n*
W	Forward one word
b	Back one word
0 (zero)	Beginning of the current line
$	End of the current line
Ctrl+u	Up one-half screen
Ctrl+d	Down one-half screen
Ctrl+f or *Page Down*	Forward one screen
Ctrl+b or *Page Up*	Back one screen

Remember that the Ctrl key combinations and the letter keys shown in Table 3-1 are designed to work in command mode. The arrow keys, which are used for moving around text, work in both command and insert mode. Try Hands-on Project 3-4 to practice using vi in command mode to move around in a file.

NOTE   Using the letter keys to move the cursor can be traced to the time when UNIX/Linux used teletype terminals that had no arrow keys. Designers of vi chose the letter keys because of their relative position on the keyboard.

Deleting Text

The vi editor employs several commands for deleting text when you are in command mode. For example, to delete the text at the cursor, type *x*. Use *dd* in command mode to delete the current line. Use *dw* to delete a word or to delete from the middle of a word to the end of the word. To delete more than one character, combine the delete commands with the cursor movement commands you learned in the preceding section. Table 3-2 summarizes the most common delete commands.

Table 3-2 vi editor's delete commands

Command	Purpose
x	Delete the character at the cursor.
dd	Delete the current line (putting it in a buffer so it can also be pasted back into the file).
dw	Delete the word starting at the cursor. If the cursor is in the middle of the word, delete from the cursor to the end of the word.
d$	Delete from the cursor to the end of the line.
d0	Delete from the cursor to the start of the line.

The command to delete a line, *dd*, actually places deleted lines in a buffer. You can then use the command *p* to paste deleted (cut) lines elsewhere in the text. (Position the cursor where you want to paste the information.) To copy and paste text, use the "yank" command, *yy*, to copy the lines. After yanking the lines you want to paste elsewhere, move the cursor, and type *p* to paste the text in the current location. You learn more about the *p* and *yy* commands in later sections of this chapter.

Hands-on Project 3-5 gives you the opportunity to practice using delete commands.

Undoing a Command

If you complete a command and then realize you want to reverse its effects, you can use the undo (*u*) command. For example, if you delete a few lines from a file by mistake, type *u* to restore the text.

Searching for a Pattern

You can search forward for a pattern of characters by typing a forward slash (/), typing the pattern you are seeking, and then pressing Enter. Programmers often call this a "string search." For example, suppose you want to know how many times you used the word "insure" in a file. First, go to the top of the file, type */insure*, and press Enter to find the first instance of insure. To find more instances, type *n* while you are in command mode.

When placed after the forward slash, several special characters are supported by vi when searching for a pattern. For example, the special characters \> are used to search for the next word that ends with a specific string. If you enter */te\>* you find the next word that ends with "te," such as "write" or "byte." The characters \< search for the next word that begins with a specific string, such as using */\<top* to find the next word that begins with "top," which might be "topology," for example. The ^ special character searches for the next line that begins with a specific pattern. For instance, */^However* finds the next line that starts with "However." Use a period as a wildcard to match characters. For example, */m.re* finds "more" and "mere," and */s..n* finds "seen," "soon," and "sign." Also, use brackets *[ ]* to find any of the characters between the brackets, such as */theat[er]* to find "theater" or "theatre," and */pas[st]* to find "pass" or "past." Finally, use *$* to find a line that ends with a specific character. For instance */!$* finds a line that ends with an exclamation point "!". You can type *n* after searching with any of these special

characters to find the next pattern that matches. Table 3-3 summarizes the special characters used to match a pattern.

Table 3-3   Special characters used to match a pattern

Special Character*	Purpose
\>	Searches for the next word that ends with a specific string.
\<	Searches for the next word that begins with a specific string.
.	Acts as a wildcard for one character.
[]	Finds the characters between the brackets.
$	Searches for the line that ends with a specific character.
*All of these special characters must be preceded with a slash (/) from the command mode.	

Hands-on Project 3-6 provides experience in pattern matching.

TIP

If you are in an editing session and want to review information about the file status, press Ctrl+g or Ctrl+G (you can use uppercase G or lowercase g). The status line at the bottom of the screen displays information, including line-oriented commands and error messages.

Searching and Replacing

Suppose you want to change all occurrences of "insure" in the file you are editing to "ensure." Instead of searching for "insure," and then deleting it and inserting "ensure," you can search and replace with one command. The commands you learned so far are screen-oriented. Commands that can perform more than one action (searching and replacing) are line-oriented commands and they operate in ex mode.

Screen-oriented commands execute at the location of the cursor. You do not need to tell the computer where to perform the operation because it takes place relative to the cursor. **Line-oriented commands**, on the other hand, require you to specify an exact location (an address) for the operation. Screen-oriented commands are easy to type, and their changes appear on the screen. Typing line-oriented commands is more complicated, but they can execute independently of the cursor and in more than one place in a file, saving you time and keystrokes.

A colon (:) precedes all line-oriented commands. It acts as a prompt on the status line, which is the bottom line on the screen in the vi editor. You enter line-oriented commands on the status line, and press Enter when you complete the command.

NOTE

In this chapter, all instructions for line-oriented commands include the colon as part of the command.

For example, to replace all occurrences of "insure" with "ensure," you first enter command mode (press Esc), type *:1,$s/insure/ensure/g*, and press Enter. This command means access the ex mode (*:*), beginning with the first line (*1*) to the end of the file (*$*), search for "insure," and replace it with "ensure" (*s/insure/ensure/*) everywhere it occurs on each line (g).

Try Hands-on Project 3-7 to use a line-oriented command for searching and replacing.

Saving a File and Exiting vi

As you edit a file, periodically saving your changes is a good idea. This is especially true if your computer is not on an uninterruptible power supply (UPS). A UPS is a device that provides immediate battery power to equipment during a power failure or brownout.

You can save a file in several ways. One way is to enter command mode and type *:w* to save the file without exiting. (See Figure 3-3.) If you are involved in a relatively long editing session, consider using this command every 10 minutes or so to periodically save your work. If you want to save your changes and exit right away, use *:wq* or *ZZ* from command mode. You can also use *:x* to save and exit. You should always save the file before you exit vi; otherwise, you will lose your changes. Hands-on Project 3-8 enables you to save your changes and exit an editing session.

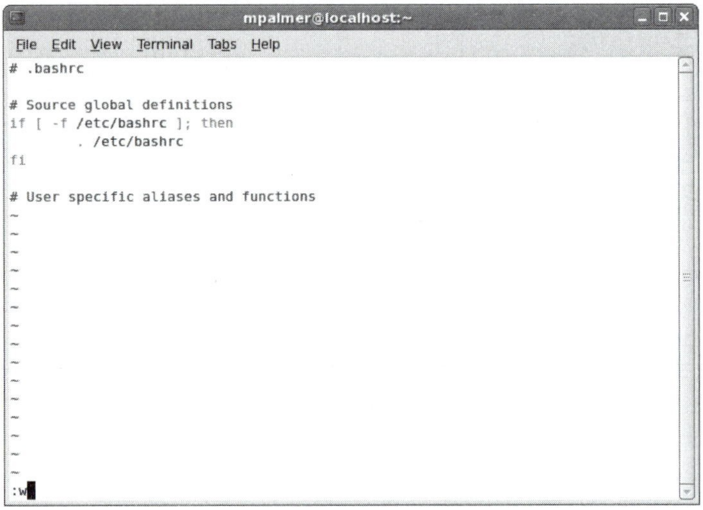

Figure 3-3   Saving without exiting

Adding Text from Another File

Sometimes, the text you want to include in one file is already part of another file. For example, suppose you already have a text file that lists customer accounts and you have another file called customerinfo that contains customer information. You want to copy the customer accounts text into the customerinfo file and make further changes to the customerinfo file. It is much easier to use the vi command to copy the text from the accounts file into the customerinfo file than it is to retype all of the text. To copy the entire contents of one file into another file: (1) use the vi editor to edit the file you want to copy into; and (2) use the command :r *filename*, where *filename* is the name of the file that contains the information you want to copy. Hands-on Project 3-9 enables you to copy from one file into another.

Leaving vi Temporarily

If you want to execute other UNIX/Linux commands while you work with vi, you can launch a shell or execute other commands from within vi. For example, suppose you're working on a text or program file and you want to leave to check the calendar for the current month. To view the calendar from command mode, type :*!cal* (a colon, an exclamation point, and the command) and press Enter. This action executes the *cal* command, and when you press Enter again, you go back into your vi editing session. Using :*!* plus a command-line command enables you to start a new shell, run the command, and then go back into the vi editor.

When you want to run several command-line commands in a different shell without first closing your vi session, use the *Ctrl+z* option to display the command line. (See Figure 3-4.) When you finish executing commands, type *fg* to go back into your vi editing session.

NOTE Using *Ctrl+z* in this context is really a function of the Bash shell, which in this example leaves the vi editor running in the background and takes you to the shell command line. When you enter *fg*, this is a shell command that brings the job you left (the vi editing session) back to the foreground.

Hands-on Project 3-10 enables you to use the :*!* and *Ctrl+z* commands from a vi editing session.

TIP You can set up a script file (a file of commands) that automatically runs when you launch vi. The file is called .exrc and is a hidden file located in your home directory. This file can be used to automatically set up your vi environment. Programmers, for example, who want to view line numbers in every editing session might create an .exrc file and include the *set number* command in the file. To learn more about scripts, see Chapters 6 and 7 ("Introduction to Shell Script Programming" and "Advanced Shell Programming").

Changing Your Display While Editing

Besides using the vi editing commands, you can also set options in vi to control editing parameters, such as using a line number display. Turn on line numbering when you want to work with a range of lines, for example, when you're deleting or cutting and pasting blocks of text. Then, you can refer to the line numbers to specify the text.

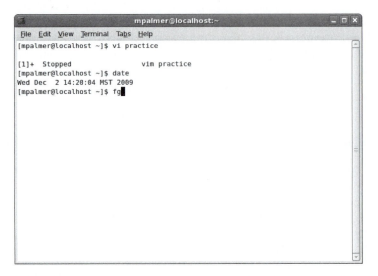

Figure 3-4 Accessing a shell command line from the vi editor

To turn on line numbering, use the *:set number* command. Then, if you want to delete lines 4 through 6, for example, it is easy to determine that these are the lines you intend to delete, and you simply use the *:4,6d* command to delete them. Try Hands-on Project 3-11 to turn on line numbering and then refer to it for deleting text.

Copying or Cutting and Pasting

You can use the *yy* command in vi to copy a specified number of lines from a file and place them on the clipboard. To cut the lines from the file and store them on the clipboard, use the *dd* command. After you use the *dd* or *yy* commands, you can use the *p* command to paste the contents in the clipboard to another location in the file. These commands are handy if you want to copy text you already typed and paste it in another location. Hands-on Project 3-12 enables you to cut text and paste it in another location within the same file.

Printing Text Files

Sometimes you want to print a file before you exit the vi editor. You can use the *lpr* (line print) shell command to print a file from vi. Type *!lpr* and then type the name of the file you want to print. Hands-on Project 3-13 enables you to print a file on which you are working in the vi editor.

You can also specify which printer you want to use via the *-P printer* option, where *printer* is the name of the printer you want to use. For example, you might have two printers, lp1 and lp2. To print the file accounts to lp2, enter *:!lpr -P lp2 accounts* and press Enter.

3

Syntax **lpr** [-option] [*filename*]

Dissection

- The argument consists of the name of the file to print.
- Options include:

  -P specifies the destination printer; you include the name of the printer just after the option.

  -# specifies the number of copies to print (up to 100 copies).

  -r deletes a print file after it is printed (saving disk space).

Canceling an Editing Session

If necessary, you can cancel an editing session and discard all the changes you made in case you change your mind. Another option is to save only the changes you made since last using the *:w* command to save a file without exiting vi. In Hands-on Project 3-14, you exit a file without saving your last change.

Getting Help in vi

You can get help in using vi at any time you are in this editor. To access the online help documentation while you are editing a file, use the *help* command. You can access help documentation after you start the vi editor by pressing Esc, then typing a colon (:), and then *help*. You access the help documentation in Hands-on Project 3-14.

You can also view documentation about vi using the *man vi* command. While you are in vi, press Esc, type *:!man vi*, and press Enter (type *q* and press Enter to go back into your editing session). Or, when you are at the shell command line and not in a vi session, type *man vi* and press Enter.

USING THE EMACS EDITOR

Emacs is another popular UNIX/Linux text editor. Unlike vi, Emacs is not modal. It does not switch from command mode to insert mode. This means that you can type a command without verifying that you are in the proper mode. Although Emacs is more complex than vi, it is more consistent. For example, you can enter most commands by pressing Alt or Ctrl key combinations.

Emacs also supports a sophisticated macro language. A **macro** is a set of commands that automates a complex task. Think of a macro as a "superinstruction." Emacs has a powerful command syntax and is extensible. Its packaged set of customized macros lets you read electronic mail and news and edit the contents of directories. You can start learning Emacs by learning its common keyboard commands. Although Emacs also supports many conventional mouse-based menu options, it is worth your time to learn the keyboard commands. When you know these, you can often navigate and use Emacs keyboard features even faster than going through menus to find the same options. Table 3-4 lists the Emacs keyboard commands.

Table 3-4   Common Emacs commands

Command	Purpose
Alt+<	Move the cursor to the beginning of the file.
Alt+>	Move the cursor to the end of the file.
Alt+b	Move the cursor back one word.
Alt+d	Delete the current word.
Alt+f	Move the cursor forward one word (moving space to space between words).
Alt+q	Reformat current paragraph using word wrap so that lines are full.
Alt+t	If the cursor is under the first character of the word, transpose the word with the preceding word; if the cursor is not under the first character, transpose the word with the following word.
Alt+u	Capitalize all letters from the cursor position in a word to the end of that word.
Alt+w	Scroll up one screen.
Alt+x doctor	Enter doctor mode to play a game in which Emacs responds to your statements with questions. Save your work first. Not all versions support this mode.
Ctrl+@	Mark the cursor location. After moving the cursor, you can move or copy text to the mark.
Ctrl+a	Move the cursor to the beginning of the line.
Ctrl+b	Move the cursor back one character.
Ctrl+d	Delete the character under the cursor.
Ctrl+e	Move the cursor to the end of the line.
Ctrl+f	Move the cursor forward one character.
Ctrl+g	Cancel the current command.
Ctrl+h	Use online help.
Ctrl+k	Delete text to the end of the line.
Ctrl+n	Move the cursor to the next line.
Ctrl+p	Move the cursor to the preceding line.
Ctrl+t	Transpose the character before the cursor and the character under the cursor.
Ctrl+v	Scroll down one screen.
Ctrl+w	Delete the marked text. Press *Ctrl+y* to restore deleted text.
Ctrl+y	Insert text from the file buffer, and place it after the cursor.
Ctrl+h, t	Run a tutorial about Emacs.
Ctrl+x, Ctrl+c	Exit Emacs.
Ctrl+x, Ctrl+s	Save the file.

Table 3-4 Common Emacs commands (continued)

Command	Purpose
Ctrl+x, u	Undo the last change.
Ctrl+Del	Delete text from the current cursor location to the end of the current word.

In most instances, Ctrl and Alt commands in Emacs are not case sensitive, so *Alt+B* and *Alt+b* are the same command.

TIP

If you are using Emacs through a remote connection, such as through SSH (see Chapter 1, "The Essence of UNIX and Linux"), try pressing *Ctrl+F10* or just *F10* to access the menu bar mode. The menu choices appear in a buffer window displayed under your main editing window. This is very useful when you cannot use the common Emacs commands through a remote connection.

Creating a New File in Emacs

Start Emacs by entering the *emacs* command in the terminal window or at a command line in UNIX/Linux. If you type a file name after this command, Emacs creates a new, blank file with that name or opens an existing file with that name. If you type *emacs* with no file name, Emacs automatically displays several introductory screens, beginning with the one shown in Figure 3-5 for Fedora. The Emacs window runs under the X Window desktop you have configured, such as GNOME.

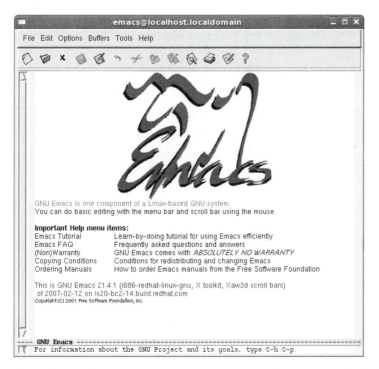

Figure 3-5 Emacs opening screen (without a file name) in Fedora with GNOME

TIP

When you start Emacs without specifying a file to open, the introductory screen display ends on a screen on which you can type notes in a buffer you do not plan to save. You can open an existing file to edit by typing Ctrl+x then Ctrl+f and entering the path and name of the file.

If you have installed a desktop, such as GNOME, there is likely to be a menu option for starting Emacs. At this writing, in Fedora and Red Hat Enterprise Linux with the GNOME desktop you can open Emacs by clicking Applications, pointing to Programming, and clicking Emacs Text Editor. In SUSE, click the Computer menu, click More Applications, click Utilities in the left pane, and click Emacs.

As Figure 3-5 illustrates, there is a menu bar at the top of the Emacs screen. When you click one of the items, such as File, a menu appears. The default menu bar has the following categories:

- *File*—Provides options for operations such as opening a file, opening a directory, saving information in a buffer, inserting information from another file, going into the split window mode, and closing the currently open file (buffer)

- *Edit*—Offers text-editing functions, such as undoing a change, cutting or copying text, pasting text, and so on

- *Options*—Provides all kinds of special options, such as syntax highlighting, region highlighting, word wrap modes, file decompression/compression, debugger options, and "mule" options that are used to set the language environment, fonts, and input method

- *Buffers*—Enables you to open any of the editor's storage buffers that currently hold information, including the text that is already in the file

- *Tools*—Provides options for compiling a program file, executing a shell command, checking the spelling of text, comparing or merging files, installing Emacs patches, reading and sending e-mail, and searching a directory

- *Help*—Provides assistance through access to manuals, a tutorial, Emacs FAQs, and the Emacs psychiatrist, which lets you ask Emacs questions

You also see an icon bar under the menu bar that provides options for the following:

- Reading a file into Emacs

- Reading a directory to access its files

- Exiting and not saving the current buffer

- Saving the contents of the current buffer to a file

- Copying the current buffer contents to a different file

- Undoing the most recent task you performed

- Cutting text

- Copying text

- Pasting text
- Searching ahead for a word pattern or string
- Printing the contents of the current buffer
- Configuring your editing preferences
- Viewing the Help menu

Navigating in Emacs

To create a new file in Emacs, type *emacs* plus the file name at the command line, such as *emacs research*. After you start Emacs, to navigate in the file, you can use either the cursor movement keys—such as the arrow keys, Page Down, Page Up, Home, and End—or Ctrl/Alt key combinations, such as *Alt+f* to move the cursor forward one word (see Table 3-4). When you want to save your work: (1) use the File menu; (2) use the icon to save the current buffer to the file; or (3) press *Ctrl+x, Ctrl+s*. Also, to exit Emacs, use the File menu, Exit Emacs option, or enter *Ctrl+x, Ctrl+c*.

In Hands-on Project 3-15, you create a file and practice saving and exiting. In Hands-on Project 3-16, you practice navigating in a file.

Deleting Information

You can use the Del or Backspace keys to delete individual characters in Emacs. Also, use *Ctrl+k* to delete to the end of a line. If you decide to undo a deletion, use *Ctrl+x, u* (do not press *Ctrl* with the *u*) to repeatedly undo each deletion. Hands-on Project 3-17 enables you to delete text and then undo your deletion.

Copying, Cutting, and Pasting Text

In Emacs, you can insert text simply by typing. You can also insert text by copying and pasting, or by cutting and pasting. Before you copy or cut text, you first need to mark the text with which to work. When you use command keys, navigate to the beginning of the text you want to replicate and press *Ctrl+Spacebar*. Next, navigate to the end of the text you want to include and press *Alt+w* to copy the text, or press *Ctrl+w* to cut the text. Next, move the cursor where you want to place the copied or cut text and press *Ctrl+y* (the *yank* command). This might sound confusing at first; the best way to learn the process is by doing it. Hands-on Project 3-18 enables you to copy and paste text in Emacs.

Searching in Emacs

Like the vi editor, Emacs lets you search for specific text. One way to search is by pressing *Ctrl+s*, entering on the status line the string of characters you want to find, and pressing *Ctrl+s* repeatedly to find each occurrence. You can also use *Ctrl+r* to search backward.

Another way to search for a string is to use the *Search forward for a string icon* or to click the Edit menu, point to Search, and click Search. In both cases, you then type the search string on the status line and press Enter. Try Hands-on Project 3-19 to search for a string.

Reformatting a File

Often, as you create a document, you want to set it up so that the lines automatically wrap around from one line to the next. Use the *Alt+q* command to turn on the word wrap feature in Emacs. Hands-on Project 3-20 teaches you to use word wrap.

Getting Help in Emacs

Emacs comes with extensive documentation and a tutorial. The Emacs tutorial is a good way to get up to speed quickly. Click the Help menu and click Emacs Tutorial; or, in most versions of Emacs, type *Ctrl+h* and then type *t*. You can also view general Emacs documentation by entering *Ctrl+h* (press this one or two times) while you are in Emacs or type *man emacs* at the command line.

CHAPTER SUMMARY

- ❏ Bits represent digital 1s and 0s. Bytes are computer characters (a series of bits) stored using numeric codes. A set of standardized codes known as ASCII codes is often used to represent characters. ASCII stands for the American Standard Code for Information Interchange. Computer files that contain only ASCII characters (bytes) are called text files.

- ❏ The vi editor is a popular choice among UNIX/Linux users. Standard editors process text files. Text files are also called ASCII files. The vi editor is a modal editor, because it works in three modes: insert, command, and ex mode. Insert mode (press *i*) lets you enter text, whereas command mode (press Esc) lets you navigate the file and modify the text. Ex mode (type *:* in command mode) is used to access an extended set of commands, including the commands to save and exit a file.

- ❏ In the vi editor's insert mode, characters you type are inserted in the file. They are not interpreted as vi commands. To exit insert mode and reenter command mode, press Esc.

- ❏ With vi, you initially edit a copy of the file placed in the computer's memory. You do not alter the file itself until you save it on disk.

- ❏ To get help for the vi editor, press Esc and enter *:help* or view the man documentation from the command line by entering *man vi*.

- ❏ The Emacs editor is a popular alternative to the vi editor and, along with vi, is included with most UNIX/Linux systems.

- ❏ Unlike vi, Emacs is not modal—it does not switch between modes. Emacs has a powerful command syntax, is extensible, and supports a sophisticated language of macro commands. A macro is a set of commands designed to simplify a complex task. Emacs' packaged set of customized macros lets you read electronic mail and news, and edit the contents of directories.

❐ You can start Emacs by typing *emacs* at the command line with or without a file name. If you enter this command and then type a file name, Emacs creates a new, blank file with that name, or opens an existing file with that name. If you type *emacs* with no file name, Emacs displays an introductory screen. You can then use a command to open an existing file or create a new file.

❐ You can use either the cursor movement keys—such as the arrow keys, Page Down, Page Up, Home, and End—or Ctrl/Alt key combinations to navigate an Emacs file.

❐ In Emacs, as well as in vi, you can undo your editing changes in sequence, even after you've made many changes.

❐ In Emacs, you can insert text simply by typing. You can also insert text by copying and pasting, or by cutting and pasting. Like the vi editor, Emacs lets you search for specific text. Emacs also has an automatic word wrap capability.

❐ For Emacs help, type *Ctrl+h* (press *t* for a tutorial) while in Emacs or use the *man emacs* command from the command line.

COMMAND SUMMARY: REVIEW OF CHAPTER 3 COMMANDS

Command	Purpose
vi commands:	
. (repeat)	Repeat your most recent change.
/	Search forward for a pattern of characters.
:!	Leave vi temporarily.
:q	Cancel an editing session.
:r	Read text from one file and add it to another.
:set	Turn on certain options, such as line numbering.
:w	Save a file and continue working.
:wq	Write changes to disk and exit vi.
:x	Save changes and exit vi.
:!lpr filename	Print a file.
i	Switch to insert mode.
p	Paste text from the buffer.
u	Undo your most recent change.
vi	Start the vi editor.
yy	Copy (yank) text to the clipboard.
ZZ	In command mode, save changes and exit vi.
Ctrl+z	Use this shell-based command (not truly a vi command) to leave vi to temporarily access the command line—use the **fg** command to return to vi.

Command	Purpose
UNIX/Linux commands:	
lpr	Print a file. -P prints to a specific printer. -# prints a specific number of copies. -r deletes the print file from disk storage.
Emacs commands: See Table 3-4	

KEY TERMS

ASCII — An acronym for American Standard Code for Information Interchange; a standard set of bit patterns organized and interpreted as alphabetic characters, decimal numbers, punctuation marks, and special characters. The code is used to translate binary numbers into ordinary language, and, therefore, makes information stored in files accessible. ASCII can represent up to 256 characters (bit patterns).

binary file — A file containing non-ASCII characters (such as machine instructions).

bit — The abbreviation for binary digit; a number composed of one of two numbers, 0 and 1. UNIX/Linux store all data in the form of binary digits. Because the computer consists of electronic circuits in either an on or off state, binary digits are perfect for representing these states.

bitmap — The rows and columns of dots or bit patterns that graphics software transforms into an infinite variety of images.

byte — The abbreviation for binary term; a string of eight binary digits or bits. These digits can be configured into patterns of bits, which, in turn, can be interpreted as alphabetic characters, decimal numbers, punctuation marks, and special characters. This is the basis for ASCII code.

command mode — A feature of a modal editor that lets you enter commands to perform editing tasks, such as moving through the file and deleting text. The UNIX/Linux vi editor is a modal editor.

compiling — A process of translating a program file into machine-readable language.

editor — A program for creating and modifying computer documents, such as program and data files.

ex mode — A text-editing command mode, currently used in the vi editor, that employs an extended set of commands initially used in an early UNIX editor called ex.

executable program file — Also called an executable; a compiled file (from a programming language) or an interpreted file (from a script) that can be run on the computer.

insert mode — A feature of a modal editor that lets you enter text. The UNIX/Linux vi editor is a modal editor.

line editor — An editor that lets you work with only one line or a group of lines at once. Although you cannot see the context of your file, you might find a line editor useful for tasks such as searching, replacing, and copying blocks of text.

line-oriented command — A command that can perform more than one action, such as searching and replacing, in more than one place in a file. When using a line-oriented command, you must specify the exact location where the action is to occur. These commands differ from screen-oriented commands, which execute relative to the location of the cursor.

machine language — The exclusive use of 0s (which mean off) and 1s (which mean on) to communicate with the computer. Years ago, programmers had to write programs in machine language, a tedious and time-consuming process.

macro — A set of commands that automates a complex task. A macro is sometimes called a superinstruction.

modal editor — A text editor that enables you to work in different modes. For example, the vi editor has three modes: insert, command, and ex.

screen editor — An editor supplied by the operating system that displays text one screen at a time and lets you move around the screen to add and change text. UNIX/Linux have two screen editors: vi and Emacs.

screen-oriented command — A command that executes relative to the position of the cursor. Screen-oriented commands are easy to type, and you can readily see their result on the screen. These commands differ from line-oriented commands, which execute independently of the location of the cursor.

text editor — A simplified word processor used to create and edit documents but that has no formatting features to boldface or center text, for example.

text file — A computer file composed entirely of ASCII characters.

Unicode — A set of bit patterns that supports up to 65,536 characters and was developed to offer more characters than ASCII for a broader range of languages, such as Chinese.

REVIEW QUESTIONS

1. You are using vi to edit a file and have just entered 12 new lines. You need to replicate the same 12 lines right after you enter them. What command-mode command can you type to replicate the lines? (Choose all that apply.)

   a. *a period (.)*

   b. *Ctrl+r*

   c. *Ctrl+R*

   d. *a dollar sign ($)*

2. Which of the following enables you to move the cursor to the left while you are in command mode in the vi editor? (Choose all that apply.)

   a. Press the right arrow key.

   b. Press the left arrow key.

   c. Press h.

   d. Press l.

3. When you started the vi editor, you forgot to specify the name for the new file you are creating. To save steps next time, how can you specify the name of a new file when you first start vi?

   a. Enter *vi -n* at the command line and then type in the file name when prompted.

   b. Enter *vi -n* and the filename, such as *vi -n myfile*.

   c. Enter *vi* and the filename, such as *vi myfile*.

   d. Enter *vi ?* and then enter the file name when you see the > prompt on the command line.

4. Your colleague has written a line of text in vi and now wants to delete the line, but save its contents in a buffer in case he decides to bring back the line he deletes. What do you recommend?

   a. While in command mode, move the cursor to the last character in the line and press *d-*.

   b. While in insert mode, move the cursor to any character in the line and press *Alt+d*.

   c. While in command mode, move the cursor to the first character in the line and press *dd*.

   d. While in insert mode, move the cursor to the last character in the line and type *:#delete*.

5. You are in the vi editor and it's now noon. Every day at noon you run a program called update, which updates a database. How can you run the program without closing your vi session?

   a. From command mode, press #, type *update*, and press Enter.

   b. From insert mode, press *Alt+* and then type *update*.

   c. From insert mode, press *&&* twice and then type *update*.

   d. From command mode, type *:!update* and press Enter.

6. While you are working on a report in vi, you decide to insert information from another text file in your home directory called summary_data. Which of the following commands (from command mode) enables you to add the contents of summary_data?

   a. *:r summary_data*

   b. *+summary_data*

   c. *add summary_data*

   d. *#copy summary_data*

7. You're editing a document using vi and you are near the end of a page. You want to quickly go back to the top of the page to check something you said. Which of the following command-line commands enables you to quickly go to the top of the page?

   a. *:top*

   b. *T*

   c. *Go1*

   d. *H*

8. You are preparing to give a training session on the vi editor. How would you describe it? (Choose all that apply.)

   a. It is modal.

   b. It is a text editor.

   c. Most UNIX/Linux distributions come with vi.

   d. It is a screen editor.

9. While working in the Emacs editor, you delete a section of text and then decide to undo your deletion. Which of the following commands should you use?

   a. Use the *Ctrl+u* command.

   b. Use the *Alt+u* command.

   c. Use the *Ctrl+x,u* command.

   d. You're stuck retyping the deleted text, because Emacs does not enable you to undelete.

10. When you copy text in Emacs, you must mark the text you want to copy by using which of the following commands?

    a. Use *Ctrl+Tab* to mark the beginning of the text and *Ctrl+Shift* to mark the end. Next press *Alt+z* to copy the text.

    b. Use *Ctrl+Spacebar* to mark the beginning of the text and *Alt+w* to mark the end as well as to copy the text.

    c. Use *:mark* to mark the beginning of the text and *:endmark* to mark the end as well as to copy the text.

    d. Use *@begin* to mark the beginning of the text and *@end* to mark the end. Next type *:copy* to copy the text.

11. You've used Emacs to write advertising copy about a new software product your company has developed. Now you find out that the name of the product has been changed slightly. What command can you use to track down all references to the old name so you can locate them?

    a. Press *Ctrl+s*.

    b. Press *Alt+f*.

    c. Type *:find*.

    d. Type *#locate*.

12. How can you find out information about the status of an editing session while in the vi editor? (Choose all that apply.)

    a. Type *:status* while in command mode.

    b. Press *Ctrl+?* while in insert mode.

    c. Press *Ctrl+g* while in command mode.

    d. Press the *Spacebar* twice while in command mode.

13. You are using the vi editor to create a list of tasks on each line and you would like an easy way to number each line (task) listed in the file. Which of the following is an easy solution?

    a. Press *Alt+F2* to turn on automatic numbering for text.

    b. When you first start vi from the command line, type *vi -n*.

    c. Enter the number 1 plus a period at the beginning of the first line, and then each new line will be numbered automatically.

    d. From command mode, enter *:set number*.

14. You have been working on a long vi text file and now you've got to rush off to a meeting. How can you quickly save your work and exit the vi editor? (Choose all that apply.)

    a. From command mode, enter *:wq*.

    b. From command mode, enter *:ZZ*.

    c. From command mode, enter *:bye*.

    d. From command mode, enter *:x*.

15. While editing a file in vi, you realize you have been spelling the word receive as recieve. How can you find all occurrences of your misspelled receive? (Choose all that apply.)

    a. From command mode, type */recieve* and press Enter.

    b. From insert mode, type *Alt+r* and enter recieve.

    c. From command mode, press *F4* and enter recieve.

    d. From insert mode, press *F7* and enter recieve.

16. As you look over the shoulder of an employee who is using the vi editor, you see her use the command *:1 $s/capitol/capital*. What does this command do?

    a. It converts all letters to capitals in the file.

    b. It changes all instances of capitol to capital.

    c. It searches to ensure that each sentence starts with an uppercase letter.

    d. It finds the last instance of capital and changes it to Capitol.

3

17. You have just pressed *Ctrl+x, Ctrl+s* in the Emacs editor thinking that this will exit Emacs, but it seems like nothing has happened. What is the problem?

    a. The *x* and the *s* are lowercase and you must instead type *X* and *S*.

    b. You have the order reversed and must instead type *Ctrl+s, Ctrl+x*.

    c. *Ctrl+x, Ctrl+s* is a command sequence that saves your file, but it does not cause Emacs to close.

    d. *Ctrl+x, Ctrl+s* is used to expand the buffer size, which is a process you don't see on the screen; and this command sequence does not exit Emacs.

18. You've just finished entering a one-page memo in Emacs and now want to quickly go to the beginning so you can reread it. What command enables you to quickly go to the beginning?

    a. *Alt+b*

    b. *Alt+H*

    c. *Go 1*

    d. *Alt+<*

19. Which of the following are menus that you would find on the menu bar in Emacs? (Choose all that apply.)

    a. View

    b. Options

    c. Edit

    d. Buffers

20. Which of the following commands enables you to use online help in Emacs?

    a. *Ctrl+?*

    b. *Ctrl+h*

    c. *?*

    d. *Ctrl+q*

21. How can you get help for using the vi editor? (Choose all that apply.)

    a. From insert mode, press *:doc.*

    b. From command mode, enter *:help.*

    c. From ex mode, enter *?doc.*

    d. From the regular command line outside of vi, enter *man vi.*

22. What is the name of a standardized bit pattern for characters and numbers that is used by most computer operating systems?

23. What is the process called compiling?

24. How can you print a file while you are in the vi editor?

25. You have started Emacs without specifying a file name for the existing file you want to open. Is there a way to specify the file name and open the file after you've started Emacs, and if so how?

HANDS-ON PROJECTS

 NOTE Hands-on Projects 3-1 through 3-14 are designed to be completed as a block of step-by-step projects in which you learn how to create and edit a file using the vi editor. These projects are performed from the command line (such as a terminal window) using your own account.

 HANDS-ON PROJECTS

Project 3-1

In this project, you start the vi editor by creating a file called textfiles to hold some basic comments about text files. This is simply a practice file to get you started learning the vi editor. It is generally best to learn on a file that is not important to your work. To open vi and create a new file, type *vi* followed by the new file's name.

To open vi and create a new file:

1. After the $ command prompt, type **vi textfiles** and press **Enter**. This starts vi and begins editing a new file called textfiles. Your screen should look similar to the one presented in Figure 3-2 earlier in this chapter.

   In the upper-left corner of your screen, you see the cursor as a solid block. The cursor indicates your current location in the file. The lines beginning with ~ are not actual lines in the file, and as you enter text on a new line, you'll see the tilde disappear from that line. Also, note that the name of your new file appears in double quotation marks on the bottom line in the screen.

2. Leave your vi editing session open for Hands-on Project 3-2.

 TIP If at any time you need to stop and later resume the following projects (through Hands-on Project 3-14) because you cannot complete them in one sitting, press *Esc*, type *:x*, and press *Enter*. When you resume, type *vi* and the file name, such as *vi textfiles*.

Project 3-2

In this project, you practice alternating between the insert and command modes in the vi editor. Next, you type text on which to practice.

To access the insert and command modes:

1. Type **i** (but do not press Enter).

    Like most vi commands, the *i* command does not appear (or echo) on your screen. The command switches you from command mode to insert mode; you don't need to press Enter to signal the command's completion. Notice that "-- INSERT --" appears at the bottom of the screen when you are in insert mode.

2. Press **Esc** to go back into command mode. What happens to the line at the bottom of the screen?

3. Press **i** to reenter insert mode.

4. Type the following text, pressing **Enter** after each line to move to the next line. Be certain that you press Enter after the final line you type to move the cursor to the next line. If you need to delete characters, press the Backspace key.

    Files contain text.
    Text contains lines.
    Lines contain characters.
    Characters form words.
    Words form text.

5. Your cursor should now be at the beginning of the sixth line with no text on that line. (See Figure 3-6.) Leave the vi editor open for Hands-on Project 3-3.

Project 3-3

In this project, you practice using the repeat command (.) to replicate the most recent changes you made to text in the vi editor.

To use the repeat command:

1. Press **Esc** to switch to command mode.

2. Type **.** (period).

    The vi editor inserts the five lines that you typed in Step 4 of Hands-on Project 3-2. Your screen should look similar to the one in Figure 3-7.

3. Keep the vi editor open for Hands-on Project 3-4.

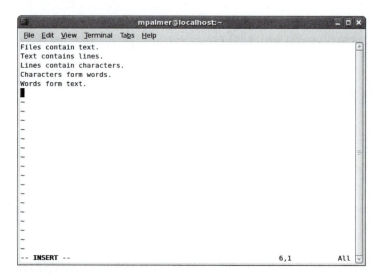

Figure 3-6   Inserting text using the vi editor

Figure 3-7   Repeating a command in the vi editor

Project 3-4

Efficiently moving the cursor to the right spot is vital to editing a file. In this project, you practice moving the cursor around the screen.

To move the cursor around the screen:

1. Press **Esc** to make certain you are in command mode.

2. Press the arrow keys to move up, right, left, and down one character at a time.

3. Type **H** to move the cursor to the upper-left corner of the screen.(*Hint*: Make certain you type uppercase letters as indicated in these steps.)

4. Type **L** to move the cursor to the last line on the screen.

5. Use the **up arrow** key to go to the beginning of the third-to-last line, which starts with "Lines." Use the **right arrow** key to go to the end of that line.

6. Type **G** to go to the beginning of the last line. This is the "go to" command. You can include a number before the G to indicate the line to which you want to move.

7. Type **2G** to move to the beginning of the second line.

8. Type **w** to go forward one word.

9. Type **b** to go back one word. Leave the vi editor open for Hands-on Project 3-5.

HANDS-ON PROJECTS

Project 3-5

People often make typing mistakes or change their mind about what to say in text. Thus the ability to delete is very important. In this project, you use the delete commands and the cursor movement keys to edit text you inserted in your file.

To edit by deleting text:

1. Press **Esc** to be certain you are in command mode.

2. Type **1G** to move to the first line of the file. You want to delete this line.

3. To delete the first line, type **dd** (but do not press Enter).

   Your file should now look like Figure 3-8.

```
                              mpalmer@localhost:~                    _  □  ✕
File  Edit  View  Terminal  Tabs  Help
Text contains lines.
Lines contain characters.
Characters form words.
Words form text.
Files contain text.
Text contains lines.
Lines contain characters.
Characters form words.
Words form text.

~
~
~
~
~
~
~
~
~
~
~
~
                                                  1,1          All
```

Figure 3-8   File after deleting the first line

4. Press **w** to go to the next word, "contains."

5. Type **dw** to delete the current word (so the line now reads "Text lines."), and then type **i** to enter insert mode.

6. Type **consistss of** between "Text" and "lines." Be certain to include the extra "s" and a space after "of."

7. Press the arrow keys to move the cursor to the extra "s" in "consistss," and then press **Esc** to switch to command mode.

8. To delete the current character (the extra "s"), type **x** (but do not press Enter).

   Your file should now look like the one in Figure 3-9.

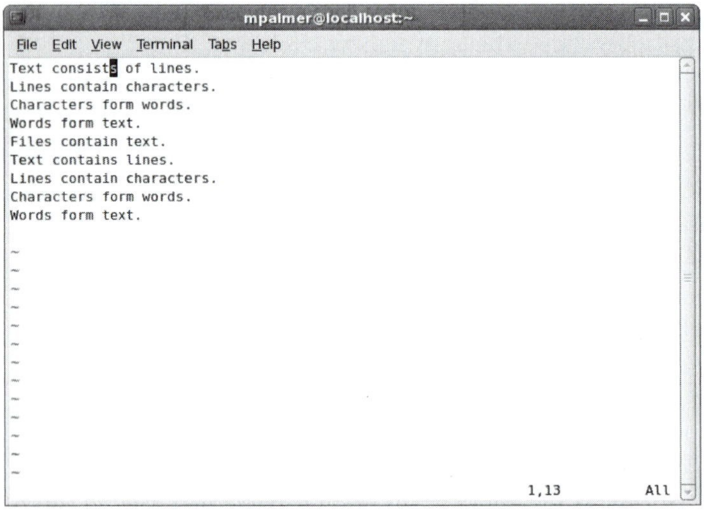

```
                          mpalmer@localhost:~                    _ □ x

 File   Edit   View   Terminal   Tabs   Help
Text consists of lines.
Lines contain characters.
Characters form words.
Words form text.
Files contain text.
Text contains lines.
Lines contain characters.
Characters form words.
Words form text.

~
~
~
~
~
~
~
~
~
~
~
~
                                            1,13         All
```

Figure 3-9   File after deleting the extra "s"

9. Now, you want to edit the sentence, "Files contain text," by deleting the last word. Type **5G** to move to the fifth line and press the right arrow key to move to the "c" in "contain."

10. Type **d$** to delete the text from the cursor to the end of the line, and then type **i** to switch to insert mode.

11. Type **consist of words.** to complete the sentence. (Be certain there is a space between "Files" and "consist" and a period after "words.")

12. Now, you can edit the next sentence by replacing the final word. Press **Esc** to switch back to command mode. Next, press the arrow keys to move to the next line down in the file and move to the initial character ("l") in the word "lines."

13. Type **d0** to delete the text from the cursor to the beginning of the line, and then type **i** to enter insert mode.

14. Type **Words form** to insert the text at the beginning of the sentence. (Make certain you have a space between "form" and "lines.")

15. Your completed edits should look like those in Figure 3-10. Leave the vi editor open for Hands-on Project 3-6.

3

```
mpalmer@localhost:~                              _ □ ✕

File  Edit  View  Terminal  Tabs  Help
Text consists of lines.
Lines contain characters.
Characters form words.
Words form text.
Files consist of words.
Words form █ines.
Lines contain characters.
Characters form words.
Words form text.
~
~
~
~
~
~
~
~
~
~
~
~
-- INSERT --                           6,12        All
```

Figure 3-10   File edits after completing Step 14

Project 3-6

Sometimes, you might consistently misspell a word or you might want to locate some text to check its accuracy. In this project, you use the vi pattern-matching capability to find specific text in a file.

To search for a pattern of text:

1. Press **Esc** to ensure you are in command mode.

2. Type **H** to move the cursor to the top of the screen.

3. Type **/cons** and press **Enter** to search for the string "cons." What happens?

4. To move the cursor to the next occurrence of "cons," press **n** (for next). What happens next?

TIP

If you had searched for "/con" instead of "/cons," you would have first found "consist" on line 1 and then "contain" on line 2. (In Fedora, "con" would be highlighted in "consists" on line 1, "contain" on line 2, "consist" on line 5, and "contain" on line 7.)

5. At this point, it is valuable to learn how to view status information for your editing session. To see file status information, press **Ctrl+g**. (You also can press **Ctrl+G**.

This is one instance in which you can use uppercase or lowercase in UNIX/Linux.) Your screen should look like the one in Figure 3-11. Leave the vi editor open for the next project.

```
                           mpalmer@localhost:~                          _ □ ✕
 File  Edit  View  Terminal  Tabs  Help
Text consists of lines.                                                      ▲
Lines contain characters.
Characters form words.
Words form text.
Files consist of words.
Words form lines.
Lines contain characters.
Characters form words.
Words form text.

~
~
~
~
~
~
~
~
~
~
"textfiles" [Modified][New file] 10 lines --50%--          5,7          All  ▼
```

Figure 3-11   vi status line appears at the bottom of the screen

Project 3-7

HANDS-ON PROJECTS

Using line-oriented editing commands can be much faster than using screen-oriented commands, particularly when you want to search and replace patterns in a file. In this project, you compare using a screen-oriented command to search for occurrences of the word "text" with using a line-oriented command. Note that the line-oriented command not only finds occurrences of "text," but it also enables you to replace specific occurrences with the word "documents."

To perform a screen-oriented search for "text":

1. Press **Esc** to make certain you are in command mode.

2. Type **H** to go to the beginning of the file.

3. Type **/text** and press **Enter**.

4. Type **n** to repeat the search. (In Fedora, you see all instances of text highlighted at the same time, with the cursor on the first instance of "text." Pressing **n** takes you to the second instance. In SUSE, only the first instance of "text" is highlighted and you press **n** to go to the next one.) How many occurrences are there of the word "text"?

To search for "text" and replace "text" with "documents" using a line-oriented command:

1. Press **Esc** to be certain you are in command mode.

2. Type **:1,$s/text/documents/g** (but do not press Enter). Note that this command means "From the first line (*1*) to the end of the file (*$*), search for "text"and replace it with "documents"(*s/text/documents/*) everywhere it occurs on each line (*g*)."

3. Press **Enter**. See Figure 3-12. Leave the vi editing session open for Hands-on Project 3-8.

3

NOTE

The word "Text" in line 1 remains unchanged because it is capitalized. By default, case matters in searches.

```
┌─────────────────────────────────────────────────────────────┐
│ ▣                     mpalmer@localhost:~              _ □ x  │
├─────────────────────────────────────────────────────────────┤
│ File  Edit  View  Terminal  Tabs  Help                       │
│ Text consists of lines.                                    ▲ │
│ Lines contain characters.                                    │
│ Characters form words.                                       │
│ Words form documents.                                        │
│ Files consist of words.                                      │
│ Words form lines.                                            │
│ Lines contain characters.                                    │
│ Characters form words.                                       │
│ ▉ords form documents.                                        │
│ ~                                                            │
│ ~                                                          ▤  │
│ ~                                                            │
│ ~                                                            │
│ ~                                                            │
│ ~                                                            │
│ ~                                                            │
│ ~                                                            │
│ ~                                                            │
│ ~                                                            │
│ :1,$s/text/documents/g                  9,1          All  ▼  │
└─────────────────────────────────────────────────────────────┘
```

Figure 3-12   Searching for and replacing text using a line-oriented edit command

HANDS-ON PROJECTS

Project 3-8

Periodically saving your work in the vi editor can help ensure that you don't lose your work if there is an unexpected power failure. Also, when you exit vi after making changes, be certain to exit using a command that saves your work prior to exiting. In this project, you practice using commands to save your work.

To save the work in your file without exiting vi:

1. Press **Esc**, if necessary, to enter command mode.

2. Type **:w** and then press **Enter** to save your changes.

To save your work and then exit:

1. From command mode, type **:x** and press **Enter**. (See Figure 3-13.)

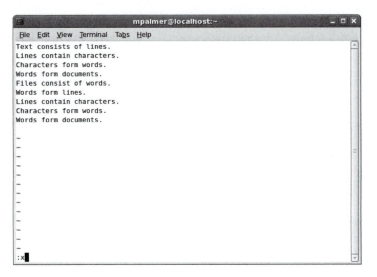

Figure 3-13   Using :x to save and then exit

Project 3-9

Copying the contents of one file into another can eliminate extra typing when you are working in UNIX/Linux. In this project, you use the vi editor to create a new file and add text to that file from the textfiles file you just saved in Hands-on Project 3-8.

To create a new file and add text from another file:

1. Type **vi practice** and press **Enter** to create a new file called practice.

2. Press **Esc** to make certain you are in command mode.

3. Type **:r textfiles** and press **Enter**.

   Your file should look like the one in Figure 3-14. The *r* command copied the text from textfiles and put it in the current file, practice. Notice the blank line at the top of the file. The status line provides information about the file you added, including its name and the number of lines and characters it contains.

4. Move the cursor to the blank line, and type **dd** to delete it.

5. Leave the practice file open for Hands-on Project 3-10.

Project 3-10

Sometimes you need to do two things at once. For instance, consider a situation in which you are working on a text file in vi and someone calls to schedule a meeting, but neither of you has a calendar handy. You can run the *cal* command, or other commands, without closing the vi editor. In this project, you learn two ways to execute commands without closing your vi editing session.

```
                         mpalmer@localhost:~              _ □ x
 File  Edit  View  Terminal  Tabs  Help
 Text consists of lines.
 Lines contain characters.
 Characters form words.
 Words form documents.
 Files consist of words.
 Words form lines.
 Lines contain characters.
 Characters form words.
 Words form documents.

 ~
 ~
 ~
 ~
 ~
 ~
 ~
 ~
 ~
 "textfiles" 10L, 210C                    2,1          All
```

Figure 3-14 Copying one file into another in the vi editor

To leave vi temporarily to view the current month's calendar:

1. Press **Esc**, if necessary, to enter command mode.

2. Type **:!cal** and press **Enter**.

   You see this month's calendar and then instructions to "Hit ENTER or type command to continue." (See Figure 3-15.)

3. Press **Enter** to return to your vi editing session in command mode.

To access the command line to execute several commands:

1. Type **Ctrl+z** to access the command line.

2. Type **ls -l** and press **Enter** to execute a command.

3. Type **pwd** and press **Enter** to execute another command.

4. Type **cat textfiles** and press **Enter** to execute a third command.

5. Type **fg** and press **Enter** to return to your vi editing session. Into what mode do you return?

6. Leave your vi editing session open for Hands-on Project 3-11.

HANDS-ON PROJECTS

Project 3-11

Line numbering can help you quickly identify specific lines that you want to edit in vi. In this project, you turn on line numbering and then use it as a reference to delete lines in the text.

To use automatic line numbering:

1. Press **Esc** to be certain you are in command mode.

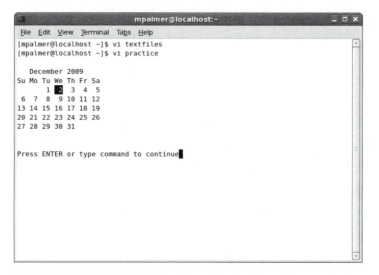

Figure 3-15 Temporarily leaving vi to run the *cal* command

2. Type **:set number** and press **Enter**. The line numbers appear on the screen. (See Figure 3-16.)

Line numbers are for reference only. They are not part of the file. Now you can use these reference numbers to delete the last three lines in the file.

3. Type **:7,9d** and press **Enter**. You've deleted lines 7 through 9 in the file.

4. Leave the practice file open for Hands-on Project 3-12.

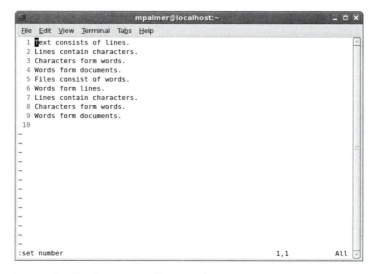

Figure 3-16 Turning on line numbering

Project 3-12

No one likes to type any more than is necessary. In this project, you learn to cut and paste text in your practice file as a way to reduce extra typing.

To cut and paste text:

1. From command mode, type **H** to move the cursor to the beginning of line 1.

2. Type **3dd** to cut the first three lines from the document and store them in the buffer.

3. Type **G** to move the cursor to the end of the file.

4. Type **p** to paste the three lines at the end of the file.

5. Leave the practice file open for Hands-on Project 3-13.

Project 3-13

In this project, you print the file you are working on, without leaving the vi editing session. Your computer should be connected to a default printer for you to complete the assignment.

To print a file:

1. Press **Esc**, if necessary, to return to command mode.

2. Type **:w** and press **Enter** to save the practice file.

3. Type **:!lpr practice** and press **Enter**. This prints the practice file in the current directory on the default printer.

4. Press Enter to return to the vi editing session.

5. Leave your vi session open for Hands-on Project 3-14.

Project 3-14

Sometimes you make changes in a document, but then decide not to save them. In this project, you make a change to the practice document and then exit without saving your change. You also learn how to view the vi help documentation.

To make an additional change, and then cancel without saving it:

1. Press **Esc**, if necessary, to access command mode.

2. With the cursor at the beginning of the top line (type **H** if it is not), type **dd** (but do not press Enter).

3. Type **:q!** and press **Enter**.

4. Type **vi practice** and press **Enter**. Notice that the sentence "Words form documents." is back in the file on line 1 because your change in Step 2 was not saved.

To view the vi help documentation:

1. Type **:help** and press **Enter** to view the help documentation. Use the **Page Down** and **Page Up** keys (or PgDn/PgUp, depending on your keyboard) to scroll through the documentation.

2. Type **:q!** and press **Enter** to leave the documentation. (In some older versions of Red Hat Enterprise Linux, this also closes the vi editor. If you are using Fedora or SUSE, proceed to Step 3 to close the editor.)

3. Type **:q!** and press **Enter** again to close the vi editor.

NOTE

In Projects 3-15 through 3-20, you practice using the Emacs editor. In these projects, you start Emacs from the command line (such as a terminal window) using your own account. If Emacs is not installed and you are using Fedora or Red Hat Enterprise Linux with the GNOME desktop, log in to root, click Applications, click Add/Remove Software, click List, check the boxes for the Emacs installation options, click Apply, and follow any remaining instructions. In SUSE, log in to root, click the Computer menu, click Install Software, select the Emacs options, click Install, and follow any remaining instructions. Ensure you have the operating system installation disks available before you install Emacs. Also, note that the Knoppix CD does not include the Emacs editor. You can obtain Emacs from *www.gnu.org/software/emacs*.

**HANDS-ON
PROJECTS**

Project 3-15

You begin using Emacs in this project by creating a new file, entering text, and then saving and closing the file.

To start Emacs and create a new file:

1. Type **emacs practice.fil** and then press **Enter**. You see the opening screen and its status bar (at the bottom of the screen), which indicates you are creating a new file.

2. To add text to the file, type the following so that your screen looks like the one in Figure 3-17:

   Files contain text.
   Text contains lines.
   Lines contain characters.
   Characters form words.
   Words form text.

3. Press **Ctrl+x** and then **Ctrl+s** to save the file. Notice that the status line reports that you wrote the file.

4. Press **Ctrl+x** and then **Ctrl+c** to exit the file.

In Emacs, you press the two Ctrl key combinations to save and exit a file.

NOTE

3

Files contain text.
Text contains lines.
Lines contain characters.
Characters form words.
Words form text.

emacs@localhost.localdomain

File Edit Options Buffers Tools Help

-u:** practice.fil   (Fundamental)--L5--All--------------------------------

Figure 3-17   Entering text in Emacs

HANDS-ON PROJECTS

Project 3-16

This project enables you to practice navigating in Emacs.

To navigate in Emacs:

1. Type **emacs practice.fil** and press **Enter**.

2. Press **Ctrl+f** to move forward one character, and then press the **right arrow** key to move forward one character at a time. Move forward by four or five characters.

3. Press **Ctrl+b** to move back one character, and then press the **left arrow** key to practice moving backward.

4. Use the **down arrow** and **up arrow** keys to move down and up through lines in the document.

5. Type **Alt+<** to go to the beginning of the file. (Use the Shift key for < on the keyboard.)

6. Type **Alt+>** to go to the end of the file. (Use the Shift key for > on the keyboard.)

7. Leave the file open for Hands-on Project 3-17.

Project 3-17

In this project, you practice deleting in Emacs and then undoing a deletion.

To delete text and undo the deletion:

1. Use the arrow keys to place the cursor on the line that begins "Lines contain...".

2. Press **Ctrl+k** to delete the current line.

3. Press **Ctrl+x** and then type **u** to undo the last change.

4. Leave the Emacs editing session open for Hands-on Project 3-18.

TIP

You can restore the text repeatedly, even after making many changes. Press *Ctrl+x*, and then press *u* as often as necessary to undo your editing commands in sequence.

Project 3-18

In this project, you copy text in Emacs and then paste the text you copied.

To copy and paste text in Emacs:

1. Move the cursor to the beginning of the sentence "Text contains lines."

2. Press **Ctrl+Spacebar**. This marks the starting point for the block of text you want to copy. You see the words "Mark set" in the status bar.

3. Press the **down arrow** and **right arrow** keys to move the cursor to the end of the text on the last line (after "...form text." — making sure you place the cursor after the period at the end of the line).

4. Press **Alt+w**. This marks the end of the text block to copy and briefly moves the cursor to the location you marked in Step 2 and then back to where you marked the end of the text. (In many versions of Emacs, you can also hold down Esc and press w to mark the end of the block.)

5. Press **Alt+>** to go to the end of the file. If necessary, press **Enter** to start a blank line after the last line ending with "...form text." Your cursor should now be at the beginning of a blank line at the end of the file.

6. Press **Ctrl+y** to paste the marked text from the clipboard into the buffer (on the screen), as shown in Figure 3-18.

To cut and paste rather than copy and paste, press *Ctrl+w* when the cursor is at the end of the block you want to cut. (See Step 4.) Then move the cursor to where you want to paste the text and press *Ctrl+y*.

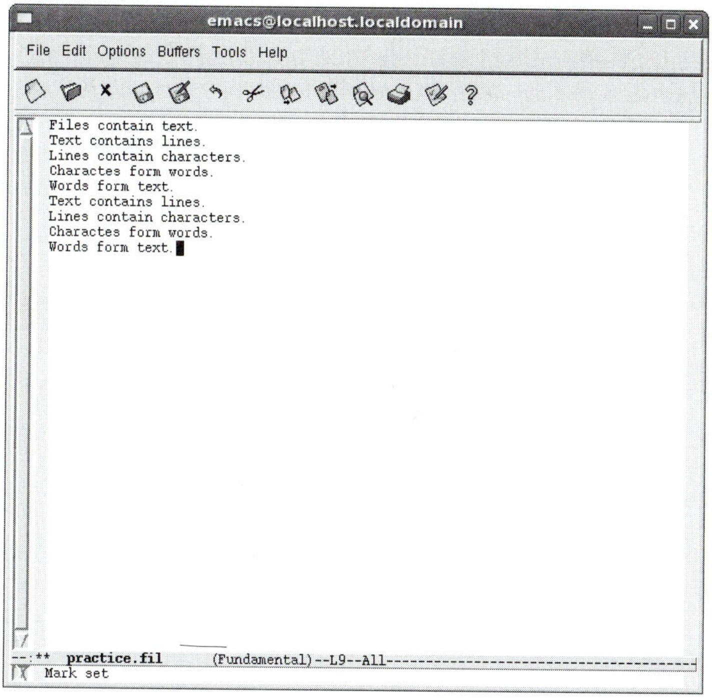

TIP

3

Figure 3-18   Copying and pasting text in Emacs

Project 3-19

HANDS-ON PROJECTS

As you use the Emacs editor, you'll discover that you often need to search for a specific pattern or string of characters. In this project, you learn two ways to perform string searches in Emacs.

To search using control key options:

1. Press **Ctrl+s**. You see the "I-search:" prompt in the status line. You can now type the text you are seeking.

2. Type **on** (but do not press Enter).

3. Press **Ctrl+s** to search for an occurrence of "on." In what word does this appear? Press **Ctrl+s** again.

4. Press **Ctrl+r** to search backward for the previous occurrence of "on."

To search using the Edit menu Search option:

1. Type **Alt+<** to move to the beginning of the file.

2. Click the **Edit** menu, point to **Search**, and click **Search....**

3. Notice that the cursor goes to the status line at the bottom of the screen.

4. Type **on** in the status line, and press **Enter**.

5. Click the **Edit** menu, point to **Search**, and click **Repeat Search** to locate the next occurrence of "on."

6. Click the **Edit** menu, point to **Search**, and click **Repeat Backwards** to search for "on" backward. Leave the Emacs editor open for Hands-on Project 3-20.

HANDS-ON
PROJECTS

Project 3-20

In this project, you turn on the word wrap feature in Emacs, so that lines automatically wrap around in the display.

To reformat your file to use word wrap:

1. Type **Alt+<** to move to the beginning of the file.

2. Press **Alt+q** to reformat the file so the lines are full of text. (See Figure 3-19. Words wrap from one line to the next.)

3. Type **Ctrl+x** and **Ctrl+s** to save the file, and then **Ctrl+x** and **Ctrl+c** to exit.

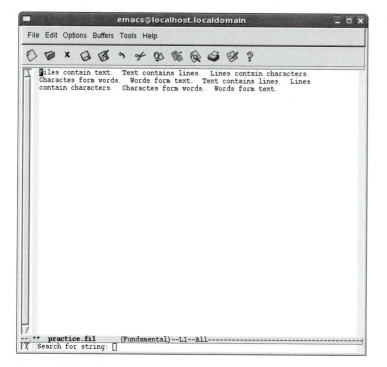

Figure 3-19 Turning on word wrap in Emacs

Discovery Exercises

1. Using the vi editor:
   - Create a document with four lines, each containing the word "today."
   - Copy the first four lines using only one command.
   - Save the file, and exit vi.
   - Reopen the document, and change "today" to "yesterday" only on the first four lines.

2. Using the vi editor:
   - Create a document called first.file, and enter a few lines of text in it. Save it.
   - Create a second document called second.file, and enter a few lines of text in it. Save it.
   - Create a third document called third.file by merging the text from the first two files.
   - Save the third file, and exit the editor.
   - Type *vi third.file* and press Enter to be certain third.file contains the text from both files.

3. Delete all text from third.file that you created using vi, and then restore it.

Use Table 3-4 to find the correct commands for performing the following basic exercises to practice using the Emacs editor.

4. Using the Emacs editor, create a new file, called sonnet, that contains the first four lines of Shakespeare's 80th Sonnet:

   O, how I faint when I of you do write,
   Knowing a better spirit doth use your name,
   And in the praise thereof spends all his might,
   To make me tongue-tied, speaking of your fame!

5. Move the cursor to any letter in the word "better" (except "b") on the second line.

6. Use the command that causes the current word to be transposed with the one that follows it. After executing the command, the line should read:

   Knowing a spirit better doth use your name,

7. Move the cursor to the word "doth" on the same line.

8. Use the command to delete the current word.

9. Move the cursor to the first character of the word "spirit" on the same line.

10. Use the command that capitalizes the letters of the word.

11. Move the cursor under the letter "y" in the word "your" on the same line.

12. Use the command that deletes the character above the cursor. The line should now read:

    Knowing a SPIRIT better use our name,

13. Move the cursor to the word "spends" on the third line.

14. Use the command that deletes text to the end of the line. The line should now read:

    And in the praise thereof

15. Move the cursor to the beginning of the first line.

16. Use the command that puts a mark at the cursor location.

17. Move the cursor to the end of the first line. Use the command that marks that particular cursor location.

18. Move the cursor to the first character of the first line.

19. Use the command that deletes marked text; that is, deletes the first line.

20. Move the cursor to the end of the file. Use the command that restores deleted text. The text that was the first line of the file is now at the end of the file. Save your work and then close the Emacs editor.

Use the vi editor with the following advanced exercises to sharpen your editing skills.

NOTE

21. Create a file with 12 lines of text. Delete the second word in the text.

22. Go to the fifth line, and insert your first and last name.

23. Remove the eighth line, and place it at the end of the file.

24. Use one command to go to the first line of the file.

25. Search for your last name.

26. Save the file, but do not exit vi.

27. Without exiting vi, temporarily execute the *ls* command to confirm that the file is saved.

28. Enter the command that causes line numbers to appear.

29. Delete lines 9 and 10.

30. Move to the line of text that contains your first and last name, cut it, and place the text in the buffer.

31. Paste the line with your first and last name in the middle of the text.

Use the Emacs editor for these more advanced exercises.

NOTE

32. Using the practice file, practice copying and pasting the text to rearrange the order of the lines.

33. Add text to the file, and practice using the cursor movement commands.

34. Replace all occurrences of the word "form" with "create."

35. Select five words and convert them to all uppercase.

36. Delete a line and then undo the deletion.

37. Transpose the first two words in each line.

38. Save the file and exit Emacs.

4

UNIX/Linux File Processing

After reading this chapter and completing the exercises, you will be able to:

♦ Explain UNIX and Linux file processing

♦ Use basic file manipulation commands to create, delete, copy, and move files and directories

♦ Employ commands to combine, cut, paste, rearrange, and sort information in files

♦ Create a script file

♦ Use the *join* command to link files using a common field

♦ Use the *awk* command to create a professional-looking report

The power of UNIX/Linux is based on its storage and handling of files. You've already learned about file systems, security, and UNIX/Linux editors. Now it's time to put your knowledge to work by manipulating files and their contents. To give you some background, this chapter starts with a short discussion of UNIX/Linux file types and file structures. Next, you learn more about using redirection operators, including how to use them to store error messages. You go on to learn file manipulation tools that you will use over and over again, either as a UNIX/Linux administrator or as an everyday user. These essential tools enable you to create, delete, copy, and move files. Other tools enable you to extract information from files to combine fields and to sort a file's contents. Finally, you learn how to assemble the information you extract from files, such as for creating reports. You also create your first script to automate a series of commands, link files with a common field, and get a first taste of the versatile *awk* command to format output.

UNIX AND LINUX FILE PROCESSING

UNIX/Linux file processing is based on the idea that files should be treated as nothing more than character sequences. This concept of a file as a series of characters offers a lot of flexibility. Because you can directly access each character, you can perform a range of editing tasks, such as correcting spelling errors and organizing information to meet your needs.

Reviewing UNIX/Linux File Types

Operating systems support several types of files. UNIX and Linux, like other operating systems, have text files, binary files, directories, and special files. As discussed in Chapter 3, "Mastering Editors," text files contain printable ASCII characters. Some users also call these regular, ordinary, or ASCII files. Text files often contain information you create and manipulate, such as a document or program source code. Binary files, also discussed in Chapter 3, contain nonprintable characters, including machine language code created from compiling a program. In UNIX/Linux, text files and binary files are considered to be **regular files**, and you will sometimes see this terminology when working with files at the command line.

Chapter 2, "Exploring the UNIX/Linux File Systems and File Security," explained that directories are system files for maintaining the structure of the file system. In Chapter 2, you also learned about device special files. Character special files are used by input/output devices for communicating one character at a time, providing what is called raw data. The first character in the file access permissions is "c," which represents the file type, a character special file. Block special files are also related to devices, such as disks, and send information using blocks of data. The first character in these files is "b." For comparison, as you learned in Chapter 2, the first character for a directory is "d," and for a normal file—not a device special file—the first character is a dash "-."

NOTE   Character special and block special files might also be called character device and block device files or character-special device and block-special device files.

Understanding File Structures

Files can be structured in several ways. For example, UNIX/Linux store data, such as letters, product records, or vendor reports, in **flat ASCII files**. The internal structure of a file depends on the kind of data it stores. A user structures a letter, for instance, using words, paragraphs, and sentences. A programmer can structure a file containing employee records using characters and words grouped together, with each individual employee record on a separate line in a file. Information about an employee in each separate line or record can be divided by separator characters or delimiters, such as colons. This type of record is called a **variable-length record**, because the length of each field bounded by colons can vary. The following is a simple example of an employee telephone record that might be stored in a flat

ASCII file and used by a human resources program. The first three fields, separated by colons, are the employee's home telephone number, consisting of the area code, prefix, and number. A human resources professional or boss might display some or all of this information in a program or report to be able to call the employee at home.

```
219:432:4567:Harrison:Joel:M:4540:Accountant:09-12-1985
```

4

Another way to create records is to have them start and stop in particular columns. For example, the area code in the previous example might start in column 1 and end in column 3. The prefix in the telephone number might go from column 5 to column 7, the last four digits in the telephone number would be in columns 9 through 12, and so on. Figure 4-1 illustrates this type of record, which is called a **fixed-length record**.

Figure 4-1   Fixed-length record

Three simple kinds of text files are unstructured ASCII characters, records, and trees. Figure 4-2 illustrates these three kinds of text files.

Figure 4-2(a) shows a file that is an unstructured sequence of bytes and is a typical example of a simple text file. This file structure gives you the most flexibility in data entry, because you can store any kind of data in any order, such as the vendor name Triumph Motors and other information related to Triumph Motors, which might be a unique vendor number, the vendor's address, and so on. However, you can only retrieve the data in the same order, which might limit its overall usefulness. For example, suppose you list the vendors (product suppliers) used by a hotel in an unstructured ASCII text file. In this format, if you want to view only vendor names or vendor numbers, you really don't have that option. You most likely will have to print the entire file contents, including address and other information for all vendors.

Figure 4-2(b) shows data as a sequence of fixed-length records, each having some internal structure. In a UNIX/Linux file, a record is a line of data, corresponding to a row. For example, in a file of names, the first line or row might contain information about a single individual, such as last name, first name, middle initial, address, and phone number. The second row would contain the same kind of data about a different person, and so on. In this structure, UNIX/Linux read the data as fixed-length records. Although you must enter data as records, you can also manipulate and retrieve the data as records. For example, you can select only certain personnel or vendor records to retrieve from the file.

The third kind of file, illustrated in Figure 4-2(c), is structured as a tree of records that can be organized as fixed-length or variable-length records. In Figure 4-2(c), each record contains a key field, such as a record number, in a specific position in the record. The key

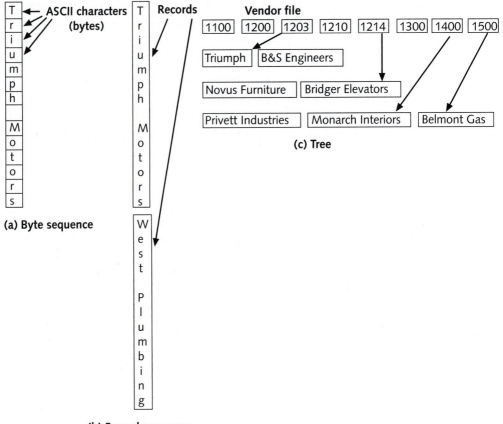

(a) Byte sequence

(b) Record sequence

(c) Tree

Figure 4-2   Three kinds of text files

field sorts the tree, so you can quickly search for a record with a particular key. For example, you can quickly find the record for Triumph Motors by searching for record #1203.

You will practice creating and manipulating different kinds of files and records in this and later chapters.

PROCESSING FILES

When performing commands, UNIX/Linux process data by receiving input from the standard input device—your keyboard, for example—and then sending it to the standard output: the monitor or console. System administrators and programmers refer to standard input as **stdin**. They refer to standard output as **stdout**. The third standard device, or file, is called standard error, or **stderr**. When UNIX/Linux detect errors in processing system tasks and user programs, they direct the errors to stderr, which, by default, is the screen.

NOTE

stdin, stdout, and stderr are defined in IEEE Std 1003.1, "Standard for Information Technology—Portable Operating System Interface (POSIX)," and the ISO 9899:1999 C language standard (for C programming). The Institute of Electrical and Electronics Engineers (IEEE) and the International Organization for Standardization (ISO) set computer-based and other standards.

4

In Chapter 1, "The Essence of UNIX and Linux," you learned about the > and >> output redirection operators. You can use these and other redirection operators to save the output of a command or program in a file or use a file as an input to a process. The redirection operators are a tool to help you process files.

Using Input and Error Redirection

You can use redirection operators (>, >>, 2>, <, and <<) to retrieve input from something other than the standard input device and to send output to something other than the standard output device.

You already used the output redirection operators in Chapter 1, when you created a new file by redirecting the output of several commands to files. Redirect output when you want to store the output of a command or program in a file. For example, recall that you can use the *ls* command to list the files in a directory, such as /home. The *ls* command sends output to stdout, which, by default, is the screen. To redirect the list to a file called homedir.list, use the redirection symbol by entering *ls > homedir.list*.

You can also redirect the input to a program or command with the < operator. For instance, a program that accepts keyboard input can be redirected to read information from a file instead. In Hands-On Project 4-1, you create a file from which the vi editor reads its commands, instead of reading them from the keyboard.

You can also use the 2> operator to redirect commands or program error messages from the screen to a file. For example, if you try to list a file or directory that does not exist, you see the following error message: No such file or directory. Assume that Fellowese is not a file or directory. If you enter *ls Fellowese 2> errors*, this places the No such file or directory error message in the errors file. Try this redirection technique in Hands-On Project 4-2.

MANIPULATING FILES

When you manipulate files, you work with the files themselves as well as their contents. This section explains how to complete the following tasks:

- Create files
- Delete files
- Remove directories
- Copy files

- Move files
- Find files
- Combine files
- Combine files through pasting
- Extract fields in files through cutting
- Sort files

Creating Files

You can create a new file by using the output redirection operator (>). You learned how to do this to redirect the *cat* command's output in Chapters 1–3. You can also use the redirection operator without a command to create an empty file by entering > and the name of the file. For example, the following command:

```
> accountsfile
```

creates an empty file called accountsfiles. Hands-On Project 4-3 enables you to create a file using the > redirection symbol.

You can also use the *touch* command to create empty files. For example, the following command creates the file accountsfile2, if the file does not already exist.

```
touch accountsfile2
```

Syntax **touch** [–options] *filename(s)*

Dissection

- Intended to change the time stamp on a file, but can also be used to create an empty file
- Useful options include:

    -a updates the access time only

    -m updates the last time the file was modified

    -c prevents the *touch* command from creating the file, if it does not already exist

---

To view time stamp information in full, use the *--full-time* option with the *ls* command, such as *ls --full-time myfile*.

The primary purpose of the *touch* command is to change a file's time stamp and date stamp. UNIX/Linux maintain the following date and time information for every file:

- *Change date and time*—The date and time the file's inode was last changed

- *Access date and time*—The date and time the file was last accessed
- *Modification date and time*—The date and time the file was last modified

TIP

Recall from Chapter 2 that an inode is a system for storing key information about files. Inode information includes the inode number, the owner of the file, the file group, the file size, the change date of the inode, the file creation date, the date the file was last modified and last read, the number of links to this inode, and the information regarding the location of the blocks in the file system in which the file is stored.

Although the *touch* command cannot alter a file's inode changed date and time, it can alter the file's access and modification dates and times. By default, it uses the current date and time for the new values. Hands-On Project 4-4 gives you experience using the *touch* command.

Deleting Files

When you no longer need a file, you can delete it using the *rm* (remove) command. If you use *rm* without options, UNIX/Linux delete the specified file without warning. Use the *-i* (interactive) option to have UNIX/Linux warn you before deleting the file. You can delete several files with similar names by using the asterisk wildcard. (See Chapter 2.) For example, if you have 10 files that all begin with the letters "test," enter *rm test** to delete all of them at one time. Hands-On Project 4-5 enables you to use the *rm* command.

Syntax **rm** [-options] *filename* or *directoryname*

Dissection

- Used to delete files or directories
- Useful options include:

  -i displays a warning prompt before deleting the file (or directory)

  -r when deleting a directory, recursively deletes its files and subdirectories (to delete a directory that is empty or that contains entries, use the *-r* option with *rm*)

Removing Directories

When you no longer need a directory, you can use the commands *rm* or *rmdir* to remove it. For example, if the directory is already empty, use *rm -r* or *rmdir*. If the directory contains files or subdirectories, use *rm -r* to delete them all. The *rm* command with the *-r* option removes a directory and everything it contains. It even removes subdirectories of subdirectories. This operation is known as recursive removal. Note that if you use *rm* alone, in many versions of UNIX/Linux, including Fedora, Red Hat Enterprise Linux, and SUSE, it does not delete a directory.

Hands-On Project 4-6 enables you to use *rmdir* to delete an empty directory and *rm -r* to delete a directory that is not empty.

Syntax **rmdir** [–options] *directoryname*

Dissection

- Used to delete directories
- A directory must be empty to delete it with the *rmdir* command.

CAUTION

Use *rm -r* with great care by first making certain you have examined all of the directory's contents and intend to delete them along with the directory. If you are just deleting an empty directory, it is safer to use the *rmdir* command in case you make a typo when you enter the name of the directory. Also, when you use rm with the *-r* option, consider using the *-i* option as well to prompt you before you delete. Additional precautions employed by some users are to (1) use *pwd* to make certain you are in the proper working directory before you delete another directory and (2) use the full path to the directory you plan to delete, because, if you mistype a name, the deletion is likely to fail rather than delete the wrong directory.

Copying Files

In Chapter 2, you were introduced to the *cp* command for copying files, which we explore further here. Its general form is as follows:

Syntax **cp** [–options] *source destination*

Dissection

- Used to copy files or directories
- Useful options include:

    -i provides a warning before *cp* writes over an existing file with the same name

    -s creates a symbolic link or name at the destination rather than a physical file (a symbolic name is a pointer to the original file, which you learn about in Chapter 6)

    -u prevents *cp* from copying over an existing file if the existing file is newer than the source file

---

The *cp* command copies the file or files specified by the source path to the location specified by the destination path. You can copy files into another directory, with the copies keeping the same names as the originals. You can also copy files into another directory, with the copies taking new names, or copy files into the same directory as the originals, with the copies taking new names.

For example, assume Tom is in his home directory (/home/tom). In this directory, he has the file reminder. Under his home directory, he has another directory, duplicates (/home/tom/duplicates). He copies the reminder file to the duplicates directory with the following command:

```
cp reminder duplicates
```

After he executes the command, a file named reminder is in the duplicates directory. It is a duplicate of the reminder file in the /home/tom directory. Tom also has the file class_of_88 in his home directory. He copies it to a file named classmates in the duplicates directory with the following command:

```
cp class_of_88 duplicates/classmates
```

After he executes the command, the file classmates is stored in the duplicates directory. Although it has a different name, it is a copy of the class_of_88 file. Tom also has a file named memo_to_boss in his home directory. He wants to make a copy of it and keep the copy in his home directory. He enters the following command:

```
cp memo_to_boss memo.safe
```

After he executes this command, the file memo.safe is stored in Tom's home directory. It is a copy of his memo_to_boss file.

You can specify multiple source files as arguments to the *cp* command. For example, Tom wants to copy the files project1, project2, and project3 to his duplicates directory. He enters the following command:

```
cp project1 project2 project3 duplicates
```

TIP

The final entry in a multiple copy (*cp*) or move (*mv*) is a directory, as in the preceding example. You learn about the move command in the next section.

After he executes the command, copies of the three files are stored in the duplicates directory.

You can also use wildcard characters with the *cp* command. For example, Tom has a directory named designs under his home directory (/home/tom/designs). He wants to copy all files in the designs directory to the duplicates directory. He enters the following command:

```
cp designs/* duplicates
```

After he executes this command, the duplicates directory contains a copy of every file in the designs directory. As this example illustrates, the *cp* command is useful not only for copying but also for preventing lost data by making backup copies of files. You use the *cp* command in Hands-On Project 4-7 to make copies in a backup directory.

Moving Files

Moving files is similar to copying them, except you remove them from one directory and store them in another. However, as insurance, a file is copied before it is moved. To move a file, use the *mv* (move) command along with the source file name and destination name. You can also use the *mv* command to rename a file by moving one file into another file with a different name.

TIP

Moving and renaming a file are essentially the same operation.

When you are moving files, using the *-i* option with the *mv* command can be a good idea so that you don't unexpectedly overwrite a destination file with the same name.

Syntax **mv** [–options] *source destination*

Dissection

- Used to move and to rename files
- Useful options include:

    -i displays a warning prompt before overwriting a file with the same name

    -u overwrites a destination file with the same name, if the source file is newer than the one in the destination

---

Hands–On Project 4-8 enables you to use the *mv* command.

Finding Files

Sometimes, you might not remember the specific location of a file you want to access. The *find* command searches for files that have a specified name. Use the *find* command to locate files that have the same name or to find a file in any directory.

Syntax **find** [*pathname*] [**-name** *filename*]

Dissection

- Used to locate files in a directory and in subdirectories

- Useful options include:

  pathname is the path name of the directory you want to search. The *find* command searches recursively; that is, it starts in the named directory and searches down through all files and subdirectories under the directory specified by *pathname*.

  -name indicates that you are searching for files with a specific *filename*. You can use wildcard characters in the file name. For example, you can use *phone** to search for all file names that begin with "phone."

  -iname works like *-name*, but ignores case. For example, if you search for *phone** as the search name, you'll find all files that begin with "phone," "Phone," "PHONE," or any combination of upper and lowercase letters.

  -mmin n displays files that have been changed within the last *n* minutes.

  -mtime n displays files that have been changed within the last *n* days.

  -size n displays files of size *n,* where the default measure for *n* is in 512-byte blocks (you can also use *nc, nk, nM,* or *nG* for bytes kilobytes, megabytes, or gigabytes, such as *find -size 2M* to find files that are 2 megabytes). For other search conditions you can use with *find*, refer to Appendix B, "Syntax Guide to UNIX/Linux Commands."

When you are using the *find* command, you can only search areas for which you have adequate permissions. As the search progresses, the *find* command might enter protected directories; you receive a "Permission denied" message each time you attempt to enter a directory for which you do not have adequate permissions. Also, when you use *find*, it is useful to note that some UNIX versions require the *-print* option after the file name to display the names of files.

Try Hands-On Project 4-9 to use the *find* command.

Combining Files

In addition to viewing and creating files, you can use the *cat* command to combine files. You combine files by using a redirection operator, but in a somewhat different format than you use to create a file. As you already know, if you enter *cat > janes_research*, you can then type information into the file and end the session by typing Ctrl+d, creating the file janes_ research. Assume that Jane has created such a file containing research results about bighorn sheep. Now assume that there is also the file marks_research, which contains Mark's research on the same topic. You can use the *cat* command to combine the contents of both files into the total_research file by entering the following:

```
cat janes_research marks_research > total_research
```

Hands-On Project 4-10 enables you to use this technique for combining files.

Combining Files with the paste Command

The *paste* command combines files side by side, whereas the *cat* command combines files end to end. When you use *paste* to combine two files into a third file, the first line of the output contains the first line of the first file followed by the first line of the second file. For example, consider a simple file, called vegetables, containing the following four lines:

```
Carrots
Spinach
Lettuce
Beans
```

Also, the bread file contains the following four lines:

```
Whole wheat
White bread
Sourdough
Pumpernickel
```

If you execute the command *paste vegetables bread > food*, the vegetables and bread files are combined, line by line, into the file food. The food file's contents are shown in Figure 4-3.

 The *paste* command normally sends its output to stdout (the screen). To capture it in a file, use the redirection operator.

TIP

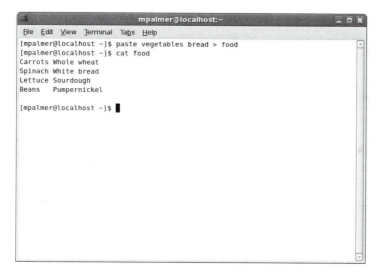

Figure 4-3   Using the *paste* command to merge files

Syntax **paste** [–options] *source files* [> *destination file*]

Dissection

- Combines the contents of one or more files to output to the screen or to another file
- By default, the pasted results appear in columns separated by tabs
- Useful options include:

  -*d* enables you to specify a different separator (other than a tab) between columns

  -*s* causes files to be pasted one after the other instead of in parallel

---

As you can see, the *paste* command is most useful when you combine files that contain columns of information. When *paste* combines items into a single line, it separates them with a tab. For example, look at the first line of the food file:

```
Carrots   Whole wheat
```

When *paste* combined "Carrots" and "Whole wheat," it inserted a tab between them. You can use the -*d* option to specify another character as a delimiter. For example, to insert a comma between the output fields instead of a tab, you would enter:

```
paste -d',' vegetables bread > food
```

After this command executes, the food file's contents are:

```
Carrots,Whole wheat
Spinach,White bread
```

```
Lettuce,Sourdough
Beans,Pumpernickel
```

Try Hands-On Project 4-11 to begin learning to use the *paste* command.

Extracting Fields Using the cut Command

You have learned that files can consist of records, fields, and characters. In some instances, you might want to retrieve some, but not all, fields in a file. Use the *cut* command to remove specific columns or fields from a file. For example, in your organization, you might have a vendors file of businesses from which you purchase supplies. The file contains a record for each vendor, and each record contains the vendor's name, street address, city, state, zip code, and telephone number; for example, Office Supplies: 2405 S.E. 17th Street: Boulder: Colorado: 80302:303-442-8800. You can use the *cut* command to quickly list only the names of vendors, such as Office Supplies, in this file. The syntax of the *cut* command is as follows:

Syntax **cut [-f** *list*] **[-d char**] [*file1 file2* . . .] or **cut [-c** *list*] [*file1 file2* . . .]

Dissection

- Removes specific columns or fields from a file

- Useful options include:

  -f specifies that you are referring to fields

  list is a comma-separated list or a hyphen-separated range of integers that specifies the field. For example, *-f 1* indicates field 1, *-f 1,14* indicates fields 1 and 14, and *-f 1-14* indicates fields 1 through 14.

  -d indicates that a specific character separates the fields

  char is the character used as the field separator (delimiter), for example, a comma. The default field delimiter is the tab character.

  file1, file2 are the files from which you want to cut columns or fields

  -c references character positions. For example, *-c 1* specifies the first character and *-c 1,14* specifies characters 1 and 14.

Recall the example vegetables and bread files discussed in the preceding section. Assume that you also have the file meats. When you use the command *paste vegetables bread meats > food*, the contents of the food file are now as follows:

```
Carrots   Whole wheat   Turkey
Spinach   White bread   Chicken
Lettuce   Sourdough     Beef
Beans     Pumpernickel  Ham
```

Next, assume that you want to extract the second column of information (the bread list) from the file and display it on the screen. You enter the following command:

```
cut -f2 food
```

The option *-f2* tells the *cut* command to extract the second field from each line. Tab delimiters separate the fields, so *cut* knows where to find the fields. The result of the *cut -f2 food* command is output to the screen, as shown in Figure 4-4.

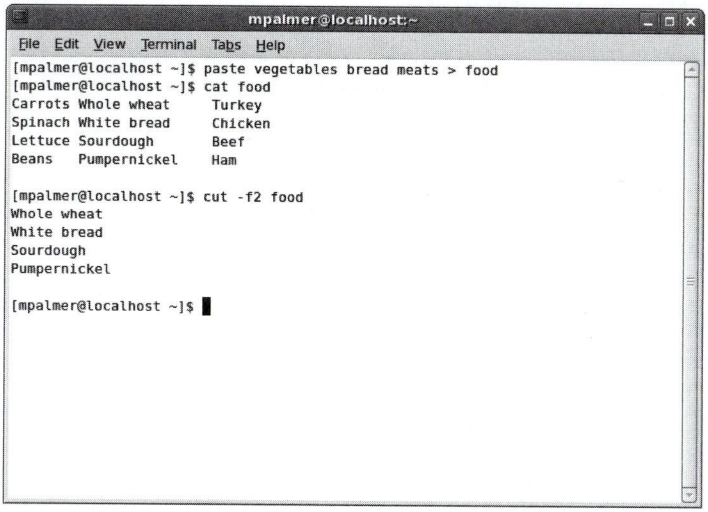

4

```
                        mpalmer@localhost:~
File  Edit  View  Terminal  Tabs  Help
[mpalmer@localhost ~]$ paste vegetables bread meats > food
[mpalmer@localhost ~]$ cat food
Carrots Whole wheat     Turkey
Spinach White bread     Chicken
Lettuce Sourdough       Beef
Beans   Pumpernickel    Ham

[mpalmer@localhost ~]$ cut -f2 food
Whole wheat
White bread
Sourdough
Pumpernickel

[mpalmer@localhost ~]$ █
```

Figure 4-4   Using the *cut* command

Another option is to extract the first and third columns from the file using the following command:

```
cut -f1,3 food
```

The result of the command is:

```
Carrots   Turkey
Spinach   Chicken
Lettuce   Beef
Beans     Ham
```

Hands-On Project 4–12 enables you to practice using the *cut* command.

Sorting Files

Use the *sort* command to sort a file's contents alphabetically or numerically. UNIX/Linux display the sorted file on the screen by default, but you can specify that you want to store the sorted data in a particular file by using a redirection operator.

Syntax **sort** [–options] [*filename*]

Dissection

■ Sorts the contents of files by individual lines

■ Useful options include:

-*k n* sorts on the key field specified by *n*

-*t* indicates that a specified character separates the fields

-*m* merges input files that have been previously sorted (does not perform a sort)

-*o* redirects output to the specified file

-*d* sorts in alphanumeric or dictionary order

-*g* sorts by numeric (general) order

-*r* sorts in reverse order

The *sort* command offers many options, which Appendix B also describes. The following is an example of its use:

```
sort file1 > file2
```

In this example, the contents of file1 are sorted and the results are stored in file2. (If the output is not redirected, *sort* displays its results on the screen.) If you are sorting a file of records and specify no options, for instance, the values in the first field of each record are sorted alphanumerically. A more complex example is as follows:

```
sort -k 3 food > sortedfood
```

This command specifies a **sorting key**. A sorting key is a field position within each line. The *sort* command sorts the lines based on the sorting key. The -*k* is the key field within the file. For instance, -*k 3* in the preceding example sorts on the third field in the food file, which is the listing of meats, and writes the results of the sort to the file sortedfood (see Figure 4-5). Notice in Figure 4-5 that the third field in the first record is Beef (and all of the records are sorted by the third field).

Hands-On Project 4-13 enables you to use the *sort* command. Also, try Hands-On Project 4-14 to use the *cat, cut, paste*, and *sort* commands in a project that puts together in one place what you have learned so far.

CREATING SCRIPT FILES

As you have seen, command-line entries can become long, depending on the number of options you need to use. You can use the shell's command-line history retrieval feature to recall and reexecute past commands. This feature can work well for you if you need to repeat commands shortly after executing them, but it is a problem if you need to perform

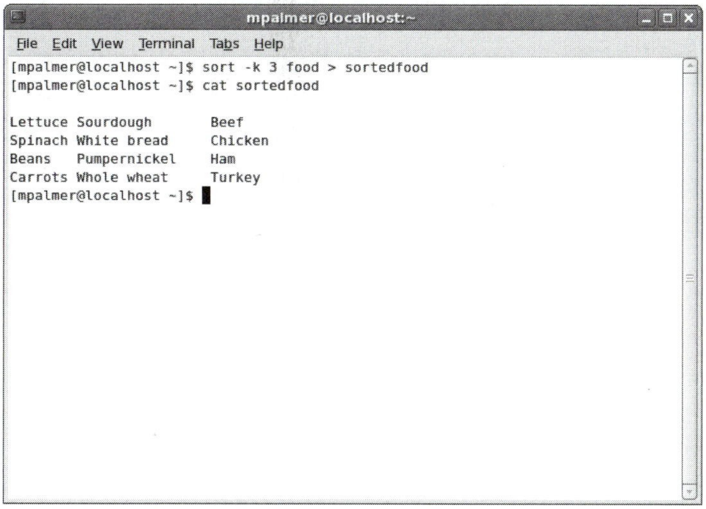

```
                            mpalmer@localhost:~
File  Edit  View  Terminal  Tabs  Help
[mpalmer@localhost ~]$ sort -k 3 food > sortedfood
[mpalmer@localhost ~]$ cat sortedfood

Lettuce Sourdough       Beef
Spinach White bread     Chicken
Beans   Pumpernickel    Ham
Carrots Whole wheat     Turkey
[mpalmer@localhost ~]$ █
```

Figure 4-5   Results of sorting on the third field in the food file

the same task a few days later. Also, there might be other people, such as an assistant or supervisor, who need to execute your stored commands and cannot access them from their own user accounts. MS-DOS and Windows users resolve this problem by creating batch files, which are files of commands that are executed when the batch file is run. UNIX/Linux users do the same: They create **shell script** files to contain command-line entries. Like MS-DOS/Windows batch files, script files contain commands that can be run sequentially as a set. For example, if you often create a specific report using a combination of the *cut*, *paste*, and *sort* commands, you can create a script file containing these commands. Instead of having to remember the exact commands and sequence each time you want to create the report, you instead execute the script file. Creating script files in this way can save you a significant amount of time and aggravation.

After you determine the exact commands and command sequence, use the vi or Emacs editor to create the script file. (See Figure 4-6.) Next, make the script file executable by using the *chmod* command with the *x* argument, as you learned in Chapter 2. Finally, use the *./* command to run a script, such as typing *./myscript* and pressing Enter to run the script file myscript.

Script files can range from the simple to the complex. In Hands-On Project 4-15, you get a basic introduction to using these files. Chapters 6 and 7, "Introduction to Shell Script Programming" and "Advanced Shell Programming," give you much more experience with script files (or scripts for short).

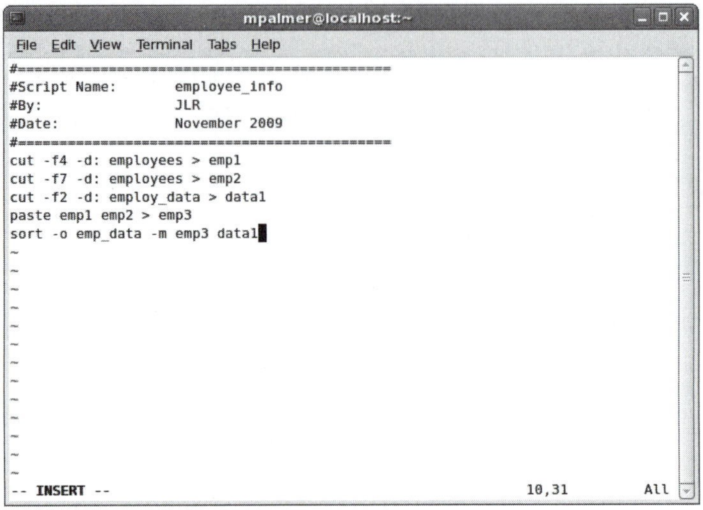

Figure 4-6 Sample script file

Using the join Command on Two Files

Sometimes, it is useful to know how to link the information in two files. You can use the *join* command to associate lines in two files on the basis of a common field in both files. If you want the results sorted, you can either sort the files on a common field before you join the information or sort on a specific field after you join the information from the files. For example, suppose you have a file that contains the employee's last name in one field, the employee's company ID in another field, and the employee's salary in the final field, as follows:

```
Brown:82:53,000
Anders:110:32,000
Caplan:174:41,000
Crow:95:36,000
```

Also, you have another file that contains each employee's last name, first name, middle initial, department, telephone number, and other information, but that file does not contain salary information, as follows:

```
Brown:LaVerne:F:Accounting Department:444-7508: . . .
Anders:Carol:M:Sales Department:444-2130: . . .
Caplan:Jason:R:Payroll Department:444-5609: . . .
Crow:Lorretta:L:Shipping Department:444-8901: . . .
```

You want to create a new third file to use for budgeting salaries that contains only the employee's last name, first name, department, and salary. To do this, you could use the *join* command to create a file with the following contents:

```
Brown:LaVerne:Accounting Department:53,000
Anders:Carol:Sales Department:32,000
Caplan:Jason:Payroll Department:41,000
Crow:Lorretta:Shipping Department:36,000
```

In this simple example, the common field for the two original files is the employee's last name. Note that in this context, the common field provides a **key** for accessing and joining the information to create a report or to create another file with the joined information. (Also refer back to Figure 4-2(c) for an example of a key-based file structure.)

NOTE

The *join* command is also associated with linking information in complex databases. The use of these databases, such as **relational databases**, is beyond the scope of this book. However, learning the *join* command to manipulate data in flat files, as used in this book, can be useful. It is used here as another file manipulation tool to complement your knowledge of the *paste*, *cut*, and *sort* commands.

Syntax **join** [–options] *file1 file2*

Dissection

- Used to associate information in two different files on the basis of a common field or key in those files

- *file1, file2* are two input files that must be sorted on the join field—the field you want to use to join the files. The join field is also called a key. You must sort the files before you can join them. When you issue the *join* command, UNIX/Linux compare the two fields. Each output line contains the common field followed by a line from file1 and then a line from file2. You can modify output using the options described next. If records with duplicate keys are in the same file, UNIX/Linux join on all of them. You can create output records for unpairable lines, for example, to append data from one file to another without losing records.

- Useful options include:

  -1 fieldnum specifies the common field in file1 on which to join

  -2 fieldnum specifies the common field in file 2 on which to join

  -o specifies a list of fields to output. The list contains blank-separated field specifiers in the form m.n, where *m* is the file number and *n* is the position of the field in the file. Thus, *-o 1.2* means "output the second field in the first file."

  -t specifies the field separator character. By default this is a blank, tab, or new line character. Multiple blanks and tabs count as one field separator.

  -a filenum produces a line for each unpairable line in the file *filenum*. (In this case, *filenum* is a 1 for *file1* or a 2 for *file2*.)

  -e str replaces the empty fields for the unpairable line in the string specified by *str*. The string is usually a code or message to indicate the condition, for example, *-e "No Vendor Record."*

Hands-On Project 4-16 gives you an opportunity to use the *join* command.

A Brief Introduction to the Awk Program

Awk, a pattern-scanning and processing language, helps to produce reports that look professional. Although you can use the *cat* and *more* commands to display the output file that you create with your *join* command, the *awk* command (which starts the Awk program when you enter it on the command line) lets you do the same thing more quickly and easily.

The name Awk is formed from the initials of its inventors, (Alfred) Aho, (Peter) Weinberger, and (Brian) Kernighan. They have provided a rich and powerful programming environment in UNIX/Linux that is well worth the effort to learn, because it can perform actions on files that range from the simple to the complex—and can be difficult to duplicate using a combination of other commands.

NOTE   In Fedora, Red Hat Enterprise Linux, SUSE and some other versions of UNIX and Linux, you actually use gawk, which includes enhancements to awk and was developed for the GNU Project by Paul Rubin and Jay Fenlason. When you type awk at the command line, you really execute gawk—or you can just type *gawk*.

Syntax **awk [- Fsep]** ['*pattern* {action} ..'] *filenames*

Dissection

- *awk* checks to see if the input records in the specified files satisfy the *pattern* and, if they do, *awk* executes the *action* associated with it. If no pattern is specified, the action affects every input record.

- *-F:* means the field separator is a colon

The *awk* command is used to look for patterns in files. After it identifies a pattern, it performs an action that you specify. One reason to learn *awk* is to have a tool at your fingertips that lets you manipulate data files very efficiently. For example, you can often do the same thing in *awk* that would take many separate commands using a combination of *paste*, *cut*, *sort*, and *join*. Another reason for learning *awk* is that you might have a project you simply can't complete using a combination of *paste*, *cut*, *sort*, and *join*, but you can complete it using *awk*.

Some of the tasks you can do with *awk* include:

- Manipulate fields and records in a data file.

- Use variables. (You learn more about variables in Chapter 6.)

- Use arithmetic, string, and logical operators. (You learn more about these types of operators in Chapters 6 and 7.)

- Execute commands from a shell script.

- Use classic programming logic, such as loops. (You learn more looping logic in Chapter 6.)

- Process and organize data into well-formatted reports.

4

Consider a basic example in which you want to print text to the screen. The following is a simple *awk* command-line sequence that illustrates the syntax:

```
awk 'BEGIN { print "This is an awk print line." }'
```

When you type this at the command line, the following appears on the screen:

```
This is an awk print line.
```

The *awk* command-line sequence to produce this output does the following things:

1. *awk* starts the Awk program to process the command-line actions.

2. The pattern is signaled by BEGIN.

3. The pattern and the action are enclosed in single quotation marks.

4. The action in the curly brackets { } is processed by the Awk program.

5. The Awk *print* command is executed to print the string inside the double quotation marks (input from the keyboard or stdin) so that it appears on the screen (stdout).

Using a more advanced example, you can use *awk* to process input from a data file and display a report as output. Consider the following sample *awk* command-line sequence:

```
awk -F: '{printf "%s\t %s\n", $1, $2}' datafile
```

In this example, the following happens:

1. *awk -F:* starts the Awk program and tells Awk that the field separator between records in the input file (datafile) is a colon.

2. The pattern and action are enclosed within the single quotation marks.

3. *printf* is a command used in the Awk program to print and format the output. (You learn more about *printf* in Chapter 5, "Advanced File Processing".) In this case, the output goes to the screen (stdout).

4. *$1* and *$2* signify that the fields to print and format are the first (*$1*) and second (*$2*) fields in the specified input file, which is datafile.

5. *datafile* is the name of the input file that contains records divided into fields.

Try Hands-On Projects 4-17 and 4-18 for a further introduction to *awk*.

awk is presented here to give you a first, experiential taste of this powerful tool. There is a lot to learn about using *awk*, and you learn more in later chapters. For now, consider this brief introduction of *awk* as a natural follow-on to your introduction to the *join* command—like a musician sight-reading new music as a rudimentary step to learning more about it. For more information about *awk*, type *man awk* to read the online documentation.

CHAPTER SUMMARY

- UNIX/Linux support regular files, directories, character special files, and block special files. Regular files contain user information. Directories are system files for maintaining the file system's structure. Character special files are related to serial input/output devices, such as printers. Block special files are related to devices, such as disks.

- Files can be structured in several ways. UNIX/Linux store data, such as letters, product records, or vendor reports, in flat ASCII files. File structures depend on the kind of data being stored. Three kinds of regular files are unstructured ASCII characters, records, and trees.

- Often, flat ASCII data files contain records and fields. They typically use one of two formats: variable-length records and fixed-length records. Variable-length records usually have fields that are separated by a delimiter, such as a colon. Fixed-length records have fields that are in specific locations, such as a column range, within a record.

- When performing commands, UNIX/Linux process data—they receive input from the standard input device and then send output to the standard output device. UNIX/Linux refer to the standard devices for input and output as stdin and stdout, respectively. By default, stdin is the keyboard and stdout is the monitor. Another standard device, stderr, refers to the error file that defaults to the monitor. Output from a command can be redirected from stdout to a disk file. Input to a command can be redirected from stdin to a disk file. The error output of a command can be redirected from stderr to a disk file.

- The *touch* command updates a file's time stamp and date stamp and creates empty files.

- The *rmdir* command removes an empty directory. Also, the *rm* command can be used to delete a file, and the *rm* command with the *-r* option can be used to delete a directory that contains files and subdirectories.

- The *cut* command extracts specific columns or fields from a file. Select the fields you want to cut by specifying their positions and separator character, or you can cut by character positions, depending on the data's organization.

- To combine two or more files, use the *paste* command. Where *cat* appends data to the end of the file, the *paste* command combines files side by side. You can also use *paste* to combine fields from two or more files.

- Use the *sort* command to sort a file's contents alphabetically or numerically. UNIX/Linux display the sorted file on the screen by default, but you can also specify that you want to store the sorted data in a particular file.

❏ To automate command processing, include commands in a script file that you can later execute as a program. Use the vi editor to create the script file, and use the *chmod* command to make it executable.

❏ Use the *join* command to extract information from two files sharing a common field. You can use this common field to join the two files. You must sort the two files on the join field—the one you want to use to join the files. The join field is also called a key. You must sort the files before you can join them.

❏ Awk is a pattern-scanning and processing language useful for creating a formatted report with a professional look. You can enter the Awk language instructions in a program file using the vi editor and call it using the *awk* command.

COMMAND SUMMARY: REVIEW OF CHAPTER 4 COMMANDS

Command	Purpose	Options Covered in This Chapter
awk	Starts the *awk* program to format output	**-F** identifies the field separator. **-f** indicates code is coming from a disk file, not the keyboard.
cat	Views the contents of a file, creates a file, merges the contents of files	
cp	Copies one or more files	**-i** provides a warning before *cp* writes over an existing file with the same name. **-s** creates a symbolic link or name at the destination rather than a physical file. **-u** prevents *cp* from copying over an existing file, if the existing file is newer than the source file.
cut	Extracts specified columns or fields from a file	**-c** refers to character positions. **-d** indicates that a specified character separates the fields. **-f** refers to fields.
find	Finds files	**-iname** specifies the name of the files you want to locate, but the search is not case sensitive. **-name** specifies the name of the files you want to locate, but the search is case sensitive. **-mmin** *n* displays files that have been changed within the last *n* minutes. **-mtime** *n* displays files that have been changed within the last *n* days. ***-size n*** displays files of size *n*.

Command	Purpose	Options Covered in This Chapter
join	Combines files having a common field	**-a** *n* produces a line for each unpairable line in file *n*. **-e** *str* replaces the empty fields for an unpairable file with the specified string. **-1** and **-2** with the field number are used to specify common fields when joining. **-o** outputs a specified list of fields. **-t** indicates that a specified character separates the fields.
mv	Moves one or more files	**-i** displays a warning prompt before overwriting a file with the same name. **-u** overwrites a destination file with the same name, if the source file is newer than the one in the destination.
paste	Combines fields from two or more files	**-d** enables you to specify a different separator (other than a tab) between columns. **-s** causes files to be pasted one after the other instead of in parallel.
rm	Removes one or more files	**-i** specifies that UNIX/Linux should request confirmation of file deletion before removing the files. **-r** specifies that directories should be recursively removed.
rmdir	Removes an empty directory	
sort	Sorts the file's contents	**-k** *n* sorts on the key field specified by *n*. **-t** indicates that a specified character separates the fields. **-m** means to merge files before sorting. **-o** redirects output to the specified file. **-d** sorts in alphanumeric or dictionary order. **-g** sorts by numeric (general) order. **-r** sorts in reverse order.
touch	Updates an existing file's time stamp and date stamp or creates empty new files	**-a** specifies that only the access date and time are to be updated. **-m** specifies that only the modification date and time are to be updated. **-c** specifies that no files are to be created.

Key Terms

fixed-length record — A record structure in a file in which each record has a specified length, as does each field in a record.

flat ASCII file — A file that you can create, manipulate, and use to store data, such as letters, product reports, or vendor records. Its organization as an unstructured sequence of bytes is typical of a text file and lends flexibility in data entry, because it can store any kind of data in any order. Any operating system can read this file type. However, because you can retrieve data only in the order you entered it, this file type's usefulness is limited. Also called an ordinary file or regular file.

key — A common field in every file record shared by each of one or more files. The common field, or key, enables you to link or join information among the files, such as for creating a report.

regular file — A UNIX/Linux reference to ASCII/text files and binary files. Also called an ordinary file.

relational database — A database that contains files that UNIX/Linux treat as tables, records that are treated as rows, and fields that are treated as columns and that can be joined to create new records. For example, using the *join* command, you can extract information from two files in a relational database that share a common field.

shell script — A text file that contains sequences of UNIX/Linux commands that do not need to be converted into machine language by a compiler.

sorting key — A field position within each line of a file that is used to sort the lines. For instance, in the command *sort -k 2 myfile*, myfile is sorted by the second field in that file. The *sort* command sorts the lines based on the sorting key.

stderr — An acronym used by programmers for standard error. When UNIX/Linux detect errors in programs and program tasks, the error messages and analyses are directed to stderr, which is often the screen (part of the IEEE Std 1003.1 specification).

stdin — An acronym used by programmers for standard input and used in programming to read input (part of the IEEE Std 1003.1 specification).

stdout — An acronym used by programmers for standard output and used in programming to write output (part of the IEEE Std 1003.1 specification).

variable-length record — A record structure in a data file in which the records can have variable lengths and are typically separated by a delimiter, such as a colon.

REVIEW QUESTIONS

1. You are starting a new year and need to create 10 empty files for your accounting system. Which of the following commands or operators enable you to quickly create these files? (Choose all that apply.)

   a. *mkfile*

   b. *>*

   c. *newfile*

   d. *;*

2. Your project team uses a group of the same files and tracks whether they are still in use by looking at the last modified date. You need to show that a series of files are still in use by changing the last modified date to today. What command do you use?

   a. *date -m*

   b. *chdate*

   c. *touch*

   d. *update*

3. Which of the following are ways in which you can structure a record containing data? (Choose all that apply.)

   a. prosasium

   b. scanned

   c. fixed-length

   d. variable-length

4. You need to delete 30 files that all start with the letters "customer," such as customer_accounts, customer_number, and so on. Which of the following commands enables you to quickly delete these files?

   a. *removeall customer*

   b. *omit customer*

   c. *-customer*

   d. *rm customer**

5. You are in your home directory and need to copy the file MemoRequest to a folder under your home directory called Memos. Which of the following commands do you use?

   a. *cp MemoRequest Memos*

   b. *duplicate MemoRequest Memos*

   c. *mv MemoRequest /*

   d. *link / Memos MemoRequest*

4

6. You have a personnel file that contains the names, addresses, and telephone numbers of all employees. The first field in the personnel file is the employee number and the second field is the employee last name. The third field is the first name and middle initial. Because there are no employees with the same last name, you want to check the file by last name to make certain all employees are included. Which of the following commands should you use?

   a. *paste -l2 personnel*

   b. *cut -f2 personnel*

   c. *capture personnel 2*

   d. *join 2.0 personnel*

7. You are doing some "house cleaning" and want to delete several empty directories. Which of the following commands can you use? (Choose all that apply.)

   a. *rmdir*

   b. *dirdel*

   c. *deldir*

   d. *clear -d*

8. You are trying to use the command *sort -t: +5 datastore*, but you get an error message each time you try it. How can you save the error message in a file called error, so you can e-mail the file to your computer support person?

   a. Enter *error sort -t: +5 datastore.*

   b. Enter *stderr sort -t: +5 datastore.*

   c. Enter *sort -t: +5 datastore << error.*

   d. Enter *sort -t: +5 datastore 2> error.*

9. Which of the following commands would you use to make a backup copy of the file AR2008?

   a. *bak AR2008*

   b. *AR2008 <<*

   c. *cp AR2008 AR2008.bak*

   d. *comp AR2008 < bak*

10. You have a lot of subdirectories under your home directory and know that you saved the file supplemental in one of them, but you are not sure which one. After you use *cd* to change to your home directory, which of the following commands enables you to search all of your subdirectories for the file?

   a. *search / supplemental*

   b. *mv -s supplemental*

   c. *dirsearch supplemental*

   d. *find -name supplemental*

11. You have created a script file called sum_report in your home directory and have made it executable. What command do you use to run the script?

    a. *./sum_report*

    b. *rm sum_report*

    c. *go sum_report*

    d. *#sum_report*

12. Standard output is referred to as which of the following?

    a. out_put

    b. stdout

    c. termout

    d. outsource

13. Which of the following conditions must be met for you to combine two files using the *join* command? (Choose all that apply.)

    a. The two files must be exactly the same length.

    b. Both files must have a field that contains a numbered identifier.

    c. The two files must have a common field, such as last name.

    d. Both files must use a colon as the field separator.

14. Which of the following commands can you use to sort the file vendor_name and display the results on the screen?

    a. *sort > vendor_name*

    b. *sort vendor_name <*

    c. *sort vendor_name stdin*

    d. *sort vendor_name*

15. When you use the *paste* command, columns of information are separated by a tab. However, your boss wants the columns separated by a colon. What option enables you to specify the colon as the separator?

    a. *-s:*

    b. *-d:*

    c. *--sep :*

    d. *--div:*

16. You are examining your addresses file, which contains the first and last names of people you know as well as their street address, city, state, zip code, and telephone number. You want to print a list of last names, which is field 1, and telephone numbers, which is field 7. Which of the following commands enables you to print this list?

    a. *cat 1:7 addresses*

    b. *sort -t: 1-7 addresses*

    c. *cut -f1,7 addresses*

    d. *paste r:1:7 addresses*

4

17. You keep a yearly record of the birds you've seen in your town. The name of the file is birds. The file contains the following fields: name (field 1), markings (field 2), year(s) viewed (field 3), and location (field 4). You want to review the contents of the file, sorted by location. Which of the following commands do you use?

    a. *sort -k 4 birds*

    b. *sort birds >4*

    c. *paste birds -s:45*

    d. *cut birds .4*

18. Which of the following can be accomplished with the *mv* command? (Choose all that apply.)

    a. move a file

    b. modify the contents of a file

    c. rename a file

    d. change a file's owner

19. Your boss asks you to create a professional-looking report from the contents of two files. Which of the following tools enables you to produce a polished report?

    a. *cat*

    b. *awk*

    c. *touch*

    d. *finetouch*

20. What command enables you to sort the contents of a file in reverse order?

    a. *cut -r*

    b. *paste -b*

    c. *sort -t*

    d. *sort -r*

21. You want to combine two files, data07 and data08, into a file called data_all. Which of the following commands do you use?

    a. *cut data07 + data08 2>> data_all*

    b. *paste data07/data08 to data_all*

    c. *sort data 07 data08 <<2 data_all*

    d. *cat data07 data08 > data_all*

22. How can you use the *touch* command to create four new files called sum, datanew, results, and calcs (using one command line)?

23. Create a command that sorts on the second field in the file addresses and then writes the sorted results to the new file, sorted_addresses.

24. Create a command that enables you to copy all of the files in the spreadsheets directory to the accounts directory (when both directories are first-level directories under your home directory and you are currently in your home directory).

25. You play guitar and keep two files on your computer. One file, called strings, lists the different brands of strings you keep on hand. Another file, called music, lists the music books and scores you own. When you enter the command *paste strings music*, what happens?

HANDS-ON PROJECTS

Remember that you can type *clear* and press Enter at the end of any project to start with a fresh screen display.

TIP

HANDS-ON PROJECTS

Project 4-1

You can handle input and output in UNIX/Linux in many ways. In this project, you create a file that feeds commands into the vi editor. (For this and all projects in the chapter, log in using your own account, rather than logging in as root.)

To create a file from which the vi editor reads commands:

1. Use the vi editor to create and then save the file testfile containing the following text (ensure that you don't enter a blank line after the last line):

   ```
   This is line 1.
   This is line 2.
   This is line 3.
   This is line 4.
   ```

2. Type **cat testfile** and press **Enter** to check your work.

3. Next, using the vi editor, create and save another text file named **commands** with one line containing the following vi commands: **2GddGp:x**. (See Figure 4-7.)

```
                        mpalmer@localhost:~              _ □ x
  File  Edit  View  Terminal  Tabs  Help
  2GddGp:x█                                                    ▲
  ~
  ~
  ~
  ~
  ~
  ~
  ~
  ~
  ~
  ~
  ~
  ~
  ~
  ~
  ~
  ~
  -- INSERT --                              1,9         All   ▼
```

Figure 4-7   Using vi to create the commands file

4. Type **cat commands** and press **Enter** to verify the contents of the commands file.

5. Type **vi testfile < commands** and press **Enter**. (Because the input is from a file and not the keyboard, you might see a warning that the input is not from a terminal. Simply ignore the warning.) This loads testfile into the vi editor and redirects vi's input to the text in the commands file. The text in the commands file is treated as commands typed on the keyboard.

6. Type **cat testfile** and press **Enter**. You see the contents of testfile after the vi commands execute. The contents are:

```
This is line 1.
This is line 3.
This is line 4.
This is line 2.
```

Project 4-2

In this project, you use the 2> redirection operator to write an error message to a file.

To redirect an error message:

1. Force the *ls* command to display an error message by giving it an invalid argument. Assuming you have no file or directory in your home directory named oops, type **ls oops** and press **Enter**. You see the following error message:

```
ls: oops: No such file or directory
```

2. Redirect the error output of the *ls* command. Type **ls oops 2> errfile** and press **Enter**. There is no output on the screen.

3. Type **cat errfile** and press **Enter**. You see errfile's contents:

   ```
   ls: oops: No such file or directory
   ```

4. See Figure 4-8.

Figure 4-8   Creating the errfile and viewing its contents

HANDS-ON PROJECTS

Project 4-3

In this project, you practice using the > redirector to create an empty file.

To create an empty file:

1. Type **> newfile1** and press **Enter**. This creates an empty file called newfile1.

2. To list the new file, type **ls –l newfile1** and press **Enter**.

3. You see only the information listed next, where jean is your user name.

   ```
   -rw-r--r-- 1 jean jean    0 Nov 1 16:57 newfile1
   ```

4. To create another new file, type **> newfile2** and press **Enter**.

HANDS-ON PROJECTS

Project 4-4

This project shows you how to use the *touch* command to create a file and to change its time stamp.

To create a file and alter its date/time stamp with the *touch* command:

1. Type **touch newfile3** and press **Enter**. This command creates the file newfile3.

2. Type **ls –l newfile3** and press **Enter**. You see a long listing for the newfile3 file. Note its modification date and time.

3. Wait at least one minute.

4. Type **touch newfile3** and press **Enter**. This updates the file's access and modification date stamp and time stamp with the system date and time.

5. Type **ls –l newfile3** and press **Enter**. Look at the file's modification time. It should be different now. (Figure 4-9 shows the time stamp changed after 10 minutes.)

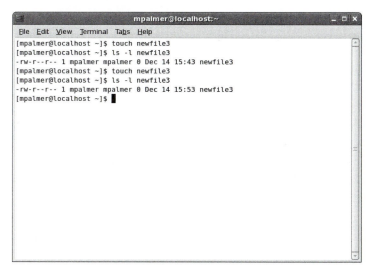

Figure 4-9 Using *touch* to create a file and change its time stamp

Project 4-5

In this project, you delete two of the files you created previously.

To delete a file from the current directory:

1. Type **rm newfile1** and press **Enter**. This permanently deletes newfile1 from the current directory.

2. Type **rm –i newfile2** and press **Enter**. You see the message, rm: remove regular empty file 'newfile2'?

3. Type **y** for yes and press **Enter**.

To delete a group of files using wildcards:

1. You can specify multiple file names as arguments to the *touch* command. Type **touch file1 file2 file3 filegood filebad** and press **Enter**. This command creates these files: file1, file2, file3, filegood, and filebad.

2. Type **ls file*** and press **Enter**. You see the listing for the files you created in Step 1.

3. Type **rm file*** and press **Enter**.

4. Type **ls file*** and press **Enter**. The files have been erased. (See Figure 4-10.)

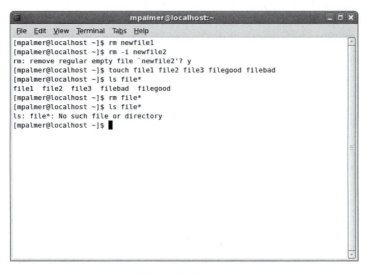

```
                              mpalmer@localhost:~
File  Edit  View  Terminal  Tabs  Help
[mpalmer@localhost ~]$ rm newfile1
[mpalmer@localhost ~]$ rm -i newfile2
rm: remove regular empty file `newfile2'? y
[mpalmer@localhost ~]$ touch file1 file2 file3 filegood filebad
[mpalmer@localhost ~]$ ls file*
file1  file2  file3  filebad  filegood
[mpalmer@localhost ~]$ rm file*
[mpalmer@localhost ~]$ ls file*
ls: file*: No such file or directory
[mpalmer@localhost ~]$
```

Figure 4-10   Deleting files with the *rm* command

HANDS-ON PROJECTS

Project 4-6

In this project, you create a directory and then use the *rmdir* command to remove it. Then, you use the *rm* command to delete a directory that contains subdirectories.

To create a directory and then remove it with the *rmdir* command:

1. Type **mkdir newdir** and press **Enter**. This creates a new directory named newdir.

2. Use a relative path with the *touch* command to create a new file in the newdir directory. Type **touch newdir/newfile** and press **Enter**. This creates the file newfile in the newdir directory.

3. Type **ls newdir** and press **Enter** to see a listing of the newfile file.

4. To attempt to remove the directory, type **rmdir newdir** and press **Enter**. You see an error message similar to:

   ```
   rmdir: newdir: Directory not empty
   ```

5. Use a relative path with the *rm* command to delete newfile. Type **rm newdir/newfile** and press **Enter**.

6. The directory is now empty. Type **rmdir newdir** and press **Enter**.

7. Type **ls** and press **Enter**. The newdir directory is no longer there.

To recursively remove a directory with several subdirectories:

1. Create a directory with several subdirectories. Type **mkdir company** and press **Enter**. Type **mkdir company/sales** and press **Enter**. Type **mkdir company/marketing** and press **Enter**. Type **mkdir company/accounting** and press **Enter**.

2. Create three empty files in the company directory. Type **touch company/file1 company/file2 company/file3** and press **Enter**.

4

TIP

The commands you type next in Step 3 are very similar. You can reduce your typing by using the up arrow key to recall the first command and then modify it.

3. Copy the files to the other directories by doing the following:

    ◌ Type **cp company/file1 company/file2 company/file3 company/sales** and press **Enter**.

    ◌ Type **cp company/file1 company/file2 company/file3 company/marketing** and press **Enter**.

    ◌ Type **cp company/file1 company/file2 company/file3 company/accounting** and press **Enter**.

4. Use the *ls* command to verify that the files were copied into all three directories.

5. Remove the company directory and everything it contains. Type **rm –r company** and press **Enter**.

6. Type **ls** and press **Enter**. The company directory is removed.

HANDS-ON
PROJECTS

Project 4-7

The *cp* command is especially useful for preventing data loss; you can use it to make backup copies of your files. In this project, you create three new files, and then copy them to a different directory Then, you duplicate one file and give it a different name.

To create three files and copy them to a directory:

1. If you do not already have a subdirectory called source, be certain you're in your home directory and then create the directory. Type **mkdir source** and then press **Enter**.

2. To create three files in your home directory, type **> file1** and press **Enter**, type **> file2** and press **Enter**, and then type **> file3** and press **Enter**.

3. Now, you can copy the three files to the source directory. Type **cp file1 file2 file3 source** and press **Enter**. (Or to save time, you can type **cp file* source**.)

4. Next, copy one of the files and give it a different name, so you can distinguish it as a backup file. Type **cp file1 file1.bak** and press **Enter**. (See Figure 4-11.)

Now your working directory contains two files with identical contents but different names.

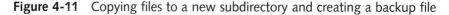

```
                        mpalmer@localhost:~                    _ □ x
File  Edit  View  Terminal  Tabs  Help
[mpalmer@localhost ~]$ mkdir source
[mpalmer@localhost ~]$ > file1
[mpalmer@localhost ~]$ > file2
[mpalmer@localhost ~]$ > file3
[mpalmer@localhost ~]$ cp file* source
[mpalmer@localhost ~]$ cp file1 file1.bak
[mpalmer@localhost ~]$ █
```

Figure 4-11   Copying files to a new subdirectory and creating a backup file

HANDS-ON PROJECTS

Project 4-8

In this project, you use the *mv* command to practice moving files.

To move a file from one directory to another:

1. To create the new file thisfile in your home directory, type **> thisfile** and then press **Enter**.

2. Type **mv thisfile source** and press **Enter** to move the new file to the source directory.

3. Type **ls** and press **Enter**. thisfile is not listed. Type **ls source** and press **Enter**. You see thisfile listed.

4. To move more than one file, type the file names before the directory name. For example, type **mv file1 file1.bak source** and press **Enter**.

5. To create the new file my_file, type **> my_file** and press **Enter**.

6. To rename my_file to your_file, type **mv my_file your_file** and press **Enter**.

7. Type **ls** and press **Enter**. You see your_file listed, but my_file is not listed.

Project 4-9

In this project, you use the *find* command to find every file named file1 in the /home directory and all its subdirectories.

To find a file:

1. Type **find /home –name file1** and press **Enter**.

2. In what directories do you find the file? If there are other users on the system, can you view their home directories to see if file1 exists there?

> Although Linux does not require it, some UNIX versions require the *-print* option after the file name to display the names of files the *find* command locates.
>
> **TIP**

Project 4-10

In the next projects, you practice creating simple data files to gain initial experience in manipulating those files using UNIX/Linux commands. For this project, you begin by using the *cat* command with a redirection operator to practice creating and combining the product1 and product2 files and to further explore the versatility of the redirection operator. The basic files that you work with, in this instance, are sample product description files, with each record (line) containing the name of the product (in the first field) and a number to further help identify that product (in the second field). Figure 4-12 illustrates a conceptual example of the contents of the two files you create.

```
File name: product1

Lobby Furniture          1201
Ballroom Specialties     1221
Poolside Carts           1320
Formal Dining Specials   1340
Reservation Logs         1410
```

```
File name: product2

Plumbing Supplies        1423
Office Equipment         1361
Carpeting Services       1395
Auto Maintenance         1544
Pianos and Violins       1416
```

Figure 4-12 Two sample product description files

To use the *cat* command to combine files:

1. Type **cat > product1** and press **Enter**.

2. Type the following text, pressing **Enter** at the end of each line:

```
Lobby Furniture:1201
Ballroom Specialties:1221
Poolside Carts:1320
Formal Dining Specials:1340
Reservation Logs:1410
```

3. Press **Ctrl+d**.

4. Now, you can redirect the output of *cat* to create the product2 file in your home directory. This file also contains two colon-separated fields.

5. After the command prompt, type **cat > product2** and press **Enter**.

6. Type the following text, pressing **Enter** at the end of each line:

```
Plumbing Supplies:1423
Office Equipment:1361
Carpeting Services:1395
Auto Maintenance:1544
Pianos and Violins:1416
```

7. Press **Ctrl+d**.

8. Now, you can combine the two files in a master products file. After the $ command prompt, type **cat product1 product2 > products3** and press **Enter**.

9. To list the contents of products, type **more products3** and press **Enter**. You see the following list (see Figure 4-13 for the entire command sequence):

```
Lobby Furniture:1201
Ballroom Specialties:1221
Poolside Carts:1320
Formal Dining Specials:1340
Reservation Logs:1410
Plumbing Supplies:1423
Office Equipment:1361
Carpeting Services:1395
Auto Maintenance:1544
Pianos and Violins:1416
```

```
[icon] mpalmer@localhost:~                    [_][□][X]
File  Edit  View  Terminal  Tabs  Help
Lobby Furniture:1201
Ballroom Specialties:1221
Poolside Carts:1320
Formal Dining Specials:1340
Reservation Logs:1410
[mpalmer@localhost ~]$ cat > product2
Plumbing Supplies:1423
Office Equipment:1361
Carpeting Services:1395
Auto Maintenance:1544
Pianos and Violins:1416
[mpalmer@localhost ~]$ cat product1 product2 > products3
[mpalmer@localhost ~]$ more products3
Lobby Furniture:1201
Ballroom Specialties:1221
Poolside Carts:1320
Formal Dining Specials:1340
Reservation Logs:1410
Plumbing Supplies:1423
Office Equipment:1361
Carpeting Services:1395
Auto Maintenance:1544
Pianos and Violins:1416
[mpalmer@localhost ~]$ ▮
```

Figure 4-13   Creating and combining files with the *cat* command

Project 4-11

In Hands-On Project 4-10, you learned how to combine files using the *cat* command. In this project, you combine files using a different method, the *paste* command. Here, you combine the two product files you created in Project 4-10 to display the records in these files in two separate columns.

To use the *paste* command to combine files:

1. Type **clear** and press **Enter** to clear the screen, if you are continuing directly from Project 4-10.

2. Type **paste product1 product2** and press **Enter**.

   This command-line sequence means "combine the file called product1 with the file called product2 and show the results on the screen using a separate column for the contents of each file" (see Figure 4-14). The columns appear uneven, because the records in the files are of different lengths and are separated into columns by tab characters (which you don't see on the screen).

3. How can you write the output of the *paste* command to a file instead of to the screen in this example?

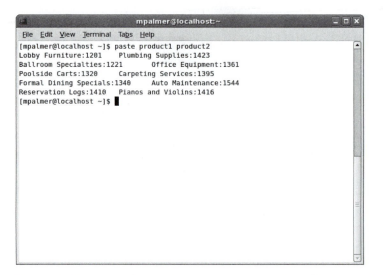

Figure 4-14   Using the *paste* command to combine files

Project 4-12

The *cut* command offers versatility in manipulating and presenting the contents of basic data files. In this project, you begin by creating two files: corp_phones1 and corp_phones2. The corp_phones1 file includes five records of variable size, and a colon separates each field in the record. Figure 4-2(c), shown earlier in the chapter, illustrates this type of file structure. The corp_phones2 file also includes five records of fixed length, illustrated in Figure 4-2(b). Figure 4-15 illustrates the contents of the two files. You can use the *cut* command with either file to extract a list of names.

To create the corp_phones1 and corp_phones2 files:

1. Use the vi or Emacs editor to create the file **corp_phones1**.

2. Type the following lines of text, exactly as they appear. Press **Enter** at the end of each line:

   ```
   219:432:4567:Harrison:Joel:M:4540:Accountant:09-12-1985
   219:432:4587:Mitchell:Barbara:C:4541:Admin Asst:12-14-1995
   219:432:4589:Olson:Timothy:H:4544:Supervisor:06-30-1983
   219:432:4591:Moore:Sarah:H:4500:Dept Manager:08-01-1978
   219:432:4527:Polk:John:S:4520:Accountant:09-22-1998
   ```

3. Save the file, and create a new file named **corp_phones2**.

4. Type the following lines of text, exactly as they appear. Consult Figure 4-15 for the precise position of each character. Press **Enter** at the end of each line. In this file, you are creating fixed-length records, which means that each field must start in a specific column and exactly line up under one another. For example, the telephone area code

```
File name:  corp_phones1 (Variable-length Records - fields separated by colon :)

219:432:4567:Harrison:Joel:M:4540:Accountant:09-12-1985
219:432:4587:Mitchell:Barbara:C:4541:Admin Asst:12-14-1995
219:432:4589:Olson:Timothy:H:4544:Supervisor:06-30-1983
219:432:4591:Moore:Sarah:H:4500:Dept Manager:08-01-1978
219:432:4527:Polk:John:S:4520:Accountant:09-22-1998

Storage space = 279 bytes
```

```
File name:  corp_phones2 (Fixed-length records)

Character positions
1-3 5-7 9-12 14-25        26-35    36 38-41 43-58           59-68
===============================================================
219 432 4567 Harrison     Joel     M 4540 Accountant        09-12-1985
219 432 4587 Mitchell     Barbara  C 4541 Admin Asst        12-14-1995
219 432 4589 Olson        Timothy  H 4544 Supervisor        06-30-1983
219 432 4591 Moore        Sarah    H 4500 Dept Manager      08-01-1978
219 432 4527 Polk         John     S 4520 Accountant        09-22-1998

Storage space = 345 bytes
```

Figure 4-15   Two versions of a sample telephone file structure for a company

219 is in columns 1 through 3. The person's last name starts in column 14 and can go through column 25.

```
219 432 4567 Harrison Joel     M 4540 Accountant     09-12-1985
219 432 4587 Mitchell Barbara  C 4541 Admin Asst     12-14-1995
219 432 4589 Olson    Timothy  H 4544 Supervisor     06-30-1983
219 432 4591 Moore    Sarah    H 4500 Dept Manager   08-01-1978
219 432 4527 Polk     John     S 4520 Accountant     09-22-1998
```

5. Save the file, and exit the editor.

Next, you extract the first and last names from the corp_phones1 file. This file includes variable-length records and fields separated by colon characters. You can select the fields you want to cut by specifying their positions and separator character (which is a colon in this case).

To use the *cut* command to extract fields from variable-length records:

1. Type **cut -f4-6 -d: corp_phones1** and press **Enter**.

   This command means "cut the fields (*-f*) in positions four through six (*4–6*) that the colon character (*-d:*) delimits in the corp_phones1 file."

   You see the list of names:

```
Harrison:Joel:M
Mitchell:Barbara:C
Olson:Timothy:H
Moore:Sarah:H
Polk:John:S
```

Now, you extract the first and last names from the corp_phones2 file. This file includes fixed-length records, instead of records containing colons to separate the fields, so you can cut by specifying character positions.

To use the *cut* command to extract fields from fixed-length records:

1. Type **cut -c14-25,26-35,36 corp_phones2** and press **Enter**.

   This command means "cut the characters (*-c*) in positions 14 through 25, 26 through 35, and position 36 (*14–25,26–35,36*) in the corp_phones2 file."

   You see the list of names:

   ```
   Harrison    Joel        M
   Mitchell    Barbara     C
   Olson       Timothy     H
   Moore       Sarah       H
   Polk        John        S
   ```

   Also, see Figure 4-16 for an example of how your screen will look after using the *cut* command on the corp_phones1 and then the corp_phones2 files.

 Be certain not to include a space in the code sequence after the dash (-) options in the cut command. For example, the correct syntax is *cut* (space) *-c14-25,26-35,36* (space) *corp_phones2*.

TIP

```
                        mpalmer@localhost:~                    _ □ ×
File  Edit  View  Terminal  Tabs  Help
[mpalmer@localhost ~]$ cut -f4-6 -d: corp_phones1
Harrison:Joel:M
Mitchell:Barbara:C
Olson:Timothy:H
Moore:Sarah:H
Polk:John:S

[mpalmer@localhost ~]$ cut -c14-25,26-35,36 corp_phones2
Harrison    Joel      M
Mitchell    Barbara   C
Olson       Timothy   H
Moore       Sarah     H
Polk        John      S

[mpalmer@localhost ~]$ █
```

Figure 4-16   Comparing the *cut* command results of a variable- versus a fixed-length file

Using the *cut* command with variable-length or fixed-length records produces similar results. Cutting from fixed-length records creates a more legible display but requires more storage space. For example, corp_phones2 requires about 345 bytes, and corp_phones1 requires about 279.

Project 4-13

Sorting the corp_phones1 and corp_phones2 files you created in Hands-On Project 4-12 is relatively easy because you can refer to field numbers. In the first two steps of this project, you sort the corp_phones1 file by last name and first name, respectively. In the third and fourth steps, you do the same thing with corp_phones2. Notice that the output of these four steps goes to stdout (the screen). The final step uses the *-o* option, instead of output redirection, to write the sorted output to a new disk file, sorted_phones.

In earlier versions of UNIX/Linux, you had to specify character positions of fields to sort a fixed-length file, such as the corp_phones2 file in our project examples. This was done by using the *+F.C* option, where *F* is the number of the field and *.C* is the character position. The *+F.C* option is still available in some systems, but it is easier to use the *-k* option.

To sort the corp_phones1 file:

1. After the $ prompt, type **sort –t: –k 4 corp_phones1** and press **Enter**.

    In this example, the *-t* option indicates the separator character between fields, which is a colon (:). The *-k* option specifies sorting on the fourth field, or the last name field in this instance. You see the following on your screen:

    ```
    219:432:4567:Harrison:Joel:M:4540:Accountant:09-12-1985
    219:432:4587:Mitchell:Barbara:C:4541:Admin Asst:12-14-1995
    219:432:4591:Moore:Sarah:H:4500:Dept Manager:08-01-1978
    219:432:4589:Olson:Timothy:H:4544:Supervisor:06-30-1983
    219:432:4567:Polk:John:S:4520:Accountant:09-22-1998
    ```

2. Type **sort –t: –k 5 corp_phones1** and press **Enter**.

    This sorts the variable-length records (*-t:* indicates that the fields are delimited by a colon) starting at the first name field (*-k 5*). You see the following on your screen:

    ```
    219:432:4587:Mitchell:Barbara:C:4541:Admin Asst:12-14-1995
    219:432:4567:Harrison:Joel:M:4540:Accountant:09-12-1985
    219:432:4567:Polk:John:S:4520:Accountant:09-22-1998
    219:432:4591:Moore:Sarah:H:4500:Dept Manager:08-01-1978
    219:432:4589:Olson:Timothy:H:4544:Supervisor:06-30-1983
    ```

3. Type **sort –k 4 corp_phones2** and press **Enter**.

This sorts the fixed-length file by last name, starting at the fourth field. In this example, no separator is specified, because fixed-length files don't use a separator. You see the following on your screen:

```
219 432 4567 Harrison  Joel     M 4540 Accountant    09-12-1985
219 432 4587 Mitchell  Barbara  C 4541 Admin Asst    12-14-1995
219 432 4591 Moore     Sarah    H 4500 Dept Manager  08-01-1978
219 432 4589 Olson     Timothy  H 4544 Supervisor    06-30-1983
219 432 4527 Polk      John     S 4520 Accountant    09-22-1998
```

4. Type **sort –k 5 corp_phones2** and press **Enter**.

This sorts the file by first name, starting at the fifth field. You see the following on your screen:

```
219 432 4587 Mitchell  Barbara  C 4541 Admin Asst    12-14-1995
219 432 4567 Harrison  Joel     M 4540 Accountant    09-12-1985
219 432 4527 Polk      John     S 4520 Accountant    09-22-1998
219 432 4591 Moore     Sarah    H 4500 Dept Manager  08-01-1978
219 432 4589 Olson     Timothy  H 4544 Supervisor    06-30-1983
```

5. Type **clear** and press **Enter** to clear the screen for easier viewing.

6. To sort by first name and create the output file sorted_phones, type **sort –t: –k 5 –o sorted_phones corp_phones1** and press **Enter**. This sorts the corp_phones1 file by first name and creates an output file, sorted_phones. Type **cat sorted_phones** and press **Enter** to verify that you successfully created the sorted_phones file. (See Figure 4-17.)

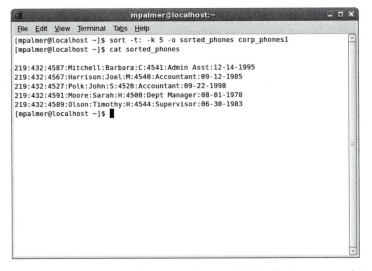

Figure 4-17 Sorting the corp_phones1 file by first name and storing the result in sorted_phones

Project 4-14

In this project, you use the many file-processing tools you've learned, to help reinforce your knowledge to this point. First, use the *cat* command to create the vendors file. The records in the vendors file consist of two colon-separated fields: the vendor number and vendor name.

4

To create the vendors file:

1. Type **cat > vendors** and press **Enter**.

2. Type the following text, pressing **Enter** at the end of each line:

   ```
   1201:Cromwell Interiors
   1221:Design Extras Inc.
   1320:Piedmont Plastics Inc.
   1340:Morgan Catering Service Ltd.
   1350:Pullman Elevators
   1360:Johnson Office Products
   ```

3. Press **Ctrl+d**.

In the next steps, use the *cat* command to create the products file. The records in the products file consist of three colon-separated fields: the product number, the product description, and the vendor number.

To create the products file:

1. Type **cat > products** and press **Enter**.

2. Type the following text, pressing **Enter** at the end of each line, including the last line (use all zeros in the first and last fields, including in S0107, for example):

   ```
   S0107:Lobby Furniture:1201
   S0109:Ballroom Specialties:1221
   S0110:Poolside Carts:1320
   S0130:Formal Dining Specials:1340
   S0201:Reservation Logs:1410
   ```

3. Type **Ctrl+d** to end the *cat* command.

4. Figure 4-18 shows conceptual examples of the vendors and products files you have created.

Now use the *cut*, *paste*, and *sort* commands to create a single-example vendor report. You start by using the *cut* command to extract product descriptions and vendor numbers from the products file and storing them in separate files, p1 and p2. Then extract vendor numbers and names from the vendors file, and store them in v1 and v2. Use the *paste* command to combine the two vendor files (v1 and v2) in a third file, v3. Then combine the two product files (p1 and p2) in a file called p3. Sort and merge the v3 and p3 files, and send their output to the vrep file, the vendor report.

To use the *cut*, *paste*, and *sort* commands to create a report:

1. Type **cut –f2 –d: products > p1** and press **Enter**.

```
File name: vendors

Vendor  Vendor Name
Number
================================
1201:Cromwell Interiors
1221:Design Extras Inc.
1320:Piedmont Plastics Inc.
1340:Morgan Catering Service Ltd.
1350:Pullman Elevators
1360:Johnson Office Products
```

```
File name: products

Prod      Product      Vendor
Number    Description  Number
================================
S0107:Lobby Furniture:1201
S0109:Ballroom Specialties:1221
S0110:Poolside Carts:1320
S0130:Formal Dining Specials:1340
S0201:Reservation Logs:1410
```

Figure 4-18   Vendors and products files

This means "extract the data from the second field delimited by a colon in the products file, and store it in the p1 file." It stores these product descriptions in the p1 file (remember you can use the *cat* command to verify the contents):

```
Lobby Furniture
Ballroom Specialties
Poolside Carts
Formal Dining Specials
Reservation Logs
```

2. Type **cut –f3 –d: products > p2** and press **Enter**.

This means "extract the data from the third field delimited by a colon in the products file, and store it in the p2 file." It stores these vendor numbers in the p2 file:

```
1201
1221
1320
1340
1410
```

3. Type **cut –f1 –d: vendors > v1** and press **Enter**.

This means "extract the data from the first field delimited by a colon in the vendors file, and store it in the v1 file." It stores these vendor numbers in the v1 file:

```
1201
1221
1320
1340
1350
1360
```

4

4. Type **cut –f2 –d: vendors > v2** and press **Enter**.

This means "extract the data from the second field delimited by a colon in the vendors file, and store it in the v2 file." It stores these product descriptions in the v2 file:

```
Cromwell Interiors
Design Extras Inc.
Piedmont Plastics Inc.
Morgan Catering Service Ltd.
Pullman Elevators
Johnson Office Products
```

5. Type **paste v1 v2 > v3** and press **Enter**.

This means "combine the data in v1 and v2, and direct it to the file v3. It stores these vendor numbers and product descriptions in the v3 file:

```
1201 Cromwell Interiors
1221 Design Extras Inc.
1320 Piedmont Plastics Inc.
1340 Morgan Catering Service Ltd.
1350 Pullman Elevators
1360 Johnson Office Products
```

6. Type **paste p2 p1 > p3** and press **Enter**.

This means "combine the data in p2 and p1, and direct it to a file called p3." It stores these vendor numbers and product descriptions in the p3 file:

```
1201 Lobby Furniture
1221 Ballroom Specialties
1320 Poolside Carts
1340 Formal Dining Specials
1410 Reservation Logs
```

7. Type **sort –o vrep –m v3 p3** and press **Enter**.

This means "merge the data in v3 and p3, and direct the output to a file called vrep." It stores these vendor numbers and product descriptions in the vrep file:

```
1201 Cromwell Interiors
1201 Lobby Furniture
1221 Ballroom Specialties
1221 Design Extras Inc.
1320 Piedmont Plastics Inc.
1320 Poolside Carts
1340 Formal Dining Specials
```

```
1340 Morgan Catering Service Ltd.
1350 Pullman Elevators
1360 Johnson Office Products
1410 Reservation Logs
```

At this point, your screen should look similar to Figure 4-19. In one project, you have accomplished quite a lot. You've used the *cat* command to create files and used the *cut*, *paste*, and *sort* commands to extract information from the files, combine the information, and then sort and merge the information into a new file.

```
mpalmer@localhost:~                                          _ □ ×

File  Edit  View  Terminal  Tabs  Help
[mpalmer@localhost ~]$ cat > vendors
1201:Cromwell Interiors
1221:Design Extras Inc.
1320:Piedmont Plastics Inc.
1340:Morgan Catering Service Ltd.
1350:Pullman Elevators
1360:Johnson Office Products
[mpalmer@localhost ~]$ cat > products
S0107:Lobby Furniture:1201
S0109:Ballroom Specialties:1221
S0110:Poolside Carts:1320
S0130:Formal Dining Specials:1340
S0201:Reservation Logs:1410
[mpalmer@localhost ~]$ cut -f2 -d: products > p1
[mpalmer@localhost ~]$ cut -f3 -d: products > p2
[mpalmer@localhost ~]$ cut -f1 -d: vendors > v1
[mpalmer@localhost ~]$ cut -f2 -d: vendors > v2
[mpalmer@localhost ~]$ paste v1 v2 > v3
[mpalmer@localhost ~]$ paste p2 p1 > p3
[mpalmer@localhost ~]$ sort -o vrep -m v3 p3
[mpalmer@localhost ~]$ █
```

Figure 4-19   Using *cat, cut, paste,* and *sort* together to create and process files

Project 4-15

You might encounter many situations in which you must process files and create reports in the same way. You might do this on a weekly basis, for example, as the contents of files change and you want to create new reports or informational files to have on hand. Creating a script gives you a way to remember and reuse a sequence of commands that you can run over and over again. In this project, you create a simple script to process the products and vendors files and write your results to the vrep file.

To use the vi editor to create a script:

1. Use the vi editor to create your script file. Type **vi ven_report** and press **Enter**.

2. The vi editor starts and creates a new file, ven_report.

3. Enter insert mode (press **i**), and then type the following, pressing **Enter** at the end of every line:

```
cut -f2 -d: products > p1
cut -f3 -d: products > p2
cut -f1 -d: vendors > v1
cut -f2 -d: vendors > v2
paste v1 v2 > v3
paste p2 p1 > p3
sort -o vrep -m v3 p3
```

These are the same commands you used in Hands-On Project 4-14 to create the vrep vendor report. Figure 4-20 illustrates how the vi editor screen should look after you have entered the commands.

4. Press **Esc**.

5. Type **:wq** or **:x** and press **Enter** to exit the vi editor.

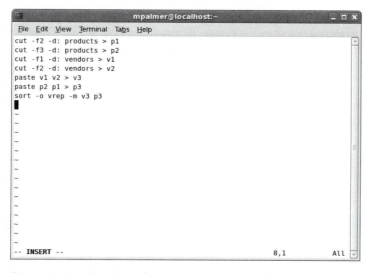

Figure 4-20 Creating the ven_report script file using the vi editor

Now, you can make the script executable with the *chmod* command. The *chmod* command sets file permissions. In the example that follows, the *chmod* command and its *ugo+x* option make the ven_report file executable by users (owners), group, and others.

To make the script executable:

1. Type **chmod ugo+x ven_report** and press **Enter**.

   (See Chapter 2 for more information on the *chmod* command.)

2. Type **rm vrep** and press **Enter** to delete the vrep file you created in Hands-On Project 4-14. Next, to ensure the script works, type **./ven_report** and press **Enter**. (The ./ command enables you to run a script.)

3. Type **cat vrep** and press **Enter** to verify the vrep file contents look identical to those shown in Step 7 of Hands-On Project 4-14.

NOTE

In addition to making a shell script executable, it is a good idea to specify the shell for which the script is designed to run. For example, if you have designed a script for the Bash shell, you can place #!/bin/bash as the first line in the script. You learn how to do this in Chapter 7.

HANDS-ON PROJECTS

Project 4-16

The products and vendors files that you have created offer an opportunity to begin exploring what you can do with the *join* command. This command is potentially more complex than many you have learned so far. In this project, you get a start in using the *join* command by creating a sample vendor report from the products and vendors files.

To use the *join* command to create a report:

1. Type **join –a1 –e "No Products" –1 1 –2 3 –o '1.2 2.2' –t: vendors products > vreport ; cat vreport** and press **Enter**. (Remember that if you make a typing mistake, you can use the up arrow to recall a command, press the left arrow key to correct the mistake, and then run the command again.)

In this command, the *-1* and *-2* options indicate the first or second specified file, such as vendors or products. The numbers following *-1* and *-2* specify field numbers used for the join or match. Here, you use the first field of the vendors file to join the third field of the products file.

The *-a* option tells the command to print a line for each unpairable line in the file number. In this case, a line prints for each vendor record that does not match a product record.

The *-e* option lets you display a message for the unmatched (*-a1*) record, such as "No Products."

The *-o* option sets the fields that will be output when a match is made.

The *1.2* indicates that field two of the vendors file is to be output along with *2.2*, field two of the products file.

The *-t* option specifies the field separator, the colon. This *join* command redirects its output to a new file, vreport. The *cat* command displays the output on the screen.

See Figure 4-21 to view the output of the report.

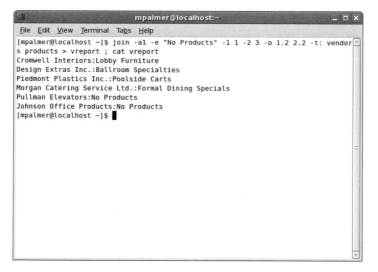

Figure 4-21   vreport output from the *join* command

HANDS-ON
PROJECTS

Project 4-17

This project gives you a brief introduction to using the *awk* command for creating a more polished vendor report than in Hands-On Project 4-16 and gives you a glimpse of the next step in creating reports.

To generate and format the vendor report:

1. Type **awk –F: '{printf "%-28s\t %s\n", $1, $2}' vreport** and then press **Enter**.

   You see the vendor report, including vendor names and product descriptions, as illustrated in Figure 4-22.

The parts of the *awk* command you typed in Step 1 are:

▢ *awk -F:* calls the Awk program and identifies the field separator as a colon.

▢ *'{printf "%-28s\t %s\n", $1, $2}'* represents the action to take on each line that is read in. Single quotation marks enclose the action.

▢ *printf* is a print formatting function from the C programming language. It lets you specify an edit pattern for the output. The code inside the double quotation marks defines this pattern. The code immediately following the % tells how to align the field to be printed. The - sign specifies left alignment. The number that follows, *28*, indicates how many characters you want to display. The trailing *s* means that the field consists of nonnumeric characters, also called a string. The \t inserts a tab character into the edit pattern. The *%s* specifies that another string field should be printed. You do not need to specify the string length in this case, because it is the last field printed (the product name). The \n specifies to skip a line after printing each output record. The *$1* and *$2*, separated with a comma, indicate that the first and second fields in the input file should be placed in the edit pattern where the two *s* characters appear. The first field is the vendor name, and the second is the product description. (You learn much more about *printf* in Chapter 10, "Developing UNIX/Linux Applications in C and C++"; it is presented here to provide you a brief introduction on which to build as you progress through the book.)

❑ *vreport* is the name of the input file.

```
[mpalmer@localhost ~]$ awk -F: '{printf "%-28s\t %s\n", $1, $2}' vreport
Cromwell Interiors          Lobby Furniture
Design Extras Inc.          Ballroom Specialties
Piedmont Plastics Inc.      Poolside Carts
Morgan Catering Service Ltd. Formal Dining Specials
Pullman Elevators           No Products
Johnson Office Products     No Products
[mpalmer@localhost ~]$ 
```

Figure 4-22 Vendor report created via the *awk* command

HANDS-ON PROJECTS

Project 4-18

To refine and automate the vendor report, you can create a shell script that uses the *awk* command. This new script, however, includes only the *awk* command, not a series of separate commands. You then call the Awk program using *awk* with the *-f* option. This option tells Awk that the code is coming from a disk file, not from the keyboard. You present the action statements inside the Awk program file, in a different way, which resembles programming code. The program file includes additional lines needed to print a heading and the current date for the report.

The next steps show what happens when you enter the Awk program in a file like this. You use the *FS* variable to tell the program what the field separator is—in this example, a colon. *FS* is one of many variables that *awk* uses to advise the program about the file being processed. Other codes you see here set up an initial activity that executes once when the program loads. *BEGIN* followed by the opening curly brace ({) indicates this opening activity. The closing curly brace (}) marks the end of actions performed when the program first loads. These actions print the headings, date, and dash lines that separate the heading from the body of the report.

To create the *awk* script:

1. Type **vi awrp** and press **Enter** to start the vi editor and create the file awrp. Press **i** to start insert mode.

2. Type the following code. (*Note*: In the seventh line of code, enter 52 equal signs, keeping them on the same line as shown in Figure 4-23.)

```
BEGIN {
        { FS = ":"}
        { print "\t\tVendors and Products\n" }
        { "date" | getline d }
        { printf "\t  %s\n",d }
        { print "Vendor Name\t\t\t Product Names\n" }
        { print"====================================\n" }
}
{ printf "%-28s\t%s\n",$1, $2 }
```

In the code you have typed, the *getline* option is used. *Getline* is designed to read input. In this case, it reads the date and places it into the *d* variable, which then is printed via the *printf* command.

Your vi edit session should look like the one in Figure 4-23.

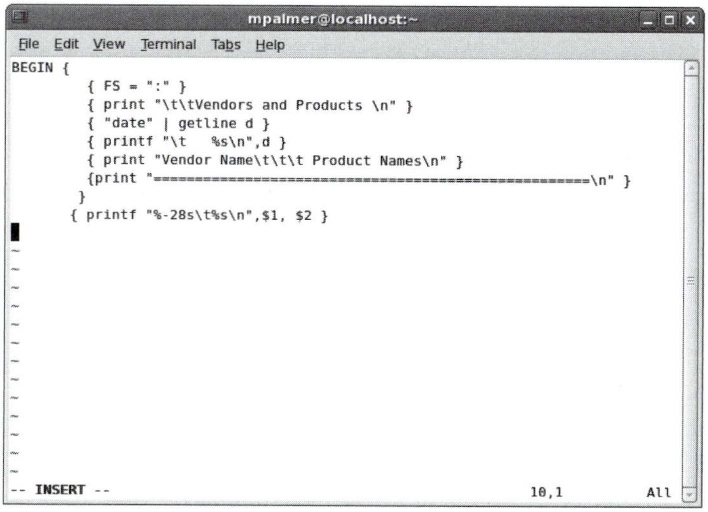

Figure 4-23   Creating the awrp file using the vi editor

3. Press **Esc**.

4. Type **:wq** or **:x** and press **Enter** to exit the vi editor.

5. Type **awk -f awrp vreport > v_report** and press **Enter**.

   This means "using the Awk program, combine the fields from the awrp file with the fields from the vreport file, and send them to a new file called v_report."

6. Type **cat v_report** and press **Enter**. Your screen should look similar to Figure 4-24.

7. To print the report on the default printer, type **lpr v_report** and press **Enter**.

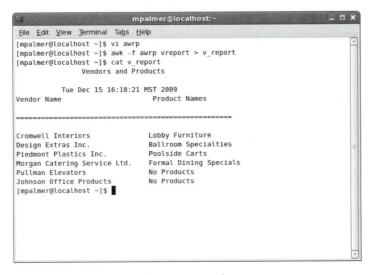

Figure 4-24   Viewing the contents of v_report

DISCOVERY EXERCISES

1. How can you create a file called history by using a redirection operator?

2. Wait one minute or more and then change the time stamp on the history file you just created.

3. Back up the history file to the file history.bak.

4. Sort the corp_phones1 file by the last four digits of the phone number.

5. Create and use a command that displays only the last names and telephone numbers (omitting the area code) of people in the corp_phones2 file. Place a space between the telephone number and the last name.

6. Assume you have a subdirectory named datafiles directly under your current working directory, and you have two files named data1 and data2 in your current directory. What command can you use to copy the data1 and data2 files from your current working directory to the datafiles directory?

7. Assume you have four files: accounts1, accounts2, accounts3, and accounts4. Write the *paste* command that combines these files and separates the fields on each line with a "/" character, displaying the results to the screen.

8. How would you perform the action in Exercise 7, but write the results to the file total_accounts?

9. Assume you have 10 subdirectories and you want to locate all files that end with the extension ".c". What command can you use to search all 10 of your subdirectories for this file?

10. After you create a script file, what are the next steps to run it?

11. Change the *awk* script that you created earlier so that the column headings are "Vendor" and "Product" and the name of the report is "Vendor Data."

12. Create the subdirectory mytest. Copy a file into your new subdirectory. Delete the mytest subdirectory and its contents using one command.

13. Use the *cut* command to create a file called descriptions that contains only the product descriptions from the products file you created earlier in this chapter.

14. You are worried about copying over an existing or newer file in another directory when you use the *move* command. What are your options in this situation?

15. What command enables you to find all empty files in your source directory?

16. How can you find all files in your home directory that were modified in the last seven days?

17. How can you put the contents of each line of the product1 file side by side with the contents of the product2 file, but with only a dash between them instead of a tab?

18. Make a copy of the corp_phones2 file and call it testcorp. Next, create a single-line command that enables you to cut characters in the fifth column of the testcorp file and paste them back to the first column in the same file. (*Hint:* Two good solutions exist, one in which you use a semicolon and one with more finesse in which you use a pipe character.)

19. How can you use a command you have learned in this chapter to list the names of all users on your system? (*Hint:* Find out the name of the file in which user information is stored.)

20. Type *who* and press **Enter** to view a list of logged-in users, along with other information. Now use the *who* command (which you learned about in Chapter 1) with a command you learned in this chapter to view who is logged in, but to suppress all other information that normally accompanies the *who* command.

5

ADVANCED FILE PROCESSING

After reading this chapter and completing the exercises, you will be able to:

♦ Use the pipe operator to redirect the output of one command to another command

♦ Use the *grep* command to search for a specified pattern in a file

♦ Use the *uniq* command to remove duplicate lines from a file

♦ Use the *comm* and *diff* commands to compare two files

♦ Use the *wc* command to count words, characters, and lines in a file

♦ Use manipulation and transformation commands, which include *sed*, *tr*, and *pr*

♦ Design a new file-processing application by creating, testing, and running shell scripts

---

With file-processing commands, you can manage files through sorting, cutting, formatting, translating, comparing, and using other processing techniques. Your UNIX/Linux abilities are strengthened from knowing the versatility of these commands. In this chapter, you learn many new file-processing, selection, manipulation, and transformation commands to put into your expanding toolbox.

You begin by learning new file-processing commands and progress to using more complex manipulation and format commands. In the second portion of the chapter, you put your knowledge to work by designing an application in a step-by-step process. The beginning steps involve designing a file structure. Next, you use commands to determine ways to extract information from the files. Then, you build small shell scripts of commands and test each one. After you have the small scripts individually built, you combine them into a larger application that you run.

NOTE   Some of the capabilities that you discover in this chapter can also be performed using graphical utilities from a GUI-based desktop, such as GNOME or KDE. By learning how to use these capabilities through commands instead of GUI tools, you often have the advantage of being able to do more—and do it faster. Also, you can often perform actions from the command line that you cannot perform with the same versatility from a GUI desktop tool.

ADVANCING YOUR FILE-PROCESSING SKILLS

In Chapter 4, "UNIX/Linux File Processing," you learned to use several UNIX/Linux commands to extract and organize information from existing files and transform that information into a useful format. Now you build on those skills and learn to use new file-processing commands and operators. The commands you use for file processing can be organized into two categories: selection commands and manipulation and transformation commands.

Selection commands focus on extracting specific information from files, such as using the *comm* command to compare file contents. Table 5-1 lists the selection commands you have already mastered plus new commands you learn in this chapter.

Table 5-1   Selection commands

Command	Purpose
comm	Compares sorted files and shows differences
cut	Selects columns (fields)
diff	Compares and selects differences in two files
grep	Selects lines or rows
head	Selects lines from the beginning of a file
tail	Selects lines from the end of a file
uniq	Selects unique lines or rows (typically preceded by a sort)
wc	Counts characters, words, or lines in a file

Manipulation and transformation commands alter and transform extracted information into useful and appealing formats. Table 5-2 lists these commands.

Table 5-2   Manipulation and transformation commands

Command	Purpose
awk	Invokes Awk, a processing and pattern-scanning language
cat	Concatenates files
chmod	Changes the security mode of a file or directory
join	Joins two files, matching row by row
paste	Pastes multiple files, column by column
pr	Formats and prints
sed	Edits data streams

Table 5-2 Manipulation and transformation commands (continued)

Command	Purpose
sort	Sorts and merges multiple files
tr	Translates and deletes character by character

USING THE SELECTION COMMANDS

5

You used the *head* and *tail* commands in Chapter 1, "The Essence of UNIX and Linux," and the *cut* command in Chapter 4. You also learned to use redirection operators. Now you learn a new redirection operator, called a pipe, and work with the *grep, diff, uniq, comm,* and *wc* commands for processing files.

NOTE

See Appendix B, "Syntax Guide to UNIX/Linux Commands," for additional information about these commands.

Using the Pipe Operator

As you have learned, most UNIX/Linux commands take their input from stdin (the standard input device) and send their output to stdout (the standard output device). You have also used the > operator to redirect a command's output from the screen to a file, and you have used the < operator to redirect a command's input from the keyboard to a file. The **pipe operator (|)** redirects the output of one command to the input of another command. The pipe operator is used in the following way:

```
first_command | second_command
```

The pipe operator connects the output of the first command with the input of the second command. For example, when you list the contents of a large directory, such as /etc or /sbin using the *ls -l* command, the output races across the screen and you really see only the end of the listing. If you are using a terminal window, you might be able to use the scroll bar to go backward through the listing, but this might not be as convenient as other ways to view the output, or the terminal window or command-line access on your system might not support fully scrolling back. An alternative is to pipe output of the *ls -l* command to use as input of the *more* command. For example, when you enter the following command using the pipe operator, you can view the contents of the /sbin directory one screen at a time and use the spacebar to advance to the next screen.

```
ls -l /sbin | more
```

Hands-on Project 5-1 enables you to use the pipe operator for a directory listing.

TIP

You can also use the *less* command with a directory to view its contents one screen at a time, such as *less /sbin*.

The pipe operator can connect several commands on the same command line, in the following manner:

```
first_command | second_command | third_command ...
```

This technique can be useful, for example, when you want to list and then sort in reverse order the contents of a large directory and display the result one screen at a time, as shown in Figure 5-1 for the contents of the /etc directory. Try Hands-on Project 5-2 to use the pipe operator to combine commands on one line.

```
mpalmer@localhost:~
File  Edit  View  Terminal  Tabs  Help
[mpalmer@localhost ~]$ ls /etc | sort -r | more
yum.repos.d
yum.conf
yum
yp.conf
xml
xinetd.d
xdg
X11
wvdial.conf
wpa_supplicant
wgetrc
warnquota.conf
virc
vimrc
updatedb.conf
udev
termcap
syslog.conf
sysctl.conf
sysconfig
sudoers
subversion
stunnel
--More--
```

Figure 5-1   Combining commands using the pipe operator

Using the grep Command

Use the *grep* command to search for a specified pattern in a file, such as a particular word or phrase. UNIX/Linux find and then display the line containing the pattern you specify.

Syntax **grep** [-options] *pattern* [*filename*]

Dissection

- Finds and displays lines containing a particular search pattern
- Can be used on text and binary regular files
- Can search multiple files in one command
- Useful options include:

    -i ignores case

    -l lists only file names

    -c counts the number of lines instead of showing them

    -r searches through files under all subdirectories

    -n includes the line number for each line found

    -v displays only lines that don't contain the search pattern

---

NOTE

Three typical meanings are associated with *grep*: Global Regular Expression Print, Global Regular Expression Parser, and Get Regular Expression Processing.

Consider a situation in which you have written a document for a company in which you refer multiple times to the Computer Resources Committee. Further, your company's management is contemplating broadening the focus of the committee and calling it the Computer and Telecommunications Resources Committee. When company management asks you to determine how often existing company documentation in the /documentation directory refers to the Computer Resources Committee, you can use the *grep* command to find out. Here is an example of what you would enter:

```
grep -r Computer Resources Committee /documentation
```

In some cases, when you use *grep*, it is helpful to enter the character pattern you are trying to find in single or double quotes. For example, this is true when you are looking for two or more words, so that the words can be distinguished from a file, as in the command: *grep 'red hat' operating_system*. In this example, 'red hat' is the character pattern and operating_system is the file you are searching. If you enter *red hat* without quotes you are likely to get an error because *grep* interprets hat as a file name. In Hands-on Project 5-3, you use the *grep* command to search for and extract specific text.

NOTE

Many UNIX/Linux systems offer a combination of four grep-type commands: *grep*, *egrep*, *fgrep*, and *zgrep*. For example, besides *grep* there is *egrep* (also executed as *grep -E*), which is used for "extended" or more complex expressions. *fgrep* (or *grep -F* on most systems) searches for fixed or text strings only and not expressions. *zgrep* is used to perform searches on files that are compressed or zipped.

Using the uniq Command

The *uniq* command removes duplicate lines from a file. Because it compares only consecutive lines, the *uniq* command requires sorted input. The syntax of the *uniq* command is as follows:

Syntax **uniq** [–options] [*file1* > *file2*]

Dissection

- Removes consecutive duplicate lines from one file and writes the result to another file
- Useful options include:

    –u outputs only the lines of the source file that are not duplicated

    –d outputs one copy of each line that has a duplicate, and does not show unique lines

    –i ignores case

    –c starts each line by showing the number of each instance

---

In its simplest form, the *uniq* command removes successive identical lines or rows from a file. For example, consider a simple file called parts that contains the following entries:

          muffler

          muffler

          shocks

          alternator

          battery

          battery

          radiator

          radiator

          coil

          spark plugs

          spark plugs

          coil

You can use the *uniq* command to create an output file called inventory that removes all the successive duplicates. The command to use is as follows (see Figure 5-2):

```
uniq parts > inventory
```

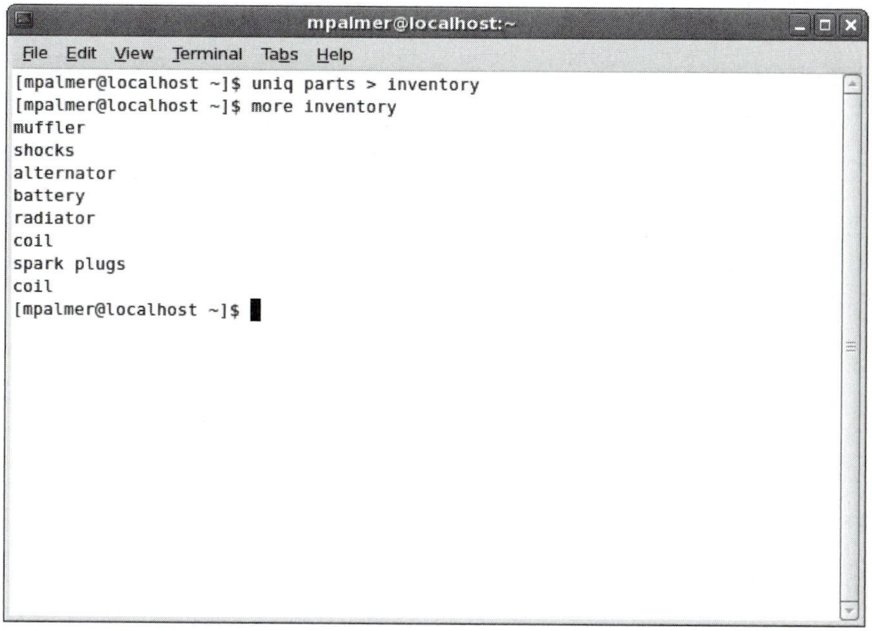

Figure 5-2   Using *uniq* to remove duplicate entries and create a new output file

Notice in Figure 5-2 that coil is still listed twice. This is because in the original parts file, the two occurrences of coil are not successive. In the parts file, the first instance of coil is just before the first listing for spark plugs, and the second instance of coil is after the second instance of spark plugs.

The *-u* option instructs *uniq* to generate as output only the lines of the source file that are not duplicated successively. (If a line is repeated successively, it is not generated as output.) Here is an example (see Figure 5-3):

```
uniq -u parts > single_items
```

In Figure 5-3, coil is also listed twice because in the original parts file, the two occurrences of coil are not successive.

The *-d* option instructs *uniq* to generate as output one copy of each line that has a successive duplicate line. Unduplicated lines are not generated as output. Here is an example:

```
uniq -d parts > multi_items
```

Hands-on Project 5-4 enables you to use the *uniq* command.

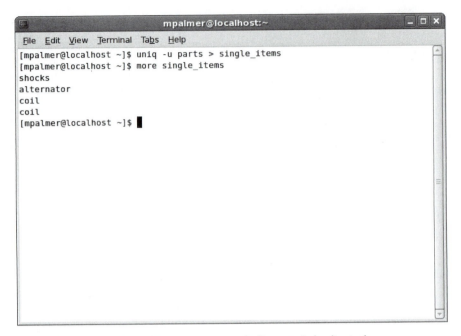

Figure 5-3 Creating a file containing only lines not duplicated

Using the comm Command

Like the *uniq* command, the *comm* command identifies duplicate lines. Unlike the *uniq* command, it doesn't delete duplicates, and it works with two files rather than one. The *comm* command locates identical lines within two identically sorted files. It compares lines common to file1 and file2, and produces three-column output:

- The first column contains lines found only in file1.
- The second column contains lines found only in file2.
- The third column contains lines found in both file1 and file2.

The syntax of *comm* is as follows:

Syntax **comm** [–options] *file1 file2*

Dissection

- Compares two sorted files for common lines and generates three columns of output to show which lines are unique to each file and which are common to both files

- Useful options include:

  -1 do not display lines that are only in file1

  -2 do not display lines that are only in file2

  -3 do not display lines appearing in both file1 and file2

Hands-on Project 5-5 uses the *comm* command.

5

Using the diff Command

The *diff* command shows lines that differ between two files and is commonly used to determine the minimal set of changes needed to convert file1 to file2. The command's output displays the line(s) that differ. Differing text in file1 is preceded by the less-than symbol (<), and for file2 is preceded by the greater-than symbol (>).

Syntax **diff** [-options] *file1 file2*

Dissection

- Shows lines that differ between two files
- Useful options include:

  -b ignores blanks that repeat

  -B does not compare for blank lines

  -i ignores case

  -c shows lines surrounding the line that differs (for context)

  -y display the differences side-by-side in columns

Consider a comparison of two files, zoo1 and zoo2, that contain variable-length records of food supplies for zoo animals. You create these files in Hands-on Project 5-4, and they contain the following lines. File zoo1 contains:

```
Monkeys:Bananas:2000:850.00
Lions:Raw Meat:4000:1245.50
Lions:Raw Meat:4000:1245.50
Camels:Vegetables:2300:564.75
Elephants:Hay:120000:1105.75
Elephants:Hay:120000:1105.75
```

File zoo2 contains:

```
Monkeys:Bananas:2000:850.00
Lions:Raw Meat:4000:1245.50
Camels:Vegetables:2300:564.75
Elephants:Hay:120000:1105.75
```

When you enter *diff zoo1 zoo2*, the first lines of output are as follows:

```
3d2
< Lions:Raw Meat:4000:1245.50
```

In this example line of output, the code *3d2* indicates that to make the files the same, you need to delete the third line in file1, so file1 matches file2. The *d* means delete, the *3* means the third line from file1, and the *2* means that file1 and file2 will be the same up to, but not including, line 2.

In another example, assume that you reverse the order of the files in the comparison by entering *diff zoo2 zoo1* and the first lines of output are as follows:

```
2a3
> Lions:Raw Meat:4000:1245.50
```

The code *2a3* indicates you need to add a line to file1, so file1 matches file2. The *a* means to add a line or lines to file1. The *3* means line 3 is to be added from file1 to file2. The *2* indicates that the line must be added in file2 following line 2.

The *diff* command is an example of a command that is easier to understand after you use it. Try Hands-on Project 5-6 to further explore how this command works.

Using the wc Command

Use the *wc* command to count the number of lines (option *-l*), words (option *-w*), and bytes or characters (option *-c*) in text files. You can specify all three options in the command line, such as *-lwc* or any other combination. If you enter the command without options, you see counts of lines, words, and characters in that order. (See Figure 5-4.)

Syntax **wc** [–options] [*files*]

Dissection

- Calculates the line, word, and byte count of the specified file(s)
- Useful options include:

  -c shows byte count

  -l shows line count

  -w shows word count

Hands-on Project 5-7 gives you experience using the *wc* command.

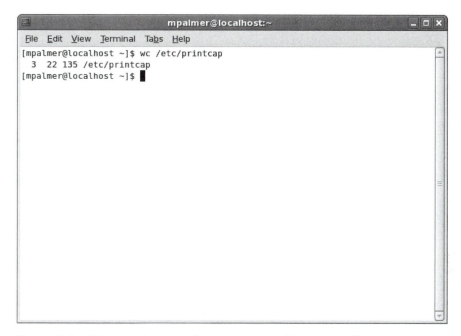

Figure 5-4   Using *wc* to count lines, words, and bytes in a file

USING MANIPULATION AND TRANSFORMATION COMMANDS

In addition to the commands that you learned in Chapter 4 that are used to manipulate and format data, you can also use the *sed*, *tr*, and *pr* commands to edit and transform data's appearance before you display or print it.

Introducing the sed Command

When you want to make global changes to large files, you need a different kind of tool than an interactive editor, such as vi and Emacs. Another UNIX/Linux editor, *sed*, is designed specifically for this purpose, and is sometimes called a stream editor because input to *sed* is rendered in standard output (to display on the screen). The minimum requirements to run *sed* are an input file and a command that lets *sed* know what actions to apply to the file. *sed* commands have two general forms: (1) provided as part of the command line and (2) provided as input from a script file.

Syntax **sed** [-options] [*command*] [*file(s)*]
    sed [-options] [-*f scriptfile*] [*file(s)*]

Dissection

- *sed* is a stream editor that can be used on one or more files, and is particularly useful for making global changes on large files.

- The first form lets you specify an editing command on the command line.

- The second form lets you specify a script file containing *sed* commands.

- Useful options include:

  d deletes lines specified by the *-n* option (no hyphen in front of the *d* option)

  p prints to output the lines specified by the *-n* option (no hyphen in front of the *p* option)

  s substitutes specified text (no hyphen in front of this *s* option)

  a appends text (no hyphen in front of this option)

  -e specifies multiple commands on a command line

  -n specifies line numbers on which to work

For example, you can use *sed* to work with a new file, to display only certain lines—such as only lines 3 and 4—and then to work on or replace only those lines. You learn to use *sed* in this way by working through Hands-on Project 5-8, entering the edit commands from the command line.

To append new lines in *sed*, you must use the *a* command. This command appends lines after the specified line number. Like all other *sed* commands, it operates on all lines in the file if you do not specify a line number. In Hands-on Project 5-9, you create and manipulate a document's contents by using the *a* command from a script.

Translating Characters Using the tr Command

The *tr* or translate command (also called the translate characters command) copies data from the standard input to the standard output, substituting or deleting characters specified by options and patterns. The patterns are strings and the strings are sets of characters.

Syntax **tr** [-options] [*"string1" "string2"*]

Dissection

- In its simplest form, *tr* translates each character in *string1* into the character in the corresponding position in *string2*. The strings typically need to be "quoted" with either single or double quotation marks.

- Useful options include:

  –d deletes characters

  –s substitutes or replaces characters

A popular use of *tr* is to convert lowercase characters to uppercase characters. For example, you can translate the contents of a file from lowercase to uppercase characters by using [a–z] to specify the lowercase characters and [A–Z] to specify the uppercase characters. Other commonly used applications are to use the *-d* option to delete characters and *-s* to replace or substitute characters.

When translating characters, you often need to use either single quotation marks or double quotation marks in the command line around the characters you intend to translate. Consider the following examples:

```
tr "c" " " < constants
```

and

```
tr 'c' ' ' < constants
```

Both of these commands accomplish the same thing. They replace all occurrences of the letter "c" with one blank space in the file constants (the input file), and display the translated result to the screen.

You use the *tr* command in Hands-on Project 5-10.

Using the pr Command to Format Your Output

The *pr* command prints the specified files on the standard output in paginated form. If you do not specify any files or you specify a file name of "–", *pr* reads the standard input.

By default, *pr* formats the specified files into single-column pages of 66 lines. Each page has a five-line header, which, by default, contains the current file's name, its last modification date, the current page, and a five-line trailer consisting of blank lines.

Syntax **pr** [–options] [*file* ...]

Dissection

- Formats one or more files by providing pagination, columns, and column heads
- Common options include:

  –h (header format) lets you customize your header lines

  –d double-spaces output

  –l n sets the number of lines per page

Hands-on Project 5-11 enables you to use the *pr* command.

DESIGNING A NEW FILE-PROCESSING APPLICATION

One reason for learning UNIX/Linux selection, manipulation, and transformation commands is to develop an application. Whether you are creating an application for yourself or for others, the most important phase in developing a new application is creating a design. The design defines the information an application needs to produce. The design also defines how to organize this information into files, records, and fields, which are called **logical structures** because each represents a logical entity, such as a payroll file, an employee pay record, or a field for an employee Social Security number. Files consist of records, and records consist of fields. You learned about records and fields in Chapter 4.

This chapter gives you a preliminary look at developing an application by starting with record design considerations. How you set up records in a file can influence what you can do with an application. It also affects the ways in which you can use selection, manipulation, and transformation commands. If you pack the file with more information or fields than are needed, you make accessing data for a specific purpose inefficient or difficult. If you fail to include data that is needed, the application has limited value to the user, and the versatility of data-handling commands is underused.

Another consideration when you design records is how specific fields in one file might have particular importance for data handling. As you learned in Chapter 4, some fields can be used as key fields. These fields are important for enabling useful sorts and for linking the contents of two or more files through the *join* command. For example, by placing an employee's last name in a separate field without the first name and middle initial, you can sort on the last name or use the last name as a common field between two files you want to link.

Some organizations also give employees or students a special ID that can be used in records, such as in human resources or student information records. This ID can be a valuable key field for sorting, selecting, joining, and handling all types of information. For example, in a four-character ID, the first two characters might represent a department and the second two might represent the individual employee in that department. A user or programmer can use this field to sort employee records by department in a report. Another option is to use the *grep* command to create a specialized report for a particular department. A last name or ID field can also make it easier to evaluate duplicate records using the *uniq* and *comm* commands.

In this portion of the book, you begin by considering record design and key fields. Next, you apply this information and you use the tools you have learned to create an example Programmer Activity Status Report, such as might be developed for a company or organization. The report will show programmers' names and the number of projects on which each programmer is working. As you work your way through the next sections, be certain to stop and perform the Hands-on Projects referenced in each section before you move on to the next section.

In the following sections, you start by learning file, record, and field design, and then use the selection, manipulation, and transformation commands to select, manipulate, and format information—all in preparation for formulating the Programmer Activity Status Report. You also learn more about shell scripts—how to use them in an application and how to run them using alternate methods. Finally, you create and test scripts that implement your knowledge and culminate in the Programmer Activity Status Report.

Designing Records

The first task in the record design phase is to define the fields in the records. These definitions take the form of a **record layout** that identifies each field by name and data type (such as numeric or nonnumeric). Design the file record to store only those fields relevant to the record's primary purpose. For example, to design your Programmer Activity Status Report in the Hands-on Projects, you need two files: one for programmer information and another for project information. You include a field for the programmer's name in the programmer file record and a field for the project description in the project file record. However, you do not store a programmer's name in a project file, even though the programmer might be assigned to the project. Also, you do not store project names in the programmer files. This structure is intended to give you an idea of how actual data files might be set up, so that each type of file can be used for a different purpose in a larger system of files and programs.

Allocating the space needed for only the necessary fields of the records keeps records brief and to the point. Short records, like short sentences, are easier to understand. Likewise, the simpler you make your application, the better it performs. However, you also want to be certain to include a field that uniquely identifies each record in the file. For instance, the programmer file record in this example includes a programmer number field to separate programmers who might have the same name.

The programmer number field in the programmer file record should be numeric. Numeric fields are preferable to nonnumeric fields for uniquely identifying records because the computer interprets numbers faster than nonnumeric data in the fields. The project record can use a nonnumeric project code to uniquely identify each project record, such as EA-100.

Linking Files with Keys

As you learned in Chapter 4, multiple files can be joined by a key—a common field shared by each of the linked files. Another important task in the design phase is to plan a way to join files, if necessary. For example, the programmer-project application uses the programmer's number to link the programmer to the project file. In Hands-on Project 5-12, you create two data files, the programmer and the project files, that both contain the programmer's number field for use as a key on which to manipulate and join data.

Before you begin to consider the process of creating files for the Programmer Activity Status Report project, review the record layouts for the programmer and project files illustrated in Figure 5-5.

Programmer file – record layout

Field name	Data type	Example
programmer_number	Numeric	101
lname	Alpha	Johnson
fname	Alpha	John
midinit	Alpha	K
salary	Numeric	39000

Field separator is a colon :

Sample record:

101:Johnson:John:K:39000

Project file – record layout

Field name	Data type	Example
project_code	Alpha	EA-100
project_status	Numeric	1 (*See Note)
project_name	Alpha	Reservation Plus
programmer_number	Numeric	110

Field separator is a colon :

Sample record:

EA-100:1:Reservation Plus:110

*Note: Project status codes 1=Unscheduled 2=Started 3=Completed 4=Canceled

Figure 5-5   Programmer and project file record layouts

A sampling of records for the programmer file is as follows:

```
101:Johnson:John:K:39000
102:King:Mary:K:39800
103:Brown:Gretchen:K:35000
104:Adams:Betty:C:42000
. . .
```

In this record design, the first field contains the programmer number, such as 101 in the first record. The programmer number is included as a key field to allow all kinds of data handling, such as using the *sort*, *comm*, and *join* commands—as you do in Hands-on Project 5-15, for example. The next three fields include the programmer's last name, first name, and middle initial. Dividing the full name into three fields opens the way for many data-handling techniques, including sorting by last name or using all three fields for identifying duplicate records. The final field contains the employee's salary, which can be useful for printing salary information reports related to employee evaluations and raises.

A sampling of the records for the project file created in Hands-on Project 5-12 is as follows:

```
EA-100:1:Reservation Plus:110
EA-100:1:Reservation Plus:103
EA-100:1:Reservation Plus:107
EA-100:1:Reservation Plus:109
. . .
```

The first field in the record is a code to identify a specific project, such as EA-100. An organization might use such a code to not only identify the project, but also to identify the persons, project team, department, division, or subsidiary who requests the project. In this example, the first two letters (EA) represent the department and the last three digits (100) represent the unique project number for that department. The second field contains the project status:

- 1=Unscheduled
- 2=Started
- 3=Completed
- 4=Cancelled

The third field contains the name of the project, such as "Reservation Plus." The fourth field is the programmer number to show which programmer is working on that project. One reason the programmer number is important to the records in the project file is that it can be used as a key field to link specific information in the project file with information in the programmer file.

Creating the Programmer and Project Files

Now that you have reviewed the basic elements of designing and linking records, you can begin the steps to implement your application design. Recall from Chapters 2 and 3 ("Exploring the UNIX/Linux File Systems and File Security" and "Mastering Editors") that UNIX/Linux file processing can use flat files. Working with these files is easy, because you can create and manipulate them with text editors, such as vi and Emacs. The flowchart in Figure 5-6 provides an overview and analysis of programmer project assignments as derived from the programmer and project files used in this example.

A first step in this process is to create the programmer and project files and fill them with records, which you do in Hands-on Project 5-12. The files use a variable-record format, with a colon between each field as the delimiter.

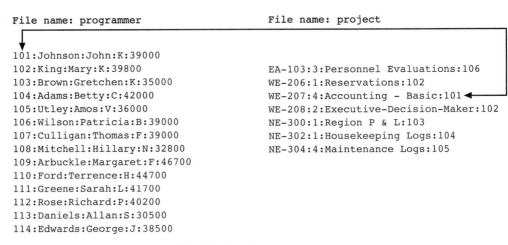

```
File name: programmer                    File name: project

101:Johnson:John:K:39000
102:King:Mary:K:39800                     EA-103:3:Personnel Evaluations:106
103:Brown:Gretchen:K:35000                WE-206:1:Reservations:102
104:Adams:Betty:C:42000                   WE-207:4:Accounting - Basic:101
105:Utley:Amos:V:36000                    WE-208:2:Executive-Decision-Maker:102
106:Wilson:Patricia:B:39000               NE-300:1:Region P & L:103
107:Culligan:Thomas:F:39000               NE-302:1:Housekeeping Logs:104
108:Mitchell:Hillary:N:32800              NE-304:4:Maintenance Logs:105
109:Arbuckle:Margaret:F:46700
110:Ford:Terrence:H:44700
111:Greene:Sarah:L:41700
112:Rose:Richard:P:40200
113:Daniels:Allan:S:30500
114:Edwards:George:J:38500
```

Flowchart Logic

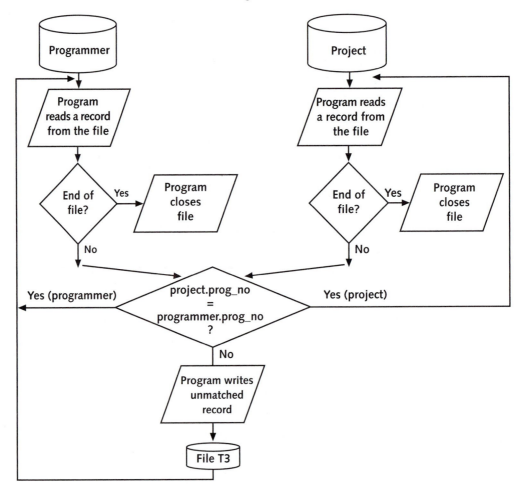

Figure 5-6 Overview and analysis of programmer assignments

As you read these sections, plan to complete each Hands-on Project as it is mentioned before reading further.

NOTE

Formatting Output

Chapter 4 introduced the *awk* command and Awk programming language, which simplify preparation of formatted output. You get another introductory lesson in using *awk* here, because the *printf* capability in *awk* can be very powerful for creating a polished report for an application—and specifically for the Programmer Activity Status Report you are developing in the Hands-on Projects. As you have learned, Awk is a full-featured programming language and could have a chapter unto itself. The limited presentation in this chapter gives you another glimpse of Awk by introducing the use of the *printf* function within the *awk* command, which formats output. The *printf* function has the following syntax:

Syntax **printf** (*format, $expr1, $expr2, $expr3*)

Dissection

- *format* is always required. It is an expression with a string value that contains literal text and specifications of how to format expressions in the argument list. Each specification begins with a percentage character (%), which identifies the code that follows as a modifier (- to left-justify; *width* to set size; *.prec* to set maximum string width or digits to the right of the decimal point; *s* for an array of characters (string); *d* for a decimal integer; *f* for a floating-point decimal number). Enclosed in double quotation marks (" "), *format* is often referred to as a mask that overlays the data fields going into it.

- *$expr1, $expr2, $expr3* represent data fields. These expressions typically take the form $1, $2, $3, and so on. In the programmer file, the expression $1 indicates the programmer number (the first field), $2 indicates the programmer's last name (the second field), and $3 indicates the programmer's first name (the third field).

You can use the *awk* command and *printf* function to print the following information from the programmer file: programmer number, programmer last name, and programmer first name, all left-justified. The command line to accomplish this is:

```
awk -F: '{printf "%d %-12.12s %-10.10s\n", $1, $2, $3}' programmer
```

Hands-on Project 5-13 enables you to use this command on the programmer file. Each % symbol in the format string corresponds with a $ field, as follows:

- *%d* indicates that field $1 (programmer number) is to appear in decimal digits.

- *%-12.12s* indicates that field $2 (programmer name) is to appear as a string. The hyphen (-) specifies the string is to be left-justified. The 12.12 indicates the string should appear in a field padded to 12 spaces, with a maximum size of 12 spaces.

- *%-10.10s* indicates that field $3 (programmer salary) is to appear as a string. The hyphen (-) specifies the string is to be left-justified. The 10.10 indicates the string should appear in a field padded to 10 spaces, with a maximum size of 10 spaces.

The spaces that appear in the format string are printed exactly where they appear in relation to the *awk* and *printf* parameters—a space is between each % parameter (that is, after %d), for example, but spaces after each field designator, such as after $1, are, in this one case, optional. The trailing \n tells *awk* to skip a line after displaying the three fields. See Figure 5-7 for an example of the output of the report from this *awk* command.

```
mpalmer@localhost:~
File  Edit  View  Terminal  Tabs  Help
[mpalmer@localhost ~]$ awk -F: '{printf "%d %-12.12s %-10.10s\n", $1, $2, $3}' p
rogrammer
101 Johnson      John
102 King         Mary
103 Brown        Gretchen
104 Adams        Betty
105 Utley        Amos
106 Wilson       Patricia
107 Culligan     Thomas
108 Mitchell     Hillary
109 Arbuckle     Margaret
110 Ford         Terrence
111 Greene       Sarah
112 Rose         Richard
113 Daniels      Allan
114 Edwards      George
[mpalmer@localhost ~]$
```

Figure 5-7   *awk* report using *printf* to display the three fields

The *awk* command provides a shortcut when compared to other UNIX/Linux file-processing commands, when you need to extract and format data fields for output. For example, although it takes a few lines of code, you can use the *cut*, *paste*, and *cat* commands to extract and display the programmers' last names and salaries. As an alternative, you can do the same thing using a one-line *awk* command. Hands-on Project 5-14 enables you to compare using both techniques. Also, try Hands-on Project 5-15 for more experience using the *cut*, *sort*, *uniq*, *comm*, and *join* commands.

Using a Shell Script to Implement the Application

The report-generating application you are developing in the Hands-on Projects consists of many separate commands that must run in a certain order. As you recall from Chapter 4, you can create a script file to simplify the application. You store commands in a script file, which in effect becomes a program. When you develop an application, you should usually test and debug each command before you place it in your script file. You can use the vi or Emacs editor to create script files. (Chapters 6 and 7, "Introduction to Shell Script Programming" and "Advanced Shell Programming," cover shell script programming in more detail.)

A shell script should contain not only the commands to execute, but also comments to identify and explain the shell script so that users or programmers other than the script's author can understand how it works. Comments also enable the original author to remember the logic of the script over time. Use the pound (#) character in script files to mark comments. This tells the shell that the words following # are a comment, not a UNIX/Linux command. Hands-on Project 5-16 enables you to build a shell script for a set of commands that create a temporary file showing information about the number of programs on which programmers are currently working. This script and temporary file will become a part of the process used to produce the Programmer Activity Status Report.

Running a Shell Script

You can run a shell script in virtually any shell that you have on your system. In this book, you use the Bourne Again Shell, or Bash, which is commonly used in Linux systems. In different shells, some incompatibilities often exist in terms of the exact use, syntax, and options associated with commands. One advantage to using the Bash shell is that it accepts more variations in command structures than the original Bourne shell; Bash is a freeware derivative of the Bourne and Korn shells.

When you create a shell script to run in Bash, you can immediately run the script by typing *sh* (to call the Bash shell interpreter) and then the name of the script, as follows:

```
sh testscript
```

Another advantage of using *sh* is that you can accompany it with several debugging options to help you troubleshoot problems with your script. (You learn more about these debugging options in Chapter 6.) For your beginning experiences with shell scripts in this chapter, you use *sh* simply to run your scripts.

NOTE
In UNIX systems, *sh* calls the shell command interpreter for the shell that is the default to the particular UNIX system. In Linux, including Fedora, Red Hat Enterprise Linux, and SUSE, you can use either *sh* or *bash* to run a shell script and call the Bash shell interpreter. In these systems, *sh* is actually a link to the Bash shell.

Another way to run a shell script, which you learn more about in Chapter 6 (and already got a glimpse of in Hands-on Project 4-15 in Chapter 4), is to make it executable by using the x permission and then typing ./ prior to the script name when you run the script itself. In addition, when you write a script, it is advisable to specify with what shell the script is intended to be used. You do this by including a command—such as *#!/bin/bash* for the Bash shell—on the first line of the script. Chapter 7 shows you how to implement this practice as your shell scripts become more advanced.

In Hands-on Project 5-17, you use the *sh* command to run the script created in Hands-on Project 5-16. In Hands-on Projects 5-18 and 5-19, you create and run scripts that are the next steps in creating the final Programmer Activity Status Report.

Putting It All Together to Produce the Report

An effective way to develop applications is to combine small scripts into a larger script file. In this way, it is easier to complete a large task by dividing it into a series of smaller ones—a basic programming rule. Also, through this approach, you can test each small script to ensure it works. In Hands-on Projects 5-16 through 5-19, you create, execute, and test individual small scripts in the process of preparing to create a Programmer Activity Status Report. After the scripts are tested, you can place the contents of each smaller script into a larger script file in the proper sequence to produce the final Programmer Activity Status Report. Hands-on Project 5-20 pulls together your smaller projects into one large task to generate the report.

CHAPTER SUMMARY

- The UNIX/Linux file-processing commands can be organized into two categories: (1) selection commands and (2) manipulation and transformation commands. Selection commands extract information. Manipulation and transformation commands alter and transform extracted information into useful and appealing formats.

- The *grep* command searches for a specific pattern in a file.

- The *uniq* command removes duplicate lines from a file. You must sort the file because *uniq* compares only consecutive lines.

- The *comm* command compares lines common to two different files, file1 and file2, and produces three-column output that reports variances between the files.

- The *diff* command attempts to determine the minimum set of changes needed to convert the contents of one file to match the contents of another file.

- When you want to know the byte, word, or line count in a file, use the *wc* command.

- The *sed* command is a stream editor designed to make global changes to large files. Minimum requirements to run *sed* are an input file and a command that tells *sed* what actions to apply to the file. Input to the *sed* action can be from the command line or through a script file.

- The *tr* command copies data read from the standard input to the standard output, substituting or deleting the characters specified by options and patterns.

- The *pr* command prints the standard output in pages.

❑ The design of a file–processing application reflects what the application needs to produce. The design also defines how to organize information into files, records, and fields, which are also called logical structures.

❑ Use a record layout to identify each field by name and data type (numeric or nonnumeric). Design file records to store only those fields relevant to each record's primary purpose.

❑ Shell scripts should contain commands to execute and comments to identify and explain the script. The pound (#) character is used in script files for comments.

❑ Write shell scripts in stages so that you can test each part before combining them into one script. Using small shell scripts and combining them in a final shell script file is an effective way to develop applications.

5

Command Summary: Review of Chapter 5 Commands

Command	Purpose	Options Covered in This Chapter
comm	Compares and outputs lines common to two files	-1 do not display lines that are only in file1 -2 do not display lines that are only in file2 -3 do not display lines appearing in both file1 and file2
diff	Compares two files and determines which lines differ	-b ignores blanks that repeat -B does not compare for blank lines -i ignores case -c shows lines surrounding the line that differs (for context) -y displays the differences side-by-side in columns
grep	Selects lines or rows	-i ignores case -l lists only file names -c only counts the number of lines matching the pattern instead of showing them -r searches through files under all subdirectories -n includes the line number for each line found -v displays only lines that don't contain the search pattern
pr	Formats a specified file	-d double-spaces the output -h customizes the header line -l *n* sets the number of lines per page

Command	Purpose	Options Covered in This Chapter
printf	Tells the Awk program what action to take for formatting and printing information	
sed	Specifies an editing command or a script file containing sed commands	a\ appends text after a line p displays lines d deletes specified text s substitutes specified text -e specifies multiple commands on one line -n indicates line numbers on which to work
sh	Executes a shell script	
tr	Translates characters	-d deletes input characters found in string1 from the output -s checks for sequences of string1 repeated consecutive times
uniq	Removes duplicate lines to create unique output	-u outputs only the lines of the source file that are not duplicated -d outputs one copy of each line that has a duplicate, and does not show unique lines -i ignores case -c starts each line by showing the number of each instance
wc	Counts the number of lines, bytes, or words in a file	-c counts the number of bytes or characters -l counts the number of lines -w counts the number of words

Key Terms

logical structure — The organization of information in files, records, and fields, each of which represents a logical entity, such as a payroll file, an employee's pay record, or an employee's Social Security number.

manipulation and transformation commands — A group of commands that alter and format extracted information so that it's useful and can be presented in a way that is appealing and easy to understand.

pipe operator (|) — The operator that redirects the output of one command to the input of another command.

record layout — A program and data file design step that identifies the fields, types of records, and data types to be used in data files.

selection commands — The file-processing commands that are used to extract information.

REVIEW QUESTIONS

1. You have just finished a 25-page paper that you have written using Emacs. The file containing the paper is called /assignments/data_sources. After your instructor has briefly looked at the paper, she recommends that you change all instances of the reference "data is" to "data are" before you submit it. Which of the following commands can you use to locate these references in the file for a quick assessment of how much you have to change?

   a. *find - i 'data is' /assignments/data_sources*

   b. *test /assignments/data_sources "data is"*

   c. *grep "data is" /assignments/data_sources*

   d. *scan -t data is /assignments/data_sources*

2. You are interested in determining the number of words in your /assignments/data_sources file mentioned in Question 1. Which of the following commands should you use?

   a. *wc -w /assignments/data_sources*

   b. *wc -m /assignments/data_sources*

   c. *counter /assignments/data_sources*

   d. *counter -c /assignments/data_sources*

3. Which of the following are examples of manipulation and transformation commands? (Choose all that apply.)

   a. *sed*

   b. *pr*

   c. *join*

   d. *paste*

4. Which of the following is true of the pipe operator? (Choose all that apply.)

   a. Only one pipe operator can be used on a single command line.

   b. It is used to perform division on the results of a numerical command operator.

   c. It is used instead of the colon (:) for entering multiple commands

   d. It redirects the output of one command to the input of another command.

5. Because the data was formatted the same in two inventory files, you decided to combine their contents into one file. Now you want to determine if there are duplicate entries on consecutive lines in the new file. Which of the following commands enables you to find the duplicate entries?

   a. *dup*

   b. *pr*

   c. *uniq*

   d. *cat*

6. Your friend is using the command *comm entryfile*, but is getting an error message. What is the problem? (Choose all that apply.)

   a. entryfile contains only numbers, but the *comm* command must be used on a file with text.

   b. It is necessary to use either the *-m* or *-t* option with the *comm* command.

   c. entryfile is too long, because the *comm* command can only be used on a file under 100 KB in size.

   d. It is necessary to specify two files when you use the *comm* command.

7. Your boss is trying to import the customers file into her spreadsheet program, but the data goes into the spreadsheet incorrectly. This is because the fields are separated by dashes (-) and the spreadsheet program requires the fields to be separated by colons (:). Which of the following commands can you use to convert the customers file?

   a. *replace - : customers*

   b. *tr "-" ":" < customers*

   c. *sed %- %: > customers*

   d. *cat -r -/: customers*

8. How can you link multiple files to manipulate the data in those files?

   a. with a linker

   b. with a project field

   c. with a common or key field

   d. with an operator entry

9. While in the Bash shell, you have written a simple script file and now want to execute the script. Which of the following commands enables you to run the script?

   a. *sh*

   b. *go*

   c. *ex*

   d. *!!*

10. You are using the *grep* command, but it is only searching through files in your immediate home directory. What option enables you to search through subdirectories below your home directory?

   a. *-s*

   b. *--sub*

   c. *-c*

   d. *-r*

11. Your software has a bug in that it enables you to create a vendors file in which there are duplicate entries of vendors. Which of the following methods enables you to remove the duplicate vendors in this text file?

    a. Sort the file and then use the *comm* command to remove the duplicates, inputting the result into the same file.

    b. Sort the file in reverse order and then use the *dump* command to remove the duplicates.

    c. Sort the file and then use the *uniq* command to remove the duplicates, inputting the result in a new file.

    d. Reverse sort the file, use the *join* command, and output the results back into the vendors file.

12. Each time you list the files in your home directory, the output scrolls by so fast you can't read it. Which of the following enables you to view the output one screen at a time?

    a. *cat -pause*

    b. *ls -l | more*

    c. *window ls -a*

    d. *dir < display*

13. You are creating a file to send over the Internet via a satellite connection that only allows you to send files under 250 KB. Which of the following commands enables you to determine the number of bytes in the file before you try to send it?

    a. *cat -s*

    b. *tr -b*

    c. *counter -k*

    d. *wc -c*

14. In the command *sed -f fixit notes > instructions*, what is "fixit"?

    a. a script file

    b. an operator

    c. a function

    d. a formatting interpreter

15. When you design a record layout, you should do which of the following? (Choose all that apply.)

    a. identify each field by data type

    b. plan to delimit fields using a dash

    c. identify each field by name

    d. store only fields relevant to the record's purpose

16. What *sed* command option enables you to append new text to a file?

    a. *p*

    b. *-n*

    c. *a*

    d. *|add*

17. Your boss has two salary scale files, salary and salary1, and wants to compare their contents side by side to see if there are any differences in the files. Which of the following commands should he use?

    a. *diff -S salary > salary1*

    b. *comm salary salary1*

    c. *uniq salary < salary1*

    d. *sed --comp salary salary1*

18. When you use the *pr* command how can you limit the output to only a screen full of text to view. (Choose all that apply.)

    a. Maximize your terminal window to hold 24 lines.

    b. Pipe the output into *more*.

    c. Use the *-l 23* option.

    d. Pipe the *less* command into the *more* command.

19. When you use the Awk *printf* capability, what does the dollar sign ($) represent?

    a. a field size limit

    b. a multiplier

    c. a command to put text in lowercase

    d. a data field

20. Your boss is trying to delete the word "difficult" as it appears in a text file containing his speech about motivation. The name of the file is motivate. When he decides to use the *tr* command to delete this word, it instead deletes characters throughout the text. Which of the following commands is he likely to have used?

    a. *tr -d "difficult" < motivate*

    b. *tr difficult motivate*

    c. *tr -o 'difficult' > motivate*

    d. *tr --eliminate difficult motivate*

21. When you enter the command *grep Linux /info/Linux_features | head*, what is the maximum number of lines that will be displayed?

    a. 24 lines

    b. 23 lines

    c. 15 lines

    d. 10 lines

22. List four examples of selection commands.

23. What is the general format for using the pipe operator?

24. Briefly explain what you can accomplish with the *sed* command.

25. You want to create a file of your friends' and relatives' names, addresses, telephone numbers, and other information. When you mention this to your sister-in-law, she recommends having separate fields for the first, middle, and last names. Briefly explain why this is a good idea.

5

HANDS-ON PROJECTS

 Complete these projects from the command line, such as from a terminal window, and log in using your own account and home directory.

NOTE

HANDS-ON PROJECTS

Project 5-1

The pipe operator directs the output of one command to the input of another. In UNIX/Linux, this operator is very useful for combining commands on one line and yielding output that is easier to read or use. In this project, you use the pipe operator to direct the output of the *ls* command to the input of the *more* command so you can more easily view the contents of a large directory.

To redirect the output of the *ls* command to the *more* command:

1. Type **ls –l /etc** and press **Enter**. Notice that the output of the command scrolls by quickly.

2. Type **ls –l /etc | more** and press **Enter**. (See Figure 5-8.)

3. Notice the output fills the screen and pauses with the prompt "More" displayed on the bottom line. Each time you press the spacebar, the output advances to the next screen. Press the **spacebar** to scroll a screen at a time or press **Enter** to advance one line at a time until the command has finished. You also can type **q** at any point to exit the display of the directory contents.

HANDS-ON PROJECTS

Project 5-2

The pipe operator enables you to combine multiple commands on a single line. In this project, you pipe the contents of a directory listing into the *sort* command and then pipe the result into the *more* command.

```
                            mpalmer@localhost:~                          _ □ X
 File  Edit  View  Terminal  Tabs  Help
total 3536
-rw-r--r--  1 root root    15346 Oct  1  2006 a2ps.cfg
-rw-r--r--  1 root root     2562 Oct  1  2006 a2ps-site.cfg
drwxr-xr-x  4 root root     4096 Mar  2  2007 acpi
-rw-r--r--  1 root root       47 Dec 20 17:20 adjtime
-rw-r--r--  1 root root     1512 Apr 25  2005 aliases
-rw-r-----  1 root smmsp   12288 Dec 21 13:34 aliases.db
drwxr-xr-x  4 root root     4096 Mar  2  2007 alsa
drwxr-xr-x  2 root root     4096 Dec  1 16:57 alternatives
-rw-r--r--  1 root root      298 Sep 29  2006 anacrontab
-rw-r--r--  1 root root     6286 Dec 20 17:20 asound.state
-rw-------  1 root root        1 Aug 23  2006 at.deny
-rw-------  1 root root     2479 Oct  7  2006 autofs_ldap_auth.conf
-rw-r--r--  1 root root      560 Oct  7  2006 auto.master
-rw-r--r--  1 root root      581 Oct  7  2006 auto.misc
-rwxr-xr-x  1 root root     1292 Oct  7  2006 auto.net
-rwxr-xr-x  1 root root      558 Oct  7  2006 auto.smb
drwxr-xr-x  4 root root     4096 Mar  2  2007 avahi
-rw-r--r--  1 root root     1361 Mar 21  2006 bashrc
drwxr-xr-x  2 root root     4096 Mar  2  2007 beagle
drwxr-xr-x  2 root root     4096 Dec 21 13:34 blkid
drwxr-xr-x  2 root root     4096 Mar  2  2007 bluetooth
drwxr-xr-x  2 root root     4096 Mar  2  2007 bonobo-activation
--More--
```

Figure 5-8   Piping *ls -l* into *more*

To connect several commands with the pipe operator:

1. Type **ls /etc|sort –r|more** and press **Enter**. This command redirects the directory listing of the /etc directory to the *sort -r* command. *sort -r* sorts the directory listing in reverse order. The *sort* command's output is redirected to the *more* command.

2. After you execute the command, you should see the directory listing of /etc in reverse order. (Refer back to Figure 5-1.)

3. Press the **spacebar** until the displayed output is finished.

Project 5-3

In this project, you use several features of the *grep* command and you learn to combine it with the *head* command for more manageable output. As you recall from Chapter 1, you can use the *head* command to retrieve the first 10 lines of a file. You can combine the *grep* and *head* commands to retrieve only the first 10 lines containing the word or phrase. For example, here you use *grep* with *head* to find the first 10 lines in /etc/termcap that contain the characters "IBM." (Knoppix does not have the /etc/termcap file used in this project. Consult with your instructor about using a suitable file with Knoppix.)

To display lines in a file containing a particular word or phrase:

1. To see all the lines in the /etc/termcap file that contain the characters "IBM," type **grep IBM /etc/termcap**, and press **Enter**. Many lines fit the criteria, and the output scrolls by quickly.

2. Redirect the output of the *grep* command to the input of the *more* command. Type **grep IBM /etc/termcap | more** and press **Enter**. (Remember, you can recall and then add on to commands used previously by pressing the up arrow.) (See Figure 5-9.)

```
mpalmer@localhost:~

File  Edit  View  Terminal  Tabs  Help

# The IBM PC alternate character set.  Plug this into any Intel console entry.
# Define IBM PC keypad keys for vi as per MS-Kermit while using ANSI.SYS.
# ":kh=\E[Y:".  Added IBM-PC forms characters and highlights, they match
ibmpcx|xenix|ibmx|IBM PC xenix console display:\
origpc3|origibmpc3|IBM PC 386BSD Console:\
oldpc3|oldibmpc3|old IBM PC BSD/386 Console:\
bsdos-pc|IBM PC BSD/OS Console:\
# with little  snowflake or star characters (IBM PC ROM character \017 = ^O)
# IBMPC Kermit 1.2.
pckermit|pckermit12|UCB IBMPC Kermit 1.2:\
        :is=K2 UCB IBMPC Kermit 1.2  8-30-84\n:tc=kermit:
# IBMPC Kermit 1.20
pckermit120|UCB IBMPC Kermit 1.20:\
        :is=\EO\Eq\EJ\EY7 K3 UCB IBMPC Kermit 1.20  12-19-84\n:\
# MS-DOS Kermit 2.27 for the IBMPC
msk227|mskermit227|MS-DOS Kermit 2.27 for the IBMPC:\
        :is=\EO\Eq\EG\Ew\EJ\EY7 K4 MS Kermit 2.27 for the IBMPC 3-17-85\n:\
# MS-DOS Kermit 2.27 UCB 227.14 for the IBM PC
msk22714|mskermit22714|UCB MS-DOS Kermit 2.27 UCB 227.14 IBM PC:\
        :is=\EO\Eq\EG\Ev\EJ\EY7 K6 MS Kermit 2.27 UCB 227.14 IBM PC 3-17-85\n:\
# low 7 bits of the IBM-PC display-memory attribute.  Bletch.
rbcomm|IBM PC with RBcomm and EMACS keybindings:\
rbcomm-nam|IBM PC with RBcomm without autowrap:\
--More--
```

Figure 5-9   Using the *grep* command with the *more* command

3. Press the **spacebar** until the command output is finished.

4. Type **clear** and press **Enter** to clear the screen.

5. Redirect the output of the *grep* command to the *head* command. Type **grep IBM /etc/termcap|head** and press **Enter**.

The command that you typed in Step 5 told *grep* to look for "IBM" in the /etc/termcap file, and then display the first 10 lines that are found. See Figure 5-10 for an example of the command's results.

The *grep* command's options and wildcard support allow powerful search operations. In the next set of steps, you learn more about these options, such as performing searches on the basis of capitalization and by ignoring capitalization. You also learn to search using wildcard and metacharacter options to extend the range of your searching.

To expand the *grep* command's search capabilities through its options and regular expression support:

1. To see each line in the /etc/termcap file that contains the word "Linux," type **grep Linux /etc/termcap**, and press **Enter**. (Be certain to capitalize the "L" in Linux.)

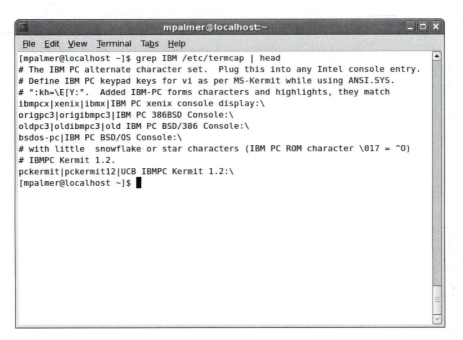

Figure 5-10 Using *grep* with *head*

2. Some lines in the file contain the word "linux" (with a lowercase l). The search you performed in Step 1 only displayed the lines that contain "Linux." The *-i* option tells grep to ignore the case of the search characters. Type **grep –i linux /etc/termcap** and press **Enter**. You see the lines that contain either "Linux" or "linux."

3. Type **clear** and press **Enter** for better viewing of the next step.

4. The *grep* command supports regular expression characters in the search string. To see all the lines of the /etc/termcap file that start with "lin" followed by any set of characters, type **grep –i "^lin" /etc/termcap**, and press **Enter**. (See Figure 5-11.)

NOTE

The ^ character is a special *grep* expression called a metacharacter. Its purpose is to search for words that begin with the string that immediately follows it. In Step 4, the ^ character is searching for words that begin with the string "lin".

5. The *grep* command can process multiple files one after another. Type **grep linux /etc/*** and press **Enter**. You see the lines that contain "linux" from all the files in the /etc directory.

6. Type **clear** and press **Enter**.

7. The *-l* (lowercase L) option instructs *grep* to display only the names of the files that contain the search string. Type **grep –l linux /etc/*** and press **Enter**. You see the

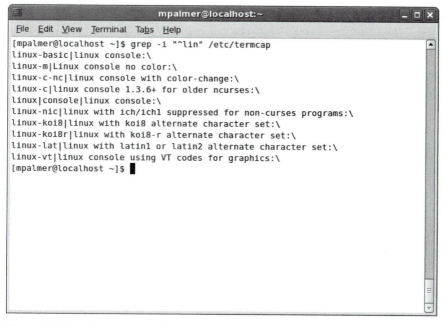

Figure 5-11 Using a metacharacter for a *grep* search

names of the files in the /etc directory that contain "linux." For what files is information displayed?

8. Type **clear** and press **Enter**.

The *grep* command also searches files for phrases that contain spaces, as long as the phrase is specified on the command line inside quotation marks. For example, *grep* can search for the phrase "IBM PC," as demonstrated in the next set of steps.

To search a file for a phrase:

1. Type **grep "IBM PC" /etc/termcap** and press **Enter**. You see all lines in the /etc/termcap file that contain the phrase IBM PC.

2. Type **clear** and press **Enter**.

In the previous examples, *grep* searches the file specified on the command line. *grep* can also take its input from another command, through the pipe operator.

To redirect the output of a command to the *grep* command:

1. Type **ls /etc | grep magic** and press **Enter**. You see a list of the files whose names contain the word "magic."

2. Type **clear** and press **Enter**.

Project 5-4

This project illustrates common uses of the *uniq* command. To perform the project, start by using the vi editor to create a new file, zoo1, in your working directory. This is a simple data file example, containing variable-length records that list animal names, food descriptions, pounds eaten daily, and food costs. Type the duplicate records in Step 1 as shown. After you create the file, use the *uniq* command to remove the duplicate records.

To remove duplicate lines with the *uniq* command:

1. Type **vi zoo1** and press **Enter** to open the vi editor. Press **i** and type the following text, pressing **Enter** at the end of each line except the final line:

```
Monkeys:Bananas:2000:850.00
Lions:Raw Meat:4000:1245.50
Lions:Raw Meat:4000:1245.50
Camels:Vegetables:2300:564.75
Elephants:Hay:120000:1105.75
Elephants:Hay:120000:1105.75
```

2. Press **Esc** to switch to command mode. Type **:wq** or **:x** and press **Enter**.

3. To use *uniq* to remove duplicate lines from the zoo1 file and use the output redirection operator to create the new file zoo2, type **uniq zoo1 > zoo2**, and press **Enter**.

4. Type **cat zoo2** and press **Enter**.

5. You see the contents of zoo2 as listed next. Notice that the *uniq* command removed the duplicate lines.

```
Monkeys:Bananas:2000:850.00
Lions:Raw Meat:4000:1245.50
Camels:Vegetables:2300:564.75
Elephants:Hay:120000:1105.75
```

Project 5-5

In this project, you explore the *comm* command. You start by creating the file my_list. Next, you duplicate the file, and then use the *comm* command to compare the two files.

To use the *comm* command to compare files:

1. To create the file my_list, at the command prompt, type **cat > my_list** and press **Enter**.

2. Type the following text, pressing **Enter** at the end of each line:

```
Football
Basketball
Skates
Soccer ball
```

3. Press **Ctrl+d**.

4. To copy my_list to a second file, your_list, type **cp my_list your_list**, and press **Enter**.

5. Now use the *comm* command to compare my_list to your_list. Type **comm my_list your_list** and press **Enter**.

6. You see the three-column output. (Note that the text showing column headings is inserted for your reference. This text does not appear on your screen.) Notice that the lines in the third column are those that both files contain. (How your columns line up will vary depending on the operating system.) The files are identical.

```
Column 1  Column 2  Column 3
                    Football
                    Basketball
                    Skates
                    Soccer ball
```

7. Now add a new line to my_list. Type **cat >> my_list** and press **Enter**.

8. Type **Golf ball** and press **Enter**.

9. Press **Ctrl+d**.

10. Use *comm* to compare my_list to your_list again. Type **comm my_list your_list** and press **Enter**.

11. You see the three-column output, with the unique new line in my_list in column 1. (Again note that your columns might line up differently.)

```
Column 1         Column 2         Column 3
                                  Football
                                  Basketball
                                  Skates
                                  Soccer ball
Golf ball
```

12. Add a new line to your_list. Type **cat >> your_list** and press **Enter**.

13. Type **Tennis ball** and press **Enter**.

14. Press **Ctrl+d**.

15. Type **comm my_list your_list** and then press **Enter** for another comparison. (See Figure 5-12.)

Project 5-6

In this project, you use the *diff* command to compare the contents of the zoo1 and zoo2 files you created previously in Hands-on Project 5-4.

To use *diff* to find differences between two files:

1. Review the contents of zoo1 and zoo2 by typing **more zoo1 zoo2** and pressing **Enter**. Press the **spacebar** to see the second file's contents. (See Figure 5-13.)

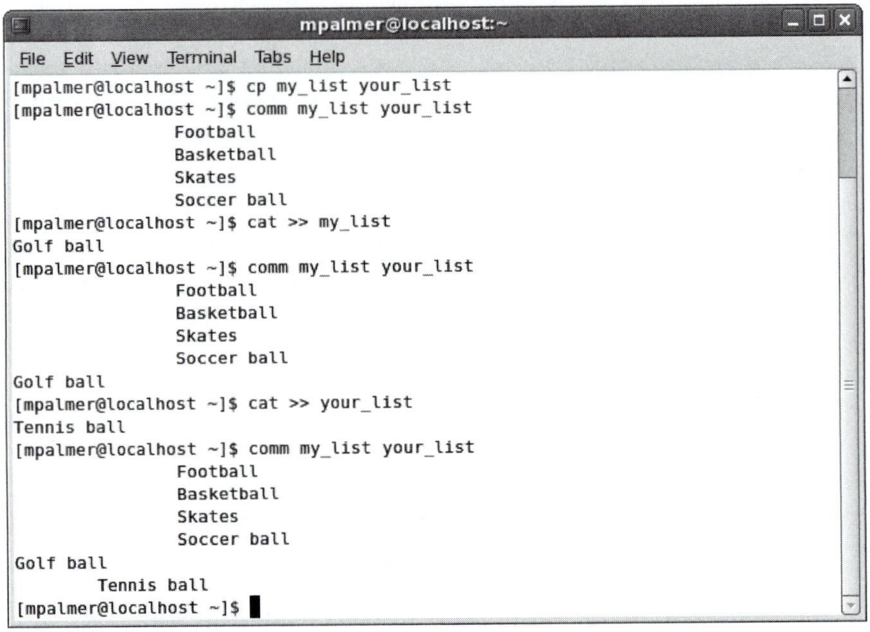

```
mpalmer@localhost:~
File  Edit  View  Terminal  Tabs  Help
[mpalmer@localhost ~]$ cp my_list your_list
[mpalmer@localhost ~]$ comm my_list your_list
                Football
                Basketball
                Skates
                Soccer ball
[mpalmer@localhost ~]$ cat >> my_list
Golf ball
[mpalmer@localhost ~]$ comm my_list your_list
                Football
                Basketball
                Skates
                Soccer ball
Golf ball
[mpalmer@localhost ~]$ cat >> your_list
Tennis ball
[mpalmer@localhost ~]$ comm my_list your_list
                Football
                Basketball
                Skates
                Soccer ball
Golf ball
        Tennis ball
[mpalmer@localhost ~]$ 
```

Figure 5-12   Comparing files using *comm*

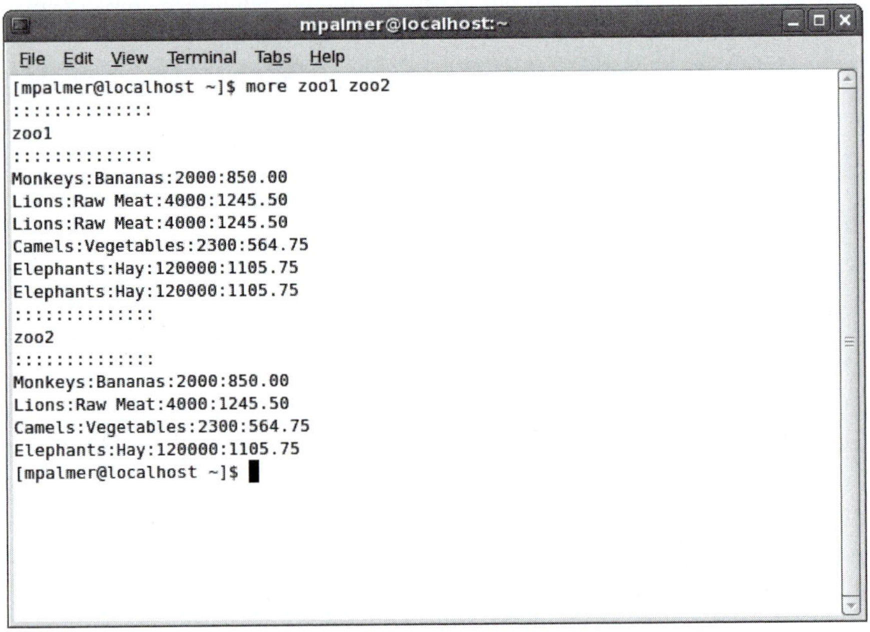

```
mpalmer@localhost:~
File  Edit  View  Terminal  Tabs  Help
[mpalmer@localhost ~]$ more zoo1 zoo2
::::::::::::::
zoo1
::::::::::::::
Monkeys:Bananas:2000:850.00
Lions:Raw Meat:4000:1245.50
Lions:Raw Meat:4000:1245.50
Camels:Vegetables:2300:564.75
Elephants:Hay:120000:1105.75
Elephants:Hay:120000:1105.75
::::::::::::::
zoo2
::::::::::::::
Monkeys:Bananas:2000:850.00
Lions:Raw Meat:4000:1245.50
Camels:Vegetables:2300:564.75
Elephants:Hay:120000:1105.75
[mpalmer@localhost ~]$ 
```

Figure 5-13   Viewing the contents of the zoo1 and zoo2 files

2. Type **diff zoo1 zoo2** and press **Enter**.

3. You see this information:

```
3d2
< Lions:Raw Meat:4000:1245.50
6d4
< Elephants:Hay:120000:1105.75
```

This means that you need to delete the third and sixth lines from zoo1 so the file matches zoo2. (Note that in some versions of UNIX/Linux, you might see *5d4* instead of *6d4* because another way to match the files is to delete the fifth line in zoo1, which is the same as the sixth line.)

4. To reverse the comparison order, type **diff zoo2 zoo1**, and press **Enter**. You see this information:

```
2a3
> Lions:Raw Meat:4000:1245.50
4a6
> Elephants:Hay:120000:1105.75
```

This means that you need to add the two lines shown in zoo2, so the file matches zoo1. You would add the third line of zoo1 to go after the second line in zoo2. And, you would add the sixth line of zoo1 to go after the fourth line of zoo2.

HANDS-ON PROJECTS

Project 5-7

In this project, you use the *wc* command to count the number of lines in a new file called counters.

To create a file and count its lines:

1. Type **cat > counters** and press **Enter**.

2. Type this text, pressing **Enter** at the end of each line:

   Linux is a full featured UNIX clone.
   Linux is available in free and commercial versions.

3. Type **Ctrl+d**.

4. To find the number of lines in counters, type **wc -l counters**, and press **Enter**. UNIX/Linux report that the file contains two lines.

5. To find the number of bytes in counters, type **wc -c counters**, and press **Enter**. UNIX/Linux report that the file contains 89 bytes.

6. To find the number of words in counters, type **wc -w counters**, and press **Enter**. UNIX/Linux report that the file contains 15 words.

7. To count words, characters, and lines in counters, type **wc -lwc counters**, and press **Enter**. UNIX/Linux report the counts for lines (2), words (15), and bytes (89). (Note that if you enter *wc counters*, you get the same output as entering *wc -lwc counters*.) See Figure 5-14 to view the output of the *wc* command.

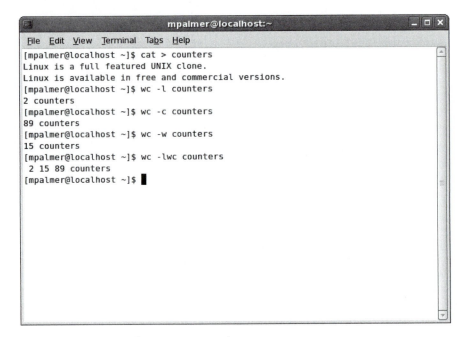

Figure 5-14   Using the *wc* command

Project 5-8

sed is a stream editor that enables you to work on specific lines in a file and modify their contents. In this project, you use *sed* to display specific lines and edit a file that you create. The focus of this project is on using *sed* commands from the command line.

To use *sed* to manipulate a file:

1. Create the new file, unix_stuff, in your working directory by using the vi or Emacs editor. The unix_stuff file should contain the following lines (press **Enter** after typing each line—excluding after the final line—to have five lines of text):

   ```
   Although UNIX supports other database systems,
   UNIX has never abandoned the idea of working with
   flat files. Flat files are those that are based on pure
   text with standard ASCII codes. Flat files
   can be read by any operating system.
   ```

2. To display only lines 3 and 4, type **sed –n 3,4p unix_stuff**, and press **Enter**. (The *-n* option prevents *sed* from displaying any lines except those specified with the *p* command.)

   This means "find lines numbered (*-n*) 3 and 4 in the file unix_stuff and display them (*p*)."

You see lines 3 and 4:

```
flat files. Flat files are those that are based on pure
text with standard ASCII codes. Flat files
```

3. In *sed*, you can place two commands on one line. If you want to delete lines 3 and 4 and then display the file, you must use the *-e* option to specify multiple commands on the same line. To delete lines 3 and 4 from unix_stuff and display the results, type **sed –n –e 3,4d –e p unix_stuff**, and press **Enter**.

You see this text:

```
Although UNIX supports other database systems,
UNIX has never abandoned the idea of working with
can be read by any operating system.
```

Lines 3 and 4 are not actually deleted from the file, but simply filtered out so that they are not displayed on the output to the screen.

4. To display only lines containing the word "Flat," type **sed –n /Flat/p unix_stuff**, and press **Enter**.

You see this text:

```
flat files. Flat files are those that are based on pure
text with standard ASCII codes. Flat files
```

5. To replace all instances of the word "Flat" with "Text," type **sed –n s/Flat/Text/p unix_stuff**, and press **Enter**. (Be certain that you capitalize the words "Flat" and "Text".) The *s* command substitutes one string of characters for another.

You see the following text. (See Figure 5-15.)

```
flat files. Text files are those that are based on pure
text with standard ASCII codes. Text files
```

HANDS-ON PROJECTS

Project 5-9

You continue working with the *sed* command in this project, so that you learn how to append lines from one file to another. First, you use the vi editor to create a new script file, more_stuff. You use the append command, *a*, in the more_stuff file with the lines to be appended by *sed* to the file unix_stuff. (You could accomplish the same outcome by using *cat more_stuff >> unix_stuff*, but the purpose here is to show you the versatility of *sed*.) You must terminate each line, except for the final line of the file being added, with a backslash character. In this project, the *$* preceding the *a\\* symbol tells *sed* to append more_stuff to unix_stuff after the final line in unix_stuff; without *$*, *sed* repeatedly adds all the lines in more_stuff after each line in unix_stuff.

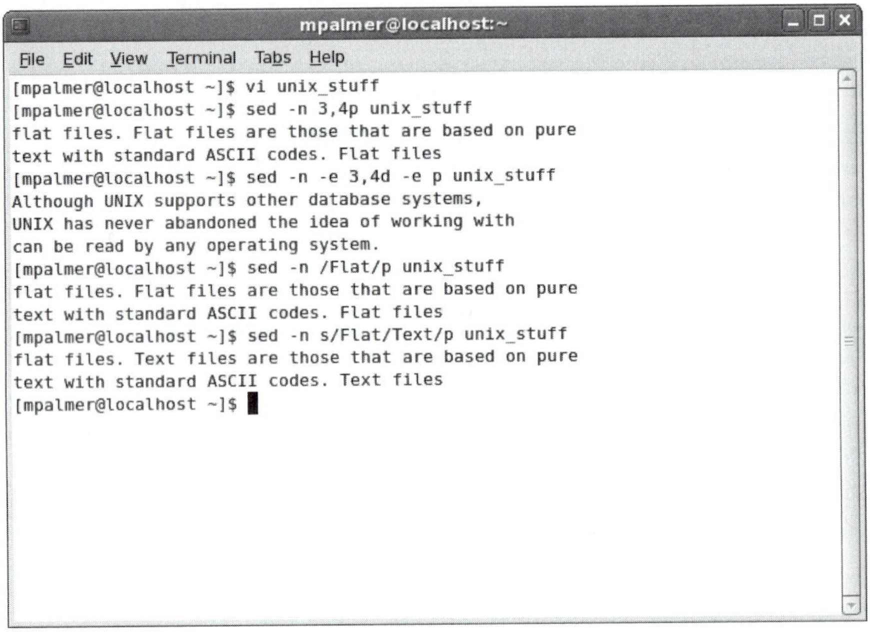

Figure 5-15 Using *sed* to display and edit the output of the unix_stuff file

To create a script file to append lines to another file using *sed*:

1. Use the vi editor to create the script file more_stuff to have the following lines (press **i** to go into the insert mode and press **Enter** at the end of each line, except at the end of the final line):

   ```
   $a\
   Informix and Oracle, two major relational database\
   companies have installed their RDBMS packages on UNIX\
   systems for many years.
   ```

2. After you enter the information, press **Esc** to switch to command mode. Type **:wq** or **:x** and press **Enter** to save the file and exit vi.

3. To use the *sed* command to run the script file, type **sed –f more_stuff unix_stuff**, and press **Enter**.

   You see the following text. (See Figure 5-16.)

   ```
   Although UNIX supports other database systems,
   UNIX has never abandoned the idea of working with
   flat files. Flat files are those that are based on pure
   text with standard ASCII codes. Flat files
   can be read by any operating system.
   Informix and Oracle, two major relational database
   companies have installed their RDBMS packages on UNIX
   systems for many years.
   ```

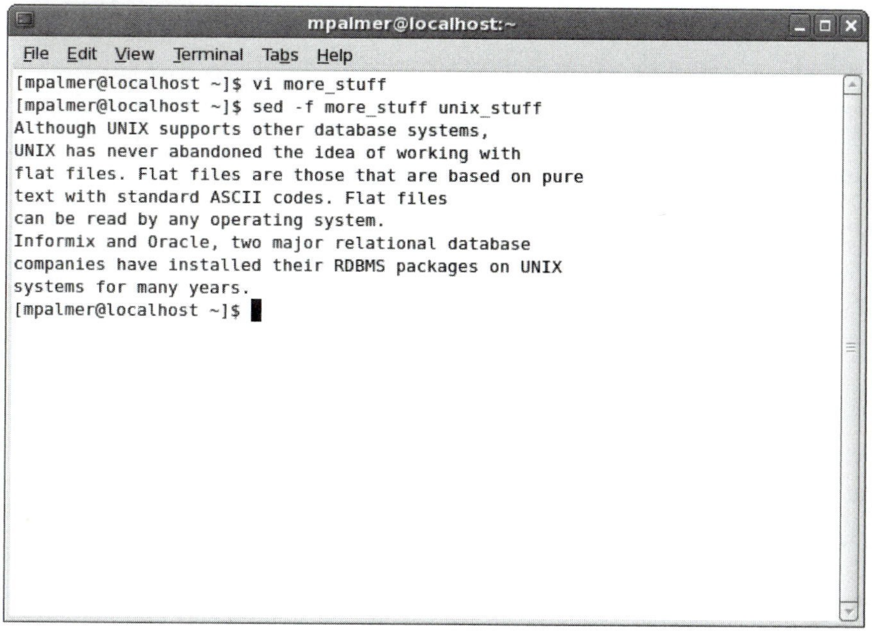

Figure 5-16   Creating and running a script to use *sed*

4. Use vi to create the file stuff_replace. Press **i** to go into the insert mode and insert the following *sed* commands into the file:

```
s/UNIX/Linux/
s/abandoned/given up/
s/standard/regular/
```

The lines in the file instruct *sed* to replace all occurrences of "UNIX" with "Linux," "abandoned" with "given up," and "standard" with "regular."

After you enter the lines, press **Esc** to switch to command mode. Type **:wq** or **:x** and press **Enter**.

5. Type **clear** and press **Enter** to clear your work area on the screen.

6. Execute *sed*, with the script file you created in Step 4, on the unix_stuff file. Redirect *sed*'s output to the file unix_stuff 2. Type **sed –f stuff_replace unix_stuff > unix_stuff 2** and press **Enter**.

7. Type **cat unix_stuff 2** and press **Enter**. You see the file with the changes specified by the stuff_replace script file, as shown in Figure 5-17.

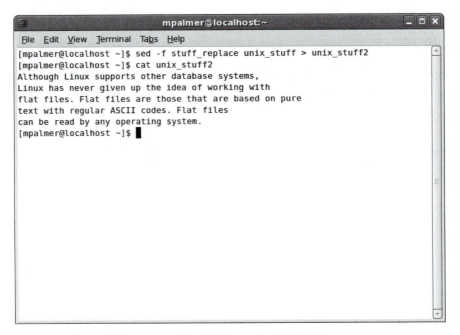

Figure 5-17   *sed* changes written to the unix_stuff2 file

Project 5-10

The *tr* command is used to translate characters in files, such as converting from lowercase to uppercase letters, deleting specified characters, and replacing characters. In this project, you do all of these in the following steps. You use the counters file you created in Hands-on Project 5-7.

To translate lowercase characters to uppercase characters in the file counters:

1. Type **tr [a-z] [A-Z] < counters** and press **Enter**.

   You see these lines:

   ```
   LINUX IS A FULL FEATURED UNIX CLONE.
   LINUX IS AVAILABLE IN FREE AND COMMERCIAL VERSIONS.
   ```

You can also use the *-d* option with the *tr* command to delete input characters found in *string1* from the output. This is helpful when you need to remove an erroneous character from the file.

To delete specified characters from the counters file:

1. To delete the characters "full" from the output, type **tr -d "full" < counters**, and press **Enter**.

   You see this text:

   ```
   Linx is a eatred UNIX cone.
   Linx is avaiabe in ree and commercia versions.
   ```

Notice that the command deleted all characters in "full"—every f, u, and l from the output—rather than occurrences of the word "full." (See Figure 5-18.)

```
mpalmer@localhost:~
File  Edit  View  Terminal  Tabs  Help
[mpalmer@localhost ~]$ tr [a-z] [A-Z] < counters
LINUX IS A FULL FEATURED UNIX CLONE.
LINUX IS AVAILABLE IN FREE AND COMMERCIAL VERSIONS.
[mpalmer@localhost ~]$ tr -d "full" < counters
Linx is a  eatred UNIX cone.
Linx is avaiabe in ree and commercia versions.
[mpalmer@localhost ~]$
```

Figure 5-18 Using *tr* to translate characters in a file

The *-s* option of the *tr* command checks for sequences of a character or string of characters repeated several consecutive times. When this happens, *tr* replaces the sequence of repeated characters with the character or string you specify. For example, use the *-s* option when you need to change a field delimiter in a flat file from one character to another. For instance, in the file zoo2, use *tr* to replace the field delimiter ":" with a space character, " ". First, use *cat* to display the file.

To replace characters in the file counters:

1. Type **cat zoo2** and press **Enter**.

   You see this text:

   ```
   Monkeys:Bananas:2000:850.00
   Lions:Raw Meat:4000:1245.50
   Camels:Vegetables:2300:564.75
   Elephants:Hay:120000:1105.75
   ```

2. Type **tr –s ":" " "** **< zoo2** and press **Enter**.

You see this text:

```
Monkeys Bananas 2000 850.00
Lions Raw Meat 4000 1245.50
Camels Vegetables 2300 564.75
Elephants Hay 120000 1105.75
```

Project 5-11

In this project, you employ the *pr* command to format the unix_stuff file that you created in Hands-on Project 5-8. You use the pipe operator (|) to send the output to the *more* command so that the output screen does not flash by too fast to read.

To format a file:

1. Type **pr –h "UNIX Files & Databases" < unix_stuff | more** and press **Enter**. Type **q** to exit after you have viewed the text display.

   Now, you can type the same command, but add the *-l 23* option to limit the number of lines per page to 23. Because the standard number of lines on most monitors is 24, you do not need to send the output to the *more* or *less* commands to hold the screen.

2. Type **pr –l 23 –h "UNIX Files & Databases" < unix_stuff** and press **Enter**. See Figure 5-19 to view how the screen should look.

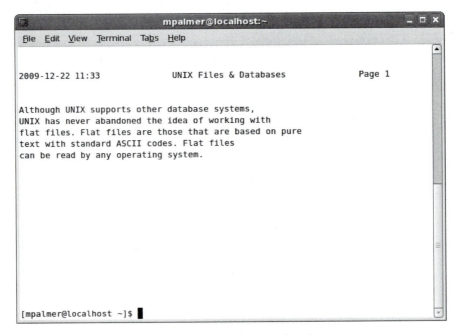

Figure 5-19 Results of the *pr* command using the *-l* option

HANDS-ON PROJECTS

Project 5-12

Beginning with this project, you now start a series of related projects to design and implement various programmer and project reports, building up to creating a polished Programmer Activity Status Report. In this project, you create two files to be used for reporting, the programmer and project files.

To create the programmer file:

1. Type **vi programmer** and press **Enter**.

2. Type **i** to switch to insert mode, and then type the following text, pressing **Enter** at the end of each line except for the final line:

```
101:Johnson:John:K:39000
102:King:Mary:K:39800
103:Brown:Gretchen:K:35000
104:Adams:Betty:C:42000
105:Utley:Amos:V:36000
106:Wilson:Patricia:B:39000
107:Culligan:Thomas:F:39000
108:Mitchell:Hillary:N:32800
109:Arbuckle:Margaret:F:46700
110:Ford:Terrence:H:44700
111:Greene:Sarah:L:41700
112:Rose:Richard:P:40200
113:Daniels:Allan:S:30500
114:Edwards:George:J:38500
```

3. Press **Esc** to switch to command mode.

4. Type **:wq** or **:x** and press **Enter** to write the file and exit vi.

To create the project file:

1. Type **vi project** and press **Enter**.

2. Type **i** to switch to insert mode, and type the following text, pressing **Enter** at the end of each line except for the final line:

```
EA-100:1:Reservation Plus:110
EA-100:1:Reservation Plus:103
EA-100:1:Reservation Plus:107
EA-100:1:Reservation Plus:109
EA-101:2:Accounting-Revenues Version 4:105
EA-101:2:Accounting-Revenues Version 4:112
EA-102:4:Purchasing System:110
EA-103:3:Personnel Evaluations:106
WE-206:1:Reservations:102
WE-207:4:Accounting - Basic:101
WE-208:2:Executive-Decision-Maker:102
NE-300:1:Region P & L:103
NE-302:1:Housekeeping Logs:104
NE-304:4:Maintenance Logs:105
```

5

3. Press **Esc** to switch to command mode.

4. Type **:wq** or **:x** and press **Enter** to write the file and exit from vi.

Project 5-13

In this project, you use the *awk* command to print a preliminary report of the contents of the programmer file you created in Hands-on Project 5-12.

To print the fields in the programmer file using *awk*:

1. Type **awk –F: '{printf "%d %-12.12s %-10.10s\n", $1, $2, $3}' programmer** and press **Enter** (use a single quotation mark around the curly brackets and not a back quote). See Figure 5-7 for an example of the output.

Spacing is very important for this command. Note that there is a single space after awk, -F:, '{printf, "%d, %-12.12s, %-10.10s\n", and $1, $2, $3}'. Also, be certain you type curly brackets and not straight ones.

Project 5-14

For this project, you compare creating a report of programmer information using three command lines and temporary files via the *cut*, *paste*, and *more* commands, to using one *awk* command line and no temporary files. In the first set of steps, you start by using the *cut* command to extract the last name (field 2) from the programmer file, and store the output in the temp1 file. Next, you use the *cut* command to extract the salary (field 5) from the programmer file, and store the output in temp2. Then, you use the *paste* command to combine temp1 and temp2, and create the file progsal. Finally, you use the *more* command to display the output. In the second set of steps, you can accomplish the same task with one *awk* command.

To extract and display information using *cut*, *paste*, and *more*:

1. Type **cut –f2 –d: programmer > temp1** and press **Enter**.

2. Type **cut –f5 –d: programmer > temp2** and press **Enter**.

3. Type **paste temp1 temp2 > progsal** and press **Enter**.

4. To use the *more* command to display the output, type **more progsal**, and press **Enter**.

You see output similar to the following excerpt:

```
Johnson              39000
King                 39800
Brown                35000
Adams                42000
Utley                36000
Wilson               39000
Culligan             39000
. . .
```

NOTE Note that for the longer names in the file, such as Culligan, the second column might line up differently than for the shorter names because of the tab spacing.

To accomplish the same task with one *awk* command:

1. Type **awk –F: '{printf "%–10.10s %7.0f \n", $2, $5}' programmer**, and press **Enter**.

You see output similar to the following excerpt:

```
Johnson              39000
King                 39800
Brown                35000
Adams                42000
Utley                36000
. . .
```

NOTE There are two important differences between using the *cut* and *paste* commands and using the *awk* command. First, you don't have to create three extra files when using *awk*. Second, the column display has a more even appearance when using *awk*.

HANDS-ON PROJECTS

Project 5-15

When you manipulate the information in the programmer and project fields, you can determine which programmers are not assigned a project, which is the focus of this assignment. Here, you exercise your knowledge of the *cut*, *sort*, *uniq*, *comm*, and *join* commands in one project. You select the programmer_number fields stored in the project file. These fields identify programmers who are currently assigned to projects. Refer to Figure 5-5 as you work through this project.

Start by cutting the programmer_number fields from the project file (field 4), and piping (|) the output to the *sort* command to place any duplicate numbers together. Pipe the sorted output to the *uniq* command to remove any duplicate programmer_numbers. Finally, redirect the output to a temporary file, t1. (The t1 file is a list of programmer numbers that identifies programmers who are assigned to projects.)

To select fields from the project file:

1. Type **cut –d: –f4 project | sort | uniq > t1** and press **Enter**.

2. To display the contents of t1, type **cat t1**, and press **Enter**.

   You see the list of programmer numbers:

   ```
   101
   102
   103
   104
   105
   106
   107
   109
   110
   112
   ```

   The next step is to cut the programmer_number fields (field 1) from the programmer file, and pipe the output as you did in Step 1. Call the new temporary file t2, which is a list of programmer numbers that identifies all of the programmers.

3. Type **cut –d: –f1 programmer | sort | uniq > t2** and press **Enter**.

4. To display the contents of t2, type **cat t2**, and press **Enter**.

   You see this list of programmer numbers:

   ```
   101
   102
   103
   104
   105
   106
   107
   108
   109
   110
   111
   112
   113
   114
   ```

   Now that t1 and t2 are sorted in the same order, you can match them. Use the *comm* command to select the lines from t1 that do not match lines in t2, and redirect the output to another file, t3, which lists programmer numbers of all programmers who are not assigned to projects.

5. Type **comm –13 t1 t2 > t3** and press **Enter**.

6. To display the programmer numbers for programmers who are not working on projects, type **cat t3**, and press **Enter**.

You see this list of programmer numbers:

```
108
111
113
114
```

To display the names of unassigned programmers, you can now sort the programmer file in programmer_number order, and write the output to t4.

7. Type **sort -t: -k 1 -o t4 programmer** and press **Enter**.

Now use the *join* command to match programmer_numbers in t4 and t3, and redirect the output to t5, which contains the names of all programmers who are not assigned to a project.

8. Type **join -t: -1 1 -2 1 -o 1.2 -o 1.3 -o 1.4 t4 t3 > t5** and press **Enter**.

9. To display the contents of t5, type **cat t5**, and press **Enter**.

You see the following list of programmer names:

```
Mitchell:Hillary:N
Greene:Sarah:L
Daniels:Allan:S
Edwards:George:J
```

Now, you can transform the output using the *sed* editor to eliminate the colon field separators in t5.

10. Type **sed -n 's/:/ /gp' < t5** and press **Enter**.

You see this list of programmer names:

```
Mitchell Hillary N
Greene Sarah L
Daniels Allan S
Edwards George J
```

Project 5-16

This project shows you how to add comments to your shell programs and creates a temporary file of programmer projects that will be used in subsequent projects on the way to building the Programmer Activity Status Report. You start by using the vi editor to create the new script file, which is called pact. Notice that you begin by inserting comments to identify and explain the script.

To create a script and add comments:

1. Type **vi pact** and press **Enter**.

2. Type **a** (you can type *a* as well as *i*) to switch to insert mode, and then type the following text, pressing **Enter** at the end of each line. (See Figure 5-20.)

NOTE

In Step 2, the line that starts with "cut -d: -f4..." and ends with "...> pnum" is broken into two lines to fit on this text page. When you enter the same line in the vi editor, place this all on one line as shown in Figure 5-20, or else your script will not work properly.

```
# ==========================================================
# Script Name:   pact
# By:            Your initials
# Date:          November 2009
# Purpose:       Create temporary file, pnum, to hold the
#                count of the number of projects each
#                programmer is working on. The pnum file
#                consists of:
#                prog_num and count fields
# ==========================================================
cut -d: -f4 project | sort | uniq -c | awk '{printf "%s:
  %s\n",$2,$1}' > pnum
# cut prog_num, pipe output to sort to remove duplicates
# and get count for prog/projects.
# output file with prog_number followed by count
```

3. Press **Esc** to switch to command mode.

4. Type **:x** and press **Enter** to write the file and exit from vi.

```
mpalmer@localhost:~
File  Edit  View  Terminal  Tabs  Help
# ================================================================
# Script Name:      pact
# By:               MP
# Date:             November 2009
# Purpose:          Create temporary file, pnum, to hold the
#                   count of the number of projects each
#                   programmer is working on. The pnum file
#                   consists of:
#                   prog_num and count fields
#================================================================
cut -d: -f4 project | sort | uniq -c | awk '{printf "%s: %s\n",$2,$1}' > pnum
# cut prog_num, pipe output to sort to remove duplicates
# and get count for prog/projects.
# output file with prog_number followed by count
~
~
~
~
~
~
~
~
-- INSERT --                                           14,49          All
```

Figure 5-20 Creating the pact script with comments

Project 5-17

In this project, you use the *sh* (shell) command to run the pact script from Hands-on Project 5-16. After you run the script, you use the *less* command to display the contents of the pnum file.

To run the pact script that you created earlier:

1. Type **sh pact** and press **Enter**.

2. Type **less pnum** and press **Enter** to view the contents of the pnum file that is created by the pact script.

3. You see these programmer numbers and project count fields:

```
101: 1
102: 2
103: 2
104: 1
105: 2
106: 1
107: 1
109: 1
110: 2
112: 1
```

4. Press **q** to exit the text display and return to the command line.

Project 5-18

After completing Hands-on Project 5-17, you now have a file that contains programmer numbers and the number of projects on which each programmer is working. In this project, you create a script file, pnumname, to extract the programmer names and numbers from the programmer file, and redirect the output to the file pnn.

To create another script file:

1. Type **vi pnumname** and press **Enter**.

2. Type **a** to switch to insert mode, and then type the following text, pressing **Enter** at the end of each line:

```
# =========================================================
# Script Name:   pnumname
# By:            Your initials
# Date:          November 2009
# Purpose:       Extract Programmer Numbers and Names
# =========================================================
cut -d: -f1-4 programmer | sort -t: -k 1 | uniq > pnn
# The above cuts out fields 1 through 4.
# The output is piped to a sort by programmer number.
# The sorted output is piped to uniq to remove
# duplicates.
# Uniq redirects the output to pnn.
```

3. Press **Esc** to switch to command mode.

4. Type **:wq** or **:x** and press **Enter** to write the file and exit from vi.

5. To run the shell program and use the *less* command to display the contents of pnn, type **sh pnumname**, and press **Enter**.

6. Type **less pnn** and press **Enter**.

7. You see the programmer names and numbers, with duplicates eliminated:

```
101:Johnson:John:K
102:King:Mary:K
103:Brown:Gretchen:K
104:Adams:Betty:C
105:Utley:Amos:V
106:Wilson:Patricia:B
107:Culligan:Thomas:F
108:Mitchell:Hillary:N
109:Arbuckle:Margaret:F
110:Ford:Terrence:H
111:Greene:Sarah:L
112:Rose:Richard:P
113:Daniels:Allan:S
114:Edwards:George:J
```

8. Press **q** to exit the text display.

HANDS-ON PROJECTS

Project 5-19

In this project, you create and run a script file, joinall, to join the files pnn and pnumname, and redirect the output to pactrep.

To create a script file that joins two files:

1. Type **vi joinall** and press **Enter**.

2. Type **a** to switch to insert mode, and then type the following text, pressing **Enter** at the end of each line:

```
# =======================================================
# Script Name:  joinall
# By:           Your initials
# Date:         November 2009
# Purpose:      Join pnum and pnn to create a report file
# =======================================================
# Join the files including the unassigned programmers.
# You do this by placing the programmer names (pnn) file,
# first, in the join sequence.
# =======================================================
join -t: -a1 -j1 1 -j2 1 pnn pnum > pactrep
```

3. Press **Esc** to switch to command mode.

4. Type **:wq** or **:x** and press **Enter** to write the file and exit from vi.

5. To run joinall and use *less* to display the contents of pactrep, type **sh joinall**, and press **Enter**.

6. Type **less pactrep** and press **Enter**.

7. You see the programmer names, including unassigned programmers' names:

```
101:Johnson:John:K: 1
102:King:Mary:K: 2
103:Brown:Gretchen:K: 2
104:Adams:Betty:C: 1
105:Utley:Amos:V: 2
106:Wilson:Patricia:B: 1
107:Culligan:Thomas:F: 1
108:Mitchell:Hillary:N
109:Arbuckle:Margaret:F: 1
110:Ford:Terrence:H: 2
111:Greene:Sarah:L
112:Rose:Richard:P: 1
113:Daniels:Allan:S
114:Edwards:George:J
```

8. Type **q** to exit, if necessary.

**HANDS-ON
PROJECTS**

Project 5-20

Your work in earlier projects now pays off as you create the Programmer Activity Status Report. In this project, you start by using the vi editor to create the shell script practivity. You use the *:r* command to retrieve the pact, pnumname, and joinall scripts created earlier, and place them in the practivity shell script. You then use the *dd* command in vi to remove the lines indicated in the comments.

To create the final shell script:

1. Type **vi practivity** and press **Enter**.

2. Type **a** to switch to insert mode, and then type the following text, pressing **Enter** at the end of each line:

```
# ============================================================
# Script Name:   practivity
# By:            Your initials
# Date:          November 2009
# Purpose:       Generate Programmer Activity Status Report
# ============================================================
```

3. Press **Esc** to switch to command mode.

4. To retrieve the three script files, type **:r pact**, and press **Enter**. Move the cursor to the end of the file, type **:r pnumname**, and press **Enter**. Move the cursor to the end of the file, type **:r joinall**, and press **Enter**.

5. Use the *dd* command to delete all of the imported comments, leaving only the comments entered in Step 2. For example, you could move the cursor to each line that begins with a #, and then type **dd**. You could also move the cursor to the first line beginning with a #, and then type **9dd** to delete the current line and the eight comment lines after it. Do the same for the remaining comment lines in the file.

   Besides the comments from Step 2, only these three lines should remain in the script:

   ```
   cut -d: -f4 project | sort | uniq -c | awk '{printf "%s:
   %s\n",$2, $1}' > pnum
   cut -d: -f1-4 programmer | sort -t: -k 1 | uniq > pnn
   join -t: -a1 -j1 1 -j2 1 pnn pnum > pactrep
   ```

6. Type the following in the script at the end of the file:

   ```
   # Print the report
   awk '
   BEGIN {
     { FS = ":"}
     { print "\tProgrammer Activity Status Report\n" }
     { "date" | getline d }
     { printf "\t   %s\n",d }
     { print "Prog#  \t*--Name--*                Projects\n" }
     { print "=========================================\n" }
   }
   { printf "%-s\t%-12.12s %-12.12s %s\t%d\n",
        $1, $2, $3, $4, $5 } ' pactrep
   # remove all the temporary files
    rm pnum pnn pactrep
   ```

NOTE For the column headings, create a space between Prog# and \t*--Name--* and create 16 or 17 spaces between *--Name--* and Projects. Also, type the characters very carefully, because a small mistake can prevent the script from working properly.

7. Press **Esc** to switch to command mode. Be certain the script looks similar to the one in Figure 5-21.

8. Type **:wq** or **:x** and press **Enter** to write the file and exit from vi.

9. Type **sh practivity** and press **Enter**. Figure 5-22 illustrates the report.

```
#===============================================================
# Script Name:        practivity
# By:                 MP
# Date:               November 2009
# Purpose: Generate Programmer Activity Status Report
#===============================================================
cut -d: -f4 project | sort | uniq -c | awk '{printf "%s: %s \n",$2,$1}' > pnum
cut -d: -f1-4 programmer | sort -t: -k 1 | uniq > pnn
join -t: -a1 -j1 1 -j2 1 pnn pnum > pactrep
# Print the report
awk '
BEGIN {
  { FS = ":" }
  { print "\tProgrammer Activity Status Report\n" }
  { "date" | getline d }
  { printf "\t   %s\n",d }
  { print "Prog# \t*--Name--*                   Projects\n" }
  { print "===============================================================\n"}
  }
  { printf "%-s\t%-12.12s %-12.12s %s\t%d\n",
           $1, $2, $3, $4, $5 } ' pactrep
# remove all the temporay files
 rm pnum pnn pactrep
                                                23,20        All
```

Figure 5-21   Entering the practivity script in vi

```
[mpalmer@localhost ~]$ vi practivity
[mpalmer@localhost ~]$ sh practivity
        Programmer Activity Status Report

          Thu Dec 24 09:19:43 MST 2009
Prog#    *--Name--*                   Projects


===============================================================

101     Johnson      John        K    1
102     King         Mary        K    2
103     Brown        Gretchen    K    2
104     Adams        Betty       C    1
105     Utley        Amos        V    2
106     Wilson       Patricia    B    1
107     Culligan     Thomas      F    1
108     Mitchell     Hillary     N    0
109     Arbuckle     Margaret    F    1
110     Ford         Terrence    H    2
111     Greene       Sarah       L    0
112     Rose         Richard     P    1
113     Daniels      Allan       S    0
114     Edwards      George      J    0
[mpalmer@localhost ~]$
```

Figure 5-22   Programmer Activity Status Report

Discovery Exercises

1. Use a command to find the instances in which the word "host" is used in the /etc directory.

2. What addition to the command you used in Exercise 1 can you use to slow the output to one screen at a time?

3. How can you determine the number of lines and words in the /etc/termcap file?

4. Use a command to remove the letters "o" and "a" from the my_list file you created in the Hands-on Projects—and write the output to the file changed_list.

5. Use a command to find out which lines in the my_list file contain the word "Foot."

6. Create a file called trees, containing the following individual lines:

   ```
   Oak tree
   Pine tree
   Spruce tree
   Cottonwood
   Maple tree
   ```

   Use the vi editor to create a file called more_trees, and copy in the contents of the trees file. Next, add the following trees at the end of the list.

   ```
   Redwood
   Willow tree
   ```

   Use a command to compare the trees and more_trees files and that outputs the differences in columns.

7. Use a command to compare the trees and more_trees files and show the differences in terms of individual lines that differ.

8. Determine the number of bytes in both the trees and more_trees files using a one-line command.

9. Use a command to replace the word "tree" with "plant" in the more_trees file and display the output to the screen.

10. Create a new file, CD_list, and enter these lines in the file:

    ```
    country:1000:210
    rock:1001:380
    classical:1002:52
    alternative:1003:122
    light rock:1004:151
    light rock:1004:151
    celtic:1005:44
    jazz:1006:62
    soundtracks:1007:32
    soundtracks:1007:32
    ```

Use the *sed* command and a script file to add these lines to the end of the CD_list file:

```
hard rock:1008:70
misc:1009:22
```

11. Use a command to find the duplicate lines (records) in the CD_list file.

12. Use the *uniq* command to remove the duplicate lines in the CD_list file, placing the corrected information in a file called CD_list_new.

13. In the CD_list_new file, replace the word "misc" with "other," save the changes in the file CD_list_replace, and then compare the contents of the CD_list file with the CD_list_replace file to ensure your changes are implemented.

14. Use the *grep* command to find all the lines that contain the word "celtic" in the CD_list_new file.

15. Use a command to make all letters uppercase in the CD_list_new file and save the output to a file called CD_list_uppercase.

16. Use the *sed* command on the CD_list_new file to replace the words "light rock" with "easy listening" and the word "alternative" with "experimental."

17. Create a file called software with these fields:

    □ Project Number, using the same numbers shown in the project file (which you created earlier in this chapter)

    □ Software Code, using any three-digit number

    □ Software Description, such as Excel

    Then write a small application joining records in the software file to matching records in the project file, and use the Awk program to print a report describing the software for each project you created earlier.

18. View the first 20 lines of /etc/termcap. Next use a command to change all characters in "version" to uppercase for only the first 20 lines in /etc/termcap.

19. Find a command to compare the differences between three files and that creates output for individual lines.

6

INTRODUCTION TO SHELL SCRIPT PROGRAMMING

> ## After reading this chapter and completing the exercises, you will be able to:
>
> ♦ Understand the program development cycle
> ♦ Compare UNIX/Linux shells for creating scripts
> ♦ Use shell variables, operators, and wildcard characters
> ♦ Use shell logic structures
> ♦ Employ shell scripting to create a menu
> ♦ Use commands to help debug shell scripts
> ♦ Explain ways to customize your personal environment
> ♦ Use the *trap* command
> ♦ Develop a menu-based application

S hell script programming is a greatly valued ability among UNIX and Linux users, programmers, and administrators because it gives flexibility in creating applications of all kinds. Some users create scripts to generate reports from data files. Others use scripts to create and maintain data files, such as for tracking projects, finances, or people. Still others perform system maintenance tasks through scripts, including monitoring who is logged in or backing up files.

The focus of this chapter is to develop your shell script programming skills and to show you how to build a menu-based application. You begin by getting an overview of the application you will build and of the program development cycle. Next, you learn about shell script programming tools that include using variables, operators, and logic structures. Finally, in the Hands-on Projects, you put to work what you've learned by building a menu-based application.

PREVIEWING THE APPLICATION

As you learned in Chapters 4 and 5 ("UNIX/Linux File Processing" and "Advanced File Processing"), commands such as *grep, cut, paste,* and *awk* are powerful commands for manipulating data. Although these commands are powerful, they can be difficult for nontechnical users, in part because they often must be combined in long sequences to achieve the results you want. Repeatedly executing these command sequences can be cumbersome, even for experienced technical users. You've discovered in earlier chapters that shell scripts can help eliminate these problems.

One advantage of shell scripts is that you can create them to present user-friendly screens—for example, screens that automatically issue commands such as *grep* and *awk* to extract, format, and display information. This gives nontechnical users access to powerful features of UNIX/Linux. For your own use, shell scripts save time by automating long command sequences that you must perform often.

The shell script application you develop in this chapter and enhance in Chapter 7, "Advanced Shell Programming," is a simulated employee information system that stores and displays employee data—such as you might commonly find in a human resources system in an organization. It presents a menu of operations from which the user can choose. Among other tasks, these operations automate the process of inputting, searching for, formatting, and displaying employee records. For preliminary testing, you create and use a data file that contains a sampling of employee records, similar to one that an experienced shell programmer might use for testing.

As you learn the tools needed to develop your application in this chapter, you gain experience with the following scripting and programming features of the UNIX/Linux shell:

- *Shell variables*—Your scripts often need to keep values in memory for later use. **Shell variables** temporarily store values in memory for use by a shell script. They use symbolic names that can access the values stored in memory. In this case, a **symbolic name** is a name consisting of letters, numbers, or characters and is used to reference the contents of a variable; often the name reflects a variable's purpose or contents.

- *Shell script operators*—Shell scripts support many **shell script operators**, including those for assigning the contents of a shell variable, for evaluating information, for performing mathematical operations, and for piping or redirection of input/output.

- *Logic or control structures*—Shell scripts support **logic structures** (also called **control structures**), including sequential logic (for performing a series of commands), decision logic (for branching from one point in a script to a different point), looping logic (for repeating a command several times), and case logic (for choosing an action from several possible alternatives).

In addition, you learn special commands for formatting screen output and positioning the cursor. Before you begin writing your application, it is important to understand more about the program development cycle and the basic elements of programming.

THE PROGRAM DEVELOPMENT CYCLE

The process of developing an application is known as the **program development cycle**. The steps involved in the cycle are the same whether you are writing shell scripts or high-level language programs.

The process begins by creating program specifications—the requirements the application must meet. The specifications determine what data the application takes as input, the processes that must be performed on the data, and the correct output.

After you determine the specifications, the design process begins. During this process, programmers create file formats, screen layouts, and algorithms. An **algorithm** is a sequence of procedures, programming code, or commands that result in a program or that can be used as part of a program. Programmers use a variety of tools to design complex applications. You learn about some of the tools in this chapter and about additional tools in Chapter 7.

After the design process is complete, programmers begin writing the actual code, which they must then test and debug. **Debugging** is the process of going through program code to locate errors and then fix them. When programmers find errors, they correct them and begin the testing process again. This procedure continues until the application performs satisfactorily.

Figure 6-1 illustrates the program development cycle.

Using High-Level Languages

Computer programs are instructions often written using a high-level language, such as COBOL, Visual Basic, C, or C++. A **high-level language** is a computer language that uses English-like expressions. For example, the following COBOL statement instructs the computer to add 1 to the variable COUNTER:

```
ADD 1 TO COUNTER.
```

Here is a similar statement, written in C++:

```
counter = counter + 1;
```

A program's high-level language statements are stored in a file called the **source file**. This is the file that the programmer creates with an editor such as vi or Emacs. The source file cannot execute, however, because the computer can only process instructions written in low-level machine language. As you recall from Chapter 3, "Mastering Editors," machine-language instructions are cryptic codes expressed in binary numbers. Therefore, the high-level source file must be converted into a low-level machine language file, as described next.

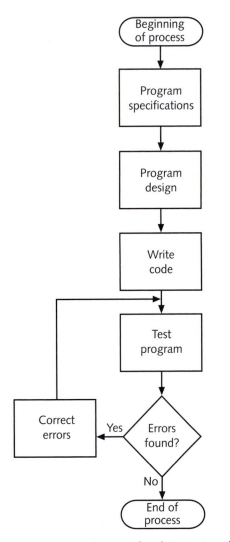

Figure 6-1 Program development cycle

The source file is converted into an executable machine-language file by a program called a compiler. The **compiler** reads the lines of code that the programmer wrote in the source file and converts them to the appropriate machine-language instructions. For example, the Linux C and C++ compilers are named *gcc* and *g++*. The following command illustrates how to compile the C++ source code file, datecalc.C, so that you can run it as the program datecalc:

```
g++ datecalc.C -o datecalc
```

In this sample command, the *-o* option followed by *datecalc* instructs the compiler to create an executable file, datecalc. The source file is datecalc.C. The command causes the compiler to translate the C++ program datecalc.C into an executable machine-language program, which is stored in the file datecalc. You learn more about C and C++ programming in Chapter 10, "Developing UNIX/Linux Applications in C and C++."

TIP

As you learn in Chapter 10, some important differences exist between C and C++ source code, and therefore it is necessary to use the correct compiler (*gcc* versus *g++*). Remember, when you invoke one of these compilers in Linux, the *gcc* compiler expects C files to have the .c extension, whereas the *g++* compiler expects C++ files to have the .C extension.

If a source file contains **syntax errors** (grammatical mistakes in program language use), it cannot be converted into an executable file. The compiler locates and reports any syntax errors, which the programmer must correct.

NOTE

After compiling, the executable program might still contain fatal run-time errors or logic errors. Fatal run-time errors cause the program to abort, for example, due to an invalid memory location specified in the program code. Logic errors cause the program to produce invalid results because of problems such as flawed mathematical statements.

Another way to accomplish programming tasks is to develop UNIX/Linux shell scripts, which you learn in this chapter.

Using UNIX/Linux Shell Scripts

First introduced in Chapter 4, UNIX/Linux shell scripts are text files that contain sequences of UNIX/Linux commands. Like high-level source files, a programmer creates shell scripts with a text editor. Unlike high-level language programs, shell scripts do not have to be converted into machine language by a compiler. This is because the UNIX/Linux shell acts as an **interpreter** when reading script files. As this interpreter reads the statements in a script file, it immediately translates them into executable instructions, and causes them to run. No executable file is produced because the interpreter translates and executes the scripted statements in one step. If a syntax error is encountered, the execution of the shell script halts.

After you create a shell script, you tell the operating system that the file can be executed. This is accomplished by using the *chmod* ("change mode") command that you learned in Chapters 2 and 4 ("Exploring the UNIX/Linux File Systems and File Security" and "UNIX/Linux File Processing,") to change the file's mode. The mode determines how the file can be used. Recall that modes can be denoted by single-letter codes: *r* (read), *w* (write), and *x* (execute). Further, the *chmod* command tells the computer who is allowed to use the file: the user or owner (*u*), the group (*g*), or all other users (*o*). For a description of the *chmod* command, see Appendix B, "Syntax Guide to UNIX/Linux Commands."

Recall from Chapter 4 that you can change the mode of a file so that UNIX/Linux recognize it as an executable program (mode x) that everyone (user, group, and others) can use. In the following example, the user is the owner of the file:

```
$ chmod ugo+x filename <Enter>
```

Alternatively, you can make a file executable for all users by entering either:

```
$ chmod a+x filename <Enter>
```

or

```
$ chmod 755 filename <Enter>
```

In *chmod a+x*, the *a* stands for all and is the same as *ugo*. Also, remember from Chapter 2 that *chmod 755* gives owner (in the first position) read, write, and execute permissions (7). It also gives group (in the second position) read and execute permissions (5), and gives others (in the third position) read and execute permissions (5).

After you make the file executable, you can run it in one of several ways:

- You can simply type the name of the script at the system command prompt. However, before this method can work, you must modify your default directory path to include the directory in which the script resides. The directory might be the source or bin directory under your home directory. If you use this method, before any script or program can be run it must be retrieved from a path identified in the **PATH variable**, which provides a list of directory locations where UNIX or Linux looks to find executable scripts or programs. You learn how to temporarily modify the PATH variable in the "Variables" section later in this chapter; you learn how to permanently modify the PATH variable in Chapter 7.

- If the script resides in your current directory, which is not in the PATH variable, you can run the script by preceding the name with a dot slash (./) to tell UNIX/Linux to look in the current directory to find it, as follows:
    ```
    $ ./filename <Enter>
    ```

- If the script does not reside in your current directory and is not in the PATH variable, you can run it by specifying the absolute path to the script. For example, if the script is in the data directory under your home directory, you can type either of the following (using Tom's home directory as an example):
    ```
    $ /home/tom/data/filename <Enter>
    ```
    or
    ```
    $ ~/data/filename <Enter>
    ```

Shell scripts run less quickly than compiled programs because the shell must interpret each UNIX/Linux command inside the executable script file before it is executed. Whether a programmer uses a script or a compiled program (such as a C++ program) is often related to several factors:

- Whether the programmer is more proficient in writing scripts than source code for a compiler

- Whether there is a need for the script or program to execute as quickly as possible, such as to reduce the load on the computer's resources when there are multiple users

- Whether the job is relatively complex; if so, a compiled program might offer more flexible options or features

Prototyping an Application

A **prototype** is a running model of your application, which lets you review the final results before committing to the design. Using a shell script to create a prototype is often the quickest and most efficient method because prototyping logic and design capabilities reside within UNIX/Linux.

After the working prototype is approved, the script can be rewritten to run faster using a compiled language such as C++. If the shell script performs well, however, you might not need to convert it to a compiled program.

Using Comments

In Chapter 5, you were introduced to using comments to provide documentation about a script. Plan to use comments in all of your scripts and programs, so that later it is easier to remember how they work.

Comment lines begin with a pound (#) symbol, such as in the following example from the pact script you created in Hands-on Project 5-16 in Chapter 5:

```
# =========================================================
# Script Name:  pact
# By:           Your initials
# Date:         November 2009
# Purpose:      Create temporary file, pnum, to hold the
#               count of the number of projects each
#               programmer is working on. The pnum file
#               consists of:
#               prog_num and count fields
# =========================================================
cut -d: -f4 project | sort | uniq -c | awk '{printf "%s:
 %s\n",$2,$1}' > pnum
# cut prog_num, pipe output to sort to remove duplicates
# and get count for prog/projects.
# output file with prog_number followed by count
```

In this example, comment lines appear at the beginning of the script and after the *cut* command. You can place comment lines anywhere in a script to provide documentation. For example, in the Hands-on Projects for this chapter, you typically place comments at the beginning of a script to show the script name, the script's author, the date the script was written, and the script's purpose. As you write code in this and later chapters, insert any additional comment lines that you believe might be helpful for later reference. Some examples of what you might comment include:

- Script name, author(s), creation date, and purpose
- Modification date(s) and the purpose of each modification
- The purpose and types of variables used (You learn about variables in this chapter.)
- Files that are accessed, created, or modified
- How logic structures work (You create logic structures in this chapter.)
- The purpose of shell functions (You create shell functions in Chapter 7.)
- How complex lines of code work
- The reasons for including specific commands

Although writing comments might take a little extra time, in the long run the comments can save you much more time when you need to modify that script or incorporate it in an application with other scripts.

THE PROGRAMMING SHELL

Before you create a script, choose the shell in which to run the script. As you learned in Chapter 1, UNIX/Linux versions support different shells and each shell has different capabilities. Also, recall that all Linux versions use the Bash shell (Bourne Again Shell) as the default shell. Table 6-1 lists the three shells that come with most Linux distributions, their derivations, and distinguishing features in relation to shell programming.

Table 6-1   Linux shells

Shell Name	Original Shell from Which Derived	Description in Terms of Shell Programming
Bash	Bourne and Korn shells	Offers strong scripting and programming language features, such as shell variables, logic structures, and math/logic expressions; combines the best features of the Bourne and Korn shells
csh/tcsh	C shell	Conforms to a scripting and programming language format; shell expressions use operators similar to those found in the C programming language
ksh/zsh	Korn shell	Is similar to the Bash shell in many respects, but also has syntax similar to that of C programming; useful if you are familiar with older Korn shell scripts

The Bash shell offers improved features over the older Bourne and Korn shells and is fully backward compatible with the Bourne shell. In addition, the Bash shell, when compared to the other shells, has a more powerful programming interface. For these reasons, you use the Bash shell for shell scripts in this book.

TIP

The manual pages in Fedora, Red Hat Enterprise Linux, and SUSE contain a generous amount of documentation about the Bash shell. Just enter *man bash* to access the documentation.

Now that you have selected the shell, it is important to learn about several basic features used by shell scripts, including variables, shell operators, and special characters.

VARIABLES

Variables use symbolic names that represent values stored in memory. The three types of variables discussed in this section are configuration variables, environment variables, and shell variables. **Configuration variables** are used to store information about the setup of the operating system, and after they are set up, you typically do not change them.

You can set up **environment variables** with initial values that you can change as needed. These variables, which UNIX/Linux read when you log in, determine many characteristics of your login session. For example, in Chapter 2 you learned about the PS1 environment variable, which determines the way your prompt appears. In addition, UNIX/Linux use environment variables to determine such things as where it should look for programs, which shell to use, and the path of your home directory.

Shell variables (defined earlier) are those you create at the command line or in a shell script. They are very useful in shell scripts for temporarily storing information.

Environment and Configuration Variables

Environment and configuration variables bear standard names, such as PS1, HOME, PATH, SHELL, USERNAME, and PWD. (Configuration and environment variables are capitalized to distinguish them from user variables.) A script file in your home directory sets the initial values of environment variables. You can use these variables to set up and personalize your login sessions. For example, you can set your PATH variable to search for the location of shell scripts that other users have created, so you can more easily execute those scripts. Table 6-2 lists standard Bash shell environment and configuration variables.

You can, at any time, use the *printenv* command to view a list of your current environment and configuration variables, which you should typically do before you change any. (See Figure 6-2.) Hands-on Project 6-1 enables you to view your environment variables.

```
                        mpalmer@localhost:~                    _ □ x
 File  Edit  View  Terminal  Tabs  Help
DESKTOP_SESSION=default
PATH=/usr/kerberos/bin:/usr/local/bin:/usr/bin:/bin:/usr/X11R6/bin:/home/mpalmer
/bin
GDM_XSERVER_LOCATION=local
INPUTRC=/etc/inputrc
PWD=/home/mpalmer
XMODIFIERS=@im=none
LANG=en_US.UTF-8
GDMSESSION=default
SSH_ASKPASS=/usr/libexec/openssh/gnome-ssh-askpass
HOME=/home/mpalmer
SHLVL=2
GNOME_DESKTOP_SESSION_ID=Default
LOGNAME=mpalmer
CVS_RSH=ssh
DBUS_SESSION_BUS_ADDRESS=unix:abstract=/tmp/dbus-5Eic33hHqQ,guid=7923394b8609ed7
983a87bc661632200
LESSOPEN=|/usr/bin/lesspipe.sh %s
DISPLAY=:0.0
G_BROKEN_FILENAMES=1
COLORTERM=gnome-terminal
XAUTHORITY=/tmp/.gdmJS8Q5U
_=/usr/bin/printenv
[mpalmer@localhost ~]$ ▊
```

Figure 6-2   Viewing the environment variable listing

Syntax **printenv** [–options] [*variable name*]

Dissection

■ Prints a listing of environment and configuration variables

■ Specifies one or more variables as arguments to view information only about those variables

---

TIP

Besides the *printenv* command, consider using the *set* command (discussed later in this chapter) with no arguments to view your current Bash shell environment, including environment variables, shell script variables, and shell functions. (You learn about shell functions in Chapter 7.) To learn more about the environment and configuration variables used on your system, type *man bash* at the command line. Scroll to the section, Shell Variables.

Table 6-2 Standard Bash shell environment and configuration variables

Name	Variable Contents	Determined by
HOME	Identifies the path name for user's home directory	System
LOGNAME	Holds the account name of the user currently logged in	System
PPID	Refers to the parent ID of the shell	System
TZ	Holds the time zone set for use by the system	System
IFS	Enables the user to specify a default delimiter for use in working with files	Redefinable
LINEND	Holds the current line number of a function or script	Redefinable
MAIL	Identifies the name of the mail file checked by the mail utility for received messages	Redefinable
MAILCHECK	Identifies the interval for checking and received mail (example: 60)	Redefinable
PATH	Holds the list of path names for directories searched for executable commands	Redefinable
PS1	Holds the primary shell prompt	Redefinable
PS2	Contains the secondary shell prompt	Redefinable
PS3 and PS4	Holds prompts used by the *set* and *select* commands	Redefinable
SHELL	Holds the path name of the program for the type of shell you are using	Redefinable
BASH	Contains the absolute path to the Bash shell, such as /bin/bash	User defined
BASH_VERSION	Holds the version number of Bash	User defined
CDPATH	Identifies the path names for directories searched by the *cd* command for subdirectories	User defined
ENV	Contains the file name containing commands to initialize the shell, as in .bashrc or .tcshrc	User defined
EUID	Holds the user identification number (UID) of the currently logged in user	User defined
EXINIT	Contains the initialization commands for the vi editor	User defined
FCEDIT	Enables you to access a range of commands in the command history file; FCEDIT is a Bash shell utility and is the variable used to specify which editor (vi by default) is used when you invoke the FC command	User defined
FIGNORE	Specifies file name suffixes to ignore when working with certain files	User defined

6

Table 6-2 Standard Bash shell environment and configuration variables (continued)

Name	Variable Contents	Determined by
FUNCNAME	Contains the name of the function that is running, or is empty if there is no shell function running	User defined
GROUPS	Identifies the current user's group memberships	User defined
HISTCMD	Contains the sequence number that the currently active command is assigned in the history index of commands that already have been used	User defined
HISTFILE	Identifies the file in which the history of the previously executed commands is stored	User defined
HISTFILESIZE	Sets the upward limit of command lines that can be stored in the file specified by the HISTFILE variable	User defined
HISTSIZE	Establishes the upward limit of commands that the Bash shell can recall	User defined
HOSTFILE	Holds the name of the file that provides the Bash shell with information about its network host name (such as *localhost.localdomain*) and IP address (such as *129.0.0.24*); if the HOSTFILE variable is empty, the system uses the file /etc/hosts by default	User defined
HOSTTYPE	Contains information about the type of computer that is hosting the Bash shell, such as i386 for an Intel-based processor	User defined
INPUTRC	Identifies the file name for the Readline start-up file overriding the default of /etc/inputrc	User defined
MACHTYPE	Identifies the type of system, including CPU, operating system, and desktop	User defined
MAILPATH	Contains a list of mail files to be checked by mail for received messages	User defined
MAILWARNING	Enables (when set) the user to determine if she has already read the mail currently in the mail file	User defined
OLDPWD	Identifies the directory accessed just before the current directory	User defined
OPTIND	Shows the index number of the argument to be processed next, when a command is run using one or more option arguments	User defined
OPTARG	Contains the last option specified when a command is run using one or more option arguments	User defined

Table 6-2   Standard Bash shell environment and configuration variables (continued)

Name	Variable Contents	Determined by
OPTERR	Enables Bash to display error messages associated with command-option arguments, if set to 1 (which is the default established each time the Bash shell is invoked)	User defined
OSTYPE	Identifies the type of operating system on which Bash is running, such as linux-gnu	User defined
PROMPT_COMMAND	Holds the command to be executed prior to displaying a primary prompt	User defined
PWD	Holds the name of the directory that is currently accessed	User defined
RANDOM	Yields a random integer each time it is called, but you must first assign a value to the RANDOM variable to properly initialize random number generation	User defined
REPLY	Specifies the line to read as input, when there is no input argument passed to the built-in shell command, which is read	User defined
SHLVL	Contains the number of times Bash is invoked plus one, such as the value 3 when there are two Bash (terminal) sessions currently running	User defined
TERM	Contains the name of the terminal type in use by the Bash shell	User defined
TIMEFORMAT	Contains the timing for pipelines	User defined
TMOUT	Enables Bash to stop or close due to inactivity at the command prompt, after waiting the number of seconds specified in the TMOUT variable (TMOUT is empty by default so that Bash does not automatically stop due to inactivity.)	User defined
UID	Holds the user identification number of the currently logged in user	User defined

Shell Variables

Shell variables are variables that you can define and manipulate for use with program commands that you employ in a shell. These are variables that are temporarily stored in memory and that you can display on the screen or use to perform specific actions in a shell script. For example, you might define the shell variable TODAY to store today's date so you can later recall it and then print it on a report generated from a shell script.

When you work with shell variables, keep in mind guidelines for handling them and for naming them. Some basic guidelines for handling shell variables are:

- Omit spaces when you assign a variable without using single or double quotation marks around its value, such as when assigning a numerical value—use *x=5* and not *x = 5*. (This type of assignment also enables you to perform mathematical operations on the assigned value.)

- To assign a variable that must contain spaces, such as a string variable, enclose the value in double or single quotation marks—use *fname="Thomas F. Berentino"* and not *fname=Thomas F. Berentino*. A **string** variable is a nonnumeric field of information treated simply as a group of characters. Numbers in a string are considered characters rather than digits.

- To reference a variable, use a dollar sign ($) in front of it or enclose it in curly brackets ({ }).

- If the variable consists of an array (a set of values), use square brackets ([ ]) to refer to a specific position of a value in an array—use *myarray[0]=value1* for the first value in the array, for example.

- Export a shell variable to make the variable available to other shell scripts (as discussed in the following section).

- After you create a shell variable, you can configure it so that it cannot be changed by entering the *readonly* command with the variable name as the argument, such as *readonly fname*.

Sample guidelines for naming shell variables are:

- Avoid using the dollar sign in a variable name, because this can create confusion with using the dollar sign to reference the shell variable.

- Use names that are descriptive of the contents or purpose of the shell variable—use *lname* for a variable to contain a person's last name, instead of *var* or *x*, for example.

- Use capitalization appropriately and consistently—for instance, if you are defining address information, use variable names such as *city*, *state*, *zip* and not *City*, *STATE*, *zip*. Note that some programmers like to use all lowercase letters or all uppercase letters for variable names. For example, many script, C, and C++ programmers prefer using all lowercase letters when possible.

- If a variable name is to consist of two or more words, use underscores between the words—use last_name and not last name, for example.

In the next section, you learn about shell operators, which are used to define and evaluate variables, such as environment and shell variables.

SHELL OPERATORS

Bash shell operators are divided into four groups:

- Defining operators
- Evaluating operators
- Arithmetic and relational operators
- Redirection operators

You learn about each of these groups of operators in the following sections. You also learn how to use the *export* command to make a variable you have defined available to a shell script. Finally, you look at how to modify the PATH environment variable to make it easier to run shell scripts.

Defining Operators

Defining operators are used to assign a value to a variable. Evaluating operators are used for actions such as determining the contents of a variable. The equal sign (=) is one of the most common operators used to define a variable. For example, assume that you want to create a variable called NAME and assign Becky as the value to be contained in the variable. You would set the variable as follows:

```
NAME=Becky
```

The variable names or values that appear to the left and right of an operator are its **operands**. The name of the variable you are setting must appear to the left of the = operator. The value of the variable you are setting must appear to the right.

NOTE Notice there are no spaces between the = operator and its operands.

Sometimes, it is necessary to assign to a variable's contents a string of characters that contain spaces, such as Becky J. Zubrow. To make this kind of assignment, you surround the variable contents with double quotation marks as follows:

```
NAME="Becky J. Zubrow"
```

Another way to assign a value to a shell variable is by using the back quote (`) operator. (The back quote is not the same as the apostrophe or single quotation mark; see the following Tip.) This operator is used to tell the shell to execute the command inside the back quotes and then store the result in the variable. For example, in the following:

```
LIST=`ls`
```

The *ls* command is executed and a listing of the current working directory is stored in the LIST variable.

TIP

On many standard keyboards, the key for the back quote operator is located in the upper-left corner under the Esc key and is combined with the tilde (~) on that key.

Evaluating Operators

When you assign a value to a variable, you might want to evaluate it by displaying its contents via an **evaluating operator**. You can use the dollar sign ($) in front of the variable along with the *echo* command to view the contents. For example, if you enter:

```
echo $NAME
```

you see the contents of the NAME variable you created earlier. You can also use the format echo "$NAME" to view the variable's contents. However, if you enter:

```
echo '$NAME'
```

using single quotation marks, the contents of NAME are suppressed and all you see is $NAME echoed on the screen.

Try Hands-on Project 6-2 to use the defining and evaluation operators.

Arithmetic and Relational Operators

Arithmetic operators consist of the familiar plus (+) for addition, minus (-) for subtraction, asterisk (*) for multiplication, and slash (/) for division. **Relational operators** compare the relationship between two values or arguments, such as greater than (>), less than (<), equal to (=), and others. Table 6-3 explains the arithmetic and relational operators. For a complete listing of arithmetic operators enter *man bash* and go to the section, ARITHMETIC EVALUATION.

Table 6-3   Examples of the shell's arithmetic and relational operators

Operator	Description	Example
-, +	Unary minus and plus	+R (denotes positive R) -R (denotes negative R)
!, ~	Logical and bitwise negation	!Y (returns 0 if Y is nonzero, returns 1 if Y is zero) ~X (reverses the bits in X)
*, /,%	Multiplication, division, and remainder	A * B (returns A times B) A / B (returns A divided by B) A % B (returns the remainder of A divided by B)
+,-	Addition, subtraction	X + Y (returns X plus Y) X - Y (returns X minus Y)
>,<	Greater than and less than	M > N (Is M greater than N?) M < N (Is M less than N?)
=,!=	Equality and inequality	Q = R (Is Q equal to R?) Q != R (Is Q not equal to R?)

When using arithmetic operators, the usual mathematical precedence rules apply: Multiplication and division are performed before addition and subtraction. For example, the value of the expression 6 + 4 * 2 is 14, not 20. Precedence can be overridden, however, by using parentheses. For example, the value of the expression (6 + 4) * 2 is 20, not 14. Other mathematical rules also apply; for example, division by zero is treated as an error.

To store arithmetic values in a variable, use the *let* statement. For example, the following command stores 14 in the variable X (See Figure 6-3 using the *echo* command to show the contents of X after using the *let* command.):

```
let X=6+4*2
```

Figure 6-3   Using *let* to set the contents of a shell variable

Notice in the preceding example that there is one space between *let* and the expression that follows it. Also, there are no spaces in the arithmetic equation following a *let* statement. In this example, there are no spaces on either side of the equal (=), plus (+), and multiplication (*) operators.

You can use shell variables as operands to arithmetic operators. Assuming the variable X has the value 14, the following command stores 18 in the variable Y:

```
let Y=X+4
```

Syntax **let** *expression with operators*

Dissection

■ Performs a given action on numbers that is specified by operators and stores the result in a shell variable

■ Parentheses are used around specific expressions if you want to alter the mathematical precedence rules or to simply ensure the result is what you intend.

---

let is a built-in command for the Bash shell. For documanetation about *let*, enter *man bash*, and scroll down to the section SHELL BUILTIN COMMANDS. Try Hands-on Project 6-3 to learn how to use the *let* command.

REDIRECTION OPERATORS

Recall that the > **redirection operator** overwrites an existing file. For example, in *cat file1 > file2*, the contents of file1 overwrite the contents of file2. If you write a shell script that uses the > operator to create a file, you might want to prevent it from overwriting important information. You can use the *set* command with the *-o noclobber* option to prevent a file from being overwritten, as in the following example:

```
$ set -o noclobber <Enter>
```

Syntax **set** [-options] [*arguments*]

Dissection

■ With no options, displays the current listing of Bash environment and shell script variables

■ Useful options include:

-a exports all variables after they are defined

-n takes commands without executing them, so you can debug errors without affecting data (Also see the *sh -n* command later in this chapter.)

-o sets a particular shell mode—when used with *noclobber* as the argument, it prevents files from being overwritten by use of the > operator

-u shows an error when there is an attempt to use an undefined variable

-v displays command lines as they are executed

---

set is another built-in command for the Bash shell. For documentation about *set*, enter *man bash*, and scroll down to the section SHELL BUILTIN COMMANDS.

TIP

If you want to save time and automatically export all shell script variables you have defined, use *set* with the -a option.

However, you can choose to overwrite a file anyway by placing a pipe character (|) after the redirection operator:

```
$ set -o noclobber    <Enter>
$ cat new_file > old_file <Enter>
  bash: old_file: cannot overwrite existing file
$ cat new_file >| old_file <Enter>
```

CAUTION

Avoid employing the -o *noclobber* option if you are using the Bash shell in the X Window interface with the KDE desktop. On some distributions, using the option in this manner can unexpectedly terminate the command-line session.

Exporting Shell Variables to the Environment

Shell scripts cannot automatically access variables created and assigned on the command line or by other shell scripts. To make a variable available to a shell script, you must use the *export* command to give it a global meaning so that it is viewed by the shell as an environment variable.

Syntax **export** [–options] [*variable names*]

Dissection

- Makes a shell variable global so that it can be accessed by other shell scripts or programs, such as shell scripts or programs called within a shell script

- Useful options include:

  -*n* undoes the export, so the variable is no longer global

  -*p* lists exported variables

---

export is a built-in Bash shell command, which means you can find help documentation by entering *man bash* and scrolling to the SHELL BUILTIN COMMANDS section. Try Hands-on Project 6-4 to use the *export* command in the Bash shell.

Modifying the PATH Variable

Just as shell variables are not universally recognized until you export them, the same is true for executing a shell script. Up to this point, you have used ./ to run a shell script. This is because the shell looks for programs in the directories specified by the PATH variable. If you are developing a shell script in a directory that is not specified in your PATH environment variable, you must type ./ in front of the shell name. If you just type the name of the shell by itself, the script doesn't run because it is not in your currently defined path—which means that the shell interpreter cannot find it to run. You need to type ./ to tell the shell interpreter to look in your current working directory.

For example, in some UNIX/Linux systems, such as Fedora, Red Hat Enterprise Linux, and SUSE, your home directory is not automatically defined in your current path. You can verify this by typing the following to see what directories are in your path:

```
echo $PATH
```

In Fedora or Red Hat Enterprise Linux, for example, you will likely see a path such as the following:

```
/usr/kerberos/bin:/usr/local/bin:/usr/bin:/bin:/usr/X11R6/bin:/
home/username/bin
```

Notice that each directory in the path is separated by a colon. Your home directory, as represented by /home/*username* is not in the path by default, but another directory, /home/*username*/bin, in which programs might be stored, is in the path by default—although the actual directory, /home/*username*/bin, might not be created by default on your system even though it is in the path.

Because new shell scripts are most often kept in the current directory while they are being tested, you should add the current working directory to the PATH variable. Here is an example command for how you can do this quickly:

```
PATH=$PATH:.
```

Remember, the shell interprets $PATH as the contents of the PATH variable. This sample command sets the PATH variable to its current contents. The colon and dot (.) add the current directory to the search path so that the shell program can locate the new program.

After you type this command, you can execute new shell scripts by simply using the name of the script without prefacing it with the ./ characters. Hands-on Project 6-5 enables you to try this.

TIP   When you type PATH=$PATH:., the current working directory is temporarily stored as part of your path only for the duration of your login session.

CAUTION

Configuring to have the current directory set in your path does involve some risk if a hacker gains access to your account while you are logged in. For example, a hacker might gain access through an open port (communication path in a network protocol). If you choose to put your current working directory in the PATH variable, be certain you have secured access to your account, such as through closing unused ports. For more Information about operating system security, including for UNIX/Linux systems, see *Guide to Operating Systems Security* (Course Technology, ISBN 0-619-16040-3).

6

MORE ABOUT WILDCARD CHARACTERS

Shell scripts frequently use the asterisk (*) and other wildcard characters (such as ? and [ ]), which help to locate information containing only a portion of a matching pattern. For example, to list all program files with names that contain a .c extension, use the following command:

```
ls *.c
```

Wildcard characters are also known as **glob** characters. If an unquoted argument contains one or more glob characters, the shell processes the argument for file name generation. Glob characters are part of **glob patterns**, which are intended to match file names and words. Special constructions that might appear in glob patterns are:

- The question mark (?) matches exactly one character, except for the backslash and period.
- The asterisk (*) matches zero or more characters in a file name.
- [*chars*] defines a class of characters. The glob pattern matches any single character in the class. A class can contain a range of characters, as in [a–z].

For example, assume the working directory contains files chap1, chap2, and chap3. The following command displays the contents of all three files:

```
more chap[1-3] <Enter>
```

The commands and variables used in shell scripts are organized into different logic structures. In the next sections, you learn how to use logic structures for effective script handling.

SHELL LOGIC STRUCTURES

Logic structures are techniques for structuring program code and affect the order in which the code is executed or how it is executed, such as looping back through the code from a particular point or jumping from one point in the code to another. The four basic logic structures needed for program development are:

- Sequential logic
- Decision logic

- Looping logic
- Case logic

Each of these logic structures is discussed in the following sections.

Sequential Logic

Sequential logic works so that commands are executed in the order in which they appear in the script or program.

For example, consider a sales manager in a company who begins each week by tallying sales information. First, she runs the tally_all program to compute the year's gross sales statistics up to the current date. Then she runs the profit_totals program to tally the profit statistics. Next, she runs the sales_breakdown report program that shows the sales performance of the 40 salespeople she manages. Finally, she runs the management_statistics report program to provide the sales statistics needed by her management. The sales manager can automate her work by creating a script that uses sequential logic, first running the tally_all program, then the profit_totals, the sales_breakdown, and the management_statistics programs. Her shell script with sequential logic would have the following sequence of commands (note that her system is set up so that all she needs to do is to enter the programs names at the commandline):

tally_all

profit_totals

sales_breakdown

management_statistics

The only break in sequence logic comes when a branch instruction changes the flow of execution by redirecting to another location in the script or program. A **branch instruction** is one that tells the program to go to a different section of code.

Many scripts are simple, straightforward command sequences. An example is the Programmer Activity Status Report script you wrote in Chapter 5, and is listed next. The shell executes the script's commands in the order they appear in the file. You use sequential logic to write this type of application.

```
#===================================================================
# Script Name:        practivity
# By:                 MP
# Date:               November 2009
# Purpose: Generate Programmer Activity Status Report
#===================================================================
cut -d: -f4 project | sort | uniq -c | awk '{printf "%s:
 %s \n",$2,$1}' > pnum
cut -d: -f1-4 programmer | sort -t: +0 -1 | uniq > pnn
join -t: -a1 -j1 1 -j2 1 pnn pnum > pactrep
```

```
# Print the report
awk '
BEGIN {
   { FS = ":" }
   { print "\tProgrammer Activity Status Report\n" }
   { "date" | getline d }
   { printf "\t   %s\n",d }
   { print "Prog# \t*--Name--*                          Projects\n" }
   { print "=============================================\n"}
}
   { printf "%-s\t%-12.12s %-12.12s %s\t%d\n",
            $1, $2, $3, $4, $5 } ' pactrep
# remove all the temporary files
rm pnum pnn pactrep
```

Hands-on Project 6-6 enables you to build a short script to demonstrate sequential logic as well as practice the *let* command, and to build expressions using constants, variables, and arithmetic operators.

Decision Logic

Decision logic enables your script or program to execute a statement or series of statements only if a certain condition exists. In this usage, a **statement** is another name for a line of code that performs an action in your program. The *if* statement is a primary decision-making logic structure in this type of logic.

In decision logic, the script is programmed to make decisions as it runs. By using the *if* statement, you can specify conditions for the script to evaluate before it makes a decision. For example, if *a* occurs, then the script does *b*; but if *x* occurs instead, then the script does *y*. Consider a situation in which a magazine publisher gives the reader two subscription choices based on price. If the reader sends in $25, then the magazine publisher gives him 12 weeks of the publication, but if the reader sends in $50 dollars, then the magazine publisher gives him 24 weeks of the publication.

Another way to use a decision structure is as a simple yes or no situation. For example, you might use a portion of a script to enable the user to continue updating a file or to close the file. When the script asks: "Do you want to continue updating (*y* or *n*)?", if you answer *y* then the script gives you a blank screen form in which to enter more information to put in the file. If instead you answer *n*, then the script closes the file and stops.

Consider, for example, the following lines of code. In this shell script, the user is asked to enter a favorite vegetable. If the user enters "broccoli," the decision logic of the program displays "Broccoli is a healthy choice." If any other vegetable is entered, the decision logic displays the line "Don't forget to eat your broccoli also."

```
echo -n "What is your favorite vegetable? "
read veg_name
if [ "$veg_name" = "broccoli" ]
then
```

```
    echo "Broccoli is a healthy choice."
else
    echo "Don't forget to eat your broccoli also."
fi
```

NOTE

Throughout the sample scripts, variables are always enclosed in double quotation marks, as in "$veg_name", "$choice", "$looptest", "$yesno", "$guess", and "$myfavorite", because of how the shell interprets variables. All shell variables, unless declared otherwise, are strings, which are arrays of alphanumeric characters. If you do not enter data in the string variables, the variables are treated as blank strings, which result in an invalid test. The enclosing double quotation marks, therefore, maintain the validity of strings, with or without data, and the test is carried out without producing an error condition.

You create and run this script in Hands-on Project 6-7. However, before you attempt the project, let's examine the contents of the script. The first statement uses the *echo* command to display a message on the screen. The *-n* option suppresses the line feed that normally appears after the message. The second statement uses the *read* command, which waits for the user to type a line of keyboard input. The input is stored in the variable specified as the *read* command's argument. The line in the script reads the user's input into the veg_name variable.

The next line begins an *if* statement. The word "if" is followed by an expression inside a set of brackets ([ ]). (The spaces on either side that separate the [and] characters from the enclosed expression are necessary.) The expression, which is tested to determine if it is true or false, compares the contents of the veg_name variable with the string broccoli. (When you use the = operator in an *if* statement's test expression, it tests its two operands for equality. In this case, the operands are the variable $veg_name and the string broccoli. If the operands are equal, the expression is true—otherwise, it is false. If the contents of the $veg_name variable are equal to broccoli, the statement that follows the word "then" is executed. In this script, it is the *echo* statement, "Broccoli is a healthy choice."

If the *if* statement's expression is false (if the contents of the $veg_name variable do not equal broccoli), the statement that follows the word "else" is executed. That statement reads, "Don't forget to eat your broccoli also." In this script, it is a different *echo* statement.

Notice the last statement, which consists of the characters "fi." *fi* ("if" spelled backward) always marks the end of an *if* or an *if...else* statement.

NOTE

When you evaluate the contents of a variable using a logic structure, such as the *if* statement, you need to define the variable first, such as through a *read* statement.

You can nest a control structure, such as an *if* statement, inside another control structure. To **nest** means that you layer statements at two or more levels under an original statement structure. For example, a script can have an *if* statement inside another *if* statement. The first *if* statement controls when the second *if* statement is executed, as in the following code sample:

```
echo -n "What is your favorite vegetable? "
read veg_name
if [ "$veg_name" = "broccoli" ]
then
    echo "Broccoli is a healthy choice."
else
    if [ "$veg_name" = "carrots" ]
    then
        echo "Carrots are great for you."
    else
        echo "Don't forget to eat your broccoli also."
    fi
fi
```

As you can see, the second *if* statement is located in the first *if* statement's *else* section. It is only executed when the first *if* statement's expression is false.

Decision logic structures, such as the *if* statement, are used in applications in which different courses of action are required, depending on the result of a command or comparison.

Looping Logic

In **looping logic**, a control structure (or loop) repeats until a specific condition exists or some action occurs. The basic idea of looping logic is to keep repeating an action until some condition is met. For example, the logic might keep printing a list of people's names until it reaches the final name on the list, prints the final name, and stops. In another example, a script might open an inventory file of mountain bike models, print the model and quantity for the first bike, do the same for the second bike, and so on until there are no more bikes listed in the file.

You learn two looping mechanisms in the sections that follow: the *for* and the *while* loop.

The For Loop

Use the *for* command to loop through a range of values. It causes a variable to take on each value in a specified set, one at a time, and perform some action while the variable contains each individual value. The loop stops after the variable has taken on the last value in the set and has performed the specified action with that value.

An example of a *for* loop is as follows:

```
for USERS in john ellen tom becky eli jill
do
   echo $USERS
done
```

In this *for* loop structure, the first line specifies the values that will be assigned, one at a time, to the USERS shell variable. Because six values are in the set, the loop repeats six times. Each time it repeats, USERS contains a different value from the set, and the statement between the *do* and *done* statements is executed. The first time around the loop, "john" is assigned to the USERS variable and is then displayed on the screen via the *echo $USERS* command. Next, "ellen" is assigned to the USERS variable and displayed. The loop continues through "tom," "becky," "eli," and "jill." After "jill" is assigned to USERS and displayed on the screen, the looping comes to an end and the *done* command is executed to end the looping logic.

Hands-on Project 6-8 enables you to use a *for* loop in a shell script.

Executing Control Structures at the Command Line

Most shell script control structures, such as the *if* and *for* statements, must be written across several lines. This does not prevent you from executing them directly on the command line, however. For example, you can enter the *for* statement at the command prompt, enter the variable name and elements to use for the variable, and press Enter. You go into a command-line processor to execute the remaining statements in the loop, pressing Enter after each statement. The shell knows more code comes after you type the first line. It displays the > prompt, indicating it is ready for the control structure's continuation. The shell reads further input lines until you type the word "done," which marks the end of the *for* loop.

In the following lines, each of the elements tennis, swimming, movies, and travel are displayed one line at a time until the loop ends after displaying travel. (See Figure 6-4.)

```
$ for myhobbies in tennis swimming movies travel <Enter>
> do <Enter>
> echo $myhobbies <Enter>
> done <Enter>
```

Hands-on Project 6-8 enables you to compare using the command line to using a shell script for executing a simple *for* loop.

Using Wildcard Characters in a Loop

The [ ] wildcard characters can be very useful in looping logic. For example, consider that you have four files that all start with the same four characters: chap1, chap2, chap3, and chap4. You can use the wildcard notation chap[1234] to output the contents of all four file names to the screen using the following statement:

```
for file in chap[1234]; do
    more $file
done
```

Notice that in the first line, two commands are combined by using the semicolon (;) character to run each on one line. Try Hands-on Project 6-9 to use brackets as wildcards.

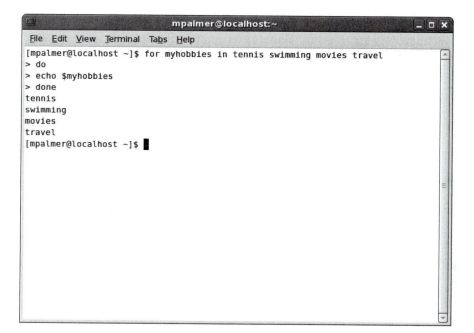

Figure 6-4   Using the *for* loop from the command line

The While Loop

A second approach to looping logic is the *while* statement. The *while* statement continues to loop and execute commands or statements as long as a given condition or set of conditions is true. As soon as the condition or conditions are false, the loop is exited at the *done* statement. The following is an example of a simple shell script that uses a *while* statement:

```
echo -n "Try to guess my favorite color:  "
read guess
while [ "$guess" != "red" ]; do
  echo "No, not that one. Try again. "; read guess
done
```

In this example, the first line asks the user to "Try to guess my favorite color: " and the user's response is read into the variable *guess*.

The *while* loop tests an expression in a manner similar to the *if* statement. As long as the statement inside the brackets is true, the statements inside the *do* and *done* statements repeat. In this example, the expression inside the brackets is "*$guess*" != "*red*", which tests to see if the *guess* variable is not equal to the string, "red". Note that *!=* is the not-equal (inequality) operator. (Refer to Table 6-3.) The *while* statement tests the two operands on either side of the *!=* operator and returns true if they are not equal. Otherwise, it returns false. In this example, the *echo* and *read* statements inside the loop repeat until the user enters red, which makes the expression "*$guess*" != "*red*" false.

Hands-on Project 6-10 gives you the opportunity to program the sample code described here and then to program a more complex example such as might be used to input name and address information in a file.

TIP

Use looping logic in the form of *for* and *while* statements in applications in which code must be repeated a determined or undetermined number of times.

Case Logic

The **case logic** structure simplifies the selection of a match when you have a list of choices. It allows your script to perform one of many actions, depending on the value of a variable.

Consider a fund raiser in which contributors receive different premiums. If someone gives $20 they get a free pen. If they give $30 they get a T-shirt and if they give $50 they get a free mug. People who give $100 get a free CD. In case logic, you can take the four types of contributions and associate each one with a different action. For example, when the user types in 30 in answer to the question, "How much did you contribute?", then the screen displays "Your free gift is a T-shirt." If the user types in 100, then the screen displays, "Your free gift is a CD." The advantage of case logic in this example is that it simplifies your work by using fewer lines—you use one *case* statement instead of several *if* statements, for example.

One common application of the case logic structure is in creating menu selections on a computer screen. A menu is a screen display that offers several choices. Consider, for example, a menu used in a human resources application in which there is a menu option to enter information for a new employee, another menu option to view employee name and address information, another menu option to view salary information, and so on. Each menu option branches to a different program. For example, if you select the option to enter information for a new employee, this starts the employee data entry program. Or, if you select to view employee salary information, a salary report program runs.

The following is a basic example of how the *case* statement works in case logic:

```
echo -n "Enter your favorite color: "; read color
  case "$color" in
    "blue")  echo "As in My Blue Heaven.";;
    "yellow") echo "As in the Yellow Sunset.";;
    "red")  echo "As in Red Rover, Red Rover.";;
    "orange") echo "As in Autumn has shades of Orange.";;
    *) echo "Sorry, I do not know that color.";;
  esac
```

In this sample script, the case structure examines the contents of the color variable, and searches for a match among the values listed. When a match is found, the statement that immediately follows the *case* value is executed. For example, if the color variable contains orange, the *echo* statement that appears after "orange") is executed: "As in Autumn has shades of Orange." If the contents of the color variable do not match any of the values listed, the statement that appears after *) is executed: "Sorry, I do not know that color."

Note the use of two semicolons (;;) that terminate the action(s) taken after the case structure matches what is being tested. Also notice that the case structure is terminated by the word "esac," which is "case" spelled backward.

As you can see, case logic is designed to pick one course of action from a list of many, depending on the contents of a variable. This is why case logic is ideal for menus, in which the user chooses one of several values. Try Hands-on Project 6-11 to program using case logic.

6

Using Shell Scripting to Create a Menu

When you create an application that consists of several shell scripts, it is often useful to create a menu with options that branch to specific scripts. You create menus in the Hands-on Projects section of this chapter. In preparation for creating a menu, you need to have one more command under your belt, the *tput* command. This is one of the less-publicized UNIX/Linux commands, but is important to know for developing an appealing and user-friendly menu presentation.

Syntax **tput** [–options] *arguments*

Dissection

- Can be used to initialize the terminal or terminal window display, position text, and position the cursor

- Useful options include:

  bold=`tput smso` offbold=`tput rmso` enables/disables boldfaced type

  clear clears the screen

  cols prints the number of columns

  cup positions the cursor and text on the screen

The *tput* command enables you to initialize the terminal display or terminal window, to place text and prompts in desired locations, and to respond to what the user selects from the menu. Some examples of what you can do with the *tput* command are:

- *tput cup 0 0* moves the cursor to row 0, column 0, which is the upper-left corner of the screen.

- *tput clear* clears the screen.

- *tput cols* prints the number of columns for the current terminal display.

- *bold=`tput smso` offbold=`tput rmso`* sets boldfaced type by setting the bold shell variable for stand-out mode sequence and by setting the offbold shell variable to turn off stand-out mode sequence.

Hands-on Project 6-12 enables you to gain experience using the *tput* command. Hands-on Project 6-15 uses the *tput* command so you can begin building a menu to use with an actual application.

DEBUGGING A SHELL SCRIPT

As you have probably discovered by this point, sometimes a shell script does not execute because there is an error in one or more commands within the script. For example, perhaps you entered a colon instead of a semicolon or left out a bracket. Another common problem is leaving out a space or not putting a space in the correct location.

Now that you have some experience developing shell scripts and have possibly encountered some problems, you can appreciate why it is important to have a tool to help you troubleshoot errors. The *sh* command that is used to run a shell script includes several options for debugging.

Syntax **sh** [–options] [*shell script*]

Dissection

- In UNIX and Linux, it calls the command interpreter for shell scripts; and in Linux, it uses the Bash shell with the command interpreter
- Useful options include:

  -n checks the syntax of a shell script, but does not execute command lines

  -v displays the lines of code while executing a shell script

  -x displays the command and arguments as a shell script is run

Two of the most commonly used *sh* options are *-v* and *-x*. The *-v* option displays the lines of code in the script as they are read by the interpreter. The *-x* option shows somewhat different information by displaying the command and accompanying arguments line by line as they are run.

By using the *sh* command with these options, you can view the shell script line by line as it is running and determine the location and nature of an error on a line when a script fails.

Try Hands-on Project 6-13 to compare *sh -v* and *sh -x* to debug a shell script.

Further, sometimes you want to test a script that updates a file, but you want to give the script a dry run without actually updating the file—particularly so that data in the file is not altered if the script fails at some point. Use the *-n* option for this purpose because it reads and checks the syntax of commands in a script, but does not execute them. For example, if you are testing a script that is designed to add new information to a file, when you run it with the *sh -n* command, the script does not actually process the information or add it to the file. If a syntax error exists, you see an error message so you know that you must fix the script before using it on live data.

Now that you have an idea of how to create a menu script, it is helpful to learn some additional shell features and commands before creating your application. You first learn more about how to customize your personal environment and how to use the *trap* command to clean up unnecessary files in your environment.

6

CUSTOMIZING YOUR PERSONAL ENVIRONMENT

When your work requirements center on computer programming and shell scripting, consider customizing your environment by modifying the initial settings in the login scripts. A **login script** is a script that runs just after you log in to your account. For example, many programmers set up a personal bin directory in which they can store and test their new programs without interfering with ongoing operations. The traditional UNIX/Linux name for directories that hold executable files is bin.

A useful tool for customizing the command environment is the alias. An **alias** is a name that represents another command. You can use aliases to simplify and automate commands you use frequently. For example, the following command sets up an alias for the *rm* command.

```
alias rm="rm -i"
```

This command causes the *rm -i* command to execute any time the user enters the *rm* command. This is a commonly used alias because it ensures that users are always prompted before the *rm* command deletes a file. The following are two other common aliases that help safeguard files:

```
alias mv="mv -i"
alias cp="cp -i"
```

Syntax **alias** [–options] [*name* = *"command"*]

Dissection

- Creates an alternate name for a command
- Useful options include:

   -p prints a list of all aliases

---

alias is a built-in Bash shell command. You can learn more about *alias* by entering *man bash* and find *alias* under the SHELL BUILTIN COMMANDS section. Hands-on Project 6-14 enables you to set aliases.

The **.bashrc file** that resides in your home directory as a hidden file (enter *ls -a* to view hidden files) can be used to establish customizations that take effect for each login session. The .bashrc script is executed each time you generate a shell, such as when you run a shell script. Any time a subshell is created, .bashrc is reexecuted. The following .bashrc file is commented to explain how you can make your own changes.

```
# .bashrc
# Source global definitions
if [ -f /etc/bashrc ]; then
     . /etc/bashrc # if any global definitions are defined
                   # run them first
alias rm='rm -i'   # make sure user is prompted before
                   # removing files
alias mv='mv -i'   # make sure user is prompted before
                   # overlaying files
set -o ignoreeof   # Do not allow Ctrl-d to log out
set -o noclobber   # Force user to enter >| to write
                   # over existing files
PS1="\w \$"        # Set prompt to show working directory
```

In addition to knowing how to customize your work environment, you should also be familiar with the *trap* command to clean your storage of temporary files.

THE TRAP COMMAND

trap is a command in the Bash shell that is used to execute another command when a specific signal is received. For example, you might use *trap* to start a new program after it detects through an operating system signal that a different program has terminated. Another example is using *trap* to end a program when *trap* receives a specific signal, such as trapping when the user types Ctrl-c and gracefully ending the currently running program.

The *trap* command is useful when you want your shell program to automatically remove any temporary files that are created when the shell script runs. The *trap* command specifies that a command, listed as the argument to *trap*, is read and executed when the shell receives a specified system signal.

Syntax **trap** [*command*] [*signal number*]

Dissection

■ When a signal is received from the operating system, the argument included with *trap* is executed.

■ Common signals used with *trap* include:

0   The completion of a shell script has occurred

1   A hang up or logout signal has been issued

2   An interrupt has been received, such as Ctrl+c

     3   A quit signal has been issued

     4   An illegal instruction has been received

     9   A termination signal has been issued

     15   A program has been ended, such as through a *kill* command

     19   A process has been stopped

     20   A process has been suspended

- Useful options include:

   -l displays a listing of signal numbers and their associated signal designations

6

Here is an example of a use for the *trap* command:

```
trap "rm ~/tmp/* 2> /dev/null; exit" 0
```

This command has two arguments: a command to be executed and a signal number from the operating system. The command *rm ~/tmp/* 2> /dev/null; exit* deletes everything in the user's tmp directory, redirects the error output of the *rm* command to the null device (so it does not appear on the screen), and issues an *exit* command to terminate the shell. The signal specified is 0, which is the operating system signal generated when a shell script is exited. So, if this sample command is part of a script file, it causes the specified *rm* command to execute when signal 0 is sent by the operating system.

The programmer often sets up ~/tmp (a subdirectory of the user's home directory) to store temporary files. When the script file exits, any files placed in ~/tmp can be removed. This is called "good housekeeping" on the part of the programmer.

The *trap* command is another example of a built-in Bash shell command. You can learn more about *trap* by entering *man bash* and finding the *trap* command listed in the SHELL BUILTIN COMMANDS section.

PUTTING IT ALL TOGETHER IN AN APPLICATION

In this chapter, you learned all of the pieces necessary to create a multifunctional application. You learned how to:

- Assign and manage variables
- Use shell operators
- Employ shell logic structures
- Use additional wildcard characters
- Use *tput* for managing screen initialization and screen text placement
- Use the *trap* command to clean up temporary files used by an application

In Hands-on Projects 6-15 through 6-20, you use the skills and knowledge you have acquired in this and previous chapters to build a multipurpose application. The application you build simulates one that an organization might use to track telephone numbers and other information about its employees. This application enables the user to input new telephone number and employee information, to print a list of telephone numbers, and to search for a specific telephone number. You build the application entirely from shell scripts. Also, to make this undertaking manageable (and be consistent with programming practices), you build the application through creating small pieces that you prototype, test, and later link together into one menu-based application.

CHAPTER SUMMARY

- ❏ A high-level language (such as C, C++, or COBOL) is a language that uses English-like expressions. A high-level language must be converted into a low-level (machine) language before the computer can execute it. Programmers use a compiler to convert the high-level language to machine language.

- ❏ An interpreter reads commands or a programming language and interprets each line into an action. A shell, such as the Bash shell, interprets UNIX/Linux shell scripts. Shell scripts do not need to be converted to machine language because the UNIX/Linux shell interprets the lines in shell scripts.

- ❏ UNIX/Linux shell scripts, created with the vi or Emacs editor, contain instructions that do not need to be written from scratch, but can be selectively chosen from the operating system's inventory of executable commands.

- ❏ Linux shells are derived from the UNIX Bourne, Korn, and C shells. The three typical Linux shells are Bash, csh/tcsh, and ksh/zsh; Bash is the most commonly used Linux shell.

- ❏ UNIX/Linux employ three types of variables: configuration, environment, and shell. Configuration variables contain setup information for the operating system. Environment variables hold information about your login session. Shell variables are created in a shell script or at the command line. The *export* command is used to make a shell variable an environment variable.

- ❏ The shell supports many operators, including ones that perform arithmetic operations.

- ❏ You can use wildcard characters in shell scripts, including the bracket ([ ]) characters. Brackets surround a set of values that can match an individual character in a name or string.

- ❏ The logic structures supported by the shell are sequential, decision, looping, and case.

- ❏ You can use the *tput* command to manage cursor placement.

- ❏ You can customize the .bashrc file that resides in your home directory to suit particular needs, such as setting alias and default shell conditions.

- ❏ You can create aliases and enter them into .bashrc to simplify commonly used commands, such as *ls -l* and *rm -i*.

- ❏ Use the *trap* command inside a script file to remove temporary files after the script file has been run (exited).

COMMAND SUMMARY: REVIEW OF CHAPTER 6 COMMANDS

Command	Purpose	Options Covered in This Chapter
alias	Establishes an alias	**-p** prints all aliases.
case. . .in. . .esac	Allows one action from a set of possible actions to be performed, depending on the value of a variable	
export	Makes a shell variable an environment variable	**-n** can be used to undo the export. **-p** lists the exported variables.
for: do. . .done	Causes a variable to take on each value in a set of values; an action is performed for each value	
if. . .then. . . else. . .fi	Causes one of two actions to be performed, depending on the condition	
let	Stores arithmetic values in a variable	
printenv	Prints a list of environment variables	
set	Displays currently set shell variables; when options are used, sets the shell environment	**-a** exports all shell variables after they are assigned. **-n** takes commands without executing them, so you can debug errors. **-o** sets a particular shell mode—when used with **noclobber** as the argument, it prevents files from being overwritten by use of the > operator. **-u** yields an error message when there is an attempt to use an undefined variable. **-v** displays command lines as they are executed.
sh	Calls the command interpreter for shell scripts	**-n** checks the syntax of a shell script, but does not execute command lines. **-v** displays the lines of code while executing a shell script. **-x** displays the command and arguments as a shell script is run.
tput cup	Moves the screen cursor to a specified row and column	
tput clear	Clears the screen	
tput cols	Prints the number of columns on the current terminal	
tput smso	Enables boldfaced output	
tput rmso	Disables boldfaced output	

6

Command	Purpose	Options Covered in This Chapter
trap	Executes a command when a specified signal is received from the operating system	-l displays a listing of signal numbers and their signal designations.
while: do. . .done	Repeats an action while a condition exists	

Key Terms

.bashrc file — A file in your home directory that you can use to customize your work environment and specify what occurs each time you log in. Each time you start a shell, that shell executes the commands in .bashrc.

algorithm — A sequence of instructions, programming code, or commands that results in a program or that can be used as part of a program.

alias — A name that represents a command. Aliases are helpful in simplifying and automating frequently used commands.

arithmetic operator — A character that represents a mathematical activity. Arithmetic operators include + (addition), - (subtraction), * (multiplication), and / (division).

branch instruction — An instruction that tells a program to go to a different section of code.

case logic — One of the four basic shell logic structures employed in program development. Using case logic, a program can perform one of many actions, depending on the value of a variable and matching results to a test. It is often used when there is a list of several choices.

compiler — A program that reads the lines of code in a source file, converts them to machine-language instructions or calls the assembler to convert them into object code, and creates a machine-language file.

configuration variable — A variable that stores information about the operating system and does not change the value.

control structures — *See* logic structures.

debugging — The process of going through program code to locate errors and then fixing them.

decision logic — One of the four basic shell logic structures used in program development. In decision logic, commands execute only if a certain condition exists. The *if* statement is an example of a coded statement that sets the condition(s) for execution.

defining operator — Used to assign a value to a variable.

environment variable — A value in a storage area that is read by UNIX/Linux when you log in. Environment variables can be used to create and store default settings, such as the shell that you use or the command prompt format you prefer.

evaluating operator — Enables you to evaluate the contents of a variable, such as by displaying the contents.

6

glob —A character used to find or match file names; similar to a wildcard. Glob characters are part of glob patterns.

glob pattern — A combination of glob characters used to find or match multiple file names.

high-level language — A computer language that uses English-like expressions. COBOL, Visual Basic (VB), C, and C++ are high-level languages.

interpreter — A UNIX/Linux shell feature that reads statements in a program file, immediately translates them into executable instructions, and then runs the instructions. Unlike a compiler, an interpreter does not produce a binary (an executable file) because it translates the instructions and runs them in a single step.

logic structures — The techniques for structuring program code that affect the order in which the code is executed or how it is executed, such as looping back through the code from a particular point or jumping from one point in the code to another. Also called control structures or control logic.

login script — A script that runs just after you log in to your account.

looping logic — One of the four basic shell logic structures used in program development. In looping logic, a control structure (or loop) repeats until some specific condition exists or some action occurs.

nest —When creating program code, a practice of layering statements at two or more levels under an original statement structure.

operand — The variable name that appears to the left of an operator or the variable value that appears to the right of an operator. For example, in NAME=Becky, NAME is the variable name, = is the operator, and Becky is the variable value. Note that no spaces separate the operator and operands.

PATH variable — A path identifier that provides a list of directory locations where UNIX/Linux look for executable programs.

program development cycle —The process of developing a program, which includes (1) creating program specifications, (2) the design process, (3) writing code, (4) testing, (5) debugging, and (6) correcting errors.

prototype — A running model, which lets programmers review a program before committing to its design.

redirection operator — An operator or symbol that changes the input or output data stream from its default direction, such as using > to redirect output to a file instead of to the screen.

relational operator — Compares the relationship between two values or arguments, such as greater than (>), less than (<), equal to (=), and others.

sequential logic — One of four basic logic structures used for program development. In sequential logic, commands execute in the order they appear in the program, except when a branch instruction changes the flow of execution.

shell script operator — The symbols used with shell scripts that define and evaluate information, that perform arithmetic actions, and that perform redirection or piping operations.

shell variable —A variable you create at the command line or in a shell script. It is valuable for use in shell scripts for storing information temporarily.

source file — A file used for storing a program's high-level language statements (code) and created by an editor such as vi or Emacs, To execute, a source file must be converted to a low-level machine language file consisting of object code.

statement — A reference to a line of code that performs an action in a program.

string — A nonnumeric field of information treated simply as a group of characters. Numbers in a string are considered characters rather than digits.

symbolic name — A name used for a variable that consists of letters, numbers, or characters, that is used to reference the contents of a variable, and that often reflects the variable's purpose or contents.

syntax error — A grammatical mistake in a source file or script. Such mistakes prevent a compiler or interpreter from converting the file into an executable file or from running the commands in the file.

Review Questions

1. Your organization routinely uses scripts, but as some employees have left, there are scripts that contain only command lines and no one is certain of their purpose. What steps can be taken to ensure a way for others to know the purpose of a script?

    a. Create text documentation of scripts and use the *scriptdoc* command to organize and display the documentation.

    b. Use the *whatis* command to create and save new documentation for scripts.

    c. Require that script writers place comment lines inside the scripts using the # symbol to begin each comment line.

    d. Require that scripts be named using the descriptive sentence naming function in UNIX/Linux.

2. Which of the following shells enables the use of scripts? (Choose all that apply.)

    a. Bash

    b. csh

    c. sea

    d. zsh

3. You frequently use the command *ls -a* and want to save time by just entering *l* to do the same thing. Which of the following commands enables you to set your system to view hidden files by only entering *l*?

    a. *put l= ls -a*

    b. *set l to ls -a*

    c. *set " ls -a" to "l"*

    d. *alias l=" ls -a"*

4. You have written a script, but when you run it there is an error. Which of the following commands can you use to debug your script? (Choose all that apply.)

   a. *debug -all*

   b. *sh -v*

   c. *./ -d*

   d. *sh -x*

5. You have written a shell program that creates four temporary files. Which of the following commands can you use to remove these files when the script has completed its work?

   a. *trap*

   b. *grep*

   c. *del*

   d. *clear*

6. Which of the following commands works well for menus used in a script? (Choose all that apply.)

   a. *do*

   b. *case*

   c. *choose*

   d. *comm*

7. You are currently in the source directory, which is the new directory you have just created for storing and running your scripts. You want to make certain that the source directory is in your default path. Which of the following commands enables you to view the current default path settings?

   a. *cat PATH*

   b. *show path*

   c. *sed PATH!*

   d. *echo $PATH*

8. You have created a script for use by your entire department in a commonly accessed directory. Only you are able to run the script, which works perfectly. Which of the following is likely to be the problem?

   a. You did not link the script.

   b. You did not give all users in your department execute permission for that script.

   c. You did not designate to share ownership of the script.

   d. There are two kinds of scripts, universal and private. You have created a private script and need to convert it to universal.

9. Your current working directory contains a series of files that start with the word "account" combined with a, b, c, d, and e, such as accounta, accountb, and so on. Which of the following commands enables you to view the contents of all of these files? (Choose all that apply.)

   a. *ls account "a -e"*

   b. *less account "a,e"*

   c. *more account[a,b,c,d,e]*

   d. *cat account{a to e}*

10. For which of the following logic structures used within a script is *fi* the final line for that logic structure? (Choose all that apply.)

    a. *loop*

    b. *case*

    c. *for*

    d. *if*

11. Which of the following are examples of arithmetic or relational operators? (Choose all that apply.)

    a. *!*

    b. *<*

    c. *%*

    d. ***

12. You have created a series of scripts that use the same environment variables. However, when you run these scripts, some of them do not seem to recognize the environment variables you have set. What is the problem?

    a. You need to use the *export* command so these variables have global use.

    b. You are creating too many environment variables, because the maximum number is five.

    c. You must use the *home* command to make these variables native to your home directory.

    d. Only the system administrator can create environment variables and you should contact her to create the ones you need to use.

13. You have spent the last two hours creating a report in a file and afterwards you use *cat* to create a new file. Unfortunately the new file name you used was the same as the name you used for the report, and now your report is gone. What should you do next time to prevent this from happening?

    a. Enter the *cat -s* command before you start.

    b. Enter the command, *set -o noclobber* before you start.

    c. Always use the *cat -m* command when you use *cat* to create a file, because this command checks to see if the file already exists.

    d. After you created the report file you should have used the *chmod a-o* command to prevent the file from being deleted or overwritten.

14. You have remotely logged into a computer running UNIX or Linux, but you are not certain about which operating system you are using. However, when you display the contents of the _____ variable it shows which operating system you are using.

    a. OP

    b. OPTIND

    c. OID

    d. OSTYPE

15. What command can you use to view the environment and configuration variables already configured on your system?

    a. *var*

    b. *envar*

    c. *printenv*

    d. *let -all*

16. Which of the following are valid expressions? (Choose all that apply.)

    a. *let x=5*9*

    b. *let x=y+10*

    c. *let m=12/4*

    d. *let r=128-80*

17. When you type *for wood maple spruce oak pine* at the command line and then press Enter, what should you type next at the > prompt?

    a. *do*

    b. *go*

    c. *fi*

    d. *term*

18. You want to store a long listing of your files in a variable called myfiles. Which of the following commands enables you to do this?

    a. *let ls -l=myfiles*

    b. *echo ls -l > myfiles*

    c. *myfiles=' ls -l'*

    d. *let ls -l > myfiles*

19. What error is in the following script code?

    ```
    case "selection" in
    " i ") ./listscript ;;
    " ii ") ./numberscript ;;
    " iii ") ./findscript ;;
    esac
    ```

    a. All references to ;; should be replaced with a back quote.

    b. There should be a dollar sign in front of selection, as in "$selection"

    c. There should be no double quote marks in the code.

    d. The code must end with the statement, "out".

20. You are working with a colleague on a script called value that updates several files. You want to test the script, but not update the files. Which of the following commands can you use?

    a. *test -noupdate value*

    b. *trap -u value*

    c. *set -u value*

    d. *sh -n value*

21. You only have to enter the name of a script to have it run, such as entering *myscript*. What setting enables you to do this?

    a. You have set the SCRIPT environment variable to 1 instead of the default 0.

    b. Right after you logged in you entered *setup scripts*.

    c. The first line in your scripts is always *run*, which enables scripts to be run in this way.

    d. You have placed the directory from which you run the scripts in your PATH variable.

22. What would you expect to find in the HOME environment variable?

23. What is the difference between a compiler and an interpreter?

24. What command would you use to place the cursor in row 10 and column 15 on the screen or in a terminal window?

25. What is the purpose of a login script?

HANDS-ON PROJECTS

Complete these projects using the command line, such as from a terminal window, and log in using your own account and home directory.

Project 6-1

6

Before setting one or more environment variables, it is a good idea to view their current configurations. In this project, you use the *printenv* command to view a list of your environment variables.

To see a list of your environment variables:

1. Your list of environment variables might be longer than the default screen or terminal window size, so it can be helpful to pipe the output into the *more* command. Type **printenv | more** and press **Enter**.

2. Record some examples of environment variables. Press the **spacebar** to advance through the listing one screen at a time.

3. Type **clear** and press **Enter** to clear the screen.

4. Next, use the *printenv* command to view the contents of two variables: SHELL and PATH. Type **printenv SHELL PATH** and press **Enter**. (See Figure 6-5.)

5. Type **clear** and press **Enter** to clear the screen for the next project.

Project 6-2

This project enables you to use the defining and evaluating operators to learn how they work. You begin by assigning a value to a variable and then view the contents of the variable you assigned. You then learn how to assign a variable that contains spaces, and you compare using single and double quotation marks to evaluate the contents of a variable. Finally, you use the back quote marks to execute a command and store the result in a variable.

To create a variable, and assign it a value:

1. Type **DOG=Shepherd** and press **Enter**.

   You've created the variable DOG and set its value to Shepherd.

To see the contents of a variable:

1. Type **echo DOG** and press **Enter**.

   You see the word "DOG."

2. To see the contents of the DOG variable, you must precede the name of the variable with a $ operator. Type **echo $DOG** and press **Enter**. You see the word "Shepherd." (See Figure 6-6.)

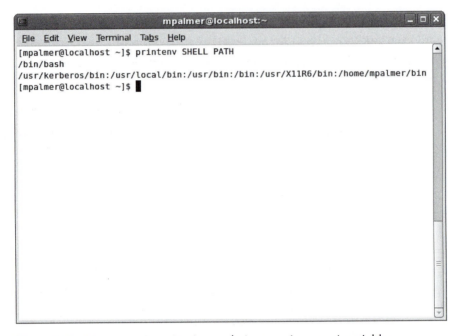

Figure 6-5   Using *printenv* to view only two environment variables

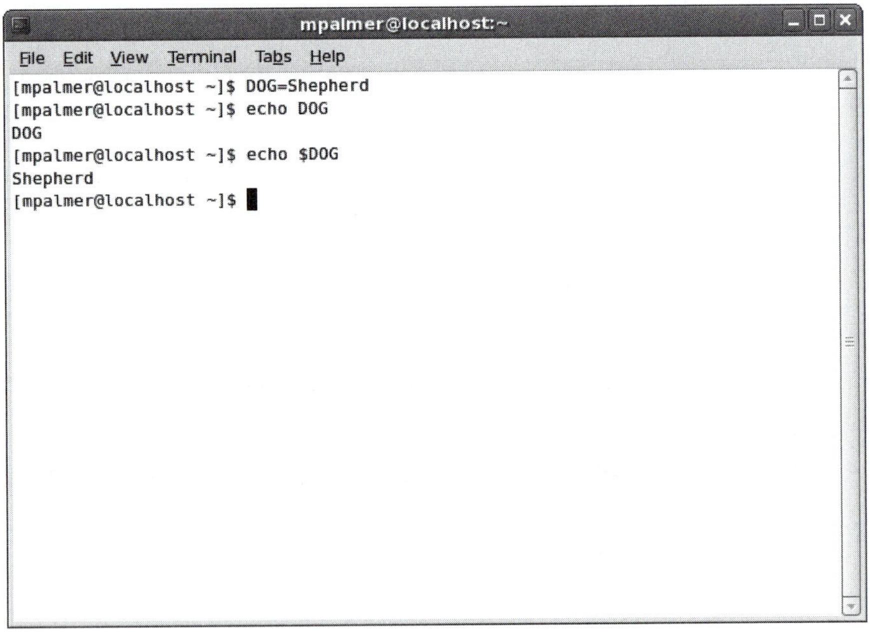

Figure 6-6   Viewing the contents of a variable

To use double quotation marks to set a variable to a string of characters containing spaces:

1. Type **MEMO="Meeting will be at noon today"** and press **Enter**.

2. Type **echo $MEMO** and press **Enter**.

   You see the contents of the MEMO variable: Meeting will be at noon today.

To demonstrate how double quotation marks do not suppress the viewing of a variable's contents, but single quotation marks do suppress the viewing:

1. Type **echo '$HOME'** and press **Enter**.

   You see $HOME on the screen.

2. Type **echo "$HOME"** and press **Enter**.

   You see the path of your home directory on the screen.

To demonstrate the back quote operator for executing a command:

1. Type **TODAY=`date`** and press **Enter**. This command creates the variable TODAY, executes the *date* command, and stores the output of the *date* command in the variable TODAY. (No output appears on the screen.)

2. Type **echo $TODAY** and press **Enter**. You see the output of the *date* command that was executed in Step 1.

3. Type **clear** and press **Enter** to clear the screen for the next project.

Project 6-3

In this project, you employ the *let* command to practice using arithmetic operators to set the contents of a shell variable. First, you use an expression with constants (no variables), and then you use an expression containing a variable.

To practice using the arithmetic operators:

1. Type **let X=10+2*7** and press **Enter**.

2. Type **echo $X** and press **Enter**. You see 24 on the screen.

3. Type **let Y=X+2*4** and press **Enter**.

4. Type **echo $Y** and press **Enter**. You see 32 on the screen, as shown in Figure 6-7.

5. Type **clear** and press **Enter** to clear the screen for the next project.

Project 6-4

In this project, you export a shell variable to make it globally recognized.

To demonstrate the use of the *export* command:

1. Type **cat > testscript** and press **Enter**.

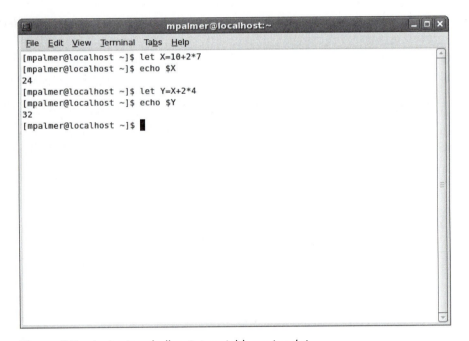

Figure 6-7 Assigning shell script variables using *let*

2. Type **echo $MY_VAR** and press **Enter**.

3. Type **Ctrl+d**. You have created a simple shell script named testscript. Its only function is to display the value of the MY_VAR variable.

4. To make the script executable, type **chmod ugo+x testscript**, and press **Enter**.

5. Type **MY_VAR=2**, and press **Enter**.

6. Type **echo $MY_VAR** and press **Enter** to confirm the preceding operation. You see 2 on the screen.

7. Next look at the list of environment variables. Type **printenv | more** and press **Enter**.

   Look carefully as you scroll through the output of the *printenv* command. You do not see the MY_VAR variable.

8. Type **clear** and press **Enter** to clear the screen.

9. Execute the shell script by typing **./testscript** and pressing **Enter**. The script displays a blank line. This is because it does not have access to the shell variable MY_VAR.

10. Make the variable available to the script by typing **export MY_VAR** and pressing **Enter**.

11. Execute the script again by typing **./testscript** and pressing **Enter**. This time, the value 2 appears. (See Figure 6-8 on the next page.)

12. Now look at your list of environment variables by typing **printenv | more** and pressing **Enter**. Again, look carefully as you scroll through the list. This time, you see MY_VAR listed.

13. Type **clear** and press **Enter** to clear the screen for the next project.

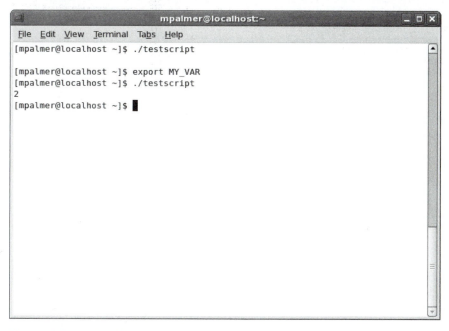

Figure 6-8 Using the *export* command

Project 6-5

In Hands-on Project 6-4, you had to use ./ before testscript because your current working directory is not in your PATH environment variable. In this project, you view the contents of the PATH variable. Next, you add the current working directory to the PATH variable and run testscript without using the ./ characters.

To see the contents of the PATH variable:

1. Type **echo $PATH** and press **Enter**.

   You see a list of directories. Notice that the path names are separated by colons (:).

To add the current working directory to the PATH variable:

1. Type **PATH=$PATH:.** and press **Enter**.

2. Type **echo $PATH** and press **Enter**. The dot (.) is now appended to the list.

3. You can now run scripts in your current working directory without typing the ./
characters before their names. Test this by typing **testscript** and pressing **Enter**. You
see testscript execute, as in Figure 6-9.

```
mpalmer@localhost:~
File  Edit  View  Terminal  Tabs  Help
[mpalmer@localhost ~]$ echo $PATH
/usr/kerberos/bin:/usr/local/bin:/usr/bin:/bin:/usr/X11R6/bin:/home/mpalmer/bin
[mpalmer@localhost ~]$ PATH=$PATH:.
[mpalmer@localhost ~]$ echo $PATH
/usr/kerberos/bin:/usr/local/bin:/usr/bin:/bin:/usr/X11R6/bin:/home/mpalmer/bin:
.
[mpalmer@localhost ~]$ testscript
2
[mpalmer@localhost ~]$ █
```

Figure 6-9   Adding your current working directory to the PATH variable to run shell scripts

Project 6-6

In this project, you gain further experience in writing a very simple shell script using
sequential logic. In these steps, you create the shell script, seqtotal.

To demonstrate sequential logic:

1. Type **vi seqtotal** and press **Enter**.

2. Type **i** to switch to vi's insert mode.

3. Type the following lines:

```
let a=1
let b=2
let c=3
let total=a+b+c
echo $total
```

4. Press **Esc** to switch to vi's command mode.

5. Type **:x** and press **Enter** to save the file and exit vi.

6. Next test the new shell script, seqtotal. (To save a few keystrokes, use the *sh* command instead of the *chmod* command.) Type **sh seqtotal** and press **Enter**.

You see the output of the script, which is 6.

Project 6-7

This project provides your first introduction to using an *if* statement in a shell script and demonstrates decision logic. In the first set of steps, you create a script using a basic *if* statement. Then, in the second set of steps, you modify your script to include an *if* statement nested within an *if* statement.

6

To demonstrate the *if* statement as well as to implement decision logic:

1. Type **vi veg_choice** and press **Enter**.

2. Type **i** to switch to vi's insert mode.

3. Type the following lines:

```
echo -n "What is your favorite vegetable? "
read veg_name
if [ "$veg_name" = "broccoli" ]
then
    echo "Broccoli is a healthy choice."
else
    echo "Don't forget to eat your broccoli also."
fi
```

4. Be certain your editing session looks like the one in Figure 6-10. Press **Esc** to switch to vi's command mode.

5. Type **:x** and press **Enter** to save the file and exit vi.

6. Make the script executable by typing **chmod ugo+x veg_choice** and pressing **Enter**. Next, run the script by typing **./veg_choice** and pressing **Enter** (if you are continuing the same terminal session from Hands-on Project 6-5, you don't need to type "./", because the PATH environment variable stil contains the current working directory.)

7. When asked to enter the name of your favorite vegetable, answer **broccoli**.

8. Run the script again and respond with **corn** or some other vegetable name.

TIP

Remember that you must use the *chmod* command first to make the script executable. Then, after the command prompt, type the path to the script plus the script's name to execute it. Another way to run the script is to use the *sh* command, as you did with the seqtotal script. Yet a third alternative after you use the *chmod* command is to add your current working directory to your path, as you learned in Hands-on Project 6-5. Then, you just enter the name of your script to run it.

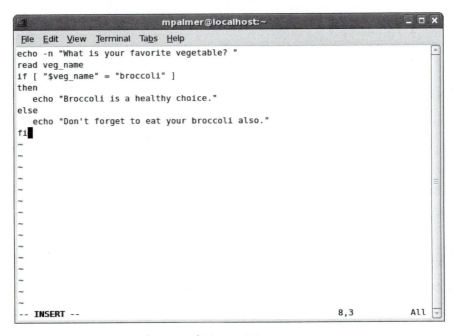

Figure 6-10 Creating the veg_choice script

To practice writing a nested *if* statement:

1. Open the veg_choice file in vi or Emacs.

2. Edit the file so it contains the following lines. (Code has been added to the *else* part of the original *if* statement. See the lines in bold.)

```
echo -n "What is your favorite vegetable? "
read veg_name
if [ "$veg_name" = "broccoli" ]
then
    echo "Broccoli is a healthy choice."
else
    if [ "$veg_name" = "carrots" ]
    then
        echo "Carrots are great for you."
         else
        echo "Don't forget to eat your broccoli also."
    fi
fi
```

3. Execute the script and respond with **carrots** when asked for your favorite vegetable. You should see the response "Carrots are great for you."

4. Type **clear** and press **Enter** to clear the screen for the next project.

Project 6-8

In this project, you learn to use a *for* loop in a shell script and on the command line, both demonstrating how looping logic works.

To demonstrate looping logic in a shell script:

1. Create the file our_users with vi or Emacs.

2. Type the following lines into the file:

```
for USERS in john ellen tom becky eli jill
do
    echo $USERS
done
```

3. Save the file and exit the editor.

4. Give the file execute permission, and run it. Your results should look similar to those shown in Figure 6-11.

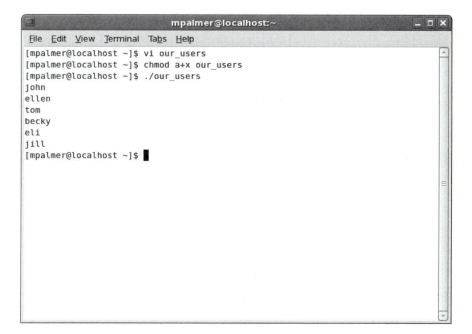

Figure 6-11   Running the our_users script to execute a sample *for* loop

To demonstrate entering the same *for* loop at the command line:

1. At the command line, enter **for USERS in john ellen tom becky eli jill** and press **Enter**.

2. At the > prompt, type **do** and press **Enter**.

3. Type **echo $USERS** and press **Enter**.

4. Type **done** and press **Enter**. What do you see on the screen?

5. Type **clear** and press **Enter** to clear the screen for the next project.

Project 6-9

In this project, you create a *for* loop and use the brackets wildcard format to loop through each element in a *for* statement, which consists of simulated book chapters. You first create the files chap1 through chap4. Next, you create a script that displays the contents of each file using the *more* command.

To create the sample chapter file and use wildcards in a *for* loop:

1. Type **cat > chap1** and press **Enter**.

2. Type **This is chapter 1** and press **Enter**.

3. Type **Ctrl+d**. The file chap1 is created.

4. Type **cat > chap2** and press **Enter**.

5. Type **This is chapter 2** and press **Enter**.

6. Type **Ctrl+d**. The file chap2 is created.

7. Type **cat > chap3** and press **Enter**.

8. Type **This is chapter 3** and press **Enter**.

9. Type **Ctrl+d**. The file chap3 is created.

10. Type **cat > chap4** and press **Enter**.

11. Type **This is chapter 4** and press **Enter**.

12. Type **Ctrl+d**. The file chap4 is created.

13. Use the vi or Emacs editor to create the shell script, chapters. The script should have these lines:

```
for file in chap[1234]; do
    more $file
done
```

14. Save the file and exit the editor.

15. Give the file execute permission, and test it. You see output similar to Figure 6-12.

Project 6-10

The *while* statement is another example of looping logic in addition to the *for* statement. In this project, you first create a shell program that contains a basic *while* statement. Next, you create a shell program as might be used for an onscreen data input form to store name and address information in a flat data file.

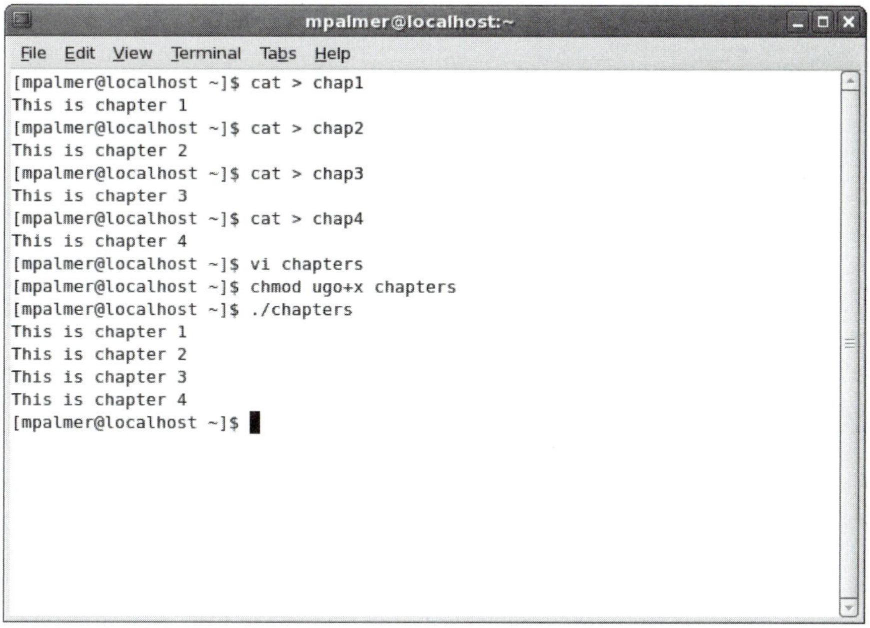

```
mpalmer@localhost:~
File  Edit  View  Terminal  Tabs  Help
[mpalmer@localhost ~]$ cat > chap1
This is chapter 1
[mpalmer@localhost ~]$ cat > chap2
This is chapter 2
[mpalmer@localhost ~]$ cat > chap3
This is chapter 3
[mpalmer@localhost ~]$ cat > chap4
This is chapter 4
[mpalmer@localhost ~]$ vi chapters
[mpalmer@localhost ~]$ chmod ugo+x chapters
[mpalmer@localhost ~]$ ./chapters
This is chapter 1
This is chapter 2
This is chapter 3
This is chapter 4
[mpalmer@localhost ~]$ █
```

6

Figure 6-12 Executing the chapters shell script

To use a basic *while* statement in a shell script:

1. Use the vi or Emacs editor to create a shell script called colors.

2. Enter the following lines of code:

```
echo -n "Try to guess my favorite color:  "
read guess
while [ "$guess" != "red" ]; do
 echo "No, not that one. Try again. "; read guess
done
```

3. Save the file and exit the editor.

4. Give the file execute permission, and test it. Type **clear** and press **Enter** to clear the screen.

Another example of the *while* statement is a data-entry form.

To create a *while* loop that serves as a data-entry form:

1. Use vi or Emacs to create a script file, nameaddr.

2. Type these lines into the file:

```
looptest=y
 while [ "$looptest" = y ]
  do
   echo -n "Enter Name: "; read name
```

```
      echo -n "Enter Street: "; read street
      echo -n "Enter City: "; read city
      echo -n "Enter State: "; read state
      echo -n "Enter Zip Code: "; read zip
      echo -n "Continue? (y)es or (n)o: "; read looptest
   done
```

3. Save the file and exit the editor.

4. Give the file execute permission, and test it. As you test the script, enter several names and addresses. When you finish, answer **n** (for no) when the script asks you, "Continue? (y)es or (n)o." (See Figure 6-13.) Type **clear** and press **Enter** to clear the screen for the next project.

```
                                    mpalmer@localhost:~                         _ □ ✕
 File  Edit  View  Terminal  Tabs  Help
 [mpalmer@localhost ~]$ vi nameaddr
 [mpalmer@localhost ~]$ chmod a+x nameaddr
 [mpalmer@localhost ~]$ ./nameaddr
 Enter Name: Sara Lopez
 Enter Street: 142 North Main Street
 Enter City: Hanover
 Enter State: NC
 Enter Zip Code: 28766
 Continue? (y)es or (n)o: y
 Enter Name: Jim Mason
 Enter Street: 722 Rutgers Lane
 Enter City: Asheville
 Enter State: NC
 Enter Zip Code: 28801
 Continue? (y)es or (n)o: n
 [mpalmer@localhost ~]$ ▮
```

Figure 6-13   Using the nameaddr script

HANDS-ON PROJECTS

Project 6-11

Case logic is often used when many choices are given through a program or when many responses can be made on the basis of one choice. In this project, you create a shell script that employs case logic to respond to your favorite color (many possible responses selected on the basis of one choice).

To demonstrate case logic:

1. Use the vi or Emacs editor to create the manycolors shell script.

   Type these lines into the file:

```
echo -n "Enter your favorite color: "; read color
 case "$color" in
   "blue")  echo "As in My Blue Heaven.";;
   "yellow") echo "As in the Yellow Sunset.";;
   "red")   echo "As in Red Rover, Red Rover.";;
   "orange") echo "As in Autumn has shades of Orange.";;
   *    ) echo "Sorry, I do not know that color.";;
 esac
```

2. Save the file and exit the editor

3. Give the file execute permission, and test it. (See Figure 6-14.)

```
mpalmer@localhost:~
File  Edit  View  Terminal  Tabs  Help
[mpalmer@localhost ~]$ vi manycolors
[mpalmer@localhost ~]$ chmod ugo+x manycolors
[mpalmer@localhost ~]$ ./manycolors
Enter your favorite color: blue
As in My Blue Heaven.
[mpalmer@localhost ~]$ ./manycolors
Enter your favorite color: yellow
As in the Yellow Sunset.
[mpalmer@localhost ~]$ ./manycolors
Enter your favorite color: orange
As in Autumn has shades of Orange.
[mpalmer@localhost ~]$ ./manycolors
Enter your favorite color: red
As in Red Rover, Red Rover.
[mpalmer@localhost ~]$ ./manycolors
Enter your favorite color: green
Sorry, I do not know that color.
[mpalmer@localhost ~]$ █
```

Figure 6-14   Using the manycolors shell script

Project 6-12

The *tput* command enables you to initialize the screen and position the cursor and text in an appealing way. This project introduces you to *tput*. First, you enter the command directly from the command line. Next, you create a sample shell script and menu to understand more about this command's capabilities.

To use *tput* directly from the command line:

1. Type the following command sequence, and press **Enter**:

```
tput clear ; tput cup 10 15 ; echo "Hello" ; tput cup 20 0
```

In the results of this command sequence, the screen clears; the cursor is positioned at row 10, column 15, on the screen; the word "Hello" is printed; and the prompt's position is row 20, column 0.

To create a sample input menu in a shell script:

1. Use the vi or Emacs editor to create a screen-management script, scrmanage, containing the following lines:

```
tput cup $1 $2  # place cursor on row and col
tput clear    # clear the screen
bold=`tput smso` # set stand-out mode - bold
offbold=`tput rmso` # reset screen - turn bold off
echo $bold      # turn bold on
tput cup 10 20; echo "Type Last Name:" # bold caption
tput cup 12 20; echo "Type First Name:" # bold caption
echo $offbold   # turn bold off
tput cup 10 41; read lastname # enter last name
tput cup 12 41; read firstname # enter first name
```

2. Save the file and exit the editor.

3. Give the file execute permission, and then test it. (See Figure 6-15.) Clear the screen for the next project.

TIP   The single back quotes around `tput smso` and `tput rmso` must be in the direction as shown or the bold/unbold command does not work. This single back quote mark is found in the upper-left corner of most keyboards, usually on the same key as the tilde (~).

HANDS-ON PROJECTS

Project 6-13

In this project, you first compare the use of the *sh -v* and *sh -x* options in terms of the output to the screen. Next, you practice debugging a shell script using *sh -v*.

To compare the results of the *sh -v* and *sh -x* options to debug a script:

1. Type **sh -v colors** (remember that colors is the script you created earlier in this chapter in which the favorite color is red), and press **Enter**.

2. Type **green** and press **Enter**.

3. Type **red** and press **Enter**. Notice that the command lines are printed.

4. Type **sh -x colors** and press **Enter**.

5. Type **green** and press **Enter**.

6. Type **red** and press **Enter**. Now, the command lines and arguments are displayed with a plus in front of them. Figure 6-16 illustrates the output of the *sh -v* and *sh -x* options.

Figure 6-15   Using *tput* in a script to produce a simple menu

```
[mpalmer@localhost ~]$ sh -v colors
echo -n "Try to guess my favorite color: "
Try to guess my favorite color: read guess
green
while [ "$guess" != "red" ] ; do
    echo "No, not that one. Try again. "; read guess
done
No, not that one. Try again.
red
[mpalmer@localhost ~]$ sh -x colors
+ echo -n 'Try to guess my favorite color: '
Try to guess my favorite color: + read guess
green
+ '[' green '!=' red ']'
+ echo 'No, not that one. Try again. '
No, not that one. Try again.
+ read guess
red
+ '[' red '!=' red ']'
[mpalmer@localhost ~]$
```

Figure 6-16   Comparing *sh -v* and *sh -x* for debugging

To practice debugging a shell script:

1. Use the vi or Emacs editor to open the colors script for editing.

2. Go to the third line and delete the closing (right) bracket (]) after "red" and then exit, saving your change.

3. Type **sh –v colors** and press **Enter**.

4. Type **green** and press **Enter**. In the final line of output, you'll see a note that shows the closing bracket is missing on line 3 of the colors script:

   ```
   colors: line 3: [: missing ']'
   ```

5. Use vi or Emacs to open the colors script and put the missing closing bracket back in.

6. Delete the **echo** command (only the word echo and not the entire command line) on the fourth line of the colors script. Close the editor and save your work.

7. Type **sh –x colors** and press **Enter**.

8. Type **green** and press **Enter**. Notice in the message that a command is missing on line 4:

   ```
   colors: line 4: No, not that one try again. : command
    not found
   ```

9. Type **red** and press **Enter** to exit the script, or press **Ctrl+z** to exit.

10. Open the colors script using the vi or Emacs editor, retype the **echo** command on line 4, and close and save your work.

Project 6-14

In this project, students learn how to create an alias.

To create an alias:

1. To create an alias called *ll* for the *ls* command, type **alias ll="ls –l"**, and press **Enter**. Now, when you use the new *ll* alias, the *ls -l* command executes automatically.

2. Test the alias by typing **ll** and pressing **Enter**. You see a long directory listing.

Project 6-15

This project is the first in a series of projects to develop a sample application that tracks telephone number and other information for employees in an organization. In this project, you first ensure that you have a source subdirectory in which to store the source files you develop. Next, you create the initial menu that users see when they execute the application. Be certain you retain the phmenu script file that you create here so you can use it in later projects.

To set up your source subdirectory:

1. In Chapter 4, you created a source subdirectory under your home directory. With your home directory as your current working directory (type **cd** and press **Enter**), type **ls** and press **Enter** to ensure that your source subdirectory exists. If it does not exist, type **mkdir source**, and press **Enter**.

2. Type **cd source** and press **Enter** to make the source directory your current working directory. Be certain you are in your source directory for all of the projects that follow in this chapter. In this way, you ensure that your application files are in one place.

To begin work on the menu for your application:

1. Use the vi or Emacs editor to enter the phmenu script shown next.

```
#============================================================
# Script Name:      phmenu
# By:               Your initials here
# Date:             Today's date
# Purpose:          A menu for the Corporate Phone List
# Command Line:     phmenu
#============================================================
loop=y
while [ "$loop" = y ]
do
 clear
 tput cup 3 12; echo "Corporate Phone Reporting Menu"
 tput cup 4 12; echo "=============================="
 tput cup 6 9; echo "P - Print Phone List"
 tput cup 7 9; echo "A - Add New Phones"
 tput cup 8 9; echo "S - Search for Phones"
 tput cup 10 9; echo "Q - Quit: "
 tput cup 10 19;
 read choice || continue
done
```

2. Save the file and exit the editor.

3. Give the file execute permission by typing **chmod a+x phmenu** and pressing **Enter**. Next, test the script by typing **./phmenu** and pressing **Enter**. (See Figure 6-17.) (You have to press **Ctrl+c** to exit the script because the Quit option has not yet been programmed.)

4. Clear the screen for the next project.

HANDS-ON PROJECTS

Project 6-16

The data file that you use for your telephone number application is called corp_phones. In this project, you ensure that the corp_phones file is created and contains some preliminary

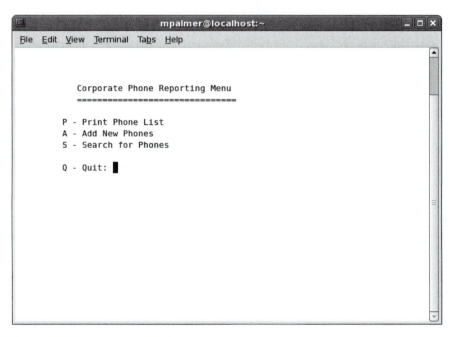

Figure 6-17 Running the phmenu script

data that is useful for testing your application as you continue to develop it. You also practice extracting information from the file by using the *grep* command.

To create the corp_phones file:

1. In Chapter 4, you created the corp_phones, corp_phones1, and corp_phones2 files in your home directory and performed projects to manipulate and alter data in those files. If those files are still in your home directory, use the **rm** command to delete them. This ensures two things: that the corp_phones file you create next has the proper information for using your new telephone number application, and that you know what is in the corp_phones file for the projects you complete in this chapter. Toward that end, some of the data you now enter is slightly different than what you used in the files you created in Chapter 4.

2. If you are in your home directory, type **cd source**, and press **Enter**. Use the **pwd** command to ensure you are in the source directory.

3. Use the vi or Emacs editor to create the corp_phones file.

4. Enter the following records in the file:

```
219-555-4567:Harrison:Joel:M:4540:Accountant:09-12-1985
219-555-4587:Mitchell:Barbara:C:4541:Admin Asst:12-14-1995
219-555-4589:Olson:Timothy:H:4544:Supervisor:06-30-1983
219-555-4591:Moore:Sarah:H:4500:Dept Manager:08-01-1978
219-555-4544:Polk:John:S:4520:Accountant:09-22-2001
219-555-4501:Robinson:Albert:J:4501:Secretary:08-12-1997
```

5. Save the file and exit the editor.

6. Type **grep 219-555-4591 corp_phones** and press **Enter** to search for a specific telephone number.

The output should look like this:

```
219-555-4591:Moore:Sarah:H:4500:Dept Manager:08-01-1978
```

7. Type **grep Accountant corp_phones** and press **Enter** to search the file for all accountants. (See Figure 6-18.)

```
                        mpalmer@localhost:~/source                     _ □ x

 File  Edit  View  Terminal  Tabs  Help
[mpalmer@localhost ~]$ cd source
[mpalmer@localhost source]$ pwd
/home/mpalmer/source
[mpalmer@localhost source]$ vi corp_phones
[mpalmer@localhost source]$ grep 219-555-4591 corp_phones
219-555-4591:Moore:Sarah:H:4500:Dept Manager:08-01-1978
[mpalmer@localhost source]$ grep Accountant corp_phones
219-555-4567:Harrison:Joel:M:4540:Accountant:09-12-1985
219-555-4544:Polk:John:S:4520:Accountant:09-22-2001
[mpalmer@localhost source]$ █
```

Figure 6-18   Working with the corp_phones data file

Project 6-17

The phmenu menu script that you created and tested in Hands-on Project 6-15 still needs some work, because it doesn't contain a way to call applications after they are selected. In this project, you solve this problem by adding case logic to the menu.

To make additions to the phone menu script:

1. If you have interrupted your development process and have just logged back in or switched to another directory, change to the source directory and use the *pwd* command to verify you are in that directory.

2. Use the vi or Emacs editor to open the phmenu file in your source directory. In the following lines, add the lines that are boldfaced to the script:

```
#=======================================================
```

```
# Script Name:         phmenu
# By:                  Your initials here
# Date:                November 2009
# Purpose:             A menu for the Corporate Phone List
# Command Line:        phmenu
#===========================================================
phonefile=~/source/corp_phones
loop=y
while [ "$loop" = y ]
do
  clear
  tput cup 3 12; echo "Corporate Phone Reporting Menu"
  tput cup 4 12; echo "=============================="
  tput cup 6 9; echo "P - Print Phone List"
  tput cup 7 9; echo "A - Add New Phones"
  tput cup 8 9; echo "S - Search for Phones"
  tput cup 10 9; echo "Q - Quit: "
  tput cup 10 19;
  read choice || continue
    case $choice in
      [Aa]) ./phoneadd ;;
      [Pp]) ./phlist1 ;;
      [Ss]) ./phonefind ;;
      [Qq]) exit ;;
      *) tput cup 14 4; echo "Invalid Code"; read choice ;;
    esac
done
```

3. Save the file and exit the editor.

4. Test the script. (Acceptable entries are A, a, P, p, S, s, V, v, Q, and q. Any other entries cause the message "Invalid Code" to appear.) Type **Ctrl+c** to exit when you are finished testing.

HANDS-ON PROJECTS

Project 6-18

It can be useful to have a way to display unformatted file data, in such a display the records appear exactly as they are stored in the data file. This enables the application developer to ensure that records are accurate and that the application is working as expected. Also, some users might be interested in viewing the raw data in a file, so they can ensure it is accurately entered. In this project, you add an option in phmenu to use the *less* command to view the contents of the corp_phones file.

To use the *less* command to view unformatted records:

1. Be certain you are in the source directory. Next, open phmenu in the editor of your choice, and add the two boldfaced lines shown below:

```
#===========================================================
# Script Name:         phmenu
```

```
# By:               Your initials here
# Date:             Today's date
# Purpose:          A menu for the Corporate Phone List
# Command Line:     phmenu
#============================================================
phonefile=~/source/corp_phones
loop=y
while [ "$loop" = y ]
do
  clear
  tput cup 3 12; echo "Corporate Phone Reporting Menu"
  tput cup 4 12; echo "=============================="
  tput cup 6 9; echo "P - Print Phone List"
  tput cup 7 9; echo "A - Add New Phones"
  tput cup 8 9; echo "S - Search for Phones"
  tput cup 9 9; echo "V - View Phone List"
  tput cup 10 9; echo "Q - Quit: "
  tput cup 10 19;
  read choice || continue
     case $choice in
       [Aa]) ./phoneadd ;;
       [Pp]) ./phlist1 ;;
       [Ss]) ./phonefind ;;
       [Vv]) less $phonefile ;;
       [Qq]) exit ;;
       *) tput cup 14 4; echo "Invalid Code"; read choice ;;
     esac
done
```

2. Save the file and exit the editor.

3. Test the script.

HANDS-ON PROJECTS

Project 6-19

In your menu design, when users enter P or p, the application should print a phone list. The *awk* program offers a good example of how the UNIX/Linux shell programmer can accelerate development because a single *awk* command can select fields from many records and display them in a specified format on the screen. In this project, you develop the phlist1 script and use *awk* to display a phone list.

To create the phlist1 script:

1. From the source directory, use the editor of your choice to create the phlist1 script as follows:

```
# ============================================================
# Script Name:   phlist1
# By:            Your initials here
# Date:          Today's date
# Purpose:       Use awk to format colon-separated fields
```

```
#                    in a flat file and display to the screen
# Command Line:    phlist1
# ============================================================
clear
tput cup 2 20; echo "Corporate Phone List"
tput cup 3 20; echo "===================="
tput cup 5 0;
awk -F: '{printf "%-12s %-12s %s\t%s %s %10.10s %s\n", $2, $3,
  $4, $1, $5, $6, $7}' corp_phones
```

2. Save the file and exit the editor.

3. Give the file execute permission by typing **chmod a+x phlist1** and pressing **Enter**. Run the script by typing **./phlist1** and pressing **Enter**. (See Figure 6-19.)

```
                    mpalmer@localhost:~/source
 File  Edit  View  Terminal  Tabs  Help

                   Corporate Phone List
                   ====================

Harrison    Joel         M     219-555-4567 4540 Accountant 09-12-1985
Mitchell    Barbara      C     219-555-4587 4541 Admin Asst 12-14-1995
Olson       Timothy      H     219-555-4589 4544 Supervisor 06-30-1983
Moore       Sarah        H     219-555-4591 4500 Dept Manag 08-01-1978
Polk        John         S     219-555-4544 4520 Accountant 09-22-2001
Robinson    Albert       J     219-555-4501 4501  Secretary 08-12-1997
[mpalmer@localhost source]$
```

Figure 6-19   Testing the phlist1 script

Project 6-20

Now, you need to develop a way to enter new telephone number information into the corp_phones file so that users can eventually build a complete data file of all employees. Notice that the phmenu script offers the option to add a phone record. To accomplish this, you develop the phoneadd script.

To create the phoneadd script for data entry:

1. Ensure you are in the source directory and then use the vi or Emacs editor to create the script phoneadd. Enter the following code:

```
# ===========================================================
# Script Name:   phoneadd
# By:            Your initials here
# Date:          Today's date
# Purpose:       A shell script that sets up a loop to add
#                new employees to the corp_phones file.
# Command Line:  phoneadd
#
# ===========================================================
trap "rm ~/tmp/* 2> /dev/null; exit" 0 1 2 3
phonefile=~/source/corp_phones
looptest=y
while [ $looptest = y ]
do
  clear
  tput cup 1 4; echo "Corporate Phone List Additions"
  tput cup 2 4; echo "=============================="
  tput cup 4 4; echo "Phone Number: "
  tput cup 5 4; echo "Last Name    : "
  tput cup 6 4; echo "First Name   : "
  tput cup 7 4; echo "Middle Init  : "
  tput cup 8 4; echo "Dept #       : "
  tput cup 9 4; echo "Job Title    : "
  tput cup 10 4; echo "Date Hired   : "
  tput cup 12 4; echo "Add Another? (y)es or (q)uit: "
  tput cup 4 18; read phonenum
  if [ "$phonenum" = "q" ]
        then
            clear; exit
  fi
  tput cup 5 18; read lname
  tput cup 6 18; read fname
  tput cup 7 18; read midinit
  tput cup 8 18; read deptno
  tput cup 9 18; read jobtitle
  tput cup 10 18; read datehired
  # Check to see if last name is not a blank before you
  # write to disk
  if [ "$lname" > "          " ]
  then
  echo "$phonenum:$lname:$fname:$midinit:$deptno:$jobtitle:$datehired" >> $phonefile
  fi
  tput cup 12 33; read looptest
  if [ "$looptest" = "q" ]
```

```
   then
      clear; exit
   fi
done
```

NOTE   Make sure you place the following statement on only one line: echo "$phonenum:$lname:$fname:$midinit:$deptno:$jobtitle:$datehired" >> $phonefile. It is wrapped on two lines here because of space limitations on the page.

2. Save the file and exit the editor. Notice the section that checks to ensure the last name is not blank. (See the comment.) This is included so that incomplete data is not written to the file. In this code, the *if* statement checks to make certain that the lname variable is greater than an empty string (has contents). If lname does have a value (a string), the contents of all of the variables—lname, fname, midinit, deptno, jobtitle, datehired—are written to the phonefile variable (corp_phones) using the *echo* command.

3. Give the file execute permission by typing **chmod a+x phoneadd** and pressing **Enter**.

4. Run the script by typing **./phoneadd** and pressing **Enter**.

5. Next, test the script by adding the following employees. (Press **Enter** after each separate field entry, for example, type 219-555-7175 and press **Enter** to go to the Last Name field.) See Figure 6-20.

```
219-555-7175 Mullins Allen L 7527 Sales Rep 02-19-2007
219-555-7176 Albertson Jeannette K 5547 DC Clerk 02-19-2007
```

6. Press **Ctrl+c** after you enter the data.

You've now created the foundation for the corporate employee telephone number application. However, you still need to address several deficiencies. For example, how can you return to a previous field as you enter the data? What happens when you enter the same employee twice? What happens if you assign a new employee a phone number that has already been assigned to someone else? In Chapter 7, you continue the development process and address these issues.

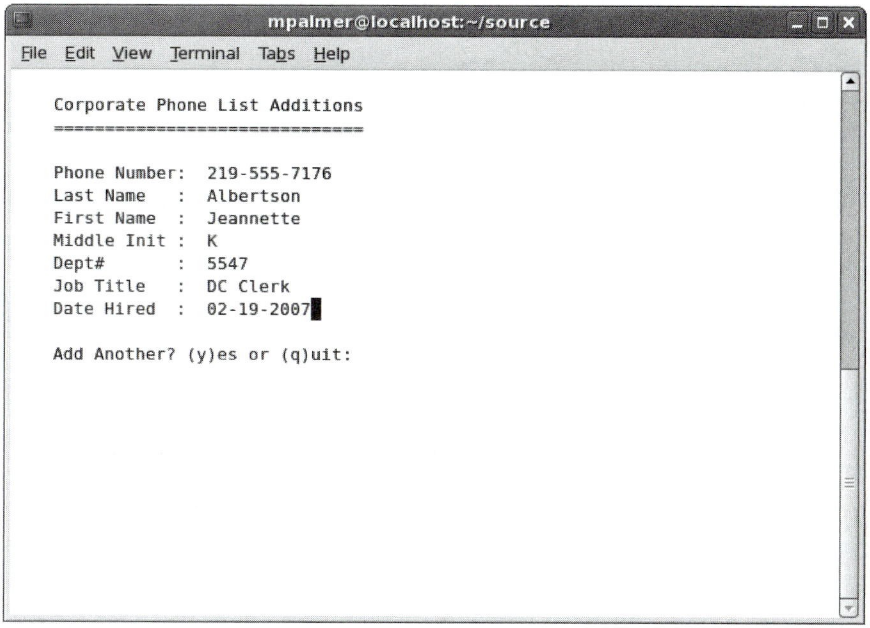

```
                       mpalmer@localhost:~/source
File  Edit  View  Terminal  Tabs  Help

    Corporate Phone List Additions
    ================================

    Phone Number:  219-555-7176
    Last Name   :  Albertson
    First Name  :  Jeannette
    Middle Init :  K
    Dept#       :  5547
    Job Title   :  DC Clerk
    Date Hired  :  02-19-2007█

    Add Another? (y)es or (q)uit:
```

Figure 6-20   Testing the phoneadd script

6

DISCOVERY EXERCISES

1. Use two different commands to display the contents of the *HOME* variable.

2. Assign the variable *t* the value of 20. Next, assign the variable *s* the value of t+30. Finally, display the contents of *t* and s to verify you have correctly defined these variables.

3. Make the *s* variable you assigned in Exercise 2 an environment variable and use the command to verify it is recognized as an environment variable.

4. Switch to your source directory. Display the contents of the PATH variable. Next, use the command to add your current working directory to the PATH variable.

5. After completing Exercise 4, run the phmenu program in the easiest way.

6. Create a variable called *iam* and assign the results of the *whoami* command to it. Display the contents of the variable to verify your results.

7. Change back to your home directory, if you are not in it. Use the *set* command to set up your working environment to prevent you from overwriting a file.

8. Create an alias called *var* that displays your environment variables.

9. At the command line, use a *for* loop that uses the variable *sandwiches* and then displays a line at a time each of the following sandwiches: chicken, ham, hummus, tomato.

10. Create a script that uses case logic to have someone guess your favorite sandwich, such as tuna.

11. Display the contents of the .bashrc file. Next use the vi editor to edit that file and put in an alias so that every time you type *list,* you see a long file listing of a directory.

12. Use a command to simulate how you would troubleshoot a problem with the sandwich script you created in Exercise 10.

13. What is wrong with the following lines of code?

    ```
    While [ "$value" = "100" ; do
         Echo "That's a large number."    Read value
    fi
    ```

14. Use the *let* command to store the value 1024 in the variable *ram.* Display the contents of *ram.*

15. Temporarily change your home directory environment variable to */home* and then use one command to go to your home directory. Change the home directory environment variable back to your regular home directory and switch to it.

16. Use the *tput* command to clear the screen and then to place the cursor in row 7, column 22.

17. Write a script that creates the following menu:

    Soup Menu

    ==========

    (t)omato

    (b)ean

    (s)quash

    Select a soup . . . (q) to quit

18. List all of the signal numbers and designations for the *trap* command. What is the designation for signal 31?

19. Modify your script from Exercise 17 so that there is a beep or bell sound when the menu is ready to take the user's input.(Hint: review the *man* documentation for the *echo* command.)

20. Is there a command that you can use to prevent shell variables from being assigned new values? If so, what is it?

ADVANCED SHELL PROGRAMMING

After reading this chapter and completing the exercises, you will be able to:

- Perform program design and analysis using flowcharts and pseudocode
- Use techniques to ensure a script is employing the correct shell
- Set the default shell
- Configure Bash login and logout scripts
- Set defaults for the vi editor
- Use the *test* command for programming functions
- Format record output
- Delete records using a script
- Set up a quick screen-clearing technique
- Create a program algorithm to solve a cursor-repositioning problem
- Develop and test a program to eliminate duplicate records
- Create shell functions and use them in a program

In the preceding chapter, you learned about the program development cycle and began developing a program to automate the maintenance of employee telephone records in the corp_phones file. You developed a menu that presents several options and a data-entry screen that allows records to be added to the file. In this chapter, you develop more advanced scripts for the employee telephone number application.

You start by learning how to plan algorithms and use flowcharts for program development. Next, you learn to create complex decision expressions with the *test* command. Also, you learn more about how to format output. For the employee telephone number application you create and enhance scripts to add code that deletes a specified record, searches for a record, adds logic to prevent duplicate data entry, and uses functions to sort and display records.

Understanding Program Design and Analysis

In Chapter 6, "Introduction to Shell Script Programming," you learned that the program development cycle begins with creating specifications for a program. Specifications enable you to determine the type of data needed for input, the processes that must be performed, and the output requirements. The next step in the program development cycle is the design process.

In the design process, a computer program is developed by analyzing the best way to achieve the desired results. Two popular and proven analysis tools are used to help you design your programs to meet the program specifications: the flowchart and pseudocode.

Flowcharting

Many organizations map each step of a process as a way to design that process. Consider the example of a corporation that decides to create a new design for the hiring process. The corporation currently has a hiring process that requires many manual operations, and the corporation wants to design a new process to automate functions and make better use of computer resources. In the design phase a committee discusses the new procedures and computer resources they want to use. Next, the committee creates a flowchart to demonstrate what will happen in each step of the process. A **flowchart** is a logic diagram that uses a set of standard symbols to visually explain the sequence of events from the start of a process to its end point.

Organizations use flowcharts to design and document all kinds of processes and procedures. Programmers also use flowcharts to map and understand a program's sequence and each action the program takes. For the programmer the flowchart provides a map through the design process to show what programs and logic must be created. It provides a way of linking what is wanted in the specifications to the program code that is to be written.

Consider, for instance, the favorite vegetable program example in Chapter 6, which is as follows:

```
echo -n "What is your favorite vegetable? "
read veg_name
if [ "$veg_name" = "broccoli" ]
then
   echo "Broccoli is a healthy choice."
else
   echo "Don't forget to eat your broccoli also."
fi
```

Figure 7-1 shows an example flowchart that you might have created prior to developing the program.

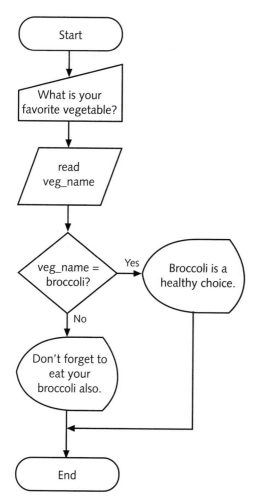

Figure 7-1   Sample flowchart

Each step in the program is represented by a symbol in the flowchart. The shape of the symbol indicates the type of operation being performed, such as input/output or a decision. Figure 7-2 shows standard flowchart symbols and their meanings.

The arrows that connect the symbols represent the direction in which the program flows. In the flowchart in Figure 7-1, the arrow after the Start terminator shows the program flowing to an operation that displays the message (in a manual input flowchart symbol), "What is your favorite vegetable?" Next, the program flows to an input operation (represented by the data symbol for input/output operations) that reads a value into veg_name. A decision structure (represented by a diamond-shaped symbol) is encountered next, and compares the veg_name variable's contents to the string, "broccoli". If the contents of veg_name equals "broccoli," the logic takes the "Yes" branch and displays "Broccoli is a healthy choice." and

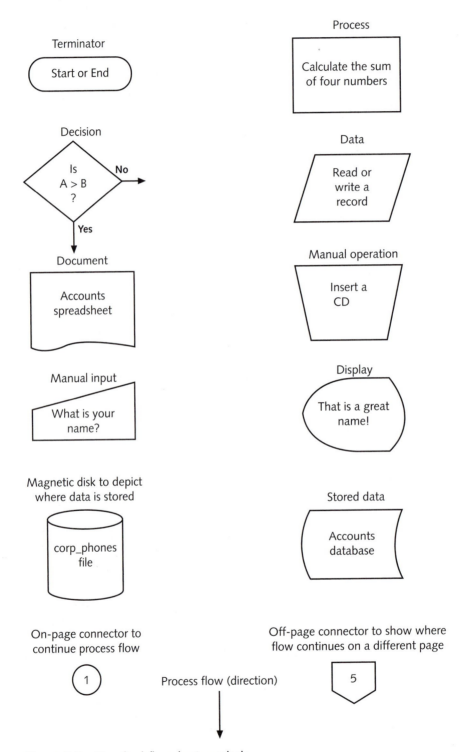

Figure 7-2 Standard flowchart symbols

then the program ends. If veg_name does not equal "broccoli," the program takes the "No" branch and displays "Don't forget to eat your broccoli also." and the program terminates.

You can manually create a flowchart using a drawing template. Flowchart templates provide the symbols that denote logical structures, input-output operations, processing operations, and the storage media that contain the files, as shown in Figure 7-2. Another way to create a flowchart is to use a flowcharting software package, such as ABC Flowcharter, Corel Flow, Microsoft Visio, or SmartDraw. Popular word-processing packages, such as OpenOffice.org Writer (with Dia Diagrams), Microsoft Word, and WordPerfect, are also equipped with flowcharting tools.

TIP You can learn more about flowcharting at these Web sites: *en.wikipedia.org/wiki/Flowchart, www.smartdraw.com/tutorials/flowcharts/tutorial_02.htm,* and *office.microsoft.com/training/training.aspx?AssetID=RC010198841033.*

7

Writing Pseudocode

After creating a flowchart, the next step in designing a program is to write **pseudocode**. Pseudocode instructions are similar to actual programming statements. Use them to create a model that you can later use as a basis for a real program. For example, here are pseudocode statements for the veg_choice program:

```
Display "What is your favorite vegetable? " on the screen
Enter data into veg_name
If veg_name is equal to "broccoli"
Then
     Display "Broccoli is a healthy choice." on the screen
Else
     Display "Don't forget to eat your broccoli also." on the
screen
End If
```

Pseudocode is a design tool only, and is never processed by the computer. Therefore, you have no strict rules to follow. The pseudocode should verbally match the symbolic logic illustrated on the flowchart. For example, Figure 7-3 shows the flowchart and pseudocode that represent a change to the phone number application you developed in Chapter 6, so that data can be reentered in a field to enable a user to go back to a field to correct an error.

In the next sections, you learn how to program the code to achieve the logic in the pseudocode example. Before you work on the program code you learn how to ensure that a script uses the correct shell and you advance your programming skills by learning the versatility of the *test* command.

TIP Many resources are available on the Internet to help you learn more about pseudocode, such as *www.infoweblinks.com/content/pseudocode.htm* and *en.wikipedia.org/wiki/Pseudocode.* Also, you can search for the word "pseudocode" and find many Internet links.

Pseudocode:

```
While entry = minus
    do
        Reposition cursor in previous field
        Enter the data
        Reposition cursor in field following the field that was
            just entered (reentered data)
        Continue testing while loop
    Done
```

Flowchart:

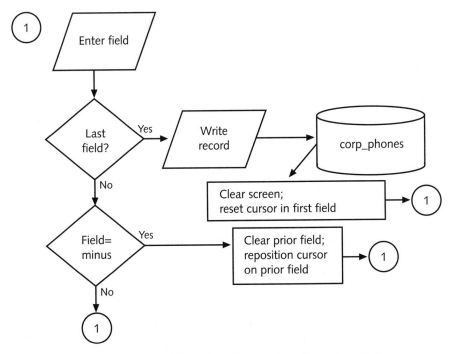

Figure 7-3   Pseudocode and flowchart for reentry of previous fields

ENSURING THE CORRECT SHELL RUNS THE SCRIPT

Each UNIX/Linux user has the freedom to choose which shell he prefers. When developing a shell script, ensure that the correct shell is used to interpret your script, because all shells do not support the same commands and programming statements.

When you create a script, include the command that sets the particular shell to use on the first line of the script. In this book we use the Bash shell. The line in the script for setting the Bash shell is:

```
#!/bin/bash
```

In the line to specify the shell, start with the # character, followed by the ! character and provide the path of the shell, such as /bin/bash for the Bash shell.

When the system reads this code line it loads the Bash shell and uses it to interpret the statements in the script file. Because many shells are provided in UNIX/Linux, you should always begin your scripts with this statement. Even if the user who runs your script is operating in a different shell, this line ensures that the script will run properly.

SETTING THE DEFAULT SHELL

For your own account, the shell that is set up by default is established by the system administrator in the /etc/passwd file. To have a specific shell set when you log in, contact your system administrator. If you are the system administrator, you can set the default shell by editing the line in the /etc/passwd file that pertains to your account. For example, if your account is trbrown, the /etc/passwd entry for your account will be similar to the following:

```
trbrown:x:500:500:Thomas Brown:/home/trbrown:/bin/bash
```

Notice that this is simply a record with variable-length fields separated by colons. The final field in the record specifies the path for the default shell set for the user's account, such as /bin/bash. By logging in as root, you can edit the /etc/passwd file employing the vi or Emacs editor. If you edit the file, consider making a backup copy before you edit it. Also, should you edit the file, *be very careful with the changes that you make*, or you might prevent yourself or someone else from logging in to the system.

Another safer way to set the default shell for an account is to use software that accompanies your system for configuring users and groups. In Fedora and Red Hat Enterprise Linux, for example, you can use the User Manager tool in the GNOME desktop. To change the default shell for your account, use these general steps:

1. Log in as root.

2. Click the System menu, point to Administration, and click Users and Groups.

3. Double-click your account in the listing of accounts.

4. In the User Properties dialog box, change the Login Shell: entry to contain the path to the shell you want as the default, such as /bin/bash (see Figure 7-4). Click OK.

5. Close the User Manager tool.

In openSUSE Linux with the GNOME desktop, you can use the YaST tool to configure users. YaST is a multifunction tool that enables you to manage openSUSE from one location. Here are the steps for using YaST:

1. Log in as root.

2. Click the Computer menu.

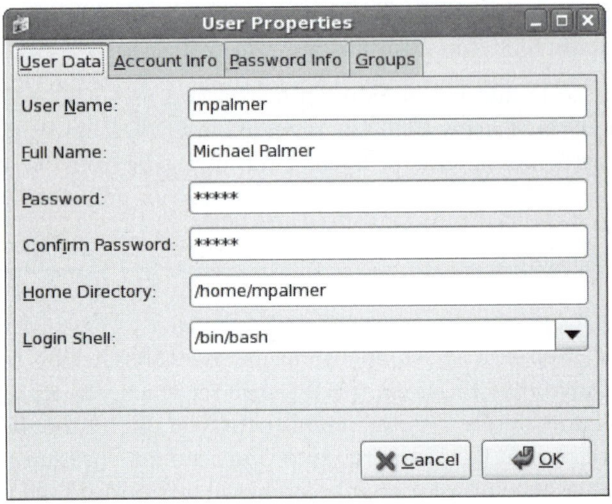

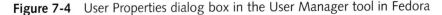

Figure 7-4   User Properties dialog box in the User Manager tool in Fedora

3. Click More Applications.

4. Click System in the left pane.

5. Click YaST (you may need to scroll down to find YaST in the list).

6. Click Security and Users in the left pane.

7. Click User Management.

8. Double-click your account name.

9. Click the Details tab.

10. Change the Login Shell entry to contain the path to the shell you want as the default shell and click Accept.

11. Click Finish.

12. Close the YaST Control Center @ *computername* window.

USING BASH LOGIN AND LOGOUT SCRIPTS

With Bash set as your shell, two scripts run automatically when you log in: .bash_profile and .bashrc. If you change to a different shell after you log in, both scripts also run as soon as you change back to the Bash shell. As you learned in Chapter 6, the .bashrc file is a hidden file contained in your home directory. The same is also true for the .bash_profile file. You can view both files by entering *cd* to ensure you are in your home directory and then entering *ls -a*.

The .bash_profile file is run each time you log in or give the command to set Bash as your current shell. It typically contains settings, such as environment variable settings, aliases, and other settings that you always want in effect when you are in the Bash shell. You can always use the vi or Emacs editor to add or modify settings in this file. Figure 7-5 shows the default .bash_profile file in Fedora.

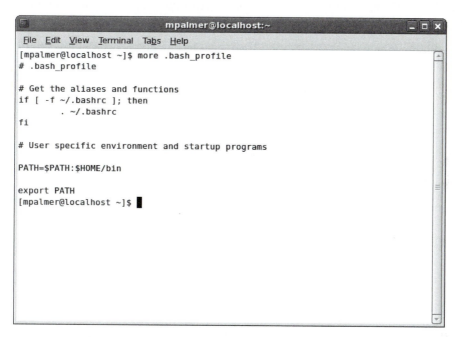

Figure 7-5   .bash_profile script file

 TIP   The .bash_profile script file is used in many UNIX/Linux systems, such as Fedora and Red Hat Enterprise Linux. However, some Linux systems, such as SUSE Linux call this the .profile file, instead.

The .bashrc file also runs when you log in using the Bash shell as the default—and when you go back into the Bash shell after temporarily using a different shell. As with the .bash_profile (or .profile) file, you can configure this file to have environment variables and other settings you want to always be in effect when you are in the Bash shell. The .bashrc file serves an additional purpose that is not shared by the .bash_profile (or .profile) file—the .bashrc file is run each time you start a Bash shell within a Bash shell, which is called running a subshell. You started a subshell, for example, in Chapter 3, "Mastering Editors," when you typed *Ctrl+z* from within the vi editor. In Chapter 3, this Bash shell command took you to the command line (in a subshell), so you could execute a command without closing your vi editing session. When pressing *Ctrl+z* started the subshell in that example, the system also ran the .bashrc script.

UNIX/Linux systems might also have an /etc/.bashrc, /etc/bashrc, or /etc/bash.bashrc file that sets default functions, variables, aliases, and other settings for all Bash shell users. In Fedora and Red Hat Enterprise Linux, two files set Bash shell defaults for all users: /etc/bashrc and /etc/profile. In SUSE these files are /etc/bash.bashrc and /etc/profile. The /etc/bashrc (or /etc/bash.bashrc) file sets default functions and aliases and the /etc/profile file sets default environment variables and startup programs. A system administrator can configure these files so there is a basic level of consistency among Bash shell users.

In addition, a .bash_logout file in each Bash user's home directory executes commands when the user logs out. (SUSE does not have a default .bash_logout file.) For example, this file often contains a line with the *clear* command to clear the terminal or terminal window screen when the user logs out. Another option is to insert an *echo* command to echo specific text to the screen, such as "It has been a pleasure working with you" or "All programs you have used are the property of this company."

Try Hands-On Project 7-1 to view the contents of the .bash_profile, .bashrc, .bash_logout, /etc/bashrc, and /etc/profile files (for Fedora and Red Hat Enterprise Linux, or similar files for SUSE and Knoppix).

Setting Defaults for Using the vi Editor

If you prefer using the vi editor, you have the option of configuring a file called .exrc in your home directory. As you learned in Chapter 3, .exrc can be used to automatically set up your vi environment. For example, if you do much script or other programming, you might want to have vi automatically display line numbers to make it easier to quickly identify a specific line of code that you want to examine or modify. Another possibility is to set the number of tab spaces when you tab to indent or nest lines of code. The following is an example of lines that you might insert when you create or modify the .exrc file:

```
set number
set tabstop=3
set shell=/bin/bash
```

In this example, when you use vi, lines are identified by line number, and when you use the Tab key, it tabs over three spaces. Also, when you start a subshell from within vi (by using the :! vi command or *Ctrl+z*), the shell used is Bash.

Using the test Command

Often when you create a script or other application program, you need to rely on the existence of one or more data files, directories, or both. In another situation, you might need to determine if one file is older than another. In yet other situations, you might need to evaluate two strings or integers. The *test* command can be used for these and several other purposes.

Syntax **test** [-options] [*argument/expression/integer*]

Dissection

- Used to analyze an expression to determine if it is true—often used in shell scripts to verify an environmental condition, such as the existence of a file

- Useful options include:

  -d tests for the existence of a specific directory

  -e tests for the existence of a file

  -r determines if the file has read permission

  -s determines if the file has some type of contents (is not empty)

  -w determines if the file has write permission

  -x determines if the file is executable

  -nt compares the first file in the argument with the second file to determine if the first file is newer

  -ot compares the first file in the argument with the second file to determine if the first file is older

  -eq compares two integers to determine if they are equal

  ! determines if an expression is false

  stringa = stringb determines if two strings are equal

NOTE

Many other options to evaluate strings, expressions, and integers are available; see Tables 7-1, 7-2, 7-3, and 7-4 for more information.

The *test* command uses operators expressed as options to perform the evaluations. Using *test*, you can:

- Perform relational tests with integers (such as equal, greater than, and less than).

- Test strings.

- Determine if a file exists and determine the type of file.

- Perform Boolean tests.

In addition, you can place the *test* command inside your shell script or execute it directly from the command line. For example, if you have the following statement in a script:

```
while [ "$furniture" != "desk" ]; do
```

you can use the *test* command to accomplish the same thing by using the following statement instead:

```
while test $furniture != "desk" ; do
```

In both statements, as long as the *furniture* variable does not equal "desk," the *while* loop continues to process.

In the following sections and in the Hands-On Projects, you learn to use *test* at both the command line and in scripts, as well as perform many different kinds of evaluations of files, directories, strings, integers, and other elements.

Performing Relational Integer Tests with the test Command

The *test* command can determine if one integer is equal to, greater than, less than, greater than or equal to, less than or equal to, or not equal to another integer. Table 7-1 describes the integer options of the *test* command.

Table 7-1   Integer options of the *test* command

Option	Meaning	Example
-eq	Equal to	*test a -eq b*
-gt	Greater than	*test a -gt b*
-lt	Less than (small L and small T)	*test a -lt b*
-ge	Greater than or equal to	*test a -ge b*
-le	Less than or equal to (small L and small E)	*test a -le b*
-ne	Not equal to	*test a -ne b*

The *test* command returns a value known as an exit status. An **exit status** is a numeric value that the command returns to the operating system when it finishes. The value of the *test* command's exit status indicates the results of the test performed. If the exit status is 0 (zero), the test result is true. An exit status of 1 indicates the test result is false.

The exit status is normally detected in a script by the *if* statement or in a looping structure. You can view the most recent command's exit status by typing the command:

```
echo $?
```

Figure 7-6 illustrates a test evaluation in which the exit status is 0 or true.

NOTE

On some systems, you must have the *test* command echo the exit code on the same line as the *test* command, as in the following example:

```
test $name = "Bjorn" ; echo $?.
```

Try Hands-On Project 7-2 to use the *test* command to evaluate integer expressions.

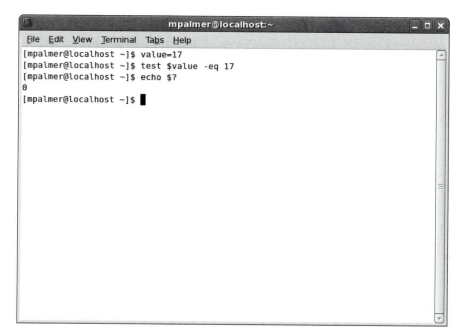

Figure 7-6   Using test to obtain an exit status of 0

Performing String Tests with the test Command

You can use the *test* command to determine if a string has a length of zero characters or a nonzero number of characters. Also, you can test two strings to determine if they are equal or not equal. These tests are useful in scripts to test the contents of variables, for example, to ensure that a variable contains a specific value. Consider a script that is intended to work on a record of an employee whose last name (the contents of the *lname* variable used in the script) is Rossetti. The script can use the *test* command to ensure that *lname* contains Rossetti. If it is not Rossetti, the script might print an error message, signaling that you need to correct an error in the script or in your employee data.

Table 7-2 describes the string testing options of the *test* command.

Table 7-2   String options with the *test* command

Option or Expression	Meaning	Example
-z	Tests for a zero-length string	*test -z string*
-n	Tests for a nonzero string length	*test -n string*
string1 = string2	Tests two strings for equality	*test string1 = string2*
string1 != string2	Tests two strings for inequality	*test string1 != string2*
string	Tests for a nonzero string length	*test string*

Hands-On Project 7-3 performs string tests from the command line.

Testing Files with the test Command

The *test* command can determine if a file exists and if it has a specified permission or attribute (such as executable, readable, writable, and directory). For example, if your script is designed to create a file and store that file in a specific directory, you might want the script to alert the user if the directory does not exist. Consider another example in which a script needs to modify the contents of a file. You can have the script use the *test* command to determine if the user has permission to write to the file before taking any action to modify the file's contents. Table 7-3 describes several of the *test* command's file evaluation options.

Table 7-3   File evaluation options of the *test* command

Option	Meaning	Example
-b	True if a file exists and is a block special file (which is a block-oriented device, such as a disk or tape drive)	test -b filename
-c	True if a file exists and is a character special file (which is a character-oriented device, such as a terminal or printer)	test -c filename
-d	True if a file exists and is a directory	test -d filename
-e	True if a file exists	test -e filename
-f	True if a file exists and is a regular file	test -f filename
-nt	Compares the first file in the argument with the second file to determine if the first file is newer	test filea -nt fileb
-ot	Compares the first file in the argument with the second file to determine if the first file is older	test filea -ot fileb
-r	True if a file exists and can be read	test -r file
-s	True if a file exists and its size is greater than zero	test -s file
-w	True if a file exists and can be written to	test -w file
-x	True if a file exists and can be executed	test -x file

Try Hands-On Project 7-4 to use *test* to evaluate the existence of a directory and a file and then test for permissions.

Performing Boolean Tests with the test Command

The *test* command's Boolean operators let you combine multiple expressions with AND and OR relationships. You can also use a Boolean negation operator. Boolean operators are named after the mathematician George Boole and refer to using a logic system to determine if something is true or false. A **Boolean operator** is a logical operator that symbolizes AND, OR, or NOT to evaluate a relationship, such as a comparison of two expressions—and the result of the evaluation is either true or false.

Consider, for example, a script that accesses a file to enable the user to view the contents of the file and then to modify the file's contents. As a first step you want the script to verify that the user has both read and write permissions for that file. In this case you can use a Boolean operator to test for read AND write permissions. Table 7-4 describes Boolean operators.

Table 7-4   Boolean operators used with the *test* command

Option	Meaning	Example
-a	Logical AND	test expression1 -a expression2
-o	Logical OR	test expression1 -o expression2
!	Logical negation	test !expression

The *-a* operator combines two expressions and tests a logical AND relationship between them. The form of the *test* command with the *-a* option is:

```
test expression1 -a expression2
```

If both expression1 and expression2 are true, the *test* command returns true (with an exit status of 0). However, if either expression1 or expression2 is false the *test* command returns false (with an exit status of 1).

The *-o* operator also combines two expressions. It tests a logical OR relationship. The form of the *test* command with the *-o* option is:

```
test expression1 -o expression2
```

If either expression1 or expression2 is true, the *test* command returns true (with an exit status of 0). However, if neither of the expressions is true, the *test* command returns false (with an exit status of 1).

The *!* operator negates the value of an expression. This means that if the expression normally causes *test* to return true, it returns false instead. Likewise, if the expression normally causes *test* to return false, it returns true instead. The form of the *test* command with the *!* operator is the following:

```
test !expression
```

In Hands-On Project 7-5 you use Boolean operators to test the permissions on a file. Also, try Hands-On Projects 7-6 through 7-8 to use the *test* command to test for your source directory and to add the command to scripts you created in Chapter 6.

FORMATTING RECORD OUTPUT

To format record output use the translate utility, *tr*. The translate utility, as you recall from Chapter 5, "Advanced File Processing," changes the standard input (characters you type at the keyboard) character by character. The standard input can also be redirected with the < operator to come from a file rather than from the keyboard. For example, the following command sends the contents of the counters file as input to the *tr* command and then converts lowercase characters to uppercase.

```
tr [a-z] [A-Z] < counters
```

TIP

The syntax of the *tr* command can vary from version to version of UNIX/Linux. For that reason, Fedora, Red Hat Enterprise Linux, and SUSE generally accept most variations. For example, you can run any of the following formats in these Linux distributions.

```
tr "[a-z]" "[A-Z]" < counters
tr '[a-z]' '[A-Z]' < counters (use single quotes, not back quotes)
tr a-z A-Z < counters
```

By using the | operator, the translate utility also works as a filter in situations in which the input comes from the output of another UNIX/Linux command. For example, the following command sends the output of the *cat* command to *tr*:

```
cat names | tr ":" " "
```

This sample command pipes (|) the contents of the names file to *tr*. The *tr* utility replaces each occurrence of the : character with a space. In this respect, the *tr* utility works like the *sed* command, except that *sed* changes the standard input string by string, not character by character.

In Hands-On Project 7-9, you format output from the corp_phones file that you have already created for your employee telephone number application. Next, in Hands-On Project 7-10, you create the phonefind script to search for and display telephone number information. The phonefind script is another piece added to your employee telephone number application and can be called from the phmenu menu script you wrote in Chapter 6.

DELETING PHONE RECORDS

In this section you review the *sed* command for use in applying to the employee telephone number application you are perfecting. Recall from Chapter 5 that *sed* takes the contents of an input file and applies actions, provided as options and arguments, to the file's contents. The results are sent to the standard output device. A simple way to delete a phone record using *sed* is with the *-d* (delete) option. Here is a pseudocode representation of the necessary steps:

```
Enter phone number
Use sed -d to delete the matching phone number and output to
a temporary file, f
Confirm acceptance
If the output is accepted, copy the temporary file f back to
corp_phones (overlaying it)
```

In Hands-On Project 7-11, you revise the phmenu script you started in Chapter 6 to implement the logic in the pseudocode presented here.

CLEARING THE SCREEN

Often when a script is designed it is important to clear the screen one or more times, such as when you first execute the script or go from one menu or screen to another. The *clear* command, which you learned in Chapter 1, "The Essence of UNIX and Linux," is a useful housekeeping utility for clearing the screen, but you can use a faster method. You can store the output of the *clear* command in a shell variable. Recall from Chapter 6 that you can store the output of a command in a variable by enclosing the command in single back quotes (use the ` character usually found in the upper-left portion of the keyboard, along with the tilde ~). For example, this command stores the output of the *date* command in the variable TODAY:

```
TODAY=`date`
```

The output of the *clear* command is a sequence of values that erases the contents of the screen. Storing these values in a variable and then echoing the contents of the variable on the screen accomplishes the same thing, but about 10 times faster. This is because the system does not have to first locate (in a directory) and execute the *clear* command—it is instead stored in a variable for immediate action.

To set up a shell variable for clearing screens you can use the following commands:

```
CLEAR=`clear`
export CLEAR
```

After you execute these commands, each time you enter the following (see Figure 7-7), the screen is quickly cleared:

```
echo $CLEAR
```

 TIP This technique is provided to show you one way in which to enable some commands in scripts to run faster. This can be important for faster response needed by those accessing a UNIX/Linux host computer over a network, a dial-up connection, or the Internet.

In Hands-On Project 7-12, you set up a shell variable and export it so you can use that variable in all of your scripts.

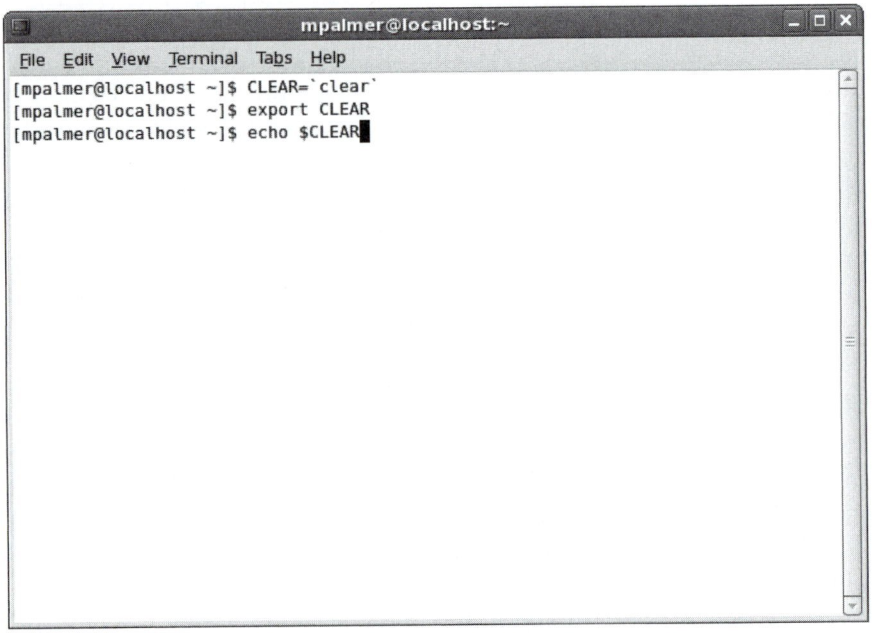

```
mpalmer@localhost:~
File  Edit  View  Terminal  Tabs  Help
[mpalmer@localhost ~]$ CLEAR=`clear`
[mpalmer@localhost ~]$ export CLEAR
[mpalmer@localhost ~]$ echo $CLEAR
```

Figure 7-7   Setting up and using a script variable to clear the screen

CREATING AN ALGORITHM TO PLACE THE CURSOR

As you continue developing your employee telephone number application, another feature
to add is the ability to return the cursor to a previous field on the screen when adding
records to the corp_phones file. For example, you can designate a particular character, such
as the minus (hyphen) character (-), to signal the script to return the cursor to the previous
field on the data-entry screen. When the user enters a minus sign and presses Enter, the
cursor is repositioned at the start of the previous field. You can make this change by editing
the phoneadd program that you've already created (which provides the user with data-entry
screens). Recall from Chapter 6 that you can do this by creating an algorithm. To review, an
algorithm is a sequence of instructions, programming code, or commands that results in a
program or that can be used as part of a larger program. Integral to the process of developing
an algorithm is to first model it through creating pseudocode, which is discussed earlier in
this chapter.

Here is the pseudocode for repositioning the cursor at the previous field when the user enters the minus sign (-):

```
Read information into field2
While field2 equals "-"
     Move cursor to position of previous field, field1
     Clear current information displayed in field1
     Read new information into field1
     If field1 = "q"
     Then
         Exit program
     End If
     Move cursor to position of field2
     Read information into field2
End While
```

The following is an example algorithm for the phoneadd program you can use to implement the pseudocode:

```
tput cup 5 18; read lname
   while test "$lname" = "-"
      do   tput cup 4 18; echo "        "
           tput cup 4 18; read phonenum
           tput cup 5 18; read lname
      done
```

This code reads the last name into the variable lname. If lname contains a minus sign (-), the cursor moves to the previous field, which contains the phone number. The value displayed for the phone number is cleared from the screen and a new value is entered into phonenum. The cursor is then moved back to the last name field and the last name is entered. The *while* statement repeats this process as long as the user types a minus sign for the last name.

NOTE   Using the *if* statement instead of the *while* statement allows only one return to the prior field. Instead you need a loop so the process repeats as long as the user enters a minus sign for the field.

Notice this *while* statement:

```
while test "$lname" = "-"
```

The argument *$lname* is enclosed in quotation marks to prevent the command from producing an error in the event the user presses just Enter or more than one word for the last name. For example, if the user enters Smith Williams for the last name, the preceding statement is interpreted as:

```
while test "Smith Williams" = "-"
```

However, if the statement is written without the quotation marks around *$lname*, the statement is interpreted as:

```
while test Smith Williams = "-"
```

This statement causes an error message because it passes too many arguments to the *test* command.

You implement this new code in Hands-On Project 7-13.

PROTECTING AGAINST ENTERING DUPLICATE DATA

Because users do not always enter valid data, a program should always check its input to ensure the user has entered acceptable information. This is known as **input validation**. For example, the corp_phones data file used by your employee telephone number application should have only one record for a given telephone number. If there are two or more records for a person and her associated telephone number, this adds confusion and can possibly result in errors.

The best approach is to create an input validation algorithm that prevents the user from adding a phone number that has already been assigned. The pseudocode and flowchart to accomplish this are shown in Figure 7-8. After you review this figure, try Hands-On Project 7-14 to add an algorithm to the phoneadd script you created earlier to perform input validation.

Pseudocode:

```
If phone number is already on file
    Then
        Display message on the screen "This number has already been assigned to: "
        Display the person's record who has the duplicate number
        Clear the screen and prepare for another entry
End if
```

Flowchart:

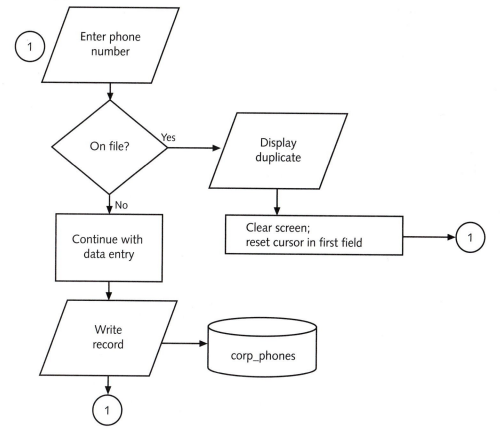

Figure 7-8   Modifications for the phoneadd script to perform input validation

USING SHELL FUNCTIONS

A **shell function** is a group of commands that is stored in memory and assigned a name. Shell scripts can use the function name to execute the commands. You can use shell functions to isolate reusable code sections, so that you do not have to duplicate algorithms throughout your program. This means that after you develop and test lines of code to perform an action, you don't have to retype those lines in several scripts. Instead, you can create one function containing those lines of code and simply call the function from different scripts. Functions are useful because they save you typing time. They also enable you to reuse lines of code that are already tested, reducing the time you spend debugging and making your code reliable.

A function name differs from a variable name because a function name is followed by a set of parentheses, while the commands that make up the function are enclosed in curly brackets. For example, look at the code for a function:

```
datenow()
{
date
}
```

The name of this sample function is "datenow." It has only one command inside its curly brackets: the *date* command. When the *datenow( )* function is executed, it calls the *date* command.

Defining a Function from the Command Line

You can define functions from the command line by first entering the name of the function and then completing the parameters to define it. Here is a replication of what you would enter to create the *datenow( )* function:

```
[martin@localhost ~]$ datenow() <Enter>
> { <Enter>
> date <Enter>
> } <Enter>
[martin@localhost ~]$
```

In these steps, you begin by entering the name of the function immediately followed by open and closed parentheses—in this example, you type *datenow( )*. When you press Enter, the shell displays the greater than prompt (>) that signifies you need to enter the parameters for the function. The first parameter you provide is an open curly bracket, to signify the start of the code or commands that the function will execute. Next, the *date* command is entered. Finally in this example, the closed curly bracket is provided to show the end of the code or commands to execute. When you press Enter after typing the closed curly bracket, the shell is ready to execute your new function when you enter it from the command line.

Functions are usually stored in script files and loaded into memory when you log in. However, you can also enter them at the command line.

Arguments are passed to functions in the same manner as any other shell procedure. The function accesses the arguments using the positional variables (also called parameters) $1 to $9. For example, $1 is the first argument given with a function, $2 is the second argument, and so on. Simply type the arguments following the command name, placing a space between each argument. For example, you can design the *datenow( )* function discussed earlier to use the argument "Today's date and time are:" and display this line before showing the date as follows:

```
[martin@localhost ~]$ datenow "Today's date and time are:"
Today's date and time are:
Mon Feb 9 21:49:45 MST 2009
```

In this example, the string, "Today's date and time are:" is an argument in the first position ($1) after the *datenow( )* function.

A shell script or function typically can accept up to nine positional parameters, $1 through $9. This means that what you enter after the script or function name is placed in a variable ($1 to $9). If you have a function called .num and you enter *.num 20 55*, 20 is the first argument and is placed in the $1 variable; 55 is the second argument and is placed in the $2 variable. The code within the .num function can then operate on the contents of $1 (in this case 20) and $2 (in this case 55).

Besides $1 through $9, other positional parameters can also be used in scripts and functions. For example, $0 contains the name of the script or function (or might have the name of the shell), whereas $* is a text string containing all of the positional variables (the contents of $1 through $9). Finally, $?, which you have used with the *test* command, is the exit status of the final command in a script or function, which is 0 if the script or function runs successfully.

Hands-On Project 7-15 enables you to create the *datenow( )* function from the command line. Then, in Hands-On Project 7-16, you redefine the *datenow( )* function to accept an argument.

Creating Functions Inside Shell Scripts

One of the best ways to improve your programming productivity is to learn how to create functions within scripts. The advantage of this approach is that you can reuse code instead of writing the same routines over and over again. This saves time and reduces errors. It also acknowledges that there are often common activities that you perform from one script to another, particularly within an application that uses several scripts, as does the employee telephone number application that you have been developing. For example, you can create functions to sort a data file, such as the corp_phones file, and use these in scripts, such as the phone listing script (phlist1) in the employee telephone number application. The phlist1 script can then call these functions to display the list of phone numbers sorted in a variety of ways.

For example, you might create the following lines in a shell script, called .myfuncs:

```
sort_name()
{
sort -k 2 -t: corp_phones
}
sort_job()
{
sort -k 6 -t: corp_phones
}
sort_dept()
{
```

```
sort -k 5 -t: corp_phones
}
```

As you can determine from these lines of code, there is one function that sorts the corp_phones file by last name, one that sorts by the job name, and one that sorts by department number (see Chapter 4, "UNIX/Linux File Processing," to review the syntax of the *sort* command).

By placing these functions in the .myfuncs file, you create a file that is hidden unless you enter *ls -a* to view it. As a next step, you can execute the .myfuncs script each time you log in by starting it from your .bash_profile or .bashrc login script; or, you can simply run .myfuncs from the command line. Either method loads all your functions into memory just as you load environment variables.

In Hands-On Project 7-17, you create the sort functions in the .myfuncs file. Then in Hands-On Project 7-18, you start .myfuncs from the command line and also place it in your .bashrc login script. Finally, in Hands-On Project 7-19, you employ your new functions as a finishing touch on your employee telephone number application.

TROUBLESHOOTING A SHELL SCRIPT

Most shell script writers at some point encounter problems that require troubleshooting. As you gain more experience writing scripts, you'll be able to more quickly troubleshoot any problems. You might look upon troubleshooting as a way to further tune your script writing skills. You'll retain lessons learned from troubleshooting and be able to apply them to making more foolproof scripts.

Here are some tips to help you troubleshoot a script:

1. Ensure that you have assigned execute permissions to the script, such as *chmod a+x* or *chmod a+rx* (or *chmod 755*).

2. Be certain you've included on the first line of the script a command to specify the shell to use, such as *# !/ bin/bash*.

3. Use the *sh -n, -v,* and *-x* troubleshooting options as you learned in Chapter 6.

4. Look for typographic errors, which are some of the most common causes of script problems.

5. Look for errors in the use of particular characters, such as the following:

    a. Omitting the semicolon between two separate commands on the same line

    b. Using single quote marks (') instead of back quote marks (`) or vice versa

    c. Omitting single or double quote marks

    d. Omitting the pound sign (#) for comments

    e. Using the wrong redirection operator, such as > instead of <

6. Check for syntax errors in the use of commands inside the script.

7. Look for the use of command options that are not supported in your distribution of UNIX/Linux. For example, the use of the +*n* option to designate a key sort field is no longer supported by the *sort* command on many systems.

8. Check looping logic to be sure it does not start with the wrong value, such as 1 instead of 0.

9. Ensure there is an exit point for your looping logic so you don't create a looping structure that never ends (goes into a continuous loop).

10. Make sure you haven't created a script that does not work for another user because that user has different environment variables or functions in their login script.

7

Chapter Summary

❑ The two most popular and proven analysis tools are the program flowchart and pseudocode. The flowchart is a logic diagram drawn using a set of standard symbols that explains the flow and the action to be taken by the program.

❑ Pseudocode is a model of a program. It is written in statements similar to your natural language.

❑ When you write a script, have the first line in the script file specify the shell, such as by entering #!/bin/bash for the Bash shell.

❑ Use the *test* command to validate the existence of directories and files as well as compare numeric and string values.

❑ The translate utility (*tr*) changes the characters typed at the keyboard, character by character, and also works as a filter when the input comes from the output of another UNIX/Linux command. Standard input can also be redirected to come from a file rather than from the keyboard.

❑ The *sed* command reads a file as its input and outputs the file's modified contents. Specify options and pass arguments to *sed* to control how the file's contents are modified.

❑ To speed clearing the screen, assign the *clear* command sequence to the shell variable CLEAR that can be set inside your login script. This clears your screen faster because it does not require a lookup sequence in a file every time it executes.

❑ Shell functions can make a shell programmer more efficient by enabling code to be reused. You can combine several functions in one shell script and then load the functions in memory for use at any time.

COMMAND SUMMARY: REVIEW OF CHAPTER 7 COMMANDS

test Command Option	Meaning	Example Command
!	Logical negation	*test !expression*
-a	Logical AND	*test expression1 -a expression2*
-b	Tests if a file exists and is a block special file (which is a block-oriented device, such as a disk or tape drive)	*test -b file*
-c	Tests if a file exists and is a character special file (which is a character-oriented device, such as a terminal or printer)	*test -c file*
-d	True if a file exists and is a directory	*test -d file*
-e	True if a file exists	*test -e file*
-eq	Equal to	*test a -eq b*
-f	Tests if a file exists and is a regular file	*test -f file*
-ge	Greater than or equal to	*test a -ge b*
-gt	Greater than	*test a -gt b*
-le	Less than or equal to	*test a -le b*
-lt	Less than	*test a -lt b*
-n	Tests for a nonzero string length	*test -n string*
-ne	Not equal to	*test a -ne b*
-o	Logical OR	*test expression1 -o expression2*
-r	True if a file exists and is readable	*test -r file*
-s	True if a file exists and has a size greater than zero	*test -s file*
string	Tests for a nonzero string length	*test string*
string1 = string2	Tests two strings for equality	*test string1 = string2*
string1 != string2	Tests two strings for inequality	*test string1 != string2*
-w	True if a file exists and is writable	*test -w file*
-x	True if a file exists and is executable	*test -x file*
-z	Tests for a zero-length string	*test -z string*

KEY TERMS

Boolean operator — A logical operator that symbolizes AND, OR, or NOT to evaluate a relationship, such as a comparison of two expressions—and the result of the evaluation is either true or false.

exit status — A numeric value that the *test* command returns to the operating system when *test* finishes performing an evaluation of an expression, string, integer, or other information. If the exit status is 0 (zero), the test result is true. An exit status of 1 indicates the test result is false.

flowchart — A logic diagram that uses a set of standard symbols to explain the logic in a program's sequence and each action performed in the sequence.

input validation — A process a program performs to ensure that the user has entered acceptable information, such as preventing a user from entering a duplicate record in a data file.

pseudocode —The instructions that are similar to actual programming statements. Used to create a model that might later become the basis for a program.

shell function — A group of commands stored in memory and assigned a name. Shell functions simplify the program code. For example, you can include a function's name within a shell script so the function's commands execute as part of the script. You can also use shell functions to store reusable code sections, so that you do not need to duplicate them.

7

REVIEW QUESTIONS

1. You have been asked to write a script for use by the faculty at the engineering school at your college. The script you write uses the Bash shell, but some faculty members often use a different shell in their work. How can you best ensure that the Bash shell is invoked when this script is run?

    a. Have the script print a warning to the screen that it requires the Bash shell.

    b. Have the system administrator adjust all faculty accounts so the Bash shell is the default.

    c. Enter the line # !/ bin/bash as the first line in the script.

    d. Create a function for all faculty user accounts that prevents use of shells other than Bash.

2. Which of the following script statements accomplishes the same thing as the statement: *while ["$part" != "alternator"] ; do* ? (Choose all that apply.)

    a. *while $part <! "alternator" | do test*

    b. *while test $part != "alternator" ; do*

    c. *for test $part > "alternator" ; do*

    d. *test $part -eq "alternator" | do*

3. Your shell script, called .filetests, contains several functions used to run tests on files, such as to determine if a file is empty or has the correct permissions. Which of the following is/are true about .filetests? (Choose all that apply.)

    a. You can load the file's functions into memory by entering . .filetests.

    b. This is a hidden file.

    c. You can run the functions in the file by entering *!. filetests*.

    d. This is a character special file.

4. When you enter *echo $CLR* your screen clears very quickly. Which of the following commands must you have entered previously to enable use of *echo $CLR* to clear the screen?

   a. *set =:clear*

   b. *let clear=CLR*

   c. *$clear=CLR*

   d. *CLR=`clear`*

5. Your company has assigned you to revise 22 scripts. Since you use the vi editor, how can you set it to automatically display lines as numbered so it is easier for you to work on these revisions?

   a. Create a vi macro that enables you view the lines as numbered when you press *n* in the command mode.

   b. Create the .exrc file in your home directory so this file contains the line: *set number*.

   c. Type *set_lines* and press *Enter* before you start vi.

   d. Press # while you are in the ex mode in vi.

6. You use the same five shell functions every day and are looking for a way to ensure they are available as soon as you log into your account. What can you do?

   a. Make them residual system variables.

   b. Make them permanent environment variables.

   c. Load them via your login script.

   d. Make them permanent functions by adding them to the /func directory.

7. When you enter *test -d tmp ; echo $?*, you see a 0 displayed on the screen. What does this mean?

   a. The tmp file is empty.

   b. The tmp file contains over 1 MB.

   c. The tmp directory exists.

   d. The tmp directory is empty.

8. What does a down arrow represent in a flowchart?

   a. process flow

   b. manual input

   c. stored data

   d. display

9. Which of the following are examples of Boolean operators used with the *test* command? (Choose all that apply.)

   a. *-a* for a logical AND

   b. *-m* for a partial MERGE

   c. *-n* for logical NEGATION

   d. *-o* for a logical OR

10. You have a specialized data file, called customers, in which the fields in the file are separated by the character ^. You want to view this file with a colon between the fields before you convert it to remove the ^ characters and insert colons. Which of the following commands enables you to view the file in this way?

   a. *insert -t : ^ | customers*

   b. *test - i [^] [:] customers*

   c. *cat customers | tr "^" ":"*

   d. *sub ':' '^' > customers*

11. Which of the following statements enables you to determine if the variable, called value, is less than 750?

   a. *echo $value -l 750*

   b. *comm value$ to 750*

   c. *test $value - lt 750*

   d. *test "value" >! 750*

12. Some Linux systems use the _____ script to perform the same actions each time a user logs out of her account.

   a. .bash_logout

   b. .bash_rc

   c. /bin/bashout

   d. /etc/logoff_bash

13. You have recently met with your company's budget committee about creating a script to for producing the same budget reports at the end of each month. Because this is an important undertaking you've started by creating a flowchart. What step should you take next?

   a. Immediately write the functions you'll need for the script.

   b. Create a menu script.

   c. Find the three most important fields in the Budget file that you can use as keys

   d. Write pseudocode before you create the actual script.

7

14. Which of the following are examples of symbols you might use in a flowchart? (Choose all that apply.)

    a. decision

    b. document

    c. data

    d. magnetic disk

15. The script you are creating takes data input to use for updating a file. Before taking the data input, you want the script to verify that the file to be updated, called clients, exists and that the script user has permission to write to that file. Which of the following statements enables you to do this?

    a. *string -w clients*

    b. *test -w clients*

    c. *chmod -all clients*

    d. *tr -ew clients*

16. When working on the script in Question 15, which of the following should you consider?

    a. output strength

    b. input validation

    c. functional reciprocation

    d. user vacillation

17. Each month your business manually deletes specific records for employees who have left the company. You have been asked to write a script to automate this process. Which of the following commands works well for deleting records in a file?

    a. *cut -a*

    b. *purge -d*

    c. *trdel -r*

    d. *sed -d*

18. In which of the following files would a system administrator set the default shell used by your account?

    a. .shell

    b. /home/shell

    c. /etc/passwd

    d. /home

19. Which of the following characters are placed right after a function name when you create a shell function?

    a. ( )

    b. !#

    c. [[

    d. //

20. When you create a shell function from the command line, what character do you enter at the first > prompt just after you declare the function's name?

    a. "

    b. {

    c. '

    d. $

21. What symbol is typically used at the start and end of a flowchart?

    a. terminator

    b. display

    c. connector

    d. manual operation

22. What is an exit status and with what command is it used?

23. In your organization everyone uses the Bash shell in Red Hat Enterprise Linux and all users use the same aliases and shell functions. In what file or files can the system administrator place these aliases and functions so they are available to all users?

24. Create a statement that enables you to determine if the file /source/results is newer than the file /data/results.

25. Create a simple function that determines if the string variable, text, contains no characters (is of zero length).

HANDS-ON PROJECTS

NOTE

Complete these projects using the command line, such as a terminal window, using the Bash shell, and using your own account. Use your home directory unless otherwise directed.

Project 7-1

When you use the Bash shell, it is valuable to view the contents of the files that it uses for your startup environment: .bash_profile, .bashrc, .bash_logout, /etc/bashrc, and /etc/profile (for Fedora and Red Hat Enterprise Linux). In this project, you view those files (or the equivalent files in SUSE and Knoppix Linux).

To view the files affecting the Bash environment:

1. If you are using Fedora or Red Hat Enterprise Linux, type **more .bash_profile .bashrc .bash_logout /etc/bashrc /etc/profile** and press **Enter**. If you are using SUSE, type **more .profile .bashrc/etc/bash.bashrc/etc/profile** and press **Enter** (SUSE does not have a .bash_logout file). Or in Knoppix, type **more .bashrc /etc/bash.bashrc/etc/profile** and press **Enter** (Knoppix does not have the files, .profile and .bash_logout). (If you prefer, you can use the *cat*, *more*, or *less* commands for one file at a time.)

2. Press the **Spacebar** to advance through the contents of the files.

Project 7-2

The *test* command enables you to evaluate many types of conditions, including providing a comparison of integers. In this project, you evaluate integer expressions from the command line.

To use the *test* command with integer expressions:

1. Create the variable number with the value 122 by typing the command **number=122** and pressing **Enter**.

2. Type **test $number -eq 122** and press **Enter**.

3. Type **echo $?** and press **Enter**. The result displayed on your screen is 0, as in the following example:

```
[beth@localhost ~]$ number=122
[beth@localhost ~]$ test $number -eq 122
[beth@localhost ~]$ echo $?
0
```

The *echo $?* command displays the exit status of the most recent command executed. In this example, the *test* command returns the exit status 0, indicating the expression *$number -eq 122* is true. This means the variable number (*$number*) is equal to 122.

4. Type **test $number -gt 142** and press **Enter**.

5. Type **echo $?** and press **Enter**. This time, the result should be 1 (false) because 122 is not greater than (-gt) 142.

6. Type **value=51** and press **Enter**.

7. Type **test $number -lt $value** and press **Enter**.

8. Type **echo $?** and press **Enter**. The result of the test that appears on your screen is now 1:

```
[beth@localhost ~]$ value=51
[beth@localhost ~]$ test $number -lt $value
[beth@localhost ~]$ echo $?
1
```

In this example, the *test* command returns the exit status 1, indicating the expression *$number -lt $value* is false. This means *$number* is not less than *$value*.

Project 7-3

In this project, you use the *test* command to evaluate the contents of strings.

To use the *test* command's string evaluation capabilities:

1. Type **lname="Rossetti"** and press **Enter**.

2. Type **test $lname = "Rossetti"** and press **Enter**.

3. Type **echo $?** and press **Enter**. The result shown on your screen is 0:

```
[beth@localhost ~]$ lname="Rossetti"
[beth@localhost ~]$ test $lname = "Rossetti"
[beth@localhost ~]$ echo $?
0
```

In this example, the *test* command returns the exit status 0, indicating the expression *$lname = "Rossetti"* is true. This means *$lname* and *"Rossetti"* are equal.

4. Type **test $lname != "Hanson"** and press **Enter**.

5. Type **echo $?** and press **Enter**. Your screen looks similar to the following:

```
[beth@localhost ~]$ test $lname != "Hanson"
[beth@localhost ~]$ echo $?
0
```

In this case, the *test* command returns the exit status 0, indicating the expression *$lname != "Hanson"* is true. This means *$lname* and *"Hanson"* are not equal.

6. Type **test –z $lname** and press **Enter**.

7. Type **echo $?** and press **Enter**. Your screen looks similar to the following:

```
[beth@localhost ~]$ test -z $lname
[beth@localhost ~]$ echo $?
1
```

The final *test* command in the preceding example returns the exit status 1, indicating the expression *-z $lname* is false. This means the string *$lname* is not zero length.

Project 7-4

In this project, you learn how to use the *test* command to evaluate files and directories.

To use the *test* command's file-testing capabilities:

1. Type **mkdir test_directory** and press **Enter** to create a directory.

2. Type **test –d test_directory** and press **Enter**.

3. Type **echo $?** and press **Enter**. You should see an exit status of 0 to show that it is true the test_directory exists.

4. Type **touch test_file** and press **Enter** to create an empty file named test_file.

5. Type **ls –l test_file** and press **Enter** to view the permissions for test_file. The permissions should look similar to the following:

```
[beth@localhost ~]$ ls -l test_file
-rw-r--r-- 1  beth      beth          0 Feb 8 12:43 test_file
```

6. Notice that the file has read and write permissions for you, the owner.

7. Next type **test –x test_file** and press **Enter**.

8. Type **echo $?** and press **Enter**. Your screen looks similar to the following:

```
[beth@localhost ~]$ test -x test_file
[beth@localhost ~]$ echo $?
1
```

The *test* command returns an exit status of 1 because test_file is not executable.

9. Type **test –r test_file** and press **Enter**.

10. Type **echo $?** and press **Enter**. Your screen should be similar to the following:

```
[beth@localhost ~]$ test -r test_file
[beth@localhost ~]$ echo $?
0
```

The *test* command now returns an exit status of 0, indicating test_file is readable.

Project 7-5

At times, it is useful to determine if two expressions are both true or if one or the other of two expressions are true by employing the *test* command with Boolean operators. In this project, you use Boolean operators to test the relationship of expressions for AND, OR, or NOT outcomes.

To use the *test* command's Boolean operators:

1. Recall that the test_file file you created in Hands-On Project 7-4 has read and write permissions. You can use Boolean operators to test for both permissions at once. Type **test –r test_file –a –w test_file** and press **Enter**.

This command tests two expressions using an AND relationship: *-r test_file* and *-w test_file*. If both expressions are true, the *test* command returns true.

2. Type **echo $?** and press **Enter**. The results on your screen look similar to the following:

```
[beth@localhost ~]$ test -r test_file -a -w test_file
[beth@localhost ~]$ echo $?
0
```

The *test* command returns an exit status of 0, indicating that test_file is readable and writable.

3. Type **test –x test_file –o –r test_file** and press **Enter**.

This command tests two expressions using an OR relationship: *-x test_file* and *-r test_file*. If either of these expressions is true, the *test* command returns true.

4. Type **echo $?** and press **Enter**. The results on your screen look similar to the following:

```
[beth@localhost ~]$ test -x test_file -o -r test_file
[beth@localhost ~]$ echo $?
0
```

The *test* command returns an exit status of 0, indicating that test_file is either executable OR readable.

5. Type **test ! –r test_file** and press **Enter**.

This command negates the result of the expression *-r test_file*. If the expression is true, the *test* command returns false. Likewise, if the expression is false, the *test* command returns true.

6. Type **echo $?** and press **Enter**. Your screen looks similar to the following:

```
[beth@localhost ~]$ test ! -r test_file
[beth@localhost ~]$ echo $?
1
```

The *test* command returns an exit status of 1, indicating the expression *! -r test_file* is false.

Project 7-6

So far, your use of the *test* command has been for more theoretical applications. In this project, you use the *test* command to verify your working environment. You next use the *test* command to verify the source directory you created in Chapter 4 and used in Chapter 6 for developing the telephone number and employee information application. Be certain you have the source directory and the applications you developed in Chapter 6 for the remaining projects in this chapter. If not, go back to Chapter 6 to create them.

To verify that your source directory exists:

1. Type **test –d source ; echo $?** and press **Enter**. This command determines if the source directory exists and if it is a directory. Because the *echo $?* command is included on the same line, the exit status appears immediately after you press Enter.

   The exit status should be 0 to show you have a source directory. If not, use the *mkdir* command to create the source directory.

2. In Chapter 6, you created the file corp_phones and the shell scripts phmenu and phoneadd. Verify that you have the corp_phones file. Next type **cd ~/source** and press **Enter** to make source your working directory. Type **test –e corp_phones ; echo $?** and press **Enter**. If you see the exit status 0, the file exists. If not, go back to Chapter 6 to create it (or see your instructor for help).

3. Repeat the *test –e* command for the phmenu, phoneadd, and phlist1 files in the source directory. If you don't have them, go back to Chapter 6 to create them (or see your instructor for help).

4. To permanently add the /home/*username*/source directory to your PATH variable (where *username* is your login name), so that it takes effect each time you log in, you can edit your .bash_profile file. First type **cd** and press **Enter** to return to your home directory. Use the vi editor to open the .bash_profile (or the .profile in SUSE or .bashrc in Knoppix) file.

5. Move the cursor to the line that reads:

   `PATH=$PATH:$HOME/bin`

6. Type **i** to switch to insert mode. Type **:$HOME/source** (include the colon) at the end of the line. (See Figure 7-9.)

7. Press **Esc**, type **:x** or **:wq**, and then press **Enter** to save the file and exit the editor.

8. To make the new PATH value take effect, log out and then log back in.

9. After you log back in, type **echo $PATH**, and press **Enter**. At the end of the paths listed on the screen, you should see the path you just added. Note that now you can run scripts from the source directory by typing only the script name.

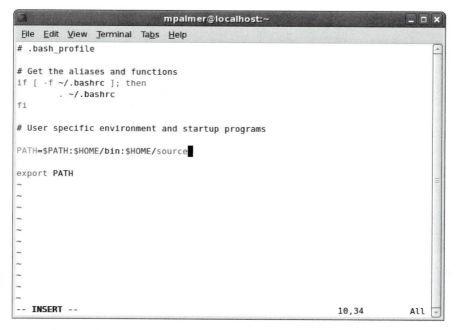

Figure 7-9 Adding your source directory to the path in the .bash_profile script file

Project 7-7

Now that you have some practice using the *test* command from the command line, it is time to apply your knowledge to a script file. Once again, recall the favorite vegetable script, veg_choice, you wrote and modified in Chapter 6, Hands-On Project 6-7:

```
echo -n "What is your favorite vegetable? "
read veg_name
if [ "$veg_name" = "broccoli" ]
then
    echo "Broccoli is a healthy choice."
else
    if [ "$veg_name" = "carrots" ]
    then
        echo "Carrots are great for you."
    else
        echo "Don't forget to eat your broccoli also."
    fi
fi
```

In this project, you modify an *if* statement in the script so it uses the *test* command. When done, the program runs identically as it did before.

To modify the veg_choice script to use *test*:

1. Type **cd** to ensure you are in your home directory. Load the veg_choice file into vi or Emacs.

2. Change the line that reads:

   ```
   if [ "$veg_name" = "broccoli" ]
   ```

   to this:

   if test $veg_name = "broccoli"

   Your screen should look similar to Figure 7-10.

3. Save the file and exit the editor.

4. Test the script by executing it. Type **broccoli** and press **Enter** when asked "What is your favorite vegetable?" The output of the script should be similar to the following:

   ```
   [beth@localhost ~]$ ./veg_choice
   What is your favorite vegetable? broccoli
   Broccoli is a healthy choice.
   ```

5. Type **clear** and press **Enter** to clear the screen for the next project.

```
mpalmer@localhost:~
File  Edit  View  Terminal  Tabs  Help
echo -n "What is your favorite vegetable? "
read veg_name
if test $veg_name = "broccoli"
then
   echo "Broccoli is a healthy choice."
else
   if [ "$veg_name" = "carrots" ]
   then
      echo "Carrots are great for you."
   else
      echo "Don't forget to eat your broccoli also."
   fi
fi
~
~
~
~
~
~
~
~
~
~
-- INSERT --                                    3,31         All
```

Figure 7-10   Using the *test* command in the veg_choice script

Project 7-8

In this project, you modify a *while* loop so it uses the *test* command.

To modify a *while* loop to use the *test* command:

1. Recall the script in your home directory named colors, which you wrote in Chapter 6. It repeatedly asks the user to guess its favorite color, until the user guesses

HANDS-ON
PROJECTS

the color red. The code for the colors script is as follows (it uses a *while* loop until the *guess* variable contains the word red):

```
echo -n "Try to guess my favorite color: "
read guess
while [ "$guess" != "red" ]; do
 echo "No, not that one. Try again. "; read guess
done
```

2. Load the colors script file into vi or Emacs.

3. Change the line that reads:

```
while [ "$guess" != "red" ]; do
```

to this:

while test $guess != "red" ; do

4. Save the file and exit the editor.

5. Test the script. Figure 7-11 shows sample output of the program.

6. Type **clear** and press **Enter** to clear the screen.

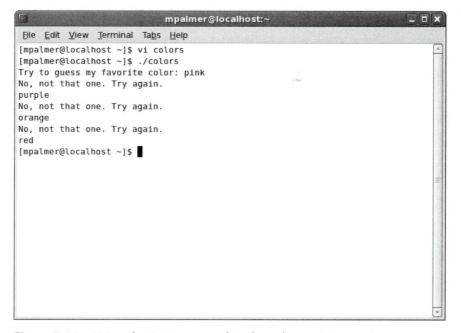

Figure 7-11   Using the *test* command in the colors script

Project 7-9

You can use the *tr* utility to change lowercase characters to uppercase, as well as to replace colon characters with spaces. In this project, you use both the *grep* and *tr* commands to learn how to remove the colon when you display records in the corp_phones file on which you worked in Chapter 6.

To format the contents of a file using the *grep* and *tr* commands:

1. Type **cd ~/source** and press **Enter** to change to the source directory.

2. Use the *grep* command to retrieve a record from the corp_phones file that matches the phone number 219-555-4501, and then pipe (using the | symbol) the output to *tr* to replace the colon characters in the record with space characters. Type **grep 219-555-4501 corp_phones | tr ':' ' '** and then press **Enter**. The output on your screen looks similar to the following:

   ```
   [mpalmer@localhost source]$ grep 219-555-4501 corp_phones
    | tr ':' ' '
   219-555-4501 Robinson Albert J 4501 Secretary 08-12-1997
   ```

3. Change lowercase characters to uppercase in the corp_phones file by typing **cat corp_phones | tr '[a-z]' '[A-Z]'** and then pressing **Enter**. Your screen looks similar to Figure 7-12. (Your results might look slightly different because of differences in test data entered in previous Hands-On Projects.)

```
                     mpalmer@localhost:~/source
File  Edit  View  Terminal  Tabs  Help
[mpalmer@localhost ~]$ cd ~/source
[mpalmer@localhost source]$ grep 219-555-4501 corp_phones | tr ':' ' '
219-555-4501 Robinson Albert J 4501 Secretary 08-12-1997
[mpalmer@localhost source]$ cat corp_phones | tr '[a-z]' '[A-Z]'
219-555-4567:HARRISON:JOEL:M:4540:ACCOUNTANT:09-12-1985
219-555-4587:MITCHELL:BARBARA:C:4541:ADMIN ASST:12-14-1995
219-555-4589:OLSON:TIMOTHY:H:4544:SUPERVISOR:06-30-1983
219-555-4591:MOORE:SARAH:H:4500:DEPT MANAGER:08-01-1978
219-555-4544:POLK:JOHN:S:4520:ACCOUNTANT:09-22-2001
219-555-4501:ROBINSON:ALBERT:J:4501:SECRETARY:08-12-1997
219-555-7175:MULLINS:ALLEN:L:7527:SALES REP:02-19-2007
219-555-7176:ALBERTSON:JEANNETTE:K:5547:DC CLERK:02-19-2007
[mpalmer@localhost source]$
```

Figure 7-12   Formatting the contents of the corp_phones file

Project 7-10

The combined use of the *tr* and *grep* commands that you used in Hands-On Project 7-9 can be used to create a new script for your employee telephone number application. Recall from Chapter 6 that the phmenu script you created in that chapter has an S option on the menu to "Search for Phones," but you did not create a script to perform such a search. In this project, you create a script for that option that searches for a specific telephone number and displays the employee information associated with it.

To add record-searching capability to your program:

1. The phmenu program is already equipped to call the script phonefind when the user selects S from the menu. This command instructs the program to search for a phone number. Make certain your current working directory is the source directory. Next use the vi or Emacs editor to create the phonefind script by typing the following:

```
#!/bin/bash
#=========================================================
# Script Name: phonefind
# By:          Your initials here
# Date         Today's date
# Purpose:     Searches for a specified record in the
#              corp_phones file
#=========================================================
phonefile=~/source/corp_phones
clear
tput cup 5 1
echo "Enter phone number to search for: "
tput cup 5 35
read number
echo
grep $number $phonefile | tr ':' ' '
echo
echo "Press ENTER to continue..."
read continue
```

2. Save the file and exit the editor.

3. Type **chmod a+x phonefind** and press **Enter** to make the file executable, and then test the script by searching for the number 219-555-7175. Your screen should look similar to Figure 7-13.

4. Press **Enter** to exit the phonefind script after you display the telephone number information.

7

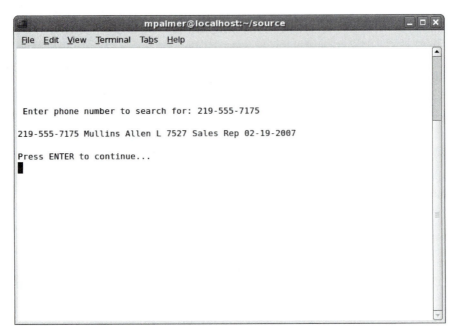

Figure 7-13   Running the phonefind script

Project 7-11

With what you have learned so far, now is a good time to revise the phmenu script you created in Chapter 6 to include the option to delete a record. In this revision, you use *sed* to create a temporary file called f. After you are finished using f, it is deleted near the end of the script by using the *rm f* command. To make your script more foolproof, you also use the *trap* command, as you learned in Chapter 6, to be certain the f file is deleted before starting any code. Just before the *phonefile=~/source/corp_phones* line, you insert this statement: *trap "rm ./f 2> /dev/null; exit" 0 1 3*. The advantage of this technique is that it ensures that the f file is deleted. After all, your previous run of phmenu could have aborted before deleting the f file near the end of the script.

To delete phone records by editing the phmenu program:

1. Be certain you are in the source directory. Using the vi or Emacs editor, retrieve the revised phmenu program and add the code shown in boldface:

> The code line *tput cup 18 4; echo "Accept? (y)es or (n)o: "* should be entered
> as one continuous line. It is wrapped into two lines in this example because of
> the page margin limitation.
>
> **NOTE**

```
#!/bin/bash
#========================================================
# Script Name:    phmenu
# By:             Your initials here
```

```
# Date:          Today's date
# Purpose:       A menu for the Corporate Phone List
# Command Line:  phmenu
#============================================================
trap "rm ./f 2> /dev/null; exit" 0 1 3
phonefile=~/source/corp_phones
loop=y
while test $loop = "y"
do
 clear
 tput cup 3 12; echo "Corporate Phone Reporting Menu"
 tput cup 4 12; echo "=============================="
 tput cup 6 9; echo "P - Print Phone List"
 tput cup 7 9; echo "A - Add New Phones"
 tput cup 8 9; echo "S - Search for Phones"
 tput cup 9 9; echo "V - View Phone List"
 tput cup 10 9; echo "D - Delete Phone"
 tput cup 12 9; echo "Q - Quit: "
 tput cup 12 19;
 read choice || continue
   case $choice in
      [Aa]) ./phoneadd ;;
      [Pp]) ./phlist1 ;;
      [Ss]) ./phonefind ;;
      [Vv]) clear ; less $phonefile ;;
      [Dd]) tput cup 16 4; echo "Delete Phone Record"
            tput cup 17 4; echo "Phone: "
            tput cup 17 11; read number
            tput cup 18 4; echo "Accept? (y)es
             or (n)o: "
            tput cup 18 27; read Accept
            if test $Accept = "y"
                   then
                      sed /$number/d $phonefile > f
                      cp f $phonefile
                   rm f
            fi
            ;;
      [Qq]) clear ; exit ;;
      *)tput cup 14 4; echo "Invalid Code"; read  choice ;;
   esac
done
```

2. Save the file and exit the editor. Later in Step 4, when you test the program, the menu appears and is similar to Figure 7-14.

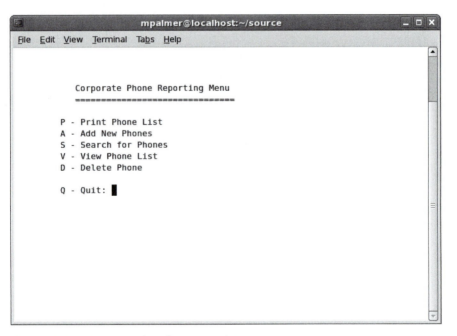

Figure 7-14 Running the phmenu script

3. Type **clear** and press **Enter** to clear the screen. Use the *more* command to display the contents of the corp_phones file in the source directory before you delete a record (type **more corp_phones** and press **Enter**). Your screen should be similar to Figure 7-15. (Remember that some of the records you added when you tested the application in Chapter 6 might be different from those in this example screen.)

4. Run the phmenu program, type **D** or **d**, press **Enter**, and test the delete option by entering the telephone number **219-555-4567**, and pressing **Enter**. Figure 7-16 shows the Delete Phone Record screen.

5. Type **y** to confirm the deletion, and then press **Enter**.

6. On the main menu, type **V** or **v** to view the phone file, and then press **Enter**. Your screen looks similar to Figure 7-17.

   Notice the record for phone number 219-555-4567 is no longer in the file.

7. Press **Q** or **q** to return to the menu, press **Q** or **q**, and then press **Enter** to exit the phmenu script.

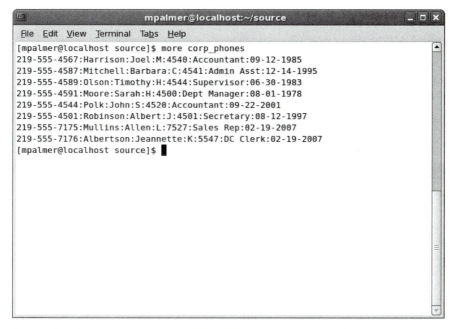

Figure 7-15 Reviewing the contents of the corp_phones file

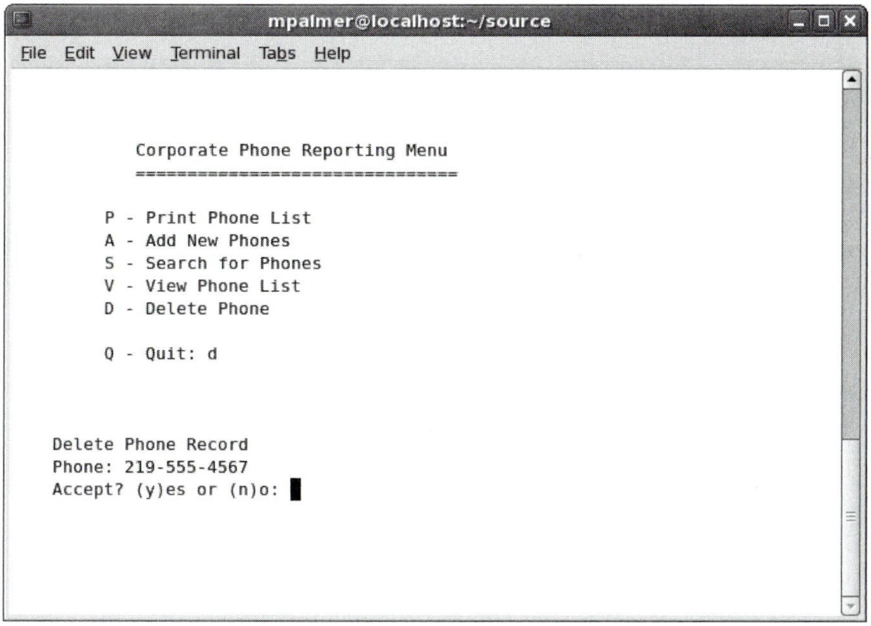

```
                mpalmer@localhost:~/source
File  Edit  View  Terminal  Tabs  Help


          Corporate Phone Reporting Menu
          ==================================

       P - Print Phone List
       A - Add New Phones
       S - Search for Phones
       V - View Phone List
       D - Delete Phone

       Q - Quit: d



   Delete Phone Record
   Phone: 219-555-4567
   Accept? (y)es or (n)o: █
```

Figure 7-16 Running the Delete Phone option

```
219-555-4587:Mitchell:Barbara:C:4541:Admin Asst:12-14-1995
219-555-4589:Olson:Timothy:H:4544:Supervisor:06-30-1983
219-555-4591:Moore:Sarah:H:4500:Dept Manager:08-01-1978
219-555-4544:Polk:John:S:4520:Accountant:09-22-2001
219-555-4501:Robinson:Albert:J:4501:Secretary:08-12-1997
219-555-7175:Mullins:Allen:L:7527:Sales Rep:02-19-2007
219-555-7176:Albertson:Jeannette:K:5547:DC Clerk:02-19-2007
/home/mpalmer/source/corp_phones (END)
```

Figure 7-17 Using the View Phone List option to verify your deletion

Project 7-12

In this project, you create a shell variable to use for quickly clearing the screen from any shell script. You start by setting up the variable from the command line to see how it works and then you add this capability to your .bashrc file for future use each time you log in using the Bash shell. (You'll most likely notice in this project that setting up this shell variable seems more cumbersome than simply entering *clear* as a stand-alone command. However, using the shell variable can be very effective when you include it in a script or program.)

To clear screens by setting a shell variable:

1. Type **cd** and press **Enter** to ensure you are in your home directory.

2. Set a shell variable, CLEAR, to the output of the *clear* command, by typing the following (use the back quote character with `clear` and not single quotation marks):

   ```
   CLEAR=`clear`
   export CLEAR
   ```

3. Use your new variable in your shell programs for a fast clear operation by typing **echo "$CLEAR"** and pressing **Enter**.

4. To make this fast clear always available, use the vi or Emacs editor to open the .bashrc file and place the following lines at the end of the file:

   ```
   CLEAR=`clear`
   export CLEAR
   ```

5. Save the file, exit, and then log out and log in again to activate the login script. Test your change to the login script by typing **echo "$CLEAR"** and then pressing **Enter**. Verify that the screen clears.

Project 7-13

In this project, you continue to enhance your employee telephone number application by adding the capability to enter the minus (-) character to reposition the cursor and reenter data in the data-entry screen. This requires making some modifications to the phoneadd data-entry script.

To allow reentry of data:

1. Type **cd ~/source** and press **Enter** to ensure you are in the source directory. Next open the phoneadd program using the vi or Emacs editor.

2. Add the following boldface code to the program. Notice that the revised code also includes your new, faster, screen clear feature. It also changes the existing *if* statements, so they use the *test* command.

TIP

For each *echo* statement that you add to the code in Step 2, be certain to place 12 blank spaces between the opening double quotation mark and the closing double quotation mark.

```
#!/bin/bash
#===========================================================
# Script Name:  phoneadd
# By:           Your initials here
# Date:         Today's date
# Purpose:      A shell script that sets up a loop to add
#               new employees to the corp_phones file.
# Command Line: phoneadd
#
#===========================================================
trap "rm ~/tmp/* 2> /dev/null; exit" 0 1 2 3
phonefile=~/source/corp_phones
looptest=y
while test "$looptest" = "y"
do
      clear
      tput cup 1 4; echo "Corporate Phone List Additions"
      tput cup 2 4; echo "=============================="
      tput cup 4 4; echo "Phone Number: "
      tput cup 5 4; echo "Last Name    :"
      tput cup 6 4; echo "First Name   :"
      tput cup 7 4; echo "Middle Init  :"
      tput cup 8 4; echo "Dept#        :"
      tput cup 9 4; echo "Job Title    :"
```

```
tput cup 10 4; echo "Date Hired :"
tput cup 12 4; echo "Add Another? (y)es or (q)uit: "
tput cup 4 18; read phonenum
if  test $phonenum = "q"
then
   clear ; exit
fi
tput cup 5 18 ; read lname
while test "$lname" = "-"
do
     tput cup 4 18 ; echo "                    "
     tput cup 4 18 ; read phonenum
     if test "$phonenum" = "q"
     then
          clear ; exit
     fi
     tput cup 5 18 ; read lname
done
tput cup 6 18 ; read fname
while test "$fname" = "-"
do
     tput cup 5 18 ; echo "                    "
     tput cup 5 18 ; read lname
     if test "$lname" = "q"
     then
          clear ; exit
     fi
     tput cup 6 18 ; read fname
done
tput cup 7 18 ; read midinit
while test "$midinit" = "-"
do
     tput cup 6 18 ; echo "                    "
     tput cup 6 18 ; read fname
     if test "$fname" = "q"
     then
          clear ; exit
     fi
     tput cup 7 18 ; read midinit
done
tput cup 8 18 ; read deptno
while test "$deptno" = "-"
do
     tput cup 7 18 ; echo "                    "
     tput cup 7 18 ; read midinit
     if test "$midinit" = "q"
     then
          clear ; exit
     fi
     tput cup 8 18 ; read deptno
```

```
        done
        tput cup 9 18 ; read jobtitle
        while test "$jobtitle" = "-"
        do
                tput cup 8 18 ; echo "                    "
                tput cup 8 18 ; read deptno
                if test "$deptno" = "q"
                then
                    clear ; exit
                fi
                tput cup 9 18 ; read jobtitle
        done
        tput cup 10 18; read datehired
        while test "$datehired" = "-"
        do
                tput cup 9 18 ; echo "                    "
                tput cup 9 18 ; read jobtitle
                if test "$jobtitle" = "q"
                then
                    clear ; exit
                fi
                tput cup 10 18 ; read datehired
        done
        #Check to see if last name is not blank before you
        #write to disk
        if  test "$lname" != ""
        then
                echo"$phonenum:$lname:$fname:$midinit:$deptno:
$jobtitle:$datehired" >> $phonefile
        fi
        tput cup 12 33 ; read looptest
        if  test "$looptest" = "q"
        then
            clear ; exit
        fi
done
```

3. Save the file and exit the editor.

4. Before you run this script, be certain that you have a tmp directory just under your home directory (/home/*username*/tmp) for storing temporary files. If you do not have a tmp directory, use the *mkdir* command to create one.

5. Execute the phoneadd script. For the phone number enter **219-555-4523** and press **Enter**. Your screen appears and is similar to Figure 7-18.

6. In the Last Name field, type the **minus sign** (-), and press **Enter**. Your cursor moves back to the Phone Number field. Your screen looks like Figure 7-19.

7. Reenter the phone number as **219-555-4511** and press **Enter**.

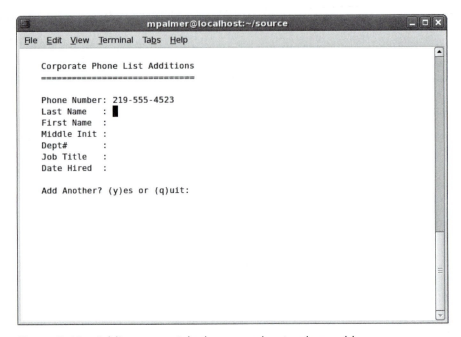

Figure 7-18   Adding a new telephone number to phoneadd

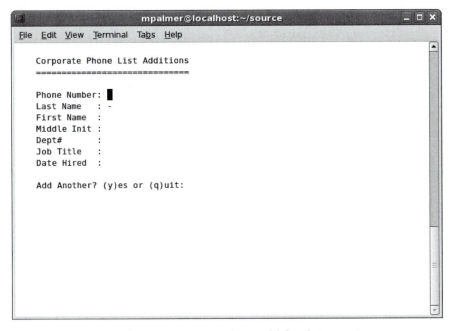

Figure 7-19   Using the minus sign in phoneadd for data reentry

8. Complete the remaining fields with the following information. As the cursor moves to each field, test the program by typing the **minus sign(-)** and pressing **Enter**. The cursor should move to the previous field each time.

Last Name: **Brooks**   Dept#: **4540**

First Name: **Sally**   Job Title: **Programmer**

Middle Init: **H**   Date Hired: **02-20-2007**

9. After you enter the date in the Date Hired field, press **Enter** to save the information to the file, and then press **q** to quit. Use the *cat* command to display the contents of the corp_phones file. The new record should appear.

Project 7-14

In this project, you further modify the phoneadd script to protect against duplicate phone numbers using a process called input validation. Review the pseudocode and flowchart in Figure 7-7 before you perform this modification.

To prevent phone number duplications via the phoneadd script:

1. Be certain you are in the source directory. Load the phoneadd script into vi or Emacs.

2. Add the boldface section of the following code to complete the revised script.

> **NOTE** Be sure to enter one continuous line for the code: *tput cup 19 1; echo "This number has already been assigned to:"*. Also, use one continuous line for the code: *tput cup 21 1; echo "Press ENTER to continue..."*. Both of these code lines are wrapped into two lines in the code example due to the margin limitations of the book.

```
#!/bin/bash
# =========================================================
# Script Name:   phoneadd
# By:            Your initials here
# Date:          Today's date
# Purpose:       A shell script that sets up a loop to add
#                new employees to the corp_phones file.
#                The code also prevents duplicate phone
#                numbers from being assigned.
# Command Line: phoneadd
#
# =========================================================
trap "rm ~/tmp/* 2> /dev/null; exit" 0 1 2 3
phonefile=~/source/corp_phones
looptest=y
while test "$looptest" = "y"
do
  clear
```

7

```
tput cup 1 4; echo "Corporate Phone List Additions"
tput cup 2 4; echo "==============================="
tput cup 4 4; echo "Phone Number:"
tput cup 5 4; echo "Last Name    :"
tput cup 6 4; echo "First Name   :"
tput cup 7 4; echo "Middle Init :"
tput cup 8 4; echo "Dept#        :"
tput cup 9 4; echo "Job Title   :"
tput cup 10 4; echo "Date Hired :"
tput cup 12 4; echo "Add Another? (y)es or (q)uit "
tput cup 4 18; read phonenum
if  test $phonenum = "q"
then
        clear ; exit
fi
# Check to see if the phone number already exists
while grep "$phonenum" $phonefile > ~/tmp/temp
do
        tput cup 19 1 ; echo "This number has already
         been assigned to: "
        tput cup 20 1 ; tr ':' ' ' < ~/tmp/temp
        tput cup 21 1 ; echo "Press ENTER to
         continue... "
        read prompt
        tput cup 4 18 ; echo "                    "
        tput cup 4 18 ; read phonenum
        if test $phonenum = "q"
        then
            clear ; exit
        fi
done
tput cup 5 18 ; read lname
        ... The remainder of the program is unchanged
```

3. Save the file and exit the editor.

4. If you have not already created a tmp directory under your home directory, create one now.

5. Run the program. Test it by entering a phone number that already exists in the file, such as **219-555-4587**, and then press **Enter**. Your screen should look like Figure 7-20.

6. Press **Enter** and press **Ctrl+z** to exit. Type **clear** and press **Enter** to clear the screen.

```
                    mpalmer@localhost:~/source

 File  Edit  View  Terminal  Tabs  Help

   Corporate Phone List Additions
   =============================

   Phone Number: 219-555-4587
   Last Name   :
   First Name  :
   Middle Init :
   Dept#       :
   Job Title   :
   Date Hired  :


   Add Another? (y)es or (q)uit:




 This number has already been assigned to:
 219-555-4587 Mitchell Barbara C 4541 Admin Asst 12-14-1995
 Press ENTER to continue...
```

Figure 7-20   Testing the input validation capability in the phoneadd script

Project 7-15

Functions can save time by enabling you to reuse lines of code in many scripts or programs. In this project, you create a simple function, called *datenow( )*, to display the current date.

To declare the simple *datenow( )* function:

1. Type **cd** and press **Enter** to change to your home directory.

2. At the command line, type **datenow( )**, and press **Enter**. Notice the prompt changes to the **>** symbol. This indicates the shell is waiting for you to type more information to complete the command you started.

3. At the > prompt, type **{**, and press **Enter**.

4. At the next > prompt, type **date**, and press **Enter**.

5. At the third > prompt, type **}**, and press **Enter**. The normal prompt now returns.

6. You have created the *datenow( )* function and stored it in the shell's memory. Call it by typing **datenow** and pressing **Enter**. (See Figure 7-21.)

7. Type **clear** and press **Enter** to clear the screen.

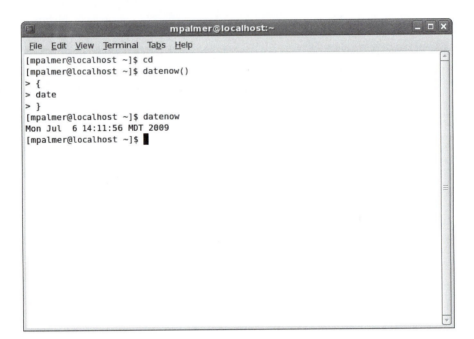

Figure 7-21 Creating the *datenow( )* function

Project 7-16

One of the most important capabilities of functions is accepting arguments. In this project, you redefine the *datenow( )* function to accept an argument.

To redefine the *datenow( )* function to accept an argument:

1. At the command line, type **datenow( )**, and press **Enter**. The commands you are about to type replace those previously stored in the *datenow( )* function in Hands-On Project 7-15.

2. At the > prompt, type **{**, and press **Enter**.

3. At the > prompt, type **echo "$1"**, and press **Enter**. When the function runs, this command displays the information passed to the function in the first argument used when you execute datenow.

4. At the > prompt, type **date**, and press **Enter**.

5. At the > prompt, type **}**, and press **Enter**. The normal prompt returns.

6. Test the function by typing **datenow "Today's date and time are:"** and pressing **Enter**. Your screen looks similar to the following:

```
[beth@localhost ~]$ datenow "Today's date and time are:"
Today's date and time are:
Mon Nov 9 21:49:45 MST 2009
```

Project 7-17

Learning to create functions in shell scripts can make you a more efficient and accurate script programmer. In this project, you create a hidden shell script called .myfuncs that includes sorting functions for use on the corp_phones file used by your employee telephone number application.

To place several functions inside a shell script:

1. Ensure you are in the source directory.

2. Use the vi or Emacs editor to create the .myfuncs file inside your source directory.

3. Enter the following functions:

```
sort_name()
  {
  sort -k 2 -t: corp_phones
  }
sort_job()
  {
  sort -k 6 -t: corp_phones
  }
sort_dept()
  {
  sort -k 5 -t: corp_phones
  }
```

4. Save the file and exit the editor.

5. Type **clear** and press **Enter**.

Project 7-18

In this project, you load the .myfuncs file into memory so its functions can be executed. To do this, you type a period (.), followed by a space, followed by the name of the file containing the functions (.myfuncs). In the second part of the project, you start the .myfuncs script from the .bashrc login script, so you can run the .myfuncs functions anytime after you log in.

To load the .myfuncs file:

1. At the command line, type **. .myfuncs** (type a **period**, press the **spacebar**, type a **period**, and type **myfuncs**), and press **Enter**. Nothing appears, but the functions are loaded into memory. Test some functions. Type **sort_dept** and press **Enter**. (See Figure 7-22; your results might look slightly different because of differences in new records entered during earlier testing.)

2. Type **sort_name** and press **Enter** to see the telephone records sorted by last name. Type **sort_job** and press **Enter** to sort the records by the job name.

```
                    mpalmer@localhost:~/source                        _ □ X
 File  Edit  View  Terminal  Tabs  Help
[mpalmer@localhost ~]$ cd source
[mpalmer@localhost source]$ vi .myfuncs
[mpalmer@localhost source]$ . .myfuncs
[mpalmer@localhost source]$ sort_dept
219-555-4591:Moore:Sarah:H:4500:Dept Manager:08-01-1978
219-555-4501:Robinson:Albert:J:4501:Secretary:08-12-1997
219-555-4544:Polk:John:S:4520:Accountant:09-22-2001
219-555-4511:Brooks:Sally:H:4540:Programmer:02-20-2007
219-555-4587:Mitchell:Barbara:C:4541:Admin Asst:12-14-1995
219-555-4589:Olson:Timothy:H:4544:Supervisor:06-30-1983
219-555-7176:Albertson:Jeannette:K:5547:DC Clerk:02-19-2007
219-555-7175:Mullins:Allen:L:7527:Sales Rep:02-19-2007
[mpalmer@localhost source]$ █
```

Figure 7-22 Using the sort_dept script function

To modify your .bashrc file to load the .myfuncs script:

1. Type **cd** to ensure you are in your home directory. Load your .bashrc file into the vi or Emacs editor.

2. At the end of the file, add the following command; be certain to put a space between the period (.) and the tilde (~):

   ```
   . ~/source/.myfuncs
   ```

3. Save the file and exit the editor.

4. Log out and log back in to load the functions.

5. Make your source directory your current working directory.

6. Test the sort_name, sort_dept, and sort_job functions.

**HANDS-ON
PROJECTS**

Project 7-19

Now, you are ready to enhance the employee telephone number application to display the telephone listing in order sorted by employees' last names. You can do this by using the sort_name function, as stored in the .myfuncs file.

To sort the phone list, you make a minor revision to the phlist1 script to load the functions, and then call sort_name to redirect the sorted output to a temporary file. The sorted temporary file serves as input to the *awk* command that displays the records. The revised code also uses the CLEAR variable you set up in Hands-On Project 7-12.

To sort the phone listing:

1. Switch to the source directory, if you are not already in it. Use the vi or Emacs editor to open the phlist1 script. Add the additions and revisions that are shown in boldface.

```
#!/bin/bash
# ========================================================
# Script Name:    phlist1
# By:             Your initials here
# Date:           Today's date
# Purpose:        Use awk to format colon-separated fields
#                 in a flat file and display to the screen
# Command Line:   phlist1
# ========================================================
echo "$CLEAR"
tput cup 2 20; echo "Corporate Phone List"
tput cup 3 20; echo "===================="
tput cup 5 0;
. .myfuncs
sort_name > sorted_phones
awk -F: ' { printf "%-12s %-12s %s\t%s %s %10.10s %s\n",
  $2, $3, $4, $1, $5, $6, $7 } ' sorted_phones
tput cup 23 1; echo "Review"
tput cup 22 8; read prompt
```

2. This code includes the .myfuncs shell script, which contains sort functions. Thus, the code works regardless of whether the .myfuncs shell script is already loaded in memory via the .bashrc file. Save the file and exit the editor.

3. Test the file by typing **phlist1** and pressing **Enter**. (See Figure 7-23.) Press **Enter** when you finish observing the screen.

```
                        mpalmer@localhost:~/source                     _ □ ×
 File  Edit  View  Terminal  Tabs  Help

                 Corporate Phone List
                 ====================

 Albertson    Jeannette    K    219-555-7176 5547    DC Clerk 02-19-2007
 Brooks       Sally        H    219-555-4511 4540 Programmer 02-20-2007
 Mitchell     Barbara      C    219-555-4587 4541 Admin Asst 12-14-1995
 Moore        Sarah        H    219-555-4591 4500 Dept Manag 08-01-1978
 Mullins      Allen        L    219-555-7175 7527    Sales Rep 02-19-2007
 Olson        Timothy      H    219-555-4589 4544 Supervisor 06-30-1983
 Polk         John         S    219-555-4544 4520 Accountant 09-22-2001
 Robinson     Albert       J    219-555-4501 4501   Secretary 08-12-1997




 Review ▮
```

Figure 7-23   Testing the phlist1 script

DISCOVERY EXERCISES

1. What are the exit statuses of the *test* commands discussed in this chapter and what do they mean?

2. Create a variable called mem_size and set its contents to 1024. Next use the *test* command to determine if the contents of mem_size are less than or equal to 512.

3. Set your shell from the command line to be the Bash shell. Then use the *echo* command to verify the contents of the shell variable. What is now contained in the shell variable?

4. After performing Exercise 3, use the *test* command to evaluate whether the shell variable contains a reference to the Bash shell and use the *echo* command to determine the result. (Note that this provides one way to verify from within a script that the script user is set up to use the Bash shell.)

5. Make certain that your home directory is your current working directory. Use the command to verify that your source directory exists. How might knowledge of this command be useful when you create scripts for yourself or others?

6. Switch to your source directory and make a copy of the corp_phones file (which will give you a valuable backup of the corp_phones file) with the name corp_phones_bak. Using the *tr* command as a filter for output from another command, display to the screen the contents of corp_phones_bak so that all uppercase letters from A to M are lowercase.

7. Make your home directory your current working directory. Use the vi or Emacs editor to open the veg_choice script you created in Chapter 6. Enter a line in that script to ensure the script uses the Bash shell. Run veg_choice to ensure your change works properly.

8. Edit the veg_choice script again, but this time change the line *if ["$veg_name" = "carrots"]* to use the *test* command.

9. Create pseudocode and a flowchart for a proposed script that does the following:

   ❑ Reads and sets the variable M

   ❑ Reads and sets the variable R

   ❑ Reads and sets the variable T

   ❑ Sums M, R, and T in the variable A

   ❑ Evaluates A to determine if it is greater than 2000

   ❑ If A is greater than 2000, prints on the screen "A is over 2000."

   ❑ If A is less than or equal to 2000, prints on the screen "A is 2000 or less."

10. Create the script for Exercise 9 and name it evaluate_*yourinitials*, such as evaluate_jp. Test your script.

11. Create a shell variable, called CALNOW, that outputs the calendar for the current month.

12. How could you set up CALNOW so that it works every time you log in using the Bash shell?

13. List the records in the corp_phones_bak file that you created earlier, so that they are displayed without colons separating the fields, but have one space between the fields instead.

14. Use the vi or Emacs editor to open the nameaddr script you created in Chapter 6. The script should look similar to the following:

```
looptest=y
 while [ "$looptest" = y ]
  do
    echo -n "Enter Name : "; read name
    echo -n "Enter Street : "; read street
    echo -n "Enter City  : "; read city
    echo -n "Enter State  : "; read state
    echo -n "Enter Zip Code: "; read zip
    echo -n "Continue? (y)es or (n)o: "; read looptest
  done
```

How can you change this script to employ the *test* command?

7

15. In your source directory, write a script called "them" in which you create a function called whoisthere that displays a listing of who is logged in and displays the column headings for the information that appears.

16. Make the contents of your script resident in memory and test your whoisthere function.

17. Modify your whoisthere function so that you can enter "These are the folks logged in:" as an argument to appear before your list of who is logged in to the system.

18. What actions do you take next to use the whoisthere function with your modifications?

19. How can you set up your new whoisthere function so that it can be run each time you log in using the Bash script?

20. Use a one-line command to strip out the telephone prefix (219-) and the colons in the corp_phones_bak file and save the result in a file called noprefix.

21. Troubleshoot the problems with the following script:

```
#================================================
Script Name: record_entry
By: TRJackson
#================================================
looptrack = y
while [ "$ looptrack " = 1 ]
do
   echo -n "Type in the account number:" read account
   echo -n "Type the first and last name:" ; read full_name
   echo -n "Type the age:" red age
   echo -n "Enter another record?" ; read looptrack
finish
```

8

EXPLORING THE UNIX/LINUX UTILITIES

After reading this chapter and completing the exercises, you will be able to:

♦ Understand many of the UNIX/Linux utilities that are available and how they are classified

♦ Use the *dd* utility to copy and convert files

♦ Monitor hard disk usage

♦ Use system status utilities

♦ Monitor and manage processes

♦ Check the spelling of text in a document

♦ Use the *cmp* command to compare the contents of two files

♦ Format text to create and use a man page

♦ Use the *dump* command to back up a system

♦ Send and receive e-mail

♦ Use basic network commands and utilities

So far in this book, you have used many practical UNIX/Linux utilities, from utilities to list files to editors for creating and modifying files to the selection, manipulation, and transformation utilities. UNIX and Linux offer a full array of utilities beyond the ones you have already learned.

In this chapter, you learn more about the utilities in UNIX/Linux. First, you survey the categories of UNIX/Linux utilities, including file-processing utilities, system status utilities, network utilities, communications utilities, security utilities, programming utilities, source code management utilities, and miscellaneous utilities. There isn't enough room in this chapter to explore all of the utilities in depth, and you have already learned to use many of the utilities listed, so the utilities are presented in summary tables. This chapter then explores a sampling of useful utilities, including the *dd* utility for copying and converting files, utilities for monitoring hard disk usage, utilities to monitor the system status and system processes, a spell-checking utility, a utility to compare files, and a utility to format text. Other utilities you learn about in this chapter include utilities to back up files, an e-mail utility, basic networking utilities, the Network File System for sharing resources, and Samba for accessing Windows-based files.

UNDERSTANDING UNIX/LINUX UTILITIES

UNIX/Linux utilities let you create and manage files, run programs, produce reports, and generally interact with the system. Beyond these basics, the utility programs offer a full range of services that let you monitor and maintain the system and recover from a wide range of errors. UNIX/Linux utilities are classified into eight major functional areas dictated by user needs: file processing, system status, networking, communications, security, programming, source code management, and miscellaneous.

UNIX/Linux utilities are programs, but they are often referred to as commands in the documentation. In this chapter, you see both "utility" and "command," depending on the command you are using.

For the sake of completeness, this chapter contains some references and commentary about utilities in general, but it concentrates on those utilities that relate to file processing, system status, e-mail, networking, backups, and miscellaneous tasks.

Utility programs are vital for working in an operating system. You have already worked with dozens of utilities, many of which are reviewed for your convenience in the tables included with this chapter. For example, you have already worked with many of the file-processing utilities, some of the system status utilities, and some of the miscellaneous utilities.

In this and later chapters, you work with additional system status, programming, and miscellaneous utilities. There are many, many UNIX/Linux utilities, and there is not room in this book to cover them all. However, you can come back to the tables in this chapter for a quick reference to utilities you have used or to find a utility for a specific task. You can learn more about these utilities using the *man* and *info* documentation options (such as *man mesg* or *info mesg*).

New utility programs are continually being added as developers find better and faster ways to make UNIX/Linux run more efficiently.

CLASSIFYING UNIX/LINUX UTILITIES

Utilities can be classified in several categories, as some work exclusively with UNIX/Linux files, others handle network tasks, and still others are designed to help programmers. File-processing utilities, listed in Table 8-1, make up the largest category. These utilities display and manipulate files.

Table 8-1   File-processing utilities

Command	Brief Description of Function
awk	Processes files
cat	Displays files (and is used with other tools to concatenate files)
cmp	Compares two files
comm	Compares sorted files, and shows differences
cp	Copies files
cpio	Copies and backs up files to an archive
cut	Selects characters or fields from input lines
dd	Copies and converts input records
diff	Compares two text files, and shows differences
dump	Backs up files
fdformat	Formats a floppy disk at a low level
file	Displays the file type
find	Finds files within file tree
fmt	Formats text very simply
grep	Matches patterns in a file
groff	Processes embedded text formatting codes
gzip	Compresses or decompresses files
head	Displays the first part of a file (first 10 lines by default)
ispell	Checks one or more files for spelling errors
less	Displays files allowing for scrolling forward and backward (pauses when screen is full)
ln	Creates a link to a file
lpr	Sends a file to a printer or printer device
ls	Lists file and directory names and attributes
man	Displays documentation for commands
mkbootdisk	Creates a CD (or floppy disk on older distributions) from which to boot a system
mkdir	Creates a new directory
mkfs	Builds a UNIX/Linux file system
mount	Mounts file systems and devices
mv	Renames and moves files and directories
newfs	Creates a new file system (used in UNIX systems in particular)
od	Formats and displays data from a file in octal, hexadecimal, and ASCII formats
paste	Concatenates files horizontally

8

Table 8-1   File-processing utilities (continued)

Command	Brief Description of Function
pr	Formats text files for printing and displays them
pwd	Shows the directory you are in
rdev	Queries or sets the root image device
restore	Restores files (from a dump)
rm	Removes files
rmdir	Removes directories
sed	Edits streams (noninteractive)
sort	Sorts or merges files
tail	Displays the last lines of files (last 10 lines by default)
tar	Copies and backs up files to a tape archive
touch	Changes file modification dates
uniq	Displays unique lines of a sorted file
wc	Counts lines, words, and bytes
whereis	Locates information about a specific file

System status utilities, listed in Table 8-2, is the second largest category. It includes utilities that display and alter the status of files, disks, and the overall system. These utilities let you know who is online, the names and status of running processes, the amount of hard disk space available, and where to find other commands you need to run.

Table 8-2   System status utilities

Command	Brief Description of Function
date	Sets and displays date and time
df	Displays the amount of free space remaining on disk
du	Summarizes file space usage
file	Determines file type (for example: shell script, executable, ASCII text, and others)
finger	Displays detailed information about users who are logged in
free	Displays amount of free and used memory in the system
edquota	Displays user disk quotas and enables them to be changed
kill	Terminates a running process
ps	Displays process status by process identification number and name
sleep	Suspends process execution for a specified time
top	Dynamically displays the status of processes in real time, focusing on those processes that are using the most CPU resources
uname	Shows information about the operating system
vmstat	Shows information about virtual memory use
w	Displays detailed information about the users who are logged in
who	Displays brief information about the users who are logged in

Network utilities, listed in Table 8-3, consist of the essential commands for communicating and sharing information on a network, as well as for viewing information about network connection status.

Table 8-3 Network utilities

Command	Brief Description of Function
ftp	Transfers files over a network
ifconfig	Sets up a network interface
netstat	Shows network connection information
nfsstat	Shows statistics for Network File System (NFS; file upload and download) activity
ping	Polls another network station (using TCP/IP); great for a fast determination about whether your network connection is working
rcp	Remotely copies a file from a network computer
rlogin	Logs in to a remote computer
route	Displays routing table information, and can be used to configure routing
rsh	Executes commands on a remote computer
showmount	Lists clients that have mounted volumes on a server
telnet	Connects to a remote computer on a network
traceroute	Shows the route along a network between the source device and the destination, such as from a computer to a server
wvdial	Controls a modem dialer for dial-up connections over a phone line

8

The communication utilities, listed in Table 8-4, handle mail and messaging tasks. These programs include some advanced features such as **Multipurpose Internet Mail Extensions (MIME)**, which is a standard that supports sending and receiving binary files in mail messages.

Table 8-4 Communications utilities

Command	Brief Description of Function
mail	Sends electronic mail messages
mesg	Denies (mesg n) or accepts (mesg y) messages
talk	Lets users simultaneously type messages to each other
wall	Sends a message to all logged in users (who have permissions set to receive messages)
write	Sends a message to another user

Security utilities, which are shown in Table 8-5, enable you to make your system safer from intrusions and help to prevent damage from viruses or malicious programs. They range from securing your files to configuring a password to establishing a firewall. A firewall is software or hardware placed between two or more networks or that can reside on a particular computer and that selectively allows or denies access via a network.

Table 8-5 Security utilities

Command	Brief Description of Function
chgrp	Changes the group associated with a file or the file's group ownership
chmod	Changes the access permissions of a file or directory
chown	Changes the owner of a file
ipchains	Manages a firewall and packet filtering (do not use if you are using *iptables* instead)
iptables	Manages a firewall and packet filtering (do not use if you are using *ipchains* instead)
passwd	Changes a password

Programming utilities, listed in Table 8-6, are designed to help users develop software projects written in C and C++ programs. You learn to use many of these utilities in Chapter 10, "Developing UNIX/Linux Applications in C and C++."

Table 8-6 Programming utilities

Command	Brief Description of Function
configure	Configures program source code automatically
g++	Compiles a C++ program
gcc	Compiles a C program
make	Maintains program source code
patch	Updates source code

Source code management utilities, which are listed in Table 8-7, are vital in a programming and development environment. When several applications developers are working on a project, you need to have ways to track programming changes. If these changes are not tracked, the changes made by one programmer might inadvertently be undone or changed by another, with unanticipated outcomes. For financial auditing requirements, you must also have ways to track programming changes to meet the demands of audit reviews. This protects programmers who work on applications that affect how money is handled, and it protects organizations. These UNIX/Linux utilities have a proven track record in managing teamwork programming, and are vital tools for scheduling and managing large-scale applications.

Table 8-7 Source code management utilities

Command	Brief Description of Function
ci	Creates changes in Revision Control Systems (RCS)
co	Retrieves an unencoded revision of an RCS file
cvs	Manages concurrent access to files in a hierarchy
rcs	Creates or changes the attributes of an RCS file
rlog	Prints a summary of the history of an RCS file

Finally, miscellaneous utilities include unique programs that perform very specific and special functions. As you can see from the descriptions in Table 8-8, these commands include providing a system calendar, scheduling events, and identifying terminals attached to the system.

Table 8-8 Miscellaneous utilities

Command	Brief Description of Function
at	Executes a command or script at a specified time
atq	Shows the jobs (commands or scripts) already scheduled to run
atrm	Enables you to remove a job (command or script) that is scheduled to run
batch	Runs a command or script, and is really a subset of the at command that takes you to the at> prompt, if you type only batch (in Fedora, Red Hat Enterprise Linux, or SUSE, a command or script is run when the system load is at an acceptable level)
cal	Displays a calendar for a month or year
cd	Changes to a directory
crontab	Schedules a command to run at a preset time
expr	Evaluates expressions (used for arithmetic and string manipulations)
fsck	Checks and fixes problems on a file system (repairs damage)
printenv	Prints environment variables
tee	Clones output stream to one or more files
tr	Replaces specified characters (a translation filter)
tty	Displays terminal path name
xargs	Converts standard output of one command into arguments for another

Now that you have surveyed the diverse utilities that are available, you are ready to use a sampling of commands that UNIX/Linux users employ frequently.

USING THE dd COMMAND

Files not only store information, but they also store it in a particular format. For example, most computers store text using ASCII codes. (Some legacy IBM mainframes, however, use EBCDIC codes to store text.) In addition to the internal codes that computers use to store information, some files store text in all uppercase letters. Likewise, other files store text in all lowercase letters. Some files include only records, where each record consists of several fields. A special character, such as a colon, separates the fields, and each record ends with a character denoting a line break. Different files have different internal formats, depending upon how the file is used.

The standard UNIX/Linux copy utility, cp, duplicates a file, but it cannot alter the format of the destination copy. When you need to copy a file and change the format of the destination copy, use the *dd* command instead of *cp*. Possessing a rich set of options that allow it to handle copies when other methods are inappropriate, the *dd* command can, for instance, handle conversions to and from legacy EBCDIC to ASCII (used on PCs). The *dd* command is frequently used for devices such as tapes, which have discrete record sizes, or for fast multisector reads from disks.

Syntax **dd** [options]

Dissection

- Copies an input file and can convert the file's contents to another format or to have different characteristics
- Useful options (these do not start with a hyphen) include:

  if= designates the input file

  of= designates the output file

  bs= specifies the block size in bytes for the input and output files

  ibs= specifies the input block size in bytes (on many systems, the default is 512 bytes)

  obs= specifies the output block size in bytes (on many systems, the default is 512 bytes)

  conv= converts the input file according to a specified designation, such as using *conv=block* to convert variable-length records to fixed-length, *conv=unblock* to convert fixed-length records to variable length, *conv=ascii* to convert EBCDIC to ASCII, *conv=lcase* to convert uppercase to lowercase, or *conv=ucase* to convert lowercase to uppercase

---

TIP

Specifying block size, an optional requirement, speeds copying, especially when copying backups to tape. On some systems, another advantage of the *dd* command is that users can access a removable medium such as a CD without first mounting it.

Hands-On Project 8-1 enables you to use the *dd* command to back up a file.

Checking Hard Disk Usage

UNIX/Linux system users, as well as the system itself, create and enlarge files. Eventually, unless files are removed, even the largest disk runs out of free space. To maintain adequate free space, you should use these basic strategies:

- Be vigilant against running dangerously low on free space by using the *df* command.

- Watch for conspicuous consumption by using the *du* command.

- Follow a routine schedule for "garbage" collection and removal by using a combination of the *find* and the *rm* commands.

Using the df Utility

The *df* utility reports the number of 1024-byte blocks that are allocated, used, and available; the percentage used; and the mount point—for mounted file systems. The reports displayed are based on the command options entered. For example, Figure 8-1 shows the *df* information in megabytes for one file system (/dev/hda2). You can be in either your account or the root account to use *df* and the other utilities described in this section, but it is recommended that you use your account for the projects in this book.

Syntax **df** [-options] [*filesystem*]

Dissection

- Displays information about how space is allocated in a file system, such as used and free space

- Useful options include:

  -h displays in "human-readable" format, such as using 29G (G is for GB) instead of 29659208

  -l displays only local file systems

  -m displays sizes in megabytes

  -t displays only the type of file system

Hands-On Project 8-2 enables you to use the *df* command.

NOTE

If you just enter *df* without specifying a file system, this shows information for all mounted file systems. Also, note that the combined used and available disk space might not total to the allocated space because the system uses some space for its own purposes.

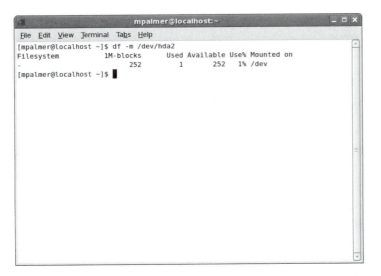

Figure 8-1   Viewing information for one file system in megabytes

Using the du Utility

The *du* utility summarizes disk usage. If you enter the command without options, you receive a report based on all file usage, starting at your current directory and progressing down through all subdirectories. File usage is expressed in the number of 512-byte blocks (default) or by the number of bytes (the *-b* option). Figure 8-2 shows the *du* command used to display information about the /etc directory in bytes.

Syntax **du** [-options] [*filesystem*]

Dissection

- Summarizes disk usage, with the default of presenting information by directory
- Useful options include:

  -a displays information for files as well as for directories

  -b displays information in bytes

  -c creates a total at the end

  -h displays information in "human-readable" format, such as using 3.7M for 3.7 million instead of 3700

  -S omits the size of subdirectories in the totals for directories

Try Hands-On Project 8-3 to use the *du* command.

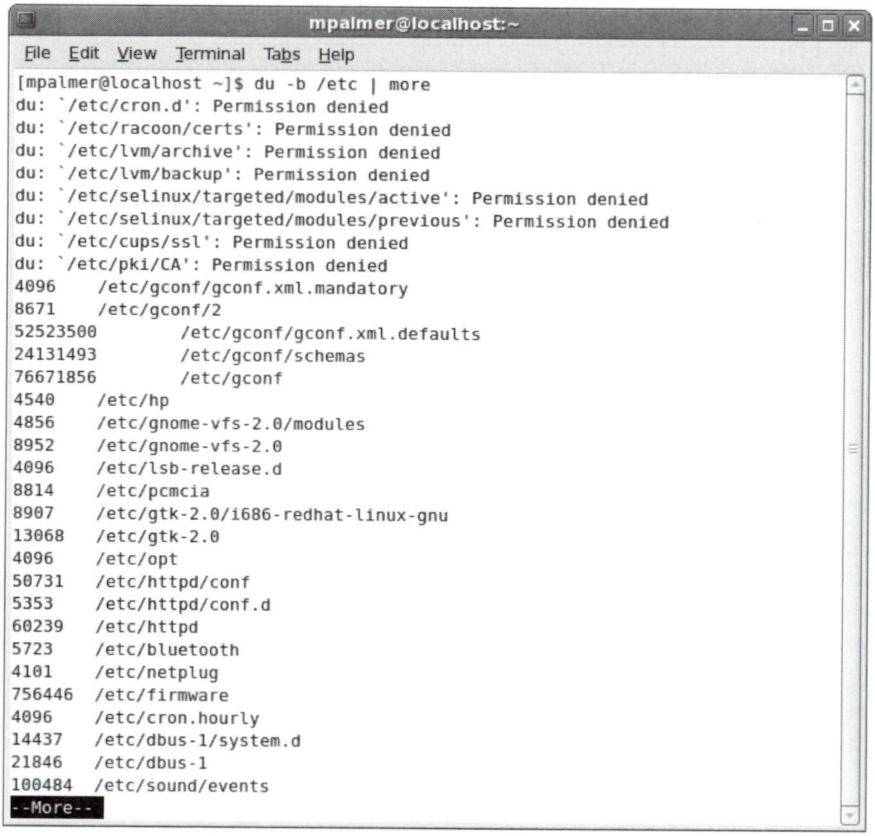
mpalmer@localhost:~
File Edit View Terminal Tabs Help
[mpalmer@localhost ~]$ du -b /etc | more
du: `/etc/cron.d': Permission denied
du: `/etc/racoon/certs': Permission denied
du: `/etc/lvm/archive': Permission denied
du: `/etc/lvm/backup': Permission denied
du: `/etc/selinux/targeted/modules/active': Permission denied
du: `/etc/selinux/targeted/modules/previous': Permission denied
du: `/etc/cups/ssl': Permission denied
du: `/etc/pki/CA': Permission denied
4096 /etc/gconf/gconf.xml.mandatory
8671 /etc/gconf/2
52523500 /etc/gconf/gconf.xml.defaults
24131493 /etc/gconf/schemas
76671856 /etc/gconf
4540 /etc/hp
4856 /etc/gnome-vfs-2.0/modules
8952 /etc/gnome-vfs-2.0
4096 /etc/lsb-release.d
8814 /etc/pcmcia
8907 /etc/gtk-2.0/i686-redhat-linux-gnu
13068 /etc/gtk-2.0
4096 /etc/opt
50731 /etc/httpd/conf
5353 /etc/httpd/conf.d
60239 /etc/httpd
5723 /etc/bluetooth
4101 /etc/netplug
756446 /etc/firmware
4096 /etc/cron.hourly
14437 /etc/dbus-1/system.d
21846 /etc/dbus-1
100484 /etc/sound/events
--More--

Figure 8-2 Viewing *du* information for the /etc directory

Removing Garbage Files

An easy way to free space in your file systems is to remove garbage files. **Garbage files** are temporary files, such as a core file, that lose their usefulness after several days. A **core file** is created when an executing program attempts to do something illegal, such as accessing another user's memory. The UNIX/Linux operating system detects the attempt and sends a signal to the program. The signal halts the offending program, and creates a copy of the program and its environment in a file named core in the current directory. The programmer who wrote the program that "dumps core" (slang for this event) might be interested in dissecting the core file with a debugging tool. However, all too often the core file simply languishes unused in some branch of the directory hierarchy. All files created this way have the same name: core.

Another file with a generic name is a.out, the default for the output of program compilation procedures. Like core files, the true identity of these generically named files often gets lost over time. You can use the *find* command to retrieve these wasteful files, and then execute the *rm* command to remove them, such as by executing the following:

```
find . "(" -name a.out -o -name core ")" -exec rm {} \;
```

You used the *find* command in earlier chapters to locate files. The preceding *find* command example locates every occurrence of the a.out and core files, and then deletes them with the *rm* command. The first argument, dot (.), tells *find* to start looking in the current directory. The argument *"(" -name a.out -o -name core ")"* uses the -o (OR) operator. It tells *find* to search for files named a.out OR core. The *-exec rm* option instructs *find* to execute the *rm* command each time it locates a file with the name being searched for. The {} characters are replaced with the matching file name. For example, when the command locates an a.out file, the {} characters are replaced with a.out, so the command *rm a.out* is executed. The \; terminates the command. You search for and remove a.out and core files in Hands-On Project 8-4.

You can locate several other garbage files with the *find* command. For example, users often name files test, temp, or tmp to indicate temporary files that might be forgotten over time and should be removed.

Using System Status Utilities

As you see from the list of command descriptions in Table 8-2, the system status commands reflect the system's performance. Although system engineers who assess the CPU's performance primarily use this data, you should at least know how to obtain this information. You can redirect the output of these commands to a file that you can then print or forward to the system administrator and system tune-up specialists.

Using the top Command

One of the most effective utilities for auditing system performance is the *top* command. The *top* command displays a listing of the most CPU-intensive tasks, such as the processor state, in real time (the display is updated every five seconds by default). This means that you can actually see what is happening inside the computer as it progresses.

Syntax **top** [options]

Dissection

- Monitors CPU-intensive tasks; options on many systems can be specified with or without a hyphen (-) preceding the option
- Useful options include:

  d specifies the delay between screen updates

  p monitors the process with the specified process id (PID)

  q causes the *top* utility to refresh without delay

  s allows the *top* utility to run in secure mode, which disables the interactive commands, such as *k* to kill a process (a good option for those not in charge of tuning the system)

  S runs *top* in cumulative mode; this mode displays the cumulative CPU time used by a process instead of the current CPU time used

  n specifies how many times to update the display

  b enables you to run in batch mode so that you can send the output to a file for later study (you must use the *n* option with the *b* option)

  i causes the *top* utility to ignore any idle processes

  c displays the command line instead of the command name only

---

While running, the *top* command supports interactive commands such as *k*, which kills a running process. The *top* utility continues to produce output until you press *q* to terminate the execution of the program.

 The simplest way for most users to run the *top* utility is to issue the command without options.

TIP

Try Hands-On Project 8-5 to use the *top* command.

Using the uptime Command

Sometimes, you might need to know how long a system has been running since you last booted it. For example, if there have been recent system problems, you might want to track how long your system has been up since the last problem requiring a reboot. The *uptime* command displays the current time, how long the system has been up, the number of users on the system, and the load average. The load average is for three intervals: the past 1 minute, 5 minutes, and 15 minutes.

Syntax **uptime**

Dissection

■ Displays how long the system has been up since the last boot

---

Using the free Command

A useful, though static, display of memory usage is generated by the *free* command. The *free* command displays the amount of free and used memory in the system. (See Figure 8-3.) The *free* command also enables you to monitor the usage of your swap space (disk space that acts like an extension of memory; see Chapter 2, "Exploring the UNIX/Linux File Systems and File Security"). By monitoring your system using *free*, you can determine if you have enough RAM for the tasks on your computer, and you can determine if your swap space is set properly. Unlike *top*, the *free* utility runs and then automatically exits.

Syntax **free** [–options]

Dissection

■ Provides statistics about free and used memory

■ Useful options include:

-*b* shows information in bytes (the default display is in kilobytes)

-*m* shows information in megabytes

-*g* shows information in gigabytes

-*s n* continuously monitors memory statistics so that you can view changes over time; the *n* value sets the interval at which *free* updates the statistics in seconds—type *Ctrl+c* to end

-*t* creates totals for RAM and swap memory statistics

Hands-On Project 8-6 enables you to use the *free* command.

```
                                mpalmer@localhost:~                          _ □ x
 File  Edit  View  Terminal  Tabs  Help
[mpalmer@localhost ~]$ free
              total        used        free      shared     buffers      cached
Mem:         514684      479724       34960           0       58504      226168
-/+ buffers/cache:       195052      319632
Swap:       1048568           0     1048568
[mpalmer@localhost ~]$ █
```

Figure 8-3   Using the *free* command to monitor memory and swap usage

Forwarding top and free Output

If you are experiencing problems with your computer, such as slow response, you might want to forward the output of the *top* and *free* commands to a computer support person for analysis. This is easily accomplished by using the > redirection symbol to store the contents in a file, as in the following command line, which provides *top* data terminating after three updates (the *n 3* option):

```
top n 3 > topdata
```

After you create the file, you might send it to a computer support person via e-mail or print the file using the *lpr* command:

```
lpr topdata
```

Try Hands-On Project 8-7 to save the results of *top* and *free* to files.

MANAGING PROCESSES

When you run a program, it starts one or more processes that are identified to the operating system through a unique number called a **process id** or **PID**. UNIX and Linux offer utilities to manage how a program is run and to monitor or kill processes used by a program. In the following sections, you learn how to run a program in the background, which means that although you do not see the program displayed in a window, it is still running behind the scenes. Also, you learn how to view what programs/processes are running on your system and how to kill a process.

Running Processes in the Background

Because UNIX/Linux is a multitasking operating system, it allows you to run programs in the background while you continue to work with other programs. For example, if you have a program that prints a lengthy report, you can run it in the background and continue working with other programs while the report is printing. As another example, you might decide to run the *top* program in the background to gather information about your system, or you might run a program in the background that schedules and starts other programs at a later time.

To run a program in the background, append the & character to the end of the command used to start the program. For example, to run the *top* program in the background, you would enter the following:

```
top&
```

Try Hands-On Project 8-8 to run a program in the background.

Monitoring Processes

Monitoring processes that are running can be valuable so you can identify which processes are active and determine if there are any you want to stop, such as processes running in the background or processes associated with programs you are no longer using. In another instance, you might start a program that runs for a long time, such as a statistics program that processes a huge amount of data. After you start the program, you might change your mind about what you want it to do, and need to stop the program so you can reset calculation parameters.

The *ps* command shows you a list of the processes currently running. When you use the command with no options, it shows a list of the processes associated with the current login session. When used with the *-A* or *-e* options, it shows a very long list of all processes running on the system, as shown in Figure 8-4.

Syntax **ps** [-options]

Dissection

- Provides a listing of the currently running processes
- Useful options include:

    -A or *-e* shows all processes currently running on the system

    -C commandname shows processes selected on the specified command name

    -p PID shows processes selected on the specified PID

    -l PID shows a long listing of information about processes

    l PID (no hyphen) shows a long listing of information about processes and has slightly different categories of display than the *-l* option

    --user shows processes by user

Hands-On Project 8-9 shows you how to use the *ps* command.

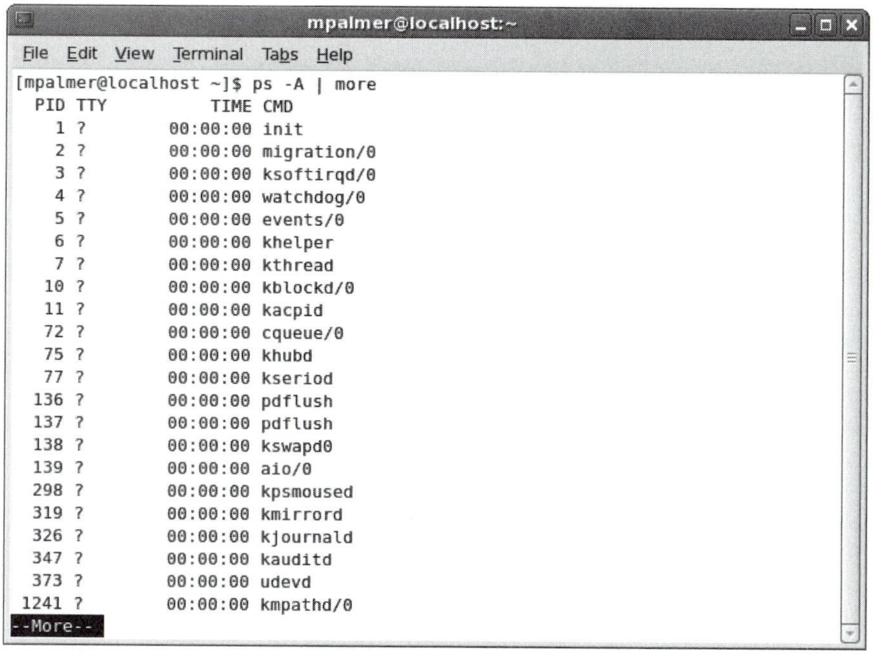

```
                          mpalmer@localhost:~                    _ □ x
File  Edit  View  Terminal  Tabs  Help
[mpalmer@localhost ~]$ ps -A | more
  PID TTY          TIME CMD
    1 ?        00:00:00 init
    2 ?        00:00:00 migration/0
    3 ?        00:00:00 ksoftirqd/0
    4 ?        00:00:00 watchdog/0
    5 ?        00:00:00 events/0
    6 ?        00:00:00 khelper
    7 ?        00:00:00 kthread
   10 ?        00:00:00 kblockd/0
   11 ?        00:00:00 kacpid
   72 ?        00:00:00 cqueue/0
   75 ?        00:00:00 khubd
   77 ?        00:00:00 kseriod
  136 ?        00:00:00 pdflush
  137 ?        00:00:00 pdflush
  138 ?        00:00:00 kswapd0
  139 ?        00:00:00 aio/0
  298 ?        00:00:00 kpsmoused
  319 ?        00:00:00 kmirrord
  326 ?        00:00:00 kjournald
  347 ?        00:00:00 kauditd
  373 ?        00:00:00 udevd
 1241 ?        00:00:00 kmpathd/0
--More--
```

Figure 8-4   Viewing all of the running processes

Killing Processes

If you are the system administrator and have root privileges, you might find it necessary to kill a user's process because its associated program is malfunctioning or using too many system resources. As a single user, you might find it necessary to kill a process that you have running in the background or one that you have started, but have changed your mind about running. Use the *kill* command plus the PID or process name as the argument to kill a process. (You, of course, can find both the PID and process name by using the *ps* command first.)

Syntax **kill** [*PID*] or **kill** [*%processname*]

Dissection

- Stops a process
- Use *kill -9* (9 is a signal number) to stop a process that does not respond to just the *kill* command

---

Hands-On Project 8-10 enables you to use the *kill* command.

Be very careful when using the *kill* command. If you kill a process that the operating system needs, you can cause disastrous results!

CAUTION

CHECKING THE SPELLING OF A DOCUMENT

If you create many plain-text documents in UNIX/Linux, it can be valuable to know how to check the spelling in those documents. For example, you might frequently create plain-text memos, e-mail messages or attachments, documentation files (such as readme files), or even papers using plain-text editors, such as vi and Emacs. You can check the spelling in such documents by using the *ispell* utility.

Syntax **ispell** [–options] *filenames*

Dissection

- Checks the spelling of words in one or more plain-text files and suggests changes
- Useful options include:

    -b creates a backup (.bak) of the original file

    -C ignores concatenated words

    -S orders the suggested substitutions from most likely to least likely

The *ispell* utility scans a text document, displays errors on the screen, and suggests other words with similar spellings as replacements for unrecognized words. A menu that appears on the bottom line of the screen shows corrective options and exit codes. (See Figure 8-5.)

In Hands-On Project 8-11, you use the *ispell* utility on a document.

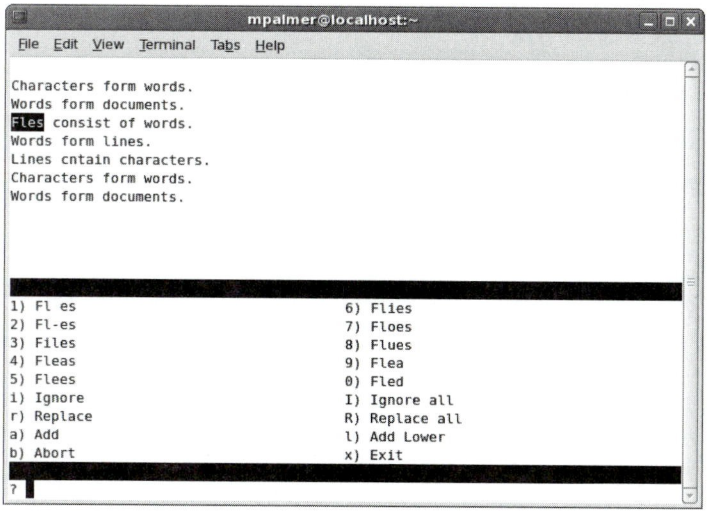

Figure 8-5 Checking the spelling in a document with *ispell*

COMPARING FILES

Suppose you have a file that you work with regularly. You make a backup copy of the file for safekeeping. Later, you want to see if the original file has changed since you made the backup copy. You can use the *cmp* utility to compare the contents of two files, and if there is a difference, the command reports the location at which the files first start to differ.

Syntax **cmp** [–options] *file1 file2*

Dissection

- Compares two files and indicates if they are different

When you compare two files, there is no output if the contents are identical. If the contents are not identical, you see a message that specifies the first byte (character) that is different between the files. For example, if you compare filea, which contains the line,

```
This is one file.
```

to fileb, which contains the following:

```
This is a different file.
```

the result from the command *cmp filea fileb* is

```
filea fileb differ: byte 9, line 1
```

Try Hands-On Project 8-12 to compare two files using the *cmp* command.

FORMATTING TEXT IN UNIX/LINUX

Text formatting in UNIX/Linux involves preparing a text file with embedded typesetting commands and then processing the marked-up text file with a computer program. This program generates commands for the output device, such as a printer, a monitor, or some other typesetter. UNIX/Linux's *nroff* and *troff* commands are often used to process the embedded typesetting commands to format the output.

UNIX/Linux users have long used the *nroff* and *troff* commands to produce manuals, corporate reports, books, and newspapers. These programs evolved from an earlier program, RUNOFF (a utility created in the late 1970s), which read pure text with embedded codes to format and print a text-enriched report. An embedded code is a special sequence of characters that is included with the regular text in the file. The special codes are not printed, but are interpreted as commands to perform text-formatting operations. For example, there are codes to produce boldface print, center text, and underline certain lines.

Using embedded codes in text to produce enriched output provides the advantage of not needing additional word-processing programs to produce documents. You can use any editor that works with text files, such as vi or Emacs. In addition, you can use added features, such as hyperlinks, to cross-reference other documents from within your document. You do need, however, an HTML browser program such as Mozilla Firefox, or UNIX/Linux utilities such as *nroff* and *troff*, to translate and execute the embedded hyperlink codes.

Linux provides *groff*, which implements the features of both *nroff* and *troff*.

Syntax **groff** [-T*dev*]

Dissection

- Text formatting utility

- Useful options include:

    -*T* designates a device type (no space between T and the device type), which specifies an output device such as ASCII to tell *groff* that the device is a typewriter-like device. The device type *dev* is for the man pages. Some other device types include *ps* for postscript printers, *dvi* for TeX dvi format, and *lj4* for an HP LaserJet4-compatible printer.

Table 8-9 lists a sampling of embedded codes supported by *groff*.

Table 8-9   Sample *groff* embedded commands

Embedded Command	Meaning
.ce *n*	Center next *n* lines
.ds C	Center
.ds R	Right-justify
.p *n*	Start a new paragraph indented *n* characters

Table 8-9 Sample *groff* embedded commands (continued)

Embedded Command	Meaning
.sa 0	Turn off justification
.sa 1	Turn on justification
.ul *n*	Underline the next *n* lines

You can use *groff* to display your own man page. The format codes consist of tags and font-change commands that control the formatting and which you type into your man page document. The tags and font-change commands consist of the following:

- The *.TH* tag indicates the man page title, as well as the date and a version number string. In the formatted man page, the version and date strings appear at the bottom of each page.

- The *.SH* tag indicates a section. (Section names usually appear in all uppercase characters on a man page.) Six common sections of a man page are:

  - NAME—The name of the command or program

  - SYNOPSIS—A brief description of the command or program

  - DESCRIPTION—A detailed description of the command or program

  - FILES—A list of files used by the command or program

  - SEE ALSO—A list of other commands or programs that are related to this one

  - BUGS—A list of known bugs

- The *.SS* tag indicates the beginning of a subsection. For example, Options is a subsection of the DESCRIPTION section.

- The *.TP* tag indicates each item in the Options subsection.

- The \fB command changes the font to boldface, the \fI command changes the font to italic, the \fR command changes the font to roman (regular text), and the \fP command changes the font to its former setting.

Try Hands-On Project 8-13 to create a man page for the phmenu script application that you completed in Chapter 7, "Advanced Shell Programming."

When you are satisfied with the man page format, you can make it available to others by copying it (while logged in as root) to one of the man page directories. All man pages are stored in subdirectories of the /usr/share/man directory (in Fedora, Red Hat Enterprise Linux, and SUSE). These subdirectories have names such as man1, man2, man3, and man4. All man pages in man1 are identified with a common suffix, .1, so phmenu.1 is copied to /usr/share/man/man1. The suffix number represents the section number of the man page.

When you request a man page using the *man* program, you specify the section number you want to see by placing the number after the name. (If you type only the name, *man* looks recursively for the page through all the subdirectories, starting with /usr/share/man/man1, and then displays the first match.) For example, if you want *man* to print the second version of the *break* command, follow the *man* command with *break 2*.

In Hands-On Project 8-14, you copy the man page you created in Hands-On Project 8-13 to the /usr/share/man/man1 directory.

NOTE

Depending on your operating system and how security is configured, you might need root privileges to copy a man page into the directories under /usr/share/man.

ARCHIVING AND BACKING UP FILES

It is good practice to periodically archive or back up files. If you find you rarely use some files, consider archiving them to CD, DVD, tape or another removable medium and storing that medium in a safe place. Archive old text documents and financial files, for example. Archiving provides a good way to make more room on your hard disks for your active files.

Another sound practice is to back up your important active files. On a system used in a business, this might include backing up spreadsheets, customer files, and word-processed or text documents. On a home system, you might back up personal documents, family financial records, photos, music files, and other important files.

NOTE

You may not need to restore files from a backup often, but when you do, it can be crucial. One family purchased a new computer and loaded hundreds of photos onto the hard drive. Within the first year, the hard drive failed and they permanently lost all of the photos because there were no backups.

For archiving or backing up files to a CD or DVD, consider obtaining GUI software that enables you to create a file system image, such as iso9660 or UDF (see Chapter 2, "Exploring the UNIX/Linux File Systems and File Security") before you copy (burn) files. Fedora, Red Hat Enterprise Linux, and SUSE come with the GNOME CD/DVD Creator GUI software that is part of the Nautilus program. Nautilus is a file manager program that is described in Chapter 11, "The X Window System." To use this software in the GNOME desktop in Fedora and Red Hat Enterprise Linux, insert a blank CD/DVD, double-click the Computer icon on the desktop, and double-click the CD/DVD drive to open the Nautilus CD/DVD Creator window. To use the GNOME CD/DVD Creator in SUSE, click Computer, click More Applications, click Multimedia in the left pane, and click Gnome CD/DVD Creator.

Using the *dump* Command

When you need to back up lots of files and directories or you want to do a full system backup, you can use the *dump* utility from the command line. The *dump* utility is often used to back up to one or more tapes and can be used to back up all files on a partition, only specified files, files that have changed by date, or files that have changed after the previous backup. Files can be backed up using a dump level that correlates a dump to a specific point in time—out of nine possible levels. *dump* level 0 is used to back up all files. Level 1 backs up only files that have changed since the level 0 dump. Level 2 backs up only files that have changed since the level 1 dump, and so on up to level 9. For example, on Saturday or Sunday when the week is done and no one is in the office, you might use *dump* level 0. Monday's *dump* might be set up as level 1, Tuesday's *dump* level 2, and so on. Using this approach, if you lost your disk drive on Thursday you would have to restore starting with the level 3 tape from Wednesday, then restore the level 2 tape from Tuesday, next the level 1 tape from Monday, and finally the level 0 tape from Saturday or Sunday.

NOTE

If you don't have many files that change, another approach is to use a dump level 0 once every week or less often.

8

Syntax **dump** [–options] *devicename and partition or filenames*

Dissection

- Backs up files and directories

- Uses 9 levels—level 0 backs up all files, level 1 backs up all files that have changed since the level 0 backup, level 2 backs up all files that have changed since the level 1 backup and so on up through level 9

- Useful options include:

  -0 through *-9* specifies the dump level

  -A filename enables you to specify an archive file on the tape that contains a table of contents so you can later determine what is on the tape

  -d density is used to specify the tape density (the default is 1600 bpi)

  -f device backs up to a specific device, such as tape drive /dev/tape

  -L label is used to place a label on the tape to describe its contents and that can be read later

  -u creates a journal entry for a successful dump in the file /etc/dumpdates or /var/lib/dumpdates (the file location may vary by UNIX/Linux distribution; the dumpdates file is useful for determining which backups have been successfully completed in the past in case you must do a restore)

For example, you might have all of your important spreadsheet, document, and financial files on the /dev/hda2 partition of your computer. The following command enables you to copy all of the files on /dev/hda2 to a tape:

```
dump -0u -f /dev/st0 /dev/hda2
```

This command tells the system to perform a level 0 (-0) dump, to create an entry in the dumpdates file (*u*), write to a SCSI tape device (*-f /dev/st0*), and back up all files from the /dev/hda2 (*/dev/hda2*) partition. (Another way that a tape device might be referenced is as /dev/tape for a device connected via a typical serial or USB connection.)

Using the *restore* Command

The *restore* command enables you to restore an entire partition or only specified files or directories from a backup medium created via the *dump* command. When you use *restore*, it by default copies back to your current working directory.

Syntax **restore** [–options] *device partition* or *filenames*

Dissection

- Restores entire file systems, specific files, and directories
- Useful options include:

  -f device or *file* specifies the device (such as a tape drive) or the file containing the backup

  -i runs the restore in an interactive mode for selecting specific files and directories to restore

  -N shows the file names and directories on the backup medium

  -r restores a file system

  -x specifies certain files or directories to be restored

To restore the tape created in the example under the "Using the *dump* Command" section, you would enter the following command:

```
restore -r -f /dev/st0
```

 If you have lost a disk drive and you need to restore a partition, you'll first need to create the partition, mount it, and then perform the restore. To create the partition in this example, you would use the command *mkfs /dev/hda2*. Next you would mount the partition, such as through the command *mount /dev/ hda2*. See Chapter 2 for more information about file systems and partitions.

When you just want to restore certain files or directories, you have the most flexibility if you use the following command (when the backup is on the tape device, /dev/tape):

```
restore -i -f /dev/tape
```

After you press Enter, the *restore* utility gives you a prompt at which you can enter instructions for what you want to do. For example, the *cd* command enables you to switch to a specific directory on the backup medium. The *ls* command gives a listing of files and subdirectories within the current working directory on the backup medium. The *add* command lets you place specific files or directories on the list of items to be restored. For example, to add the financials file you would type *add financials*.

Using *mail* to Send Mail

If you use a UNIX or Linux server or have a multiuser workstation, the *mail* utility can be very useful for communicating among account holders. This utility was first developed for BSD UNIX, but has become popular on other UNIX and many Linux systems including Fedora, Red Hat Enterprise Linux, and SUSE. Also, if the UNIX/Linux server you access has an e-mail system for handling network and Internet mail, then you may be able to use *mail* to communicate with users beyond your immediate server.

8

Syntax **mail** [-options] [*username*]

Dissection

- Enables you to send and receive mail through your computer or server
- When you read your mail, you can type *?* at the & prompt to review the commands for managing mail

To send *mail* to another user account, enter *mail* plus the account name. (To send mail beyond the computer you are logged onto, enter the user's e-mail address.) Enter the subject of your mail at the Subject: prompt. After you enter the subject you go into a text mode for entering your message. Type in a text line. Next, press Enter and fill in another line of text. Continue pressing Enter after each line until you are finished with the message. Press *Ctrl+d* to exit the text mode. At the Cc: prompt enter the name of the user you want to copy (see Figure 8-6) or leave this blank and press Enter to send the message.

To retrieve your messages, enter *mail* at the command line. You'll see a list of your messages. A new message is prefaced with an *N* (for new). If you have previously viewed that a message is waiting, but decided not to open it, the next time you use *mail*, a *U* (for unread) appears in front instead of an *N* (see Figure 8-7). The number that identifies the message follows next. To read a message, type its message number at the & prompt. To view all of the commands for managing your mail, type *?* at the & prompt and press Enter. When you want to leave the mail utility type *q* and press Enter. Try Hands-On Project 8-15 to use the *mail* command.

NOTE

Another useful command for communications is *talk*, which enables two people on the same computer (such as a server) or on different computers on a network to converse by typing messages. To find out more about *talk*, enter *man talk*.

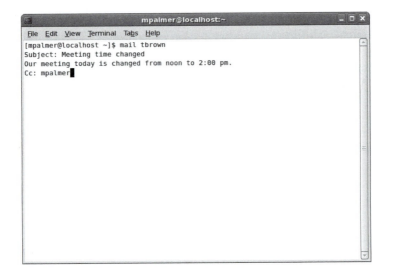

Figure 8-6   Using the *mail* command

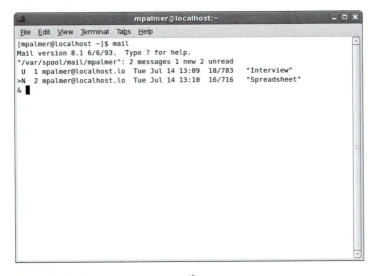

Figure 8-7   Accessing your mail

Using Networking Utilities

UNIX and Linux offer many utilities to accommodate a connection to the network. Four utilities that can be invaluable to you include:

- *ifconfig*
- *ping*

- *traceroute*

- *netstat*

You learn about each of these utilities in the next sections.

Using the ifconfig Utility

The *ifconfig* utility can be used to configure your computer's connection to the network. Another use of *ifconfig*, which is our interest for this book, is to obtain information about your network connection. For example, *ifconfig* displays your **Internet Protocol (IP) address**. The **Internet Protocol (IP)** is used to help ensure that information on a network goes to the right place. The IP address might be thought of as similar to a street address, which enables the postal carrier and your visitors to find your house.

An IP address uses a dotted decimal notation that consists of 8-bit binary numbers (octets) separated by periods used to identify a computer or network device and the network it is on. The format is as follows: 10000001.00000101.00001010.00000001, which converts to the decimal value 129.5.10.1. The first part of the address (which depends on the type of network) designates a unique identifier for a network, called the network identifier (NET_ID). For example, a school or corporation has its own NET_ID, which distinguishes its network from all others. The second part of the address is the host identifier (HOST_ID), which distinguishes a computer or network device from any other computer or device on a network.

There are times when it is important to know your IP address, which you can find out by using *ifconfig*. Besides your account name, your IP address is another means for people to find you on a network and to test communications to your computer. This utility also enables you to view basic information about how your computer is working on the network. For example, it shows the number of transmissions of data and transmission errors. If you suspect there is a problem with your network connection at your computer, you can use *ifconfig* for clues.

Syntax **ifconfig** [*network interface*]

Dissection

- Configures a network connection and is used to view information about the connection, such as the IP address

- For a computer with one network connection or interface in an Ethernet network, specify *eth0* as the interface parameter

- Useful options include:

    -a show all network interfaces including those that are not currently working

---

Hands-On Project 8-16 enables you to use *ifconfig* to determine your IP address.

Using the ping Utility

Sometimes you might wonder if the network is working or if your connection or someone else's connection is working. The *ping* utility offers a simple way to test connections. This utility polls another computer on the same network or on another network. If you poll several other computers and you get no response, then your computer might be having problems communicating or your network might be down. If you can successfully poll a computer on your network, but you cannot poll a computer or service over the Internet, then the Internet connection might be down.

You can poll a computer by entering *ping* plus the IP address of the other computer or network device that you want to poll. Some versions of *ping* also let you poll by using the computer name or computer and domain name of the device you want to poll—such as *ping rbrown@xxx.com* or *ping redhat.com*. Try Hands-On Project 8-17 to use the *ping* command.

Syntax **ping** [–options] *host*

Dissection

- Polls a computer on the same or a different network to determine if your computer is working, the network is working, or the remote computer is connected and working

- Useful options include:

  -a sounds a beep or other audible sound when receiving a response to the poll

  -c returns the number of polls

  -q displays only a summary of the results

Using the traceroute Utility

The *traceroute* utility can be used to determine the network path between point A and point B, such as the path between your computer and the computer of an associate who is in another city or state or across the Internet. The statistics from *traceroute* show the number of hops (networks or network devices) through which your communication travels. The statistics also show the time it takes in milliseconds to go from one point to the next.

You might use *traceroute* to ensure your computer is connected and working and that your network is working from point to point. It can also show if your network connection or your Internet provider is responding at a slow or fast pace. Another use of *traceroute* is to get a general idea of how efficiently your network is designed. Hands-On Project 8-18 enables you to use *traceroute*.

Syntax **traceroute** [–options] *host*

Dissection

- Tracks the route that a network communication takes from point A on a network to point B
- Provides information about the number of hops between two points (on the same or different networks) and the time it takes to go between points

Using the netstat Utility

The *netstat* utility gathers statistics and information about IP communications on a computer. Some of the information provided by *netstat* include the following:

- Network protocol communications
- Network connections established by the host computer
- Network routing information
- Information about computers remotely logged onto the host computer
- Data and communications errors

A user or server administrator might use *netstat* to monitor open ports (network communications channels on a computer). Both legitimate users and intruders may have traffic through those ports that bears watching. Through *netstat* a user or server administrator can also watch the amount of incoming and outgoing traffic. If the traffic is slow or experiencing lots of errors, this can mean there is a communication problem, such as a failing network connection. Try Hands-On Project 8-19 to use *netstat*.

Syntax **netstat** [–options] *host*

Dissection

- Monitors network traffic into and out of the host computer
- Useful options include:
  - -*a* displays statistics for all communications ports used by the transport protocol
  - -*p* shows programs in use that are related to active ports
  - -*n* displays communication via IP addresses and port numbers
  - -*s* shows a wide range of communications statistics, including errors

SHARING RESOURCES USING NETWORK FILE SYSTEM

UNIX/Linux systems enable resource sharing over a network by using **Network File System (NFS)**. NFS enables one computer running UNIX/Linux to mount a partition from another UNIX/Linux computer and then access file systems on the mounted partition as though they are local. Fedora, Red Hat Enterprise Linux, and SUSE support three versions of NFS: NFS version 2 (NFSv2) which is used on many UNIX/Linux systems, NFS version 3 (NFSv3) which is newer and offers better file and error handling than NFSv2, and NFS version 4 (NFSv4) which is the newest version at this writing. NFSv4 offers better security for the host, functions well through network security measures, offers improved performance over the Internet, and is compatible with UNIX, Linux, and Windows.

When a client mounts an NFS volume from a host, both the client and host use **remote procedure calls (RPCs)**. An RPC enables services and software on one computer to use services and software on a different computer. To use NFS in Fedora, Red Hat Enterprise Linux, and SUSE, the portmap service must be enabled (your particular Linux distribution may require additional services). This service handles the RPC request to mount a partition and makes the computer act like a server for those who access files via NFS. To start a service, use the *service* command from the root account, such as:

```
service portmap
```

Syntax **service** *servicename*

Dissection

- Runs a script that starts a service in UNIX/Linux, such as a service to enable remote procedure calls or a service to enable printing
- Services reside in the directory /etc/init.d

The security that controls which clients can use NFS on a hosting computer is handled through entries in three files: /etc/hosts.allow, /etc/hosts.deny, and /etc/exports. The /etc/hosts.allow file contains the IP addresses of the clients that are allowed to use NFS and the /etc/hosts.deny file contains computers that are not allowed to use NFS. Also, the /etc/exports file on the NFS host must contain information about which directories can be accessed by clients through NFS. For example, the /etc/exports file might contain the following lines:

```
/home/mpalmer/shared 192.168.0.72(ro)  192.168.0.84(ro)
/home/mpalmer/docs    192.168.0.72(rw)  192.168.0.41(rw)
```

In this example, on the first line the directory /home/mpalmer/shared is shared via NFS. The IP address 192.168.0.72 is the address of the host (server) computer and 192.168.0.84 is the IP address of the computer that can access the shared directory. The (ro) designates read only permission to the shared directory. On the second line, the directory /home/mpalmer/docs is shared from the host computer at IP address 192.168.0.72 and can be accessed by the client at IP address 192.168.0.41 with read and write permissions.

The purpose of this section is to give you a brief introduction to NFS so that you know of its existence. For more detailed information about setting up and using NFS visit the Web site: *nfs.sourceforge.net/nfs-howto/ar01s03.html*.

NOTE

Besides configuring the /etc/hosts.allow, /etc/hosts.deny, and /etc/exports files, the resources mounted through NFS are also protected by the permissions on the actual directories and files.

To access a shared directory through NFS, the client must use the *mount* command (from the root account), for example:

```
mount bluefin:/home/mpalmer/shared /mnt/shared
```

In this example, the directory /home/mpalmer/shared on the computer bluefin is mounted on the client as /mnt/shared.

ACCESSING MICROSOFT WINDOWS SYSTEMS THROUGH SAMBA

UNIX/Linux computers can access shared Windows system drives through the use of Samba. **Samba** is a utility that uses the Server Message Block (SMB) protocol, which is also used by Windows systems for sharing folders and printers. In Fedora, Red Hat Enterprise Linux, and SUSE, Samba is configured in the /etc/samba/smb.conf file. At this writing, to access Windows shared drives from Fedora or Red Hat Enterprise Linux with the GNOME desktop, click Places, click Network Servers, double-click Windows Network (continue clicking the appropriate icons to access a specific computer and shared folder). In SUSE (at this writing) click Computer, click More Applications, click Network Servers File Browser, and double-click Windows Network (continue clicking the appropriate icons to access a specific computer and its shared folders). In Knoppix using the KDE desktop, click the K Menu in the Panel at the bottom of the desktop, point to KNOPPIX, point to Utilities, click Samba Network Neighborhood, and browse to the Windows computer you want to access.

You can learn more about Samba and new releases of Samba at the Web site: *us3.samba.org/samba*.

NOTE

CHAPTER SUMMARY

❑ UNIX/Linux utilities are classified into eight major functional areas dictated by user needs: file processing, system status, networking, communications, security, programming, source code management, and miscellaneous tasks.

❑ Because utility programs are executed by entering their names on the command line, these programs are also referred to as commands.

❑ The *dd* command has a set of options that allows it to perform copying tasks, such as converting the contents of a file, that are not available in other copying utilities.

❑ The *df* utility checks and reports on free disk space.

❑ The *du* command checks for disk usage (consumption).

❑ You can use the *find* command to retrieve wasteful files, and then execute the *rm* command to remove them from the hard disk.

❑ The *top* and *free* utilities provide detailed views of the "internals" of the system to determine factors such as CPU and memory use.

❑ The *uptime* command shows how long a system has been up since booting.

❑ You can redirect the output of the *top* and *free* commands to a disk file to use as input for a report to the system administrator and system tune-up specialists.

❑ You can run a program in the background by appending the & operator to the end of the command line.

❑ The *ps* command displays all processes currently running.

❑ The *kill* command terminates a specific process.

❑ The utility that checks spelling, *ispell*, scans a text document for typing errors and suggests corrections.

❑ Text formatting in UNIX/Linux involves preparing a text file with embedded typesetting commands and then processing the marked-up text file with a computer program that generates commands for the output device.

❑ Text containing embedded typesetting commands is processed (read) by programs like the *nroff* and *troff* utilities or the Linux *groff* utility for formatting output.

❑ Formatted text can be created to produce man pages for new applications.

❑ Archive and back up file systems, directories, and files using the *dump* command. To restore information saved through *dump* use the *restore* command.

❑ The *mail* command is a basic utility for sending and retrieving mail on a UNIX/Linux computer.

❑ The *ifconfig*, *ping*, *traceroute*, and *netstat* commands are used on computers connected to a network for viewing information about the network connection and for troubleshooting the connection.

- Network File System (NFS) enables users to share directories and files over a network.

- Samba is a utility that enables UNIX/Linux computers to access folders and files shared on networked Windows computers.

COMMAND SUMMARY: REVIEW OF CHAPTER 8 COMMANDS

Please refer to the tables within the chapter for a command review.

Table	Shows
Table 8-1	File-processing utilities
Table 8-2	System status utilities
Table 8-3	Network utilities
Table 8-4	Communications utilities
Table 8-5	Security utilities
Table 8-6	Programming utilities
Table 8-7	Source code management utilities
Table 8-8	Miscellaneous utilities
Table 8-9	Sample *groff* embedded commands

KEY TERMS

core file — A type of garbage file created when an executing program attempts to do something illegal, such as accessing another user's memory.

garbage file — A temporary file, such as a core file, that loses its usefulness after several days.

Internet Protocol (IP) — A network protocol or communications language that handles addressing and routing of information over a network so that it reaches the correct destination.

Internet Protocol (IP) address — An address that Internet Protocol uses to locate a specific computer or device on a network. An IP address uses a dotted decimal notation that consists of 8-bit binary numbers (octets) separated by periods used to identify a computer or network device and the network it is on.

Multipurpose Internet Mail Extensions (MIME) — A communications standard that supports sending and receiving binary files in mail messages.

Network File System (NFS) — Enables file transfer and other shared services that involve computers running UNIX/Linux.

process id (PID) — An identification number that the operating system assigns to a process for managing and tracking that process.

remote procedure calls (RPCs) — Enable services and software on one computer to use services and software on a different computer.

Samba — Used by UNIX/Linux and Mac OS X systems, a utility that employs the Server Message Block (SMB) protocol, which is also used by Microsoft Windows systems for sharing folders and printers. Samba enables UNIX/Linux and Mac OS X systems to access shared Windows resources.

REVIEW QUESTIONS

1. You have obtained a new utility, called *watchit*, to monitor security on your computer, and you decide to run the utility in the background. Normally, to start the utility you would enter *watchit* at the command line. Which of the following commands enables you to start and run this utility in the background?

    a. *hide watchit*

    b. *watchit&*

    c. *sh -h watchit*

    d. *shh watchit*

2. You've obtained over a hundred large graphics files to use in publications, but you want to be sure there is enough available disk space on your computer to store these files. Which of the following commands should you use?

    a. *df*

    b. *diskfree*

    c. *ls --space*

    d. *netstat*

3. Your company is launching a marketing campaign, and to start, you've created a file called promotion in normal uppercase and lowercase letters that will be used to place text for ads on the Internet and in newspapers. When you show the promotional text to your boss, she is curious about how it would look in all uppercase letters for emphasis. Which of the following commands enables you to convert the text and save the result to the file, promotion_uppercase?

    a. *cat -u promotion | promotion_uppercase*

    b. *case [a-z] [A-Z] promotion >> promotion_uppercase*

    c. *case -u promotion > promotion_uppercase*

    d. *dd if=promotion of=promotion_uppercase conv=ucase*

4. Which of the following can you restore from a backup tape made via the *dump* command? (Choose all that apply.)

    a. a file

    b. a partition of directories and files

    c. a directory

    d. a subdirectory

5. Your network has a combination of Linux and Microsoft Windows computers. There is a Windows server that offers shared files for clients to access. Which of the following enables you to access the shared files from your Linux computer?

   a. Windows Share

   b. Network Share

   c. Samba

   d. Leopard

6. You help manage the Linux server for your department. Right now the server has no protection against power failures and there have been several power failures recently. To help make your case for a power protection device, you want to keep track of the amount of time the server has been running since the last power outage that caused it to go down. What command enables you to track how long the server has been up?

   a. *top*

   b. *uptime*

   c. *df*

   d. *boot*

7. You've purchased a new program for your computer, but the computer seems to slow down when you run the program. Which of the following commands enables you to monitor the memory usage as you run the program so you can determine if the program is a memory hog?

   a. *free*

   b. *memuse*

   c. *mu*

   d. *test*

8. You are working on a report about disk usage on your company's server to help determine if it is time to purchase additional disks. Which of the following commands enables you to obtain disk usage statistics for your report?

   a. *free -t*

   b. *dd -of*

   c. *top -d | more*

   d. *du -h | more*

9. When you create a section name in a man page, such as the DESCRIPTION section, what tag should you use just before the section name?

   a. .TH

   b. .SS

   c. \SC

   d. .SH

8

10. Which of the following are levels of backups that can be made with the *dump* command? (Choose all that apply.)

    a. 0

    b. 5

    c. 15

    d. 20

11. How can you specify which device to use for a *restore* from a backup tape created by the *dump* command?

    a. Use the *--device* option.

    b. Use the parameter, *output=devicename*.

    c. Use the *-f* option.

    d. Use the *-i* option so that you can do the restore from the interactive mode and select the device on the fly.

12. You've opened your mail on the company's server by using the *mail* command. Several messages are listed. How can you tell which ones are new or unopened messages?

    a. New messages begin with number 1 and unopened ones begin with the number 2.

    b. New or unopened messages begin with an N or a U.

    c. Both new and unopened messages begin with the tag, "unopened".

    d. New and unopened messages begin with a closed folder symbol.

13. You suspect that your computer's connection to the network is not working because you don't seem to be able to connect to the Internet through the network. Which of the following commands can help you determine if your connection is working? (Choose all that apply.)

    a. *ping*

    b. *netconnect*

    c. *df*

    d. *tr*

14. You are setting up NFS to share files on the network from your Fedora Linux computer. Which of the following is a service that must be running to enable you to use NFS for sharing files?

    a. NFSstart

    b. share

    c. portmap

    d. netlink

15. What is the command that you can use (from root) to start the service mentioned in Question 14?

    a. *service*

    b. *start*

    c. *init*

    d. *go*

16. In the following command, what is the purpose of -*o*?

    ```
    find . "( " -name a.out -o -name core ")"
    ```

    a. It tests for the existence of files.

    b. It is the "OR" operator.

    c. It directs output to the core file.

    d. It directs output to the a.out file.

17. You have a small network in your business with just a few network devices connected along with 22 Linux computers and you want to see how efficiently your network is designed. Which of the following commands can you use from different computers to determine the route information takes from one computer to another?

    a. *vmstat*

    b. *pong*

    c. *nettraffic*

    d. *traceroute*

18. Your computer is slowing down because you've started a process that is taking most of the memory and CPU resources. Which of the following commands enables you to find the process id so you can stop that process?

    a. *ps*

    b. *df*

    c. *du*

    d. *free*

19. Which of the following commands enables you to stop the process mentioned in Question 18?

    a. *bye*

    b. *kill*

    c. *ci*

    d. *tar*

8

20. Your colleague is creating a new man page to document a manufacturing process used by your company. She wants to be able to quickly view the man page as she works on it so that she can have other people view it before copying the man page into production. Which of the following commands enables her and others to periodically review her work in a format similar to the man page format?

    a. *.//*

    b. *show*

    c. *groff*

    d. *dd*

21. A user on your network has received an error message that there is another computer on the same network using the same IP address, so the user cannot access the network. You send out a message to the 18 Linux users on your network to ask that they check the IP addresses on their computers and e-mail this information to you, so that you can determine who has the duplicate IP address. What utility do you tell users to run to determine their IP addresses?

    a. *ifconfig*

    b. *ipquery*

    c. *df*

    d. *cmp*

22. Name two types of information that you can obtain using *netstat*.

23. What is the purpose of the *top* command and how can you use it to stop a process?

24. You are gathering information about the amount of disk space occupied by users' home directories. What command enables you to view a breakdown by individual directories under the /home directory? (Provide the actual command you would run and any special considerations for running it.)

25. Name two files that should be modified for security when using NFS.

HANDS-ON PROJECTS

Complete these projects using the command line, such as from a terminal window, using the Bash shell. Also, use your own account and home directory (one project requires the root or superuser password to complete the steps).

NOTE

HANDS-ON PROJECTS

Project 8-1

The *dd* command enables you to copy a file and also has the advantage that you can convert the file's contents in the process. In this project, you create a file using all uppercase characters and then convert its contents to lowercase.

To make a copy of a file and convert its contents:

1. Use the *cat* command or the editor of your choice to create a file, datafile. The file should contain the following text:

   THIS IS MY DATA FILE.

2. Make a copy of the file by typing **dd if=datafile of=datafile.bak conv=lcase** and then press **Enter**.

3. Type **cat datafile.bak** to verify your work. (See Figure 8-8.)

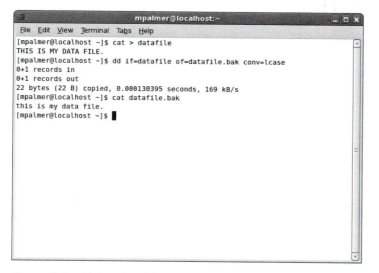

```
mpalmer@localhost:~

File  Edit  View  Terminal  Tabs  Help
[mpalmer@localhost ~]$ cat > datafile
THIS IS MY DATA FILE.
[mpalmer@localhost ~]$ dd if=datafile of=datafile.bak conv=lcase
0+1 records in
0+1 records out
22 bytes (22 B) copied, 0.000130395 seconds, 169 kB/s
[mpalmer@localhost ~]$ cat datafile.bak
this is my data file.
[mpalmer@localhost ~]$ ▮
```

Figure 8-8   Using the *dd* command

Project 8-2

In this project, you use the *df* command to determine usage of the file systems on your hard drive.

To use the *df* command to check file system usage:

1. Type **df** and then press **Enter**. (See Figure 8-9.)

2. Of course, your file systems and their statistics are different from those shown in Figure 8-9. In Figure 8-9, notice, for example, that the *df* command reports that the /dev/mapper/VolGroup00-LogVol100 file system (the default volume 1) file system has 37709304 blocks of 1 kilobytes each. There are 3415244 blocks in use, and 32347644 blocks available. Ten percent of the blocks are in use, and the file system is mounted on /. Also, notice in Figure 8-9 that there is a tmpfs file system mounted on /dev/shm. This disk space can be used like virtual memory in some UNIX and Linux systems. In Fedora and Red Hat Enterprise Linux tmpfs is configured by default via the *mount* command (it is not configured by default in SUSE or Knoppix). The actual amount of virtual memory used can expand or contract

depending on the need. tmpfs is designed to speed access to active files and is used before conventional swap space (and can swap files with less activity to swap space). Some systems use the name shmfs instead of tmpfs.

3. You can specify a file system as an argument. The statistics for that file system alone appear on the screen. Type **df /dev/hda1** (or another partitioned disk appropriate to your system) and press **Enter**. You see the disk statistics for that volume only.

4. The *-h* option causes the numbers to print in human-readable form. Instead of displaying raw numbers for size, amount of disk space used, and amount of space available, the statistics are printed in kilobyte, megabyte, or gigabyte format. Type **df -h** and then press **Enter**.

5. Type **clear** and press **Enter** to clear the screen for the next project.

```
                            mpalmer@localhost:~                       _ □ X
 File  Edit  View  Terminal  Tabs  Help
[mpalmer@localhost ~]$ df
Filesystem           1K-blocks      Used Available Use% Mounted on
/dev/mapper/VolGroup00-LogVol00
                      37709304   3415244  32347644  10% /
/dev/hda1               101086     10815     85052  12% /boot
tmpfs                   257340         0    257340   0% /dev/shm
[mpalmer@localhost ~]$
```

Figure 8-9 Using the *df* command

Project 8-3

When you want to see directory, subdirectory, and file size information, use the *du* command. In this project, you use the *du* command to learn about your disk use.

To report on disk use:

1. To receive a report on disk usage starting at your home directory, type **du | more**, and then press **Enter**. (The results of the *du* command can be lengthy, so pipe its output to the *more* command.) Figure 8-10 shows an example of the command's output.

2. The output shows the number of 512-byte blocks used in each subdirectory (including hidden subdirectories). Type **q** to exit the *more* command.

3. To view a similar report on disk usage by the number of bytes instead of by 512-byte blocks, start at your home directory, type **du -b | more**, and then press **Enter**.

```
                        mpalmer@localhost:~                    _ □ x
File  Edit  View  Terminal  Tabs  Help
220      ./.gstreamer-0.10
16       ./dept_4540
280      ./.metacity/sessions
288      ./.metacity
16       ./.redhat/esc
24       ./.redhat
32       ./corp_db
8        ./.gnome2_private
16       ./tmp
8        ./.openoffice.org2.0/user/autotext
4        ./.openoffice.org2.0/user/store
656      ./.openoffice.org2.0/user/config/imagecache
16       ./.openoffice.org2.0/user/config/soffice.cfg/modules/swriter/accelerator
/en-US
20       ./.openoffice.org2.0/user/config/soffice.cfg/modules/swriter/accelerator
4        ./.openoffice.org2.0/user/config/soffice.cfg/modules/swriter/menubar
4        ./.openoffice.org2.0/user/config/soffice.cfg/modules/swriter/images/Bitm
aps
8        ./.openoffice.org2.0/user/config/soffice.cfg/modules/swriter/images
4        ./.openoffice.org2.0/user/config/soffice.cfg/modules/swriter/statusbar
4        ./.openoffice.org2.0/user/config/soffice.cfg/modules/swriter/toolbar
44       ./.openoffice.org2.0/user/config/soffice.cfg/modules/swriter
4        ./.openoffice.org2.0/user/config/soffice.cfg/modules/StartModule/menubar
--More--
```

Figure 8-10   Results of the *du* command from a home directory

4. Type **q** to exit the *more* command.

5. Like the *df* command, the *du* command supports the *-h* option to display statistics in human-readable format. Type **du -h | more** and then press **Enter.** You can press the **Spacebar** to advance through screens or type **q** to exit the display of statistics.

Besides the *-h* option, the *du* command supports the *-x* option, which enables you to omit directories in file systems other than the one in which you are working when more than one file system is mounted.

TIP

6. Type **clear** and press **Enter.**

Project 8-4

In this project, you use the *find* command to search for and delete all occurrences of a.out and core. The steps that follow assume you have a source directory in your home directory. The test files, a.out and core, are quickly created using the *touch* command, which, when followed by the file names, creates empty files. The tilde (~) ensures that these files go into your home and source directories. You should already have a source directory for this project. If not, create a source directory under your home directory before you start.

To remove garbage files:

1. Create some garbage files, core and a.out, and place them in your home directory and in the source subdirectory under your home directory. First type **touch ~/core ; touch ~/a.out** and press **Enter** to create the files in your home directory. Next type **touch ~/source/core ; touch ~/source/a.out** and press **Enter.**

2. Verify that you are in your home directory, type **find . "(" –name a.out –o –name core ")"** and then press **Enter**. You should see a listing of the four files you created in Step 1, the core and a.out files in the home directory and in the source directory under the home directory.

3. Remove the garbage files by typing **find . "(" –name a.out –o –name core ")" –exec rm {} \;** and then pressing **Enter**.

4. Check that the files have been removed by repeating the *find* command you entered in Step 2. If the files have been removed, there is no output. (See Figure 8-11.)

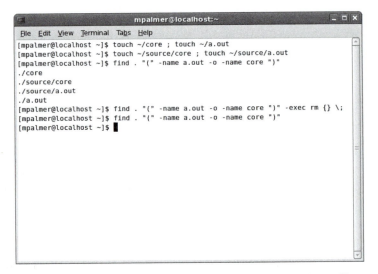

Figure 8-11   Using the *find* command to delete garbage files

HANDS-ON PROJECTS

Project 8-5

Sometimes, your system might respond slowly or seem to have delays. In these conditions, it is useful to employ the *top* command to monitor CPU use by processes and other system information, as you learn in this project.

To use the *top* utility:

1. Display the CPU activity by typing **top** and then pressing **Enter**. Your screen should look similar to Figure 8-12. (Don't forget that this display changes while on screen.)

2. The processes are shown in the order of the amount of CPU time they use. After looking at the display for a short time, press **q** to exit from the *top* utility.

3. Run the *top* utility again. Notice the far-left column of information labeled PID. This column lists the process id of each process shown. Notice the PID of the *top* command. (In Figure 8-12, the *top* command's PID is 26214. Yours is probably different.)

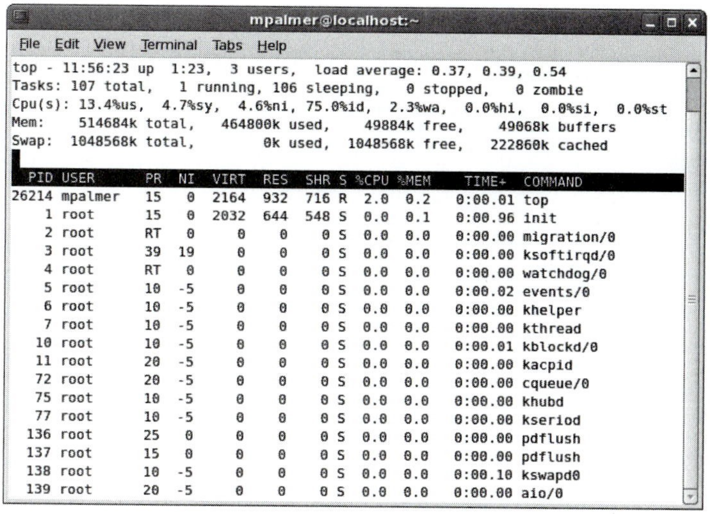

Figure 8-12   Sample *top* display

4. Press **k** to initiate the *kill* command. The *top* utility asks you to enter the PID to kill. Enter the PID of the *top* command. Press **Enter** to kill the process. (You might have to press Enter a second time to return to a command prompt.) Type **clear** and press **Enter** (you might have to execute *clear* more than once) to clear the lines from the screen. The *top* utility is no longer running.

5. Run the *top* utility in secure mode by typing **top -s** and pressing **Enter**.

6. Press **k** to initiate the *kill* command. Because top is running in secure mode, it displays the message "Unavailable in secure mode," as shown in Figure 8-13.

7. Press **q** to exit the *top* utility.

8. Type **clear** and press **Enter** to clear the screen.

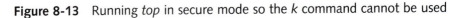

```
                              mpalmer@localhost:~                        _ □ x
 File  Edit  View  Terminal  Tabs  Help
 top - 12:02:16 up  1:29,  3 users,  load average: 0.24, 0.20, 0.40
 Tasks: 107 total,   2 running, 105 sleeping,   0 stopped,   0 zombie
 Cpu(s):  2.3%us,  0.0%sy,  0.0%ni, 97.7%id,  0.0%wa,  0.0%hi,  0.0%si,  0.0%st
 Mem:    514684k total,   468040k used,    46644k free,    49552k buffers
 Swap:  1048568k total,        0k used,  1048568k free,   224816k cached
 Unavailable in secure mode
   PID USER      PR  NI  VIRT  RES  SHR S %CPU %MEM    TIME+  COMMAND
  2338 root      15   0  103m  16m 6212 S  1.7  3.3  1:38.77 Xorg
 26250 mpalmer   15   0  2164 1004  788 R  0.3  0.2  0:00.02 top
     1 root      15   0  2032  644  548 S  0.0  0.1  0:00.96 init
     2 root      RT   0     0    0    0 S  0.0  0.0  0:00.00 migration/0
     3 root      35  19     0    0    0 S  0.0  0.0  0:00.00 ksoftirqd/0
     4 root      RT   0     0    0    0 S  0.0  0.0  0:00.00 watchdog/0
     5 root      10  -5     0    0    0 S  0.0  0.0  0:00.02 events/0
     6 root      10  -5     0    0    0 S  0.0  0.0  0:00.00 khelper
     7 root      10  -5     0    0    0 S  0.0  0.0  0:00.00 kthread
    10 root      10  -5     0    0    0 S  0.0  0.0  0:00.01 kblockd/0
    11 root      20  -5     0    0    0 S  0.0  0.0  0:00.00 kacpid
    72 root      20  -5     0    0    0 S  0.0  0.0  0:00.00 cqueue/0
    75 root      10  -5     0    0    0 S  0.0  0.0  0:00.00 khubd
    77 root      10  -5     0    0    0 S  0.0  0.0  0:00.00 kseriod
   136 root      25   0     0    0    0 S  0.0  0.0  0:00.00 pdflush
   137 root      15   0     0    0    0 S  0.0  0.0  0:00.00 pdflush
   138 root      10  -5     0    0    0 S  0.0  0.0  0:00.10 kswapd0
```

Figure 8-13   Running *top* in secure mode so the *k* command cannot be used

HANDS-ON
PROJECTS

Project 8-6

Plan to periodically monitor memory use in your computer, particularly if the computer seems to run slowly when you use specific programs. In this project, you use the *free* command to monitor memory.

To use the *free* command:

1. Type **free** and press **Enter**. The command displays the amount of total, used, and free memory. It also displays the amount of shared memory, buffer memory, and cached memory. In addition, the amount of total, used, and free swap memory is shown. By default, all amounts are shown in kilobytes.

2. Type **free -m** and press **Enter** to see the *free* command's output in megabytes.

3. Type **free -t** and press **Enter** to see memory use totals. (See Figure 8-14.)

```
                          mpalmer@localhost:~                    _ □ ×
 File  Edit  View  Terminal  Tabs  Help
[mpalmer@localhost ~]$ free
              total        used        free      shared     buffers      cached
Mem:         514684      475424       39260           0       55028      225996
-/+ buffers/cache:       194400      320284
Swap:       1048568           0     1048568
[mpalmer@localhost ~]$ free -m
              total        used        free      shared     buffers      cached
Mem:            502         464          38           0          53         220
-/+ buffers/cache:          189         312
Swap:          1023           0        1023
[mpalmer@localhost ~]$ free -t
              total        used        free      shared     buffers      cached
Mem:         514684      475352       39332           0       55048      225992
-/+ buffers/cache:       194312      320372
Swap:       1048568           0     1048568
Total:      1563252      475352     1087900
[mpalmer@localhost ~]$ █
```

Figure 8-14   Displaying memory use using different *free* command options

Project 8-7

There are times when you might want to send the results of the *top* and *free* utilities to a computer support person for help. In this project, you save the results from these utilities to different files and then print the files.

To save and print the displays generated by the *top* and *free* utilities:

1. Redirect the output of the *top* utility to a file in your current directory by typing **top > topdata** and then pressing **Enter**.

2. Wait about 10 seconds, and then press **q** to exit the *top* utility. Type **more topdata** and press **Enter** to confirm you have written the information to the topdata file. To see additional lines in the display, you may need to repeatedly press **Enter**. Type **q** to exit the *more* display of the file contents.

3. Redirect the output of the *free* utility to a file in your current directory by typing **free > freedata** and then pressing **Enter**. Type **more freedata** and press **Enter** to verify the contents of the freedata file.

4. Print the information you have saved for the computer support specialist by typing **lpr topdata**, pressing **Enter**, typing **lpr freedata**, and then pressing **Enter** again.

5. Type **clear** and press **Enter** to clear the screen.

Project 8-8

In UNIX/Linux, you can run programs in the background. In this project, you practice running the *top* program in the background.

To run a program in the background:

1. Experiment with running a program in the background by running the *top* program in the background. Type **top&** and press **Enter**.

    After you enter the command, the system reports the process id or PID (id that identifies the process) used by the program that you started in the background, such as 26851 in Figure 8-15.

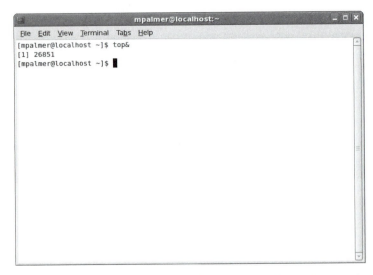

Figure 8-15   Starting the *top* utility to run in the background

    The *top* utility is running, but because it runs in the background, you see no other output.

2. Continue to run the *top* utility in the background.

Project 8-9

In this project, you learn how to use the *ps* command to view processes on your system.

To use the *ps* command:

1. Type **ps** and press **Enter**. The output of the *ps* command includes this information about each process you are running:

    ❑ PID

    ❑ Name of the terminal or station where the process started

> ❑ Amount of time the process has been running
>
> ❑ Name of the process

Notice that the *top* utility might still be running in the background, or you might see a message at the end of the *ps* display that *top* has stopped running.

2. To see a list of all processes running on the system, type **ps -A | more**, and press **Enter**.

3. Press the **spacebar** until the command finishes its output.

4. Notice that with the command options you've used so far, it is difficult to tell the status of a process, such as whether or not it has finished. Type **ps l** (that is, a lower-case letter l and not a one), and press **Enter** to see the long display. The WCHAN column shows the status of a process, such as "finish."

5. Now consider that you want to know who is running a particular process by user name. Type **ps -A u | more** and press **Enter**. (See Figure 8-16, which shows information in the middle of the listing.) Press the **spacebar** to scroll through the listing. Notice that many processes are being run by root as well as by your account.

```
                           mpalmer@localhost:~                      _ □ x
 File  Edit  View  Terminal  Tabs  Help
inary -nodaemon
root     2331  0.0  0.5  15656  2700 ?        S    10:33   0:00 /usr/sbin/gdm-b
inary -nodaemon
root     2335  0.0  0.3  16636  1768 ?        S    10:33   0:00 /usr/sbin/gdm-b
inary -nodaemon
root     2338  8.9  3.3  24408 17448 tty7     Ss+  10:33  33:09 /usr/bin/Xorg :
0 -audit 0 -auth /var/gdm/:0.Xauth -nolisten tcp vt7
mpalmer  2423  0.0  1.3  22628  6828 ?        Ss   11:04   0:00 /usr/bin/gnome-
session
mpalmer  2471  0.0  0.0   4292   500 ?        Ss   11:04   0:00 /usr/bin/ssh-ag
ent /usr/bin/dbus-launch --exit-with-session /etc/X11/xinit/Xclients
mpalmer  2474  0.0  0.1   2816   520 ?        S    11:04   0:00 /usr/bin/dbus-l
aunch --exit-with-session /etc/X11/xinit/Xclients
mpalmer  2475  0.0  0.2   3144  1284 ?        Ss   11:04   0:00 /bin/dbus-daemo
n --fork --print-pid 8 --print-address 6 --session
mpalmer  2481  0.0  0.7   7380  3676 ?        S    11:04   0:00 /usr/libexec/gc
onfd-2 5
mpalmer  2484  0.0  0.1   2536   844 ?        S    11:04   0:00 /usr/bin/gnome-
keyring-daemon
mpalmer  2486  0.0  1.3  33600  6984 ?        Rl   11:04   0:00 /usr/libexec/gn
ome-settings-daemon
mpalmer  2503  0.0  1.6  17768  8672 ?        Ss   11:04   0:08 metacity --sm-c
lient-id=default1
--More--
```

Figure 8-16   Using *ps* to view user information for all processes

Project 8-10

Sometimes, you need to stop a process, such as one running in the background or one that you no longer want to use. In this project, you use the *kill* command to stop a process.

To stop a process using the *kill* command:

1. In this step, you terminate the *top* utility that you started in Hands-On Project 8-8 and that might still be running in the background. (If you received a message that it

stopped, continue anyway for practice or restart the utility by typing **top&** and pressing **Enter**.) Type **ps** and press **Enter**. Look at the list of processes to find the *top* utility's PID.

2. Type one of these commands (both perform the same operation): **kill <*process id*>** and press **Enter**, or **kill %top** and press **Enter**.

3. Type **ps l** and press **Enter** to see a list of the processes and to check the status (look under the WCHAN column) of the *top* process.

Project 8-11

If you often work with plain-text documents, it is helpful to know about the *ispell* command for spell checking. You practice using *ispell* in this project.

To use *ispell*:

1. Use the vi or Emacs editor to create a file, and name it **document1**.

2. Enter the following text, with misspellings:

   This is a document that describes our newest and fastest machineery. Take the time to lern how to use each piece of equipment.

3. Save the file and exit the editor.

4. Scan the file for spelling errors by typing **ispell document1** and then pressing **Enter**.

5. To correct the word "machineery," look at the options at the bottom of the screen, and find the one that says "machinery," which is number 1 in Figure 8-17. Type the number of that option to correct the misspelling, or you can select the *r* (*Replace*) option, retype the word after the *With:* prompt, and press **Enter**. Notice that the word is then corrected in the text.

6. On the next screen, the next misspelled word, "lern," is highlighted. Find the correct spelling in the list at the bottom of the screen and enter the number that represents the correctly spelled word.

7. The program exits and returns you to the command line. Type **cat document1** and press **Enter**. The misspelled words have been corrected.

```
┌─────────────────────────────────────────────────────────┐
│ ▪               mpalmer@localhost:~            _ □ x │
│ File  Edit  View  Terminal  Tabs  Help                  │
├─────────────────────────────────────────────────────────┤
│                                                          │
│ This is a document that describes our newest             │
│ and fastest machineery. Take the time to lern            │
│ how to use each piece of equipment.                      │
│                                                          │
│                                                          │
│                                                          │
│                                                          │
│                                                          │
│                                                          │
│                                                          │
│ ███████████████████████████████████████████████████     │
│ 1) machinery            4) machined                      │
│ 2) machine              5) machines                      │
│ 3) machinery's          6) machine's                     │
│                                                          │
│ i) Ignore               I) Ignore all                    │
│ r) Replace              R) Replace all                   │
│ a) Add                  l) Add Lower                      │
│ b) Abort                x) Exit                          │
│ ███████████████████████████████████████████████████     │
│ ?                                                        │
└─────────────────────────────────────────────────────────┘
```

Figure 8-17   Spell checking document1

Project 8-12

In this project, you create two files and use the *cmp* command to compare the differences.

To compare two files with the *cmp* command:

1. Use the vi or Emacs editor to create the file file1, containing this text:

   This is file 1.
   It is a practice file.
   It belongs to me.

2. Save the file and exit the editor.

3. Use the editor to create the file file2, containing the text:

   This is file 2.
   It is a practice file.
   It belongs to you.

4. Save the file and exit the editor.

5. At the command line, type **cmp file1 file2**, and press **Enter**. Your screen looks similar to the following:

   ```
   [mpalmer@localhost ~]$ cmp file1 file2
   file1 file2 differ: byte 14, line 1
   ```

6. This result means that the two files differ, with the first point of difference at the 14th character in both files.

7. Type **clear** and press **Enter** to clear the screen for the next project.

Project 8-13

You can use the *groff* utility to create your own man pages to document applications that you create. In this project, you create a man page for the phmenu application you finished in Chapter 7.

To write and format a man page:

1. Verify that you are in your ~/source directory. Recall that the ~ indicates your home directory.

2. Use the vi or Emacs editor to create the file phmenu.1. Type the following text into the file:

```
.TH PHMENU 1 "November 2008" "phmenu Version 1.01"
.SH NAME
phmenu \- Menu for Dominion Employee Telephone Listings
.SH SYNOPSIS
\fB phmenu\fP
.SH DESCRIPTION
\fP Menu for maintaining employees' phones and job titles\fP.
\fP Record includes phone number, name, dept, and date-hired\fP.
.SS Options
.TP
\fB -v \fIView Phone List\fR
Display unformatted phone records.
.TP
\fB -p \fIPrint Phone List\fR
 Corporate Phones report sorted by Employee Name.
.TP
\fB -a \fIAdd Phone to List\fR
Add new phone record.
.TP
\fB -s \fISearch for Employee Phones\fR
Enter Name to search and retrieve phone record.
.TP
\fB -d \fIDelete Phone\fR
Remove phone record.
.SH FILES
.TP
\fC/home/source/corp_phones\fR
```

3. Save the file and exit the editor.

4. Test the man page by typing **groff –Tascii –man phmenu.1 | more** and then pressing **Enter**. Your screen should appear similar to Figure 8-18.

If you find any formatting discrepancies, check the dot commands and any embedded font changes against the code you typed in Step 2.

TIP

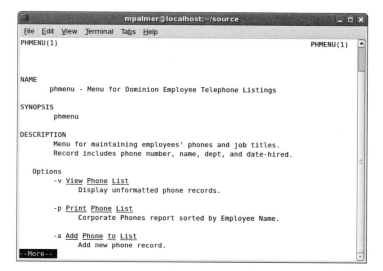

Figure 8-18   Using *groff* to view the phmenu documentation

5. Press **q** to exit the *more* command, and then test your new man page by typing **man ./phmenu.1** and then pressing **Enter**. Your screen should look similar to Figure 8-19. Type **q** to exit the man page.

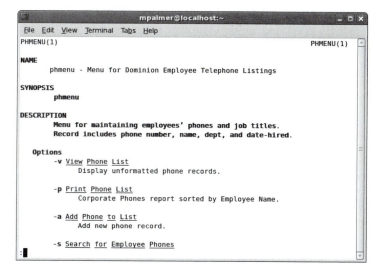

Figure 8-19   Using *man* to display the phmenu documentation

Project 8-14

In this project, you copy the man page created in Hands-On Project 8-13 into a directory so that general users can access it like any other man page. You need the root password for this project.

To copy the man page into a man page directory:

1. Verify that you are in your source directory.

2. Type **su** and then press **Enter** (to log in as superuser).

3. Enter the root password and then press **Enter**.

4. Type **cp phmenu.1 /usr/share/man/man1** to copy the man page to the man1 directory and then press **Enter**. (Check with your instructor if your system uses a different location in which to store the manual pages.)

5. To exit from superuser mode, type **exit** and then press **Enter**.

6. Test that this file has been correctly copied by typing **man phmenu** and then pressing **Enter**. Press the **spacebar** to advance through the display.

7. Type **q**.

Project 8-15

The *mail* command enables you to send and receive mail. In this project you learn how to create a message, send it to yourself, and then read the message.

To use the *mail* command:

1. Type **mail** plus your user account name, such as mail mpalmer, and press **Enter**.

2. For the Subject: line type, **Reminder**. Press **Enter**.

3. For the first line of text in the message type, **Your report is due tomorrow by noon.** Press **Enter**.

4. In the second line of text type, **Don't forget to spell check it before you send it in**. Press **Enter**.

5. Type **Ctrl+d**.

6. At the Cc: line press **Enter**.

7. Back at the regular command prompt, type **mail** and press **Enter**.

8. Look for your message, which will start with the character *N*. Notice the number to the right of the *N* which is the message's identification number. Type the number of the message at the & prompt and press **Enter**.

9. After you read the message, type **?** at the & prompt and press **Enter**.

10. Notice the commands that you can use at the & prompt.

11. Type **d** and the number of your message, such as **d 1** and press **Enter**. This deletes your message.

12. Type **h** and press **Enter** to view your active message headers and notice that the message you sent to yourself is now gone.

13. Type **q** and press **Enter** to leave mail.

14. Type **clear** and press **Enter**.

Project 8-16

Sometimes you need to know your IP address when you are connected to a network or to the Internet. This address enables others to communicate with your computer. In this project, you use the *ifconfig* utility to find your IP address and to view other information about your network connection.

On some systems you will need access to the root account or an account with superuser privileges to run *ifconfig*. However, on many systems just entering *ifconfig* from a user's account does not run the command because it is not in the default path. In Fedora, Red Hat Enterprise Linux, and SUSE you can run *ifconfig* from your account by entering */sbin/ifconfig* at the command line instead of just *ifconfig*. In other systems, such as Knoppix, you can run *ifconfig* without specifying the path because the default path to the command is already set up.

To use the *ifconfig* command:

1. In Fedora and Red Hat Enterprise Linux, at the command prompt type **/sbin/ifconfig eth0** and press **Enter** (see Figure 8-20). In Knoppix just enter **ifconfig eth0** and press **Enter**.

2. In the second line of the results, the IP address is listed to the right of inet addr: and in Figure 8-20 is the address 192.168.0.5

3. Also, notice the transmission information on the screen. RX packets: and TX packets: show the number of data packets (units) of information that have been received by your computer and transmitted from the computer. If you see lots of errors (in the hundreds) in transmitting or receiving, many dropped packets, or many overruns, this is a clue that there may be a problem with your network communications, such as the network card in your computer. Also, if you see lots of collisions (in the hundreds), this can mean that there is a problem with your network or with devices communicating on your network. (Note that some errors and collisions are normal for any network.)

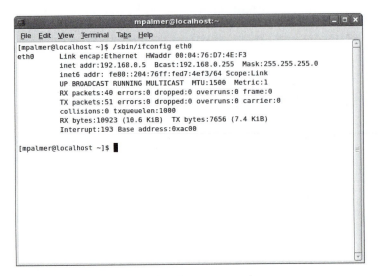

```
                           mpalmer@localhost:~
 File  Edit  View  Terminal  Tabs  Help
[mpalmer@localhost ~]$ /sbin/ifconfig eth0
eth0      Link encap:Ethernet  HWaddr 00:04:76:D7:4E:F3
          inet addr:192.168.0.5  Bcast:192.168.0.255  Mask:255.255.255.0
          inet6 addr: fe80::204:76ff:fed7:4ef3/64 Scope:Link
          UP BROADCAST RUNNING MULTICAST  MTU:1500  Metric:1
          RX packets:40 errors:0 dropped:0 overruns:0 frame:0
          TX packets:51 errors:0 dropped:0 overruns:0 carrier:0
          collisions:0 txqueuelen:1000
          RX bytes:10923 (10.6 KiB)  TX bytes:7656 (7.4 KiB)
          Interrupt:193 Base address:0xac00

[mpalmer@localhost ~]$ █
```

Figure 8-20   Using the *ifconfig* command

HANDS-ON
PROJECTS

Project 8-17

The *ping* utility is a good troubleshooting tool for determining if your connection, the network, or a remote connection is working on a network.

To use the *ping* command:

1. At the command line, type **ping –c 5** (-c 5 limits the number of polls to five) plus the IP address of your computer as you determined in Hands-On Project 8-16, such as **ping –c 5 198.168.0.210**.

2. Press **Enter**.

3. In the summary statistics, notice how many packets were sent and received.

4. Type **clear** and press **Enter**.

HANDS-ON
PROJECTS

Project 8-18

traceroute is another command that enables you to test your network and network connection. It tells you the route your communications take between your computer and another computer or server or to a destination on the Internet. Before you start, obtain a network address from your instructor of another computer or server on your network or of a server on the Internet.

To use the *traceroute* command:

1. Type **traceroute** plus your IP address and press **Enter** to view the network path to your computer (see Figure 8-21).

2. How many hops are there?

3. Type **traceroute** plus the IP address provided by your instructor.

4. How many hops do you see now?

5. Type **clear** and press **Enter**.

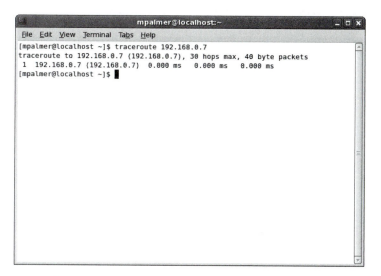

```
                         mpalmer@localhost:~
File  Edit  View  Terminal  Tabs  Help
[mpalmer@localhost ~]$ traceroute 192.168.0.7
traceroute to 192.168.0.7 (192.168.0.7), 30 hops max, 40 byte packets
 1  192.168.0.7 (192.168.0.7)  0.000 ms   0.000 ms   0.000 ms
[mpalmer@localhost ~]$
```

Figure 8-21   Using *traceroute*

Project 8-19

Use the netstat command for an array of communications statistics received at and transmitted by your computer. This utility not only provides another way for you to monitor your network connection, it also gives you information about who is connected and what they are doing (including intruders that you do not see any other way).

To use the *netstat* command:

1. Type **netstat –a** and press **Enter** to view communications across open ports on your computer. As you'll see, there is likely to be a great deal of activity.

2. Type **netstat –n** and press **Enter** to view any IP connections for other computers and other connected ports.

3. Type **netstat –s** and press **Enter** for a large compilation of communications statistics (see Figure 8-22). Scroll back, if your window allows, to view the statistics for IP communications. As you view the statistics do you see any errors, such as discarded packets?

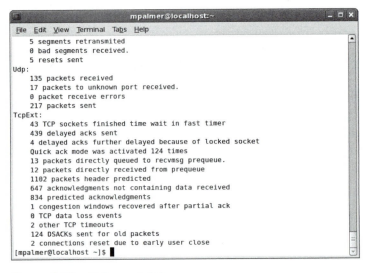

Figure 8-22 Using *netstat*

DISCOVERY EXERCISES

1. Use the *df* command to view file system use in megabytes.

2. Use the *touch* command to create the file letters. Next use the *dd* command to make a backup of the file.

3. Use the command that gives you information about swap space and memory use.

4. Start the *top* utility. Notice that *top* is listed as one of the most active processes. Determine what CPU percentage is used by running *top*. Stop the *top* utility.

5. Start the *top* utility so that it updates every 20 seconds. Now, do you see *top* in the list of the most active processes on your screen? Stop the *top* utility.

6. Use the command to determine which users have processes running on your system.

7. Log in as root and try using *ifconfig*, *netstat*, and *route*. Also, when you use *ifconfig*, record the "inet addr" (IP) value for eth0 (your Ethernet address) and for lo (your localhost loopback address), such as 127.0.0.1 for lo.

8. If you are connected to a network, use the *ping* command to *ping* one or both of the addresses you obtained in Exercise 7. Also, if you have access to an Internet connection, use the *ping* command to *ping* the GNOME Web site, using *ping gnome.org* (or use another site provided by your instructor).

9. Log out of root and back in to your own account. Type the command to determine the PID of your Bash shell session and record the PID.

10. Use the vi editor to create and save the famous_words file with the following contents (including misspellings):

    ```
    We mst all hang togther or
    Assuredly we shll all hang separately.
        -- Ben Franklin
    ```

    Make a copy of the document using the *dd* command and calling the copy famous_words.bak. Use a tool to check and correct the spelling errors in the famous_words document.

11. Use the *cmp* command to compare the famous_words and famous_words.bak files.

12. Start the *top* utility. Type ? after the utility starts. What information do you see? Press Enter and stop the *top* utility.

13. Run the *man* program in the background with the argument *df*. Record the PID of the process you have started.

14. Use the command to kill the process you started in Exercise 14.

15. Edit the phmenu.1 file, and add a new section named SEE ALSO. Under this section, list the following files:

    ```
    phoneadd
    phlist1
    ```

16. Save and test the revised phmenu.1 file using the *groff* and *man* programs.

17. Edit the phmenu.1 file, and add a new section named BUGS. Under this section, list a line that reads:

    ```
    None Known
    ```

18. Save and test the revised phmenu.1 file using the *groff* and *man* programs.

19. Edit the phmenu.1 file and add a new section named AUTHOR. Under this section, list your name. Save and test the revised file using the *groff* and *man* programs.

20. Use the command that enables you to view the documentation for *ifconfig*. Notice the many options for configuring your network connection.

21. Find out the IP address of a friend's computer or of a favorite Web site and use the command to poll that computer or Web site.

22. Use a command to view the contents of the /etc/init.d directory to see a listing of services you can start on your computer. Do you see the portmap file?

8

PERL AND CGI PROGRAMMING

After reading this chapter and completing the exercises, you will be able to:

♦ Understand the basics of the Perl language

♦ Identify and use data types in Perl scripts

♦ Understand differences between the Awk program and Perl programming

♦ Access disk files in Perl

♦ Use Perl to sort information

♦ Set up a simple HTML Web page

♦ Understand how Perl and CGI are used for creating Web pages

---

One of the strengths of UNIX and Linux is their support for scripting and programming languages that can be used to create applications, including applications for the Web. Perl is one of these languages and is well worth learning, particularly if you plan to create reports or develop Web applications. When combined with CGI, a communications protocol, Perl can be used to create interactive Web pages, such as those used when you order a product over the Internet.

This chapter gives you a basic introduction to Perl so that you understand its capabilities. You learn how to identify Perl data types, and compare Perl to Awk. As you learn more about Perl, you use it to display text, to access disk files, and to sort alphanumeric and numeric fields. At the end of this chapter, you are briefly introduced to writing Web pages using Perl, HTML, and CGI.

INTRODUCTION TO PERL

Practical Extraction and Report Language (Perl) is a free script language that runs on many operating systems, including UNIX, Linux, Windows, and Mac OS X. You can use Perl to manipulate text, display output, handle mathematical processes, and work with files. An important reason for learning Perl is that it is a popular scripting tool used for generating reports and for Web programming. Perl was released by Larry Wall in 1987 as a simple report generator, but has evolved into a staple for Web programmers.

Perl contains a blend of features found in other languages. It is very similar to the C language, but also contains features found in Awk and shell programs. Some users consider Perl to be easier to use than C. Others consider Perl to be more powerful and versatile than shell script programming.

Perl is an interpreted language, which, as you learned in Chapter 6, "Introduction to Shell Script Programming," means that statements are read and immediately executed. In contrast, a compiled language is one in which a program called a compiler converts program code into machine language instructions. In many UNIX/Linux systems, the Perl interpreter is contained in the /usr/bin directory (/usr/bin/perl).

You begin learning Perl by examining a few simple script programs, such as this one:

```
#!/usr/bin/perl
# Program name: example1.pl
print("This is a simple\n");
print("Perl program.\n");
```

The first line in the program tells the operating system to use Perl to interpret the file. Recall from Chapter 7, "Advanced Shell Programming," that when the first line of a program begins with #!, the remainder of the line is assumed to give the path of the interpreter.

The second line in the sample program is a comment that documents the name of the file. Like shell scripts, Perl programs use the # character to mark the beginning of a comment. Notice that the program name mentioned in the comment includes the extension .pl, which is an extension typically used to signify that a file (example1.pl) is a Perl script.

The third and fourth lines of the program display text on the screen. In these lines, the *print* statement displays the specified strings to stdout (the screen). The strings are enclosed in double quotation marks. The \n included at the end of the string characters means to perform a line feed, so that the next information displayed to the screen is on the next line. The program output is shown in Figure 9-1.

NOTE

If you decide to reproduce this script or others in the next group of examples, be certain to give the script files execute permissions prior to running them.

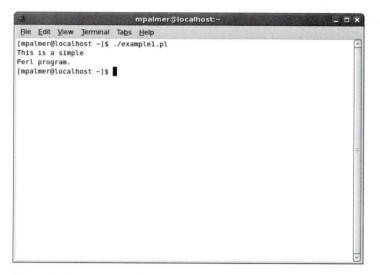

Figure 9-1   Running the example1.pl script

In this simple script, the *print* statements each have a single argument, which is displayed on the screen. The first *print* statement displays the string "This is a simple" and the \n characters advance the cursor to the beginning of the next line. The second *print* statement is similar to the first. It displays the string "Perl program." and then advances the cursor to the beginning of the next line. Notice that the two *print* statements end with a semicolon. All complete statements in Perl end with a semicolon.

NOTE   The parentheses surrounding the *print* statement's argument are optional. For example, these two statements perform the same operation:

```
print ("Hello");
print "Hello";
```

Look at a second Perl script, which uses a variable:

```
#!/usr/bin/perl
# Program name: example2.pl
$name = "Charlie";
print ("Greetings $name\n");
```

The example2.pl script uses the variable *$name*. The variable is initialized with the string "Charlie". Notice that when *$name* is inserted in the *print* statement's argument, it displays the contents of the variable, with the output displayed as follows:

```
[ellen@localhost ~]$ ./example2.pl
Greetings Charlie
```

Perl can also read input from the keyboard. The next program is an example.

```
#!/usr/bin/perl
# Program name: example3.pl
print ("Enter a number: ");
$number = <STDIN>;
print ("You entered $number\n");
```

The program's output is shown in Figure 9-2.

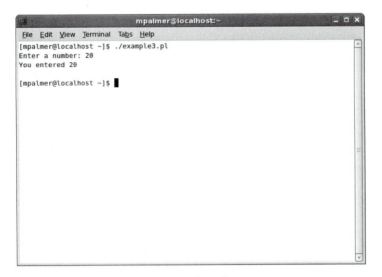

Figure 9-2   Running the example3.pl script

In Perl, <STDIN> reads input from the keyboard (remember that stdin is the standard input device). The program uses this line to assign keyboard input to the variable *$number.*

```
$number = <STDIN>
```

Like other languages, Perl offers the *if-else* statement as a decision structure. Here is an example:

```
#!/usr/bin/perl
# Program name: example4.pl
print ("Enter a number: ");
$number = <STDIN>;
if ($number == 10)
{
    print ("That is the number I was thinking of.\n");
}
else
{
    print ("You entered $number\n");
}
```

The == operator tests two numeric values for equality. The *if* statement uses the == operator to determine if *$number* is equal to 10. If it is, the block (which consists of lines of code enclosed inside a set of curly brackets) immediately following the *if* statement is executed. Otherwise, the block that follows the *else* statement is executed. The output that you see when you run the example4.pl script and enter 10 is "That is the number I was thinking of." When you enter any other number, you see the output "You entered" plus the number that you entered, as shown in Figure 9-3.

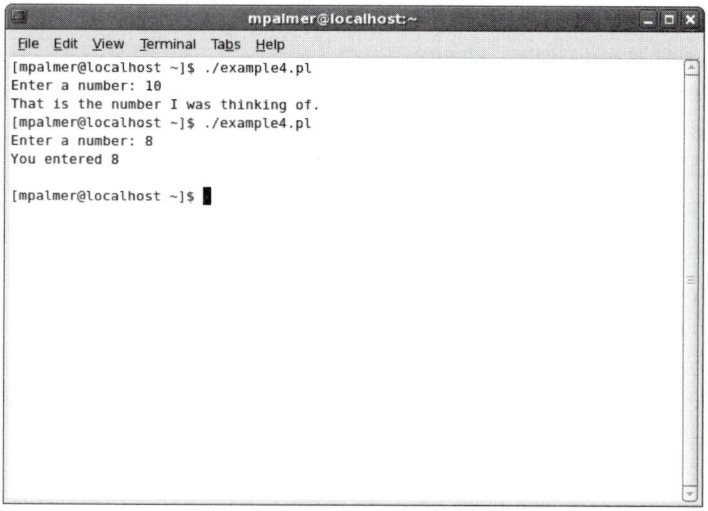

```
mpalmer@localhost:~
File  Edit  View  Terminal  Tabs  Help
[mpalmer@localhost ~]$ ./example4.pl
Enter a number: 10
That is the number I was thinking of.
[mpalmer@localhost ~]$ ./example4.pl
Enter a number: 8
You entered 8

[mpalmer@localhost ~]$
```

Figure 9-3   Running the example4.pl script

Perl also has operators that test for less than, greater than, less than or equal to, and greater than or equal to relationships. Table 9-1 shows the Perl numeric relational operators and Table 9-2 lists its string relational operators.

Table 9-1   Perl's numeric relational operators

Operator	Meaning
==	Equality
<	Less than
>	Greater than
<=	Less than or equal to
>=	Greater than or equal to
!=	Not equal to

Table 9-2   Perl's string relational operators

Operator	Meaning
eq	Equality
lt	Less than
gt	Greater than

Table 9-2   Perl's string relational operators (continued)

Operator	Meaning
le	Less than or equal to
ge	Greater than or equal to
ne	Not equal to

Notice that the numeric relational operators are symbolic, such as <= for less than or equal to, as typically is used in numeric formulas. The string relational operators are character based, such as *le* for less than or equal to. The next program demonstrates how two strings stored in two variables—*$my_name* and *$your_name*—are compared for equality using the *eq* string relational operator.

```perl
#!/usr/bin/perl
# Program name: example5.pl
$my_name = "Ellen";
$your_name = "Charlie";
if ($my_name eq $your_name)
{
        print ("Your name is the same as mine.\n");
}
else
{
        print ("Hello. My name is $my_name\n");
}
```

The output of example5.pl is as follows:

```
[ellen@localhost ~]$ ./example5.pl
Hello. My name is Ellen
```

Perl also provides standard arithmetic operators:

- + performs addition.

- - performs subtraction.

- * performs multiplication.

- / performs division.

The next program, example6.pl, demonstrates a simple arithmetic operation.

```perl
#!/usr/bin/perl
# Program name: example6.pl
$num1 = 10;
$num2 = 50;
$num3 = 12;
$average = ($num1 + $num2 + $num3) / 3;
print ("The average is $average\n");
```

When you run example6.pl, you see the following on your screen:

```
[ellen@localhost ~]$ ./example6.pl
The average is 24
```

As you can see from the preceding program, Perl also lets you group operations within parentheses. Now that you have a general understanding of Perl, let's study its data types.

IDENTIFYING DATA TYPES

The computer programmer must understand not only what is contained in files, records, and fields, but also the format in which it is stored. Are the fields of information numeric (numbers that can be processed), alphabetic (letters), or alphanumeric (a combination of letters and numbers)? How do you treat control characters, such as tab and newline? Although it might seem obvious that a data item such as a person's name cannot be added or multiplied, the programmer must write code that properly handles any and all data items that appear in a program. Otherwise, misidentified data generates processing errors. To successfully write code, programmers need to identify data types.

Data can be represented in Perl in a variety of ways. In this chapter, you learn about these types of data:

- Variables and constants

- Scalars

- Numbers

- Strings

- Arrays

- Hashes

Variables and Constants

Variables are symbolic names that represent values stored in memory. For example, the variable *$x* might hold the value 100, and *$name* might hold the sequence of characters Charlie. The value of a variable can change while the program runs. **Constants**, however, do not change value as the program runs. They are written into the program code itself. For example, this statement assigns the value of the constant 127.89 to the variable *$num*:

```
$num = 127.89
```

Scalars

In the broadest sense, data is perceived as being either numeric or nonnumeric. A nonnumeric field of information is treated simply as a string of characters (hence, the term string). Programmers associate strings with such items as a person's name, address, or license plate number. Numbers can also be used for logical analysis as well as for mathematical computations. A **scalar** is a simple variable that holds a number or a string. Scalar variable names begin with a dollar sign ($).

All of these are examples of statements that assign numeric or string values to scalar variables:

```
$x = 12;
$name = "Jill";
$pay = 12456.89;
```

Numbers

Numbers are stored inside the computer as either signed integers (as in 14321) or double-precision, floating-point values (as in 23456.85). Numeric literals (constant values versus variable values) can be either integers or floating-point values. An integer is a positive or negative whole number or zero—examples include 0, 1, -1, 20, -15, -208, and 72. A floating-point value is a real number that can be expressed as a decimal, exponential number, or number in scientific notation in which the precision of the number is related to the number's scale (such as precise up to four decimal points). These numeric representations are consistent with all programming languages, but Perl also uses an additional convention with numeric literals to improve legibility—the underscore character, as in 5_456_678_901. (Perl uses the comma as a list separator.) The underscore only works within literal numbers specified in a program, not in strings functioning as numbers or in data read from elsewhere. Similarly, hexadecimal constants are expressed with the leading 0x prefix (as in 0xfff), and octal constants are expressed with the leading 0 prefix (as in 0256).

Strings

Strings are often used for logical analysis, sorts, or searches. Strings are sequences of any types of characters (including numbers that are treated as characters rather than digits). String literals are usually delimited by either single quotation marks (' ') or double quotation marks (" "). Single-quoted strings are not subject to interpolation (except for \' and \\, used to put single quotation marks and backslashes into a single-quoted string). Interpolation refers to the mathematical process of interpreting a value between two known values on the basis of making assumptions about predictable behavior, such as guessing that the interpreted value in 1, 2, ?, 4, 5 is the number 3.

Within double quotation marks, variables are interpolated; a backslash (\) preceding a variable name is used to ensure it is not interpolated. In addition, the backslash is used to ensure a control or escape character is not interpolated. Table 9-3 lists the code and meaning for several control or escape character sequences used within double quotation marks.

Table 9-3   Perl's double-quoted string, control, and escape characters

Code	Meaning
\n	New line
\r	Carriage return

Table 9-3 Perl's double-quoted string, control, and escape characters (continued)

Code	Meaning
\t	Horizontal tab
\f	Form feed
\b	Backspace
\a	Bell (alarm)
\033	ESC in octal
\x7f	Del in hexadecimal
\cC	Ctrl+C
\\	Backslash
\"	Double quote
\u	Force next character to uppercase
\l	Force next character to lowercase
\U	Force all following characters to uppercase until \E is encountered
\L	Force all following characters to lowercase until \E is encountered
\Q	Backslash—quote all following nonalphanumeric characters until \E is encountered
\E	End \U, \L, \Q

For example, compare the use of special codes in the next program, example7.pl, with those shown in Table 9-3.

```
#!/usr/bin/perl
# Program name: example7.pl
print ("\\words\\separated\\by\\slashes\n");
print ("This is a \"quote\"\n");
print ("\Uupper case\n");
print ("\LLOWER CASE\n");
```

The program output is shown in Figure 9-4.

Arrays

Arrays are variables that store an ordered list of scalar values that are accessed with numeric subscripts, starting at zero. The variables in an array are usually of the same data type, such as types of pets, names of people, or types of cars. When stored, the items in an array typically occupy a separate line or row (as in a file or in memory) and each row is given a number to differentiate one array element from another. Consider an array of pets that contains the elements: dog, cat, parrot, and hamster. When the elements are stored, such as in a file or in memory, each type of pet is a separate line of data or row. Also, each row is typically given a number to distinguish it from all other rows. In this example, dog is stored in row number 0, cat in row 1, parrot in row 2 and hamster in row 3.

An "at" sign (@) precedes the name of an array when assigning it values. When processing the individual elements of an array, however, use the $ character. For example, the following program, example8.pl, creates the array *pets*.

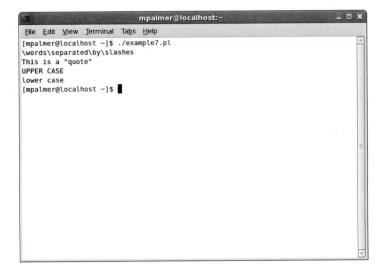

Figure 9-4 Running the example7.pl script

```
#!/usr/bin/perl
# Program name: example8.pl
@pets = ("dog", "cat", "parrot", "hamster" );
print ("My pets are:\n");
print ("$pets[0]\n");
print ("$pets[1]\n");
print ("$pets[2]\n");
print ("$pets[3]\n");
```

Figure 9-5 shows the output of the example8.pl script.

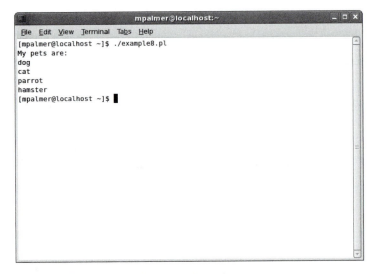

Figure 9-5 Running the example8.pl script

Hashes

A **hash** is a variable that represents a set of key/value pairs. Consider an inventory system of canned food items as an example. Each food item is assigned a value or stock keeping unit (SKU) to differentiate it from others. A can of chili might have an SKU of 0184, a can of tomato soup an SKU of 0292, and so on. The key/value pair for a can of chili is "0184, chili" and the key/value pair for can of tomato soup is "0292, tomato soup". By associating the products in this way, a company can type in the SKU and immediately see it is for a particular product or vice versa. The SKU is like a data key associated with a product (you learned about keys in Chapter 4, "UNIX/Linux File Processing").

Hash variables are preceded by a percent sign (%) when they are assigned values. To refer to a single element of a hash, use the $ character before the variable name, followed by the key associated with the value in curly brackets. For example:

```
%animals = ('Tigers', 10, 'Lions', 20, 'Bears', 30);
$animals{'Bears'}
```

returns the value 30. Another, more readable way to define this is to use the ==> operator (also called the arrow operator) to define the key/value pairs:

```
%animals = (Tigers ==> 10, Lions ==> 20, Bears ==> 30);
```

The following program, example9.pl, demonstrates the use of a hash variable.

```
#!/usr/bin/perl
# Program name: example9.pl
%animals = ('Tigers', 10, 'Lions', 20, 'Bears', 30);
print ("The animal values are:\n");
print ("$animals{'Tigers'}\n");
print ("$animals{'Lions'}\n");
print ("$animals{'Bears'}\n");
```

The program's output is as follows:

```
[ellen@localhost ~]$ ./example9.pl
The animal values are:
10
20
30
```

Now that you understand about data types, you are ready to learn more about programming using Perl. Perl's similarities and differences with other programming languages can be illustrated by comparing how the same program appears in the Awk format and in Perl.

PERL VERSUS THE AWK PROGRAM

The Awk program does not require the programmer to explicitly set up looping structures as does Perl. Perl's *while* loop, on the other hand, is almost identical to the one found in the C and C++ programming languages. The Awk program, therefore, uses fewer lines of code to resolve pattern–matching extractions than does Perl. For example, look at the following Awk program, awkcom.a, and its output. The program counts the number of comment lines that appear in the file specified on the command line. (This assumes we are skipping the path line, which, for example, is *#!/usr/bin/awk -f* in the awkcom.a file.) Figure 9-6 illustrates the output of the awkcom.a program.

```
#!/usr/bin/awk -f
# Program name: awkcom.a
# Purpose: Count the comment lines in a file.
#          Enter the file name on the command line.

END {
  print "The file has ", line_count, " comment lines."
}
/^#/ && !/^#!/  { ++line_count }  # This occurs for
  every line.
```

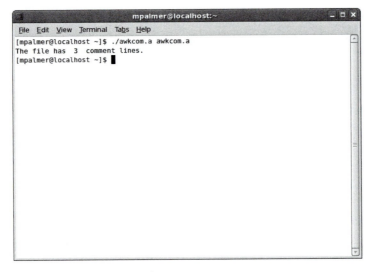

Figure 9-6   Running awkcom.a

Now compare the awkcom.a program with this Perl program:

```
#!/usr/bin/perl
# Program name: perlcom.pl
# Purpose: Count the source file's comment lines
# ==============================================
$filein = $ARGV[0];
while (<>)
{
    if (/^#/ && !/^#!/)
    {
    ++$line_count
```

```
    }
}
print ("File \"$filein\" has $line_count comment lines. \n");
```

Although the end results of both programs are very similar, you can see where the two programs differ. The Awk program uses an implicit *while* loop that automatically sends the entire contents of the file named on the command line to the pattern-matching and action part of the program. However, for the Perl program you need to build the *while* loop explicitly. The output of the perlcom.pl script is shown in Figure 9-7.

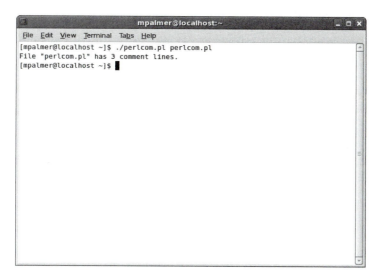

Figure 9-7   Running perlcom.pl

The first line of each program tells the shell program to run either the Awk program or the Perl program and to pass the statements in the file to the program for execution. Both programs also use the pound sign (#) to specify a comment line. Further, the pattern-matching code is the same in both programs. That is where the similarities end.

The -*f* option in the Awk program tells the shell that the program is being called with a script file that contains the *awk* commands. Note that if the -*f* option is not included, the Awk program uses the first command-line argument as its program. Recall that an Awk program contains more built-in commands to read lines from the file. All an Awk program needs is the pattern-matching conditions to select the lines. The reading of the file is implied as shown in the following code:

```
/^#/&& !/^#!/  { ++line_count }
```

An Awk program also uses BEGIN and END to control when commands execute. All statements in a BEGIN block execute before the input file is read. All statements in an END block execute after all the contents of the input file have been read. This program only needs the END pattern.

In the Perl program, the code:

```
$filein = $ARGV[0];
```

takes the name of the file on the command line (ARGV[0]) and places it in a variable so it can be referenced later. The file name originally stored in ARGV[0] from the command line is destroyed during the *while* loop.

```
while (<>)
```

The <> symbol is called the **diamond operator**. After the file is opened, you can access its data using the diamond operator. Each time it is called, it returns the next line from the file.

Curly brackets open and close a block in which you can place multiple statements:

```
if (/^#/ && !/^#!/)
{
    ++$line_count
}
```

This block tests to see if the line begins with the # character, but not with the #! characters. If true, the statement ++*$line_count* adds one to the *$line_count* variable and then closes the *if* block.

Whether the Awk program or Perl is a good choice for you is a personal decision, but either one or both should be part of your toolkit. There is no substitute for the kinds of work that either program can quickly perform with minimal code preparation. For example, you probably would not want to write a C program for a task such as scanning files for a matching pattern. However, both Perl and Awk are excellent when you are looking for the "needle in a haystack."

Both Perl and the Awk program (particularly the GNU Project's implementation of POSIX 1003.2 compliant Awk) are portable across many UNIX/Linux systems, which is an advantage because the effort to develop code on one system is not lost if you convert to another system. Also, Perl is popular as a CGI tool for Web-based applications, as you discover later in this chapter.

NOTE

Notice that we are using .a as the file extension for an Awk script. It is useful to understand and follow the common use of file extensions in UNIX/Linux. The following is a short list of typical file extensions for UNIX/Linux:

- *.a* or *.awk* for an Awk script
- *.asc* for an ASCII file
- *.bak* for a backup file
- *.c* for a C program file
- *.C*, *.cc*, or *.cpp* for a C ++ program file
- *.cgi* for a CGI script
- *.dat* for a data file
- *.gz* for a gzip compressed file
- *.log* for a log file
- *.zip* for a zip compressed file

9

How Perl Accesses Disk Files

Like most high-level programming languages, Perl uses filehandles to reference files. A **filehandle** is the name for an I/O connection between your Perl program and the operating system, and it can be used inside your program to open, read, write, and close the file. The convention is to use all uppercase letters for filehandles. In most instances, you must issue an *open* statement to open the file before you can access it. The exception to this occurs when you use the ARGV[0] variable to pass the file name to the program through the command line. In effect, you open it on the command line. As with other languages, every Perl program has three filehandles that are automatically opened: STDIN (the keyboard), STDOUT (the screen, to which the *print( )* and *write( )* statements are written by default), and STDERR (the screen, used to display error messages).

Some common methods for opening and processing external files are available. One method is illustrated in the program perlread1.pl, which passes the file name on the command line, using the standard array variable that is reserved to do just that, ARGV[0]. This Perl program displays the contents of a file. (Recall that you can also use *cat*, *less*, and *more* for doing this.) The lines of code for perlread1.pl are as follows:

```
#!/usr/bin/perl
# Program name: perlread1.pl
# Purpose: Display records in a file and count lines
$filein = $ARGV[0];
while (<>)
{
        print "$_";
        ++$line_count;
}
print ("File \"$filein\" has $line_count lines. \n");
```

The first instruction (*$filein* = *$ARGV[0]*;) saves the name of the file that is passed to the program and stores it in ARGV[0]. The *while* loop triggers the diamond operator (<>) that sequentially reads records from the file and places the value stored in ARGV[0] in the next record. This continues until the loop reaches the end of the file. When that happens, ARGV[0] contains a null (end-of-file character), so you cannot use ARGV[0] to reference the file name when the *while* loop terminates. Two commands inside the *while* loop are enclosed within curly brackets: *print "$_"* displays each record that is read and ++*$line_count* increments (counts) the records in the file. The final command, *print ("File \"$filein\" has $line_count lines. \n")*, prints the name of the file (saved in *$filein*) and the number of lines in the file. You create the perlread1.pl example in Hands-On Project 9-1.

NOTE

The Perl programming language defines a set of special variables. Among these is the $_ variable, which is the default input, output, and pattern-searching space. In the perlread1.pl program, you are using it as the default input variable. However, in the perlread1.pl program, *print "$_";* could also be written as *print;* because the $_ variable is assumed by default.

Using another method, you can open a file from within your program, as opposed to passing it on the command line. All files opened inside programs must be closed before the program terminates. Consider the following example, called perlread2.pl:

```
#!/usr/bin/perl
# Program name: perlread2.pl
# Purpose: Open disk file. Read and display the records
#          in the file. Count the number of records in
#          the file.
open (FILEIN, "students") || warn "Could not open students
 file\n";
while (<FILEIN>)
{
        print "$_";
        ++$line_count;
}
print ("File \"students\" has $line_count lines. \n");
 close (FILEIN);
```

In the perlread2.pl program, the *open( )* function appears on the first line after the comment section:

```
open (FILEIN, "students") || warn "Could not open students
 file\n";
```

Nearly all program functions are written to return a value that indicates whether the function was carried out successfully. The values returned are considered to be true or false. A true value is usually represented with a 1, and sometimes any value greater than zero. A false value is represented with a 0 (zero). The *open( )* function returns true if the file is opened successfully, and returns false if it fails to open. Opening a file can fail because the file is not found or because the file's permissions for reading and/or writing are not set. However, in

Perl, a filehandle that has not been successfully opened can still be read, but you get an immediate EOF (end-of-file signal), with no other noticeable effects. An EOF results in your program not letting you read from or write to the file because the file is not available.

The two vertical bar characters "||" are the logical OR operator. When an expression on the left of a logical OR operator returns false, the expression on the right of the operator executes. The *warn* statement on the right of the OR operator:

```
warn "Could not open students file\n";
```

is used to display an error message indicating the file did not open. The *warn* statement can either print text that you provide or it can display a system error message. Although displaying error conditions is not absolutely necessary in your programs, you should display them when it is obvious that the errors can cause subsequent problems if the program continues to run. This additional coding is especially essential in *open()* statements.

After the file is open, access to the data is made through the diamond operator (<FILEIN>). When the *while* loop reaches the end of a file, it terminates. Except for the *open()* and *close()* statements and the use of the diamond operator, the perlread2.pl program is identical to perlread1.pl. Try Hands-On Project 9-2 to create perlread2.pl.

9

USING PERL TO SORT

One of the most important tasks in managing data is organizing it into a usable format. Perl provides a powerful and flexible sort operator. It can sort string or numeric data in ascending or descending order. It even allows advanced sorting operations in which you define your own sorting routine.

Using Perl to Sort Alphanumeric Fields

Perl can be used to sort information. Consider the perlsort1.pl program, which sorts words into alphabetical order using the *sort* statement.

```
#!/usr/bin/perl
# Program name: perlsort1.pl
# Purpose: Sort a list of names contained inside an array
# Syntax: perlsort1.pl <Enter>
#===========================================================
@somelist = ("Oranges", "Apples", "Tangerines", "Pears",
  "Bananas",  "Pineapples");
@sortedlist = sort @somelist;
print "@sortedlist";
print"\n";
```

Looking at the program, the statement:

```
@somelist = ("Oranges", "Apples", "Tangerines", "Pears",
  "Bananas",  "Pineapples");
```

puts the value of (Oranges, Apples, Tangerines, Pears, Bananas, Pineapples) into @somelist. The statement:

```
@sortedlist = sort @somelist;
```

calls the Perl *sort* statement and returns the sorted output to the array variable, @sortedlist. The final two statements in the program print the sorted results and skip a line before the program terminates and returns to the command line. Hands-On Project 9-3 enables you to create and use the perlsort1.pl program.

Data is not always coded as part of the program or entered at the keyboard. Often, programs must read information from files. Consider, for example, the students file that is created in Hands-On Project 9-1 containing the names Joseph, Alice, Mary, Zona, Aaron, Barbara, and Larry. The following example demonstrates how Perl accesses the contents of the students file by passing the file name on the command line:

```
#!/usr/bin/perl
# Program name: perlsort2.pl
# Purpose: Sorts a text file alphabetically. File name is
#          entered on the command line.
# Syntax: perlsort2.pl file name <Enter>
#==========================================================
$x = 0;
while (<>)
{
        $somelist[$x] = $_;
        $x++;
}
@sortedlist = sort @somelist;
print @sortedlist;
```

The perlsort2.pl program uses the statement:

```
$x = 0;
```

to initialize a variable, x, to contain an index to the array. The first element of every array is zero (0). In the *while* loop,

```
while (<>)
{
        $somelist[$x] = $_;
        $x++;
}
```

the next line in the file is automatically copied into the $_ variable. The assignment statement:

```
$somelist[$x] = $_;
```

copies the contents of the $_ variable into an element of the array. The element is determined by the variable x, which is used as a subscript. After the assignment operation occurs, the following statement executes:

```
$x++;
```

The ++ operator adds one to its argument, so the statement increments the variable x. As a result, the first name, Aaron, is placed in *$somelist[0]*, Alice is placed in *$somelist[1]*, and so on.

The statement:

```
@sortedlist = sort @somelist;
```

sorts the array, @somelist, placing the alphabetized names into @sortedlist, and the final instruction prints the alphabetized list of students' names. Try Hands-On Project 9-4 to create the perlsort2.pl program.

Using Perl to Sort Numeric Fields

Sorting numeric fields can be done using a subroutine in which you can define comparison conditions (for example, greater than, less than, or equal to) between the data you are sorting. A **subroutine** (also called a **routine**) is a segment of code often used over and over again that can be internal or external to a program. A subroutine typically is identified by a beginning control statement, such as the *sub* statement in Perl, and a unique name that often reflects its purpose.

To sort numeric fields in the example provided here, the sort subroutine is called repeatedly, passing two elements to be compared on each call. The scalar variables a and b store the two values that are compared to select the larger value. Using the comparison operation, a return code of -1, 0, or +1 is returned, depending on whether a is less than, equal to, or greater than b, as in the following sample of code:

```
sub numbers
{
 if ($a < $b)    { -1; }
 elsif ($a == $b)    { 0; }
 else   { +1; }
}
```

When sorting numbers, you need to instruct Perl to use this sort subroutine as the comparison function, rather than the built-in ASCII ascending sort (the default). To do this, place the name of the subroutine between the keyword "sort" and the list of items to be sorted:

```
$sortednumbers = sort numbers 101, 87, 34, 12, 1, 76;
```

The statement instructs Perl to sort the values in the list by using the *numbers* subroutine to determine their order. The output is in numeric order, not ASCII order.

The numeric comparison of a and b is performed so frequently that Larry Wall, Perl's creator, developed a special Perl operator for numeric sorts, <=>. This sort operator, known as the **spaceship operator**, reduces coding requirements. To illustrate the code savings, compare the next sort subroutine using the spaceship operator with the previous one:

```
sub numbers
{
```

```
        $a <=> $b;
}
```

This *numbers* subroutine produces the same result as the first example, which uses an *if-else* statement. Perl allows an even more compact notation—the **inline sort block**, which looks like this:

```
@sortednumbers = sort { $a <=> $b; } @numberlist;
```

This statement uses the block { *$a <=> $b;* } as the sort routine. It eliminates the need for a separate subroutine. Let's examine how the following Perl program sorts numeric data:

```
#!/usr/bin/perl
# Program name: perlsort3.pl
# Purpose: Sorts numerically using a subroutine. File name
#          is entered on the command line.
# Syntax: perlsort3.pl file name <Enter>
#===========================================================
$x = 0;
while (<>)
{
   $somelist[$x] = $_;
   $x++;
}
@sortedlist = sort numbers @somelist;
print @sortedlist;
sub numbers
{
        if ($a < $b)
                { -1; }
        elsif ($a == $b)
                { 0; }
        else
                { +1; }
}
```

The perlsort3.pl program uses a sort subroutine that compares *$a* and *$b* numerically rather than textually. The program also initializes the array element index to start with the first element, 0. The *while* loop,

```
while (<>)
{
   $somelist[$x] = $_;
   $x++;
}
```

works the same as previously described, in that it reads records from a file and stores the lines inside an array.

The sort subroutine,

```
sub numbers
{
    if ($a < $b)   { -1; }
    elsif ($a == $b) { 0; }
    else { +1; }
}
```

compares the two numbers that are sequentially passed to it from the *while* loop. If the value in *$a* is less than the value in *$b*, the subroutine returns –1. If *$a* is equal to *$b*, the subroutine returns 0. Otherwise, the subroutine returns +1. For the numberlist file that contains the numbers 130, 100, 121, 101, 120, and 122 (in that order), perlsort3.pl produces the sorted output shown in Figure 9-8. In Hands-On Project 9-5, you create and run perlsort3.pl.

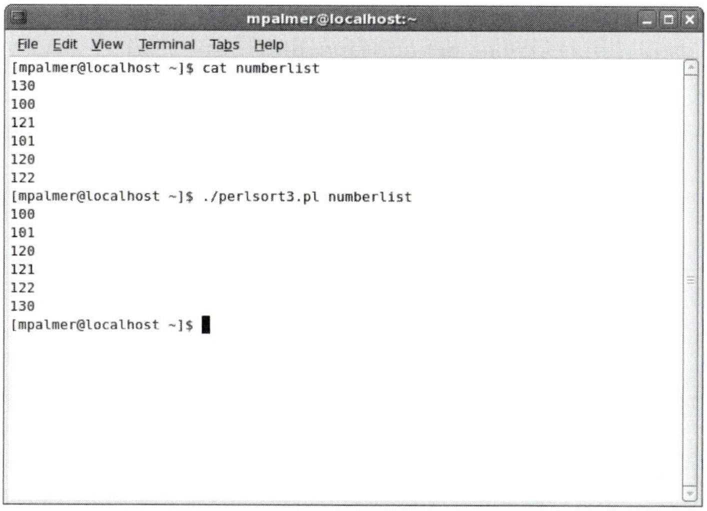

Figure 9-8   Sorted output of the numberlist file using perlsort3.pl

Sometimes, the spaceship operator can reduce coding time by replacing several lines of code. Consider the following perlsort4.pl program:

```
#!/usr/bin/perl
# Program name: perlsort4.pl
# Purpose: Sort numerically using the spaceship operator
#               (<=>)
# syntax: perlsort4.pl file name <Enter>
#=========================================================
$x = 0;
while (<>)
{
    $somelist[$x] = $_;
    $x++;
}
```

```
@sortedlist = sort numbers @somelist;
print @sortedlist;
sub numbers
{
   $a <=> $b;
}
```

In this example, the three lines of code previously used between the open and closed brackets in the *numbers* subroutine in perlsort3.pl:

```
sub numbers
{
    if ($a < $b)   { -1; }
    elsif ($a == $b) { 0; }
    else { +1; }
}
```

are replaced in perlsort4.pl by the following one line of code using the spaceship operator:

```
sub numbers
{
   $a <=> $b;
}
```

You create perlsort4.pl in Hands-On Project 9-6.

Now that you are more familiar with Perl, you learn how to create a Web page.

Setting Up a Web Page

In the next sections of this chapter, you get a very basic introduction to creating Web documents and Perl-based CGI programs. Both types of programming experiences are just a beginning, as there are entire books written about each of these areas. The purpose of this chapter is to help you experience them, get a glimpse of their uses, and entice you to seek additional experiences to learn more.

You can create a Web page using **Hypertext Markup Language (HTML)**. HTML is a format for creating documents with embedded codes known as **tags**. When the document is viewed in a Web browser, such as Firefox or Internet Explorer, the tags give the document special properties. Examples of properties include foreground and background colors, font size and color, and the placement of graphic images. In addition, HTML tags let you place **hyperlinks** in a document. A hyperlink is text or an object that, when clicked, loads another document and displays it in the browser.

After you use HTML to create a Web page, you can publish the page on a Web server. A **Web server** is a system running Web server software, such as Apache, that is connected to the Internet. The Web server software lets other users access the HTML document via the Internet.

NOTE

Apache, which is offered through the Apache Software Foundation, is really Apache HTTP Server. It is an open-source Web server software popularly used on UNIX and Linux computers. If you access the Web, you have probably also accessed a server running Apache, because at this writing the majority of Web servers run Apache. Visit the Apache Software Foundation Web site at *www.apache.org*.

You can experiment with and test HTML documents using your Linux system's loopback networking feature. The **loopback** feature allows your UNIX or Linux system to access its own internal network configuration instead of an external network. The loopback feature is installed automatically when you install Fedora, Red Hat Enterprise Linux, or SUSE for example. It uses the IP address 127.0.0.1, which is the standard designation for loopback communications. (See Discovery Exercise 7 in Chapter 8, "Exploring the UNIX/Linux Utilities.") Also, the name of the computer at the loopback address is **localhost**.

To use the loopback, you actually do not need to be connected to any network. What is more important, the loopback can emulate a real-world Web site, so you can carry out the testing and development of your new Web pages. Standalone testing of new Web pages is recommended; after fully testing your work, you can then transfer your documents to any Web server, knowing that they are ready to perform.

9

CREATING A SIMPLE WEB PAGE

You can use a visual HTML editor, such as Adobe Dreamweaver or Microsoft Expression Web, to create Web pages. These programs let you graphically construct a Web page in a "what you see is what you get" fashion. If you have no visual HTML editor, all you need is a text editor, such as vi or Emacs. You create the HTML document by typing its text and the desired embedded tags. The following is a sample HTML file:

```
<HTML>
<HEAD><TITLE>My Simple Web Page</TITLE></HEAD>
<BODY>
<H1>Just a Simple Web Page</H1>
This is a Web page with no frills!
</BODY>
</HTML>
```

All special codes contained inside angled brackets <> are tags. The first tag, <HTML>, identifies the file as an HTML document. Notice the corresponding </HTML> tag at the end of the file. Everything between the <HTML> and </HTML> tags is considered text with HTML tags. In general, most tags are used this way. One tag marks the beginning of a section, and a corresponding tag marks the end of the section.

Note that there are two parts to the code: a head and a body. The **head** contains the title, which appears on the title bar of your browser window. The **body** defines what appears within the browser window. All other tags refine the Web page's appearance. Figure 9-9 shows the Web page's appearance in the FirefoxWeb browser in Fedora.

Firefox is derived from Web browser software developed by the Mozilla Foundation (visit *www.mozilla.org* for more information).

NOTE

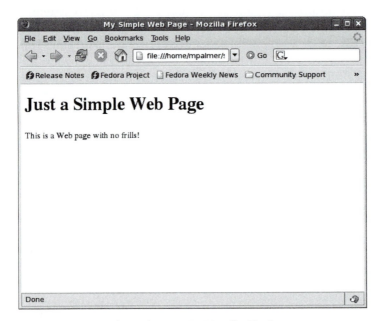

Figure 9-9   Simple Web page in Mozilla Firefox

You can use tags to set background and foreground colors and to manipulate text with such tags as <FONT SIZE=*n*>(*insert text here*)</FONT>. You can change text sizes with the heading tags, where <H1> is the largest and <H6> is the smallest. (However, note that users' browsers might also automatically change the actual text size.)

Because standard HTML ignores multiple spaces, tabs, and carriage returns, you can enclose text within <PRE></PRE> (preformatted text) tag pairs. Otherwise, any consecutive spaces, tabs, carriage returns, or combinations produce a single space. You can also use the <P> tag, which creates two line breaks, or the <BR> tag, which creates one line break. Neither tag requires a closing tag.

Browsers automatically wrap text so you don't need to worry about page widths. To center text, however, use <CENTER>(*text here*)</CENTER>. To indent from both margins, use <BLOCKQUOTE>(*text here*)</BLOCKQUOTE>. To change color, use <FONT COLOR="RGB">(*text here*)</FONT>, where RGB is the RGB color code. An RGB color code is a set of three numbers that specify a color's red, green, and blue components.

For example, the code 512218 specifies a red component of 51, a green component of 22, and a blue component of 18. The higher the number, the more intense the color component.

The following is another example of an HTML file.

```
<HTML>
<HEAD><TITLE>UNIX/Linux Programming Tools</TITLE></HEAD>
<BODY>
<H1><CENTER>My UNIX/Linux Programming Tools</CENTER></H1>
<H2>Languages</H2>
<P>Perl</P>
<P>Shell Scripts</P>
<P>C and C++</P>
<H2>Editors</H2>
<P>vi</P>
<P>Emacs</P>
<H2>Other Tools</H2>
<P>awk</P>
<P>sed</P>
</BODY>
</HTML>
```

This Web page lists UNIX/Linux programming tools under the headings Languages, Editors, and Other Tools. You create this Web page in Hands-On Project 9-7.

Now that you have some general knowledge of creating Web pages, you need to learn how to use Perl and CGI to make them interactive.

CGI OVERVIEW

Perl is the most commonly used language for **Common Gateway Interface (CGI)** programming. CGI is a protocol, or set of rules, governing how browsers and servers communicate. Here is why CGI is important. When you access a Web page that just displays information, such as the Web page you create in Hands-On Project 9-8, what happens in basic terms is that a Web client contacts a Web server and the Web page is sent to the client for display. This is an example of a Web page that is static, one in which no information is exchanged from the client.

When it is important to exchange information, such as when you order a product over the Internet, you dynamically supply information on a form. The information you provide might include your name, address, credit card number, and other information. To exchange and process a form containing information typically involves (1) using CGI for communication between the client's Web browser and the Web server and (2) a program that can be executed. The program is often a Perl script or a program written in the C language. Also, the program is often stored in a subdirectory on a Web server called cgi-bin. The programs in cgi-bin are set up to have executable permissions, such as the *x* permission in UNIX/ Linux, and also typically have *r* permissions so the client can view the associated Web page.

Any script that sends or receives information from a server needs to follow the standards specified by CGI. Thus, scripts written in Perl follow the CGI protocol. CGI Perl scripts are specifically written to get, process, and return information through your Web pages—they make Web pages interactive.

 CGI scripts can raise security concerns on a Web server. A CGI script may contain code that enables a Web intruder to snoop through or modify files in a Web directory. When you use a CGI script on a Web server, ensure that you trust the source of the script or create the script yourself and have someone check your work for security holes.

To allow your HTML document to accept input, especially where CGI rules apply, precede the input area with a description of what you want users to enter. For example, if you want users to enter cost, you use this code:

```
Total Cost? <INPUT TYPE=text NAME=cost SIZE=10>
```

In addition, consistent with transmitting information to and from Web sites, you can use the special code *INPUT TYPE=submit*, which sends out the data when a user clicks the Submit button. The destination that you want to receive the submitted information is coded into the FORM tag. The FORM tag specifies how to obtain the information to be transferred. There are two methods, GET and POST. The GET method transfers the data within the Uniform Resource Locator (URL, which provides an address to an entity on the Internet) itself. POST uses the body portion of the HTTP request to pass parameters. (You use the POST method in this chapter.)

This book is not intended to provide you with complete information about programming Perl scripts for CGI, but simply to make you aware of their relationship and potential. Various Web sites offer hundreds of prepared Perl scripts that you can use with your own Web page applications. Sample Web sites include the following:

- *www.scriptarchive.com* (offering many free CGI scripts)
- *www.extropia.com*
- *awsd.com/scripts*

The following sites provide useful Perl script and CGI information:

- *www.perl.com* (also see *www.perl.com/pub/a/doc/FAQs/cgi/perl-cgi-faq.html*)
- *www.devdaily.com/perl/edu/qanda/*
- *www.perlaccess.com*

In Hands-On Projects 9-8 and 9-9, you have an opportunity to experience Perl and CGI by first viewing a sample Web page in this format and then creating your own.

NOTE

For more in-depth information about Perl and CGI, consider the following books: *Perl Programming for the Absolute Beginner* by Jerry Lee Ford, Jr., *Perl Power! The Comprehensive Guide* by John Flynt, and *Perl Fast & Easy Web Development* by Leslie Bate.

CHAPTER SUMMARY

- Perl is used as a powerful text-manipulation tool similar to the Awk program.
- Perl is written in scripts that are translated and executed by the Perl program.
- Perl programmers need to understand how to identify data types so that their Perl programs correctly process the data. In Perl, the data types include variables and constants, scalars, strings, arrays, and hashes.
- Perl and Awk are both powerful processing languages that function in different ways and should become part of your toolkit, such as for creating versatile reports.
- Perl uses filehandles for the I/O connection between a file and Perl, such as for opening a file.
- Perl can sort both numeric and alphanumeric data. For numeric sorts, the spaceship (<=>) operator can be used to reduce coding requirements.
- HTML is used to format text for presentation in a Web page. A key to using HTML is learning to use its tags for formatting text.
- CGI (Common Gateway Interface) is a protocol or set of rules governing how browsers and servers communicate. Any script that sends or receives information from a server needs to follow the standards specified by CGI.

COMMAND SUMMARY: REVIEW OF CHAPTER 9 COMMANDS

Please refer to the tables within the chapter for a command review.

Table	Shows
Table 9-1	Perl's numeric relational operators
Table 9-2	Perl's string relational operators
Table 9-3	Perl's double-quoted string, control, and escape characters

KEY TERMS

array — A variable that stores an ordered list of scalar values that is accessed with numeric subscripts, starting at zero.

body — One of two parts of HTML code. (The other part is the head.) The body defines what appears within the browser window.

Common Gateway Interface (CGI) — A protocol or set of rules governing how browsers and servers communicate. Any script that sends information to or receives information from a server must follow these rules.

constant — A value in program code that does not change when the program runs.

diamond operator (<>) — The operator used in Perl to access data from an open file. Each time the diamond operator is used, it returns the next line from the file.

filehandle — An input/output connection between a Perl program and the operating system. It can be used inside a program to open, read, write, and close the file.

hash — A variable representing a set of key/value pairs. A percent sign (%) precedes a hash variable.

head — One of two parts of HTML code. (The other part is the body.) The head contains the title, which appears on the title bar of your browser window.

hyperlink — The text or object in a Web document that, when clicked, loads another document and displays it in the browser window.

Hypertext Markup Language (HTML) — A format for creating documents and Web pages with embedded codes known as tags.

inline sort block — A compact Perl notation that replaces an *if-else* statement and eliminates the need for a separate subroutine.

localhost — A name given to the computer that is associated with the loopback address of 127.0.0.1. *See also* loopback.

loopback — A feature that helps you experiment with and test HTML documents, or Web pages, using a UNIX or Linux system. To use localhost, you need not be connected to the Internet. Located on your PC, localhost also accesses your PC's internal network. Use localhost to ensure that networking is properly configured.

Practical Extraction and Report Language (Perl) — A scripting language that has features of C programming, shell scripting, and Awk. Created by Larry Wall in 1987 as a simple report generator, Perl has evolved to become a powerful and popular tool for creating interactive Web pages.

scalar — A simple variable that holds a number or a string. Scalar variables' names begin with a dollar sign ($).

spaceship operator (<=>) — A special Perl operator for numeric sorts that reduces coding requirements.

subroutine or **routine** — A segment of code often used over and over again that can be internal or external to a program. A subroutine typically is identified by a beginning control statement, such as the *sub* statement in Perl, and a unique name that often reflects its purpose.

tags — The code embedded in a document or Web page created with Hypertext Markup Language (HTML). When the document is viewed with a Web browser, such as Firefox or Internet Explorer, the tags give the document special properties, such as foreground and background colors, font size, and the placement of graphical elements. You can also use tags to place hyperlinks in a document.

variable — A symbolic name that represents a value stored in memory.

Web server — A system connected to the Internet running Web server software, such as Apache. The Web server software lets other users access the HTML document via the Internet.

REVIEW QUESTIONS

1. Which of the following describes Common Gateway Interface (CGI). (Choose all that apply.)

   a. It facilitates the exchange of information over the Web.

   b. It is a specialized interface for using Java scripts only.

   c. It is a security program to protect a server.

   d. It is a protocol or set of rules.

2. Your colleague is writing a Perl script and wants to determine if two strings are the same. He used the = operator, but it is not working properly. What is the problem?

   a. He should use the $!=$ operator, instead.

   b. He did not surround the strings with square brackets to show they are strings.

   c. He should use the *eq* operator, instead.

   d. He should use <EQUAL>, instead.

3. In Perl a variable that starts with $, such as *$value*, _____ . (Choose all that apply.)

   a. cannot be zero

   b. can be numeric

   c. can be nonnumeric

   d. is scalar

4. Which of the following operators is used to access data in an open file in Perl? (Choose all that apply.)

   a. #

   b. @

   c. ( )

   d. <>

5. You are training a new employee and have been asked to help him learn Perl. Which of the following statements can you use to help describe Perl? (Choose all that apply.)

   a. It is only used on UNIX and Linux systems.

   b. It is popularly used to create reports, such as business reports.

   c. It is a language that requires compiling.

   d. It can be used to manipulate text and numeric information.

9

6. You have created the following expression in Perl: *$value < 2842*. What does this expression mean?

    a. The size of the value file is 2842 kilobytes.

    b. The file 2842 is opened and given the name value for the purpose of the current Pearl script.

    c. The variable *value* is less than 2842.

    d. 2842 is written to the file called value.

7. A programmer in your group has written the following subroutine, which does not work. What is the problem?

```
run sort
{
  if ($a < $b) { -1; }
  elsif ($a == $b) { 0; }
  else { +1; }
}
```

    a. The "<" is the file handling operator and cannot be used in this context.

    b. He should replace "run" with "sub."

    c. He should remove the semicolons.

    d. He should replace "==" with "equate."

8. One of your colleagues has written a Perl script, but it does not run on some people's computers who use a different Linux distribution or who do not use the Bash shell. Which of the following might be the problem?

    a. The script does not have a beginning line that contains the path to Perl, such as *#!/usr/bin/perl*.

    b. Perl can only be run in the Bash shell.

    c. The script does not contain the line to specify it is a Perl script, which is *make= perl*.

    d. Perl does not run in the root account, which must be the account some users are accessing to run this Perl script.

9. A colleague at work has overheard you discussing the spaceship operator and is curious about what this is. What do you tell him?

    a. It refers to a Perl script that has bugs.

    b. It deletes one or more files in Perl.

    c. It is a Perl formatting editor that helps speed the writing of Perl scripts.

    d. It performs numeric sorts in Perl.

10. You are writing a Perl script that uses a segment of code over and over again, and you are tired of repeatedly typing in this code. Which of the following should you do?

    a. Create a subroutine.

    b. Use the =+= repeat operator.

    c. Use the ++ operator.

    d. Create a repeat script.

11. Which of the following are automatically opened by Perl? (Choose all that apply.)

    a. A.OUT

    b. STDOUT

    c. STDERR

    d. CORE

12. In the following statement, when is "Could not open students file" displayed?

    ```
    open (FILEIN, "students") || warn "Could not open students
     file \n" ;
    ```

    a. When open (*FILEIN, "students"*) is false.

    b. When open (*FILEIN, "students"*) is true.

    c. When the last row of data has been read from the students file.

    d. When the students file is larger then 1.5 MB.

13. When you make a Web page using HTML, what line do you start with to show that what follows after that line consists of HTML tags?

    a. #START

    b. /NEW

    c. <HTML>

    d. /BEGIN/

14. Which of the following is an example of a scalar? (Choose all that apply.)

    a. $income = 62,859;

    b. $lname = "McGregor";

    c. value = 10, Tiger;

    d. @cell* = B10;

9

15. You have written the following line in a Perl program:

    ```
    $filein = $ARGV[0];
    ```

    What is the purpose of this line?

    a. It copies a file to the ARGV directory.

    b. It closes a file.

    c. It searches for a file in all subdirectories under a directory.

    d. It saves the name of a file passed from the command line in ARGV[0].

16. In Perl, the control sequence \n is used to _____ .

    a. designate a horizontal tab

    b. designate a new line

    c. force the next character to be lowercase

    d. make a bell sound

17. You are creating a data file for an inventory system. Which of the following is a common file extension to show this is a data file?

    a. .c

    b. .dat

    c. .a

    d. .zip

18. Perl supports using which of the following logic structures? (Choose all that apply.)

    a. *if* statement

    b. *while* loop

    c. *index* jump

    d. *presort* loop

19. In Perl, strings are surrounded by which of the following? (Choose all that apply.)

    a. double commas

    b. colons

    c. percent signs

    d. single or double quotation marks

20. You colleague is creating an HTML-based Web page and wants the first line to have the largest heading size, and so he uses the tag <LARGEHEAD>. This tag isn't producing the expected result. What tag should he use instead?

    a. <FONT LARGE>

    b. <TITLE1>

    c. <H1>

    d. <P1>

21. When you assign values for an array, what character should precede the name of the array?

    a. +

    b. \A

    c. @

    d. ^

22. What arithmetic operators are used in Perl scripts?

23. What is a filehandle in Perl?

24. Name at least one difference between Perl and Awk programming.

25. Name five data types used by Perl.

9

HANDS-ON PROJECTS

 The following projects should be completed using the command line (such as from a terminal window), the Bash shell, and your own account and home directory, unless otherwise specified.

NOTE

Project 9-1

HANDS-ON PROJECTS

In this project, you create the perlread1.pl program, which illustrates how to pass a file name on the command line using the standard array variable *ARGV[0]*.

To use Perl to display the contents of a file:

1. Use the **cat** command (or the editor of your choice) to create the file **students**, containing the names **Joseph**, **Alice**, **Mary**, **Zona**, **Aaron**, **Barbara**, and **Larry**, all on a separate line. Press **Enter** after typing each name, except after Larry unless you used the *cat* command in which case you'll need to press **Enter** after typing Larry.

2. Save the file and close the editor, or if you created the file using the *cat* command, press **Ctrl+d**.

3. Use the editor of your choice to create the Perl program perlread1.pl:

```perl
#!/usr/bin/perl
# Program name: perlread1.pl
# Purpose: Display records in a file and count lines
$filein = $ARGV[0];
while (<>)
{
        print "$_";
        ++$line_count;
}
print ("File \"$filein\" has $line_count lines. \n");
```

4. Save the file and quit the editor.

5. Give the file execute permission. (Type **chmod ugo+x perlread1.pl** or **chmod a+x perlread1.pl** and press **Enter**.)

6. Test the program by typing **./perlread1.pl students** and then pressing **Enter**. Your screen should now display the contents of the students file, shown in Figure 9-10.

```
mpalmer@localhost:~
File  Edit  View  Terminal  Tabs  Help
[mpalmer@localhost ~]$ cat > students
Joseph
Alice
Mary
Zona
Aaron
Barbara
Larry
[mpalmer@localhost ~]$ vi perlread1.pl
[mpalmer@localhost ~]$ chmod ugo+x perlread1.pl
[mpalmer@localhost ~]$ ./perlread1.pl students
Joseph
Alice
Mary
Zona
Aaron
Barbara
Larry
File "students" has 7 lines
[mpalmer@localhost ~]$
```

Figure 9-10   Running perlread1.pl

Project 9-2

In this project, you create a Perl program in which you open a file from within a program.

To use Perl to open a file from within a program:

1. Use the editor of your choice to create the file perlread2.pl.

2. Enter this Perl program:

```
#!/usr/bin/perl
# Program name: perlread2.pl
# Purpose: Open disk file. Read and display the records
# in the file. Count the number of records in
# the file.
open (FILEIN, "students") || warn "Could not open
 students file\n";
while (<FILEIN>)
{
        print "$_ ";
        ++$line_count;
}
print ("File \"students\" has $line_count lines. \n");
close (FILEIN);
```

3. Save the file and quit the editor.

4. Give the file execute permission.

5. Test the program by typing .**/perlread2.pl** and then pressing **Enter**. Your output should look similar to that for the perlread1.pl script.

6. Type **clear** and press **Enter** to clear the screen for the next project.

Project 9-3

HANDS-ON PROJECTS

In this project, you use a Perl script to sort words.

To use Perl's sort statement:

1. Use the editor of your choice to create the program perlsort1.pl. Enter the following code:

```perl
#!/usr/bin/perl
# Program name: perlsort1.pl
# Purpose: Sort a list of names contained inside an array
# Syntax: perlsort1.pl <Enter>
#========================================================
@somelist = ("Oranges", "Apples", "Tangerines", "Pears",
 "Bananas", "Pineapples");
@sortedlist = sort @somelist;
print "@sortedlist";
print "\n";
```

2. Save the file and exit the editor.

3. Use the *chmod* command to grant the file execute permission.

4. Run **perlsort1.pl**. Your screen should look similar to Figure 9-11.

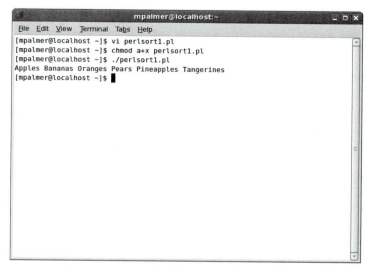

Figure 9-11   Using perlsort1.pl

5. Type **clear** and press **Enter** to clear the screen.

Project 9-4

In this project, you access and sort a file in Perl by passing the file name on the command line.

To use Perl to access a file by passing the file name on the command line:

1. Use the editor of your choice to create and save the program perlsort2.pl. Enter the following code:

```
#!/usr/bin/perl
# Program name: perlsort2.pl
# Purpose: Sorts a text file alphabetically. File name is
#          entered on the command line.
# Syntax: perlsort2.pl file name <Enter>
#============================================================
$x = 0;
while (<>)
{
        $somelist[$x] = $_;
        $x++;
}
@sortedlist = sort @somelist;
print @sortedlist;
```

2. Save the file and exit the editor.

3. Give the perlsort2.pl file execute permissions.

4. Run perlsort2.pl, using students as the test file, by typing **./perlsort2.pl students** and then pressing **Enter**. Your screen should now display the list of student names, as shown in Figure 9-12.

5. Type **clear** and press **Enter**.

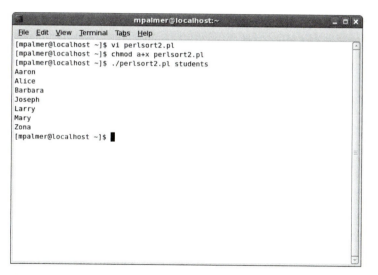

Figure 9-12   Running perlsort2.pl

Project 9-5

This project enables you to sort a numeric field using a subroutine.

To use Perl for numeric sorting:

1. Use cat, vi, or Emacs to create and save the file numberlist, containing the data **130**, **100**, **121**, **101**, **120**, and **122**. Press **Enter** after typing each number so that each one is on a separate line.

2. Use the editor of your choice to create the perlsort3.pl program. Enter the following code:

```
#!/usr/bin/perl
# Program name: perlsort3.pl
# Purpose: Sorts numerically using a subroutine. File name
#          is entered on the command line.
# Syntax: perlsort3.pl file name <Enter>
#=========================================================
$x = 0;
while (<>)
{
   $somelist[$x] = $_;
   $x++;
}
@sortedlist = sort numbers @somelist;
print @sortedlist;
sub numbers
{
      if ($a < $b)
             { -1; }
      elsif ($a == $b)
```

```
                         {  0;  }
         else
                         {  +1;  }
}
```

3. Save the file and exit the editor.

4. Use the *chmod* command to grant the file execute permission.

5. Test the program by typing **./perlsort3.pl numberlist** and then pressing **Enter**. (Refer to Figure 9-8.)

6. Type **clear** and press **Enter**.

Project 9-6

In this project, you sort the numberlist file using perlsort4.pl, which modifies the *numbers* subroutine used by perlsort3.pl to use the spaceship operator and fewer lines of code.

To use Perl's spaceship operator in the *numbers* subroutine:

1. Use the editor of your choice to create and save the program perlsort4.pl. Enter the following code:

```
#!/usr/bin/perl
# Program name: perlsort4.pl
# Purpose: Sort numerically using the spaceship operator
#          (<=>)
# syntax: perlsort4.pl file name <Enter>
#=========================================================
$x = 0;
while (<>)
{
    $somelist[$x] = $_;
    $x++;
}
@sortedlist = sort numbers @somelist;
print @sortedlist;
sub numbers
{
    $a <=> $b;
}
```

2. Save the file and exit the editor.

3. Use the *chmod* command to grant the file execute permission.

4. Test the program by typing **./perlsort4.pl numberlist** and then pressing **Enter**. Your screen (see Figure 9-13) should display the list of numbers sorted in ascending order, similar to the result of perlsort3.pl.

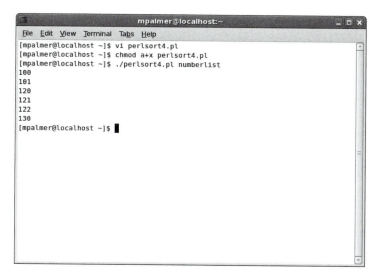

Figure 9-13   Using perlsort4.pl to sort the numberlist file

Project 9-7

HANDS-ON
PROJECTS

> **NOTE** For the examples in Projects 9-7 through 9-9, you need access to a computer that is running Fedora, Red Hat Enterprise Linux, SUSE with the GNOME desktop, or Knoppix with the KDE desktop. The Firefox Web browser should also be installed.

In this project, you create a simple HTML Web page and test it.

To create a simple Web page:

1. Use the vi or Emacs editor to create and save the UNIXtools.html file, entering the following lines:

```
<HTML>
<HEAD><TITLE>UNIX/Linux Programming Tools</TITLE></HEAD>
<BODY>
<H1><CENTER>My UNIX/Linux Programming Tools</CENTER></H1>
<H2>Languages</H2>
<P>Perl</P>
<P>Shell Scripts</P>
<P>C and C++</P>
<H2>Editors</H2>
<P>vi</P>
<P>Emacs</P>
<H2>Other Tools</H2>
<P>awk</P>
<P>sed</P>
</BODY>
</HTML>
```

2. Use the *chmod* command to grant the file execute permission.

3. In Fedora, Red Hat Enterprise Linux, or SUSE, on your desktop, double-click your home directory's icon, such as *trbrown's Home*, which opens a Window from which to view the files in your home directory. In Knoppix, click the **K Menu** and click **Home Personal Files**.

4. If necessary, use the scroll bar on the right side of the window to find the UNIXtools.html file.

5. In Fedora, Red Hat Enterprise Linux, and SUSE, double-click **UNIXtools.html** (and click **Display** in Fedora and Red Hat Enterprise Linux) to see your Web page in the Mozilla Firefox Web browser. (See Figure 9-14.) In Knoppix, right-click **UNIXtools.html**, point to **Open With**, click **Other**, click **Internet** (to list Internet applications), and double-click a Web browser, such as **Konqueror**.

6. Close all open windows.

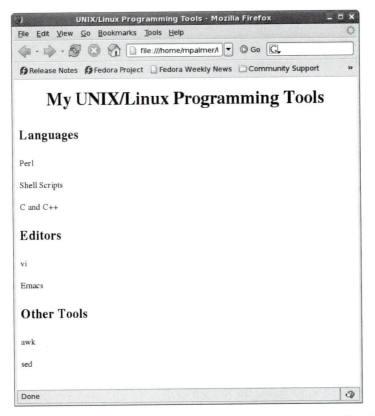

Figure 9-14 Programming tools Web page viewed in Mozilla Firefox

Project 9-8

In this project, you view a sample Web page that uses CGI and Perl to handle a form. Note that in Step 5, you need to obtain from your instructor the projest.html, projest.cgi, and subparseform.lib files. To successfully use the Submit button on your system, check with your instructor about enabling the necessary security for localhost (you can still do most of this project even without the security to use the Submit button).

To see a sample Web page:

1. Access the command line, such as by opening a terminal window.

2. From your home directory, create the cgi-bin subdirectory. Type **mkdir cgi-bin** and press **Enter**.

3. Give yourself read, write, and execute permissions to the cgi-bin subdirectory, and give group and other read and execute permissions. To do this, type **chmod 755 cgi-bin** and press **Enter**.

4. Type **cd cgi-bin** and press **Enter**.

5. See your instructor or technical support person for instructions for copying the following programs and scripts to the new directory:

   ❑ projest.html

   ❑ projest.cgi

   ❑ subparseform.lib

6. Next use the vi or Emacs editor to open the projest.html file that you copied to your working directory in Step 5. The contents of the file are:

```
<!- Program Name: projest.html ->
<HTML><HEAD><TITLE>Project Analysis</TITLE></HEAD>
<BODY>
<H2>Average Profit per Project Calculation</H2>
<FORM METHOD=POST ACTION="http://localhost/home/tom/
 cgi-bin/projest.cgi">  [continuation of previous line]
Total cost of projects last year? <INPUT TYPE=text NAME=
 projcost SIZE=10> [continuation of previous line]
Number of Projects? <INPUT TYPE=text NAME=projects SIZE=10>
Project revenue received? <INPUT TYPE=text NAME=revenue
 SIZE=10>   [continuation of previous line]
<HR><INPUT TYPE=submit NAME=submit VALUE=Submit>
<INPUT TYPE=reset NAME=reset VALUE="Start over">
</FORM></BODY></HTML>
```

7. Find the following line of code in your file:

```
<FORM METHOD=POST ACTION="http://localhost/home/tom/
 cgi-bin/projest.cgi">
```

Change the code so that it includes the specific path to where you are storing your HTML and CGI files, as shown:

```
<FORM METHOD=POST ACTION="http://path to where you are storing
  your HTML and CGI files/projest.cgi">
```

8. Save the file and exit the editor.

9. Use the *cat*, *more*, or *less* commands to view the contents of the projest.cgi and subparseform.lib files. Both of these files are really Perl scripts. The projest.cgi file contains the code used to generate the Web page. The subparseform.lib file is a Perl utility for managing the display of forms and is used by many Web programmers. When you open the projest.html file, it calls projest.cgi for this dynamic Web page. projest.cgi calls the subparseform.lib file to format the display of the form.

10. In Fedora or Red Hat Enterprise Linux with the GNOME desktop, click **Applications**, point to **Internet**, and click **Firefox Web Browser**. In SUSE with the GNOME desktop, click **Computer**, click **More Applications**, click **Internet** in the left pane, and click **Firefox**. In Knoppix with the KDE desktop, click the **K Menu**, point to **Internet**, and click **Konqueror Web Browser**.

11. In Fedora, Red Hat Enterprise Linux, and SUSE, click the **File** menu in the upper-left portion of the window in Firefox. Click **Open File**. Browse to the location of your projest.html file, such as /home/mpalmer/cgi-bin/projest.html. Select the **projest.html** file and click **Open**. In Knoppix, with the Konqueror Web browser, click the **Home Folder** link, click the **cgi-bin** subdirectory, and click **projest.html**. Use your mouse or pointing device to adjust the size of the window so that "Project revenue received?" is displayed on its own line.

12. Type **10000** in the Total cost of projects last year? text box and press **Tab** to advance to the next field. Next, type **10** in the Number of Projects? text box and press **Tab**. Finally, type **12000** in the Project revenue received? text box. The result that you see should look similar to Figure 9-15.

13. To submit the information via the Common Gateway Interface connection, you can click the **Submit** button. If you click **Submit**, the result depends on how security and network access are configured for your computer (check with your instructor). If your computer provides the access configuration to proceed, you might first see a Security Warning screen; click **Continue**. The final Perl/CGI screen then processes the information you have input and displays it (if your computer cannot connect via the loopback interface, such as because of the security at the computer or in Firefox, you'll instead see an Unable to connect screen). If you do not have the necessary access configuration, you see an Alert window showing that your connection was refused. Click **OK** if you see the Alert window.

14. Close the Web browser window.

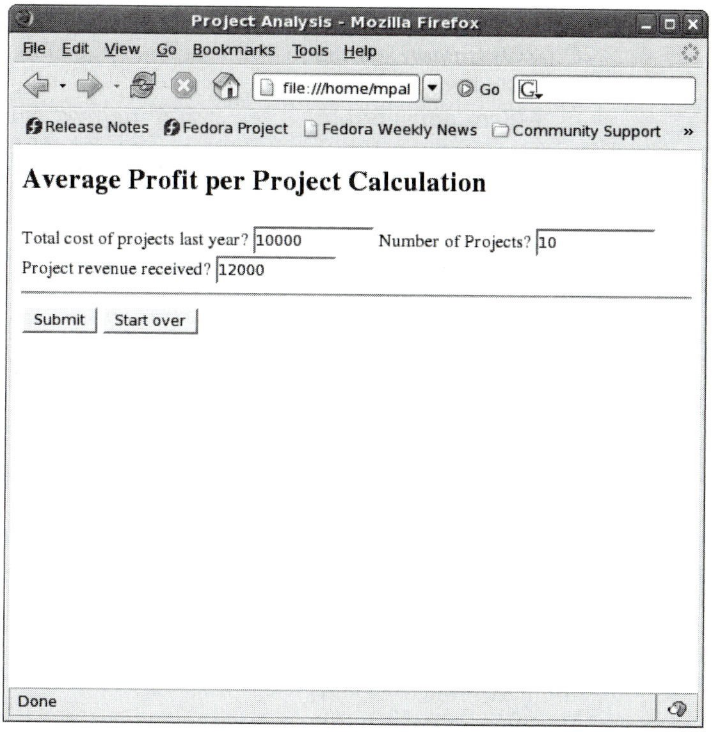

Average Profit per Project Calculation

Total cost of projects last year? 10000   Number of Projects? 10
Project revenue received? 12000

Submit | Start over

Figure 9-15   Using the projest.html Web page

HANDS-ON PROJECTS

Project 9-9

In this project, you simulate a Web page that is a form which offers hotel management customers an opportunity to order the promotional hotel management software items over the Internet. To successfully use the Submit button on your system, check with your instructor about enabling the necessary security for localhost (you can still do most of this project even without the security to use the Submit button).

To create the Web page:

1. From the command line, switch to your cgi-bin subdirectory, if you are not already in it. Use the editor of your choice to create the HTML document software.html. Enter this HTML code:

```
<!- Program Name: software.html->
<HTML><HEAD><TITLE>Practice Form</TITLE></HEAD>
<BODY BGCOLOR=WHITE>
<CENTER><H1><U>Special Software Offers</U></H1>
</CENTER>
<FORM METHOD=POST ACTION="http://localhost/your cgi-bin
 directory path/software.cgi">
<BR>
<H2><U><PRE>Special Prices     Qty</PRE></U></H2>
```

```
<FONT SIZE=5>
<PRE>Front Desk Management <INPUT TYPE=text NAME=frontdk
 SIZE=5></PRE>
<PRE>Reservation Express    <INPUT TYPE=text NAME=reserve
 SIZE=5></PRE>
<PRE>Convention Management <INPUT TYPE=text NAME=convmgt
 SIZE=5></PRE>
<HR><INPUT TYPE=submit NAME=submit VALUE=Submit>
<INPUT TYPE=reset NAME=reset VALUE="Start over">
</FORM></BODY></HTML>
```

2. Save the file in your working directory, such as your cgi-bin directory, and exit the editor. Use the *chmod* command to grant read and execute permissions to all users for the software.html file (*chmod a+rx software.html*).

3. Now use the editor to create the CGI Perl script software.cgi. Enter this code:

```
#!/usr/bin/perl
# Program name: software.cgi

require "subparseform.lib";
&Parse_Form;

$frontdk = $formdata {'frontdk'};
$reserve = $formdata {'reserve'};
$convmgt = $formdata {'convmgt'};

$qtotal = $frontdk+$reserve+$convmgt;
$tfrontdk = $frontdk*200;
$treserve = $reserve*150;
$tconvmgt = $convmgt*180;
$total = $tfrontdk+$treserve+$tconvmgt;

print "Content-type: text/html\n\n";
print "<BODY BGCOLOR=WHITE>";
print "<FONT COLOR=RED><H1><CENTER>Software
 Special</CENTER></H1></FONT><BR>";
print "<CENTER><H2><U><P>Thank you for your
 order.</P></U></H2></CENTER>";
print "<BR>";
print "<TABLE BORDER=1 BGCOLOR=CYAN ALIGN=CENTER WIDTH=300
 CELLSPACING=5>";
print "<TR><TH ALIGN=CENTER>Qty</TH>";
print "<TH ALIGN=CENTER>Software</TH>";
print "<TH ALIGN=CENTER>Total</TH></TR>";
print "<TR><TD ALIGN=CENTER>$frontdk</TD>";
print "<TD ALIGN=CENTER>Front Desk Management</TD>";
print "<TD ALIGN=CENTER>\$$tfrontdk</TD></TR>";
print "<TR><TD ALIGN=CENTER>$reserve</TD>";
print "<TD ALIGN=CENTER>Reservation Express</TD>";
print "<TD ALIGN=CENTER>\$$treserve</TD></TR>";
```

```
print "<TR><TD ALIGN=CENTER>$convmgt</TD>";
print "<TD ALIGN=CENTER>Convention Management</TD>";
print "<TD ALIGN=CENTER>\$$tconvmgt</TD></TR>";
print "<TR><TD ALIGN=CENTER>$qtotal</TD>";
print "<TD ALIGN=CENTER>Total:</TD>";
print "<TD ALIGN=CENTER>\$$total</TD></TR></TABLE>";
```

4. Save the file in your cgi-bin directory, and exit the editor.

5. Use the *chmod* command to grant the file, read and execute permissions.

Now that you have entered both the code for the Web page and CGI script, you should test your work.

To test the Web page:

1. In Fedora or Red Hat Enterprise Linux with the GNOME desktop, click **Applications**, point to **Internet**, and click **Firefox Web Browser**. In SUSE with the GNOME desktop, click **Computer**, click **More Applications**, click **Internet** in the left pane, and click **Firefox**. In Knoppix with the KDE desktop, click the **K Menu**, point to **Internet**, and click **Konqueror Web Browser**.

2. In Fedora, Red Hat Enterprise Linux, and SUSE, click the **File** menu in the Firefox Web Browser. Click **Open File**. Browse to the **cgi-bin** subdirectory containing your **software.html** file and select and open the file. In Knoppix with the Konqueror Web browser, click the **Home Folder** link, click the **cgi-bin** subdirectory, and click **software.html**.

3. Enter quantities of **10**, **15**, and **20** for the products. (See Figure 9-16.) If you have security access to connect to localhost (check with your instructor), click the **Submit** button to view a total page. (If your computer provides the access configuration to proceed, you might first see a Security Warning screen prior to the total page; click Continue.)

4. Close the Web browser window.

9

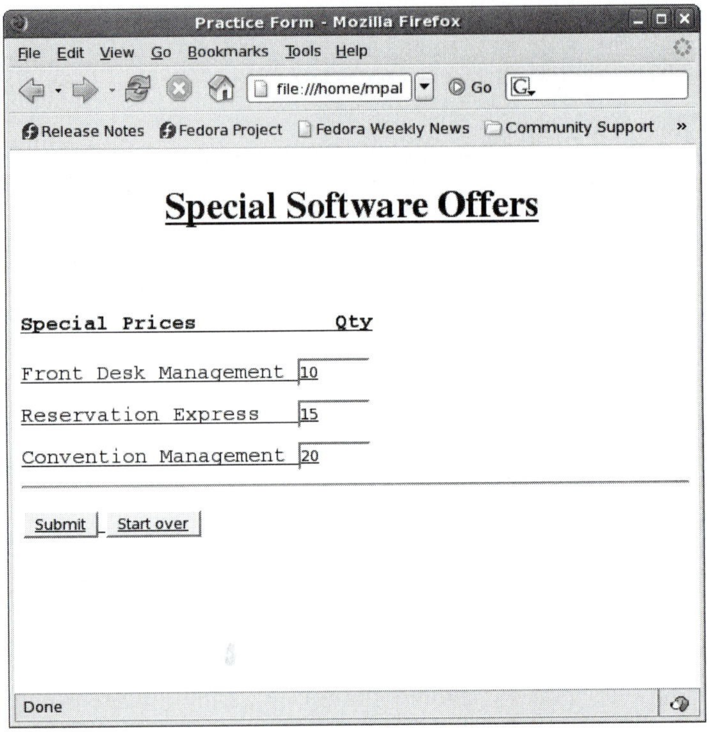

Figure 9-16   Special Software Offers Web page

DISCOVERY EXERCISES

1. Write a Perl script to display the line "Perl was developed by Larry Wall."

2. Write a Perl script in which you create a variable in the script to contain the name Beth and then have the script display "Welcome Beth."

3. Modify the script you wrote in Exercise 2 so that you prompt for the name and then display "Welcome *name*."

4. Write down four scalar variables, two of which are numeric and two that are strings.

5. Create a Perl program that uses an array of vegetables—peas, carrots, spinach, corn, beans—and in which all of the vegetables in the array are displayed to the screen.

6. Design a Perl program that sorts the last names Martin, Adams, Sandoval, Perry, Yablonsky, Brown, and Ramirez.

7. Write a Perl program that attempts to open a file that does not exist, and that prints the message "That file is nonexistent."

8. Write a Perl program that converts a value in inches to a value in centimeters and displays the result. (1 inch = 2.54 centimeters.)

9. Create a Perl program that sorts the numbers 115, 10, 19, 35, and 2 and that uses the spaceship operator to accomplish the sort.

10. Write a Perl program that contains a hash variable and displays the keys. The hash variable contains the following key and value combinations:

Key	Value
1	Martin
2	Hanson
3	Stephens
4	Rawlins

9

10

DEVELOPING UNIX/LINUX
APPLICATIONS IN C AND C++

After reading this chapter and completing the exercises, you will be able to:

♦ Understand basic elements of C programming

♦ Debug C programs

♦ Create, compile, and test C programs

♦ Use the *make* utility to revise and maintain source files

♦ Identify differences between C and C++ programming

♦ Create a simple C++ program

♦ Create a C++ program that reads a text file

♦ Create a C++ program that demonstrates how C++ enhances C functions

---

The C and C++ programming languages are very compatible with UNIX and Linux operating systems, and compilers for C and C++ are often included with UNIX/Linux. The compliers are included because you might encounter programming tasks that are difficult to perform using shell or Perl scripts—and C or C++ might provide better solutions for those tasks. This chapter offers a basic introduction to C and C++ to give you a basis for understanding their capabilities compared to those of shell and Perl scripts. The chapter is not intended to make you an accomplished C or C++ programmer, but rather to help you understand the potential of C and C++ programming in UNIX/Linux.

In this chapter, you learn how to write, compile, and execute basic C programs. You also learn how to use the *make* utility. The *make* utility is a UNIX/Linux software development tool that controls compilation as you make changes and additions to programs during their development phase. At the end of the chapter, you compare C and C++ programming and create a few simple C++ programs.

Introducing C Programming

C is the language in which UNIX was developed and refined. The original UNIX operating system was written in assembly language. **Assembly language** is a low-level language that provides maximum access to all the computer's devices, both internal and external. However, assembly language requires more coding and a greater in-depth treatment of all internal control items. The C language was partly developed to resolve the more lengthy requirements of assembly language. It has significantly reduced those requirements to a high-level set of easy-to-understand instructions. Dennis Ritchie and Brian Kernighan, two AT&T Bell Labs employees, rewrote most of UNIX using C in the early 1970s.

NOTE Ken Thompson, another AT&T Bell Labs employee, also deserves credit for his influence on the development of C. He wrote a forerunner of C, called B, in 1970 for the first UNIX system to run on the DEC PDP-7 minicomputer.

Since its inception, the C language has evolved from its original design as an operating system language to its current status as a major tool in the development of high-performance applications for general use. Because C is native to UNIX and now Linux, it works best as an application development tool, in which the operating system views the application as an extension of its core functionality. For example, **daemons** (specialized system processes, such as network printing, that run in the background) are written in C. A daemon accesses the UNIX/Linux system code just as any other part of the operating system.

C can be described, in a nutshell, as a language that uses relatively short, isolated functions to break down large, complex tasks into small and easily resolved subtasks. This function-oriented design allows programmers to create their own program functions to interact with the predefined system functions—enabling programmers to write all kinds of software applications.

Because C is a compiled language, the compiled program code cannot be viewed by examining the executable program, which provides an extra measure of security in contrast to shell and Perl scripts, in which the code can be viewed. However, the **source code** file—the file of program code you create using an editor and then compile—can be viewed if a user has permission to read the source code file, such as by using the *cat* command.

Before you create a C program, you first need to learn the basics of C programming, which are discussed in the next sections.

NOTE For this chapter, you need the C and C++ compilers installed in your workstation or server setup. In Fedora, Red Hat Enterprise Linux, and SUSE, typically they are installed in a server installation by the server administrator. If the compilers are not already installed and you have access to the root account, you can install them from the GNOME interface. In Fedora and Red Hat Enterprise Linux, click Applications, click Add/Remove Software, click List, check the boxes for the C and C++ compilers, click Apply, and follow any remaining instructions. In SUSE, log onto root, click the Computer menu, click Install Software, select the C and C++ options (such as devel_C_C++, gcc, gcc-c++, and other gcc selections) click Install, and follow any remaining instructions.(Knoppix comes with the compilers installed.)

Creating a C Program

A C program consists of separate bodies of code, known as **functions**. In other languages, bodies of code have different names, such as subroutines, routines, or procedures (you learned about subroutines in Chapter 9, "Perl and CGI Programming"). Each of these bodies of code is designed so it contributes to the execution of a single task. You put together a collection of these functions, and they become a program. Within the program, the functions call each other as needed and work to solve the problem for which the program was originally designed.

Creating a program is never done in a single step. As a programmer, you complete many phases before the program is ready to run. The first phase is to create the source code of the program. As with shell scripts and Perl programs, you use a text editor, such as vi or Emacs, to create C programs. The source code is stored in a file with the .c (lowercase c) extension. An example of such a file is simpleprogram.c.

The next phase is to execute the preprocessor and compiler. The **preprocessor** makes modifications to your program, such as including the contents of other files and creating constant values. After the preprocessor prepares your program, the compiler executes. The compiler is a program that translates the source code into **object code**, which consists of binary instructions. If you made errors, the compiler locates many of them. When this happens, you use the text editor to correct the errors and recompile the program. After the source code is compiled, it is stored by default in an executable file called a.out. Note, however, that at the time you compile the source code, you can override the default to a file name of your choice.

Many compilers translate source code into assembly code. This requires that an **assembler** be called up to translate the assembly code into object code. The compiler usually starts the assembler automatically, so you do not need to enter additional commands. Some compilers translate directly from source code into object code, skipping the assembly step. Whatever type of compiler you use, the outcome of this phase is the creation of a file that contains object code.

10

The final phase requires the use of another tool called a **linker**. This program links all the object files that belong to the program, along with any library functions the program might use. The result is an **executable file**. The entire process is depicted in Figure 10-1.

In some instances, the linker is not a separate tool because the compiler can be designed to also perform linkage, as is the case with the *gcc* compiler used in Fedora, Red Hat Enterprise Linux, and SUSE.

NOTE

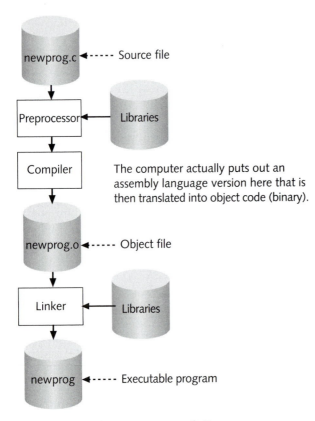

The computer actually puts out an assembly language version here that is then translated into object code (binary).

Figure 10-1   C program compilation process

C Keywords

The C language, like all programming languages, includes **keywords**. These keywords have special meanings, so you cannot use them as names for variables or functions. Table 10-1 lists the C keywords.

Table 10-1   C language keywords

Keyword	Keyword	Keyword	Keyword
auto	double	int	struct
break	else	long	switch
case	enum	register	typedef
char	extern	return	union
const	float	short	unsigned
continue	for	signed	void
default	goto	sizeof	volatile
do	if	static	while

NOTE

Table 10-1 contains standard keywords for ANSI C. GNU C adds several language extensions that include additional keywords. See the Web site *tigcc. ticalc.org/doc/gnuexts.html* for a reference to these language extensions.

10

The C Library

As you can see from Table 10-1, the C language is very small. It has no input or output facilities as part of the language. All I/O is performed through the C library. The **C library** consists of functions that perform file, screen, and keyboard operations, as well as many other tasks. For example, certain functions perform string operations, memory allocation and control, math operations, and much more. When you need to perform one of these operations in your program, you place a **function call** at the desired point. The linker joins the code of the library function with your program's object code to create the executable file.

Program Format

As mentioned earlier, C programs are made up of one or more functions. Every function must have a name, and every C program must have a function called *main()*. Here is a very simple C program:

```
int main()
{
}
```

This program does absolutely nothing, yet it contains all the elements necessary for a valid C program. The next two paragraphs examine the bare essentials of a C program.

Note the word "main" followed by a set of parentheses. (A following section, "Specifying Data Types," defines the first item—*int*.) This is the name of a function. As mentioned earlier, all C programs must have a function called *main()*. The parentheses denote that this is a function name.

On the next line is an open curly bracket. In a C program, this denotes the beginning of a block of code. The closed curly bracket on the next line denotes the end of the block of code. All functions must have an open and a closed curly bracket. The statements that normally make up the function appear between the two curly brackets. In the sample program, there are no statements; therefore, the function does nothing. The curly brackets are still required.

Including Comments

The /* symbol denotes the beginning of a comment, and the */ symbol denotes the end of a comment. The compiler ignores everything between the symbols. This example shows a C program comment:

```
/* Here is a program that does nothing. */
int main()
{
}
```

In the example, the comment "Here is a program that does nothing" appears at the top of the program. The beginning of the comment is marked with /* and the end with */. The compiler sees this program as being no different than the earlier version that had no comment.

Using the Preprocessor #include Directive

The following is a sample program that creates output:

```
/* A simple C program */
#include <stdio.h>
int main()
{
    printf("C is a programming language.\n");
    printf("C is very compatible with UNIX/Linux.\n");
}
```

Figure 10-2 shows the program's output.

In the preceding program, you see the statement:

```
#include <stdio.h>
```

This is called a **preprocessor directive**. As mentioned earlier, the preprocessor processes your program before the compiler translates it into object code. It reads your program, looking for statements that begin with the # symbol. These statements are considered preprocessor directives and cause the preprocessor to modify your source code in some way. For example, the *#include* directive causes the preprocessor to include another file in your program at the point where the *#include* directive appears.

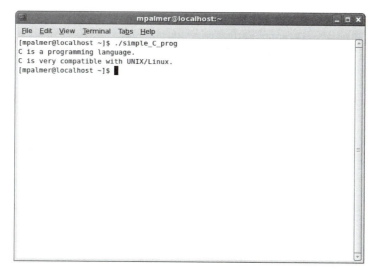

Figure 10-2   Running a simple C program

The file **stdio.h** is called a **header file** and is part of your C development system. This file contains information the compiler needs to process standard input or output statements. Any program that performs standard input or output must include the stdio header file. Because the sample program uses the *printf()* function (which performs standard output), it must include stdio.h.

The C development system includes a number of header files. All library functions require that you include a particular header file.

Specifying Data Types

Variables and constants represent data used in a C program. You must declare variables and state the type of data that the variable can hold. A variable's data type determines the upper and lower limits of its range of values. Data types with wider ranges of values occupy more memory than those with narrower ranges. The exact limits of the ranges vary among compilers and hardware platforms.

Table 10-2 shows a list of the basic data types that can be used in a C program.

Table 10-2   C data types

Data Type	Description
char	Occupies a single byte; designed to hold one character from the character set used by the running machine
int	Holds integer values; the size of an *int* variable should be the default size of an integer on the running machine, but this is not always the case
float	A single-precision, floating-point value
double	A double-precision, floating-point value

As mentioned earlier, the exact upper and lower limits of each of the value ranges for data types depends on the compiler and hardware platform being used. You can use three modifiers with *int* data types: *short*, *long*, and *unsigned*. The *short* and *long* modifiers make an integer variable smaller or larger than its default size. On some machines, a *short int* occupies half the number of bits as an *int*, and in many cases, there is no difference between a *long int* and an *int*.

Table 10-3 shows typical limits and memory requirements of C data types.

Table 10-3 Typical C data type limits and bytes occupied in memory

Data Type	Bytes	Minimum Value	Maximum Value
char	1	–128	127
unsigned char	1	0	255
short int	2	–32,768	32,767
unsigned short	2	0	65,535
int	4	–2,147,483,648	2,147,483,647
long int	4	–2,147,483,648	2,147,483,647
unsigned long	4	0	4,294,967,295
float	4	–3.4028E+38	3.4028E+38
double	8	–1.79769E+308	1.79769E+308

Character Constants

Characters are represented internally in a single byte of the computer's memory. When a character is stored in the byte, it is set to the character's code in the host character set. For example, if the machine uses ASCII codes, the letter A is stored in memory as the number 65. This is because the ASCII code for A is 65.

When you represent character data in a program as a character constant, you enclose the character in single quotation marks. Here are some examples:

```
'A'
'C'
'a'
'z'
```

Using Strings

A string is a group of characters, such as a name. Strings are stored in memory in consecutive memory locations. When you use string constants in your C program, they must be enclosed in double quotation marks. Here are some examples:

```
"Linux is a great operating system."
"Good Morning!"
"Enter your name and age."
```

Unlike higher-level languages, C does not provide a specific data type for character strings. C requires that you view strings the same way the computer does, as an array of characters. Here is how you might declare a character array to store a string:

```
char name[20];
```

This is just like declaring a *char* variable, except for the [20] appended to the variable name. It indicates that *name* should be an array of 20 characters. It is large enough to hold a string of up to 19 characters. This is because in C all strings are terminated with a null character. A **null character** is a single byte in which all bits are set to zero.

Including Identifiers

Identifiers are names given to variables and functions. When naming variables and functions, resist the temptation to use short names that do not convey the meaning of the item. Using meaningful identifiers greatly enhances the style of your program. There are only a few rules to remember:

- The first character must be a letter or an underscore (the _ character).
- After the first character, you can use letters, underscores, or digits.
- Variable names can be limited to 31 characters, and some compilers require the first 8 characters of variable names to be unique.
- Uppercase and lowercase characters are distinct.

These are all examples of legal identifiers:

- radius
- customer_name
- earnings_for_2007
- my_name

Declaring Variables

You must declare all variables before you use them in a program. A declaration begins with a data type and is followed by one or more variable names. Here is an example:

```
int days;
```

This example declares a variable named *days*. Its data type is *int*, so *days* is large enough to hold any value that fits within the range of an *int*. Notice that the declaration ends with a semicolon, as do all complete C statements.

You can declare multiple variables of the same type on the same line. Here is an example:

```
int days, months, years;
```

This example declares three variables, each of type *int*, named *days*, *months*, and *years*. Notice that commas separate the names.

You can initialize variables with values at the time they are declared by placing an equal sign after the variable name followed by a constant value. Here is an example:

```
int days = 5, months = 2, years = 10;
```

Understanding the Scope of Variables

The **scope** of a variable is the part of the program in which the variable is defined and, therefore, accessible. You can declare a variable either inside a function or any place that is not inside a function.

Variables that are declared inside a function are called **automatic variables**. These variables are local to the function in which they are declared. Here is an example:

```
/* This program declares a local variable
   in function main. The program does nothing
   else.  */
int main()
{
int days;
}
```

Here, the variable *days* is an automatic variable and is local to the function *main()*.

You can also declare a variable outside any function, as in the following example:

```
/* This program declares a global variable
   The program does nothing else.  */
int days;
int main()
{
}
```

In the preceding program, the variable is external, or global. The scope of a global variable is the entire program, beginning at the point where the declaration was made. The scope of an automatic, or local, variable is the body of the function in which it is declared.

The only place inside a function where local variables can be declared is at the beginning of the body of the function—after the open curly bracket and before any statement. You can declare global variables anywhere in a program except inside a function.

Using Math Operators

Arithmetic operators perform standard math activities, such as adding, subtracting, multiplying, and dividing the values held in variables or numbers. Table 10-4 lists the C arithmetic operators.

Table 10-4 C arithmetic operators

Operator	Meaning
+	Addition
−	Subtraction
*	Multiplication
/	Division
%	Modulus
++	Increment
--	Decrement

You can use these operators to create regular math expressions, as in the following examples:

```
x = y + 3;
num = num * 3;
days = months * 30;
```

These examples introduce the assignment operator (the equal sign). It works by assigning the value of the expression on its right to the variable whose name is on its left. In the example *days = months * 30*, the value in the variable months is multiplied by 30 and the product is stored in the variable *days*.

The final two operators shown in Table 10-4 are the **increment** (++) and **decrement** (--) **operators**. These are unary operators, which means that they work with one operand. The following example shows the variable *count* being incremented:

```
count++;
```

Likewise, this variable can be decremented by using the following statement:

```
count--;
```

The first two examples of the *count* variable show these operators in their postfix form, which means they come after the variable. You can also use them as prefix operators:

```
++count;
--count;
```

The operators behave differently depending on which form is used. For example, assume the variable *j* is set to 4. In this statement,

```
x = j++;
```

the ++ operator is used in postfix form. This means the assignment operator (=) uses the value of *j* before it is incremented. In effect, it says "set *x* equal to *j*, then increment *j*." After the operation, *x* will be equal to 4 and *j* will be equal to 5.

If the prefix form of the operator is used, you get different results:

```
x = ++j;
```

This statement says "increment *j*, then set *x* equal to *j*." Both *x* and *j* will be equal to 5 after the statement executes.

10

Generating Formatted Output with printf()

One of the most commonly used screen output library functions is *printf()*. The *f* stands for "formatted," as the function allows you to format and print several arguments of differing data types.

Syntax **printf**(*control string, expression, expression,...*);

Dissection

■ A screen output function used to format and print arguments, such as for creating reports

---

The first argument is called the **control string**. It specifies the way formatting should occur. Following the control string can be a varying number of arguments. Each of these is an expression with a value to be printed. The following is perhaps the most simple example of a *printf()* statement:

```
printf("Hello");
```

The example uses only a control string. The word *Hello* is printed on the screen. Here is another example:

```
printf("Your age is %d", 30);
```

The *%d* that appears in the control string is called a format specifier. It is not printed as part of the message, but tells *printf()* to substitute a decimal integer in its place. The decimal integer is the very next argument, the number 30. This *printf()* statement prints the following message on the screen:

```
Your age is 30
```

Although this example illustrates the usage of the *%d* format specifier, it is not very realistic. You are more likely to use it in the following manner:

```
printf("Your age is %d", age);
```

Here, *printf()* substitutes the value in the integer variable age for the *%d*. The next example prints the values of three *int* variables:

```
printf("The values are %d %d %d", num1, num2, num3);
```

This message contains the values of *num1*, *num2*, and *num3*, in that order. You can also pass arithmetic expressions to *printf()*:

```
printf("You have worked %d minutes", hours*60);
```

In fact, you can pass any valid C expression to *printf()*. However, be certain to use an appropriate format specifier. A format specifier is used to indicate the format of the data—one character, a string, or a decimal integer, for example. Table 10-5 shows a list of valid format specifiers.

Table 10-5 C format specifiers

Format Specifier	Meaning
%c	Single character
%d	Signed decimal integer
%e	Floating-point number, e notation
%E	Floating-point number, E notation
%f	Floating-point number, decimal notation
%g	Causes %f or %e to be used, whichever is shorter
%G	Causes %f or %E to be used, whichever is shorter
%i	Signed decimal integer
%o	Unsigned octal integer
%p	Pointer
%s	Character string
%u	Unsigned decimal integer
%x	Unsigned hex integer using digits 0-f
%X	Unsigned hex integer using digits 0-F
%%	Print a percent sign

TIP

The *printf* function is a powerful and versatile tool for programmers. However, it is important to be aware that a malicious user may in some instances be able to use format specifiers for *printf* to launch a format string attack on a computer that can crash the computer or possibly run a malicious program. The C and C++ compilers included with Linux systems come with options programmers can use to test the security of *printf* statements. Some examples of these options are *-Wformat*, *-Wformat-security*, *-Wall* and *-Wno-format-extra-args*, all of which are used with the *gcc* or *g++* comands when compiling a program.

Using the C Compiler

The command for the C compiler in Linux operating systems is *gcc*. In some other versions of UNIX, the C compiler is executed by using the *cc* command.

Syntax **gcc** [–options] *filename*

Dissection

- Compiles a C source code file

- Useful options include:

  -o enables you to specify an output file (a.out is the default)

  -c compiles the source code file and creates a linkable object code file (with a file name you specify that ends in .o, such as creating the linkable object code file abs_main.o from the source code file abs_main.c)

-*Wall* enables several error checking mechanisms to give you warnings about possible formatting and commenting problems

-*Wformat* provides warnings about problems with *printf* and *scanf* formatting

-*Wformat-security* warns of possible security problems when using *printf* and *scanf*

-*Wno-format-extra-args* warns of unused arguments contained in *printf* and *scanf*

In Linux, if you enter *gcc simple_program.c,* where *simple_program.c* is the source file, the default executable file is called *a.out.* Many programmers use the -o option to specify a name for the executable file. For example, if you enter *gcc simple_program.c -o simple_program,* then the executable file is called *simple_program.* (Another way to use the –o option in this example is to enter *gcc -o simple_program simple_program.c.*)

There are many options and ways to use *gcc* that go beyond the scope of this brief introduction to C programming. To learn more about using the C compiler in Linux, enter *man gcc* or *info gcc* at the command prompt. If you are using the *cc* command in UNIX, enter *man cc* to learn more.

At this point, you have learned enough C programming basics to write a simple program. Try Hands-On Project 10-1 to create a simple program.

Using the if Statement

The *if* statement allows your program to make decisions depending on whether a condition is true or false.

Syntax **if** *(condition) statement*

Dissection

- Used in a program to follow a decision path on the basis of whether a condition is true or false

If the condition is true, the statement is performed. Here is an example:

```
if (weight > 1000) printf("You have exceeded the limit.");
```

If the variable *weight* contains a value greater than 1000, the *printf()* statement executes.

Sometimes, you might need to execute more than one line of code if a condition is true. C allows you to substitute a block of code for the single statement, when necessary. The following is an example:

```
if (weight > 1000)
{
        printf("Warning!\n");
        printf("You have exceeded the limit.\n");
```

```
        printf("Please remove some weight.\n");
}
```

The preceding program segment causes the three *printf()* statements to execute if *weight* is greater than 1000.

The *if-else* construct allows your program to do one thing if a condition is true and another if it is false. Here is an example:

```
if (hours > 40)
    printf("You can go home now.");
else printf("Keep working!");
```

The *Keep working!* message prints only when the condition (hours > 40) is false. The following is an example using blocks of code:

```
if (hours > 40)
{
    printf("Go home.\n");
    printf("You deserve it!");
}
else
{
    printf("Keep working!\n");
    printf("Stop playing with the computer.");
}
```

Hands-On Project 10-2 enables you to create a simple program using an *if-else* statement.

Using C Loops

Loops in C are similar to those you have used in shell scripts and Perl programs. C provides three looping mechanisms: the *for* loop, the *while* loop, and the *do-while* loop. Using the *for* loop is best when you know the number of times that the loop is to perform. If it is unclear how many times the loop should perform, use the *while* or *do-while* loop.

Here is an example of the *for* loop:

```
for (count = 0; count < 100; count++)
    printf("Hello\n");
```

This loop means the message *Hello* will print 100 times. Following the word *for* is a set of parentheses containing three arguments. The arguments are separated by semicolons.

The first argument is the initialization. The variable *count* is being used to track the number of times the loop has run. The initialization is a statement that is executed before the first time through the loop. In the preceding example, the initialization stores the number zero in *count*.

The second argument is the test condition. The *for* loop executes as long as the test condition is true. It is evaluated before each iteration of the loop. If the condition is true, the iteration is performed. Otherwise, the loop terminates. In the example, the loop performs as long as *count* is less than 100.

The third argument is the update. It is performed at the end of each iteration. In the example, the loop increments the variable *count*.

The following program segment shows an example of the *while* loop:

```
x = 0;
while (x++ < 100)
    printf("x is equal to %d\n", x);
```

This loop repeats while *x* is less than 100. The next example illustrates a *do-while* loop, which is very similar to the *while* loop.

```
x = 0;
do
      printf("x is equal to %d\n", x);
while (x++ < 100);
```

The difference between the *while* loop and the *do-while* loop is that the *while* loop tests its condition before each iteration, and the *do-while* loop tests after each iteration. When you use the *do-while* loop, you must be certain there will be at least one iteration (it will successfully execute one time) to avoid an error condition.

In Hands-On Project 10-3, you create a C program that uses a *for* loop.

Defining Functions

When you define a function, you declare the function's name and create the lines of code that make up the function's block of code. You also state what data type is returned from the function (if any). The following is an example:

```
void message()
{
   printf("Greetings from the function message.");
   printf("Have a nice day.");
}
```

The word *void* indicates that this function does not return a value. The name of the function is *message*. A set of parentheses follows the name. This function has only two statements, both *printf()* statements. The function might appear in a complete program as:

```
#include <stdio.h>
void message();
int main()
{
    message();
}
void message()
{
    printf("Greetings from the function message.\n");
```

```
        printf("Have a nice day.\n");
}
```

The line under the *include* statement that reads

```
void message();
```

is called a **function prototype**. It tells the compiler about the function before the code for the function is fully defined. The word "void" means that this function returns no data. *Void* functions in C are like subroutines in the Fortran programming language or procedures in Pascal. They are merely modules of code that perform some task.

After the function prototype comes the function *main()*. The *main()* function includes only one line, which reads:

```
message();
```

This is a function call. You call a function by placing its name, followed by a set of parentheses and a semicolon, at the desired place in the program. This causes the program's control to pass to the function. When the program returns from the function, it resumes execution at the next statement after the function call.

After main is the definition of the function *message()*. The output of the program is:

```
[stephen@localhost ~] $ ./func1
Greetings from the function message.
Have a nice day.
```

Using Function Arguments

Sometimes, it is necessary to pass information to a function. A value passed to a function is called an argument. Arguments are stored in special automatic variables. The following is an example.

```
void print_square(int val);
{
    printf("\nThe square is %d", val*val);
}
```

This function takes an *int* argument. When it receives the argument, the function stores the argument in the variable *val*. The *printf()* statement causes the value of the expression *val*val* to print. What follows is a complete program that uses the function:

```
#include <stdio.h>
void print_square(int val)
main()
{
  int num = 5;
  print_square(num);
}

void print_square(int val)
```

10

```
{
  printf("\nThe square is %d\n", val*val);
}
```

The output of the program is:

```
[stephen@localhost ~]$ ./func2

The square is 25
```

Using Function Return Values

In addition to accepting arguments, functions might also return a value. This means you can make function calls part of arithmetic operations and assignments. For example, suppose you have a function called *triple()*. It is designed to take an *int* argument and return that value multiplied by three. You could use the function call in a manner such as:

```
y = triple(x);
```

The function receives the value in *x*, triples it, and then returns this value. The preceding statement stores the return value in a variable called *y*. The following is what the *triple()* function might look like:

```
int triple(int num)
{
    return(num * 3);
}
```

The function is defined as an *int* function. This means that it returns an *int* value. You can place a call to this function anywhere in your program where an *int* is expected. The function takes a single argument, which is also an *int*. In this function, the argument is stored in the variable *num*. This function's block of code has only one line:

```
return(num * 3);
```

This is the *return()* function. It is used to return a value back to the calling part of the program. In this example, the value of *num * 3* is returned. The next sample program demonstrates the function:

```
#include <stdio.h>
int triple(int num);
int main()
{
    int x = 6, y;
    y = triple(x);
    printf("%d tripled is %d.\n", x, y);
}
int triple(int num)
{
    return (num * 3);
}
```

The program's output is:

```
[stephen@localhost ~]$ ./func3
6 tripled is 18.
```

Try Hands-On Project 10-4 to create functions that accept arguments and return a value.

Working with Files in C

Files are continuous streams of data. They are typically stored on disk. Many file operations are sequential, meaning they work from the beginning of the file to the end of the file. When the file is opened, you are working with the beginning of the file. Every time a byte is read from or written to the file, your current position in the file is moved forward by one byte.

File Pointers

C file input/output is designed to use file pointers, which point to a predefined structure that contains information about the file. The structure template is found in stdio.h. You must declare a file pointer to use the I/O package. The following is an example:

```
FILE *fp;
```

This declares *fp* as a file pointer. It is used with various file access functions.

Opening and Closing Files

Before you can use a file, it must be opened. The library function for opening a file is *fopen()*, as in the following example:

```
fp = fopen("myfile.dat", "r");
```

The *fopen()* function takes two arguments: the file name and the access mode. This example opens a file named myfile.dat. The "*r*" means that the file is opened for reading. The following statement uses the "*w*" access mode for writing:

```
fp = fopen("myfile.dat", "w");
```

The *fopen()* function returns a file pointer. If the file cannot be opened, it returns a NULL pointer (a pointer to address zero). The following code block is one way you can test to see if the file was opened:

```
if ((fp = fopen("myfile.dat", "r")) ==NULL)
{
    printf("Error opening myfile.dat\n");
}
```

The opposite of opening a file is closing it. When a file is closed, its buffers are flushed, ensuring that all data were properly written to it. The *fclose()* function is used to close files that were opened by *fopen*. Here is an example:

```
fclose(fp);
```

10

Performing File Input/Output

C provides many functions for reading and writing files. In this chapter, you concentrate on two: *fgetc* and *fputc*. The two functions, *fgetc()* and *fputc()*, perform character input/output on files. The following is an example of *fgetc()*:

```
ch = fgetc(fp);
```

fgetc() reads a single character from the file and points to it. The character is read from the current position. Character output is performed with *fputc()* as in the following example:

```
fputc(ch, fp);
```

In this example, the character stored in *ch* is written to the current position of the file referenced by *fp*.

Testing for the End of File

Use the *feof()* function to determine if the end-of-file marker has been encountered during an input operation, as illustrated in the next example:

```
if (feof(fp))
    fclose(fp);
```

The *feof()* function returns a nonzero value if the end-of-file marker was encountered. Otherwise, it returns zero.

Now that you have a basic understanding of file operations in C, you are ready to practice writing a program in Hands-On Project 10-5 that performs file input/output.

Using the make Utility to Maintain Program Source Files

You might often work with a program that has many files of source code. For example, the absolute program you create in Hands-On Project 10-4 can be divided into two files. The following is the code for the absolute.c program.

```
#include <stdio.h>
int absolute(int num);
int main()
{
    int x = -12, y;
    y = absolute(x);
    printf("The absolute value of %d is %d\n", x, y);
}
int absolute(int num)
{
    if (num < 0)
        return (-num);
    else
        return (num);
}
```

If you were to divide this program into two files, one file can hold the function *main()* and another can hold the function *absolute()*. One file, called abs_func.c, might be written as follows:

```
int absolute(int num)
{
    if (num < 0)
        return (-num);
    else
        return (num);
}
```

A second file, called abs_main.c, might contain the following lines of code:

```
#include <stdio.h>
int absolute(int num);
int main()
{
    int x = -12, y;
    y = absolute(x);
    printf("The absolute value of %d is %d\n", x, y);
}
```

The advantage of creating two files can be that you break down the code into smaller, easier-to-understand modules that can be combined in different ways with other modules. In this example, the two files can then be compiled and linked together into one executable program. Try Hands-On Project 10-6 to practice this programming technique.

As you develop multimodule programs, such as the absolute.c program, and make changes, you must compile the programs repeatedly. However, with multimodule source files, such as in the two-file example, you only need to compile those source files in which you made changes. The linker then links the newly generated object-code files with previously compiled object code, thereby creating a new executable file. However, keeping track of what needs to be recompiled and what does not can become an overwhelming task when the program involves dozens of files of source code. This is where the *make* utility helps.

The *make* utility tracks what needs to be recompiled by using the time stamp field for each source file. All you have to do is create a control file, called the **makefile** (which is actually a file named makefile), for the *make* utility to use. The control file lists all your source files and their relationships to each other. These relationships are expressed in the form of targets and dependencies. A target file depends on another file to determine if any action needs to be taken to rebuild the target file. (The ultimate target file is, of course, the executable file that results from linking all the object files together.) The dependent files are source files, such as the .c source files, or .h files that serve as headers to be included within the source files.

10

Syntax **make** [–options] *filenames*

Dissection

- A utility for maintaining updates to multiple programs in a project; uses a control file called a makefile

- Useful options include:

  -f specifies the name of the makefile

NOTE

More options associated with *make* are beyond the scope of this book. To view the *make* documentation, enter *man make* or *info make*.

The makefile must exist in the current directory. It feeds the *make* utility all it needs to know to recompile any changed modules and then relink the objects to produce a new executable program. You can also give the makefile another name, such as make_abs. To do this, you need to enter the *-f* option followed by the name of the makefile. This is useful when you are developing more than one application from within the same directory.

The contents of make_abs, an example of a makefile, are:

```
abs_main.o: abs_main.c
    gcc -c abs_main.c
abs_func.o: abs_func.c
    gcc -c abs_func.c
abs2: abs_main.o abs_func.o
    gcc abs_main.o abs_func.o -o abs2
```

NOTE

To make this file work properly, use a tab character to indent the lines beginning with gcc. If you use the *make* command and see an invalid separator message, for example, the error can often be corrected by replacing the blank spaces in front of the *gcc* command in your *make* file with one tab (delete the spaces in front of gcc and press the Tab key once).

Two types of lines are shown in the file: dependencies and commands. The first line is a dependency, and the second line is a command:

```
abs_main.o: abs_main.c
    gcc -c abs_main.c
```

The first line establishes a dependency between abs_main.o and abs_main.c. If abs_main.c is newer than abs_main.o, the command on the second line executes (rebuilding abs_main.o). The *-c* option after the *gcc* command on the second line instructs the compiler to create a linkable object code file (in this case the abs_main.o file).

The third and fourth lines, as well as the fifth and sixth lines, establish similar dependencies and commands.

The command-line entry to build the abs2 program using the makefile is:

```
make -f make_abs abs2
```

The *-f* option instructs *make* to read the file make_abs instead of makefile. After executing the command, you can run the abs2 program. Figure 10-3 shows the output of the *make* command and the abs2 program.

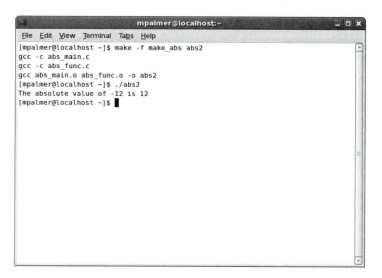

Figure 10-3   Making and running the abs2 executable file

If you forget whether you have made changes since the last time you ran the program, you can use *make* to check the source files' time stamps, and rebuild the program if necessary. The *make* utility does not recompile if the program is current, and displays a message that the makefile is up to date, as shown in the following:

```
[stephen@localhost ~]$ make -f make_abs abs2
make: 'abs2' is up to date.
```

The *make* utility follows a set of rules, both defaults and user defined. In general, a *make* rule has the following:

- A target, the name of the file you want to make (in the previous example, the target is abs2)

- One or more dependencies, the files upon which the target depends

- An action, a shell command that creates the target

Now that you have learned the structure of a makefile, you can create a simple multimodule C project by trying Hands-On Project 10-7.

After writing a simple program in C, the next step is to learn how to debug your program.

10

DEBUGGING YOUR PROGRAM

Typical errors for new C programmers include using incorrect syntax, such as forgetting to terminate a statement with a semicolon. Or, because almost everything you type into a C program is in lowercase, your program might have a case-sensitive error. Here is an example of what you might see on the screen if you omit a closing quotation mark inside a *printf* command:

```
simple.c:10: unterminated string or character constant
simple.c:10: possible real start of unterminated constant
simple.c:4:10: missing terminating " character
simple.c:5: error: syntax error before '}' token
```

The compiler generally produces more error lines than the number of mistakes it finds in the code. The compiler reports the error lines and any surrounding lines affected by the mistake(s).

NOTE   Remember that every time you modify (correct or add text to) your program source file, you must recompile the program to create a new executable program.

To correct syntax errors within your programs, use the following steps:

1. Write down the line number of each error and a brief description.

2. Edit your source file, moving your cursor to the first line number the compiler reports.

3. Within the source file, correct the error, and then move the cursor to the next line number. Most editors display the current line number to help you locate specific lines within the file.

4. After correcting errors, save and recompile the file.

TIP   When you first compile a program in C or C++ you may well see an unnerving number of compiler errors. Always keep in mind that there may only be one or two actual errors in your code, far fewer than the number of errors reported. The source of the error messages is often something simple, such as leaving out a semicolon, omitting a closing bracket, or a single instance of a misspelled variable. When you debug your program and fix an error or two, go ahead and recompile it to see if all of the error messages go away. This can save you time and frustration rather than trying to solve the meaning of every error message.

Now that you understand how to write and debug simple C programs, you are ready to create interactive programs that read input from the keyboard.

CREATING A C PROGRAM TO ACCEPT INPUT

You can draw from many standard library functions to accept input, that is, characters entered using the keyboard. Some, such as *getchar()*, are character-oriented, whereas others, such as *scanf()*, are field-oriented. This section concentrates on *scanf()*.

Unlike many other library input functions, *scanf()* can be used to input values of a variety of data types.

Syntax **scanf** (control string, expression, expression,...)

Dissection

- Reads input, such as from the keyboard or from stdin, according to a specified format

---

The *scanf()* function uses a control string with format specifiers in a manner similar to *printf()*. The arguments that follow the control string are the addresses of variables where the input is to be stored. Consider the following example:

```
scanf("%d", &age);
```

The *%d* format specifier works just like it does for *printf()*. Here, it indicates that *scanf()* should interpret the input value as a decimal integer.

The *&age* argument tells *scanf()* to store the input value in the variable age. The & is the address operator. When used with a general variable, it returns the memory address where this variable is located. The *scanf()* function needs the address of a variable to store an input value there. The next example shows how *scanf()* can be used to input a string:

```
scanf("%s", city);
```

Notice that this example does not use the & operator. Anytime you use the name of an array, it resolves to the address of the first element. It would be an error to use the & operator with the name of an array.

The format specifiers for *scanf()* are generally the same as those used with *printf()*. Table 10-6 shows the format specifiers for *scanf()*.

Table 10-6 scanf() format specifiers

Format Specifier	Interpretation
%c	Single character
%d	Signed decimal integer
%e, %f, %g	Floating-point number
%E, %G	Floating-point number
%i	Signed decimal integer
%o	Unsigned octal integer
%P	Pointer

10

Table 10-6 scanf() format specifiers (continued)

Format Specifier	Interpretation
%s	String; ignores leading whitespace characters, then reads until it encounters another whitespace character
%u	Unsigned decimal integer
%x, %X	Unsigned hex integer

Table 10-7 shows a list of modifiers you can use with *scanf()* format specifiers.

Table 10-7 Modifiers for scanf() format specifiers

Modifier	Meaning
h	Used to indicate a *short int* or *short unsigned int*, for example, "%hd"
l	Used to indicate a *long int* or *long unsigned int*, for example, "%ld"; also used to indicate a *double*, for example, "%lf"
L	Used to indicate a *long double*, for example, "%Lf"

Although it rarely contributes to a program's user-friendliness, the *scanf()* statement can accept multiple inputs. Here is an example:

```
scanf("%d %f %d", &x, &y, &z);
```

The preceding statement accepts values in the variables *x*, *y*, and *z*, which are *int*, *float*, and *int*, respectively. While typing values, the user must separate the three values with whitespace characters. Whitespace characters are spaces, tabs, and newlines.

Now try Hands-On Project 10-8 to write a C program to accept input from a keyboard using *scanf()*.

This concludes your introduction to C programming. You have learned some fundamentals of programming in C, including working with files, using the *make* utility to maintain program source files, debugging your programs, and creating a program to accept input. At this point, try Hands-On Projects 10-9 and 10-10, which enable you to put together what you have learned about C programming to create a program to encrypt information and then write a program to decrypt information.

INTRODUCING C++ PROGRAMMING

C++ is a programming language developed by Bjarne Stroustrup at AT&T Bell Labs. It builds on the C language to add object-oriented programming capabilities. Typically, C++ is best learned after you have been programming in C for a while. With C++, you can do "more with less" after you learn its nuances. Functions, the building blocks of C programming, are incorporated in C++ with added dimensions such as **function overloading**, which makes the functions respond to more than one set of criteria and conditions.

C and C++ are similar in many ways. For example, programs in both languages start with the *main()* function and call other functions that include blocks of instructions enclosed within curly brackets. Both languages support compiler directives, such as *#include* and *#define*. In Linux, the C++ compiler is called from the *g++* command; in many UNIX versions, it is called using the *cc* command. Also, the *g++* command supports using the -o option to name the executable file, such as by entering *g++ myprogram.C -o myprogram* to compile the myprogram.C source code file into the executable file, myprogram.

NOTE One important distinction should be made about C++ programs. You can place your variable declarations anywhere inside the program, before or after the instructions. This is not true of C programs, in which program variables must precede all the instructions.

The major differences between the two languages become evident when you start using the C++ enhancements and class structures, which depart dramatically from standard C procedures. C follows procedural principles, whereas C++ primarily follows object-oriented programming principles while still allowing procedural programming methods. Procedural programming follows long-standing traditions that separate the data to be processed from the procedures that process that data. Procedural techniques require that the data fields be named and defined by data types (integers, characters, strings, floating decimals, and a variety of structures and arrays) before any processing begins. **Object-oriented programming**, on the other hand, uses objects for handling data—allowing the data to be described by name and type anywhere in the program. It is more significant that C++ programs introduce objects as a new data **class**. An **object** is a collection of data and a set of operations, called **methods**, which manipulate the data. Unlike standard C functions, C++ methods are part of the object to which they belong, not the program.

Other more minor differences between C and C++ concern the name of the compiler (Linux calls the C++ compiler g++) and the suffix attached to a C++ source file, often .C or .cpp.

CREATING A SIMPLE C++ PROGRAM

To illustrate the similarity between C and C++, consider a short program, simple.C, which displays a message on the screen exactly as the C program simple.c does. The differences between the two languages start with the *#include <iostream>* instead of *#include <stdio.h>* statement. (In later versions of C++, the compiler complains if you use the older form: *<iostream.h>*.) Also, after *<iostream>*, you place the line, *using namespace std;*. Another difference is the use of the *cout* I/O stream object instead of *printf()*. Consider the following program:

```
//==========================================================
// Program Name:  simple.C
// By:            MP
// Purpose:       First program in C++ showing how to
//                produce output
```

10

```
//=========================================================
#include <iostream>
using namespace std;
int main(void)
{
  cout << "C++ is a programming language.\n";
  cout << "Like C, C++ is compatible with UNIX/Linux.\n";
}
```

NOTE

For reading input from the keyboard, C++ uses *cin* instead of *scanf()* although C++ also recognizes and compiles *scanf()* lines.

Looking at the program, notice that C++ uses // to denote a comment line. (You can also use C's /* and */ to enclose comments in your C++ program.) Recall that comments help to identify and describe the program for all who need to review the program. Comments are ignored by the compiler and do not cause the computer to perform any action when the program runs.

Furthermore, note that the standard library functions for I/O are found in *iostream* instead of stdio.h, as in the C program, and the line *using namespace std* is added. Another difference between the C and C++ programs is the use of *cout* in the C++ program, as mentioned earlier. In Hands-On Project 10-11, you create, compile, and execute the code in the simple.C file.

To continue the comparison between C and C++, you next see how a C++ program reads and displays the information in a file.

CREATING A C++ PROGRAM THAT READS A TEXT FILE

You learn further differences between C and C++ by examining the following C++ program, which reads a text file:

```
//=========================================================
// Program Name: fileread.C
// By:           MP
// Purpose:      A C++ program that reads the contents
//               of a file
//=========================================================
#include <iostream>
#include <fstream>
using namespace std;
int main(void)
{
    ifstream file("testfile");
    char record_in[256];
    if (file.fail())
        cout << "Error opening file.\n";
```

```
  else
  {
    while (!file.eof())
    {
      file.getline(record_in, sizeof(record_in));
      if (file.good())
          cout << record_in << endl;
    }
  }
}
```

There are several differences in the way C and C++ handle file operations. For example, the following code:

```
ifstream file ("testfile");
```

tells the compiler to use the *ifstream* class (object) to perform file input and output operations. The identifier file follows the class name. This statement is similar to the following C statement:

```
FILE *file;
```

Further, the *file.fail()* function is a part of the *ifstream* class and reports an invalid condition with the file access. The *endl* stream manipulator causes the screen output to skip a line, similar to \n in the C language.

The *file.getline()* function reads in a line from the file and stores it in the buffer *record_in* for subsequent processing. The *file.good()* flag is a component of the *ifstream* class and is used to determine if the record accessed contains data.

Try Hands-On Project 10-12 to create and use the fileread.C program.

Now that you have an understanding of how C++ is similar to C, in the next section you see how C++ provides additional enhancements.

10

How C++ Enhances C Functions

C++ creates a way to define a function so that it can handle multiple sets of criteria; as you learned, this feature is called function overloading. Whereas C functions are quite flexible, function overloading adds considerably to the overall functions' use by expanding the function definition to accept varying kinds and numbers of parameters. During compilation, the C++ compiler determines which function to call based on the number and types of parameters the calling statement passes to the function. For example, consider the following code that overloads a function to access the system date in two different ways:

```
//========================================================
// Program Name: datestuf.C
// By:           MP
// Purpose:      Shows you two ways to access the
//               system date
```

```
//=======================================================
#include <iostream>
#include <ctime>
using namespace std;
void display_time(const struct tm *tim)
{
    cout << "1. It is now " << asctime(tim);
}
void display_time(const time_t *tim)
{
    cout << "2. It is now " << ctime(tim);
}
int main(void)
{
    time_t tim = time(NULL);
    struct tm *ltim = localtime(&tim);
    display_time(ltim);
    display_time(&tim);
}
```

The *#include <ctime>* statement calls the C++ <ctime> library that consists of date types, structures, and functions for manipulating the time and date. Notice how the same function name is used for the different calls to the different date types that are contained in <ctime>. One is a structure (*struct tm*); the other is a date type for storing calendar time (*time_t*).

```
void display_time (const struct tm *tim)
void display_time (const time_t *tim)
```

In the line *cout << "1. It is now " << asctime(tim);*, you see that *asctime()* is a function included in <ctime> that is used with *struct tm* to yield the local time and date. In the line *cout << "2. It is now " << ctime(tim);*, you see that *ctime()* is a function in <ctime> that is used with *time_t* to yield the local time and date.

The program is able to distinguish which function to use based on the date type being passed to it.

```
Display_time(ltim);   Uses the structure type
Display_time(&tim);   Uses the time_t type
```

Hands-On Project 10-13 enables you to create the datestuf.C program.

CHAPTER SUMMARY

- ❑ The C language concentrates on how best to create commands and expressions that can be elegantly formed from operators and operands.

- ❑ C programs often consist of separate source files called program modules that are compiled separately into object code and linked to the other object codes that make up the program.

- The C program structure begins with the execution of instructions located inside a *main()* function, which calls other functions that contain more instructions.

- The *make* utility is used to maintain the application's source files. The default *make* control file is called makefile.

- An important difference between C and C++ is that C follows procedural principles and C++ primarily follows object-oriented programming principles.

- The standard stream library used by C++ is *iostream*.

- C++ provides two statements for standard input and standard output: *cin* and *cout*, respectively. These are defined in the class libraries contained in <iostream>.

- C++ offers a way to define a function so that it can handle multiple sets of criteria through a process called function overloading.

COMMAND SUMMARY: REVIEW OF CHAPTER 10 COMMANDS

Command	Purpose	Options Covered in This Chapter
g++	Compiles a C++ source code file	-o enables you to specify an output file.
gcc	Compiles a C source code file	-o enables you to specify an output file. -c compiles the source code file and creates a linkable object code file.
make	Maintains updates to multiple programs in a project	-f specifies the name of the makefile.
printf()	Formats and prints arguments, such as for creating reports	
scanf()	Used to input values of a variety of data types.	

Please refer to the tables within the chapter for additional command review.

Table	Shows
Table 10-1	C language keywords
Table 10-2	C data types
Table 10-3	Typical C data type limits and bytes occupied in memory
Table 10-4	C arithmetic operators
Table 10-5	C format specifiers
Table 10-6	*scanf()* format specifiers (C language)
Table 10-7	Modifiers for *scanf()* format specifiers

KEY TERMS

assembler — The program that is called by a compiler to translate assembly code into object code.

assembly language — A low-level language that provides maximum access to all the computer's devices, both internal and external. Writing an assembly language program requires a great deal of coding and time.

automatic variable — A variable declared inside a function and local to the function in which it is declared.

C — A programming language developed in part to overcome the disadvantages of assembly language programming, which requires a great deal of coding and time. The result is a high-level set of easy-to-understand instructions. UNIX was originally written in assembly language but further developed and refined in C, largely due to the efforts of Dennis Ritchie and Brian Kernighan of AT&T Bell Labs.

C++ — A programming language developed by Bjarne Stroustrup of AT&T Bell Labs. Stroustrup added object-oriented capabilities and other features to the C language.

C library — A collection of functions that perform file, screen, and keyboard operations, and many other tasks. To perform or include one of these functions in your program, you insert a function call at the appropriate location in your file.

class — A data structure in the C++ programming language that enables the programmer to create abstract data types. In this context, an abstract data type is one defined by the programmer for a specific programming task.

control string — An argument that specifies how formatting should occur when using the screen output library function *printf()*.

daemon — A specialized system process that runs in the background. A daemon accesses UNIX/Linux system code like any other part of the operating system.

decrement operator (--) — A C/C++ arithmetic operator that decreases the value of a variable by a specified amount.

executable file — A usable program, the result of the program development cycle.

function — A separate body of code designed to contribute to the execution of a single task. You can put together a number of functions to create a program. In some languages, functions are called subroutines or procedures.

function call — A feature that you insert in the appropriate location of a program file to specify and use one of the functions in the C/C++ library or a user-defined function.

function overloading — A feature of the C++ programming language that lets functions respond to more than one set of criteria and conditions.

function prototype — A C program statement line that tells the C compiler about a function before the code for the function is fully defined.

header file — A file containing the information the compiler needs to process standard input or output statements.

identifiers — The names given to variables and functions.

increment operator (++) — A C/C++ arithmetic operator that increases the value of a variable by a specified amount.

keywords — The components of all programming languages; these words have special meaning and must not be used as variable or function names.

linker — In program development, the tool used after the compiler to link all object files that belong to the program and any library programs the program might use.

main( ) — A required function in a C or C++ program. A C/C++ program is made up of one or more functions. Every function must have a name, and every C/C++ program must have a function called main().

makefile — A file used with the *make* utility that contains instructions for a project consisting of multiple source and executable files.

method — A set of operations that manipulate data; a part of the new data class, objects, used in the C++ programming language.

null character — A single byte whose bits are all set to zero.

object code — The binary instructions translated from program source code by a compiler.

object-oriented programming — A method of programming that uses objects for programming and handling data—allowing the data to be described by name and type anywhere in the program.

objects — A new data class introduced in the C++ programming language. An object is a collection of data and a set of operations called methods that manipulate data.

preprocessor — The routine that is used after initial application development and before the compiler to make necessary modifications to the program and to include the contents of other files.

preprocessor directive — A statement that you place in your program to instruct the preprocessor to modify your source code in some way. A preprocessor directive always begins with the # symbol. An example is *#include*, which tells the preprocessor to include another file or library in your program.

scope — The part of the program in which a variable is defined and accessible. The scope can be either inside or outside a function.

source code — The program code that you create using an editor and that either is interpreted, if you are using an interpreted programming language, or is compiled, if you are using a compiled language.

stdio.h — A header file that is part of the C programming language development system. This file contains information the compiler needs to process standard input or output statements. Any C program that performs standard input or output must include the stdio.h header file.

REVIEW QUESTIONS

1. A new programmer whom you are training is writing a C program and wants to place comment lines in the program. Which of the following characters should be used at the beginning and end of the comments?

   a. Use # at the beginning and end of the comments.

   b. Place *!#* at the beginning of each new comment line and *#!* at the end.

   c. Place *(* at the beginning and *)* at the end of the comments.

   d. Use */** at the beginning of the comments and **/* at the end.

2. You've written a C program, but are now getting an error message about the use of standard input and output statements when you compile the program. Which of the following might be the cause?

   a. You omitted the preprocessor directive for the file stdio.h.

   b. You forgot to declare the print I/O as a char data type.

   c. Your computer is not configured to use I/O.

   d. You did not specify an object file for your program.

3. Which of the following is in the proper format for a character constant? (Choose all that apply.)

   a. C!

   b. <c>

   c. 'C'

   d. 'c'

4. Which of the following are performed by functions in the C library? (Choose all that apply.)

   a. screen operations

   b. memory allocation operations

   c. file operations

   d. math operations

5. A daemon is a _____.

   a. source code program for using the C compiler

   b. log file to track compiler errors

   c. specialized system process that runs in the background

   d. memory management process for automatically deleting unused swap space when a C++ program has ended

6. A colleague of yours is just learning to use the C compiler in Linux. When she tries to compile a program called firststart.c using *gcc firststart.c* she is expecting the executable file to have the name firststart, but there is no firststart file. What is the executable file's name?

   a. c.file

   b. a.out

   c. prog.o

   d. file$.o

7. You have written a C program using the variables *num, enum, sum,* and *long.* When you compile the program you get an error message about using a variable the compiler finds unacceptable. Which of the following is likely to be the problem?

    a. These variables must be declared inside a function instead of at the beginning of the program code.

    b. C does not allow you to declare more than three variables.

    c. *enum* and *long* are keywords and cannot be used as variables.

    d. Variables must be declared in alphabetic order, but you have used the order *num, enum, sum,* and *long.*

8. Which of the following are examples of data types in the C language? (Choose all that apply.)

    a. whole

    b. int

    c. double

    d. float

9. Which of the following is the right way to use the string constant, Enter your ID:, in the C language?

    a. ~ Enter your ID:~

    b. \ Enter your ID:

    c. >> Enter your ID:

    d. "Enter your ID:"

10. Which of the following functions must be in a C program? (Choose all that apply.)

    a. *start.io ( )*

    b. *main( )*

    c. *run( )*

    d. *absolute( )*

11. Which of the following statements enables you to print *File updated.* on the screen when a C++ program is finished?

    a. *cout << "File updated.\n";*

    b. *cout >> File updated./n*

    c. scanf *~File updated.*

    d. *scanf >> File updated.\n;*

10

12. Which of the following are important characteristics of C++ programming? (Choose all that apply.)

    a. elimination of hexadecimal variables

    b. object-oriented programming

    c. use of classes for specialized programming needs

    d. designation of file size before opening a file

13. Your program to calculate values in physics requires working with positive and negative whole numbers between –14,242 and 12,528. What data types would you use to work with these numbers in a C program?

    a. unsigned short

    b. char

    c. short int

    d. signed whole

14. In your C program, you want to use a *while* loop and decrement the value, *counter*, each time the program goes through the *while* loop. Which of the following operators enables you to decrement the value in *counter*?

    a. *counter #-1;*

    b. *dec01 counter;*

    c. *++counter;*

    d. *counter--;*

15. Which of the following functions is used to open a file in the C language?

    a. *file.o( )*

    b. *scan( )*

    c. *fopen( )*

    d. *void( )*

16. What started as a simple C program has now turned into several program modules as you have refined it over the past several months. The problem is that now you do not always remember which modules you have changed at what time. What should you do?

    a. Make the modification date part of the each program's name.

    b. Use the *track( )* version tracking function.

    c. Use the C language file logging capability to track version changes.

    d. Use the *make* utility and create makefiles.

17. What compiler is started by using the *g++* command?

    a. the C++ compiler

    b. the preprocessor compiler

    c. the object and binary linker compiler

    d. the C compiler

18. The programmer you are training wants to write code to determine when the end of a file has been reached. Which of the following can he use?

    a. *putc*

    b. *feof( )*

    c. *end( )*

    d. *filemarker*

19. Your C++ program needs to access the system date in different ways. Which of the following enables you to do this?

    a. *time.d*

    b. <ctime> library

    c. const time subroutine

    d. *time( )*

20. Which of the following is an acceptable way to insert a comment line in a C++ program? (Choose all that apply.)

    a. *// Program Name: calc.C*

    b. *# Program Name: calc.C*

    c. *rem Program Name: calc.C*

    d. *\ Program Name: calc.C*

21. What character shows that you are starting a block of code in the C and C++ languages?

    a. ~

    b. `

    c. {

    d. <

22. What is an automatic variable?

23. Name a function that enables you to read the contents of a file and another function that enables you to write to the file in the C language.

24. What are three examples of looping logic structures that can be used in the C language?

25. Most programmers have to do some debugging of a C or C++ program at some point. Suggest a series of steps to follow when debugging a program.

10

HANDS-ON PROJECTS

For the following projects, log into your own account and use your home directory. Also, access the command line, such as through a terminal window.

Project 10-1

In this project, you create and run a simple C program.

To write a simple C program:

1. Use the vi or Emacs editor to create and save the file **inches.c**. (Remember that the C compiler uses the .c extension to identify a file containing C source code.) Enter this code:

```
/* This program converts 10 feet to inches. */

#include <stdio.h>

int main()
{
    int inches, feet;
    feet = 10;
    inches = feet * 12;
    printf("There are %d inches in %d feet.\n", inches,
     feet);
}
```

2. Save the program and exit the editor.

3. The C compiler is executed by the *gcc* command in Linux. Type **gcc inches.c** and press **Enter**. If you typed the program correctly, you see no messages. If you see error messages, load the program into the editor, and correct the mistake.

4. By default, the compiler stores the executable program in a file named a.out. Execute a.out by typing **./a.out** and pressing **Enter**. Your screen looks similar to Figure 10-4.

5. You can specify the name of the executable file with the *-o* option. Type **gcc -o inches inches.c** and press **Enter**. The command compiles the inches.c file and stores the executable code in a file named inches.

As you learned when *gcc* was first introduced in this chapter, you can put the *-o filename* option before the name of the file you are compiling, as in *gcc -o inches inches.c* or after the name of the file you are compiling, such as *gcc inches.c -o inches*.

6. Run the inches program by typing **./inches** and pressing **Enter**.

7. Type **clear** and press **Enter** to clear the screen for the next project.

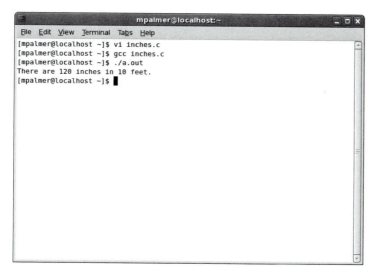

```
[mpalmer@localhost ~]$ vi inches.c
[mpalmer@localhost ~]$ gcc inches.c
[mpalmer@localhost ~]$ ./a.out
There are 120 inches in 10 feet.
[mpalmer@localhost ~]$
```

Figure 10-4   Running a.out

Project 10-2

In this project, you create a C program that uses an *if-else* statement.

To use the C *if-else* statement:

1. Create the file **radius.c** with your choice of editor. Enter the following C code:

```
/* This program calculates the area of a circle */
#include <stdio.h>
int main()
{
    float radius = 50, area;
    area = 3.14159 * radius * radius;
    if (area > 100)
        printf("The area, %f, is too large.\n", area);
    else
        printf("The area, %f, is within limits.\n", area);
}
```

2. Save the file and exit the editor.

3. Compile the program by typing **gcc –o radius radius.c** and pressing **Enter**. If you see error messages, edit the file, and correct your mistakes.

4. Execute the program by typing **./radius** and pressing **Enter** (see Figure 10-5).

5. Type **clear** and press **Enter** to clear the screen.

10

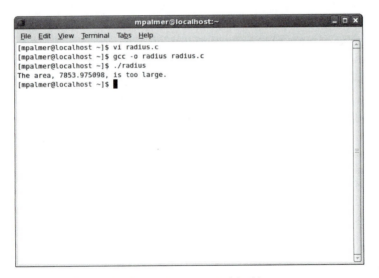

Figure 10-5   Using the radius executable file

Project 10-3

In this project, you create a C program using a *for* loop.

To practice using a C *for* loop:

1. Use the editor of your choice to create the file **rain.c**, entering this C code:

```
/* rain.c  */
#include <stdio.h>
int main()
{
    int rain, total_rain = 0;
    for (rain = 0; rain < 10; rain++)
    {
        printf("We have had %d inches of rain.\n", rain);
        total_rain = total_rain + rain;
    }
    printf("We have had a total ");
    printf("of %d inches of rain.\n", total_rain);
}
```

2. Save the file and exit the editor.

3. Compile the program and store the executable code in a file named **rain**.

4. Run the program. Your screen should look similar to Figure 10-6.

5. Type **clear** and press **Enter** to clear the screen.

```
                        mpalmer@localhost:~
File  Edit  View  Terminal  Tabs  Help
[mpalmer@localhost ~]$ vi rain.c
[mpalmer@localhost ~]$ gcc -o rain rain.c
[mpalmer@localhost ~]$ ./rain
We have had 0 inches of rain.
We have had 1 inches of rain.
We have had 2 inches of rain.
We have had 3 inches of rain.
We have had 4 inches of rain.
We have had 5 inches of rain.
We have had 6 inches of rain.
We have had 7 inches of rain.
We have had 8 inches of rain.
We have had 9 inches of rain.
We have had a total of 45 inches of rain.
[mpalmer@localhost ~]$
```

Figure 10-6   Using the rain executable file

**HANDS-ON
PROJECTS**

Project 10-4

Functions can be powerful tools in C programming. In this program, you create two functions that accept arguments and return a value.

To practice writing functions that accept arguments and return a value:

1. Use the editor of your choice to create the file **absolute.c**. Enter the following code:

```
#include <stdio.h>
int absolute(int num);
int main()
{
    int x = -12, y;
    y = absolute(x);
    printf("The absolute value of %d is %d\n", x, y);
}
int absolute(int num)
{
    if (num < 0)
        return (-num);
    else
        return (num);
}
```

2. Save the file and exit the editor.

3. Compile the program and save the executable code in a file named **absolute**.

4. Run the program to test it (see Figure 10-7).

5. Type **clear** and press **Enter** to clear the screen for the next project.

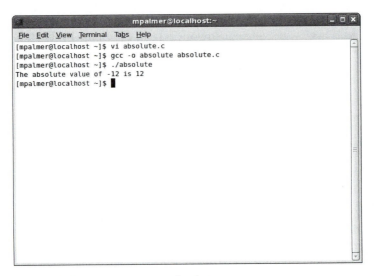

Figure 10-7   Executing the absolute program

HANDS-ON PROJECTS

Project 10-5

In this project, you create a C program that performs file input and output.

To perform file input/output:

1. Use the editor of your choice to create the file **buildfile.c**. Enter the following code in the file:

```
#include <stdio.h>
int main()
{
    FILE *out_file;
    int count = 0;
    char msg[] = "This was created by a C program.\n";
    if ((out_file = fopen("testfile", "w")) == NULL)
    {
        printf("Error opening file.\n");
    }
    while (count < 33)
    {
        fputc(msg[count], out_file);
        count++;
    }
    fclose(out_file);
}
```

2. Save the program and exit the editor.

3. Compile the program and save the executable in a file named **buildfile**.

4. Run the **buildfile** program. The program creates another file, testfile.

5. To see the contents of testfile, type **cat testfile** and press **Enter** (see Figure 10-8).

6. Type **clear** and press **Enter** to clear the screen.

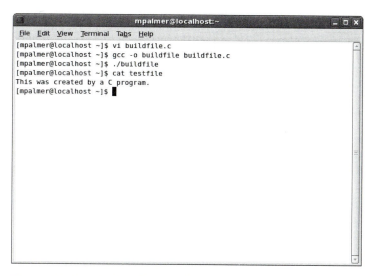

Figure 10-8   Viewing the testfile contents

Project 10-6

In this project, you create two files (refer to the functions in Project 10-4, which are now split into two files in this project) and link them together into one executable file.

To compile and link two files:

1. Use the editor of your choice to create the file **abs_func.c** and enter the following code:

```
int absolute(int num)
{
    if (num < 0)
        return (-num);
    else
            return (num);
}
```

2. Save the file.

3. Create the file **abs_main.c**. Enter this code:

```
#include <stdio.h>
int absolute(int num);
int main()
{
    int x = -12, y;
```

```
        y = absolute(x);
        printf("The absolute value of %d is %d\n", x, y);
}
```

4. Save the file and exit the editor.

5. Compile and link the two programs by typing **gcc abs_main.c abs_func.c -o abs** and then press **Enter**. The compiler separately compiles abs_main.c and abs_func.c. Their object files are linked together, and the executable code is stored in the file abs.

6. Run the **abs** program (see Figure 10-9).

7. Type **clear** and press **Enter** to clear the screen.

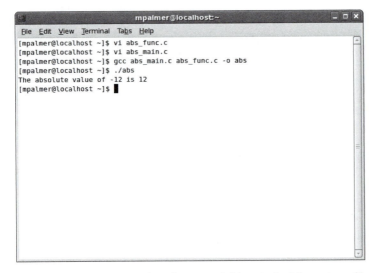

Figure 10-9   Running the abs executable created from two files

HANDS-ON
PROJECTS

Project 10-7

In this project, you use the *make* utility and a makefile to create a multimodule C project.

To create a simple multimodule C project:

1. Use the editor of your choice to create the file **square_func.c**, entering the following code in the file:

```
int square(int number)
{
        return (number * number);
}
```

2. Save the file.

3. Next create the file **square_main.c**. Enter the following code:

```
#include <stdio.h>
int square(int number);
int main()
{
    int count, sq;
    for (count = 1; count < 11; count++)
    {
        sq = square(count);
        printf("The square of %d is %d\n", count, sq);
    }
}
```

4. Save the file.

5. Next create a makefile named **make_square**. Enter the following text:

```
square_func.o: square_func.c
(press Tab)gcc -c square_func.c
square_main.o: square_main.c
  (Tab)gcc -c square_main.c
square: square_func.o square_main.o
  (Tab)gcc square_func.o square_main.o -o square
```

NOTE In some UNIX/Linux versions of the *make* command, such as in Fedora, Red Hat Enterprise Linux, and SUSE, you must place a tab character before each command line that calls the *gcc* compiler. If you do not, the *make* command returns an error.

6. Save the file and exit the editor.

7. Build the program by typing **make –f make_square square** and pressing **Enter**. (If you have errors, load the incorrect module into the editor and correct your mistakes.)

8. Run the program. Your screen should look similar to Figure 10-10.

9. Type **clear** and press **Enter** to clear the screen for the next project.

10

```
                        mpalmer@localhost:~                    _ □ ×
File  Edit  View  Terminal  Tabs  Help
[mpalmer@localhost ~]$ vi square_func.c
[mpalmer@localhost ~]$ vi square_main.c
[mpalmer@localhost ~]$ vi make_square
[mpalmer@localhost ~]$ make -f make_square square
gcc -c square_func.c
gcc -c square_main.c
gcc square_func.o square_main.o -o square
[mpalmer@localhost ~]$ ./square
The square of 1 is 1
The square of 2 is 4
The square of 3 is 9
The square of 4 is 16
The square of 5 is 25
The square of 6 is 36
The square of 7 is 49
The square of 8 is 64
The square of 9 is 81
The square of 10 is 100
[mpalmer@localhost ~]$ █
```

Figure 10-10   Building and running the square executable file

Project 10-8

In this project, you use *scanf()* in a C program to accept input from the keyboard.

To use scanf() to accept keyboard input:

1. Use the editor of your choice to create a file named **keyboard.c** and enter the following lines of code:

```c
/*==========================================================
Program Name: keyboard.c
Purpose:        Enter data using the keyboard
========================================================== */
#include <stdio.h> /* the standard input/output library */
int main()
  {
    char string[50]; /* a string field */
    float my_money; /* a floating decimal field */
    int weight; /* an integer field */
    printf("\nEnter your First Name: ");
    scanf("%s", string);
    printf("\nEnter your Desired Monthly Income: ");
    scanf("%f",&my_money);
    printf("\nEnter your friend's weight: ");
    scanf("%d",&weight);
    printf("\n\n Recap\n");
    printf("I am %s and I wish to have %6.2f per month",
     string, my_money);
    printf("\nI never would have guessed your friend weighs
     %d lbs", weight);
    printf("\n\n");
  }
```

2. Save the file and exit the editor.

3. Compile the program by typing **gcc keyboard.c -o keyboard** and then press **Enter**.

4. Execute the program by typing **./keyboard** and then press **Enter**. Provide answers to the questions on the screen (see Figure 10-11).

5. Type **clear** and press **Enter** to clear the screen.

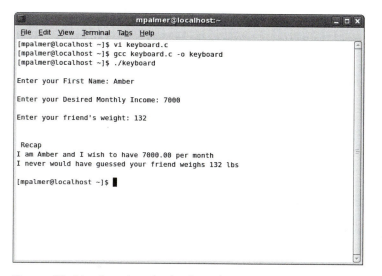

```
mpalmer@localhost:~
File  Edit  View  Terminal  Tabs  Help
[mpalmer@localhost ~]$ vi keyboard.c
[mpalmer@localhost ~]$ gcc keyboard.c -o keyboard
[mpalmer@localhost ~]$ ./keyboard

Enter your First Name: Amber

Enter your Desired Monthly Income: 7000

Enter your friend's weight: 132


 Recap
I am Amber and I wish to have 7000.00 per month
I never would have guessed your friend weighs 132 lbs

[mpalmer@localhost ~]$ █
```

Figure 10-11 Running the keyboard executable file

Project 10-9

If a file contains sensitive information, you might wish to encrypt it so others cannot read its contents. When a file is encrypted, its contents are encoded or modified in such a way that the original contents are not distinguishable. A formula is used to perform the encryption so that a complementary decryption algorithm can restore the file to its original contents. In this project, you use your knowledge of C programming to create an encoding program. The program you create opens a file, reads a character from the file, adds 10 to the character's ASCII value, and then writes the character to a second file. This procedure repeats until all characters in the file have been read, modified, and written to the second file. The second file is an encoded version of the first file. After you complete this project, you create the programs to decode information in the next project.

To create the encoding program:

1. Use the editor of your choice to create the file **encode.c** and enter the following lines of code in the file:

```c
#include <stdio.h>

void encode_file(FILE *, FILE *);
int main()
{
    FILE *in_file, *out_file;
    char infile_name[81], outfile_name[81], input;
    printf("Enter the name of the file to encode: ");
    scanf("%s", infile_name);
    if ((in_file = fopen(infile_name, "r") ) == NULL)
    {
            printf("Error opening %s\n", infile_name);
    }
    printf("Enter the output file name: ");
    scanf("%s", outfile_name);
    if ((out_file = fopen(outfile_name, "w") ) == NULL)
    {
            printf("Error opening %s\n", outfile_name);
    }
    encode_file(in_file, out_file);
    printf("The file has been encoded.\n");
    fclose(in_file);
    fclose(out_file);
}
```

2. Save the file.

3. Create the file **encode_file.c** and enter the following code:

```c
#include <stdio.h>
void encode_file(FILE *in_file, FILE *out_file)
{
  char input;
  while (!feof(in_file))
  {
   input = fgetc(in_file);
      input += 10;
          fputc(input, out_file);
  }
}
```

4. Save the file.

5. Type **clear** and press **Enter** to clear the screen, if you haven't done this already.

Project 10-10

In this project, the decoding program works opposite to the way the encoding program works. It reads a character from the encrypted file, subtracts 10 from its ASCII code, and writes the character out to another file. This procedure repeats until all encrypted characters have been converted to their original state and stored in the second file.

To create the decrypting program:

1. Use an editor to create the file **decode.c** and enter the following code:

```
#include <stdio.h>
void decode_file(FILE *, FILE *);
int main()
{
  FILE *in_file, *out_file;
  char infile_name[81], outfile_name[81], input;
  printf("Enter the name of the file to decode: ");
  scanf("%s", infile_name);
  if ((in_file = fopen(infile_name, "r") ) == NULL)
  {
        printf("Error opening %s\n", infile_name);
  }
  printf("Enter the output file name: ");
  scanf("%s", outfile_name);
  if ((out_file = fopen(outfile_name, "w") ) == NULL)
  {
        printf("Error opening %s\n", outfile_name);
  }
  decode_file(in_file, out_file);
  printf("The file has been decoded.\n");
  fclose(in_file);
  fclose(out_file);
}
```

2. Save the file.

3. Use an editor to create the file **decode_file.c**. Enter the following code:

```
#include <stdio.h>
void decode_file(FILE *in_file, FILE *out_file)
{
  while (!feof(in_file))
  {
   char input;
   input = fgetc(in_file);
   input -= 10;
     fputc(input, out_file);
  }
}
```

10

4. Save the file. You are now ready to create the makefiles for both the encode and decode programs.

5. Enter the following code in the editor, and save it in the file **encode_make** (remember to press the Tab key for the 2nd, 4th, and 6th lines that begin with *gcc*):

```
encode: encode.o encode_file.o
        gcc encode.o encode_file.o -o encode
encode.o: encode.c
        gcc -c encode.c
encode_file.o: encode_file.c
        gcc -c encode_file.c
```

6. Create a file named **decode_make**, and enter this code (press the Tab key to indent the 2nd, 4th, and 6th lines):

```
decode: decode.o decode_file.o
        gcc decode.o decode_file.o -o decode
decode.o: decode.c
        gcc -c decode.c
decode_file.o: decode_file.c
        gcc -c decode_file.c
```

7. Save the file. You are ready to build the programs.

8. Type **make -f encode_make** and press **Enter**.

9. Type **make -f decode_make** and press **Enter**. Your screen should resemble Figure 10-12.

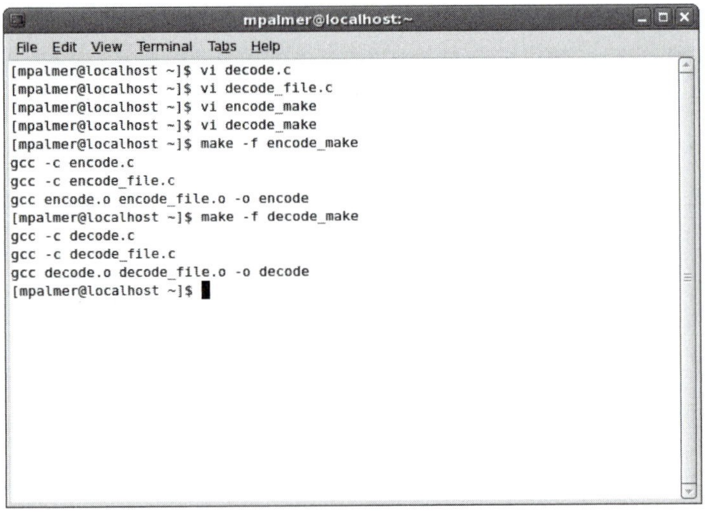

```
mpalmer@localhost:~
File  Edit  View  Terminal  Tabs  Help
[mpalmer@localhost ~]$ vi decode.c
[mpalmer@localhost ~]$ vi decode_file.c
[mpalmer@localhost ~]$ vi encode_make
[mpalmer@localhost ~]$ vi decode_make
[mpalmer@localhost ~]$ make -f encode_make
gcc -c encode.c
gcc -c encode_file.c
gcc encode.o encode_file.o -o encode
[mpalmer@localhost ~]$ make -f decode_make
gcc -c decode.c
gcc -c decode_file.c
gcc decode.o decode_file.o -o decode
[mpalmer@localhost ~]$
```

Figure 10-12   Running the makefiles

You test the encode program by encrypting the testfile that you created in the file I/O exercise. The file contains the string "This was created by a C program."

10. Type **clear** and press **Enter** to clear the screen.

11. Type **./encode** and press **Enter**. Your screen appears similar to Figure 10-13.

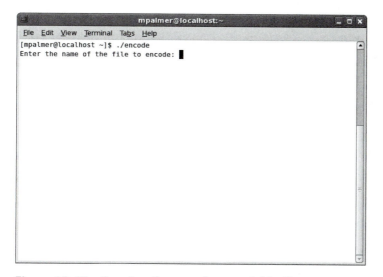

Figure 10-13   Running the encode executable file

12. In response to the prompt, type **testfile** and press **Enter**.

13. The program now asks for the name of the output file.

14. Type **secret_file** and press **Enter**. The contents of testfile have been encoded and stored in secret_file.

15. Use the **cat** command to look at the contents of secret_file. Your screen looks similar to Figure 10-14.

16. Type **clear** and press **Enter**.

17. Run the decode program by typing **./decode** and pressing **Enter**. The program asks you to enter the name of the file to decode.

18. Type **secret_file** and press **Enter**. Next, the program asks you to enter the output file name.

19. Type **normal_file** and press **Enter**. The contents of secret_file have been decoded and stored in normal_file.

20. Use the **cat** command to look at the contents of normal_file. Your screen should look similar to Figure 10-15. In some cases, you might see a couple of residual encoded characters, which appear before the prompt and represent the end-of-file marker from the encoded file. You need not be concerned with their appearance.

21. Type **clear** and press **Enter** to clear the screen.

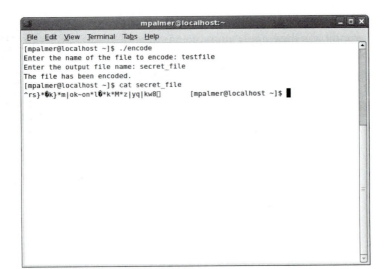

Figure 10-14   Results of running encode

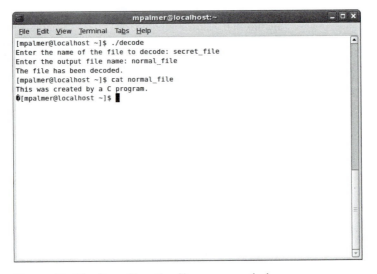

Figure 10-15   Decoding the file you encoded

Project 10-11

In this project, you create a simple C++ program.

To write a C++ program:

1. Use the editor of your choice to create the **simple.C** file. Enter the following code:

```
//=========================================================
// Program Name: simple.C
// By:              Your initials here
// Purpose:         First program in C++ showing how to
//                  produce output
```

```
//=========================================================
#include <iostream>
using namespace std;
int main(void)
{
  cout << "C++ is a programming language.\n";
  cout << "Like C, C++ is compatible with UNIX/Linux.\n";
}
```

2. Save the **simple.C** file and exit the editor.

3. Use the C++ compiler to create a program called sim_plus by typing **g++ simple.C -o sim_plus** and then press **Enter**.

4. Run **sim_plus**. Your screen should look similar to Figure 10-16.

5. Type **clear** and press **Enter** to clear the screen for the next project.

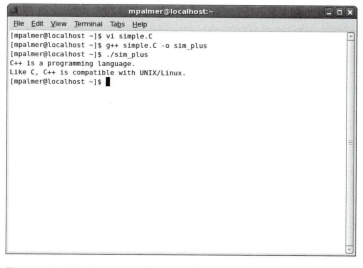

10

Figure 10-16   Running the sim_plus executable file

Project 10-12

Reading a file is important for C++ programming. In this project, you create a C++ program that reads the contents of the file, testfile, that you have worked with in previous projects.

To create a C++ program that reads a text file:

1. Use the editor of your choice to create the file **fileread.C**. Enter the following code:

```
//=========================================================
// Program Name: fileread.C
// By:           Your initials here
// Purpose:      A C++ program that reads the contents
```

```
//                      of a file
//=======================================================
#include <iostream>
#include <fstream>
using namespace std;
int main(void)
{
    ifstream file("testfile");
    char record_in[256];
    if (file.fail())
        cout << "Error opening file.\n";
    else
    {
        while (!file.eof())
        {
            file.getline(record_in, sizeof(record_in));
            if (file.good())
                cout << record_in << endl;
        }
    }
}
```

2. Save the file and exit the editor.

3. Use the g++ compiler to create an executable program called fileread.

4. Test the **fileread** program (see Figure 10-17).

5. Type **clear** and press **Enter** to clear the screen.

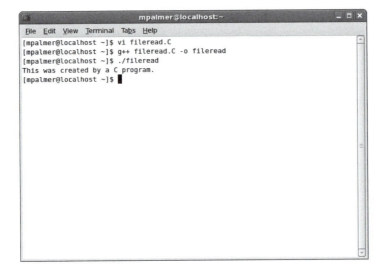

Figure 10-17   Testing the fileread program

Project 10-13

In this project, you use function overloading to determine the system time.

To use function overloading:

1. Use the editor of your choice to type the contents of **datestuf.C**. (When you enter the statement *cout << "1. It is now " << asctime(tim);*, be certain to enter the number one after the first double quotation mark and not the letter l.)

```
//=========================================================
// Program Name: datestuf.C
// By:           Your initials here
// Purpose:      Shows you two ways to access the
//               system date
//=========================================================
#include <iostream>
#include <ctime>
using namespace std;
void display_time(const struct tm *tim)
{
    cout << "1. It is now " << asctime(tim);
}
void display_time(const time_t *tim)
{
    cout << "2. It is now " << ctime(tim);
}
int main(void)
{
    time_t tim = time(NULL);
    struct tm *ltim = localtime(&tim);
    display_time(ltim);
    display_time(&tim);
}
```

2. Save the file and then exit the editor.

3. Compile datestuf.C by typing **g++ datestuf.C –o datestuf** and then press **Enter**.

4. Test the program. Your screen should be similar to Figure 10-18.

5. If you are using a terminal window, close it and log off.

10

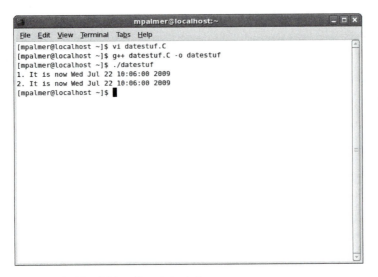

Figure 10-18   Using the datestuf program

Discovery Exercises

NOTE

After you write each program in the following exercises, compile the program and test it.

1. Write a C program called fedora.c that displays the line "Fedora is a version of Linux."

2. Create a simple C program which declares the variable number as a local variable that is an integer.

3. Modify the rain.c program you created in this chapter so that when all inches of rain are added together, the total is 136 inches.

4. Write a C program in which a prompt asks for your first name, and after you enter your first name the program displays it.

5. Write a C program in which you enter a number and then the program calculates and displays that number cubed.

6. Create a C program that lets you input a positive integer and that then tells you if it is a prime number or if it can be divided by 2.

7. Create a C program in which the user enters the outside temperature in Fahrenheit. If the temperature is 60 or over, print a comment that states "It is just fine outside." If the temperature is under 60, print a comment that states "It's not so warm outside."

8. Write a small C++ program that writes to the screen the make and model of the car or bicycle you own (or one that you wish to own).

9. Rewrite the C program keyboard.c (that you created earlier in this chapter) to compile as a C++ program.

10. Create a C++ program that tests to see if the file accounts exists and prints a message to say whether the file exists.

10

11

THE X WINDOW SYSTEM

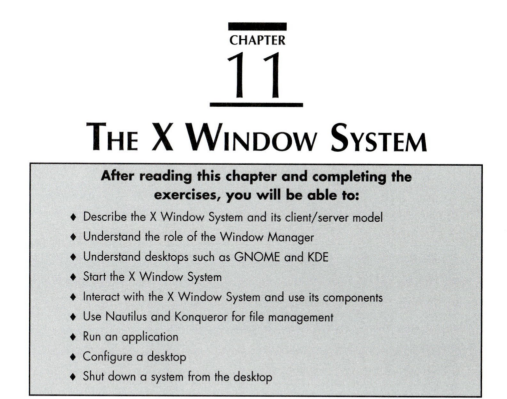

After reading this chapter and completing the exercises, you will be able to:

♦ Describe the X Window System and its client/server model

♦ Understand the role of the Window Manager

♦ Understand desktops such as GNOME and KDE

♦ Start the X Window System

♦ Interact with the X Window System and use its components

♦ Use Nautilus and Konqueror for file management

♦ Run an application

♦ Configure a desktop

♦ Shut down a system from the desktop

So far in this book, you have been working at the UNIX/Linux command line or from a terminal window. UNIX and Linux also offer the ability to use the X Window interface to provide a rich GUI experience for your work. In this chapter, you learn about X Window and about elements that can be used with it, including Window Managers and desktops. You focus on learning the popular GNOME and KDE desktops, including using windows, the Nautilus application in GNOME, Konqueror in KDE, and personalizing your desktop.

WHAT IS THE X WINDOW SYSTEM?

The **X Window System** is a GUI that runs on Linux and many UNIX operating systems. Like Windows and Macintosh operating systems, it provides an easy-to-use, graphical method of operating the computer. Programmers can also develop applications that run on the X Window System and support GUI components, such as windows, dialog boxes, buttons, and pull-down menus. Figure 11-1 shows an X Window screen in Fedora using the GNOME desktop with two windows open at the same time. Figure 11-2 shows an X Window screen in Knoppix using the KDE desktop (you learn about the GNOME and KDE desktops later in this chapter).

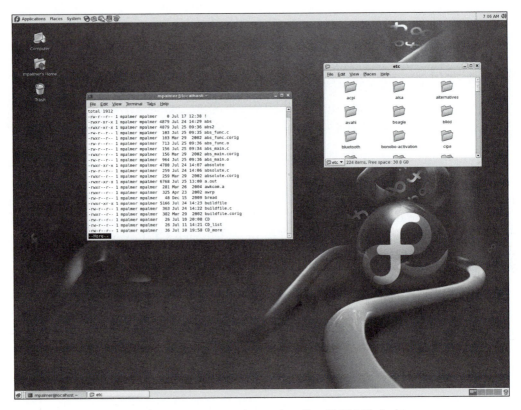

Figure 11-1   An X Window screen in Fedora using the GNOME desktop

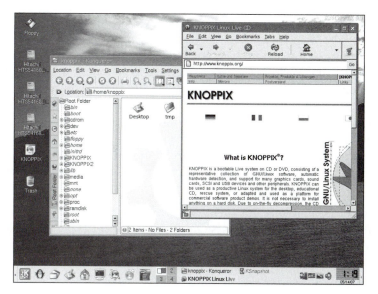

Figure 11-2   An X Window screen in Knoppix using the KDE desktop

11

The X Window System was originally developed at the Massachusetts Institute of Technology (MIT). It was created so different brands of hardware, running different variations of UNIX, would all look and feel the same to the user. It was also designed to run applications across a network consisting of different types of computers. The system developed at MIT, currently in its eleventh version, is appropriately called **X11**. At this writing, seven releases of X11 are available, with the current release called R7.2.0 (X11R7). To find out more about X11, go to the source at *www.x.org*. You can also download the latest version at this Web site.

XFree86 is a free version of X11 that was ported from non–PC-based UNIX computers to run on PCs. XFree86 is compatible with Linux, which is commonly used on PCs. You can learn more about XFree86 and obtain the latest release at *www.xfree86.org*.

NOTE

When you **port** software, you are adapting it from one type of computer or operating system to run on a different computer or operating system. A significant advantage of UNIX/Linux systems is that the operating systems and the associated software are generally adapted to work in nearly the same way when moved from less powerful (Intel-type) computers to more powerful computers (RISC-based or even mainframes), and vice versa. This characteristic is called **scalability**—the ability to port software to more or less powerful machines.

NOTE

Fedora, Red Hat Enterprise Linux, SUSE, and Knoppix are Linux systems that combine features of XFree86 and X11R7.

X Window Clients and Servers

Although you can easily use the X Window System to run programs stored on your local computer, you can also run applications over a network. X Window uses a client/server model in which a program can run on one computer but display its output on another. For example, suppose you have a network with two computers: system A and system B. On system A, you can start and run a program that resides on system B. Although you see the program running in a window on system A, it might actually be executing on system B. This interaction is transparent to you on system A; you might not know the program is actually running on a different computer. In addition, systems A and B can be different types of computers, each running a different variation of UNIX/Linux.

In X Window network terminology, the underlying desktop system from which you run a program is called the **X server**. The system that hosts and executes the program is called the **X client**.

In normal network terminology, the server is the system that hosts a program, and the client is the system that is run by the user. In X Window jargon, the terms client and server mean the opposite. The terms are reversed because the **NOTE** X Window server (on the desktop) performs operations requested by the client (on the host system). For example, the client might request that the server display a window or ask the server to move a window to a different position on the screen.

Two popular X server approaches for Windows-based PCs are X-Win32 and X-Win32 Flash from Starnet Communications. Both of these systems enable a computer running a Windows operating system, such as Windows XP or Vista, to remotely connect to a UNIX/Linux computer. X-Win32 is software that is loaded onto the PC and X-Win32 Flash comes pre-installed on a flash drive that is plugged into a PC's USB port. The Windows PC with this software displays an X Window type of GUI with windows, menus, and other features. Also, the remote connection is handled through SSH for secure communications. You can learn more about X-Win32 and X-Win32 flash at *www.starnet.com*.

Another popular X server system is Exceed from Hummingbird Connectivity. The Exceed X server applications are targeted to enable remote GUI access to UNIX/Linux computers for UNIX/Linux and Windows desktop users. Exceed also includes software for sharing resources between systems using NFS (see Chapter 2, "Exploring the UNIX/Linux File Systems and File Security"). Visit *connectivity.hummingbird.com/home/connectivity.html* to learn more about Exceed.

USING WINDOW MANAGERS

Like the UNIX operating system itself, the X Window System is layered and built from components. At the top layer is the Window Manager. The **Window Manager** controls how windows appear and how users control them. In many respects, the Window Manager is to the X Window System as the shell is to UNIX/Linux: Each provides the user an interface to the underlying components.

Many Window Managers have been developed, and most of them are available for free. Linux supports over 50 different ones. Table 11-1 presents some common Window Managers currently in use.

Table 11-1 Common Window Managers

Window Manager	Description
AnotherLevel	Based on the fvwm Window Manager and often used with some Red Hat versions of Linux
Blackbox	A lightweight or "minimalist" window manager written for speed and intended to manage windows only (no icons or shortcuts)
CDE	Common Desktop Environment, for large and small computers using open systems
Enlightenment	Popular Window Manager sometimes called E; also often used with Fedora and Red Hat versions of Linux
FluxBox	Similar to Blackbox and offers see-through windows, window tabs and title bar configuration options (fully compatible with KDE and partially compatiable with GNOME)
fvwm	Virtual Window Manager, a full featured virtual desktop and window system for X Window
fvwm95	Version of fvwm with a Windows 95 look and feel
gwm	Generic Window Manager (based on the Window Object-Oriented Language [WOOL])
IceWM	Window Manager developed in C++ that is designed for speed and compliance with the GNOME desktop
kwm	Window Manager used by KDE
lwm	Lightweight Window Manager that offers a minimal presence with no icons, no button bars, and that cannot be configured
olwm	Open Look Window Manager, which was orginally on Sun computers, but later Sun switched to mwm, CDE, and GNOME
Metacity	Window Manager developed by Havoc Pennington with Red Hat; used in Red Hat versions and Fedora; integrates well with the GNOME desktop
mwm	Motif Window Manager, used on some commercial UNIX systems including Sun computers
Oroborus	Theme-based Window Manager
sawfish	Window Manager compatible with the LISP programming language, and provides a desktop that has little clutter from icons

11

Table 11-1   Common Window Managers (continued)

Window Manager	Description
twm	Tab Window Manager or Tom's Window Manager
Window Maker	Window Manager that provides support for the GNUstep Desktop Environment

NOTE   Many of the Window Managers shown in Table 11-1 are compatible with the X Window GNOME desktop discussed in the next section. These Window Managers include Enlightenment, IceWM, fvwm, fvwm95, Metacity, Oroborus, sawfish, and Window Maker. Also, three popular "lightweight" window managers are listed: Blackbox, Fluxbox, and lwm. These are for users who want a faster booting and faster running system that uses fewer resources for the GUI by enabling fewer GUI options. To learn more about these and other Window Managers, visit the Web site *www.xwinman.org*.

USING A DESKTOP

When you use the X Window System and a Window Manager in UNIX/Linux, these are also accompanied by a desktop. The **desktop** provides the specific GUI appearance, software applications, and other resources that you use. The desktop works hand-in-hand with a Window Manager. For example, the desktop includes a space on the screen in which to open and use windows. It enables you to create and place icons in your screen's **workspace** from which to start programs or windows, and it can include other features that you can customize to match the way in which you work.

Many desktops can be used on a UNIX/Linux system, but two of the most popular (both come with most Linux systems) are GNOME and KDE.

Using GNOME

The **GNU Network Object Model Environment (GNOME)**, a product of the **GNU Project**, is a desktop environment that is used along with a Window Manager. Fedora and Red Hat Enterprise Linux install GNOME (pronounced "guh-nome") by default. However, Fedora, Red Hat Enterprise Linux, and SUSE all enable you to install either GNOME or KDE.

NOTE   The GNU Project is an organization that focuses on developing a free, UNIX-like operating system named GNU. The Linux kernel is used in many GNU distributions. The project's Web site is *www.gnu.org*. You can learn more about GNOME at *www.gnome.org*.

GNOME is considered by many to be very user-friendly and at this writing enjoys more popularity on UNIX/Linux desktops in the United States than the runner-up, which is KDE. Besides its user-friendly approach, GNOME is popular because many applications are written for it, including file-access applications, office applications, and general utilities.

Using KDE

KDE is another popular desktop that is an alternative to GNOME or that can be installed along with GNOME so that you can use both GNOME and KDE utilities. KDE is more popular internationally than GNOME and offers a broader range of drag-and-drop capabilities. KDE is currently growing in use in the United States.

Like GNOME, KDE is intended to provide UNIX/Linux users with a graphical point-and-click experience that is similar to Microsoft Windows and Mac OS. Both KDE and GNOME are compatible with X11 and with a variety of Window Managers—taking advantage of navigating UNIX/Linux through icons, windows, and other graphical features.

 You can learn more about KDE by going to the KDE organization's Web site at *www.kde.org.*

TIP

Starting the X Window System

11

If your system does not start the X Window System automatically, you can start it by using the *startx* command from the command line.

Syntax **startx** [–options]

Dissection

■ This command starts the X Window System.

■ The specific options and arguments available depend on which version of X Window is installed. At the command line, enter *man startx* or *info startx* to determine the options you can use.

Typically, you would not use *startx* from the terminal window, because use of a terminal window means that a desktop is already started. *startx* is intended for a computer or login session that does not automatically boot into X Window, for example. The general steps for starting the X Window System from a command prompt are as follows:

1. Log in to your account or into the root account.

2. From the command line, type *startx* and press Enter.

Your desktop should look similar to Figure 11-1 or 11-2, but with either a startup window open or no windows opened, instead of the two windows shown.

Configuring Linux to Automatically Start the X Window System

If your system does not automatically start the X Window System, you can configure it to do so. This is accomplished by modifying the following line in the file /etc/inittab:

`id:3:initdefault:`

The number in this line establishes the operating system's default **runlevel**, or mode of operation, at 3. Runlevel 3 is full multiuser mode. To have X Window start automatically, the runlevel should be raised to 5 (*id:5:initdefault:*), as shown in Figure 11-3. Doing so causes the system to start in X11 mode, which automatically starts the X Window System. Table 11-2 lists the runlevels for Linux systems.

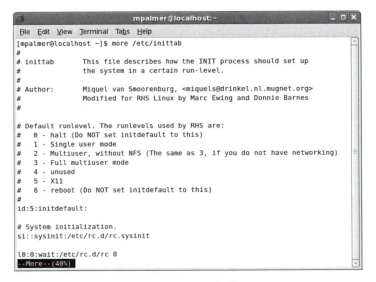

Figure 11-3   Viewing the /etc/inittab file

 NOTE   Configuring your system requires superuser privileges. You must be able to log in as root to change the runlevel. Also, if you opt to change the runlevel, first use the *cp* command to make a backup of the /etc/inittab file before you use an editor to change its contents, such as by entering *cp inittab inittab.bak*.

Hands-On Project 11-1 enables you to view the runlevel setting on your system.

Table 11-2   Runlevels for Linux systems

Runlevel	Explanation
0	Halt (shuts the system down; NEVER use this in the /etc/inittab file)
1	Single-user mode for administrative purposes via the root account
2	Multiuser mode, but network services are not enabled
3	Multiuser mode with network services enabled and nongraphical access
4	Not used

Table 11-2   Runlevels for Linux systems (continued)

Runlevel	Explanation
5	Multiuser mode enabling graphical access via X Window
6	Reboot (shuts the system down and reboots; NEVER use this in the /etc/inittab file)

TIP

On some systems, you can use the *runlevel* command from the root account to determine the current runlevel. Also, you can use the *telinit* command to change the runlevel. Fedora, Red Hat Enterprise Linux, SUSE, and Knoppix all support the *runlevel* and *telinit* commands. In all systems except Knoppix, you must be logged on as root to use the commands.

Now that you know how to start the X Window System, you are ready to learn how to navigate it and control its common components.

INTERACTING WITH THE X WINDOW SYSTEM USING GNOME

11

You interact with the X Window environment through its many components, including the GNOME and KDE desktops. In this section you learn about GNOME and later in the chapter you learn about KDE. Figure 11-4 shows the GNOME desktop, with its major components labeled.

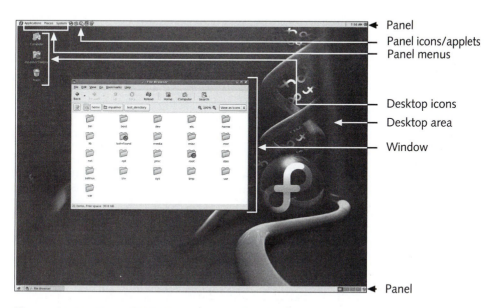

Figure 11-4   Major GNOME components in Fedora

The following list describes the components in Figure 11-4:

- *Icons*—A number of **icons**, or small images, are on the desktop. Each causes an action to take place when activated. You activate an icon by positioning the mouse pointer over it and clicking the left mouse button.

- *Panel*—This component is a strip that runs across the top and bottom of the screen, and includes menus and a number of icons (mainly in the top Panel). For example, in Fedora and Red Hat Enterprise Linux, the top Panel menus include Applications, Places, and System. The Applications menu displays categories of applications that you can access, such as Accessories, Office, and Programming. The Places menu enables you to access local files/directories, the CD/DVD drive, and network servers and resources. There is also a powerful Search option in the Places menu. The System menu has options to manage the system, find help, and log out or shut down. In SUSE there is one bottom panel by default that includes the comprehensive Computer menu from which to access all programs and utilities. Each icon in the Panel invokes an **applet** when activated. An applet is a small application written specifically to be placed on the Panel.

- *Windows*—Every program, application, or applet that runs under the X Window System runs in a window. Windows have many of their own components, which you learn about in this chapter.

- *Desktop area*—This is the background area that holds the windows and icons you are working with during your X Window session.

Now that you can identify the major components of the GNOME screen, you learn to interact with each one in the following sections.

Interacting with Windows

Windows have their own components, as shown in Figure 11-5.

A description of the window components follows:

- *Title bar*—At the top of the window border is a title bar. The title bar lists the name of the window or the application running in the window.

- *Window Menu button*—On the left side of the title bar is the Window Menu button. Click this button to see a menu offering several useful window operations.

- *Minimize Window* (or *Iconify*) *button*—Click this button to collapse the window into a small icon. The icon appears in a section of the Panel in a rectangular box in an area of the Pager called the Window List (the Pager is described later in this chapter). The program in the window is still running, but is hidden from sight.

- *Maximize/Unmaximize Window button*—Click this button to alternately expand the window to fill the screen and reduce the window to its original size.

- *Close Window button*—Click this button to close the window and terminate the application running in it.

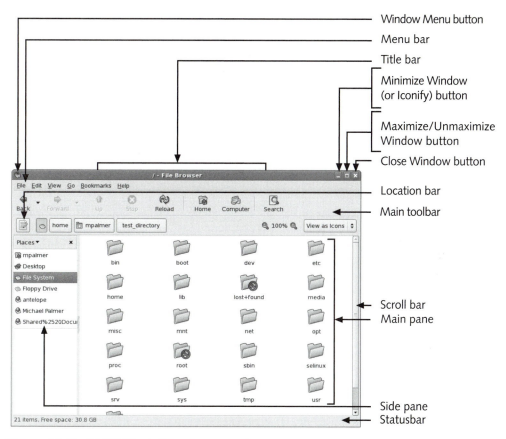

Figure 11-5   GNOME window components

- *Side pane*—This pane contains information about the window, or the window contents currently selected. It might also contain additional options, such as buttons or tabs, depending on what is active in the window. (You can also choose not to display the side pane.)

- *Menu bar*—Under the title bar, you find menu items that are appropriate to the purpose of the window, such as a File menu from which you can open a new window or close the current one. (You can choose not to display the menu bar.)

- *Main toolbar*—Under the menu bar is the main toolbar, which contains buttons for activities appropriate to the window, such as a Back button to go back to the previous window display. In some cases, buttons are deactivated because they do not currently apply. For example, the Forward button is deactivated in Figure 11-5 because there are no recent windows to go forward to.

- *Location bar*—This bar, generally located under the main toolbar, enables you to access a particular location, such as a directory or a URL (address) for a Web site (click the location icon on the far left side of the location bar to see a box in which to enter a URL).

- *Scroll bar*—If a window contains more information than it can display, you see a scroll bar. The scroll bar, which is similar to scroll bars in Microsoft Windows operating systems, lets you scroll through all the window's content.

- *Statusbar*—This bar shows status information related to your current actions, such as the name and size of a file on which you have selected to work or the number of items and free space in the main pane.

- *Main pane or View pane*—This pane shows the main display information. For example, if the window is used to view files, you see the actual files in the Main pane.

Many GNOME window components appear and function exactly like their counterparts in a Windows-based system, such as Windows XP or Vista. If you are already comfortable with one of these systems, you should be comfortable with most window operations in GNOME.

You can configure a window to display or not display any of the following: side pane, main toolbar, location bar, or statusbar. To hide any or a combination of these bars, click the View menu in the menu bar, and select to hide the appropriate bar by removing the check mark near it. Repeat this process until you have made all of your selections.

Now try Hands-On Project 11-2 to practice using these and other features in a GNOME window.

More About the Window Menu Button

The Window Menu button provides several useful capabilities that merit further explanation. When you click the Window Menu button, you see the following options:

- *Minimize*—Makes the screen disappear into the Panel.

- *Maximize/Unmaximize*—Causes the window to expand to the full size of the screen or shrink back to its original size.

- *On Top*—Places the window on top of other open windows (turns on or off).

- *Move*—Enables you to move/drag the window to another location on the desktop.

- *Resize*—Enables you to customize the size of the window by using your mouse to drag in or out the top, bottom, and sides.

- *Close*—Terminates the application and closes the window.

- *Always on Visible Workspace/Only on This Workspace*—Opens the current window to all GNOME workspaces. GNOME enables you to have several workspaces, each appearing as a separate desktop. In this way, if you have too many windows open in one workspace, you can open a window to another workspace, or to all workspaces. When you open a window to another workspace, the desktop is clean, other than the window (or other windows) you have open in that workspace. Fedora and Red Hat Enterprise Linux support four workspaces by default (workspace 1, workspace 2, workspace 3, workspace 4), which is like having four different desktops on which to work. If you think of a desktop as a desk, this means you have four different desks on which to work. When one gets too piled up with work, you can move to another desk that is empty or that has fewer piles. To see what is open in your workspaces, press *Ctrl+Alt* along with the right, left, up, and down arrows to go to different workspaces, or click the box for that workspace in the Panel. Try Hands-On Project 11-3 to use and access workspaces.

- *Move to Workspace Right*—Opens the window to the next workspace on the right (for example, if you are in the first workspace it transfers the window to the second workspace).

- *Move to Workspace Left*—Opens the window to the previous workspace or the workspace on the left (for example, if you are in the second workspace it moves the window to the first workspace, but you won't see this option if you are already in the first workspace).

- *Move to Another Workspace*—Opens the window to any of the other three workspaces you are not currently in, so that if you are in workspace 1 you can open the window to any of the workspaces 2, 3, or 4.

NOTE

The workspaces are shown in the bottom Panel as four side-by-side rectangles. You can also click one of the rectangles to open that workspace. When you click the Window Menu button, the workspace you are currently in is the one that is deactivated in the menu. At this writing, workspaces are not available by default in SUSE Linux, but you can install them.

Hands-On Projects 11-2 and 11-3 enable you to use the Window Menu button.

Interacting with the Panel

The **Panel** in Fedora and Red Hat Enterprise Linux appears, by default, at the top of the desktop and another Panel is at the bottom. The top Panel contains menus and icons on the left side. It also has a clock and a volume control icon (if your system has speakers) on the right side (see Figure 11-6). The bottom Panel contains a button on the left side to hide all windows and on the right side it contains access to the four workspaces you learned about in the last section (if you haven't tried Hands-On Project 11-3 yet, do the project now to learn how to use the workspaces from the bottom Panel).

Applications Places System	12:18 PM

Figure 11-6   The GNOME top Panel in Fedora

The Applications menu is a good starting place to access software that you can run on your system. When you access the Applications menu, you see submenus and programs that you can open. Submenus are indicated by a right-pointing arrow. Some examples of submenus include: Accessories, Games, Internet, Office, Programming, Sound & Video, and System Tools. To view the contents of a submenu, click the Applications menu on the Panel, and then point to the submenu. Try Hands-On Project 11-4 to use the Applications menu and open submenus.

To the right of the Applications menu is the Places menu. The Places menu has options to:

- Open your home folder
- Access items on the desktop
- Open storage devices and file systems on the computer
- Create a CD/DVD
- Access network servers and resources
- Perform a fast search for a specific item
- Access recently opened documents

The System menu is to the right of the Places menu and contains the following options:

- A submenu for setting preferences on the computer
- A submenu for administering the computer
- An option to obtain help
- A option to find out about GNOME
- An option to learn more about the operating system
- An option to lock the screen when you temporarily leave the computer
- An option to log off the currently open account
- An option to suspend the computer's operation
- An option to shutdown the computer (if the account has this authority)

Icons that might typically appear to the right of the menus in the Panel include the following:

- A globe with a mouse wrapped around it to open the Mozilla Firefox Web browser.
- A stamp and letter to launch Evolution Email.
- A pen and paper to start OpenOffice.org Writer, a word processor, which is part of the OpenOffice.org suite of office programs.
- A slide and bar chart of different colors from which to start OpenOffice.org Impress to create slide presentations.
- A spreadsheet and circle chart to start OpenOffice.org Calc for creating spreadsheets.
- Various other icons depending on your particular system, including a clock on the right-most side of the top Panel.

TIP You can determine the nature of an icon on the top or bottom Panel (other than the rectangles representing workspaces) by pointing to it and reading the brief explanation or screentip. Also, the icons in your Panel will depend on the system you are using, so you might see different icons.

Using Nautilus

GNOME offers a powerful file management tool called **Nautilus** (or Nautilus File Manager) that enables you to manage files and folders. Through Nautilus, you can:

- View files and folders.
- Create new folders.
- Delete and move files and folders.
- Copy and paste files and folders.
- Configure permissions.
- Open a file or start a program.
- Access the Internet.
- Set a bookmark to return to a specific file, folder, or Internet location.

One of the easiest ways to start Nautilus is to double-click the desktop icon for your home directory, which is labeled with your user name plus the word Home, for example, *mpalmer's Home*. Figure 11-7 shows the opened Nautilus window with minimal toolbars. Another way to open Nautilus into your home directory in a full-featured file browser mode is to click Applications, point to System Tools, and click File Browser.

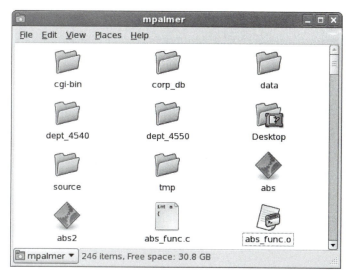

Figure 11-7   Using Nautilus

Try Hands-On Projects 11-5, 11-6, and 11-7 to use Nautilus File Browser.

CONFIGURING THE DESKTOP

You can customize many aspects of the X Window System. In this section, you learn to personalize your desktop environment by changing the background image and specifying a screensaver. Then, you learn to configure the items on the Panel and add new applets to it. Finally, you learn to add a new Panel to you desktop.

Changing the Background

The background is the desktop area behind all windows and icons. You can change the color of the desktop or specify a graphic image, called wallpaper, to be used as a background. Changing the desktop background in GNOME simply involves right-clicking a blank area in the desktop and then selecting Change Desktop Background. GNOME offers many picture files from which to select for the background, or you can use your own picture file (typically, the picture files are in .png format).

Try Hands-On Project 11-8 to change the desktop background.

Changing the Screensaver

You can use the X Window screensaver to deter unauthorized use of a server or workstation by requiring a password. When the screensaver is active and locked, it does not deactivate until the user enters a login password. If you have access to sensitive information, you should strongly consider implementing a screensaver and activating the screensaver lock feature. For example, to configure a screensaver in Fedora and Red Hat Enterprise Linux, click the System menu, point to Preferences, and click Screensaver. In SUSE click the Computer menu, click Control Center, and click Screensaver. Use Hands-On Project 11-9 to configure a screensaver for your system.

Configuring the Panel

You can configure almost every aspect of the GNOME Panel. For example, you might want to add an icon or applet to the Panel from which to run a program, or you might decide to rearrange the placement of icons on the Panel to better match the way you work. You can even add programs you have written to start them from the Panel.

In another example, you can move the Panel so that it is located at the top of the desktop or on the side. The following are general steps for moving the location of the top Panel in Fedora and Red Hat Enterprise Linux, or the bottom panel in SUSE:

1. Move your pointer into a blank area of the Panel.

2. In Fedora and Red Hat Enterprise Linux click and hold down the mouse button while you drag the top Panel to the right side of the desktop and then release the mouse button (see Figure 11-8). In SUSE, right-click a blank area in the bottom Panel and ensure Allow Panel to be Moved appears in the menu, and if it does not appear click Lock Panel Position to change the movement setting. Drag the bottom Panel to the right side of the desktop. This action locates the Panel on the right side of the desktop. Another option is to drag a Panel to a different location, such as to the left side of the desktop.

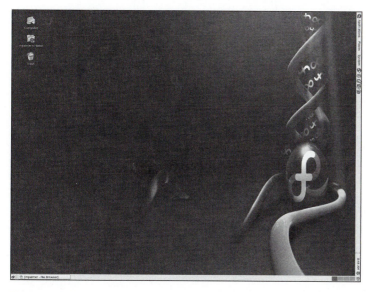

Figure 11-8   Changing the location of the top Panel in Fedora

Try Hands-On Projects 11-10, 11-11, and 11-12 to configure the Panel.

Adding a Menu to the Panel

There might be a menu within the Applications menu (in Fedora and Red Hat Enterprise Linux) or Computer menu (in SUSE) that you want to add directly to the Panel so you can access that menu without first opening the Applications or Computer menu. For example, if you frequently use the OpenOffice.org applications, you can put the Office menu on the Panel. Try Hands-On Project 11-13 to place a menu on the Panel.

Adding a New Panel

You can create a new Panel in addition to having one or more Panels already in place. This capability enables you to further customize your desktop for the way you prefer to work. For example, you might have default Panels located at the top and bottom of the desktop with the default icons and applets, and you might add a new Panel to the right side of the desktop containing icons to launch specific programs you run frequently. The general steps for adding a new Panel are as follows:

1. Right-click an open space on an existing Panel.

2. Click New Panel.

3. If you want to change the location of the new Panel, click and drag it to the new location, such as to the right side of the desktop.

4. Right-click the new Panel, click Add to Panel, and select what you want to place on the Panel, such as by double-clicking Application Launcher to add an icon from which to open a specific program.

SHUTTING DOWN FROM THE GNOME DESKTOP

When you use the GNOME desktop, proper shutdown is important to ensure that all files are closed and to protect the integrity of file systems. For example, in Fedora and Red Hat Enterprise Linux, click the System menu and click Shut Down to properly shut down your computer. In SUSE, click the Computer menu, click Log Out, and click Shut down. Try Hands-On Project 11-14 to learn about logging out and shutting down your system.

On some UNIX/Linux systems, you also have an option to press Ctrl+Alt+Del to shut down.

NOTE

INTERACTING WITH THE X WINDOW SYSTEM USING KDE

KDE is another desktop that enjoys wide use with X Window. Like GNOME, KDE provides access to your computer's resources through a GUI that includes menus, icons, desktop workspace, and drag-and-drop features. The specific look and feel of KDE may be a little different from GNOME, but what you can accomplish with the KDE desktop is very similar. KDE typically comes with more free or open-source software including utilities, multimedia, graphics, and other open source software (you learn about open source software later in this chapter.) Figure 11-9 illustrates the KDE desktop on Knoppix Linux.

Here are the descriptions of the components in Figure 11-9:

- *Icons*—Similar to GNOME, KDE uses a number of icons on the desktop. Each icon actives a program or opens a window. Move your cursor over any icon to see a small help box that names the icon and provides a brief description of its purpose.

- *Kicker*—In KDE, there is a **Kicker** that provides similar functions to the Panel in GNOME. By default the Kicker appears across the bottom of the desktop. The Kicker contains icons that invoke applets or applications.

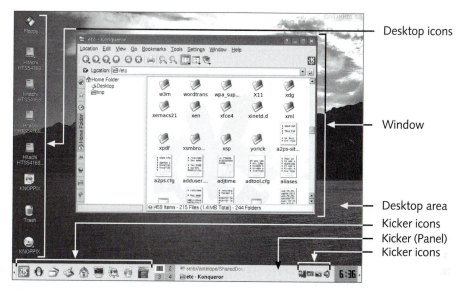

- Desktop icons
- Window
- Desktop area
- Kicker icons
- Kicker (Panel)
- Kicker icons

Figure 11-9   Major KDE components

11

- *Windows*—Programs, applications, and applets run under X Window via a window. One of the most commonly used windows is the Konqueror which is a file and Internet browser.

- *Desktop area*—This is the background area on the desktop in which you can customize your own wallpaper (background scene), access and place icons, open windows, and perform work and entertainment activities.

Try Hands-On Project 11-15 for an introduction to the KDE desktop.

Interacting with Konqueror

Much of the work in KDE is accomplished through **Konqueror**, which provides similar functions for KDE as Nautilus does for GNOME. Konqueror is a combined file manager, Web browser, and document viewer. To supplement these functions, you can use **Konqueror I/O (KIO) plugins**, which add new functionality to the native capabilities of Konqueror. For example, there is a KIO plugin to access zipped (compressed) files and another KIO plugin to view the contents of an audio CD. There are network KIO plugins for transferring files and viewing shared Windows folders via Samba (you learned about Samba in Chapter 8, "Exploring the UNIX/Linux Utilities").

Figure 11-10 shows an example Konqueror window with the components labeled.

A description of the Konqueror window components includes:

- *Title bar*—At the top of the window border is a title bar. In Konqueror, the title bar shows the application name (Konqueror) and what it is viewing, such as the /etc directory as shown in Figure 11-10.

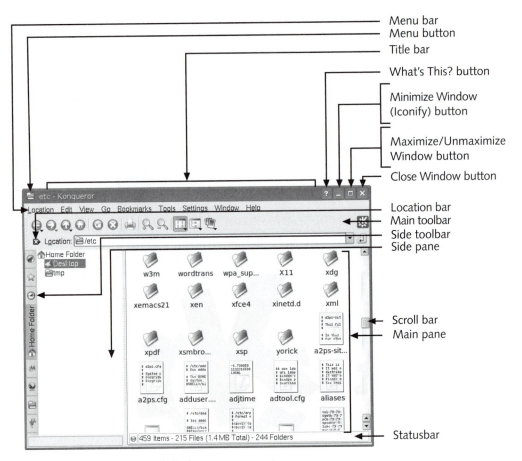

Figure 11-10   Konqueror Window components

- *Menu button*—On the left side of the title bar is the Menu button, which looks like an open folder. This button enables you to relocate Konqueror to another part of the desktop; to have the window show on top of other windows; to move the Konqueror window to any of the four desktops in KDE; to maximize, minimize, or resize the window; to shade the window; and to configure other aspects of the window's behavior.

- *Minimize Window* (or *Iconify*) *button*—Click this button to collapse the window into a small icon. The icon appears in the Kicker at the bottom of the desktop. The program in the window is still running, but is hidden from sight.

- *Maximize/Unmaximize Window button*—Click this button to alternately expand the window to fill the screen and reduce the window to its original size.

- *Close Window button*—Click this button to close the window and terminate the application running in it.

- *What's This? Button*—Click this button and then move the cursor to an icon or function in the Konqueror window to see a short description of its purpose.

- *Side pane*—This pane contains information that is determined by which icon is currently selected in the side toolbar.

- *Side toolbar*—This toolbar contains icons that set up the display of information in the side pane. For example, if you click the Home Folder icon (the default) you view the home folder contents (as in Figure 11-10) in the side pane. If you click the Root Folder icon, you see the contents of the root folder in the side pane. When you click the Bookmark icon, the side pane shows locations you have bookmarked to come back to in Konqueror.

- *Menu bar*—Under the title bar, you find menu items in the menu bar that are appropriate to the purpose of the window, such as a Location menu from which you can open a new window or open a particular directory or file.

- *Main toolbar*—Under the menu bar is the main toolbar, which contains buttons for activities appropriate to the window, such as a Back button to go back to the previous window display. In some cases, buttons are deactivated because they do not currently apply.

- *Location bar*—Found under the main toolbar, the location bar enables you to access a particular location, such as a directory or a URL (address) for a Web site. When you click the down arrow on the location bar, you can view other locations you have recently visited.

- *Scroll bar*—When a window contains more information than it can display, you see a scroll bar so you can scroll up or down through that information.

- *Status bar*—This bar shows status information related to your current actions, such as the number of files and folders within a folder and their total size.

- *Main pane*—This pane shows the main display information. For example, if the window is used to view files in a folder, you see the files in the main pane. Depending on what you are doing currently, you may also see the contents of a Web site or the text in a document file.

In Hands-On Project 11-16, you explore Konqueror in KDE.

You can learn more about Konqueror through the Web site: *www. konqueror.org.*

NOTE

Interacting with Kicker

Kicker is similar to the Panel in GNOME and the Taskbar in Microsoft Windows. On most Linux distributions with X Window and the KDE desktop, Kicker is at the bottom of the desktop and appears as shown in Figure 11-11.

NOTE
Kicker and Panel are sometimes used interchangeably in KDE, but in this chapter Kicker is used for consistency with other KDE utilities that begin with the letter "K."

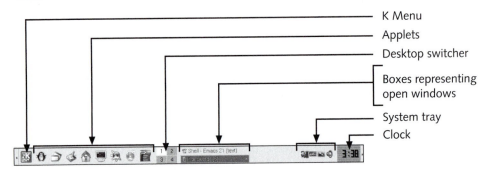

K Menu

Applets

Desktop switcher

Boxes representing open windows

System tray

Clock

Figure 11-11 Kicker in the Knoppix KDE desktop

Within Kicker are the following elements:

- *K Menu*—The primary default menu on the KDE desktop and provides comprehensive access to applications, submenus that list multiple applications, and actions, such as opening a Run Command box to issue a command. (Hands-On Project 11-15 enables you to use K Menu.)

- *Applets*—To the right of the K Menu are applets to start commonly used programs such as a listing of open windows, access to the home folder, the Konsole terminal window, Konqueror, and OpenOffice.org office applications.

- *Desktop switcher*—Next to the applets is the desktop switcher that consists of four squares representing the four desktops you can use within KDE. If Desktop 1 is full of open windows, click the Desktop 2, 3, or 4 square to switch to a desktop that is not crowded with open windows. Four desktops is the default, but you can configure fewer or more desktops.

- *Boxes representing started windows*—A started window is represented in Kicker within a box labeled for that open window. If the box's label is bold, that means the window is viewable on the desktop and if the label is not bold, the window is minimized into Kicker and not viewable on the desktop.

- *System tray*—This is an area in Kicker that contains small icons for opening key utilities, such as a utility to adjust display parameters and another to control the volume on speakers.

- *Clock*—The right-most area in Kicker displays a digital clock by default.

You can customize Kicker in several ways. For example, you can drag Kicker so that it appears on the right or left side of the desktop or on the top. You have the option to add or remove applets to Kicker to match the way your work. You can add additional Kicker panels to the desktop, so you have a Kicker at the top and the bottom, for example.

In Hands-On Project 11-17 you learn how to use and customize Kicker.

Configuring the KDE Desktop

As is true in X Window with GNOME, you can customize the KDE desktop in X Window. In the next sections you learn how to change the desktop background, the screensaver, and how to create additional desktops beyond the four already set up by default.

Changing the Background in KDE

Linux distributions with KDE often come with several desktop background selections that are well worth exploring for their diversity. You can change the background by right-clicking in an unused portion of the desktop and clicking Configure Desktop. This action starts the Configure – KDesktop utility as shown in Figure 11-12. Click Background selection in the side pane (which is the default). To view the wallpaper options for your desktop, click the down arrow in the Picture box or click the Get New Wallpapers button (for more wallpaper that you can download from the Internet).

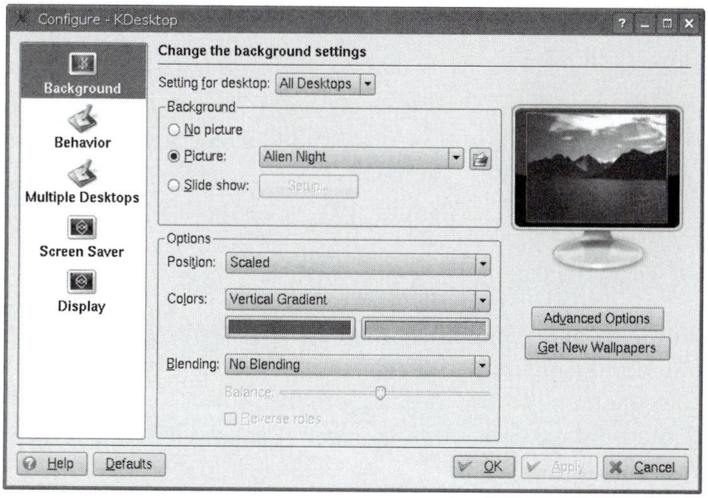

Figure 11-12   Using the Configure – KDesktop utility

Configuring the Screensaver

As you learned earlier in this chapter, configuring a screensaver is a first line of defense for protecting your computer from an intruder. Also, KDE offers a huge selection of interesting screen savers that are fun to check out. By using the Configure – KDesktop utility you can choose a screensaver that matches your tastes and set it up so that it requires a password after it starts. Use the Screen Saver option to set up your screensaver preferences.

Configuring Additional Desktops

KDE is set by default to enable four desktops that you can access through Kicker. However, you can configure fewer than four desktops or up to 20 different desktops, depending on how you use your computer. The number of desktops is configured from the Configure − KDesktop utility by clicking Multiple Desktops in the side pane. Having multiple desktops can truly make you more productive and is worth investigating.

Try Hands-On Project 11-18 to use the Configure − KDesktop utility to set up your background, screensaver, and number of desktops.

Shutting Down from the KDE Desktop

Proper shutdown of the KDE desktop is as important as properly shutting down GNOME. This ensures that all of your open program and system files are properly closed and kept intact. The general steps for logging off your account or shutting down the system (if you have authority to shut down) are as follows:

1. Click the K Menu.
2. Click Log Out.
3. To log out of your current session click End Current Session, or to shut down the computer click Turn Off Computer.

OPENOFFICE.ORG AND OPEN SOURCE SOFTWARE

OpenOffice.org is a suite of office productivity software with applications similar to those in Microsoft Office. An important difference is that OpenOffice.org is **open source software**, which means it's free to the user, and any user can join the project to work on new features. Users can download the latest versions from *www.openoffice.org*. They can also make copies and give them to others at no charge.

There is a very large body of open source software available for UNIX/Linux systems. To learn about the open-source initiative visit *www.opensource.org*. Also, a good starting point to obtain open-source software is *www.gnu.org*.

The suite of applications in OpenOffice.org are developed by hundreds of project members all over the world. Members of the OpenOffice.org project contribute in all kinds of ways from making code more efficient, to adding new features, to creating patches, to marketing the end product. As a grassroots project, this office suite is continuously evolving through the efforts of users to meet the needs of users.

Many UNIX and Linux distributions come with the OpenOffice.org suite, including Fedora, Red Hat Enterprise Linux (with commercial modifications), SUSE, and Knoppix.

OpenOffice.org is also available for Windows and Mac OS systems. In general you can transport files between OpenOffice.org and Microsoft Office programs by saving the files with the appropriate extensions, such as saving an OpenOffice document with the .doc extension for use with Microsoft Word. OpenOffice.org comes with tools or wizards to provide step-by-step guidance through a particular process, for example creating a letter or setting up a spreadsheet or database.

The program elements of OpenOffice.org include:

- *Writer*—A complete word processor for writing short or book-length documents.

- *Calc*—A spreadsheet program for managing numbers and data.

- *Impress*—A program for creating presentations including slide shows, drawings, outlines, handouts and others; and also includes diagramming tools, animation capabilities, and 3D effects.

- *Draw*—A drawing package for creating graphics and diagrams that supports 3D graphics and multiple formatting techniques.

- *Math*—A mathematical equation tool used to set up and solve mathematical equations.

- *Base*—A tool for creating and maintaining databases so that you can generate tables, indexes, and queries and reports, and perform other functions typically available in robust database software.

11

CHAPTER SUMMARY

- ❑ The X Window System is a graphical user interface, or GUI, that runs on many UNIX and Linux systems. It allows users to run applications transparently across a network.

- ❑ The X Window System is built in layers. The top layer, with which the user interacts, is called the Window Manager.

- ❑ Use the *startx* command at the command line to start the X Window System. A line can be added in the /etc/inittab file to direct Linux to start the X Window System automatically.

- ❑ The GNOME environment consists of icons, Panels, windows, and the desktop area.

- ❑ You resize, move, minimize, maximize, and close a window by interacting with its border, title bar, and buttons.

- ❑ The GNOME Panel provides access to menus, icons, Workspace Switcher (to access workspaces), and other utilities.

- ❑ Nautilus in GNOME is a graphical application for managing your directories and files and for navigating the file system.

- ❑ Your desktop background can be customized to include a picture or to display a particular color.

❑ Configuring a desktop screensaver gives you privacy and security when you leave your computer.

❑ You can customize the Panel by adding and moving applet icons. You can even add icons that launch your own programs.

❑ If you frequently use a specific GNOME menu, such as one to start office software, you can place that menu on the Panel to save steps, rather than accessing it through the Applications or Computer menus in systems using GNOME.

❑ KDE is another popular desktop similar in functionality to GNOME.

❑ The major KDE components include icons, the Kicker, windows, and a desktop area on which to work.

❑ The KDE Kicker is similar to the Panel in GNOME and includes K Menu, applets, Desktop Switcher, boxes for started windows, system tray, and a clock (the default setup). You can customize Kicker in ways similar to the Panel in GNOME.

❑ In KDE the application for managing files and folders is Konqueror.

❑ KDE enables you to customize the desktop background, screen saver, and other features.

COMMAND SUMMARY: REVIEW OF CHAPTER 11 COMMANDS

Command	Purpose
startx	Starts the X Window System graphical interface

KEY TERMS

applet — Usually a program or small software application that is represented by an icon. In the X Window GNOME and KDE desktops, an applet can be placed on the Panel or the Kicker for fast access.

desktop — The overall screen display and software that provides the specific GUI appearance and includes software applications and other resources for a UNIX/Linux system that has X Window installed, and works hand in hand with a Window Manager.

GNU Network Object Model Environment (GNOME) — A desktop environment produced by the GNU Project and that must be used with a Window Manager.

GNU Project — An organization created to develop a free, UNIX-like operating system named GNU.

icon — A small graphic symbol in a GUI that represents a program or an action that can be started by clicking or double-clicking the symbol.

KDE — A popular desktop environment for X Window that must be used with a Window Manager.

Kicker — A bar appearing on the KDE desktop that contains icons, applets, menus, and other elements that can be used to start programs or display windows in KDE. *Also see* Panel.

Konqueror — An application that opens into a window and enables the user to manage files, browse the network and Internet, and view documents.

Konqueror I/O (KIO) plugins — Programs and utilities that add new functionality to the native capabilities of the Konqueror browser and file manager.

Nautilus — An application that opens into a window and is used to manage files and folders. Also called Nautilus File Manager.

open source software — Software and accompanying source code that is available to the general public free of charge.

Panel — A bar in the the GNOME desktop that contains icons and applets for opening menus or applications. *Also see* Kicker.

port — The process of adapting software so that it can be moved from one type of computer or operating system to another.

runlevel — The level of function at which a UNIX/Linux system is running. On Linux systems, runlevels go from 0 to 6. Also called a system state or mode.

scalability — The capability for a computer operating system to be used on smaller computers, such as those with a single Intel-type processor, and on larger computers, such as those with 64-bit or RISC processors or even mainframes.

Window Manager — The top layer of the X Window System and the user's interface to the system's components. It controls how windows appear and how users control them.

workspace — An area on the desktop in which you can place icons, open windows, and add Panels or Kickers. Desktops such as GNOME and KDE offer four virtual workspaces by default and enable you to switch from one to another using the Workspace Switcher.

X client — In X Window network terminology, the system that hosts and executes a program.

X server — In X Window network terminology, the desktop system from which the user runs a program.

X Window System — A GUI that runs on Linux and many UNIX operating systems.

X11 — The eleventh version of the X Window System.

XFree86 — A version of X11 that was ported to the PC and on Linux.

11

REVIEW QUESTIONS

1. Your department is developing its own set of marketing applications. In a meeting, a member of the department asks whether a menu can be set up in the GNOME desktop for easy access to the new applications. What is your response?

   a. A menu can be set up and launched from a Panel in GNOME.

   b. A menu can be set up only through use of third-party software called CUSTOMIZE.

   c. Menus are run by default from the Start menu on the bottom Panel.

   d. GNOME does not support the setup of custom menus and so you recommend using KDE, which does.

2. Once in a while after your system has been improperly shut down, such as during a power outage, it reboots into the command line. After you log in, what command can you use to start X Window and your desktop?

   a. *gui*

   b. *xwin*

   c. *startx*

   d. *run gui*

3. You want to delete several old files in your home directory. Which of the following is a good tool to use for this purpose in GNOME?

   a. Nautilus

   b. System Tray

   c. My Computer

   d. GNUFile

4. Which of the following is a good tool to use for finding and deleting files in KDE? (Choose all that apply.)

   a. KFiler

   b. Kabinet

   c. Knop

   d. Konqueror

5. Which of the following are Window Managers that can be used with X Window? (Choose all that apply.)

   a. fvwm

   b. sawfish

   c. kwm

   d. Window Maker

6. A new inventory specialist in your company inherited a computer that has KDE installed, but the operating system boots into the command line instead of starting KDE automatically. What can the inventory specialist do to have her computer go into KDE automatically at startup?

   a. Press Ctrl+g while the system is booting.

   b. Press Alt+g while the system is booting.

   c. Change the .bashrc file to contain the ./KDE command.

   d. Edit the /etc/inittab file to have the line *id:5:initdefault:*.

7. Which of the following would you find in the Kicker in KDE by default? (Choose all that apply.)

   a. applets

   b. system monitor button

   c. network connect launcher

   d. K Menu

8. The colleague at the desk next to you has the habit of turning the power off on his computer at the end of the day by turning off the power strip—even though he has windows still open on his computer's desktop. Which of the following is a better way to shut down the computer?

   a. Press Ctrl+Del.

   b. Use a menu option in GNOME or KDE to shut down the computer.

   c. Open a terminal window and enter *stopGNOME* or *stopKDE* to properly shut down windows and files.

   d. Open a terminal window and enter *stopit!*.

9. Sometimes when you walk away from your desk and come back you find your work associate from a nearby cubicle using the Internet on your computer, because he says your connection is faster. How can you best protect your computer from this type of intrusion?

   a. Use the Panel's *postit* program to display the note, Please do not use my computer while I'm away.

   b. Set up a screensaver and have it lock your computer when it is activated.

   c. Turn off your monitor when you get up, but leave the CPU on.

   d. Set the Panel or Kicker to hide mode.

10. In which locations can you have a Panel in GNOME? (Choose all that apply.)

    a. at the top of the desktop

    b. at the bottom of the desktop

    c. on the left side of the desktop

    d. on the right side of the desktop

11. You currently have four open windows in KDE and are out of space on your desktop. Because you are feverishly working on a project, you need to leave all four windows open and start three new windows to access other data and programs. What can you do to make your work easier?

    a. Use the link option to link another computer to yours.

    b. You have no choice; you must keep the maximum open windows to four in KDE, so you have to delay opening a new window until you are finished with one that is currently open.

    c. Open the new windows on another desktop.

    d. Invoke the window switcher to tile your windows for easer viewing.

12. When you have the default GNOME desktop set up, how can you quickly access the contents of your home directory?

    a. Double-click a blank area on the Panel.

    b. Double-click a blank spot in the desktop area.

    c. Right-click the Applications or Computer menu.

    d. Double-click the icon that is labeled with your account name and the word Home.

13. You want to use a more lively desktop background than the one installed by default via KDE. How can you set up a new desktop background?

    a. Click the Kicker in a blank area and click Change Background.

    b. Right-click an open spot in your current desktop background and click Configure Desktop.

    c. Open a terminal window and enter the *desk* command plus the name of the file you want to use for the background, such as *zingers.png*.

    d. Click the background and drag it into the trash, which causes the Background Configure tool to start so you can choose a new desktop.

14. Which of the following are options available from the Windows Menu button in a GNOME window? (Choose all that apply.)

    a. Minimize

    b. Move

    c. Calibrate

    d. Place as applet in Panel

15. Another name for the X Window system is _____.

    a. Win

    b. GNUWin

    c. Sysw.1

    d. X11

16. When you run X Window over the network for the purpose of running applications on a remote computer, you use which of the following essential elements? (Choose all that apply.)

    a. Net Logon

    b. Port software

    c. X client

    d. X server

17. Your new colleague is tuning the performance of her computer and is planning to set the runlevel to 6 to speed it up. What is your advice?

    a. A runlevel of 6 is too slow because it should be at a minimum of 8.

    b. The runlevel affects only the speed of displaying windows. She should instead set the CPU level to 6 for better performance.

    c. The runlevel should never be set to 6.

    d. 6 is the ideal setting for the runlevel.

18. A new user in your organization is just starting to use Linux with the GNOME desktop. She has opened a window, but is unsure of how to close it. What should she do?

    a. Press Ctrl+e.

    b. Click the Close Window button.

    c. Drag the window off of the desktop.

    d. Right-click the window and click End on the shortcut menu.

19. Which of the following enables you to access a Web page from KDE?

    a. Konqueror

    b. KWeb

    c. Knop

    d. Web Explorer

20. A Window Manager does which of the following? (Choose all that apply.)

    a. controls how windows appear in the X Window system

    b. limits the number of open windows to four because of memory constraints in X Window

    c. is the top layer of the X Window system

    d. establishes how users control windows in the X Window system

21. Which of the following would you find in the title bar of a window in GNOME? (Choose all that apply.)

    a. file launcher icon

    b. maximize/unmaximize window button

    c. application menu button

    d. home folder access button

22. What is open source software?

23. What version of X Window has been ported to PC-based UNIX and Linux computers?

24. What is the purpose of an applet?

25. Name a file manager in either GNOME or KDE and suggest five things you can accomplish with it.

HANDS-ON PROJECTS

Project 11-1

If your system does not automatically boot into X Window, check the /etc/inittab file. In this project, you view the /etc/inittab file to determine the current setting for system initialization. For this project, you need to access the command line, such as by using a terminal window from your own account.

To view the contents of /etc/inittab:

1. Type **more /etc/inittab** and press **Enter**. What is the number in the *id:x:initdefault:* line (where *x* represents the number)? To start X Window, the number should be *5*. If your system does not start X Window, the number is likely to be *3* (for multiuser). Notice the documentation about the runlevels that can be set up for your system.

2. Type **q** to exit the *more* command.

3. If necessary, close the terminal window.

Hands-On Projects 2-14 all require that you have the GNOME desktop installed and started. Also, use your own account from which to complete the projects.

NOTE

Project 11-2

In this project, you work with an open window in GNOME. You begin by resizing a window. Next, you practice moving and then placing a window on top. In the third set of steps, you practice opening a pop-up Help menu. Finally, you practice minimizing, maximizing, and closing a window.

To practice resizing a window:

1. In Fedora or Red Hat Enterprise Linux, click **Applications**, point to **System Tools**, and click **File Browser**. (This opens the Nautilus File Browser in GNOME.) In SUSE double-click the folder on the desktop labeled with your account name and the word Home, such as *mpalmer's Home*.

2. Move the mouse pointer to the right edge of the window border. The pointer becomes a horizontal, double-headed arrow. Click and hold the left mouse button while dragging the mouse pointer to the right. You see the window expand horizontally. Drag the mouse pointer back to the left, and the window shrinks horizontally. Release the mouse button to stop resizing the window.

3. Move the mouse pointer to the bottom edge of the window. The pointer becomes a vertical, double-headed arrow. Click and hold the left mouse button as you move the pointer, first up and then down. The window expands and shrinks vertically.

4. Move the mouse pointer to the lower-right corner of the window. The pointer becomes a slanted, double-headed arrow. Click and hold the left mouse button while dragging the mouse pointer toward the lower-right corner of the screen. The window expands both horizontally and vertically. Drag the pointer back toward the upper-left corner of the screen, and the window shrinks horizontally and vertically.

5. Release the mouse button to stop resizing the window. Leave the window open for the next set of steps.

Other basic window operations include moving or placing the window on top of all other windows.

To practice moving a window or placing it on top:

1. Move the mouse pointer to the window's title bar.

2. Click and hold the left mouse button as you drag the mouse pointer across the screen. The window moves to follow the mouse pointer.

3. Release the mouse button to stop moving the window.

4. Click the **Window Menu** button in the upper-left corner of the window and click **Move**. Do not press a mouse button. Move the cursor and notice that the window moves with it. Click the left mouse button to stop movement of the window.

5. Click the **Window Menu** button in the uppermost left corner of the window in the title bar. Click **On Top**.

6. Click **Applications**, point to **Accessories**, and click **Terminal** (or open another window of your choice).

7. Try moving the window you opened over the File Browser window. Notice that the File Browser window always stays on top.

8. Click the **Window Menu** button in the File Browser window and click **On Top** (to turn off this option). Now click and drag the other open window over the File Browser window. Notice that the other window is now on top. Close the other window (such as the terminal window).

Some window components offer context-sensitive, pop-up Help boxes or screentips. These are useful for discovering the purpose of a button or another component.

To practice using the pop-up Help boxes:

1. Position the mouse pointer on the window's toolbar.

2. Move the pointer to a button that is activated (has regular print instead of lighter print), such as the **Home** or **Computer** button.

3. After a brief moment, a screentip describing the purpose of that button pops up.

4. Perform this action with other active buttons on the window, and discover their use.

11

By now, you have probably realized that pointing to an object on the screen and clicking the left mouse button carries out most operations. From this point forward, this action is called "clicking." Actions that require you to click the right mouse button are called "right-clicking."

TIP

The Minimize Window, Maximize/Unmaximize Window, and Close Window buttons are at the upper-right corner of the window. In this project, you use these to adjust the window's size and to terminate the window's application.

Refer to Figure 11-5 to review each button's location.

TIP

To practice using the Minimize Window, Maximize/Unmaximize Window, and Close Window buttons:

1. Click the **Minimize Window** button. The window disappears from the desktop.

2. The File Browser window is still running, however. Look at the Panel located at the bottom of the screen. You'll see a button in the Panel with File Browser (preceded by the name of the folder or device you are accessing, such as your home folder's name).

3. Click the button in the bottom Panel, such as **[mpalmer – File Browser]**. You see the window reappear.

4. Click the **Maximize Window** button. The window expands to fill the entire screen.

5. Click the **Unmaximize Window** button. The window shrinks back to its previous size.

6. Click the **Close Window** button. The application terminates, and its window disappears from the screen.

HANDS-ON PROJECTS

Project 11-3

Using workspaces is like having multiple desktops. If one desktop is cluttered, you can go to a different workspace to use a desktop that is not as cluttered. In this project, you learn how to use different workspaces in GNOME (workspaces are used in Fedora and Red Hat Enterprise Linux, but not by default in SUSE, thus the following steps exclude SUSE).

To practice using multiple workspaces:

1. Click **Applications**, point to **System Tools**, and click **File Browser**.

2. Click the **Window Menu** button in the upper-left corner of the window.

3. Click **Move to Workspace Right**. Notice that the window disappears because it is now in Workspace 2 and you are currently in Workspace 1.

4. Double-click the **Trash** icon on the desktop.

5. Click the **Window Menu** button.

6. Point to **Move to Another Workspace** and click **Workspace 4**.

7. Notice the four rectangles on the right side of the bottom Panel (see Figure 11-13). This is called the Workspace Switcher. The left-most rectangle is highlighted because it represents the currently active workspace, which is workspace 1.

Workspaces

Figure 11-13   Workspaces shown on the bottom Panel

8. In the Workspace Switcher, click the rectangle for Workspace 2 (the second rectangle from the left). You are now in Workspace 2 and you see the File Browser window. Also, notice in the Panel that the square representing Workspace 2 is now highlighted.

9. Press **Ctrl+Alt+right arrow** two times to go to Workspace 4 and view the open Trash window. Close the Trash Window.

10. Press **Ctrl+Alt+left arrow** two times to go back to Workspace 2. Close the File Browser window.

11. Press **Ctrl+Alt+left arrow** to go to Workspace 1.

12. Close any open windows.

TIP

When you delete a folder or file using Nautilus File Browser in GNOME, that folder or file is placed in the Trash, from which it can be recovered. When you delete a folder or file using a command such as *rm* at the command line, it is not placed in the Trash for optional recovery on most systems.

HANDS-ON PROJECTS

Project 11-4

The GNOME Applications or Computer menu offers access to a wide range of submenus and programs. In this project, you learn about using the Applications or Computer menu.

To use the Applications menu in Fedora or Red Hat Enterprise Linux:

1. Click the **Applications menu** on the top Panel.

2. Notice that items followed by an arrow contain submenus. Position the mouse pointer over each of these to see the submenu appear. For example, when you point to Accessories, you see a list of submenu items from which to select.

3. Point to **Accessories** and click **Calculator** to practice starting an application.

4. Close the Calculator window.

11

To use the Computer Menu in SUSE:

1. Click the **Computer** menu in the Panel at the bottom of the desktop.

2. Click **More Applications**.

3. Notice the categories of applications in the side (left) pane, such as New Applications, Games, Graphics, Internet, and so on.

4. Click each category in the side pane and observe the associated applications in the main pane.

5. Click the **Multimedia** category in the side pane.

6. Click **Dictionary** in the main pane to practice opening an application.

7. Close the application window you just opened.

HANDS-ON PROJECTS

Project 11-5

Nautilus is a file management tool that is included with the GNOME desktop. Through Nautilus, you can view, delete, move, copy, and perform other operations on files and folders. In this project, you open Nautilus to explore its features.

To explore features in Nautilus:

1. In Fedora and Red Hat Enterprise Linux, click **Applications**, point to **System Tools**, and click **File Browser**. In SUSE double-click the icon on the desktop for your home folder, such as *mpalmer's Home* (there is the same icon in Fedora and Red Hat Enterprise Linux, but on some systems it does not start the full-featured version of the File Browser).

2. Be certain the window is not maximized. (Click the **Unmaximize Window** button if it is.) Click the **View** menu and be certain that **View as Icons** is selected. If it is not selected, click **View as Icons** so that your window display shows folder and file icons.

3. If there is more to see in your home directory than can fit in the window, use the scroll bar on the right side of the window to scroll through the contents of your home directory.

4. Click the **File** menu and click **Create Folder**.

5. Enter the word **test** plus your initials for the folder's name, such as *testmp*, and press **Enter**.

6. Double-click the **folder** you created to open it.

7. Click the **Up** button on the toolbar to go back to your home directory.

8. Click the **Back** button on the toolbar to return to the folder you created.

9. Click the **Forward** button on the toolbar to return to your home directory.

10. Double-click **File System** in the side pane. You should now see the contents of the / root-level folder. Double-click the **etc** folder to open it, as shown in Figure 11-14.

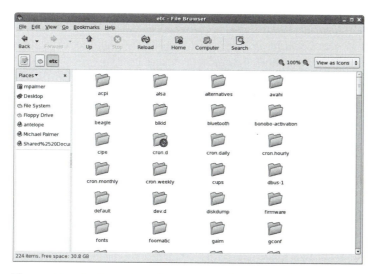

Figure 11-14 Using Nautilus to view the /etc folder in Fedora

11. Scroll to find the inittab file in the /etc directory (the same file you viewed in Project 11-1). Double-click the **inittab** file to open a new window that shows the file's contents (see Figure 11-15). Close the window showing the inittab contents.

```
#
# inittab       This file describes how the INIT process should set up
#               the system in a certain run-level.
#
# Author:       Miquel van Smoorenburg, <miquels@drinkel.nl.mugnet.org>
#               Modified for RHS Linux by Marc Ewing and Donnie Barnes
#

# Default runlevel. The runlevels used by RHS are:
#   0 - halt (Do NOT set initdefault to this)
#   1 - Single user mode
#   2 - Multiuser, without NFS (The same as 3, if you do not have
networking)
#   3 - Full multiuser mode
#   4 - unused
#   5 - X11
#   6 - reboot (Do NOT set initdefault to this)
#
id:5:initdefault:
```

Figure 11-15 Viewing the contents of the /etc/inittab file in Fedora

12. Click the **Home** button on the toolbar to return to your home directory. Leave Nautilus open for the next project.

Project 11-6

Nautilus File Browser also provides convenient methods for creating, copying, renaming, and deleting files, which you use in this project.

To create, copy, rename, and delete files:

1. Verify that Nautilus File Browser is still open to your home directory.

2. Click **File**, point to **Create Document**, and click **Empty File**. Type **testno1** and press **Enter**. Repeat the same process to create the **testno2** and **testno3** files.

3. Right-click **testno1** and notice the options on the menu.

4. Click **Copy**.

5. Scroll to and double-click the **test** directory you created in Project 11-5.

6. Move the cursor to a blank spot in the file listing on the right side of the window. Right-click the blank spot, and click **Paste**. You should see the testno1 file copied to the test directory. Now, the original **testno1** file is in your home directory and a copy of it is in your test directory.

7. Find and right-click the **testno1** file in your test directory. Delete the file by clicking **Move to Trash**.

8. Click the **Home** button to return to your home directory.

9. Use the scroll bar to find **testno2** and then right-click it. Click **Cut**.

10. Scroll to and then double-click the test directory you created in Project 11-5. Move the cursor to a blank spot in the File view on the right side of the screen, right-click the blank spot, and click **Paste**. Now, the testno2 file is moved from your home directory to your test directory. Verify this by finding the testno2 file in your test directory. Next click the **Back** button to go to your home directory, and verify that testno2 is not there.

11. Find the testno3 file in your home directory. Now, you can rename it by right-clicking **testno3** and clicking **Rename**.

12. Notice that the file name is now highlighted with a box around it. Type the name **testno4** and press **Enter**. Notice that the name is now changed to testno4. Point to an empty location in the window, and click so that the testno4 file is no longer highlighted.

13. Use the scroll bar, if necessary, to find the testno1 and testno4 files in your home directory. Press and hold **Ctrl** and click **testno1** and then click **testno4** so that both files are highlighted. Release the **Ctrl** key, then press the **Delete** (or **Del**) key to delete both files.

14. Open your test directory and delete the testno2 file that you moved from your home directory. Click the **Home** button to return to your home directory and leave Nautilus open for the next project.

When you are in the View as Icons mode (click the View menu and then click View as Icons), you can select multiple files by holding down the Shift or Ctrl keys and then clicking each file you want to select. If you are in the View as List mode (click the View menu and then click View as List), when you select a file and then hold down the Shift key while selecting another file, you also select all the files whose names appear between the two selected files. Also, while in the View as List mode, you can hold down the Ctrl key while selecting files to add them to your selection one at a time.

TIP

HANDS-ON PROJECTS

Project 11-7

In this project, you use Nautilus File Browser to configure the permissions on a folder.

To configure permissions using Nautilus File Browser:

1. Be certain Nautilus File Browser is open to your home directory.

2. Find the test directory that you created in Project 11-5. Right-click the directory and click **Properties**.

3. Click the **Permissions** tab (see Figure 11-16).

4. Find the Group section and click the up and down arrows for the **Folder Access** box. Click **Create and delete files**. Click the up and down arrows for the **File Access** box for Group. Click **Read and write**. Find the Others section under the Group section and click the up and down arrows for the **Folder Access** box. Click **None**. Click **Close**.

5. Right-click your test folder again and click **Properties**. Click the **Permissions** button and notice that the changes you made are now in effect. Click **Close**.

6. Click your test folder and press **Delete** (or **Del**) to delete it.

7. Close Nautilus File Browser.

HANDS-ON PROJECTS

Project 11-8

In this project, you change the desktop background.

To change the background:

1. Right-click a blank area on the desktop.

2. Click **Change Desktop Background**.

3. Scroll through the **Desktop Wallpaper** and click one you like such as **GNOME Curves**.

4. Click **Close** in the Fedora and Red Hat Enterprise Linux or click **Finish** in SUSE.

11

testmp Properties

Basic | Emblems | Permissions | Open With | Notes

Owner: mpalmer - Michael Palmer

Folder Access: Create and delete files

File Access: ---

Group: mpalmer

Folder Access: Access files

File Access: ---

Others

Folder Access: Access files

File Access: ---

Execute: ☐ Allow executing file as program

SELinux Context: file_t

Last changed: Thu 30 Jul 2009 05:58:17 AM MDT

Apply permissions to enclosed files

Help   ✕ Close

Figure 11-16   Viewing the Permissions tab

HANDS-ON PROJECTS

Project 11-9

Using a screensaver not only gives you some privacy when you are not using your system, but it can enable you to password protect your system when you leave your computer for a period of time. In this project, you configure a screensaver in GNOME.

To select and configure a screensaver:

1. In Fedora and Red Hat Enterprise Linux click the **System** menu, point to **Preferences**, and click **Screensaver**. In SUSE click the **Computer** menu, click **Control Center**, and click **Screensaver**.

2. Select a screensaver image that you want to use under **Screensaver theme:**.

3. Move the slider bar for **Regard the computer as idle after:** to **7** minutes (or adjust to your preference).

4. Ensure the box is checked for **Activate screensaver when computer is idle**.

5. If it isn't checked, click the box for **Lock screen when screensaver is active**. This means that after the screensaver has started, the screen is locked and you must enter

your user name and password to return to your login session and your open work on the desktop. The security advantage is that while you are away from your desk, your open work is protected until you return.

6. Click **Close** to save your changes (Close the Control Center window, if you are using SUSE.).

Project 11-10

In this project, you learn to adjust the position of icons on the Panel. Note that for Hands-On Projects 11-10, 11-11, and 11-12, the same steps work for Fedora, Red Hat Enterprise Linux, and SUSE.

To adjust the position of icons on the Panel:

1. Right-click an applet icon on the Panel, such as the printer icon.

2. On the menu, click **Move**. The mouse pointer becomes a four-way arrow.

3. Drag the mouse pointer to the left or right. As you do, the icon moves along the Panel.

4. When you decide where you want to move the icon, click the mouse. The icon stays in its current position.

Project 11-11

You can use several other applets in addition to those that appear on the Panel by default. In this project, you learn how to add applets to the Panel.

To add applets to the Panel:

1. Position the mouse pointer over any part of the Panel (on the top or bottom of the desktop) not occupied by an icon, and right-click.

2. On the menu, point to **Add to Panel**. Scroll to find **Lock Screen** and click this option to add to the Panel. Click the **Add** button. This places a lock icon on the Panel for a utility that enables you to lock your desktop when you step away from your computer. Close the Add to Panel window.

3. Click the **Lock** icon and wait a few moments until your screensaver is displayed and then press any key. When you see the login screen, provide the password to your account and click **Unlock** to access the desktop.

4. To remove the new icon, right-click the **Lock** icon, and click **Remove From Panel**.

Project 11-12

In addition to the available applets, you can also add your own programs as applets to the Panel. In this project, you place the phoneadd script you developed in Chapters 6 and 7 ("Introduction to Shell Script Programming" and "Advanced Shell Programming," respectively) on the Panel.

To add the phoneadd script to the Panel as an applet:

1. You need to add a launcher applet to the Panel. A launcher executes another program when you click its icon. Right-click the **Panel** (at the top or bottom of the desktop), click **Add to Panel**, and double-click **Custom Application Launcher**.

2. For the Type: text box, click the up and down arrows and select **Application in Terminal**.

3. In the Name: text box, type **phoneadd Script**.

4. In the Command text box, type **./source/phoneadd.**

5. In the Comment: text box, type **Adds a phone number to the corp_phones file**.

6. Your window should now look similar to Figure 11-17.

Figure 11-17   Create Launcher window

7. Click the **No Icon** button. The Browse icons window appears.

8. Scroll through the set of icons. When you see one you want to use for the phoneadd script, click it, and then click **OK**.

9. In the Create Launcher window, click **OK**. The icon you selected appears on the Panel.

10. Position the mouse pointer over the phoneadd icon, but do not click it yet. After a moment, a Help box appears with the text you entered in the Create Launcher applet Name and Comment boxes.

11. Click the icon. The script file executes in a terminal window. The window looks similar to Figure 11-18.

12. Close the terminal window and any other open windows.

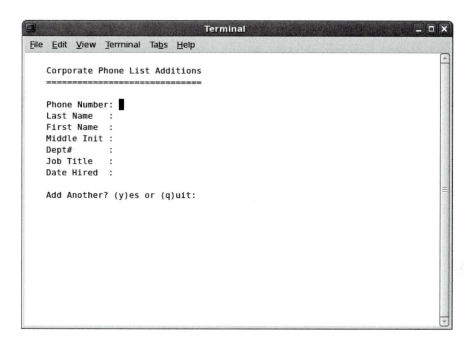

Figure 11-18   phoneadd script window

Project 11-13

In this project, you place the Office menu on the Panel.

HANDS-ON PROJECTS

To place the Office menu on the Panel:

1. Right-click the **Panel** (at the top or bottom of the desktop), click **Add to Panel**, click **Application Launcher**, and click the **Forward** button.

2. In Fedora and Red Hat Enterprise Linux, notice that the same submenus appear as you see from the Applications menu. In SUSE, you see the same application categories as when you click Computer and More Applications, plus the Control Center and YaST applications.

3. Click **Office** and click the **Add** button.

4. A new Office icon is added to the Panel.

5. Click the new **Office** icon and you'll see a menu of office applications that you can start, such as a word processor or spreadsheet application, or you'll see additional submenus (depending on the Linux distribution).

Project 11-14

Proper logout is important for any operating system, including UNIX/Linux. In this project, you use the GNOME desktop to log out of your system.

To log out and shut down a system:

1. In Fedora and Red Hat Enterprise Linux, click the **System** menu. On the menu notice there are options to log out of your account, and if your account has the right privileges, to shut down the system.

2. In SUSE, click the **Computer** menu and click **Log Out**. In the Are you sure you want to log out? window, notice there are four options:

   □ *Log out*—Does not shut down the system and enables you or another user to log back in

   □ *Shut down*—Logs out and properly shuts down the system

   □ *Restart the computer*—Logs out, shuts down, and reboots the system

   □ *Suspend the computer*—puts the computer in a suspeneded operations mode

3. When you are ready to log out and shut down, use the mouse clicks that are appropriate for your system as discussed in Step 1 or Step 2.

The following projects are included to enable you to learn about the KDE desktop. You can use the Knoppix CD that comes with this book to complete the projects. Knoppix can be run from most PCs by inserting the CD in a CD/DVD drive and booting from that drive. See Appendix C, "How to Install Fedora and How to Use the Knoppix CD" for further information about using Knoppix.

Project 11-15

The KDE desktop is another example of a desktop you can use in X Window. In this project you learn to use the K Menu to access applications and you use icons on the KDE desktop.

To briefly explore the KDE desktop:

1. Locate the **Kicker** at the bottom of the desktop.

2. Click the **K Menu** on the far-most left side of the Kicker.

3. You'll see three sections of items that you can access as follows:

   □ *Recently Used Applications*—shows the applications you have started most recently, so you can quickly return to any of these. (This section will not appear if you have just installed your system, just booted from the Knoppix CD, or have not yet run any applications.)

◻ *All Applications*—mostly consists of submenus you can open to start a specific application, but also contains applications like Control Center to set up KDE and Find Files/Folders which opens a window from which to access your files.

◻ *Actions*—lists actions you can take immediately, such as setting up bookmarks for places you frequently visit or running a command.

4. Point to each submenu under All Applications to quickly view the applications you can start within that submenu.

5. Start an application of your choice, such as an editor or a graphics application.

6. Close the application you started in Step 5.

7. Click one of the icons on the desktop, such as an icon that opens the files on a disk drive or click the Trash icon to view if there are any files that have been discarded.

8. Close any open windows.

HANDS-ON PROJECTS

Project 11-16

In this project, you examine Konqueror in the KDE desktop.

11

To use Konqueror:

1. Click the **K Menu** in the Kicker and click an option to view your home files, such as **Home Personal Files** in Knoppix.

2. Move your cursor over each button on the main toolbar and pause long enough to see the brief description of the button's purpose.

3. Move your cursor over each button on the side toolbar and pause to see the description for each button.

4. In the location bar, enter **/etc**, and press **Enter**. You'll see the files and folders in the /etc folder.

5. If you have Internet access, type the following URL in the location bar, **http://www.konqueror.org** and press **Enter** to view the Web site for Konqueror.

6. If it is not already selected, click the **Home Folder** button in the side toolbar. You'll see the contents of your home folder in the side pane.

7. Click the **Root Folder** button in the side toolbar. Now you see the folders under /. Click the **/dev** folder to view its contents in the main pane.

8. Click the **Services** button in the side toolbar to view a list of submenus or applications you can start from Konqueror. Click one of the submenus, such as *Office* (see Figure 11-19 for an example). Notice that the OpenOffice.org applications you can start are now displayed in the main pane. Move your cursor over different application icons to see a summary box about the application. Click one of the applications to start it, such as *OpenOffice.org Calc.*.(If this is the first time one of these applications has been used, follow the steps in the wizard to initialize the application.)

Figure 11-19 Viewing the contents displayed via the Services button on the side toolbar

9. Close the window for the application you started in Step 8.

10. Click the **Menu** button in the title bar (on the far left side).

11. Notice the options on the menu.

12. Point to **Advanced** on the menu. This presents another menu of options, such as the option to Keep Above Others (have the window stay on top of other windows) or Keep Below Others (have the window stay behind or under other windows).

13. From the title bar's Menu button, point to **To Desktop**, and notice that this option enables you to move the Konqueror window to any of the four desktops or to all of the desktops.

14. Click the **Tools** button on the menu bar. Notice that there are options to open a terminal window and to find a file on your computer, in addition to other options.

15. Click **Open Terminal** to start a terminal window. Close the terminal window after it appears.

16. Click the **Go** button in the menu bar and click **Applications**. In the main pane, you'll notice the same submenus that you saw in Step 8 when you clicked the Services button on the side toolbar.

17. Close the Konqueror window.

HANDS-ON PROJECTS

Project 11-17

Customizing the Kicker in the KDE desktop can help make you more productive. You learn how to use and customize the Kicker in this project.

To use and customize Kicker:

1. If you have the icon, click **Konsole** to instantly open a terminal window. Close Konsole.

2. If you have it, click the **Home** icon in Kicker to quickly open Konqueror to display your home folder.

3. In Konqueror, click the **Menu** button in the title bar, point to **To Desktop**, and click <u>4</u> **Desktop 4**.

4. In Desktop Switcher, click the **Desktop 4** square to go to Desktop 4 to see the open Konqueror window on that desktop. Close Konqueror.

5. In Desktop Switcher, click the **Desktop 1** square to return to Desktop 1.

6. Right-click Kicker in an open area.

7. Click **Add Applet to Panel**.

8. Select an applet to add that is not already in Kicker, such as *Find* or *Recent Documents*. (Find is a quick search utility and Recent Documents shows the documents you have accessed recently so you can open any one of them). Double-click the applet you want to add to Kicker.

9. Close the Add Applet – KDE Panel box.

10. Now remove the applet you added. Right-click the Kicker in a blank area, point to **Remove From Panel**, point to **Applet**, and click the name of the applet, such as *Find* or *Recent Documents*.

11. Next, you try adding an application to Kicker. Right-click Kicker in a blank area and point to **Add Application to Panel**.

12. Click **Control Center** (or add a different application if you do not have Control Center—Control Center centralizes utilities in one place for configuring your system). Note that some applications are accessed by first pointing to open an application submenu.

13. Click the icon for Control Center (or another application you added to Kicker) to start that application. Close the application's window after it opens (or first take a few minutes to explore the capabilities of Control Center and then close it).

14. Right-click the **Control Center** icon (or the icon for another application you added) in Kicker and click **Remove Control Center Button**.

Project 11-18

Use the Configure – KDesktop utility to set up your desktop background, screensaver, and desktops. In this project you learn to configure all three elements of your desktop.

To use configure the background, screensaver, and number of desktops:

1. Right-click an open space in the KDE desktop.

2. Click **Configure Desktop** to start the Configure – KDesktop utility.

3. Ensure that Background is selected in the left pane.

4. Click the down arrow in the **Picture** box.

5. Scroll through the list of wallpapers and click the ones you want to view as possibilities. You'll see example clips in the right pane.

6. Select a wallpaper and click **Apply**.

7. Click **Screen Saver** in the left pane.

8. Scroll through the categories of screensavers, such as Banners & Pictures, Desktop Distortions, Flying Things, Fractals, and so on (your specific categories may differ).

9. Select a category by clicking the plus sign in front of it. Select a few possibilities to see them displayed in the right pane.

10. Once you decide on a screensaver, click it and click **Apply**.

11. Click the box for **Start automatically** and set the After: box to **7** min (if it is not already set for 7 minutes). This causes the screensaver to start after 7 minutes of inactivity at your computer.

12. Click the box for **Require password to stop** and set the After: box for **90** sec which means that you have to enter your account password if the screensaver has been going for 90 seconds or longer (see Figure 11-20).

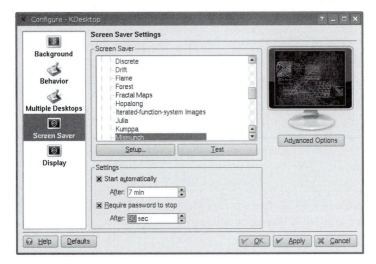

Figure 11-20   Configuring the screensaver in KDE

13. Click **Apply**.

14. Click **Multiple Desktops** in the left pane.

15. Move the Number of desktops: slider bar to **5**.

16. Click **Apply**. Notice that there are now five boxes in the desktop switcher in the Kicker.

17. Click **Behavior** in the left pane and notice the options you can configure.

18. Click **Display** in the left pane and observe the options to configure.

19. Close the Configure – KDesktop window.

DISCOVERY EXERCISES

1. If you have the GNOME desktop, open the Applications or Computer menu and find at least five menus or programs that you can start. If you are using KDE, open the K Menu and record five menus or programs that you can start.

2. In your system, right-click the desktop and record the options on the menu that you see.

3. Use two ways to open your home directory.

4. Right-click the Panel or Kicker and view its properties. How can you set the Panel or Kicker to automatically hide when not in use?

5. How can you empty the Trash in GNOME or KDE?

6. Determine what spreadsheet programs are installed on your system.

7. Add a new Panel or Kicker to your desktop and then delete it.

8. How can you remove an icon on a Panel or the Kicker?

9. Determine how to move an icon on a Panel or the Kicker.

10. Determine where you can start a Samba-based application to enable you to view Windows computers on your local network.

11. Create two applets in the Panel or in the Kicker—an applet to enable you to log out of your current session and an applet to enable you to run a command-line command.

12. Open the Emacs editor into a window on the desktop without using a terminal window to start it. (Note that the Knoppix CD does not have the Emacs editor because of space limitations.)

11

A

HOW TO ACCESS A UNIX/LINUX OPERATING SYSTEM

As you learned in Chapter 1, "The Essence of UNIX and Linux," you can access a computer running UNIX or Linux by using a directly connected terminal or a remotely connected computer using Telnet or Secure Shell (SSH). A terminal is a CPU-less monitor and keyboard that is directly connected to the UNIX or Linux computer using specialized communications equipment. A remotely connected computer is connected through a telecommunications or network connection (or a combination of these). Many operating systems support remote connections of computers through Telnet, SSH, or both. For example, you can remotely access a UNIX/Linux workstation or server from a remote Fedora computer by using Telnet or SSH. Your remote computer might also be running Windows XP/Vista and Telnet or Mac OS X and SSH.

A UNIX/Linux class at a school also might have one Red Hat Enterprise Linux server that students access from a lab of computers running Fedora or Windows XP/Vista and Telnet. In another example, an on-call system administrator who has a Mac OS X computer at home might use SSH to connect to and troubleshoot a UNIX or Linux server.

Accessing UNIX/Linux Computers from an Attached Terminal

Terminals have largely been replaced by PCs, but there are still contexts in which terminals are used because they are cheaper than PCs. As you learned in Chapter 1, "The Essence of UNIX and Linux," a terminal is a device that connects to a server or host, but consists of only a monitor and keyboard and has no CPU. When you use a terminal to access a UNIX/Linux system, you only need to turn on the terminal and press a key on the keyboard to begin your session. At the login prompt, enter your assigned user name and password to begin your session. Depending on your terminal and administrator, you might see either a graphical user interface (GUI) or text-mode login screen.

One advantage of using a terminal is the relative ease of beginning the session. Another advantage is how convenient it is to replace a malfunctioning terminal and have the user continue a session, virtually uninterrupted.

Using Telnet

The Telnet protocol can be used by one remote computer to access another over a network or the Internet. Telnet specifies how sessions are created, how data is passed, and how an interactive shell or prompt is displayed to the remote user. Telnet has been around a long time, with relatively few changes to the protocol.

Telnet has been implemented on a huge variety of systems for the purpose of establishing a session on a remote host. The different systems that use Telnet all adhere to a standard that determines how a system sends or generates the correct signals from the Telnet client to the corresponding Telnet daemon or server. Both the client and the server must understand and support at least a base level of the protocol for communications to be established and a session granted.

Systems normally run Telnet over TCP/IP connections, with a few systems supporting Telnet over IPX (a protocol used by older Novell servers). Regardless of the systems' traditional role, such as a user's workstation and a file server, all UNIX/Linux systems have the capability to be used as a client and to perform the role of a server. In fact, it's common for an administrator to connect to a server-class machine for administrative work using a Telnet client computer. The only restrictions are the software running on the machines and the security measures that have been implemented. An account and password are also needed.

Telnet uses TCP (or UDP) port 23 to send and receive its data. On a computer running UNIX/Linux, Windows XP/Vista, or Windows Server 2003/2008, the Telnet service should be started and enabled through that computer's firewall.

CAUTION   For all remote computing, SSH is strongly recommended. Telnet is included in this book since some organizations still use it. Also, Telnet is offered by default in Windows systems instead of SSH. However, because of security concerns, many organizations have discontinued the use of Telnet. Auditors of business and other financial departments strongly discourage using Telnet. If you use Telnet, it is important to recognize that transmissions are not encrypted, so it should be used only in a trusted environment, such as on a local network protected from outside traffic by a router.

USING SSH

As mentioned in Chapter 1, SSH was created to provide more sophisticated security than Telnet, such as providing encrypted authentication and communications.

SSH was developed in 1995 by Tatu Ylönen of the Helsinki University of Technology in Finland in response to a network security attack. SSH uses public key encryption, which is really a combination of public key and private key encryption that can be used over an unsecured connection. Public key encryption uses the Diffie/Hellman encryption algorithm, which is based in the use of prime numbers. SSH is also compatible with tunneling, a security technique used on the popular virtual private networks to create a secure "tunnel" of communications through a larger network. Two other advantages of SSH are that it is very compatible with X Window and it uses a secure network protocol for file transfers.

SSH is particularly suited to UNIX/Linux systems, including Mac OS X, because pipes can be used with applications for redirection through the command prompt. As you will recall, a pipe is an operator that redirects the output of one command to the input of another command using the following syntax:

```
first_command | second_command
```

When an application runs, its output can be redirected as input for SSH-secured FTP transfers of files over a network or the Internet, for example. Fedora, Red Hat Enterprise Linux, and SUSE use OpenSSH, which is primarily developed by the Open BSD Project for free use on UNIX/Linux systems. You can learn more about OpenSSH and obtain the latest version at *www.openssh.com*.

For commercial and non-commercial versions of SSH consider SSH Communications Security at *www.ssh.com*. SSH Communications Security is the company established by Tatu Ylönen to further develop SSH. If you are using a Windows operating system, you can obtain SSH for Windows at either *www.openssh.com* or *www.ssh.com*. Figure A-1 illustrates the SSH login screen using a version of SSH from SSH Communications Security.

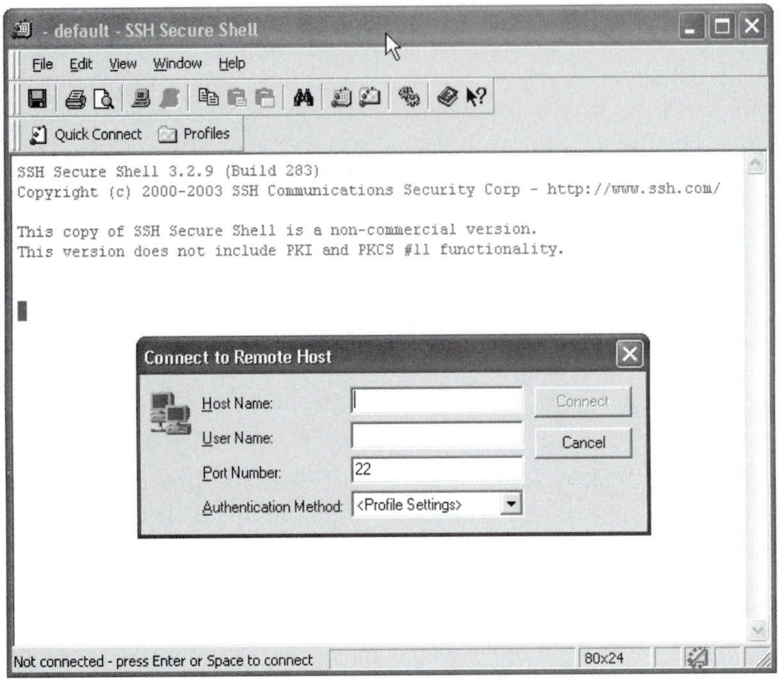

Figure A-1   Login screen for SSH from SSH Communications Security

ACCESSING A UNIX/LINUX SYSTEM FROM A MICROSOFT WINDOWS COMPUTER

When accessing a UNIX/Linux system from a computer running Microsoft Windows, you can use the version of Telnet that comes with the operating system or you can obtain other utilities from a third party. For example, one popular utility is PuTTY, which can be obtained at *www.chiark.greenend.org.uk/~sgtatham/putty*. This appendix focuses on the Telnet version that comes with Windows operating systems.

All versions of Microsoft Windows—from Windows for Workgroups to Windows XP/Vista to Windows Server 2003/2008—have access to TCP/IP networking, either natively or as an add-on. If the computer already has TCP/IP loaded, you can use the existing address and utilities to attach to a remote UNIX/Linux computer.

For example, if you are using a Microsoft Windows XP or Vista computer in the computer lab at your school to access the Internet, it's very likely that this computer can also be used, as is, to telnet to a remote host. To successfully connect, you need to know the IP address or host name of the UNIX/Linux computer that allows Telnet sessions.

On a Windows XP/Vista or Windows Server 2003/2008 computer that is configured for TCP/IP access, three tasks are generally involved in using Telnet:

1. Configure the Telnet service.

2. Enable the firewall security for Telnet.

3. Open a Command Prompt window and start Telnet.

Configuring the Telnet Service

Before you can use Telnet, you must start the Telnet service in Windows XP or Windows Server 2003. In Windows XP and Windows Server 2003, you can either start the service manually or configure the service to start automatically when you log in. In Windows Vista and Windows Server 2008, you simply need to install Telnet.

The following general steps are for configuring the Telnet service in Windows XP Professional and Windows Server 2003 to start automatically at login and show you how to start the service immediately:

1. Log in to an account that has Administrator privileges.

2. Click Start, right-click My Computer, and click Manage.

3. Double-click Services and Applications in the left pane.

4. Click Services in the left pane.

5. Double-click Telnet in the right pane.

6. If the Startup type is not set to Automatic (and you want to start it automatically when you boot the computer), click the down arrow for Startup type, and select Automatic.

7. If the Service status shows Stopped, click the Start button to start the Telnet service.

8. Click OK.

9. Close the Computer Management dialog box.

10. Log out of Windows

In Windows Vista and Windows Server 2008, it is necessary to install the Telnet Client software. Use the following steps to install Telnet Client:

1. Click Start, click Control Panel, and click Programs.

2. Under Programs and Features, click Turn Windows features on or off.

3. If you see a window asking for permission to continue, click Continue.

4. You may need to wait a minute or two while the Windows Features box builds the list of features.

5. Scroll to find Telnet Client and check the box, if it is not already checked.

6. Click OK.

7. Close the Control Panel > Programs > window.

Starting a Telnet Session

To start a Telnet session, first open a Command Prompt window and then use the Telnet command at the prompt. You need the IP address or host name for the computer you want to access, as well as an account name and password for that account on the remote computer. The following general steps are for accessing a remote computer via Telnet in Windows XP/Vista or Windows Server 2003/2008:

1. Click Start, point to All Programs, point to Accessories, and click Command Prompt.

2. Type *telnet* and the name and domain or IP address of the remote UNIX/Linux computer, such as *telnet 192.200.10.8.* Press Enter. If prompted, read the security warning message, then type y and press Enter to connect.

3. Type the account name and then press Enter.

4. Type the password and then press Enter.

NOTE You practiced connecting through Telnet in Hands-On Project 1-1 in Chapter 1. Also, Telnet services and the firewall on the remote computer must be configured in advance to allow access. See the next section for details about how to enable access at the remote computer when it is running Fedora or Red Hat Enterprise Linux.

USING A UNIX/LINUX COMPUTER TO PROVIDE ACCESS OR TO ACCESS ANOTHER COMPUTER

Because you are using the same general program and access structure, connecting to a UNIX/Linux Telnet server from a UNIX/Linux client is relatively uncomplicated. The Telnet client application is almost always installed and available on the workstation, unless specifically uninstalled or removed as a security measure.

Where Is My Telnet or SSH Client Program?

Finding the Telnet client on your UNIX/Linux computer is quite simple. On a UNIX/Linux computer, use the *which* command to see the first occurrence of a Telnet executable in your path. The *which* command also shows you all instances of any queried command in your path; for example, in Fedora, Red Hat Enterprise Linux, and SUSE entering *which -a telnet* yields the following display:

```
[robert@localhost ~]$ which -a telnet
/usr/bin/telnet
[robert@localhost ~]$
```

If you have the Kerberos version of Telnet installed for authentication security, you might also see the following:

```
[robert@localhost ~]$ which -a telnet
/usr/kerberos/bin/telnet
/usr/bin/telnet
[robert@localhost ~]$
```

The output in the second example shows two instances of the *telnet* command. The first instance is for the Kerberos version of Telnet. In the second instance, the */usr/bin* location exists for systems that don't have Kerberos installed (the default for Fedora and Red Hat Enterprise Linux). Kerberos is a security mechanism that helps systems and users more securely authenticate their user name and password across a wide area network (WAN) or across the Internet, without the security risks typically associated with programs such as Telnet and FTP.

You can also use the *which* command to determine the location of SSH by entering *which -a ssh*, which by default displays */usr/bin/ssh*. SSH uses a combination of RSA (named after the authors Rivest, Shamir, and Adleman) and digital certificates for secure authentication and communications.

Enabling Telnet and SSH

Typically, you can take the same steps on both the remote UNIX/Linux computer to which you want to connect and on the UNIX/Linux computer from which you are connecting. These steps include the following:

1. Configure the routing table to contain the IP addresses and host names of both computers.

2. Configure the firewall to allow Telnet, SSH, or both types of communications.

The general steps for configuring the routing table in Fedora and Red Hat Enterprise Linux are as follows (do this on both the computer acting as the server and on the client):

1. Log in as root.

2. Click Applications, point to Accessories, and click Terminal to open a terminal window.

3. Type *ifconfig* and press Enter. Record the inet addr and mask information for eth0. This provides the IP address and subnet mask for the computer. To facilitate loopback access, such as for the Hands-On Projects in Chapter 9, also record the lo (loopback) information—which should be 127.0.0.1 for the inet addr and 255.0.0.0 for the subnet mask. Close the terminal window.

4. Click the System menu, point to Administration, and click Network.

5. Double-click the Ethernet device (eth0) shown as Active (this is usually high-lighted by default).

6. Click the Route tab.

7. Click the Add button.

8. Enter the address (IP address) and subnet mask you recorded in Step 3 for your network card (eth0). Also, provide the gateway address, if you have it (check with your network administrator). Click OK. (In addition, for a loop-back connection, repeat Step 7 and this step, entering the address and subnet mask information for lo, the loopback information, from Step 3.)

9. Click the Add button. Enter the address and subnet mask of the other computer used in the connection (you can find this information by using Step 3 from the root account on that computer). Click OK. Click OK again.

10. Close the Network Configuration dialog box. Click Yes to save the changes. Click OK in the information window.

11. Shut down and reboot the computer to ensure the changes take effect.

To configure the routing table in SUSE:

1. Log in to the root account.

2. Click the Computer menu and click Control Center.

3. Click Configure Network in the left pane.

4. You may need to wait a few moments as your network is initialized.

5. Click User Controlled with Network Manager and click Next.

6. Ensure that your network card is highlighted and click Edit.

7. Click Routing.

8. Click Expert Configuration.

9. Click the Add button.

10. Enter the IP address of the destination computer, the gateway address, and the netmask (subnet mask). In this case the destination computer is a computer that the current computer will connect to or that will connect to it.

11. Click OK.

12. Repeat steps 9 through 11 for other computers that will connect to this computer.

13. When you are finished adding information to the routing table, click OK.

14. Click Next.

15. Click Finish.

16. Close any open windows.

17. Shut down and reboot the computer.

A

To configure the firewall for Telnet and SSH access in Fedora and Red Hat Enterprise Linux (do this on both the computer acting as the server and on the client):

1. Log in as root.

2. Click the System menu, point to Administration, and click Security Level and Firewall.

3. If the firewall is disabled, enable it by clicking the up and down arrows for the Firewall: box and selecting Enable.

4. Ensure the SSH and Telnet check boxes are checked.

5. Click OK.

6. Log out as root.

To configure the firewall for SSH (Telnet is not an option in the firewall) in SUSE:

1. Log in to the root account.

2. Click the Computer menu.

3. Click Control Center.

4. Click System in the left pane.

5. Click YaST.

6. Click Security and Users in the left pane of the YaST window.

7. Click Firewall in the right pane.

8. Click Allowed Services in the left pane, and ensure that SSH is listed under the Allowed Service column. If SSH is not listed, open the Service to Allow list box and select SSH. Click the Add button.

9. Click Next.

10. Click Accept.

11. Close any open windows and log out of root.

NOTE   An additional step to enable network and Internet access on the computer to which you are connecting is to configure the /etc/hosts.allow file from the root account. Create a separate line giving the IP address, host and domain name, and host name for each computer that will connect. For example, to configure the file for loopback access, provide the following line in the file:

```
127.0.0.1      localhost.local.domain      localhost
```

Connecting via Telnet or SSH

You connect using Telnet or SSH by accessing the command line and entering either *telnet* or *ssh* plus the IP address or host and domain name for the computer to which you want to connect. The general steps for connecting through Telnet or SSH are as follows:

1. Log in to the account from which you want to connect.

2. Access the command line or a terminal window.

3. To connect using Telnet at the command prompt, type *telnet* plus the IP address or the host name of the computer to which you want to connect, such as *telnet 192.29.20.19* or *telnet jphost*, and press Enter. Next enter the account name and then the password for the account. To connect using SSH and the account name on the command line, enter *ssh -l* plus the account name and host name, such as *ssh -l rtbrown jphost* and press Enter. Next provide the password. Or, to connect using the IP address and no account name on the command line, enter *ssh* and the IP address, such as *ssh 192.29.20.19*. Next enter the account name and then the password.

NOTE

If this is a first-time connection and you are asked whether you want to continue connecting, type *yes* and press Enter. Also, note that you practiced using SSH in Hands-On Project 1-2 in Chapter 1.

Using Mac OS X and SSH to Access a Remote Computer

SSH is the preferred method for remote access using Mac OS X. Complete the following three steps to use SSH in Mac OS X (Panther or Tiger):

1. Enable Remote Login as a service.

2. Enable Remote Login – SSH (22) through the firewall.

3. Access a terminal window to use SSH.

Enabling Remote Login as a Service and Through the Firewall

In Mac OS X Panther or Tiger, when you enable Remote Login as a service, you also enable SSH access through the Mac OS X firewall (when the firewall is in use, which is typically the case). The general steps for enabling the Remote Login service are as follows:

1. Open System Preferences by clicking its icon in the Dock at the bottom of the desktop. Another way to open System Preferences, if its icon has been removed from the Dock, is to click the Go menu at the top of the desktop, click Applications, and double-click System Preferences.

2. In the Internet & Network section, click the Sharing icon.

3. Click the Services tab, if it is not already selected.

4. Be certain that the check box for Remote Login is checked.

5. Click the Firewall tab and be certain that Remote Login – SSH is selected. (In Mac OS X Panther, the option is Remote Login -- SSH (22). 22 is the port that SSH uses in the TCP or UDP protocol for SSH network communications.). Note that when SSH is enabled as a service, it is also automatically enabled in the firewall.

6. Close the Sharing dialog box.

7. Close the Applications window if it is open.

Using SSH via a Terminal Window

Because Mac OS X is built on BSD UNIX, you can use a terminal window and command-line commands as in other UNIX/Linux systems. The general steps for connecting to a remote computer using the Mac OS X terminal window and SSH in Mac OS X Panther or Tiger are as follows:

1. Click the Go menu at the top of the desktop, click Utilities, and double-click Terminal.

2. At the command line, enter *ssh* and the IP address of the remote computer, and then enter the account name and the password. If necessary, type *yes* and press Enter to continue. Another option is to enter *ssh -l* plus the account name and host name, such as *ssh -l rtbrown jphost*, and then enter the password.

NOTE   You can find out more about SSH in a UNIX/Linux system, including Mac OS X, by accessing the command line in a terminal window and entering *man ssh*. The same applies to Telnet, for which you can enter *man telnet*.

APPENDIX

B

SYNTAX GUIDE TO UNIX/LINUX COMMANDS

This appendix is a quick reference for essential UNIX/Linux utilities available on most systems.

Table B-1 lists the commands alphabetically, including the command name, its purpose, and useful options. Table B-2 lists the UNIX/Linux utilities by category. Table B-3 summarizes the vi editor commands, and Table B-4 summarizes the Emacs editor commands. The UNIX/Linux command syntax uses the format diagrammed in Figure B-1.

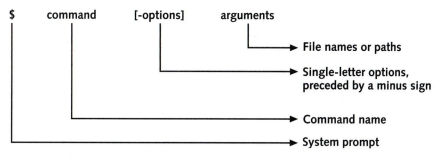

Figure B-1 Command syntax format

For example, to use the *ls* command to see a directory's contents and use the *-a* option to view hidden files plus the *-l* option to view a long listing of file detail, you would enter:

ls -al or *ls -a -l*

In another example, to make a backup copy using the *cp* command of the file myorginalfile.txt to the file clonecopy.txt (where the file names are arguments), you would enter:

cp myorginalfile.txt clonecopy.txt

Table B-1   Common UNIX/Linux commands

Command	Purpose	Useful Options and Examples
alias	Creates an alias for a command	Include in the .bashrc file for access each time you log in; example: **alias dir='ls -1'**. **-p** prints all aliases.
awk	Starts the Awk program to format output	**-f** indicates code is coming from a disk file, not the keyboard. **-F** specifies the field separator.
cal	Shows the system calendar for a specified year or month	**-1** shows a single month. **-3** shows three months beginning with the previous month. **-j** displays the calendar in Julian date format. **-s** shows Sunday as the first day in the week. **-m** shows Monday as the first day in the week. **-y** shows all of the months for the current year.
cat	Creates files, concatenates files, or can be used to display the contents of files	**cat -n** displays line numbers. **cat** *filename* displays the contents of a file. **cat >** *filename* creates a new file or enables you to overwrite the contents of an existing file. **cat >>** *filename* creates a new file or enables you to add information to an existing file. **cat** *file1 file2* **>** *file3* concatenates two existing files into one new file.
cd	Changes directories	**cd** by itself takes the user to his home directory. **.** Changes to the current working directory. **..** Changes to the parent directory.
chmod	Changes security mode of a file or directory (r: read, w: write, x: executable); sets file permissions for specified users (u: user, g: group, o: others, a: all)	**+** assigns permissions. **-** removes permissions. **chmod a+x** sets the execute bit for owner, group, and other (all).
clear	Clears the screen	Commonly aliased to **cls**; see the alias command.
comm	Compares sorted files and shows differences	**comm** *file1 file2* compares the files line by line. **-1** does not display unique lines in the first file. **-2** does not display unique lines in the second file. **-3** does not display unique lines in both files.

Table B-1   Common UNIX/Linux commands (continued)

Command	Purpose	Useful Options and Examples
cp	Copies files from one directory to another	**-b** makes a backup of the destination file, if an original one already exists (so you have a backup if overwriting a file). **-i** requests confirmation if the target file already exists. **-r** copies directories to a new directory. **-s** creates a symbolic link or name at the destination rather than a physical file. **-u** overwrites an existing file only if the source is newer than the file in the current destination.
cut	Selects and extracts specified columns or fields from a file	**-c** specifies the character position. **-d** specifies the field separator. **-f** specifies the field position.
date	Displays the system date	**-u** displays the time in Greenwich Mean Time.
diff	Compares and selects differences in two files or directories	**diff** */dir1 /dir2* compares the file entries in both directories and shows only the missing files for each directory. **-b** ignores blanks that repeat. **-B** does not compare for blank lines. **-i** ignores case. **-c** shows lines surrounding the line that differs (for context). **-y** displays the differences side-by-side in columns.
. (dot)	Represents the current directory (the "." is a link to the inode for the current directory)	Used mostly in specifying that something happened in the current directory; for example, **cp** */dir/file* **.** copies the file to the current directory.
.. (dot dot)	Represents the parent directory (the ".." is a link to the inode for the parent directory)	Used for changing to a different directory, either the parent of the current (**cd ..**) or up one directory and down a different tree (**cd** *../dir2/dir3*).
echo	Displays the specified arguments on the output device	**echo** *$VAR*, where *VAR* is the variable name, echoes the data from an environment variable to standard output; can also be used in scripts and programs.
emacs	Starts the Emacs editor	
exit or logout	Logs out of your current session	**Ctrl+d** also logs the user out of a session or a subshell and back to the parent shell.

Table B-1   Common UNIX/Linux commands (continued)

Command	Purpose	Useful Options and Examples
export	Makes a variable an environment variable; and exports a specified list of variables to other shells	**-n** can be used to undo the export. **-p** lists the exported variables.
find	Locates files that match a given value	**-amin** *n* finds files accessed more recently than *n* minutes ago. **-atime** *n* finds files last accessed *n**24 hours ago. **-fstype** *type* finds files that exist only on the specified file system type, such as ext3. **-iname** *pattern* finds files with names that match a pattern. **-inum** *inode#* finds files with inodes that match *inode*. **-name** specifies the name of the files you want to locate but the search is case sensitive. **-mmim** *m* displays files that have been changed within the last *n* minutes. **-mtime** *n* displays files that have been changed within the last *n* days. **-size** *n* displays files of size *n*. **-user** *uname* finds files owned by user matching *uname*.
fuser	Displays the process ID (PID) of processes using a given resource	Useful for finding which users have mounted a drive that needs maintenance; for example, fuser –vu /mnt shows all processes accessing a resource and their associated user names.
grep	Selects lines or rows that match a specified pattern	**-c** only counts the number of lines matching the pattern instead of showing them. **-i** ignores case. **-l** lists only file names that contain the pattern. **-L** lists only file names that do not contain the pattern. **-n** displays line numbers. **-r** searches through files under all subdirectories. **-v** displays lines in a file that do not match the specified pattern.
head	Displays the first few lines of a file	Shows the first 10 lines by default. **-n** *n* displays the first *n* lines of the specified file.
history	Lists all the commands contained in the bash history file	Bash history file is .bash_history by default and resides in the user's home directory; default number of last commands kept in the history file is 500.

Table B-1   Common UNIX/Linux commands (continued)

Command	Purpose	Useful Options and Examples
join	Combines files having a common field	**-1** *fieldnum* specifies the common field in file 1 on which to join. **-2** *fieldnum* specifies the common field in file 2 on which to join. **-a** *n* produces a line for each unpairable line in file *n*, where *n* = 1 or 2. **-e** *string* replaces the empty fields for the unpairable line with the string specified by *string*. **-o** specifies a list of fields to be output. **-t** specifies the field separator character. By default, this is a blank, tab, or newline character. Multiple blanks and tabs count as one field separator.
kill	Ends a process	**-9** destructively ends a process. **-HUP** causes the service or daemon to stop (hang up) and restart, which causes the rereading of its configuration files; often used to make changes to a running service.
last	Shows the login history of all users on the system	**-a** displays the host name from which the user connected. **-d** shows the corresponding IP address for remotes.
less	Scrolls long files to screen	Allows for scrolling up and down in a file, whereas the *more* command only allows advancing down a file.
let	Stores the results of arithmetic operations in a variable	
ln	Creates symbolic or hard links to files	By default, creates a hard link, which is another name for a particular inode. **-s** creates a symbolic link to a file, like a shortcut.
lpr	Prints a file	**-P** *printer* prints on a specified printer. **#***n* prints a specified number of copies of the file. **-r** deletes a print file after it is printed.
ls	Lists a directory's contents, including its files and subdirectories	**-a** lists hidden files. **-l** lists files in long format, showing detailed information. **-r** lists files in reverse alphabetic order. **-s** shows the size of each file. **-S** sorts the listing by file size. **-t** sorts by the time when the file or directory was last modified. **-X** sorts by extension.

B

Table B-1 Common UNIX/Linux commands (continued)

Command	Purpose	Useful Options and Examples
lspci	Displays information about all PCI buses on the system (but you must be logged in as root)	**-v** is verbose output. **-vv** is very verbose output. **-t** shows a tree-like structure of PCI bus/devices.
man	Displays the online manual for the specified command	**-d** prints information for debugging. **-f** gives a short description of the command (same as using the *whatis* command). **-K** finds a certain string by searching through all of the *man* information. **-t** formats the output for printing using ghostscript.
mkdir	Makes a new directory	**-v** verifies the file is made.
more	Displays a long file one screen at a time	Pressing the spacebar advances one screen at a time; pressing Enter advances one line at a time.
mount	Connects the file system to the directory tree in the specified location	**-r** indicates that the mounted partition's device is read-only. **-a** mounts all possible file systems from /etc/fstab. **-t** specifies the type of file system to mount.
mv	Moves or renames files	**-f** never prompts before overwriting existing files and directories. **-i** displays a warning prompt before overwriting a file with the same name. **-u** overwrites a destination file with the same name, if the source file is newer than the one in the destination.
passwd	Changes your UNIX/Linux password	Users can change only their own password; the root user can change others' passwords. **-e** expires a password causing the user to have to recreate it. **-l** locks an account. **-S** displays the password status of an account.
paste	Combines the contents of one or more files to output to the screen or to another file (by default, the pasted results appear in columns separated by tabs)	**-d** enables you to specify a different separator (other than a tab) between columns. **-s** causes files to be pasted one after the other instead of in parallel.

Table B-1 Common UNIX/Linux commands (continued)

Command	Purpose	Useful Options and Examples
pr	Formats a specified file before printing or viewing	**-a** displays output in columns across the page, one line per column. **-d** double-spaces the output. **-h** customizes the header line. **-l***n* sets the number of lines per page.
printenv	Prints a list of environment variables	
printf	Tells the Awk program what action to take for formatting and printing information	
ps	Shows processes on a system	**-a** shows all running processes. **-u** shows the user associated with a process. **-x** shows background system processes.
pwd	Displays your current path	
rm	Removes a file	**-i** requests confirmation before deleting a file. **-r** deletes a specified directory and its contents.
rmdir	Removes a directory	**-v** provides a message to verify the directory is removed.
sed	Specifies an editing command or a script file containing *sed* commands	**-a** \ appends text after a line or a script file containing *sed* commands. **-d** deletes specified text. **-e** specifies multiple commands on one line. **-n** indicates line numbers on which to work. **-p** displays lines. **-s** substitutes specified text.
set	Establishes specific operational conditions in the Bash shell	**-a** exports all shell variables after they are assigned. **-n** takes commands without executing them, so you can debug errors. **-o** sets a particular shell mode—when used with *noclobber* as the argument, it prevents files from being overwritten by use of the > operator. **-u** yields an error message when there is an attempt to use an undefined variable. **-v** displays command lines as they are executed.
sh	Executes a shell script	Makes using **./** or **#!/bin/sh** unnecessary. **-n** reads commands without executing them. **-v** displays lines of code as executed. **-x** displays commands and arguments as executed.

Table B-1   Common UNIX/Linux commands (continued)

Command	Purpose	Useful Options and Examples
sort	Sorts and merges multiple files	**+** designates the position that follows an offset (+) as a character position, not a field position. **-b** ignores leading blank characters. **-d** sorts in dictionary order. **-f** ignores differences based on uppercase and lowercase. **-g** sorts by numeric (general) order. **-k** *n* sorts on the key field specified by *n*. **-m** merges input files that have been previously sorted (does not perform a sort). **-n** sorts numbers arithmetically. **-o** redirects output to the specified file. **-r** sorts in reverse order. **-t** indicates that a specified character separates the fields.
startx	Starts the X Window System	
tail	Displays the last few lines of a file	By default, displays the last 10 lines of a file. **-n** *n* displays the last *n* lines of the specified file.
test	Compares values and validates file existence	**!** tests for logical negation. **-a** tests for a logical AND relationship. **-b** tests if a file exists and is a block special file (which is a block-oriented device, such as a disk or tape drive). **-c** tests if a file exists and is a character special file (that is, a character-oriented device, such as a terminal or printer). **-d** tests if a file exists and is a directory. **-e** tests if a file exists. **-eq** tests if equal to. **-f** tests if a file exists and is a regular file. **-ge** tests if greater than or equal to. **-gt** tests if greater than. **-le** tests if less than or equal to. **-lt** tests if less than. **-n** tests for a nonzero string length. **-ne** tests if not equal to. **-o** tests for a logical OR relationship. **-r** tests if a file exists and is readable. **-s** tests if a file exists and its size is greater than zero. **string** tests for a nonzero string length. *string1 = string2* tests two strings for equality. *string1 != string2* tests two strings for inequality. **-w** tests if a file exists and is writable. **-x** tests if a file exists and is executable. **-z** tests for a zero-length string.

Table B-1   Common UNIX/Linux commands (continued)

Command	Purpose	Useful Options and Examples
top	Displays a list of the most CPU-intensive tasks	**-c** displays the command that initiated each process. **-i** ignores any idle processes. **-q** displays output continually, with no delay between outputs. (Use with caution! Try the spacebar for periodic updates.) **-s** causes the *top* command to run in secure mode, disabling its interactive commands. **-S** runs *top* in cumulative mode, which displays the cumulative CPU time used by a process.
touch	Changes a file's time and date stamp	**-a** specifies that only the access date and time are to be updated. **-m** specifies that only the modification date and time are to be updated. **-c** specifies that no files are to be created.
tput	Formats screen text	**clear** clears the screen. **cols** prints the number of columns on the current terminal. **cup** moves the screen cursor to a specified row and column. **rmso** disables boldface output. **smso** enables boldface output.
tr	Translates characters	**-d** deletes input characters found in string1 from the output. **-s** checks for sequences of string1 repeated consecutive times.
trap	Executes a command when a specified signal is received from the operating system	**-l** displays a listing of signal numbers and their signal designations.
tty	Displays terminal pathname	
umask	Sets file permissions for multiple files	
umount	Disconnects the file system partitions from the directory tree	If mounted or being accessed by another user, see the *fuser* command to force unmounting of the resource.
uniq	Removes consecutive duplicate lines from one file and writes the result to another file	**-u** outputs only the lines of the source file that are not duplicated. **-d** outputs one copy of each line that has a duplicate, and does not show unique lines. **-i** ignores case. **-c** starts each line by showing the number of each instance.

B

Table B-1   Common UNIX/Linux commands (continued)

Command	Purpose	Useful Options and Examples
wc	Counts the number of lines, bytes, or words in a file	**-c** counts the number of bytes or characters. **-l** counts the number of lines. **-w** counts the number of words.
whatis	Displays a brief description of a command	
whereis	Locates source, binary, and manual entries for the specified string or command	**-b** searches for binary entries only. **-m** searches for manual entries only. **-s** searches for source entries only.
w	Displays users currently on the system	Shows user's originating host, idle time, her current command, CPU utilization, and login time.
who	Shows who is currently logged in to a system	**-b** verifies when the system was last booted. **-H** displays column headings. **-q** displays a quick list of users. **-u** displays session idle times.

Table B-2   UNIX/Linux utilities by category

Command	Brief Description of Function
File-Processing Utilities	
awk	Processes files
cat	Displays files (and is used with other tools to concatenate files)
cmp	Compares two files
comm	Compares sorted files, and shows differences
cp	Copies files
cpio	Copies and backs up files to an archive
cut	Selects characters or fields from input lines
dd	Copies and converts input records
diff	Compares two text files, and shows differences
dump	Backs up files
fdformat	Formats a floppy disk at a low level
file	Displays the file type
find	Finds files within file tree
fmt	Formats text very simply
grep	Matches patterns in a file
groff	Processes embedded text formatting codes
gzip	Compresses or decompresses files
head	Displays the first part of a file (first 10 lines by default)
ispell	Checks one or more files for spelling errors (on some systems, this command might not be documented via the *man* command)

Table B-2   UNIX/Linux utilities by category (continued)

Command	Brief Description of Function
less	Displays files allowing for scrolling forward and backward (pauses when screen is full)
ln	Creates a link to a file
lpr	Sends a file to a printer or printer device
ls	Lists file and directory names and attributes
man	Displays documentation for commands
mkbootdisk	Creates a CD (or floppy disk on older distributions) from which to boot a system
mkdir	Creates a new directory
mkfs	Builds a UNIX/Linux file system
more	Displays the contents of a file allowing for scrolling forward (pauses when screen is full)
mount	Mounts file systems and devices
mv	Renames and moves files and directories
newfs	Creates a new file system (used in UNIX systems in particular)
od	Formats and displays data from a file in octal, hexadecimal, and ASCII formats
paste	Combines the contents of one or more files to output to the screen or to another file (by default, the pasted results appear in columns separated by tabs)
pr	Formats text files for printing and displays them
pwd	Shows the directory you are in
rdev	Queries or sets the root image device
restore	Restores files (from a dump)
rm	Removes files
rmdir	Removes directories
sed	Edits streams (noninteractive)
sort	Sorts or merges files
tail	Displays the last lines of files (last 10 lines by default)
tar	Copies and backs up files to a tape archive
touch	Changes file modification dates and times (and can be used to create a new file)
uniq	Displays unique lines of a sorted file
wc	Counts lines, words, and bytes
whereis	Locates information about a specific file
System Status Utilities	
date	Sets and displays date and time
df	Displays the amount of free space remaining on disk
du	Summarizes file space usage
file	Determines file type (for example, shell script, executable, ASCII text, and others)
finger	Displays detailed information about users who are logged in
free	Displays amount of free and used memory in the system

Table B-2   UNIX/Linux utilities by category (continued)

Command	Brief Description of Function
edquota	Displays user disk quotas and enables them to be changed
kill	Terminates a running process
ps	Displays process status by process identification number and name
sleep	Suspends execution for a specified time
top	Dynamically displays the status of processes in real time, focusing on those processes that are using the most CPU resources
uname	Shows information about the operating system (use the -r option to determine your kernel version)
vmstat	Shows information about virtual memory use
w	Displays detailed information about the users who are logged in
who	Displays brief information about the users who are logged in
Network Utilities	
ftp	Transfers files over a network
ifconfig	Sets up a network interface
netstat	Shows network connection information
nfsstat	Shows statistics for Network File System (NFS; file upload and download) activity
ping	Polls another network station (using TCP/IP); great for a fast determination about whether your network connection is working
rcp	Remotely copies a file from a network computer
rlogin	Logs in to a remote computer
route	Displays routing table information, and can be used to configure routing
rsh	Executes commands on a remote computer
showmount	Lists clients that have mounted volumes on a server
telnet	Connects to a remote computer on a network
traceroute	Shows the route along a network between the source device and the destination, such as from a computer to a server
wvdial	Controls a modem dialer for dial-up connections over a phone line
Communications Utilities	
mail	Sends electronic mail messages
mesg	Denies (mesg n) or accepts (mesg y) messages
talk	Lets users simultaneously type messages to each other
wall	Sends a message to all logged in users (who have permissions set to receive messages)
write	Sends a message to another user
Security Utilities	
chgrp	Changes the group associated with a file or the file's group ownership
chmod	Changes the access permissions of a file or directory
chown	Changes the owner of a file
ipchains	Manages a firewall and packet filtering (do not use if you are using *iptables* instead)
iptables	Manages a firewall and packet filtering (do not use if you are using *ipchains* instead)

Table B-2   UNIX/Linux utilities by category (continued)

Command	Brief Description of Function
passwd	Changes a password
Programming Utilities	
configure	Configures program source code automatically
g++	Compiles a C++ program
gcc	Compiles a C program
make	Maintains program source code
patch	Updates source code
Source Code Management Utilities	
ci	Creates changes in Revision Control Systems (RCS)
co	Retrieves an unencoded revision of an RCS file
cvs	Manages concurrent access to files in a hierarchy
rcs	Creates or changes the attributes of an RCS file
rlog	Prints a summary of the history of an RCS file
Miscellaneous Utilities	
at	Executes a command or script at a specified time
atq	Shows the jobs (commands or scripts) already scheduled to run
atrm	Enables you to remove a job (command or script) that is scheduled to run
batch	Runs a command or script, and is really a subset of the *at* command that takes you to the *at>* prompt, if you type only *batch* (in Fedora, Red Hat Enterprise Linux, and SUSE, a command or script is run when the system load is at an acceptable level)
cal	Displays a calendar for a month or year
cd	Changes to a directory
crontab	Schedules a command to run at a preset time
expr	Evaluates expressions (used for arithmetic and string manipulations)
fsck	Checks and fixes problems on a file system (repairs damage)
printenv	Prints environment variables
tee	Clones output stream to one or more files
tr	Replaces specified characters (a translation filter)
tty	Displays terminal pathname
xargs	Converts standard output of one command into arguments for another

Table B-3   vi editor commands

Command	Purpose
:!	Leaves vi temporarily
$	Goes to the end of the line
. (repeat)	Repeats your most recent change
/	Searches forward for a pattern of characters
0 (zero)	Goes to the beginning of the line
d$ or D	Deletes from the cursor to the end of the line
d0	Deletes from the cursor to the start of the line
dd	Deletes the current line

Table B-3 vi editor commands (continued)

Command	Purpose
dw	Deletes the word starting at the cursor; if the cursor is in the middle of the word, deletes from the cursor to the end of the word
H	Goes to the upper-left corner of the screen
i	Switches to insert mode
L	Goes to the last line on the screen
p	Pastes text from the clipboard
:q	Cancels an editing session
:q!	Cancels an editing session and exits
:r	Reads text from one file and adds it to another
:set	Turns on certain options, such as line numbering
u	Undoes your most recent change
:w	Saves a file and continues working
:wq	Writes changes to disk and exits vi
:x	Saves changes and exits vi
x	Deletes the character at the cursor location
yy	Copies (yanks) text to the clipboard
ZZ	In command mode, saves changes and exits vi

Table B-4 Emacs editor commands

Command	Purpose
Alt Commands	
Alt+<	Moves the cursor to the beginning of the file
Alt+>	Moves the cursor to the end of the file
Alt+b	Moves the cursor back one word
Alt+d	Deletes the current word
Alt+f	Moves the cursor forward one word (moving space to space between words)
Alt+q	Reformats current paragraph using word wrap so that lines are full
Alt+t	If the cursor is under the first character of the word, transposes the word with the preceding word; if the cursor is not under the first character, transposes the word with the following word
Alt+u	Capitalizes all letters from the cursor position in a word to the end of that word
Alt+w	Marks the end of a text block to copy (after you have marked the start of text with *Ctrl+spacebar*) and briefly scrolls up to where you set the beginning mark
Alt+x doctor	Enters doctor mode to play a game in which Emacs responds to your statements with questions (Save your work first. Not all versions support this mode)
Ctrl Commands	
Ctrl+@	Marks the cursor location; after moving the cursor, you can move or copy text to the mark
Ctrl+a	Moves the cursor to the beginning of the line

Table B-4 Emacs editor commands (continued)

Command	Purpose
Ctrl+b	Moves the cursor back one character
Ctrl+d	Deletes the character under the cursor
Ctrl+e	Moves the cursor to the end of the line
Ctrl+f	Moves the cursor forward one character
Ctrl+g	Cancels the current command
Ctrl+h	Runs online help
Ctrl+k	Deletes text to the end of the line
Ctrl+n	Moves the cursor to the next line
Ctrl+p	Moves the cursor to the preceding line
Ctrl+t	Transposes the character before the cursor and the character under the cursor
Ctrl+v	Scrolls down one screen
Ctrl+w	Deletes the marked text; press *Ctrl+y* to restore deleted text
Ctrl+y	Inserts text from the file buffer, and places it after the cursor
Ctrl+h, t	Runs a tutorial about Emacs
Ctrl+x, Ctrl+c	Exits Emacs
Ctrl+x, Ctrl+s	Saves the file
Ctrl+x, u	Undoes the last change
Ctrl+Del	Deletes text from the current cursor location to the end of the current word
Ctrl+spacebar	Marks the beginning of text, such as to copy the text (use *Alt+w* to mark the end of the text)

B

HOW TO INSTALL FEDORA AND HOW TO USE THE KNOPPIX CD

This book comes bundled with the Fedora and Knoppix software needed to complete the Hands-On Projects at the end of each chapter. Fedora can be installed from the DVD included with the book, and Knoppix can be run from the included CD without having to be installed on your computer. Fedora is a project sponsored by Red Hat to accomplish the following objectives: (1) to provide a free version of Linux and (2) to create a public testing environment for the Red Hat Enterprise Linux products. New options, software, and the latest versions of the GNOME and KDE X Window desktops are typically included in Fedora. The newly developed Fedora elements that are well-received through public testing are considered for incorporation into future releases of Red Hat Enterprise Linux. However, the basic Linux operating system is retained in Fedora.

Knoppix was developed by Klaus Knopper for educational and professional use. It is open source software, which means that it is freely distributed. The Knoppix CD contains the Linux operating system, plus a host of software including X Window and the KDE desktop (see Chapter 11, "The X Window System"), the Konqueror file manager and Web browser, OpenOffice.org office suite, and many other open source applications.

For readers of this book, Fedora and Knoppix offer a way to learn UNIX/Linux and use some of the most current UNIX/Linux applications—all for free. Also, through using these free distributions, you learn the basic Linux skills that can be applied to Red Hat Enterprise Linux and other UNIX/Linux versions. For example, when you use Fedora for the command-line Hands-On Projects in this book, typically the same steps apply to Red Hat Enterprise Linux and other UNIX/Linux versions. For instance, the commands that you execute in the terminal window, such as *ls* or *cat*, work the same way in Fedora as in Red Hat Enterprise Linux (and virtually all other versions of UNIX/Linux). For the GNOME-based Hands-On Projects in Chapter 11, "The X Window System," typically the same or similar steps also apply in Fedora as in other UNIX/Linux systems that use the GNOME desktop. However, the appearance of some GUI screens might be a little different, depending on which version of GNOME is used in an operating system.

HOW TO INSTALL FEDORA

The Fedora installation DVD accompanies this book. Because Fedora is on a rapid development track, you can also download the latest version of Fedora at *fedoraproject.org*. In this appendix, you learn how to install Fedora for workstation functions, using GNOME as the primary desktop.

Some new users have the option to install Fedora on a computer already running another operating system, such as another version of UNIX, Linux, or Microsoft Windows. If you have 5 to 6 GB or more of unused disk space or a second hard drive, you can install Fedora in that space so that your computer can be booted either into your existing operating system or Fedora. Another option, of course, is to let the Fedora installation completely overwrite the operating system you are currently using, so that the computer can only boot into Fedora. Consider all of the ramifications of these two choices before you start the Fedora installation.

Preparing for Installation

You should perform several steps prior to the Fedora installation:

1. Back up your present system before you start. If you perform a dual-boot installation and there is a problem, you'll still have a way to restore your system. If you plan to have a computer only with Fedora, backing up before you start enables you to restore your present files and applications, either later on the same computer or on a different computer.

2. Gather information about your computer (see the following, complete list).

3. Configure the BIOS setup to boot from the DVD drive (and change the configuration back to what it was after you complete the installation).

Fedora will do its best to identify your system's components, but if you have very new components or ones that are proprietary, Fedora might need your help in identifying certain

C

components (particularly the display card). A list of information you should obtain before you install Fedora follows:

- The type and size of your hard drive(s).

- The amount of memory in your system.

- The type of DVD drive in your system (especially if it has an IDE, SCSI, or other interface).

- The brand and model of your video card (very important to know).

- The amount of video memory on your video card.

- The brand and model of your monitor, as well as the monitor's vertical and horizontal sync ranges (you can find this information in the monitor's manual).

- The type of mouse you are using (PS/2 or serial, two buttons or three).

- If your computer has a SCSI adapter, its brand and model.

- The printer type you will use, if any. You also need to know how the printer connects to the computer. If you will print through a network, you need all the correct network connection information for the printer.

Also, if your computer is on a network, you need to know:

- The type of network card in your computer.

- Your computer's IP address configuration information. You need to determine if your computer has a static IP address or if it uses BOOTP or DHCP. You also need to know the IP address of your default gateway and primary name server. (If you have a secondary and tertiary name server, you need those IP addresses as well.) Your network administrator can provide all this information.

Finally, for the version of Fedora included with this book, it is recommended that your computer have the following:

- 500 MHz or higher CPU (the faster the CPU, the faster the response in Fedora)

- 128 MB or more of RAM

- 5 GB or more disk space

- DVD or CD/DVD drive

- Mouse or pointing device

Installing Fedora

The steps for installing Fedora are as follows:

1. Boot the system from the Fedora installation DVD.

2. Press Enter to use the graphical mode installation.

3. Select Skip (use the right arrow key), and press Enter. (Choosing Skip bypasses the test of the DVD from which you are performing the installation. If you think your DVD may be damaged, however, select to test it instead.)

4. Click Next (or choose OK and press Enter, if you are not in the full graphical mode because you have less than 256 MB of memory in your computer).

5. Use the up or down arrow key to select the language, such as English. Click Next (or choose OK and press Enter).

6. Use the arrow keys to select the keyboard configuration, such as U.S. English, and click Next (or choose OK and press Enter).

7. Whether Fedora automatically detects your mouse at this point depends on the hardware in your system. If Fedora displays a configuration screen for the mouse, select the mouse configuration (or use the default selection), such as Wheel Mouse (PS/2), and click Next (or choose OK and press Enter).

8. Depending on how Fedora detects the hardware in your system, you might see the Monitor Configuration screen, particularly if the installation software cannot detect your monitor. If you see this screen, select your monitor from the list, and click Next (or choose OK and press Enter).

9. If you have an earlier version of Fedora installed on your computer, you see an Upgrade Examine screen, on which you click Upgrade an existing installation or Install Fedora Core. For the sake of learning all of the options for an installation, select Install Fedora Core (if you see this screen) and click Next (or choose OK and press Enter).

10. If you see different installation types available, select Workstation and click Next (or choose OK and press Enter).

11. If you have more than one hard drive, such as hda and hdb, select the drive on which to create the operating system. On the same screen, choose the method of partitioning from the following:

    - Remove all partitions on selected drive and create default layout.

    - Remove linux partitions on selected drive and create default layout.

    - Use free space on selected drives and create default layout.

    - Create custom layout.

    (If you want to keep an existing Windows system intact on your computer and have determined in advance that you have enough disk space for Fedora, select Use free space on selected drives and create default layout.) After you make your selection, click Next (or choose OK and press Enter). Select Yes to proceed.

12. When asked if you want to review the partition layout select Yes. Notice the partition scheme, including for partitions containing the ext file system, swap, and others (if you are creating a dual boot system you'll see a partition for ntfs, also). Select Next (or choose OK and press Enter). (However, note that you

can edit the partition scheme by selecting Edit—but if this is your first installation it is best to use the default scheme and click Next or select OK and press Enter.)

13. If your computer has under 256 MB of memory, you'll see a Low Memory box to create swap space immediately. If you see this screen, select Yes.

14. If your computer has 256 MB of RAM or more, one screen is displayed from which to choose whether or not to use the GRUB boot loader. Select to use the GRUB boot loader, but do not choose to use a boot loader password and click Next (or select OK and press Enter). If your computer has under 256 MB of memory, you'll see several screens relating to the the GRUB boot loader. On the first screen select to use the boot loader and click Next (or select OK and press Enter). On the next screen to configure the boot loader, click Next (or select OK and press Enter). On the screen to enable you to use a boot loader password, do not select to use a password and click Next (or select OK and press Enter).

15. If you see a screen allowing you to choose the partition from which to boot from GRUB, click Next (or select OK and press Enter). (When the computer is turned on you can select which system partition to boot on a dual boot computer, such a Fedora and Windows.) Also, if you see a screen from which to select the location for the boot loader, use the default and click Next (or select OK and press Enter).

16. Use the defaults for the Network Configuration. Also, for configuring the hostname, select automatically via DHCP if your computer is on a network in which host names are automatically assigned. If your computer is not on a larger network, such as a home computer, select manually and provide a host name for your computer. Click Next (or choose OK and press Enter). (Note that if your computer has less than 256 MB of RAM, the network configuration and the hostname configuration options will appear on two screens.)

17. Select the time zone and click Next (or choose OK and press Enter).

18. Enter the root password (use six characters or more). Confirm the password and click Next (or choose OK and press Enter).

19. Select to install the Office and Productivity and the Software Development packages (limit your choices to only these for this installation). Click Next (or select OK and press Enter).

20. Click Next to start the installation process. The Required Install Media window may be displayed to tell you which installation media (the DVD) you need to have ready. Click or select Continue.

21. The installer checks software package dependencies.

22. You'll see a message that a log of the installation will be written to /root/install.log. Click Next (or select OK and press Enter).

23. You may see a screen that displays the installation media to have ready, which is the Fedora Core 6 installation DVD (if you were using multiple CDs, the screen would list the CDs needed, which would be the Fedora Core 6 CDs #1, #2, and #3). Select Continue.

24. The installer formats the disk(s) and begins installing packages.

25. (If you were using multiple CDs instead of one DVD, the installer at this point would show a request for each CD. After inserting the CD you would select OK.)

26. Remove the disc in the CD/DVD drive and click Reboot.

27. If you have configured a dual-boot system, select the Fedora Core option.

28. On the Welcome screen, click Forward.

29. Read the License Agreement. If you agree, click Yes, I agree to the License Agreement, and then click Forward.

30. Use the defaults for the Firewall and click Forward.

31. Use the defaults for the SELinux screen and click Forward.

32. Reconfigure the date and time, if necessary. Click Forward.

33. Depending on your hardware configuration, you might see a screen to adjust the display settings. If you see this screen, configure the display settings, and then click Forward.

34. Complete the Username, Full Name, Password, and Password Confirmation text boxes to create an account that you can use in addition to the root account. Click Forward.

35. If a sound card is installed, you may be asked if you want to test it. Click Finish and go to Step 37.

36. If no sound card is installed on your system click Finish.

37. Log in to your new system using the root account or the additional account you created, and proceed to use the system.

USING THE KNOPPIX CD

Knoppix is included on a CD with this book to make it easy for you to access and experiment with a Linux distribution that is based on Debian GNU/Linux. The UNIX/Linux commands you learn in this book can be used in Knoppix. There is nothing to install; just boot your computer from the CD.

C

System Requirements for the Knoppix CD

Knoppix is designed to run on most common PCs with Intel/AMD-based processors. The requirements are the following (hard disk space is not mentioned because you don't use the hard disk):

- An i486 Pentium type of processor or faster
- A bootable CD or CD/DVD drive
- 32 MB of RAM for the command-line mode or 96 MB of RAM for the GUI mode to use the KDE desktop
- Standard keyboard and graphics card (Knoppix recognizes most hardware systems)
- Mouse or pointing device

Loading the Knoppix CD

Before you insert the Knoppix CD, find out how to enable your computer to boot from the CD or CD/DVD drive. Many computers have a function key that you can press when you first turn on the PC. For example, if you have a Dell computer press F12 several times right after you turn on the PC to see a menu list of boot options. On other computers press F1, Del, or another key combination. Check your computer's documentation for the exact key combination. Another way to set your computer to boot from the CD or CD/DVD drive is to configure the boot drive sequence in your computer's BIOS. On many computers when first started, you see on the screen a key combination that you can use to enter the BIOS setup menu. For other computers you'll have to check the computer's documentation about how to start the BIOS setup menu. When you set up the BIOS, configure the boot sequence so that the computer tries first to boot from the CD or CD/DVD drive. Have the hard disk as the second boot device in the boot sequence.

NOTE If you changed the boot sequence in the BIOS you can leave it in this order even after you are done using Knoppix—unless you want your computer to boot faster without first checking to see if there is a bootable CD or DVD in its CD/DVD drive. For fastest booting when you are done with Knoppix, change the BIOS so that the hard disk is first in the boot sequence.

After your computer is set up to boot from the CD or CD/DVD drive, follow these steps:

1. Turn on the computer and boot into your regular operating system.
2. Insert the Knoppix CD.
3. Shut down the computer.
4. Turn on the computer (press the appropriate key, if necessary, to boot from the CD or CD/DVD drive) and boot from the Knoppix CD.
5. Press Enter when you see the initial Knoppix screen.

6. Your system will progress through the boot sequence from the CD. If you have speakers, during bootup you'll hear the computer say, "Initiating startup sequence."

7. The KNOPPIX INFO window enables you to select which language to use, such as clicking EN for English. Note that English is the default on the CD included with this book, so you can close the window without making a selection if you want to use English.

8. Close the KNOPPIX INFO window, if you haven't already.

9. Start using Knoppix and the KDE desktop.

To open a terminal window in Knoppix:

1. Find the Kicker (Panel) at the bottom of the screen, which contains a number of icons and a clock.

2. In the Kicker, click the Konsole Terminal Program icon (it looks like a computer monitor).

To shut down Knoppix:

1. Click the K Menu in the Kicker at the bottom of the screen.

2. Click Log Out.

3. Click Turn Off Computer.

4. Remove the Knoppix CD when your CD or CD/DVD tray opens.

5. Close the tray and press Enter to complete the shutdown.

Saving Your Files on Removable Media

Because Knoppix runs from your CD/DVD drive, you cannot save files you have created on that drive. Also, it is not recommended that you save your files on the hard drive on your computer, which is why Knoppix by default is configured to prevent you from writing to a hard drive. However, to save your files created for the Hands-On Projects in this book, you can write them to a USB flash drive, a floppy drive (on an older computer), or a second CD/DVD drive. Of these options, using a USB drive is likely to be the most versatile choice.

When you save files to another medium, keep in mind that your home directory in Knoppix is /home/knoppix. You can access your home directory using the following steps:

1. Click the K Menu in the KDE desktop. (The K Menu is on the left side of the Kicker or Panel at the bottom of the screen.)

2. Click Home Personal Files. (Another method to access your home directory is to omit Step 1 and click the Home icon in the Kicker.)

3. The Konqueror file browser opens from which you can drag and drop files to copy them.

C

To copy files to a USB flash-type drive:

NOTE By default a USB drive is set as read-only. Step 3 below shows you how to configure the drive to be writable.

1. The easiest way to ensure your USB drive is detected is to insert it before you boot the computer, because it will be automatically mounted. However, if you need to insert it after you boot the computer, you'll see a configuration window open. Ensure that Open in New Window is selected and click OK. This should mount your USB drive and you'll see its icon on the desktop. Right-click the new icon and check the menu for the option, Unmount, which means your drive is mounted. If instead you see Mount, click this menu option to mount your drive.

2. If necessary, right-click the USB drive's icon on the desktop to see the menu of options.

3. Click Change read/write mode and click Yes in the Window that says Do you want to change partition /dev/sdb1 (vfat) to be writable? (If you previously enabled the write mode during your work session the message will say, Do you want to change partition /dev/sdb1 (vfat) to be read-only? In this case you should select No.)

4. To copy a file to the USB drive, click its icon on the desktop to view the drive's contents. Also, open your home folder using the steps described earlier. Drag the files you want to copy from your home folder's window to the USB drive's window.

5. If you want to remove the USB drive while the computer is still on, right-click the drive's icon and click Unmount.

NOTE Do not attempt to run script, perl, CGI, C, and C++ programs you have created in Knoppix on a Windows computer. However, you can use Wordpad in Windows to open text files and view their contents. (Windows Notepad does not correctly format text files created in Linux.)

To copy files to a floppy disk:

1. Insert the disk.

2. Click the Floppy icon on the desktop to view the disk's contents.

3. Drag the files you want to copy from your home directory's window to the floppy disk's window.

4. Ensure the floppy disk's drive light has gone out before your remove the disk.

NOTE In some cases you may need to manually mount and unmount the floppy disk. To mount the disk, first insert it, right-click the floppy disk's icon and click Mount. To unmount the disk before removing it, right-click the disk's icon and click Unmount—then remove the disk.

CAUTION In some cases your system may not recognize the filesystem of the floppy disk you insert. If this is the case, try inserting the disk before you start the computer. Another option is to manually specify the file system and mount the disk via the command line by entering *mount -t vfat /dev/fd0 /mnt/floppy*. You can *unmount* a floppy disk by entering *umount /mnt/floppy*.

To copy files to a CD or DVD drive (using a CD-R, CD-RW, DVD-R, or DVD+R disc):

1. Open Konqueror to your home directory and select the files and folders to be written to CD/DVD. You can select multiple files and folders by holding down the Ctrl key as you click each selection.

2. Right-click the highlighted selections.

3. Click Actions.

4. Click Create Data CD with K3b. (You may see a window to verify or configure the speed of your drive. Select the appropriate speed and click OK.)

5. Wait for a moment while the K3b program starts.

6. The Current Projects pane shows the files and folders you have selected to copy. You can add more files or folders by dragging them into the Current Projects pane.

7. Click the Burn button in the Current Projects pane.

8. Notice on the Writing tab that you can manually set the speed of the drive or leave it for the system to automatically detect the speed. In most cases it is best to leave the Speed: setting at Auto.

9. Click the Filesystem tab. If you want to make the CD/DVD readable in Windows, ensure that Generate Joliet extensions is selected. If you only plan to use your CD/DVD in UNIX/Linux, then you do not need to make this selection. Further, ensure that Generate Rock Ridge extensions is selected (a default selection). Rock Ridge extensions add POSIX compliancy to files so they are constructed to be compatible with all types of UNIX/Linux systems.

10. Click Burn.

11. You'll see a screen that enables you to follow the progress of the copy. When the copying is done, the CD/DVD is ejected.

12. Click Close to return to the K3b window. Close all open windows.

Useful Knoppix Tips

Like any operating system, Knoppix has some features that are good to know. Here are some tips to help as you use Knoppix:

- There is no password for the root account in Knoppix. When you log into the root account leave the password box empty.

- The KDE desktop in Knoppix contains icons for each of your computer's hard drives. You can view their contents, but by default you cannot write to the hard drives. It is possible to configure Knoppix to write to a hard drive, but it is safer not to because your hard drive's operating system, such as Windows, is not compatible with the Knoppix file system.

- If you have a second CD or CD/DVD drive there is an icon on the desktop that enables you to write to it. The same is true if you have a floppy drive.

- Every file you save in Knoppix is saved to a special memory space in RAM and not to the Knoppix CD. This means each time you shut down Knoppix, YOU'LL LOSE ALL FILES YOU HAVE SAVED. You can, however, write files to a second CD/DVD drive, to a floppy drive, or to another computer in your network. If you want to save files to a Windows computer on your network (such as to your instructor's computer or a server), click the Knoppix icon in the Kicker, point to Utilities, click Samba Network Neighborhood, and locate the computer on which to save files. You can use Konqueror to copy a file from Knoppix to a Windows computer available through Samba. To start Konqueror, click the K menu in the Kicker and click Home Personal Files (to open your home folder).

- The Knoppix CD comes with the OpenOffice.org office software. Consider giving it a try. In fact, you'll find many other open-source applications to try on the Knoppix CD. Visit *www.knoppix.org* and *www.knoppix.net* to learn more about Knoppix.

- The Knoppix CD does not come with the Emacs editor described in Chapter 3, "Mastering Editors." However, one way to use the Emacs editor is to download it from the Internet and put it on a USB flash-type of drive and run it from the USB flash drive. To obtain a copy of Emacs, visit *www.gnu.org/software/emacs* and download a version that runs in Linux. (Another option is to download a version of Emacs that runs in Windows and practice using Emacs from a Windows-based computer.)

D

UNIX/Linux Variants

A UNIX/Linux variant is simply one of the many different versions or distributions of UNIX/Linux. There are well over 100 UNIX/Linux variants that run on different kinds of computers. This appendix does not attempt to list all of the variants, but instead focuses on providing an overview of some of the most popular.

One reason why UNIX/Linux has proliferated into so many variants is because much of the operating system kernel and UNIX/Linux software are written in portable languages, such as C and C++. Another reason for the popularity of UNIX/Linux is that TCP/IP (Transmission Control Protocol/Internet Protocol), the main protocol of the Internet and of general networking, was built in to UNIX/Linux systems in the early 1980s—at the same time TCP/IP was adopted for the international network that has become the Internet. Most other operating systems did not implement full TCP/IP capabilities until much later. A third reason why UNIX/Linux has evolved into so many variants is that the basic kernel source code is publicly available, instead of being a trade secret, as is true of proprietary operating systems such as Windows. This characteristic makes it easier for vendors to adapt hardware to UNIX/Linux systems and for software creators to offer a huge range of applications, many of which are free.

POPULAR VERSIONS OF UNIX/LINUX

Most versions of UNIX/Linux follow one (or a combination) of two standards: the Berkeley System Distribution (BSD) standard and the System V release 4 (SVR4) standard.

The BSD standard grew out of the efforts of several professors and students at the University of California at Berkeley. This group of professors and students developed the BSD 3 version of UNIX/Linux and then the BSD 4 version. In the early 1990s, their work evolved into a commercial enterprise through the newly formed company, Berkeley Software Design. Two popular features of UNIX/Linux that you have learned about in this book, the vi editor and the C shell, grew out of the BSD version of UNIX/Linux. Visit *www.bsd.org* for links to BSD UNIX resources.

The System V version has roots in the work done by Bell Labs at AT&T. From the mid-1970s through the late 1980s, Bell Labs developed System V. Eventually, this version of UNIX/Linux was taken over by an AT&T subsidiary company called UNIX/Linux Systems Laboratories. In the early 1990s, UNIX/Linux Systems Laboratories joined with Novell to port a version of UNIX/Linux to Intel processors. Not only was UNIX/Linux ported to popular PCs through their work, but also this version of UNIX/Linux initiated a GUI interface for UNIX/Linux, called UNIX/Linux Desktop. Before long, UNIX/Linux Systems Laboratories was taken over by Novell. In the mid-1990s, Novell decided to de-emphasize its UNIX/Linux operations and sold them to a company called Santa Cruz Operation (SCO), which today as The SCO Group offers a System V commercial product called UnixWare. You can learn more about UnixWare at *www.sco.com*.

Today, many computer and operating system vendors provide commercial UNIX/Linux distributions. In addition, independent groups provide free UNIX/Linux systems. Table D-1 lists a sampling of the popular commercial systems; Table D-2 lists some of the free systems.

Table D-1 Popular commercial UNIX/Linux variants

Version	Manufacturer	Origin	Information on the Web
AIX and AIX 5L	IBM	A combination of SVR4 and BSD	*www.ibm.com* or *www.03.ibm.com/ servers/aix*
Darwin (MAC OS X)	Apple Computers	BSD	*www.apple.com*
Hewlett Packard UNIX (HP-UX)	Hewlett Packard	SVR4	*www.hp.com*
IRIX	Silicon Graphics	SVR4	*www.sgi.com* or *www. sgi.com/products/ software/irix*
LynxOS	LynxWorks	SVR4	*www.lynxworks.com*
Mandriva Linux	Mandriva	A combination of SVR4 and BSD	*www.mandriva.com*

Table D-1 Popular commercial UNIX/Linux variants (continued)

Version	Manufacturer	Origin	Information on the Web
Red Hat Enterprise Linux	Red Hat	SVR4	*www.redhat.com*
OpenServer	The SCO Group, Inc.	SVR4	*www.sco.com*
Solaris	Sun Microsystems	SVR4	*www.sun.com*
SUSE Linux Enterprise	Novell	SVR4	*www.novell.com/linux*
Tru64 UNIX	Hewlett Packard	SVR4	*h30097.www3.hp.com*
Turbolinux	Turbolinux, Inc.	SVR4	*www.turbolinux.com*
UnixWare	The SCO Group, Inc.	SVR4	*www.sco.com*
VxWorks	Wind River Systems	BSD	*www.windriver.com*

Table D-2 Popular free UNIX/Linux variants

Version	Source	Origin	Information on the Web
Fedora Linux	Sponsored by Red Hat	SVR4	*fedoraproject.org/index.html*
Debian GNU/Linux	Debian	BSD	*www.debian.org*
FreeBSD	The FreeBSD Project	BSD	*www.freebsd.org*
Gentoo	Gentoo Linux	SVR4	*www.gentoo.org*
Linux	Available from many sources	SVR4	*www.linux.org*
HURD	GNU	BSD	*www.gnu.org/software/hurd/hurd.html*
Knoppix	Klaus Knopper	BSD	*www.knoppix.org*
NetBSD	NetBSD Project	BSD	*www.netbsd.org*
OpenBSD	The OpenBSD Project	BSD	*www.openbsd.org*
openSUSE	openSUSE.org	BSD	*www.opensuse.org*
Ubuntu	Ubuntu	BSD	*www.ubuntu.com*

NOTE
There are many, many Linux distributions, both free and commercial. To see a list of Linux distributions visit *www.en.wikipedia.org/wiki/List_of_Linux_distributions*. After you visit this Web site you'll very likely be impressed with the world-wide efforts devoted to Linux development.

Many similarities exist between versions of UNIX/Linux. For example, they all offer full TCP/IP network compatibility. All versions of UNIX/Linux have layered components that make up the operating system (see Chapter 1, "The Essence of UNIX and Linux"), and they all use shells as command-line interpreters. In fact, virtually every version of UNIX/Linux supports the Bourne shell, and many support the C and Bash shells.

All UNIX/Linux versions come with at least one text editor, such as vi, Emacs, or both, and they use similar file and text manipulation utilities. UNIX/Linux variants use a similar hierarchical file system that employs permissions for file security. In addition, UNIX/Linux systems support a variety of software compilers, particularly C, C++, LISP, and Pascal. They also permit shell scripting and enable Perl and CGI scripts.

The differences between versions of UNIX/Linux are generally evident in some differences in commands and in the hardware platforms they use. These differences are explored in the next two sections.

UNIX/Linux Command Differences

Many of the UNIX/Linux command differences stem from whether a system is based on BSD or System V. However, command differences are also related to enhancements or changes that particular vendors have made to commands. For example, in IBM's AIX, the command to create a new user is *mkuser*; in FreeBSD, the command is *adduser*, and in Linux, the command is *useradd*. To delete a user in these systems, you use *rmuser* in AIX, *rmuser* in FreeBSD, and *userdel* in Linux.

Sometimes, the command-line differences are not in the commands that are supported, but in the options associated with a command. For example, in BSD-based systems, the *ls -s* command usually shows the file size in kilobytes, whereas the same command shows the file size in 512 blocks in SVR4 systems. To display the processor type in Fedora, Red Hat Enterprise Linux, or SUSE, you type *uname -m*, but in Solaris, you type *uname -imp*.

Table D-3 provides information on how commands can be similar or different among these systems: AIX (based on BSD and SVR4), Linux (based on SVR4 and BSD), and Solaris (based on SVR4).

NOTE In some instances in Table D-3, several commands accomplish the same purpose in a single operating system. In these cases, the commands are separated by commas. For example, four commands can be used to print a file in AIX: *lp*, *lpr*, *enq*, and *qprt*.

Table D-3 UNIX/Linux commands of AIX, Linux, and Solaris

Activity	Command in AIX	Command in Linux	Command in Solaris
Print a file	lp, lpr, enq, qprt	lpr	lp, lpr
Show the size of the swap file	lsps -a, vmstat	free, vmstat	swap -l, vmstat
Show processes	ps	ps	ps
Configure a network interface card	ifconfig	ifconfig	ifconfig
Change information associated with a user's account	chuser -a	usermod	usermod

Table D-3   UNIX/Linux commands of AIX, Linux, and Solaris (continued)

Activity	Command in AIX	Command in Linux	Command in Solaris
View information in a print queue	lpq, lpstat, qchk, enq -A	lpq	lpstat
List all of the software packages installed	lslpp -L all	rpm -qa	pkginfo
Initiate paging (virtual memory)	swapon -a	swapon -a	swap -a

UNIX/Linux Hardware Platforms

Some of the UNIX/Linux variants, such as Hewlett Packard's HP-UX, are particularly targeted for high-end, powerful RISC (Reduced Instruction Set Computer) processors or the supercharged Intel Itanium processors.

A RISC processor is fast and powerful because it requires fewer instructions for common operations and it has portions of the CPU that are dedicated to specific functions. The Itanium processor is built from the basic RISC architecture, but it includes EPIC (Explicitly Parallel Instruction Computing), which is the capability to predict upcoming processor operations on the basis of tracking previous operations. The Itanium processor also has larger processor work areas than non-EPIC RISC processors.

NOTE   Both the RISC and Itanium processors have a 64-bit architecture instead of the slower, 32-bit architecture of non-Itanium, Intel-class processors. However, Intel and AMD have introduced a family of new 64-bit processors suitable for UNIX, Linux, and Windows systems. In fact, Microsoft has announced that the Windows systems developed after Windows Vista will only run on 64-bit processors.

Other UNIX/Linux variants, such as Fedora, Red Hat Enterprise Linux, and SUSE Linux function well on 32- or 64-bit Intel-class servers and workstations. Also, Darwin UNIX is well-tailored for Macintosh computers.

Of the UNIX/Linux variants, distributions of Linux have proven to be especially versatile in terms of hardware compatibility. Besides Intel-class processors, Linux has been adapted to run on IBM mainframe and minicomputers, Hewlett Packard RISC-based computers, Sun workstations, HP/Compaq/DEC alpha computers, Silicon Graphics workstations, and many others.

Table D-4 is a list of some typical hardware configurations that can be used with UNIX/Linux operating systems. Note that as each UNIX/Linux distribution evolves, more scalability is built in so that different processors can be used. When you obtain a UNIX/

Linux distribution, ensure that you match the distribution version with the type of processor you use, 32-bit or 64-bit.

Table D-4 A sampling of UNIX/Linux systems and typical hardware compatibility

UNIX/Linux Version	Typical Hardware
AIX and AIX 5L	IBM RISC-based pSeries, iSeries, zSeries, and eSeries servers and the older RISC-based RS/6000 workstations and servers
Fedora	Intel-class and AMD 32- and 64-bit processors
HP-UX	RISC-based and Itanium processors in HP workstations and servers
IRIX	Silicon Graphics RISC-based computers, including the Silicon Graphics Fuel, O2, Octane2, and Origin workstations, servers, and supercomputers
Linux from Silicon Graphics	Intel Itanium processor in the Silicon Graphics 750 and the Altrix computers
Mac OS X and Darwin	Apple RISC-based PowerPC, G3, G4, and G5 computers, plus Intel 32- and 64-bit Core 2 Duo processors
Red Hat Enterprise Linux	Intel-class and AMD 32- and 64-bit processors
Sun Solaris	RISC-based UltraSPARC processor in Sun UltraSPARC workstations and servers, Sun Fire servers, Sun Ray workstations, and Intel-class and AMD 32- and 64-bit processors
SUSE Linux	Intel-class and AMD 32- and 64-bit processors
Turbolinux	Intel-class and AMD 32- and 64-bit processors
UnixWare and OpenServer	Intel-class and AMD 32- and 64-bit processors

CHOOSING A UNIX/LINUX VARIANT

When it comes to selecting any operating system, the best advice is to:

1. Understand the requirements of what you want to accomplish and what application software is needed to meet those requirements.

2. Select the operating system on which the software can run.

3. Select the hardware that is appropriate to the operating system and software needs.

For example, if you need to perform professional computing that requires using lots of graphics for publishing, one good choice is a Mac OS X system. If you are engaging in personal computing and want to use an Intel-based or AMD computer, a free or commercial distribution of Linux is often an appropriate selection. If the application requirement is to have a powerful server for a complex accounting system, AIX, HP-UX, or Sun Solaris on a RISC or Itanium computer might be needed; or Red Hat Enterprise Linux or SUSE may be options on a 64-bit Intel/AMD processor. In fact, as new Intel and AMD 64-bit processors have come out, some companies are migrating from traditional large-scale UNIX systems to Red Hat Enterprise Linux and SUSE Linux Enterprise.

One significant advantage to selecting any UNIX/Linux variant is the element of portability. If you start with one UNIX/Linux variant and its associated hardware platform, but later find you need to scale up to a different UNIX/Linux variant and platform, the chances are very good that you can port most or all of your initial investment in application software. Another advantage is that users trained in one UNIX/Linux variant can quickly adapt to a different variant, so you do not lose your training investment either.

As you can see, there is a variant of UNIX/Linux to help you accomplish nearly any type of computing task and on a wide range of computers—which is the single, most impressive advantage of UNIX/Linux.

D

E

UNIX/LINUX SECURITY: NETWORK AND INTERNET CONNECTIVITY

With the use of a powerful and flexible system comes the responsibility to ensure that the system is not easily broken into and misused. This appendix focuses on the security needs of running a standard UNIX/Linux installation and the steps you can take to make your computer secure.

SECURITY HARDENING

Security hardening is the process of taking a default system installation and making that system more secure, harder to break into, and, therefore, less likely to be exploited. You should understand the different levels of security hardening available. This appendix focuses on security at the workstation or server as the most likely and efficient way for you to protect the systems for which you are responsible. The other types of security—network and organizational—are beyond the scope of this book.

The steps to secure your systems include the following:

1. Implementing physical system security
2. Defining and publishing the security policy
3. Ensuring password security
4. Managing unnecessary services
5. Viewing log files on a regular basis
6. Keeping up with security fixes and patches
7. Monitoring your system automatically
8. Securing your folders and files

Implementing Physical System Security

Can a person who is not a system administrator walk up to your server and physically touch it? If yes, why? If a computer is important and you want it to be as secure as possible, it should be secured in a cabinet or other enclosure such as a locked room. Setting a BIOS password, locking the case, putting up a security camera that is above and pointing down at the computer, disabling the CD/DVD drive access internally, and keeping the cleaning staff out of the server room are great ways to increase your physical system security.

Physical security is just as important for desktop users as it is for server operators. Although you normally would not turn off a server computer at night due to its role, you can shut down a desktop computer, log out of your session, or use a locking screensaver to secure your desktop at night or when you are away for more than a moment. For example, Chapter 11, "The X Window System," explains how to set up a locking screensaver.

Defining and Publishing the Security Policy

If an action is not allowed, it's denied. This should be your standard security policy. Many examples of well-designed security policies are available on the Internet and in security manuals. Use them as a reference as you build your own.

Building your own security policy is easy when you take it task by task. The sections that follow are examples of tasks that might be included in a security policy. Also, one of the best resources for security information and policy templates is the SANS Institute, which can be found at *www.sans.org*.

Your policy should be reasonable and regularly seen by the subjects who are governed by it. Post a copy in your company's break room or on a bulletin board. Also, e-mail the security policy to company members or make it available over the network, such as in an Acrobat PDF file. Also, send reminders about the location of the policy and notify users about updates to the policy.

Ensuring Password Security

One of the most important keys to system security is having hard-to-guess passwords. This is called using a "strong" password that employs the following guidelines:

- Is six or more characters in length
- Does not contain a regular word, such as one found in the dictionary, or a name of a person or place
- Does not contain more than two or three letters already employed in the user account name
- Uses a hard-to-guess combination of uppercase and lowercase letters, numbers, and nonalphanumeric characters (nonalphanumeric characters include characters such as *, &, ^, !, #, +, =, %, and $)

Also, if you are the system administrator, it is important to understand how user account and password information is stored in your system. When the user logs in to access resources, the password file is checked to permit login authorization. The password file (/etc/passwd) contains the following kinds of information:

- The user name
- An encrypted password or a reference to a shadow file, a file associated with the password file that makes it difficult for intruders to determine the passwords of others (if the shadow file capability is turned on)
- The user identification number (UID), which can be a number as large as 60000
- A group identification number (GID) with which the user name is associated
- Information about the user, such as a description or the user's job
- The location of the user's home directory
- A command that is executed as the user logs in, which is usually the shell to start

Typically, the /etc/passwd file must be readable to all users to permit them to log in. Fortunately, many UNIX/Linux systems enable you to place the encrypted password in the shadow (/etc/shadow) file instead of in the /etc/passwd file, so that the /etc/passwd file only contains a pointer to the /etc/shadow file. The /etc/shadow file is normally available only to the system administrator for better security. Besides passwords for accounts, the shadow file contains password restriction information that includes the following:

- The minimum and the maximum number of days between password changes
- Information on when the password was last changed
- Warning information about when a password will expire
- Amount of time that the account can be inactive before access is prohibited

When you set up your system, plan to use the /etc/shadow file capabilities. In Fedora and Red Hat Enterprise Linux, for example, you can do this in the GNOME desktop by using the following general steps:

1. Log in as root.
2. Click the System menu, point to Administration, and click Authentication.
3. Click the Options tab, if it is not already displayed.
4. Check the Use Shadow Passwords check box, if it is not already selected.
5. Click OK.

In SUSE, the /etc/shadow file is automatically configured for use by the user authentication module called pam_unix2.so.

In conjunction with the use of the /etc/shadow file, plan to use password restriction options, such as requiring that users change their passwords at specific intervals. You can use these options either with the command-line utility to create the user account, such as Linux's *useradd* command (check your man pages for information), or with the desktop tool used to create user accounts, such as the User Manager in Fedora and Red Hat Enterprise Linux and the User Management option in SUSE's YaST system management tool. Also, encourage users to regularly change their own passwords using the appropriate command-line utility, such as *passwd* in Linux.

Managing Unnecessary Services

When your system is connected to a network, one way an intruder can access or compromise your system is through using a service that you do not typically use. You can increase the security on your system by stopping services that are not in use. For example, if you use SSH instead of Telnet for remote communications, consider stopping the Telnet service. When you use the GNOME desktop, you can access the Services Configuration tool in Fedora and Red Hat Enterprise Linux for starting or stopping a service. You can also use the tool to completely delete a service, add a new service, or configure the run level of a service. In SUSE you use the System Services (Runlevel) tool to enable or disable services.

The steps for accessing the Services Configuration tool in Fedora and Red Hat Enterprise Linux with GNOME are as follows:

1. Log in as root.

2. Click the System menu, point to Administration, and click Services.

3. Ensure that the Background Services tab is selected. Click any service in the left pane to see a description of the service and determine if the service is running (the service's status).

4. Use the Start or Stop buttons to start or stop a particular service that you've selected in the left pane.

To use the System Services (Runlevel) tool in SUSE:

1. Log in as root.

2. Click the Computer menu.

3. Click Control Center.

4. Click System in the left pane.

5. Click YaST in the right pane.

6. Click System in the left pane of the YaST window.

7. Click System Services (Runlevel) in the right pane of YaST (you may need to scroll to find this selection).

8. Notice that the Enabled column shows whether a service is enabled or disabled. Also, you can click a particular service to view a more complete description in the bottom of the window.

9. To enable or disable a service, click the service and then click the Enable or Disable button.

10. Click Finish when you are done and close any remaining windows.

Viewing Log Files on a Regular Basis

Linux has many useful log files that provide all kinds of information about your system and about security. Some show only boot messages, some warn of security issues, and many simply write to the log file when a given action, error, or event occurs. All are valuable sources of system information and should be examined regularly.

The default location for log files in Linux is the /var/log/ directory. Because our focus is on security, let's look at some of the most useful logs your system keeps by default:

- *boot.log*—Lists messages from the boot process

E

- *cron*—Shows information about cron tasks (cron refers to the crond daemon that runs many ordinary tasks and applications in UNIX/Linux)

- *error_log*—Lists information about system and application errors and is typically found in the directory /var/log/cups

- *maillog*—Contains mail server activities

- *messages*—Lists messages from the system, such as indications of problems, changes to run levels, I/O activities, networking activities, and when services are started or stopped

- *secure*—Provides messages relating to security

- *Xorg.O.log*—Provides messages relating to the X Window interface

In Fedora and Red Hat Enterprise Linux with the GNOME desktop, you can view several of these logs using the following steps:

1. Log into root.

2. Click the System menu, point to Administration, and click System Log.

3. The individual logs are listed in the left pane.

4. Click any log, such as messages, to view its contents in the right pane.

5. Close the window when you are finished.

To view the logs in SUSE:

1. Log in as root.

2. Click the Computer menu.

3. Click Control Center.

4. Click System in the left pane.

5. Click YaST in the right pane.

6. Click Miscellaneous in the left pane of the YaST window.

7. Click View System Log (to see the messages log by default).

8. Close the window when you are finished.

Keeping Up with Security Fixes and Patches

For many operating systems, the operating system provider offers updates for security and other fixes or enhancements. Keeping current on security updates is one of the best methods for ensuring the security of your system. Often, updates are provided to close security holes recently discovered or to foil a new virus or other malicious software.

Fedora, Red Hat Enterprise Linux, and SUSE all have tools to enable you to obtain operating system updates and patches. To obtain the updates, you need an Internet connection and you should have already registered your operating system. The general steps for starting the update process in Fedora and Red Hat Enterprise Linux are as follows:

1. Log on as root.

2. Click the Applications menu, point to System Tools, and click Software Updater.

3. Select the updates to install and click Apply Updates.

NOTE

Fedora and Red Hat Enterprise Linux also come with an update alert feature. When a new security update is available, you see an icon near the clock in the top Panel. Click the icon or wait for a warning notice box from the icon to appear from which you can click the Apply Updates button.

The general steps for accessing updates and patches in SUSE are:

1. Log in as root.

2. Click the Computer menu.

3. Click Control Center.

4. Click System in the left pane.

5. Click YaST in the right pane.

6. Click Software in the left pane in the YaST window.

7. Click Online Update.

8. Select the updates to install and click Accept.

Monitoring Your System Automatically

Plan to regularly monitor your system for possible security problems. You can automate many of the functions of monitoring by using the tools already installed on your system. To illustrate, this section walks you through automating system monitoring by regularly capturing information from the *top* command (see Chapter 8, "Exploring the UNIX/Linux Utilities").

To get a system snapshot on an hourly basis using the *crontab* utility, the *top* utility, and the *mail* command:

1. Log in as the root user.

2. Access the command line, such as by opening a terminal window.

3. Edit the crontab file by typing *crontab -e*.

4. When the file opens in vi, press the *i* on your keyboard to begin inserting text.

5. On a single line, type the following (the period is not part of the command):
   * 0-23 * * 1-5 top -nl | mail root.

   This causes the system to run the *top* command one time every hour, Monday through Friday, for every week in the month and year. The system e-mails the output of this command to you, the root user. Be certain to check your inbox using the *mail* command (see Chapter 8).

6. Press the Esc key, type *:wq* and then press Enter to exit the file.

7. Your system should return a text message similar to the following:

   ```
   no contab for root - using an empty one
   crontab: installing new crontab
   ```

You can also use many other commands in addition to the *top* command. Here is a list of several useful commands:

- *vmstat*—This command shows the current state of the processor, the memory, the swap space, the I/O system, the system, and the CPU.

- *netstat*—The *netstat* command can show you many things about the network connections to your computer. In particular, use *netstat -s* for statistics on all loaded protocols. Also, without the *-s* option, *netstat* shows the users connecting, their originating addresses, and the ports and protocols they are using to connect. See Chapter 8 for more about *netstat*.

- *ps*—Consider regularly using *ps -aux*. This shows the current state of all system processes, including all background processes that are being run by daemons.

- *pstree*—This command is used with various options. It can show all processes in a tree-like format that helps you visualize what's responsible for what processes. It also assists in eliminating some security risks associated with giving too many permissions to users.

Use the man pages to find out more about these commands.

NOTE

Securing Your Folders and Files

When you set up a system or create a new folder or file, be certain that you use the proper security. Good folder and file security ensures that only authorized users access information or run specific programs. Use the *chmod* command, as you learned in Chapter 2, "Exploring the UNIX/Linux File Systems and File Security," to configure security on folders and files. Typically, if specific users do not need access to a folder or file, you should ensure that they have no permissions on that folder or file. Also, for those who need access, give them only the appropriate permissions to match the type of access they require. This step protects both those who should have access and those who should not.

Using Kerberos Authentication

One way to harden security on a network is to use Kerberos authentication. Kerberos is a security system developed by the Massachusetts Institute of Technology to enable two parties on an open network to communicate without interception from an intruder, by creating a unique encryption key for each communication session. Note however, that other computers with which you communicate on the network must also be configured for Kerberos.

The general steps to enable Kerberos in Fedora or Red Hat Enterprise Linux are as follows:

1. Log into root.

2. Click the System menu.

3. Point to Administration and click Authentication.

4. Access the Authentication tab and check the Enable Kerberos Support check box. Also click the Configure Kerberos button to configure the authentication for your particular site and click OK.

5. Close the Authentication Configuration window.

The general steps for enabling Kerberos in SUSE are:

1. Log into root.

2. Click the Computer menu.

3. Click Control Center.

4. Click System in the left pane.

5. Click YaST in the right pane.

6. Click Security and Users in the left pane of the YaST window.

7. Click User Management in the right pane.

8. Click the Expert Options button.

9. Click Authentication and User Sources.

10. Click the Configure button.

11. Click Kerberos (you may need to click Continue, insert one or more of the SUSE CDs/DVDs, and click OK for each CD/DVD to install the software packages for Kerberos).

12. Click Use Kerberos.

13. Complete the Basic Kerberos Setting parameters to match your site.

14. Click Finish.

15. Close all windows when you are finished configuring Kerberos.

Glossary

.bashrc file — A file in your home directory that you can use to customize your work environment and specify what occurs each time you log in. Each time you start a shell, that shell executes the commands in .bashrc.

/boot partition — A partition that is used to store the operating system files that compose the kernel.

/home partition — A partition that is on the home directory and provides storage space for all users' directories. A separate section of the hard disk, it protects and insulates users' personal files from the UNIX/Linux operating system software.

/usr partition — A partition in which to store some or all of the nonkernel operating system programs that will be accessed by users.

/var partition — A partition that holds temporarily created files, such as files used for printing documents and log files used to record monitoring and administration data.

absolute path — A pathname that begins at the root file system directory and lists all subdirectories to the destination file.

algorithm — A sequence of instructions, programming code, or commands that results in a program or that can be used as part of a program.

alias — A name that represents a command. Aliases are helpful in simplifying and automating frequently used commands.

applet — Usually a program or small software application that is represented by an icon. In the X Window GNOME and KDE desktops, an applet can be placed on the Panel or the Kicker for fast access.

argument — Text that provides UNIX/Linux with additional information for executing a command. On the command line, an argument name follows an option name, and a space separates the two. Examples of arguments are file and directory names.

arithmetic operator — A character that represents a mathematical activity. Arithmetic operators include + (addition), - (subtraction), * (multiplication), and / (division).

array — A variable that stores an ordered list of scalar values that is accessed with numeric subscripts, starting at zero.

ASCII — An acronym for American Standard Code for Information Interchange, a standard set of bit patterns organized and interpreted as alphabetic characters, decimal numbers, punctuation marks, and special characters. The code is used to translate binary numbers into ordinary language, and, therefore, makes information stored in files accessible. ASCII can represent up to 256 characters (bit patterns).

assembler — The program that is called by a compiler to translate assembly code into object code.

assembly language — A low-level language that provides maximum access to all the computer's devices, both internal and external. Writing an assembly language program requires a great deal of coding and time.

authentication — The process of verifying that a user is authorized to access a particular computer, server, network, or network resource, such as Telnet or FTP.

automatic variable — A variable declared inside a function and local to the function in which it is declared.

Bash shell — A UNIX/Linux command interpreter (and the default Linux shell). Incorporates the best features of the Bourne shell and the Korn shell. Its name is an acronym for "Bourne Again Shell."

Berkeley Software Distribution (BSD) — A distribution of UNIX developed through the University of California at Berkeley, which first distributed the BSD UNIX version in 1975.

binaries — The programs residing in the /bin directory and elsewhere that are needed to start the system and perform other essential tasks. *See also* executables.

binary file — A file containing non-ASCII characters (such as machine instructions).

bit — The abbreviation for binary digit, a number composed of one of two numbers, 0 and 1. UNIX/Linux store all data in the form of binary digits. Because the computer consists of electronic circuits in either an on or off state, binary digits are perfect for representing these states.

bitmap — The rows and columns of dots or bit patterns that graphics software transforms into an infinite variety of images.

block special file — In UNIX/Linux, a file used to manage random access devices that involve handling blocks of data, including CD/DVD drives, hard disk drives, tape drives, and other storage devices. Also called a block device file.

body — One of two parts of HTML code. (The other part is the head.) The body defines what appears within the browser window.

Boolean operator — A logical operator that symbolizes AND, OR, or NOT to evaluate a relationship, such as a comparison of two expressions—and the result of the evaluation is either true or false.

bootstrap loader — A utility residing in the /boot directory that starts the operating system.

Bourne shell — The first UNIX/Linux command interpreter, developed at AT&T Bell Labs by Stephen Bourne.

branch instruction — An instruction that tells a program to go to a different section of code.

byte — The abbreviation for binary term; a string of eight binary digits or bits. These digits can be configured into patterns of bits, which, in turn, can be interpreted as alphabetic characters, decimal numbers, punctuation marks, and special characters. This is the basis for ASCII code.

C — A programming language developed in part to overcome the disadvantages of assembly language programming, which requires a great deal of coding and time. The result is a high-level set of easy-to-understand instructions. UNIX was originally written in assembly language but further developed and refined in C, largely due to the efforts of Dennis Ritchie and Brian Kernighan of AT&T Bell Labs.

C library — A collection of functions that perform file, screen, and keyboard operations, and many other tasks. To perform or include one of these functions in your program, you insert a function call at the appropriate location in your file.

C shell — A UNIX/Linux command interpreter designed for C programmers.

C++ — A programming language developed by Bjarne Stroustrup of AT&T Bell Labs. Stroustrup added object-oriented capabilities and other features to the C language.

case logic — One of the four basic shell logic structures employed in program development. Using case logic, a program can perform one of many actions, depending on the value of a variable and matching results to a test. It is often used when there is a list of several choices.

case sensitive — A property that distinguishes uppercase letters from lowercase letters—for example, *John* differs from *john*. UNIX is case sensitive.

character special file — A UNIX/Linux I/O management file used to handle byte-by-byte streams of data, such as through serial or USB connections, including terminals, printers, and network communications. Also called a character device file.

child — A subdirectory created and stored within a (parent) directory.

class — A data structure in the C++ programming language that enables the programmer to create abstract data types. In this context, an abstract data type is one defined by the programmer for a specific programming task.

client — A computer on a network running programs or accessing files from a mainframe, network server, or host computer.

command — Text typed after the command-line prompt that requests that the computer take a specific action.

command line — The onscreen location for typing commands.

command mode — A feature of a modal editor that lets you enter commands to perform editing tasks, such as moving through the file and deleting text. The UNIX/Linux vi editor is a modal editor.

Common Gateway Interface (CGI) — A protocol or set of rules governing how browsers and servers communicate. Any script that sends information to or receives information from a server must follow these rules.

compiler — A program that reads the lines of code in a source file, converts them to machine-language instructions or calls the assembler to convert them into object code, and creates a machine-language file.

compiling — A process of translating a program file into machine-readable language.

configuration variable — A variable that stores information about the operating system and does not change the value.

constant — A value in program code that does not change when the program runs.

control string — An argument that specifies how formatting should occur when using the screen output library function *printf()*.

control structures — *See* logic structures.

core file — A type of garbage file created when an executing program attempts to do something illegal, such as accessing another user's memory.

daemon — A specialized system process that runs in the background. A daemon accesses UNIX/Linux system code like any other part of the operating system.

debugging — The process of going through program code to locate errors and then fixing them.

decision logic — One of the four basic shell logic structures used in program development. In decision logic, commands execute only if a certain condition exists. The *if* statement is an example of a coded statement that sets the condition(s) for execution.

decrement operator (--) — A C/C++ arithmetic operator that decreases the value of a variable by a specified amount.

defining operator — Used to assign a value to a variable.

desktop — The overall screen display and software that provides the specific GUI appearance and includes software applications and other resources for a UNIX/Linux system that has X Window installed—and works hand in hand with a Window Manager.

device special file — A file used in UNIX/Linux for managing I/O devices. It can be one of two types: *block special file* or *character special file*.

diamond operator (<>) — The operator used in Perl to access data from an open file. Each time the diamond operator is used, it returns the next line from the file.

directory — A special type of file that can contain other files and directories. Directory files store the names of regular files and other directories, called *subdirectories*.

domain name — A name that identifies a grouping of computer resources on a network. Internet-based domain names consist of three parts: a top-level domain (such as a country or organization type), a subdomain name (such as a business or college name), and a host name (such as the name of a host computer).

editor — A program for creating and modifying computer documents, such as program and data files.

Enhanced IDE (EIDE) — An improved version of IDE that offers faster data transfer speeds and is commonly used in modern computers. *See also* Integrated Drive Electronics.

environment variable — A value in a storage area that is read by UNIX/Linux when you log in. Environment variables can be used to create and store default settings, such as the shell that you use or the command prompt format you prefer.

evaluating operator — Enables you to evaluate the contents of a variable, such as by displaying the contents.

ex mode — A text-editing command mode, currently used in the vi editor, that employs an extended set of commands initially used in an early UNIX editor called ex.

executable file — A usable program, the result of the program development cycle.

executable program file — Also called an executable; a compiled file (from a programming language) or an interpreted file (from a script) that can be run on the computer.

executables — The programs residing in the /bin directory that are needed to start the system and perform other essential tasks. *See also* binaries.

exit status — A numeric value that the *test* command returns to the operating system when *test* finishes performing an evaluation of an expression, string, integer, or other information. If the exit status is 0 (zero), the test result is true. An exit status of 1 indicates the test result is false.

extended file system (ext or ext fs) — The file system designed for Linux that is installed, by default, in Linux operating systems. It enables the use of the full range of built-in Linux commands, file manipulation, and security. Released in 1992, ext had some bugs and supported only files of up to 2 GB. In 1993, the second extended file system (ext2 or ext2 fs) was designed to fix the bugs in ext, and supported files up to 4 TB. In 2001, ext3 (or ext3 fs) was introduced to enable journaling for file and data recovery. ext4 was introduced in 2006, enabling a single volume to hold up to 1 exabyte of data and supporting the use of extents. ext, ext2, ext3, and ext4 support file names up to 255 characters.

extent — A portion of a disk, such as a block or series of blocks, that is reserved for a file and that represents contiguous space, so that as the file grows, all of it remains in the same location on disk. The use of extents reduces file fragmentation on a disk, which reduces disk wear and the time it takes to retrieve information.

file — The basic component for data storage.

file system — An operating system's way of organizing files on mass storage devices, such as hard and floppy disks. The organization is hierarchical and resembles an inverted tree. In the branching structure, top-level files (or folders or directories) contain other files, which in turn contain other files.

File Transfer Protocol (FTP) — An Internet protocol for sending and receiving files.

filehandle — An input/output connection between a Perl program and the operating system. It can be used inside a program to open, read, write, and close the file.

fixed-length record — A record structure in a file in which each record has a specified length, as does each field in a record.

flat ASCII file — A file that you can create, manipulate, and use to store data, such as letters, product reports, or vendor records. Its organization as an unstructured sequence of bytes is typical of a text file and lends flexibility in data entry, because it can store any kind of data in any order. Any operating system can read this file type. However, because you can retrieve data only in the order you entered it, this file type's usefulness is limited. Also called an ordinary file or regular file.

flowchart — A logic diagram that uses a set of standard symbols to explain the logic in a program's sequence and each action performed in the sequence.

function — A separate body of code designed to contribute to the execution of a single task. You can put together a number of functions to create a program. In some languages, functions are called subroutines or procedures.

function call — A feature that you insert in the appropriate location of a program file to specify and use one of the functions in the C/C++ library or a user-defined function.

function overloading — A feature of the C++ programming language that lets functions respond to more than one set of criteria and conditions.

function prototype — A C program statement line that tells the C compiler about a function before the code for the function is fully defined.

garbage file — A temporary file, such as a core file, that loses its usefulness after several days.

glob — A character used to find or match file names; similar to a wildcard. Glob characters are part of glob patterns.

glob pattern — A combination of glob characters used to find or match multiple file names.

GNU Network Object Model Environment (GNOME) — A desktop environment produced by the GNU Project and that must be used with a Window Manager.

GNU Project — An organization created to develop a free, UNIX-like operating system named GNU.

graphical user interface (GUI) — Software that transforms bitmaps into an infinite variety of images, so that when you use an operating system you see graphical images.

group id (GID) — A number used to identify a group of users.

hash — A variable representing a set of key/value pairs. A percent sign (%) precedes a hash variable.

head — One of two parts of HTML code. (The other part is the body.) The head contains the title, which appears on the title bar of your browser window.

header file — A file containing the information the compiler needs to process standard input or output statements.

hidden file — A file that the operating system uses to keep configuration information, among other purposes. The name of a hidden file begins with a dot.

high-level language — A computer language that uses English-like expressions. COBOL, Visual Basic (VB), C, and C++ are high-level languages.

host — *See* server.

hot fixes — The ability to automatically move data on damaged portions of disks to areas that are not damaged.

hyperlink — The text or object in a Web document that, when clicked, loads another document and displays it in the browser window.

Hypertext Markup Language (HTML) — A format for creating documents and Web pages with embedded codes known as tags.

icon — A small graphic symbol in a GUI that represents a program or an action that can be started by clicking or double-clicking the symbol.

identifiers — The names given to variables and functions.

increment operator (++) — A C/C++ arithmetic operator that increases the value of a variable by a specified amount.

information node or **inode** — A system for storing essential information about directories and files. Inode information includes (1) the name of a directory or file, (2) general information about that directory/file, and (3) information (a pointer) about how to locate the directory/file on a disk partition.

inline sort block — A compact Perl notation that replaces an *if-else* statement and eliminates the need for a separate subroutine.

input validation — A process a program performs to ensure that the user has entered acceptable information, such as preventing a user from entering a duplicate record in a data file.

insert mode — A feature of a modal editor that lets you enter text. The UNIX/Linux vi editor is a modal editor.

Integrated Drive Electronics (IDE) — Sometimes called Integrated Device Electronics, the most popular electronic hard disk interface for personal computers. This is the same as the ANSI Advanced Technology Attachment (ATA) standard.

Internet Protocol (IP) — A network protocol or communications language that handles addressing and routing of information over a network so that it reaches the correct destination.

Internet Protocol (IP) address — A set of four numbers (for the commonly used IP version 4) separated by periods—for example, 172.16.1.61—and used to identify and access remote computers on a network or over the Internet.

interpreter — A UNIX/Linux shell feature that reads statements in a program file, immediately translates them into executable instructions, and then runs the instructions. Unlike a compiler, an interpreter does not produce a binary (an executable file) because it translates the instructions and runs them in a single step.

journaling — The process of keeping chronological records of data or transactions so that if a system crashes without warning, the data or transactions can be reconstructed or backed up to avoid data loss or information that is not properly synchronized.

KDE — A popular desktop environment for X Window that must be used with a Window Manager.

kernel — The basic operating system, which interacts directly with the hardware and services user programs.

Kernel mode — A means of accessing the kernel. Its use is limited to the system administrator to prevent unauthorized actions from interfering with the hardware that supports the entire UNIX/Linux structure.

key — A common field in every file record shared by each of one or more files. The common field, or key, enables you to link or join information among the files, such as for creating a report.

keywords — The components of all programming languages; these words have special meaning and must not be used as variable or function names.

Kicker — A bar appearing on the KDE desktop that contains icons, applets, menus, and other elements that can be used to start programs or display windows in KDE. *Also see* Panel.

Konqueror — An application that opens into a window and enables the user to manage files, browse the network and Internet, and view documents.

Konqueror I/O (KIO) plugin — Programs and utilities that add new functionality to the native capabilities of the Konqueror browser and file manager.

Korn shell — A UNIX/Linux command interpreter that offers more features than the original Bourne shell. Developed by David Korn at AT&T Bell Laboratories.

line editor — An editor that lets you work with only one line or a group of lines at once. Although you cannot see the context of your file, you might find a line editor useful for tasks such as searching, replacing, and copying blocks of text.

line-oriented command — A command that can perform more than one action, such as searching and replacing, in more than one place in a file. When using a line-oriented command, you must specify the exact location where the action is to occur. These commands differ from screen-oriented commands, which execute relative to the location of the cursor.

linker — In program development, the tool used after the compiler to link all object files that belong to the program and any library programs the program might use.

localhost — A name given to the computer that is associated with the loopback address of 127.0.0.1. *See also* loopback.

log in — A process that protects privacy and safeguards a multiuser system by requiring each user to type a user name and password before using the system.

logic structures — The techniques for structuring program code that affect the order in which the code is executed or how it is executed, such as looping back through the code from a particular point or jumping from one point in the code to another. Also called control structures or control logic.

logical structure — The organization of information in files, records, and fields, each of which represents a logical entity, such as a payroll file, an employee's pay record, or an employee's Social Security number.

login script — A script that runs just after you log in to your account.

loopback — A feature that helps you experiment with and test HTML documents, or Web pages, using a UNIX or Linux system. To use localhost, you need not be connected to the Internet. Located on your PC, localhost also accesses your PC's internal network. Use localhost to ensure that networking is properly configured.

looping logic — One of the four basic shell logic structures used in program development. In looping logic, a control structure (or loop) repeats until some specific condition exists or some action occurs.

machine language — The exclusive use of 0s (which mean off) and 1s (which mean on) to communicate with the computer. Years ago, programmers had to write programs in machine language, a tedious and time-consuming process.

macro — A set of commands that automates a complex task. A macro is sometimes called a superinstruction.

main() — A required function in a C or C++ program. A C/C++ program is made up of one or more functions. Every function must have a name, and every C/C++ program must have a function called main().

mainframe — A large computer that has historically offered extensive processing, mass storage, and client access for industrial-strength computing. Mainframes are still in use today, but many have been replaced by PC-type computers that are designed as servers with powerful processing and disk storage capabilities.

makefile — A file used with the *make* utility that contains instructions for a project consisting of multiple source and executable files.

man pages — The online manual pages for UNIX/ Linux commands and programs that can be accessed by entering *man* plus the name of the command or program.

manipulation and transformation commands — A group of commands that alter and format extracted information so that it's useful and can be presented in a way that is appealing and easy to understand.

method — A set of operations that manipulate data; a part of the new data class, objects, used in the C++ programming language.

modal editor — A text editor that enables you to work in different modes. For example, the vi editor has three modes: insert, command, and ex.

mount — The process of connecting a file system to the directory tree structure, making that directory accessible.

Multipurpose Internet Mail Extensions (MIME) — A communications standard that supports sending and receiving binary files in mail messages.

multitasking system — An operating system that enables a computer to run two or more programs at the same time.

multiuser system — A system in which many people can simultaneously access and share a server computer's resources. To protect privacy and safeguard the system, each user must type a user name and password in order to use, or log in to, the system. UNIX and Linux are multiuser systems.

Nautilus — An application that opens into a window and is used to manage files and folders. Also called Nautilus File Manager.

nest — When creating program code, a practice of layering statements at two or more levels under an original statement structure.

network — A group of computers connected by network cable or wireless communications to allow many users to share computer resources and files. It combines the convenience and familiarity of the personal computer with the processing power of a mainframe.

Network File System (NFS) — Enables file transfer and other shared services that involve computers running UNIX/Linux.

null character — A single byte whose bits are all set to zero.

object code — The binary instructions translated from program source code by a compiler.

object-oriented programming — A method of programming that uses objects for programming and handling data—allowing the data to be described by name and type anywhere in the program.

objects — A new data class introduced in the C++ programming language. An object is a collection of data and a set of operations called methods that manipulate data.

open source software — Software and accompanying source code that is available to the general public free of charge.

operand — The variable name that appears to the left of an operator or the variable value that appears to the right of an operator. For example, in NAME=Becky, NAME is the variable name, = is the operator, and Becky is the variable value. Note that no spaces separate the operator and operands.

operating system (OS) — The most fundamental computer program, it controls all the computer's resources and provides the base upon which application programs can be used or written.

options — The additional capabilities you can use with a UNIX/Linux command.

ordinary user — Any person who uses the system, except the system administrator or superuser.

output redirection operator — The greater-than sign (>) is one example of a redirection operator. Typing > after a command that produces output creates a new file or overwrites an existing file and then sends output to a disk file, rather than to the monitor.

Panel — A bar in the the GNOME desktop that contains icons and applets for opening menus or applications. *Also see* Kicker.

parent — The directory in which a subdirectory (child) is created and stored.

partition — A separate section of a disk that holds a file system and that is created so activity and problems occurring in other partitions do not affect it.

PATH variable — A path identifier that provides a list of directory locations where UNIX/Linux look for executable programs.

pathname — A means of specifying a file or directory that includes the names of directories and subdirectories on the branches of the tree structure. A forward slash (/) separates each directory name. For example, the pathname of the file phones (the destination file) in the source directory of Jean's directory within the /home directory is /home/jean/source/phones.

peer-to-peer network — A networking configuration in which each computer system on the network is both a client and a server. Data and programs reside on individual systems, so users do not depend on a central server. The advantage of a peer-to-peer network is that if one computer fails, the others continue to operate.

peripherals — The equipment connected to a computer via electronic interfaces. Examples include hard disk and CD/DVD disc drives, printers, and keyboards.

permission — A specific privilege to access and manipulate a directory or file, for example, the privilege to read a file.

personal computer (PC) — A single, stand-alone machine, such as a desktop or laptop computer, that performs all input, output, processing, and storage operations.

physical file system — A section of the hard disk that has been formatted to hold files.

pipe operator (|) — The operator that redirects the output of one command to the input of another command.

port — The process of adapting software so that it can be moved from one type of computer or operating system to another.

portability — A characteristic of an operating system that allows the system to be used in a number of different environments, particularly on different types of computers. UNIX and Linux are portable operating systems.

Portable Operating System Interface for UNIX (POSIX) — Standards developed by experts from industry, academia, and government through the Institute of Electrical and Electronics Engineers (IEEE) for the portability of applications, including the standardization of UNIX features.

Practical Extraction and Report Language (Perl) — A scripting language that has features of C programming, shell scripting, and Awk. Created by Larry Wall in 1987 as a simple report generator, Perl has evolved to become a powerful and popular tool for creating interactive Web pages.

preprocessor — The routine that is used after initial application development and before the compiler to make necessary modifications to the program and to include the contents of other files.

preprocessor directive — A statement that you place in your program to instruct the preprocessor to modify your source code in some way. A preprocessor directive always begins with the # symbol. An example is *#include*, which tells the preprocessor to include another file or library in your program.

process id (PID) — An identification number that the operating system assigns to a process for managing and tracking that process.

program development cycle — The process of developing a program, which includes (1) creating program specifications, (2) the design process, (3) writing code, (4) testing, (5) debugging, and (6) correcting errors.

prototype — A running model, which lets programmers review a program before committing to its design.

pseudocode — The instructions that are similar to actual programming statements. Used to create a model that might later become the basis for a program.

record layout — A program and data file design step that identifies the fields, types of records, and data types to be used in data files.

redirection operator — An operator or symbol that changes the input or output data stream from its default direction, such as using > to redirect output to a file instead of to the screen.

regular file — A UNIX/Linux reference to ASCII/text files and binary files. Also called an ordinary file.

relational database — A database that contains files that UNIX/Linux treat as tables, records that are treated as rows, and fields that are treated as columns and that can be joined to create new records. For example,

using the *join* command, you can extract information from two files in a relational database that share a common field.

relational operator — Compares the relationship between two values or arguments, such as greater than (>), less than (<), equal to (=), and others.

relative path — A pathname that begins at the current working directory and lists all subdirectories to the destination file.

remote procedure calls (RPCs) — Enable services and software on one computer to use services and software on a different computer.

root — The system administrator's unique user name, a reference to the system administrator's ownership of the root account and unlimited system privileges. Also, root has two other meanings: (1) the basis of the tree-like structure of the UNIX/Linux file system and the name of the file (root directory) located at this level and (2) the home directory for the root account.

root file system directory — The main or parent directory (/) for all other directories (the highest level of the file system); also can refer to the directory in which the system administrator's files are stored (/root).

runlevel — The level of function at which a UNIX/Linux system is running. On Linux systems, runlevels go from 0 to 6. Also called a system state or mode.

Samba — Used by UNIX/Linux and Mac OS X systems, a utility that employs the Server Message Block (SMB) protocol, which is also used by Microsoft Windows systems for sharing folders and printers. Samba enables UNIX/Linux and Mac OS X systems to access shared Windows resources.

scalability — The capability for a computer operating system to be used on smaller computers, such as those with a single Intel-type processor, and on larger computers, such as those with 64-bit or RISC processors or even mainframes.

scalar — A simple variable that holds a number or a string. Scalar variables' names begin with a dollar sign ($).

scope — The part of the program in which a variable is defined and accessible. The scope can be either inside or outside a function.

screen editor — An editor supplied by the operating system that displays text one screen at a time and lets you move around the screen to add and change text. UNIX/Linux have two screen editors: vi and Emacs.

screen-oriented command — A command that executes relative to the position of the cursor. Screen-oriented commands are easy to type, and you can readily see their result on the screen. These commands differ from line-oriented commands, which execute independently of the location of the cursor.

Secure Shell (SSH) — A form of authentication developed for UNIX/Linux systems to provide authentication security for TCP/IP applications, including FTP and Telnet.

selection commands — The file-processing commands that are used to extract information.

sequential logic — One of four basic logic structures used for program development. In sequential logic, commands execute in the order they appear in the program, except when a branch instruction changes the flow of execution.

server — The computer that has a network operating system and, as a result, can accept and respond to requests from user programs running on other computers (called clients) in the network. Also called a host.

server operating system — An operating system that controls the operations of a server or host computer, which accepts and responds to requests from user programs running on other computers (called clients) on the network.

server-based network — A centralized approach to networking, in which client computers' data and programs reside on the server.

set group ID (SGID) bit — Enables the owner of a program to keep full ownership, but also gives members of a group temporary ownership while executing that program.

set user ID (SUID) bit — Enables the owner of a program to retain full ownership, but also gives an ordinary user temporary ownership while executing that program.

shared library images — The files residing in the /lib directory that programmers use to share code, rather than copying this code into their programs. Doing so makes their programs smaller and faster.

shell — An interface between the user and the operating system.

shell function — A group of commands stored in memory and assigned a name. Shell functions simplify the program code. For example, you can include a function's name within a shell script so the function's commands execute as part of the script. You can also use shell functions to store reusable code sections, so that you do not need to duplicate them.

shell script — A text file that contains sequences of UNIX/Linux commands that do not need to be converted into machine language by a compiler.

shell script operator — The symbols used with shell scripts that define and evaluate information, that perform arithmetic actions, and that perform redirection or piping operations.

shell variable — A variable you create at the command line or in a shell script. It is valuable for use in shell scripts for storing information temporarily.

Small Computer System Interface (SCSI) — Pronounced "*scuzzy*," a popular and fast electronic hard disk interface commonly used on network servers. SCSI is actually a set of standards that defines various aspects of fast communications with a hard disk.

sorting key — A field position within each line of a file that is used to sort the lines. For instance, in the command *sort -k 2 myfile*, myfile is sorted by the second field in that file. The *sort* command sorts the lines based on the sorting key.

source code — The program code that you create using an editor and that either is interpreted, if you are using an interpreted programming language, or is compiled, if you are using a compiled language.

source file — A file used for storing a program's high-level language statements (code) and created by an editor such as vi or Emacs. To execute, a source file must be converted to a low-level machine language file consisting of object code.

spaceship operator (<=>) — A special Perl operator for numeric sorts that reduces coding requirements.

statement — A reference to a line of code that performs an action in a program.

stderr — An acronym used by programmers for standard error. When UNIX/Linux detect errors in programs and program tasks, the error messages and analyses are directed to stderr, which is often the screen (part of the IEEE Std 1003.1 specification).

stdin — An acronym used by programmers for standard input and used in programming to read input (part of the IEEE Std 1003.1 specification).

stdio.h — A header file that is part of the C programming language development system. This file contains information the compiler needs so that it can process standard input or output statements. Any C program that performs standard input or output must include the stdio.h header file.

stdout — An acronym used by programmers for standard output and used in programming to write output (part of the IEEE Std 1003.1 specification).

sticky bit — An executable permission that either causes a program to stay resident in memory (on older UNIX/Linux systems) or ensures that only root or the owner can delete or rename a file (on newer systems).

string — A nonnumeric field of information treated simply as a group of characters. Numbers in a string are considered characters rather than digits.

subdirectory — A directory under a higher or parent directory.

subroutine or routine — A segment of code often used over and over again that can be internal or external to a program. A subroutine typically is identified by a beginning control statement, such as the *sub* statement in Perl, and a unique name that often reflects its purpose.

superblock — A special data block on a partition that contains information about the layout of blocks. This information is the key to finding anything on the file system, and it should never change.

superuser — *See* system administrator.

swap partition — A section of the hard disk separated from other sections so that it functions as an extension of memory, which means it supports virtual memory. A computer system can use the space in this partition to swap information between disk and RAM so the computer runs faster and more efficiently.

symbolic link — A name or file name that points to and lets you access a file using a different name in the same directory or a file using the same or a different name in a different directory.

symbolic name — A name used for a variable that consists of letters, numbers, or characters, that is used to reference the contents of a variable, and that often reflects the variable's purpose or contents.

syntax — A command's format, wording, options, and arguments.

syntax error — A grammatical mistake in a source file or script. Such mistakes prevent a compiler or interpreter from converting the file into an executable file or from running the commands in the file.

system administrator — A user who has an account that can manage the system by adding new users, deleting old accounts, and ensuring that the system performs services well and efficiently for all users.

System V (SysV) — A version of UNIX originating from AT&T Bell Labs and first released as System 3 in the early 1980s as a commercial version of UNIX. Today, commercial and free versions based on System V are available.

tags — The code embedded in a document or Web page created with Hypertext Markup Language (HTML). When the document is viewed with a Web browser, such as Firefox or Internet Explorer, the tags give the document special properties, such as foreground and background colors, font size, and the placement of graphical elements. You can also use tags to place hyperlinks in a document.

Telnet — An Internet terminal emulation program.

terminal — A device that connects to a server or host, but consists only of a monitor and keyboard and has no CPU. Sometimes called a dumb terminal.

terminal window — A special window that is opened from a UNIX or Linux GUI desktop and that enables you to enter commands using a shell, such as the Bash shell.

text editor — A simplified word processor used to create and edit documents but that has no formatting features to boldface or center text, for example.

text file — A computer file composed entirely of ASCII characters.

Unicode — A set of bit patterns that supports up to 65,536 characters and was developed to offer more characters than ASCII for a broader range of languages, such as Chinese.

UNIX file system (ufs) — A hierarchical (tree structure) file system supported in most versions of UNIX/Linux. It is expandable, supports large storage, provides excellent security, is reliable, and employs information nodes (inodes).

User mode — A means of accessing the areas of a system where program software resides.

utility — A program that performs useful operations such as copying files, listing directories, and communicating with other users. Unlike other operating system programs, a utility is an add-on and not part of the UNIX/Linux shell, nor a component of the kernel.

variable — A symbolic name that represents a value stored in memory.

variable-length record — A record structure in a data file in which the records can have variable lengths and are typically separated by a delimiter, such as a colon.

virtual file system — A system that occupies no disk space, such as the /proc directory. The virtual file system references and lets you obtain information about which programs and processes are running on a computer.

virtual memory — A memory resource supported by the swap partition, in which the system can swap information between disk and RAM, allowing the computer to run faster and more efficiently.

virtual storage — The storage that might be allocated via different disks or file systems (or both), but that is transparently accessible as storage to the operating system and users.

Web server — A system connected to the Internet running Web server software, such as Apache. The Web server software lets other users access the HTML document via the Internet.

wildcard — A special character that can stand for any other character or, in some cases, a group of characters and is often used in an argument, such as *ls file.**.

Window Manager — The top layer of the X Window System and the user's interface to the system's components. It controls how windows appear and how users control them.

workspace — An area on the desktop in which you can place icons, open windows, and add Panels or Kickers. Desktops such as GNOME and KDE offer four virtual workspaces by default and enable you to switch from one to another using the Workspace Switcher.

X client — In X Window network terminology, the system that hosts and executes a program.

X server — In X Window network terminology, the desktop system from which the user runs a program.

X Window System — A GUI that runs on Linux and many UNIX operating systems.

X11 — The eleventh version of the X Window System.

XFree86 — A version of X11 that was ported to the PC and on Linux.

Index

Symbols

+ (addition) operator, 515
asterisk (*) character, 79–80, 291
caret (^) character, 244–245
: (colon), 119
{} (curly brackets), 509–510
(decrement) operator, 515, 536
/ (division) operator, 515
$ (dollar sign), 24, 284
/ (forward slash), 58, 72
++ (increment) operator, 515, 536
- (minus) character, 385–389, 515
% (modulus) operator, 515
* (multiplication) operator, 515
. (period), 116
| (pipe) operator, 215–216, 236, 241–242
(pound) symbol, 24, 277, 510
? (question mark), 79–80, 291
; (semicolon), 222–223
<=> (sort) operator, 475–478
/* symbol, 510
~ (tilde), 72, 106, 115
! character, 364
./ character, 289–290, 317–318
$_ variable, 472
== operator, 461

A

a\ command, 224
.a file extension, 471
-a option, 364
absolute paths, 75–76, 90, 101–102
addition (+) operator, 515
+ (addition) operator, 472
Advanced Technology Attachment (ATA), 59
algorithms, 273, 306
    for cursor placement, 356–358
    input validation, 358–359
alias, 306
alias command, 301–302, 305, 328, 626
alphanumeric fields, sorting, 473–475
American National Standards Institute (ANSI), 59
a.out file, 410, 507
Apache server, 478–479
applets, 572, 588, 603
applications
    creating in C, 506–527
    developing file-processing, 226–234
    program development cycle, 273–278
    prototyping, 277
archive files, 420–423
arguments
    command, 14, 15

defined, 29
    passing to functions, 360–361, 392, 521–522
arithmetic operators, 286–288, 306, 514–515
arrays, 284, 465–466, 483
.asc file extension, 471
ASCII character set, 112, 113, 130
ASCII files, 112, 158
assemblers, 507, 536
assembly language, 506, 536
asterisk (*) character, 79–80, 291
AT&T Bell Labs, 5–6, 506
authentication, 5, 669
    defined, 29
    SSH and, 12
automatic variables, 514, 536
awk command, 176–179, 207–210, 214, 626
    displaying records with, 333–334
    printing output with, 231–232, 258, 259
Awk programming language, 176–178, 231
    vs. Perl, 467–471

B

B language, 506
-b option, 364
back quote operator, 286
background, desktop, 578, 585, 601–602, 609–610